PHL

54060000191428

KT-584-538

THE
PAUL HAMLYN
LIBRARY

DONATED BY
THE PAUL HAMLYN
FOUNDATION
TO THE
BRITISH MUSEUM

opened December 2000

WITHDRAWN

EATING AND DRINKING IN
ROMAN BRITAIN

What were the eating and drinking habits of the inhabitants of Britain during the Roman period? Drawing on evidence from a large number of archaeological excavations, this fascinating new study shows how varied these habits were in different regions and amongst different communities and challenges the idea that there was any one single way of being Roman or native. Integrating a range of archaeological sources, including pottery, metalwork and environmental evidence such as animal bone and seeds, this book illuminates eating and drinking choices, providing invaluable insights into how those communities regarded their world. The book contains sections on the nature of the different types of evidence used and how they can be analysed. It will be a useful guide to all archaeologists, and those who wish to learn about the strengths and weaknesses of these materials and how best to use them.

HILARY COOL is a professional archaeologist who, for the past ten years, has run her own business providing post-excavation services to the professional sector. She is also a director of Barbican Research Associates, a company specialising in writing up backlog sites. Her publications include *The Roman Cemetery at Brougham, Cumbria* (2004) and (with J. Price) *Roman Vessel Glass from Excavations at Colchester 1971–1985* (1995).

EATING AND DRINKING IN ROMAN BRITAIN

H. E. M. COOL

CAMBRIDGE
UNIVERSITY PRESS

CAMBRIDGE UNIVERSITY PRESS
Cambridge, New York, Melbourne, Madrid, Cape Town, Singapore, São Paulo

Cambridge University Press
The Edinburgh Building, Cambridge CB2 2RU, UK

Published in the United States of America by Cambridge University Press, New York

www.cambridge.org
Information on this title: www.cambridge.org/9780521003278

© Cambridge University Press 2006

This publication is in copyright. Subject to statutory exception
and to the provisions of relevant collective licensing agreements,
no reproduction of any part may take place without
the written permission of Cambridge University Press.

First published 2006

Printed in the United Kingdom at the University Press, Cambridge

A catalogue record for this publication is available from the British Library

ISBN-13 978-0-521-80276-5 hardback
ISBN-10 0-521-80276-8 hardback
ISBN-13 978-0-521-00327-8 paperback
ISBN-10 0-521-00327-X paperback

Cambridge University Press has no responsibility for the persistence or accuracy of URLs for
external or third-party internet websites referred to in this book, and does not guarantee that
any content on such websites is, or will remain, accurate or appropriate.

THE
BRITISH
MUSEUM
THE PAUL HAMLYN LIBRARY
WITHDRAWN

For Mike
who has patiently lived with me and the Romans for a very long time

Contents

Figures

Tables

Preface

I decided to write this book as it combined three of my great interests in life – food, drink and Roman Britain. Whilst few people would be surprised at the first two, a passion for the third would raise eyebrows in many archaeological circles. For much of my professional life just as real men didn't eat quiche, so real archaeologists didn't do Roman Britain. For Classical archaeologists, the province of *Britannia* was a distant excrescence, far from the 'proper' archaeology of the Mediterranean lands. Within British archaeology, it was seen as the preserve of arcane specialisms pursuing their own agendas far from where the theoretical action was. Whilst theory has now come to Roman Britain, it is still an uncomfortable place for many. Modern tastes wish to do away with anything that recalls colonialism, whilst rising nationalisms prefer not to engage with periods when Britain was self-evidently part of a wider world. Prehistory is still a safer, more comfortable and purer world for archaeologists to play in.

This is a great pity as Roman Britain is a very strange place, much stranger than the many popular books written about it would lead one to think. It is fully worthy of being studied in its own right, but that has to be done on its own terms. This involves knowing how to interpret all the data relating to it. The problem with Roman Britain is that there are just too many things. Too much pottery, too much metalwork, too many animal bones. People tend to be overwhelmed by the sheer volume. They deal with it by picking out the occasional morsel, and hoping the rest will go away. This book is offered as a kind of hitchhiker's guide to those who would like to explore this material, but who lose the will to live when faced with the reams of specialist reports that even a minor excavation can generate. It shows, I hope, how these reports can be used to explore different facets of the past. I have chosen to explore eating and drinking

because not only does it interest me but, as the celebrated gourmet and bon viveur Brillat-Savarin said 'Tell me what you eat, and I will tell you what you are'. Where better to start exploring Roman Britain?
Bon appetit!

Acknowledgements

A book like this depends on the work of the specialists who have sorted, identified, analysed and published the multitude of items on which it is based. Their names are mentioned in the footnotes, but I would like to put on record my thanks here, and my apologies too if I have misrepresented them.

Over the years I have benefited from discussions with many people. Those who have kindly answered questions specifically to do with this book include Richard Brewer, Peter Davenport, Brenda Dickinson, Jerry Evans, Andrew (Bone) Jones, Ruth Leary, Scott Martin, Quita Mould, Stephanie Ratkái, Paul Sealey and Vivien Swan. Special thanks are due to Ruth and Scott, who made the results of currently unpublished work available to me; and to Bone for reading the sections pertaining to fish. Jerry has been particularly generous with unpublished work and useful discussion. I'm sure he won't agree with what I've made of it all, but I hope he'll enjoy the result. Alex Smith and Oxford Archaeology kindly allowed me to refer to the results of the Claydon Pike excavations in advance of full publication and provided additional details.

Jaye Pont is thanked for her invaluable guidance in matters pertaining to illustration software, and I am grateful to the West Yorkshire Archaeological Service (via Chris Philo) and the Winchester Excavation Committee (via Professor Martin Biddle) for providing figs. 9.1 and 17.4.

I would like to thank Cambridge University Press for publishing the book, and the two editors who have overseen it, Jessica Kuper and Simon Whitmore. Simon is owed special thanks for his forbearance over its much delayed appearance. I am most grateful also to Sarah Parker, Joanna Breeze and Gwynneth Drabble for their work in preparing the book for publication.

Mike Baxter provided fig. 15.1 and read the final draft which was much improved by his comments. He has also provided constant encouragement and support during the book's prolonged gestation, and indeed for much longer than that. So, as is only right, this book is for him.

The final stages of preparing the manuscript have been enlivened by listening to the Test Match Special commentary of the thrilling 2005 England – Australia Ashes series. It has been most distracting – many thanks to the players of both teams and the commentators.

CHAPTER I

Apéritif

This is a book that takes that most common question 'What shall we have for dinner?' and uses it to explore the communities that lived in Britain during the first half of the first millennium AD (a period that will hereafter be called Roman Britain as a convenient shorthand). Subject-matter such as this has not always been thought very respectable. Certainly it has not been considered central to the story of Roman Britain. Yet in many ways there is no better way of understanding past societies. Eating and drinking are frequently about much more than sustaining life by the ingestion of sufficient calories. What you can and cannot eat, who you can and cannot eat it with, tends not to be so much a matter of personal choice, as the result of social conditioning. By studying the eating patterns of a society, you enter areas far beyond the mere nutritional. Eating and drinking rituals will quite frequently take you into the realms of religious beliefs, class, gender relationships, and ethnicity. Or, as Brillat-Savarin said more succinctly, 'Tell me what you eat, and I will tell you what you are'.[1]

The information that can be used for this study is entirely dependent on archaeological exploration. The scanty ancient sources that have traditionally underpinned the study of Roman Britain are virtually silent on the topic; and, when they do say anything relevant, can generally be shown to be unreliable witnesses. Archaeology, by contrast, produces data in almost embarrassing abundance. We have so much information that the problem is how best to use it, not just to explore eating habits, but also any other topic of interest. Most of these data are in the specialist contributions analysing and cataloguing the things found during excavation. These lurk behind the structural narratives of excavation reports like the submerged part of an iceberg, and are a seriously underused

---

[1] Brillat-Savarin 1826, 4th aphorism.

resource. I do not consider it an overstatement to say that they are where Roman Britain resides though, being a specialist myself, it might be considered that I am prejudiced. The patterns seen in the artefact and environmental reports often cut across preconceived notions of how life was lived in Britain during the earlier first millennium AD. It is my aim to bring this information to wider attention and, in doing so, demonstrate how it can be used.

If the specialist reports are so important, why are they so underused? The answer lies in the fact that this knowledge base developed as a service industry providing excavators with the information they needed to understand the structural narrative. It was generally very highly focused towards the provision of dating evidence because of the way Romano-British studies developed. There is a long history of studying the province stretching back to the antiquaries of the eighteenth century such as Stukely and Horsley. For many years the preferred approach was to use the archaeology as an illustration of the meagre historical record derived from the ancient sources. The role of the army, and the changing military dispositions, took centre stage. For this the overwhelming need was to be able to date sites, and to identify the different periods when particular forts were occupied. This led to a hierarchy of esteem with the finds that were either intrinsically dateable, or which could be dated, valued over those perceived as not providing this information. So, much attention was devoted to coins and inscriptions, which often come with their dates written on them. Dated typologies of pottery could be built up using the stratigraphic associations with these independently dated items, and the pottery could be used to date contexts without coins or inscriptions.

Over the past two or three decades, attention has shifted much more towards how provincial society developed. Ways of looking at the province have been much influenced by broader, theoretical approaches of the type loosely described as post-processual. Though these approaches look at much wider issues than the previous military – historical approach, what is still wanted by excavators is the dating that can be provided by the finds, and such information about the trade and exchange networks of the site as the material can provide.

The specialists who produce the reports naturally structure their work to the requirements of their 'client', the person writing up the excavations. The end result of this can easily be seen by glancing at most pottery reports. There will frequently be detailed considerations of the decorated and stamped samian sherds and the stamped mortaria, as these are perceived as best being able to give the types of dates needed. The rest of the pottery will often be dealt with in a more summary way. The most favoured route currently is to prepare fabric and vessel type series, then quantify and summarise the assemblage according to these criteria, as this will help to provide information about the trade and exchange networks.

Increasingly whilst providing this basic, but ultimately rather boring, information, wider aspects of what the data are telling us are buried in the better specialist reports. This has been going on for some time but much of the wider archaeological community seems unaware of it. This is probably because few people read excavation reports from cover to cover. They will gut them for such information that is directly relevant to what they are working on, and hope that the author of the excavation mono-graph will have extracted the 'best bits' of the specialist reports for the overview. In my experience of writing and publishing specialist reports for over a quarter of a century, this is a misguided hope. It is a rare report that explores the interactions between all aspects of the data. It is the aim of this book to explore such interactions to show what a richly textured picture of the past comes about when this is done.

It has to be admitted that the picture is still a very patchy one. In part this comes about because some areas and types of site have seen relatively little work. Until the advent of developer-funded archaeology, for example, rural sites other than villas were seriously neglected.[2] Some of the gaps result from inadequate specialist reporting. This can come about for various reasons. Sometimes it is because work on the specialist cat-egories is seen as an optional extra. Funds are not invested in various categories, or it is decided not to report fully on the material. Sometimes they are inadequate because certain conventions of reporting have arisen. In some areas the reports appear to be written mainly for the handful of fellow specialists who work in the field, blithely ignoring the fact that the ultimate aim must be to enable the integration of their information with all the rest of the data from the site. It is hoped that excavators and specialists reading this book will come to appreciate the gains that result from a full integration of all the material, and will perhaps mend their ways if necessary.

This book can be regarded as being structured in three parts. The next four chapters introduce the sources of the evidence. The first three of these are strictly archaeological and look at the food itself, the packaging it came in, and the results of ingesting the food as demonstrated by skeletal

---

[2] Hingley 2000, 150–1, Table 10.3; James 2003, 5–6, Illus. 1.

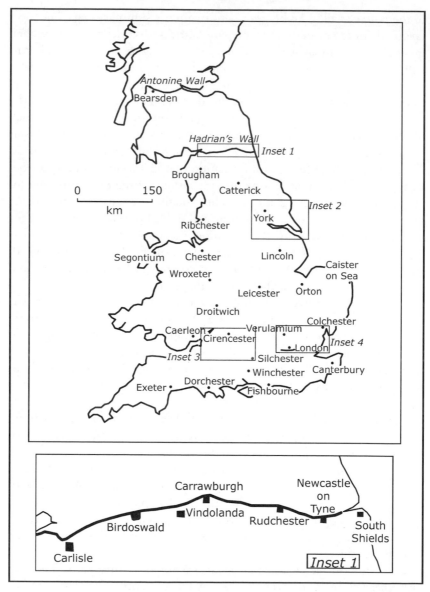

Figure 1.1. Map showing the principal sites mentioned in the text.

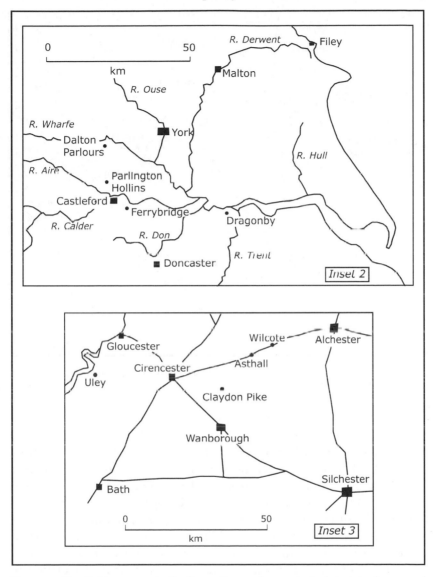

Figure 1.2. Detailed insets 2 and 3 for fig. 1.1. Inset 2 shows principal rivers in the area and inset 3 the main Roman roads.

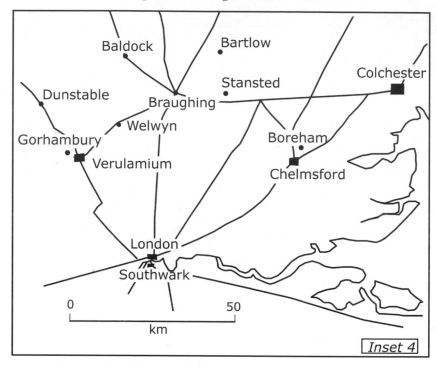

Figure 1.3. Detailed inset 4 for fig. 1.1 showing the main Roman roads.

remains. The biases inherent in these sources will be examined, and the ways in which the different types of finds are generally studied will be discussed. This first part concludes with a consideration of the written evidence (Chapter 5). Some of this is archaeological and directly relevant to Roman Britain, such as the accounts and shopping lists recovered from Vindolanda. Most of the ancient literary sources are not directly relevant to the province as they relate to the Mediterranean world, a very different social milieu. It is useful to look at them because they do provide a background to the lifestyles of at least some of the elite population in the province.

The second and third parts look at the data in two different ways. Chapters 6 to 15 look at general patterns seen in the ingredients available and favoured, and cooking techniques. It starts with basic information about the kitchen and utensils, and moves through the major food categories to finish with drink. This section takes as its model classic works in the culinary repertoire that explore the cuisine of particular parts of the world such as Elizabeth David's *French Provincial Cookery,* Marcella Hazan's *Essentials of Classic Italian Cooking* and Rosemary Brissenden's *South East Asian Food.* This section exploits data from a wide variety of sites. In the third section (Chapters 16–19) the focus shifts to particular sites at particular times to explore the tastes of different communities. These case studies demonstrate how different strands of information can be combined to show how life was changing.

The chronological scope of the book ranges from the late pre-Roman Iron Age, when the influence of Rome was being felt in the south-east, until the fifth century when a new social environment was developing. The geographical range is that part of Britain that had extended periods within the Roman province, i.e. the mainland to approximately the Antonine Wall on the Forth – Clyde isthmus.

Finally, a few words about conventions used are appropriate. The term 'finds' will be used as a convenient shorthand to represent both artefactual and ecofactual material. The book is heavily dependent on a very large number of specialist reports, but to keep the references within publishable bounds the full details of each one cannot be given. In the footnotes the convention has been adopted of citing the specialist by name and the editor or author of the monograph; thus 'Mould in Wilson 2002a'. In the references the details of the publication will be found under Wilson 2002a. The sources used for each table will be found in Appendix 1, and the locations of the main sites mentioned in the text are shown in figs. 1.1–1.3.

CHAPTER 2

The food itself

INTRODUCTION

The main direct sources of information about food come from animal bones and plant seeds. The types of meat and varieties of vegetables and fruit consumed will be considered later in the book. Here the various factors that govern the type of information that can be extracted from this material, and the biases that are inherent in its study, will be discussed. The opportunity will also be taken to consider the question of quantification. Knowing how much of a commodity has been found at a site is essential if comparisons of consumption patterns on different sites are to be made. Finally in this chapter, the nature of rubbish disposal will be considered.

ANIMAL BONES

The biases that affect animal bone assemblages can be divided into two broad categories relating to what can actually survive, and how what survives is excavated and subsequently studied.

What survives depends very much on the soil conditions in which the material was deposited. Bone does not survive well in acidic soils, and in extreme cases can disappear in its entirety.[1] The acidity of a soil is measured on the pH scale from 1 (extremely acid) to 14 (extremely alkaline), and below a value of 6 the mineral that makes up bone becomes extremely soluble. Soil acidity can vary greatly over small areas depending on husbandry, drift geology, and whether or not deposits are waterlogged. This is well demonstrated at Catterick where extensive excavations in and around the Roman town have produced conditions ranging from very good to so bad that no bone was recovered.[2] Even within a site there may

[1] Mays 1998: 17.   [2] Stallibrass in Wilson 2002b: 392.

8

be differential survival according to what type of feature the bones are deposited in. On a site with otherwise good preservation, it was possible to show that sheep and pig bones survived far better in pits than they did in ditch fills,[3] probably because they were not being exposed to the elements and to scavenging animals. Dogs can have a noticeable impact on a bone assemblage when they ingest the more succulent bones.[4] It is also suspected that the bones of different species may decay at differential rates,[5] though in the words of one eminent specialist 'the decay of buried bone is complex, and still not well understood'.[6] With all of these factors to keep in mind, it is not surprising that most animal bone reports devote some time to assessing the site formation processes that may have influenced the assemblage that survives.

One of the most important developments in archaeological methodology over the past quarter century has been the routine sieving of samples of deposits. The sample is generally disaggregated in water, and then passed through a series of sieves of increasingly fine mesh size. Such a process is vital if plant remains of the type discussed in the next section are to be recovered, and it is also very important for the study of animal bone. It has long been appreciated that hand collection on site results in a very biased assemblage favouring large fragments, often from large animals. To evaluate fish and bird consumption large-scale sieving is vital,[7] but it can also be important for some other types of meat. The consumption of suckling pig can only be evaluated if sites have been sieved, as the bones of this delicacy are rarely recovered by hand collection.[8]

As will be obvious from this, comparing assemblages from different sites to build up a picture of who was eating what and at what time, has to be done with some care. There would be little useful information gained if the assemblage from a site with good preservation that had been sieved was compared with one where only hand collection had been carried out, even if the preservation was equally good. An additional problem arises with quantification, because assemblages can only be directly compared if they have been counted in the same way.

Counting things that are habitually found in a broken state, like animal bone and pottery, is not simple. Counting fragments is unsatisfactory as the same amount of bone may end up being found in different numbers of fragments on two sites depending on butchery practice and

[3] Maltby 1981: 165 Table 2.   [4] O'Connor 2000: 22.
[5] King 1978: 210.   [6] O'Connor 2000: 25.
[7] Coy 1989: Table 2.   [8] O'Connor 1989: 17.

site formation processes. As a very simple example we can imagine a long bone from a steer. On site A this is removed during butchery as an intact bone and disposed of in a pit where it remains undisturbed until excavated. On site B a similar bone may be chopped into six pieces to remove the marrow and the pieces then thrown into a ditch. One of these may be removed by a dog and be further fragmented into four pieces by a combination of chewing and people walking on the fragments where the dog leaves them. In total there are ten fragments of this bone from site B. Simple fragment count would indicate that there was ten times the amount of bone on site B as on site A, but of course this would not be true.

Even though these problems have long been recognised, a considerable amount of fragment-count data exists in the animal bone literature. The commonly used Number of Identified Specimens (NISP) measure falls into this category. This has the added problem that the number of bones is not identical in all animals. Pigs have more teeth and toes than cattle, whilst goats can only be identified from a limited number of elements.[9]

To overcome this a variety of counting strategies have been devised by animal bone specialists.[10] One method is to calculate the minimum number of individuals represented; but any calculation of minimum numbers, be it for animal bone, pottery or any other category of find, is only useful for comparing the numbers of things of different sorts in a single assemblage. Minimum numbers have been shown to be very dependent on the size of an assemblage,[11] and so are not a useful measure when comparing different assemblages with each other.

A more useful measure is to count different elements of the skeleton based on identifying different diagnostic zones. This has the advantage that it not only allows comparison between assemblages, but also allows the investigation of what sort of consumption was going on at different sites. As a simple example, a site where the assemblage is dominated by bones from the heads and feet of cattle is likely to be an abattoir, as these are the elements often removed with the hide after the animal is slaughtered. The value of this method of quantification was shown in a study that incorporated a large number of animal bone assemblages from London. It was possible to show a pattern that could be interpreted as slaughter and hide removal taking place in the countryside, then transfer of the carcasses to primary butchery sites within the city. At those the

---

[9] See O'Connor 2001: 54–7.   [10] O'Connor 2001: 57–67.   [11] Orton 1993.

removal and disposal of the vertebrae could be observed as the carcase was butchered into joints. Finally, another set of sites could be identified which were associated with a high proportion of bones relating to prime meat joints, presumably the waste from the kitchens where they were consumed.[12]

The number of assemblages quantified by the zonal method is, alas, limited; and this book makes use of many assemblages quantified in far from ideal ways. The method of quantification will be stated, and the various drawbacks should always be borne in mind.

PLANT REMAINS

Most archaeological sites in Britain other than those with very acidic soil will produce debris from meat consumption in the form of bones. The recovery of the vegetable part of the diet tends to be much more erratic. Plant remains are generally recovered only if they have been deposited in a damp or waterlogged environment, if they have been burnt, or if they have been mineralised. Again, this is a source of evidence that is only recovered when systematic sampling and flotation is undertaken.

In waterlogged deposits the normal processes of decay are arrested because of the lack of oxygen. What tends to be preserved are the seeds, pips and stones. Whether a site produces any evidence like this clearly depends on the depositional circumstances. Mineralised remains are also reliant on the type of context, as mineralisation takes place when organic parts of seeds and stones are replaced by calcium phosphate through exposure to urine and lime.[13] Latrine pits are ideal sources for such remains.

Plant remains preserved by burning tend to be more widespread, as once burnt they are not subject to decay and can be recovered from most soil types. The level of burning has to be relatively gentle as otherwise they will be burnt to ash. Burnt plant remains relating to diet are normally in the form of seeds, as various processes involved in preparing them for consumption require the application of heat. Not all cereals result in clean grain when threshed. The glume wheats (emmer and spelt) break into separate spikelets where the grains are still enclosed and have to be released from the glume. This is generally done by parching (heating) and pounding the grain.[14] Malting grain to make beer also requires heat to

---

[12] Moreno Garcia *et al.* 1996; Orton 1996.   [13] Greig 1982: 49.   [14] Hillmann 1981.

be applied. Here the grain has to be germinated so that the proteins it contains are converted to enzymes, which in turn convert the starch into soluble sugars which can be fermented to produce beer. Germination has to be halted at a point that optimises the amount of enzyme in the grain, and this is done by the application of a gentle heat.[15]

As large quantities of grain will have been heated for cleaning and malting purposes, charred plant remains tend to be biased towards cereals, but other food stuffs can also be preserved as chance contaminants. The residues from cleaning crops (straw, chaff and weeds) were often regarded as a useful fuel, and some carbonised deposits found in kilns and corn driers are clearly fuel rather than accurately reflecting the quality of a processed crop.[16]

Various other events can lead to the preservation of foodstuffs by charring. Sometimes food stores are burnt down and, though the overall temperature of the fire would be sufficient to reduce most of the contents to ash, some material may well be merely charred if it was covered by ash at an early stage. This would have prevented oxygen reaching it and thus complete combustion. This is what clearly occurred at several venues at Colchester when it was destroyed during the Boudican rising in AD 60/1. Here fruit has been recorded, as well as fully processed grain.[17] Foodstuffs were also placed on funeral pyres and again, though much would have been fully consumed by the fire, some will survive as charred remains.[18] A particularly good example of this was associated with a burial in Southwark where dates, figs and almonds had been amongst the pyre goods, as well as barley and wheat.[19]

The types of food crop being grown can be investigated by using pollen analysis, though in general this is not as useful a resource as might be hoped. Typical analysed sequences tend to come from bogs, and are often far from cultivation sites. As the pollen of some species such as cereals does not travel over any great distance such sequences, though ideal for mapping general vegetation change through time, are of limited use for exploring the food crops produced.[20] In some circumstances, pollen analysis of samples gathered on archaeological sites can be of great value. It was from the pollen found in bedding trenches at Wollaston that it was possible to show that they had been used for vines, and to demonstrate conclusively for the first time that vineyards had been present in Roman

---

[15] Protz 1995: 10–11. [16] van der Veen 1991: 305.
[17] Murphy in Crummy 1984: 40 and 108. [18] Bouby and Marinval 2004: 77–8.
[19] Mackinder 2000: 12. [20] Huntley 2000: 68.

Britain.[21] Another intriguing use of pollen analysis was to suggest the presence of honey in a pit at Castleford.[22]

RESIDUES

Traces of foodstuffs can be trapped in the walls of pottery vessels in which they were stored or cooked, and this is potentially a very important source of information. Animal fats and plant oils are preserved as lipids and, if the pottery fragment is crushed, these can be extracted or dissolved and their molecular chemistry analysed by the technique of gas chromatography. The results are compared with modern flora and fauna to identify what was in the vessel.[23] Unfortunately, despite the large amounts of Romano-British pottery that are found every year, such techniques have rarely been applied to it. Where analyses do exist, many were carried out in the early days of lipid analysis.[24] Developments in the technique mean that some early analyses are suspect,[25] and there is a great need for new programmes of analysis. Why the methodology has not been more widely applied to Roman pottery is an interesting question. Possibly it arises from the assumption that we know what vessels were being used for. This is actually far from true, as will be explored in the case of mortaria in Chapter 6.

WHEN IS RUBBISH NOT RUBBISH?

Archaeology deals with the detritus of people's lives, but alas rubbish disposal is not a simple thing. Earlier in this chapter we saw that the type of context in which rubbish was disposed can have an important bearing on the type of evidence that survives. There is also the question of what the rubbish relates to. An ideal world would be one where the rubbish generated by a household would be neatly deposited in rubbish pits close to the house. Though this does occasionally happen, there was obviously often a more organised rubbish-disposal system also in place, so that the rubbish from a variety of different sources was mixed together. To complicate this matter still further, it is appropriate to consider here the phenomenon of structured deposition. Up to the 1980s it is fair to say that rubbish was simply rubbish to most Roman archaeologists. The things

[21] Meadows 1996.
[22] Bastow in Abramson *et al.* 1999: 173.
[23] Evershed *et al.* 2001.
[24] For example Evans, John and Going in Going 1987: 91.
[25] Evershed *et al.* 2001: 332.

dug up were regarded as broken and worn-out items that that had simply been disposed of. This was merely to impose our own cultural standards on the past. We had refuse collectors who arrived to take the detritus away each week; what could be more obvious than sensible people such as the Romans would have done the same? Increasingly it came to be appreciated that what is and isn't rubbish is very much a construct of the society you live in. Works exploring this within an archaeological context were appearing in the late 1970s and early 1980s.[26] This made people look afresh at what previously had been considered as unproblematic rubbish deposits.[27] Coming from a different intellectual tradition, the eminent Romano-British archaeologist Ralph Merrifield was also drawing attention to the fact that 'rubbish pits' often contained unusually complete items and odd combinations of things. He suggested that these were deliberately deposited items, and the motivation behind such deposits lay in the realms of ritual and magic rather than simply rubbish disposal.[28]

As the data were re-examined, it became apparent that a phenomenon now referred to as structured deposition was taking place. This was where items were deliberately placed in pits or ditches, often to mark a change or cessation of use. This activity had its origins in the prehistoric period, but there is no doubt that it was widespread in Roman Britain as well.[29] This means that data need to undergo an additional layer of interrogation. Obviously, if they come from such a deposit, they may not relate to the daily eating practices of the inhabitants of the site, but instead may be special produce appropriate for a deity.

---

[26] For example Hodder 1982.   [27] For example Hill 1989: 20.
[28] Merrifield 1987.   [29] Fulford 2001.

CHAPTER 3

The packaging

INTRODUCTION

It is useful to think about packaging according to the material it is made of: whether it is an organic material such as wood, or an inorganic one such as pottery. If the latter, there are no problems of survival and the material may be found on any sort of site. If the former, waterlogged deposits or at least damp, anaerobic ones will be required to preserve them, so their survival will be an exception rather than the rule. It is likely that much packaging was made from organic materials. Grain would have been most conveniently transported in sacks, fruit in baskets. Fragments of these sorts of containers survive only rarely, and even when they do, it is not possible to say what they contained. Pottery containers occur on many sites and some even have graffiti or inscriptions that identify the contents. Such containers will dominate discussion in this chapter, but it should always be borne in mind that they will have only accounted for a fraction of the food packaging that would have been used. That said, the information that can be gleaned from the principal pottery containers – amphorae – is invaluable for exploring the long-distance trade in luxury foodstuffs such as wine and oil.

AMPHORAE

Amphorae were large pottery vessels used to transport primarily liquid contents such as wine, oil and fish sauce over long distances: other contents could include preserved fruits, and occasionally things that were not food.[1] They are studied primarily by considering the shape of the vessel, and the fabric it is made from. Various forms of information were also written on them, and these can be used to identify the contents. It has

---

[1] Borgard and Cavalier 2003.

long been clear that different shapes were used to transport different commodities (Fig. 3.1). Unfortunately, there is no one generally agreed typology for amphora shapes, and nomenclature is not simple. Amphorae can be identified according to both systematic typologies such as that of Heinrich Dressel, and according to a type specimen named after the site on which it was first identified. In this book the different types will be referred to by the Peacock and Williams[2] typology numbers, as that work provides cross references to the names given to a form in other typologies. Where appropriate, reference will also be made to the commonest name used for a type in the British literature.

Pottery fabrics reflect the place where the vessel was made because different inclusions in the clay may only be found in particular regions. Some fabrics may be identified easily in the hand specimen. A notable example of this is the fabric of the amphorae from the Campanian region of Italy, a notable source of good wine. It is very distinctive as it appears to be full of black sand (green augite crystals).[3] Other fabrics need to be studied by taking a thin section and studying it under the microscope. Studying otherwise undiagnostic body fragments in this way allows them to be assigned to the area they were made in. It does not always allow them to be assigned to a particular type as, if a region makes a variety of commodities transported in amphorae, the fabric of all of them is likely to be the same or very similar. This is a particular problem for amphorae from southern Spain which was a major exporter of both olive oil and salted fish products.

Identifying what was in a particular amphora form can be established by a combination of strands of evidence. Amphorae can have written information on the exterior in the form of stamps made before the vessel was fired, and painted inscriptions made after. Some of this information relates to the production of the amphora itself, but the painted inscriptions (known as *tituli picti*) relate to the contents giving the weight and the item being transported. Just occasionally, they also name the place of origin.[4] Unfortunately, painted inscriptions need good preservation conditions to survive. So, though it is likely that the majority of amphorae would have been labelled, such inscriptions are not common. Another useful source of information about contents come from shipwrecks, as vessels can be found with the contents intact. An interesting example of this was an amphora found in the Thames which had clearly been

---

[2] Peacock and Williams 1986, hereafter PW.   [3] PW: 87.   [4] PW: 10–14.

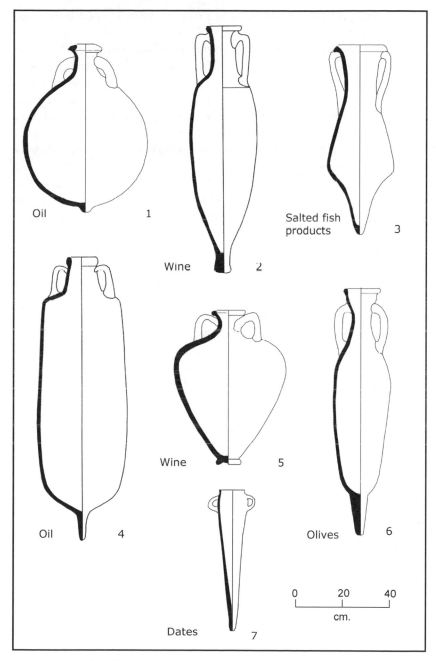

Oil 1

Wine 2

Salted fish products 3

Oil 4

Wine 5

Olives 6

Dates 7

0   20   40

cm.

Figure 3.1. Amphora forms and their main contents. 1: Dressel 20 / PW25. 2: Dressel 2/4 / PW10. 3: PW18. 4: North African / PW35. 5: PW27. 6: London 555. 7: 'Carrot' / PW 12. (After Tyers 1996.) Scale 1 : 16.

transporting preserved olives from Spain as it still contained over 6,000 olive stones.[5]

It used to be considered that an important distinction was whether or not the inside of the vessel was coated with resin. Such coatings were known from the ancient sources to be a typical treatment for the inside of vessels involved in making and transporting wine.[6] Ongoing scientific work using such techniques as gas chromatography has detected such linings on amphorae used to transport olive oil and fish sauces,[7] and so the presence of a resin lining cannot now be taken as diagnostic that the contents were wine.

As with animal bone assemblages, there are problems with comparing the quantities of amphorae from different sites. They can be found virtually entire in shipwrecks and in burials, but on most sites amphorae are found as fragments. The specialists who study this material are divided on the best method of quantification. Some favour weight, some favour minimum numbers, and some still use sherd count. Only weight fulfils the criteria that allow comparisons across sites because measures of minimum numbers are very much dependent on the size of the assemblage, and sherd count on site formation processes. The value of usefully quantifying pottery assemblages may be appreciated by an inspection of Table 3.1.

Table 3.1 has been derived from sites that were occupied throughout the Roman period. and which have had all of their pottery quantified,

Table 3.1. *Amphorae as a proportion of total pottery assemblages at various types of sites.*

Site	Type	Weight (kg)	Amphora (%)
Bainesse	Military	253.6	27.8
Leicester	Urban	7621.3	18.1
Lincoln	Urban	318.0	11.7
Alchester	Small town – suburban	536.7	11.1
Kingscote	Rural	497.4	8.2
Ivy Chimneys	Rural religious	379.6	5.4
Asthall	Roadside	144.0	4.9
Chignal	Villa	253.3	2.3

[5] Sealey and Tyers 1989.   [6] Sealey 1985: 129.
[7] Paper presented at the 33rd International Symposium on Archaeometry, Amsterdam in 2002 by A. Redford C. Heron.

Table 3.2. *Size and capacities of some of the commoner amphora forms found on British sites.*

Type	Also known as	Contents	Average Capacity (litres)	Weight range (kg)	Date (centuries)
PW 25	Dressel 20	Oil	60–65	24.5–37.2	1st – 3rd
PW 34	North African	Oil	60	14.0–17.5	2nd – 4th
PW 10	Dressel 2–4	Wine	26–34	12–16.5	1st – 2nd
PW 27	Gallic	Wine	26–37	10–15	1st – 3rd
PW 16–19	Salazon	Fish sauce	14–18 and 27–33		1st – 2nd
PW 15	Haltern 70	*Defrutum*	30	15.5–20.5	1st

including other specialist wares such as mortaria and samian. The picture it is painting reflects the situation in the third century and earlier, as the supply of amphora-borne commodities to Britain declined markedly after that. By including the whole pottery assemblage it is possible to get a broad picture, and overcome the problem of residuality. The rows of the table have been ordered by how large a proportion of the assemblage amphorae form. As can be seen from the second column, this figure is a very good indication of what sort of settlement the assemblage is coming from. It suggests that amphora-borne commodities did not commonly reach all parts of society, unless the rural sites were regularly purchasing them in repackaged form.

The different types of amphorae varied in size and weight as may be seen in Table 3.2. Given the size of the large oil amphora of Dressel Type 20, it is always to be expected that these will dominate the amphora assemblage from any site; but the varying proportions of other types present do provide an insight into consumption patterns. One factor that does have to be considered is that the later amphorae may be lighter than the earlier ones, despite having a similar capacity. This is most marked in the olive oil amphorae, but is also noted for the wine amphorae. The implications of this will be considered later in relation to patterns of olive oil importation.[8]

OTHER CERAMIC VESSELS

Occasionally other ceramic vessels have graffiti on them that allow the contents to be identified such as the jar that appears to record it held 1,884

---

[8] See p. 63.

coriander seeds[9] found at Vindolanda, but in comparison to the amphorae, these are a very minor source of information.

WOODEN BARRELS

It is clear that large wooden barrels were also used for long distance transport, and various sculpted reliefs show them being hauled on wagons. The best preserved barrels have survived because they were reused to line wells and this naturally biases the sample to very large examples. Ones recovered from Silchester, for example, are estimated to have held approximately 900 litres of liquid, but smaller ones are also known. Oak barrels found in a third-century wreck at Guernsey had capacities of 85 and 35 litres.[10] Unlike amphorae, the brands and inscriptions found on barrels were not used to indicate origin or content. Where it is possible to identify the wood the large barrels are made from, it is often found to be from species that grow in the Alps or Pyrenees.[11] The assumption is that they were used to ship wine from Gaul or Spain. If so, and it seems reasonable, then it indicates bulk shipment on a different scale to that provided by amphorae. As can be seen from Table 3.2, the two commonest types of wine amphorae (PW Classes 10 and 27) found in Britain have been estimated to have capacities in the region of 30 litres.[12] The Silchester barrels would have held thirty times that amount.

[9] RIB II.8 no. 2503.1.   [10] Rule and Monaghan 1993: 99.
[11] RIB II.4, p. 1.   [12] Sealey 1985: 10 Table 2.

CHAPTER 4

The human remains

INTRODUCTION

How well or poorly nourished people are can lead to changes in the bones. So study of the skeleton can give indications about the food consumed. This chapter explores the sort of information that can be gathered. It will look at the biases in the record and at how rich and poor diets may manifest themselves. This information will then be used to explore the nutritional history of various late Roman communities.

Human bones suffer from the same limitations with respect to preservation as animal bones do. Any inhumation cemetery on acid soil will not preserve skeletons. An even more important bias is to do with chronology. Many communities in the earlier Roman period cremated their dead. Though it is now possible to gain much useful information from cremated remains regarding the age, sex, and pathological conditions of the deceased,[1] this is a relatively new departure in Romano-British studies. The bulk of the cremated dead have never been examined in this way. Most information comes from people who were inhumed. Inhumation became increasingly popular as time progressed, and much of our evidence stems from the third and fourth centuries. Inhumation was practised earlier, and some people were still being cremated in the fourth century; but we know far more about the nutritional health of the later Roman population than we do about that of the people of the later Iron Age and early Roman period.

EVIDENCE FOR RICH DIETS

Aetiology, or causes of observed changes in bones, often has more than one source; and the food eaten is just one of them. In the case of diffuse

---

[1] See for example McKinley in Barber and Bowsher 2000: 264–77.

idiopathic skeletal hyperostosis (DISH) it seems to be generally accepted that it is associated with obesity and diabetes.[2] The disease results in much new bone formation and the gradual and complete fusing of the spine. It generally affects those older than fifty, and males are more liable to suffer from it than females.

Gout has long been associated with a rich diet and during some points of its history sufferers have seen it as a mark of distinction.[3] The disease is associated with the production of excessive uric acid, and results in the erosion of joint surfaces, mainly in the hands, feet, elbows and knees. In 90% of cases the big toe is involved. Again, it generally affects people over fifty, but affects men twenty times as often as it affects women.[4] There is a genetic predisposition towards the condition, but it is also clear that the ingestion of high quantities of lead can be a factor in its onset. It has been suggested that for the Roman period one of the sources of lead poisoning might have been the consumption of the sweet syrup *defrutum*,[5] as this was made by boiling down grape must in lead cauldrons.[6] The syrup was used both in its own right, and as a preservative for such items as olives.[7] It would have been an imported delicacy, and to be expected in the diets of those prone to overindulging themselves. There is a problem, though, with associating fourth-century gout sufferers with the consumption of such products as the evidence suggests trade in them had ceased by then.[8]

Syrups and other sweet things could be expected to lead to caries in teeth, but not all caries noted are the result of a sweet diet. They can result if there is poor dental hygiene and food is trapped between teeth. In those cases the food can break down into soluble sugars, even though the diet was relatively sugar-free. This was demonstrated in the East Cemetery in London where the teeth of 310 individuals were studied and 7% were found to be carious. The teeth affected tended to be the ones at the back of the mouth which are most difficult to clean. Over 90% of the caries observed were mild and this too suggested a lack of sweet items in the diet.[9] Where caries are combined with other indications of a rich diet it seems reasonable to conclude the condition depended on the sort of food eaten, rather than merely poor dental hygiene. A good case illustrating this was found in the cemetery at Dover Street, Southwark where a woman

---

[2] Roberts and Manchester 1995: 120–1.   [3] Porter and Rousseau 1998: 71.
[4] Roberts and Manchester 1995: 122–3.   [5] Molleson in Farwell and Molleson 1993: 193.
[6] Columella XII.19.   [7] Sealey 1985: 63.
[8] See p. 68.   [9] Conheeney in Barber and Bowsher 2000: 283.

aged between 25 and 45 was diagnosed as showing incipient signs of DISH.[10] Only 16 of her teeth remained but 4 of these showed caries. She had been buried with a rite that involved packing the grave with chalk. Such graves appear to be a fashionable burial ritual for the elite in the late Roman period;[11] and so the supposition that this individual was wealthy enough to indulge in a rich diet, including sweet things, seems likely.

EVIDENCE FOR POOR DIETS

Again, it has to be said that the observed changes in bone which seem to suggest a poor diet can have more than one cause; and it may be that sometimes the signs of poor nutrition are the result of illness which did not allow a person to take nourishment from their food. There are two regularly observed conditions that may indicate that an individual was not well nourished when young. Both result in changes to the bones of the skull and teeth which remain present in the adult.

Enamel hypoplasia is observed on teeth, and consists of defects in the enamel such as lines and pits. The stress that gives rise to them can be caused either by nutritional deficiencies or by illness.[12] It can manifest itself as a response to weaning. Cribra orbitalia is a condition where pits form on the surface of the orbital roof of the skull. The generally accepted aetiology is anaemia caused by a deficiency of iron. The changes are thought to come about when the body attempts to produce more blood cells in the marrow to compensate for the lack of iron.[13] It may be noted that some osteologists are still unconvinced of this link.[14] Iron is found in such foods as red meat, legumes and shellfish. Anaemia can be caused by a diet deficient in iron. It can also be caused by illness, and as a result of an individual suffering from a heavy parasite burden.[15] Environmental reports often report the background presence of whipworm of a size appropriate to humans suggesting that some individuals would have suffered in this way.[16]

Vitamin deficiencies can also be seen in the bones. Vitamin D is necessary for the mineralisation of bones, and a deficiency can lead

---

[10] MacKinder 2000: 45 burial 27.   [11] Philpott 1991: 92.
[12] Roberts and Manchester 1995: 58.   [13] Roberts and Manchester 1995: 167.
[14] Waldron in Davies *et al.* 2002: 153.   [15] Molleson in Farwell and Molleson 1993: 178.
[16] See, for example, Jones and Hutchinson in McCarthy 1991: 70; Boyer in Connor and Buckley 1999: 344.

to rickets. Though some of this vitamin is acquired through the diet, 90% of an individual's needs can be created by the skin if exposed to sunlight.[17] Vitamin C is acquired from fresh fruit and vegetables. A deficiency will lead to scurvy, which may manifest itself in the skeleton in the form of the deposition of new bone. It is also likely to lead to periodontal disease because the gums swell and bleed.[18] Scurvy is not often diagnosed in ancient populations, but some authorities have suggested that periostitis may reflect a Vitamin C deficiency.[19] This condition results in plaque-like new bone formation.[20] The cause is not fully understood, and it could come about as a result of repeated minor traumas. It is frequently observed in shin bones; a part of the body often subject to casual knocks and blows. Vitamin C deficiency is probably under-diagnosed in the Romano-British population. In the medieval period scurvy was endemic during winter in northern Europe due to the scarcity of fresh fruit and vegetables,[21] and similar conditions must have applied in Britain during the Roman period.

A WELL-FED POPULATION?

There is now sufficient evidence to start exploring the nutritional health of the late Roman population. Wherever possible the data presented are of third- or fourth-century date, though it is not always possible to extract subsets of data of that date for the important cemetery at Poundbury. The people buried in the cemeteries considered would have lived in a variety of environments. Those from London, Cirencester, Colchester and Poundbury lived in large towns. The people from Dunstable and Alchester lived in small towns, and the other sites are rural ones. It is not possible to compare all aspects of the population across all of the sites, as the level of reporting varies, but a general picture can be built up.

It is clear that how tall people grow to be depends, in part, on how well nourished they are when growing. One way of exploring this is to look at the mean male height and the difference between the heights of the male and female populations (sexual dimorphism). Populations with a low availability of protein tend to have a low mean male height and a low degree of sexual dimorphism.[22] As a guide it has been proposed that 1.6 m

[17] Roberts and Manchester 1995: 173.   [18] Roberts and Manchester 1995: 171.
[19] Molleson in Farwell and Molleson 1993: 189.   [20] Roberts and Manchester 1995: 130.
[21] Waldron 1989: 57.   [22] Molleson in Farwell and Molleson 1993: 184.

Table 4.1. *Mean stature of adults in eight late Roman cemeteries.*

Site	Date (century)	Male (number)	Male (mean)	Female (number)	Female (mean)
London East	2nd–4th	unknown	1.69	unknown	1.58
Cirencester	3rd–4th	107	1.69	44	1.58
Dunstable	3rd–4th	33	1.68	24	1.60
Poundbury	4th	341	1.66	360	1.61
Alington Avenue	4th	29	1.66	15	1.58
Maiden Castle Road	4th	6	1.67	6	1.59
Colchester	4th	85	1.68	59	1.56
Bradley Hill	Late 4th	10	1.69	10	1.59

should be regarded as short and 1.7 m as tall.[23] Table 4.1 shows the mean heights of the adult populations in eight cemeteries. As can be seen, none of the mean male heights are particularly low and sexual dimorphism is generally well pronounced with the possible exception of Poundbury. On the whole the figures suggest that these populations did not suffer regular food shortages, and there was adequate protein in the diet of the young.

Table 4.2 shows the incidence of caries, enamel hypoplasia and cribra orbitalia. In general the caries rates are quite low reflecting the lack of sugary foods, but the incidence at Poundbury stands out as being exceptional. The author of the report suggested the reason for this might be the result of the number of elderly people in cemetery.[24] At the site 12% were aged over 55, and the caries rate rose with age. The other large cemeteries, though, also have noticeable elderly communities. At Butt Road, Colchester, 6% of the individuals to whom an age could be assigned were over 50, at Cirencester 7% were over 53, and in the East Cemetery in London 13% were over 45. All of these sites have markedly lower rates of caries, and so the argument based on the demography at Poundbury does not seem a convincing reason for the discrepancy seen there.

Molleson[25] also noted that susceptibility to caries in later life depended on the nutrition received during infancy and childhood; and it seems very likely that, at Poundbury, this is the reason for the unusually high caries

[23] Roberts and Manchester 1995: 26.   [24] Molleson in Farwell and Molleson 1993: 183.
[25] Molleson in Farwell and Molleson 1993: 184.

Table 4.2. *Incidence of dental caries, enamel hypoplasia and cribra orbitalia. The number columns refer either to total teeth or individuals for which the percentage could be calculated. Blank fields indicate the numbers were not given, but percentages were. The total population for Poundbury was 1442 individuals.*

Site	Date	Caries Rate		Enamel hypoplasia		Cribra orbitalia	
	(century)	(%)	No.	(%)	No.	(%)	No.
London East	2nd–4th	7.3	2031	*c.* 10.0	294	>5.0	—
Cirencester	3rd–4th	5.1	3251	24.0	178	17.7	—
Dunstable	3rd–4th	3.8	1187	—	—	—	—
Chignall	3rd–4th	—	—	30.5	36	22.0	36
Poundbury	1st–4th	15.8	—	38.5	—	28.0	—
Alington Avenue	1st–4th	2.6	1954	—	—	2.7	109
Colchester	4th	3.9	3665	27.2	235	9.9	262
Alchester	4th	1.0	496	12.5	24	13.0	30

rate. The incidence of cribra orbitalia and enamel hypoplasia is also noticeably higher at the site, possibly reflecting nutritional stress in childhood. The lower sexual dimorphism seen in height at Poundbury has been commented on, and this too may be part of this pattern. Why the population at Poundbury should suffer in this way is unknown but there is other evidence at the cemetery that young children failed to thrive,[26] and it might be suspected that how they were fed had an impact upon them.

The way in which the Poundbury population seems to differentiate itself from the rest of the sites reminds us that Roman Britain was not a homogenous mass. It was full of different groups leading different life-styles which undoubtedly would have included different ways of feeding themselves and their children. The figures for Poundbury are especially interesting when compared to a small rural cemetery also outside Dorchester (Maiden Castle Road). Only twenty-two individuals were recovered but there were no examples of enamel hypoplasia recovered, and caries was restricted to one tooth in one individual.[27] Is the difference observed a simple one between a healthy country life and an unhealthy

---

[26] Molleson in Farwell and Molleson 1993: 176.   [27] Rogers in Smith *et al.* 1997: 156.

urban one; or are we perhaps looking at preferences at the level of the family unit?

Family burial plots within the Butt Road cemetery at Colchester have been suggested on the basis of similarity of burial ritual and genetic traits.[28] In the cemetery it was found cribra orbitalia and enamel hypoplasia tended to cluster in the proposed family plots,[29] and were not spread across the cemetery. In one complex, clearly reused over some time, individuals with enamel hypoplasia were found throughout the sequence.[30] Excluding the neonates and the individuals whose skeletons did not survive, thirty individuals were buried in this complex, ten of whom show the condition. This gives an incidence of 33% comparable to the Poundbury figures. The small cemetery at the Chignall villa also shows a high rate, and again one might hypothesise that these individuals would have been part of the same family group. Given the association of enamel hypoplasia with weaning, it is interesting to speculate that here we may have indications of particular child rearing habits, not necessarily shared with the neighbouring families. Was it the tradition to wean them early, and perhaps onto inappropriate food? It is clear from the ancient authors that the weaning food of choice in the Mediterranean world was cereal based, and that some mothers started to wean children after as little as six weeks.[31] Modern advice is not to move babies onto solid foods until about six months and then to start with purees of fresh fruit and vegetables.

It is probable that more could be learnt about early infant-feeding habits, but at present the data are not always presented in such a way that the information can be extracted. The incidence of enamel hypoplasia is rarely presented according to the sex of the individual. It would be interesting to know if it affected both sexes equally, with the implication that the feeding regime for both boys and girls was the same. At Butt Road, Colchester, it did,[32] but more data are clearly needed.

It might be suspected that some at least of the population suffered from a lack of fresh food during the winter months. Given that it is thought that scurvy is under-diagnosed,[33] it is difficult to assess the level of the problem. If we take Vitamin C deficiency to be one of the causes of periostitis, then some people in urban populations probably did have

[28] Crummy, N. *et al.* 1993: 92.   [29] Crummy, N. *et al.* 1993: Figs. 2.42–2.43.
[30] Crummy, N. *et al.* 1993: 93.   [31] Garnsey 1999: 107.
[32] Pinter-Bellows in Crummy, N. *et al.* 1993: 88.   [33] Roberts and Manchester 1995: 173.

Table 4.3. *The incidence of DISH in sexed individuals over the age of 45 at Poundbury.*

	Male	Female	Total
With DISH	11	0	11
Without DISH	84	129	213
Total	95	129	224

inadequate access to fresh fruit and vegetables. At Cirencester the condition affected 10–12% of the individuals examined[34] and a similar figure has been noted for the East Cemetery in London.[35] Again some communities appear to have avoided it. At Butt Road, Colchester only 1% of the individuals were affected.[36]

Overindulgence in a rich diet can also be detected, generally in the elderly. Gout has been recorded at Cirencester,[37] Poundbury[38] and in the East Cemetery in London.[39] Given the nature of the disease it is unsurprising that the cases identified are those of males, and it is of little help in distinguishing different eating patterns between the sexes. DISH, by contrast, occurs both in males and females though not equally; in modern North American populations the ratio is 65 : 35. The condition is regularly observed in Romano-British populations, but unfortunately is not always quantified. When it is, an interesting pattern can emerge.

At Poundbury eleven cases were observed, all male.[40] The incidence in the older population is shown in Table 4.3. Assuming the ancient population was susceptible to the condition in the same proportion as the modern one, this pattern can be explored statistically via a modified form of the chi-square statistic, and this shows that the condition does seem to affect males disproportionately at Poundbury.[41] It could be taken as suggesting that males were far more likely to overeat than females. There is independent evidence that at least two of the males with DISH did indeed have a rich diet. Three of the skeletons with DISH formed part of

[34] Wells in McWhirr *et al.* 1982: 182.   [35] Conheeney in Barber and Bowsher 2000: 286.
[36] Pinter-Bellows in Crummy, N. *et al.* 1993: 77.   [37] Wells in McWhirr *et al.* 1982: 191.
[38] Molleson in Farwell and Molleson 1993: Table 43.
[39] Conheeney in Barber and Bowsher 2000: 286.
[40] Molleson in Farwell and Molleson 1993: 194, Tables 46 and 60.
[41] Cool and Baxter 2005

a programme to investigate the food sources by stable-isotope analysis.[42] Two of the individuals clearly ate more foodstuffs derived from the sea than the bulk of the population. Interestingly one of the Poundbury gout sufferers also did. As will be seen in chapter 12, fish does not appear to have formed a major part of the diet of the bulk of the population, and there is some evidence to suggest this may have been an elite delicacy.

In other cemeteries DISH has been identified in female skeletons, sometimes where the burial rite suggests the individual was a member of the elite, as in the case of the woman buried at Southwark discussed above. It would be of some interest to quantify the incidence at other cemeteries in a similar way to that done in Table 4.3 as it might tell us whether the females of elite families had an equal access to rich delicacies. Poundbury stands out as unusual in many respects, and it would probably not be fair to condemn only the male element of the elite population as gluttons on its evidence.

The evidence would seem to suggest that for most of the populations examined, there was adequate nourishment though some parts of the communities such as young children may have been at risk. It is also clear that currently the evidence human bones provide for what different groups of people were eating is an underused resource. In some cases this is because of particular reporting conventions such as not distinguishing the sexes of the people with enamel hypoplasia. In others it is because techniques such as stable-isotope analysis are relatively new[43] and Romano-British skeletons have rarely been subjected to them. Certainly the latter technique with its ability to identify the eaters of marine food, most probably an elite preference, will be a most useful tool.

---

[42] Richards *et al.* 1998.   [43] Mays 1998: 182–90.

CHAPTER 5

Written evidence

INTRODUCTION

Direct written evidence for the food and drink of Roman Britain consists of the labels on packaging such as amphorae discussed in Chapter 3, and the information preserved on writing tablets found in the province. Indirect evidence comes from the ancient literary sources, many of which touch on matters of food and drink. This chapter will consider the sort of information captured in the writing tablets, and the ancient sources. The opportunity will also be taken to consider the nature of the well-developed food culture that the Roman elite at the centre of Empire clearly enjoyed, and whether some of the inhabitants of Britain were able to partake of it.

WRITING TABLETS

Two different forms of writing media were used in Roman Britain. Both were made of wood and thus require damp environments to survive. One has long been recognised and understood. These are the stylus tablets which consist of rectangular sheets of wood with narrow, raised borders around each edge. The recessed area was filled with black wax, and this could be written on with a stylus which removed the wax to reveal the pale wood below. When these tablets are found, the wax has generally disappeared but sometimes the stylus had scored deeply enough to leave traces of the writing on the wood. Many of these documents seem to recount legal or official transactions. Of these, one from London describing an enquiry into the ownership of a wood in Kent[1] is a good example, but personal letters are also known.[2] The contents of many tablets have not yet been read because the traces of writing consist of a palimpsest of

---

[1] Tomlin 1996 [2] RIB II 4 no 2443 7

different messages. So far, no information about food and drink has been recovered on a stylus tablet, but that does not mean that they were not used for shopping lists, household inventories etc. It is possible that the current bias towards legal documents is the result of those tablets being used once only. More humble household ones may exist, but their messages are lost in the jumble of reuse.

The other form of writing tablet was written on using an ink pen. These tablets were thin sheets of wood about 1 to 3mm thick, and the size of a modern postcard. When found, the traces of the writing can quickly fade. The full significance of what these slips of wood were only became apparent when large numbers of them were found during excavations at Vindolanda in 1973–5; and conservators at the British Museum developed techniques to preserve both the tablets and the writing. Excavations at the site have continued to produce these ink tablets, and there is now a large corpus of information available.[3]

Similar ink tablets have also been found elsewhere, for example at Caerleon[4] and Carlisle;[5] but the Vindolanda tablets remain by far the largest group found anywhere in the empire. They are one of the greatest treasures ever to have been uncovered by archaeology in Britain. They relate to a relatively short period in the life of a fort that lies just to the south of Hadrian's Wall. The waterlogged conditions that allowed them to survive apply to the earliest phases of the fort from c. AD 90 to 130. Vindolanda was a frontier fort at the extreme edge of the empire. It was garrisoned at this time by auxiliary units who came originally from Batavia, the area in modern Belgium and the Netherlands at the mouths of the rivers Rhine and Scheldt.[6] It is important to realise that the documents relate to the lives not of native Britons, nor of 'Romans' from the heart of empire, but to a Germanic military unit. Native Britons appear only occasionally, and then are disparaged as *Brittunculi* (wretched Britons).[7] The governor of the province, and similar high-ranking people, are distant presences.[8]

All sorts of information is preserved. There are personal letters including an invitation to a birthday party, official military inventories and movement orders, household inventories, shopping lists and children's

---

[3] Bowman and Thomas 1994; 2003. The definitive publication is now the website http://vindolanda. csad.ox.ac.uk – last accessed August 2006 – where developments in photography and digital imaging that make revised readings possible are reported.

[4] Hassall and Tomlin 1986: 450–2.   [5] Tomlin 1998.   [6] Bowman 1993: 26.

[7] Bowman and Thomas 1994: 106 no. 164.   [8] Bowman and Thomas 1994: 200 no. 225.

writing exercises. The lists of provisions include items such as pepper[9] which is very hard to find in the archaeological record. They provide a unique window onto the northern frontier at the end of the first century, and a start has already been made in attempting to use them to explore the military diet.[10] It would be fascinating to compare the inventories with the bones and plant remains preserved on the site. The damp conditions that preserved the writing tablet has also preserved much other organic material. This, alas, is currently impossible because the definitive publications of the sites have not yet appeared and only tantalising summaries are available.[11] It is much to be hoped that the reports will, eventually, appear. It would be a tragedy if the writing tablets were to remain divorced from the rest of the material culture relating to life at Vindolanda.

ANCIENT SOURCES

There is a great deal of information about food and drink scattered through the texts that have survived from antiquity. This is of variable value when exploring what was consumed in Roman Britain, as it relates to the Mediterranean heartlands of the empire where different foodstuffs were available. It is probably most useful when providing information about the food known to have been imported via amphorae. The encyclopaedic *Naturalis Historia* (Natural History) of Pliny the Elder, who died in the eruption of Vesuvius in AD 79, provides an overview of the different wine-producing areas and the quality of the products. This allows us to get some insights into how the wine, whose origins we can identify from first-century amphorae, would have been regarded by the people who drank it. Treatises on farming such as Columella's *De Re Rustica* written in the 60s provide information about how wine was customarily made, and how produce could be preserved. Such texts help us to interpret finds such as the amphora found in the Thames full of olive stones;[12] for they indicate that far from being preserved in brine or olive oil, as would be the modern practice, the olives had been packed in a very sweet syrup made from grape juice.

The doctors of antiquity viewed diet as an important medical tool. The works of such eminent practitioners as Galen, who wrote in the second half of the second century, and Dioscorides, who was a contemporary of Pliny the Elder, provide much useful information; not just on how food

---

[9] Bowman and Thomas 1994: 135 no. 184.   [10] Pearce 2002.
[11] Seaward in van Driel Murray *et al.* 1993: 91–119.   [12] Sealey and Tyers 1989.

and drink were used as treatments, but also how they were prepared. One of the most detailed descriptions of how *garum,* the fish sauce that will be discussed in Chapter 7, was made, comes from a work entitled *De Medicina et de Virtute Herbarum* (On medicine and the worth of plants) attributed to the third-century writer Gargilius Martialis.[13]

The only recipe book to survive in anything close to entirety is *De Re Coquinaria* (On Cookery) attributed to Apicius. Quite when the work was written, or who wrote it, is unknown.[14] The earliest manuscripts extant are of ninth century date, but the Latin they are written in dates to the later fourth century. The three legendary gourmets called Apicius lived much earlier; one during the first century BC, the second in the mid-first century AD and the third slightly later during the early second century. It is not known whether any of these individuals were directly connected with any parts of the work. Even if some parts of it can be attributed to one or the other of them, other parts were clearly written later as there are recipes named for the emperor Commodus who reigned in the mid-second century. It seems best to regard the book as a compilation to whom the name Apicius, synonymous with good living, became attached. It is a practical cookbook rather than a literary work; and was clearly aimed at an audience that was expected to know how to cook. The recipes give lists of ingredients but rarely quantities, and the cooking instructions can be very abbreviated. It can still be used as a practical guide, and forms a mainstay of many modern recipe books that attempt to recreate the dishes of antiquity.

It is clear that in the Ancient World there were many more recipe books in existence. Rome inherited and developed the culinary traditions of Greece, and with it the culinary literature. Much of this is now lost, with titles and fragments known only from passing references in the *Deipnosophistai* by Athenaeus. This work was written in the early third century AD in the style of discussions between dinner guests, and contains many excerpts from lost works. From these we can discover that by the third century BC, books were being written on particular aspects of cooking, and were providing recipes for regional specialities.[15] What survives is what medieval scribes chose to copy. Generally food, and matters pertaining to it, were not seen as matters suitable for serious study, so it is probable that a disproportionate number of works dealing with food did not survive. There is a fascinating chapter of recipes for cakes and

---

[13] Gozzini Giacosa 1992: 27; on the author see Curtis 1991: 11–12.
[14] Edwards 1984: ix–xiii; Gozzini Giacosa 1992: 7–8.   [15] Dalby 1996: 160.

doughnuts in *De Agricultura* (On Farming) written by the stern moralist Cato in the mid-second century BC.[16] One suspects that had he chosen to write instead *On Cakes*, not even his eminence would have preserved the work for posterity.

Recipes and references to food can often be found in literary works, and sometimes the recipes are detailed enough to be used directly in the kitchen. A poem attributed to Virgil called *Moretum*, after the dish of cheese pounded together with herbs and garlic, provides a recipe often reproduced almost verbatim in modern recipe books.[17] Literary works have to be used with some caution if they are to be pressed into service as evidence of how people of the Roman world actually ate. It is obvious, even from a superficial reading, that the dinner party given by Trimalchio as described by Petronius in the *Satyricon* is a satire on the nouveaux riches and, as such, is exaggerated for effect. In many other works, too, food is clearly being used as a metaphor; and Gowers has pointed out that despite the large number of texts dealing with meals that have survived, there is 'no straightforward, detailed description of a normal Roman meal'.[18] The types of dishes and the menus described are present for literary reasons. Rich food can stand for a bloated literary style, whilst a wholesome diet is the equivalent of literary restraint. What may appear to be a straightforward recipe for a sauce made with refined ingredients, can also be read as the poet's reflections on the type of satire that is needed for the age he is living in.[19]

That Latin literature of all sorts was so saturated with references to food is clearly an indication that the Roman world had what has been termed a differentiated cuisine.[20] This develops when a society is stratified culturally as well as politically. It has been suggested it requires access to a variety of foodstuffs, not just the locally available, a discerning and sizeable community of adventurous eaters, and a well-developed agricultural system. The habit of using literacy for a wide range of purposes, practical as well as literary and religious, is also important, as such a cuisine needs a body of recipes that can be developed by specialists. The cooks of the elite, and not just the elite themselves, need to be able to read. The Latin of Apicius's cookbook is relevant here. It is written in Vulgar Latin used by people of little formal education.[21] Clearly not everyone who lives in a society with a differentiated cuisine will eat exotic

---

[16] Cato: 72–84. For the character of the author see Holland 2003: 190–1.
[17] Dalby and Grainger 1996: 85–6.   [18] Gowers 1993: 7.   [19] Gowers 1993: 157.
[20] Goody 1982: 98–99.   [21] Dalby 1996: 179.

and elaborate dishes; but it could be expected that those at the higher end of society might, from time to time at least. To what extent did the higher levels of Roman cuisine spread to Britain?

Such a question can only really be discussed at the end of the book, but there is one aspect that can be considered here and that is the level of literacy in the province. Was it confined to a small subset of the population, or was it more widespread? There are three different strands of evidence that can be considered. They are provided by graffiti, styli and curse tablets.

Graffiti survives scratched on fragments of pottery and tiles. On pottery vessels the words scratched are generally personal names indicating own-ership of the vessel; and it is noticeable that finewares, especially plain samian vessels, were so labelled. An interesting study has shown that the incidence of graffiti seemed to be dependent on site type, with forts and their *vici* having a higher level than small towns and rural sites. It was suggested that this probably reflected levels of literacy, with the implica-tion it failed to penetrate the countryside to any great extent.[22] The alternative explanation that it was at the bigger sites that there was a greater possibility of personal possessions being stolen or borrowed was considered but rejected.

Styli for use with wax writing tablets were most commonly made of iron. In the past they were not particularly common finds. The current practice of routinely X-radiographing iron finds from excavations has greatly improved the recovery rates. X-radiography reveals the object hidden in the rusty corrosion, and it has to be suspected that previously some of the corroded fragments identified as nails were probably styli. When the types of sites on which styli are found are examined it is found that they are present at all levels of the settlement hierarchy, including rural sites.[23] It is always possible that the inhabitants of rural sites were using styli for some function other than writing, but the evidence of the curse tablets seems to support the idea that at least some part of the rural population was literate.

Curse tablets are inscriptions scratched onto pieces of lead or lead alloy. The messages are petitions to the deities; generally in the form of offering the god some reward if they exact revenge on the person who has done the petitioner wrong. Lead is a soft metal, and messages can be written on it with an implement like a stylus without great difficulty. In comparison

---

[22] Evans 1987. [23] Cool and Baxter 2002: 375.

to the rest of the empire, the Romano-British population seem to have been particularly fond of denouncing their fellows in this way. They have been found at a variety of temples across the province. The greatest number that have been read so far were recovered from the Sacred Spring in the great Temple complex at Bath, and belonged to the later second to fourth centuries. Study of the handwriting has suggested that the tablets were not written by scribes, but very probably by the individual making the petition.[24] This led the epigrapher who studied the tablets to conclude that a respectable number of people at Bath could read and write. Bath was a spa town and so it might be suggested it would have attracted a disproportionate number of upper-class, literate visitors. The same cannot be said of the rural hilltop temple at Uley where an equally large number of tablets have been found. Fewer of these have yet been read, but again it seems that different hands are represented.[25]

The styli and the curse tablets suggest that literacy spread into the rural, presumably British, population. They do not indicate that it was confined to the forts and major towns, where it might have been restricted to an incomer group. The apparent conflict with the graffiti evidence may be because security was a more important issue in the towns and especially the forts. Being literate does not necessarily mean that you can read and write fluently; but it does fulfil our need for cooks to have a practical literacy as far as recipes went. Obviously few houses will have had a shelf of cookbooks, but the possibility that some did cannot be excluded; and this may have been amongst the Romano-British elite living in their comfortable villas, as well as in the senatorial and equestrian households of commanding officers and administrators.

---

[24] Tomlin in Cunliffe 1988: 101.   [25] Tomlin in Woodward and Leech 1993: 117.

CHAPTER 6

Kitchen and dining basics: techniques and utensils

INTRODUCTION

The next eleven chapters explore the utensils and ingredients we have evidence for, and what the general patterns in the data are. This chapter concentrates on the objects used to prepare and cook food, the types of heat sources available, and how the food was served. By examining the types of sites things are found on, it is possible to start developing a picture of how cooking practices varied over time, and between different groups of the population. These objects also provide a salutary warning against assuming that vessels of similar shape will necessarily have the same function in different cultural milieus.

POTS AND PANS

In many areas of Roman Britain, though not in all, pottery vessels were central to cooking. As will be discussed in Chapter 16, this in itself marks a major change with what had been common practice in the Iron Age. Unfortunately, despite the tons of pottery excavated and published each year, this is not as helpful a source of information as it could be. The concentration on using it to date sites means that considerations of what it was actually used for are often overlooked. Vessels that are regularly used to cook food on hearths and over open fires can be expected to develop coatings of sooty deposits. Vessels used as kettles to heat water can be expected to build up deposits of limescale in hard water areas. However, it is a rare report that systematically records this. Table 6.1 has been prepared to show what types of vessels are regularly sooted and/or burnt. The sites have been selected because the information was recorded, rather than because they provide a representative sample; though they do span a range of rural, small urban and military sites.

Table 6.1. *Incidence of sooting, burning and limescale on different categories of pottery vessels.*

		Beaker	Flagon	Dish	Bowl	Mortaria	Jar	Lid
Baldock	Number	53	41	55	159	56	268	10
	Sooted %	0	2	4	8	4	9	0
	Burnt %	2	2	4	6	21	9	30
	Lime %	—	—	—	—	—	6	—
Dalton Parlours	Number	0	0	12	16	14	18	1
	Sooted %	—	—	17	6	14	39	0
	Burnt %	—	—	0	6	0	0	0
	Lime %	—	—	—	—	—	3	—
West Yorkshire	Number	0	0	9	14	10	70	0
	Sooted %	—	—	22	7	0	33	—
	Burnt %	—	—	11	0	30	1	—
Warrington	Number	37	20	47	131	86	296	9
	Sooted %	3	0	2	0	0	2	0
	Burnt %	5	5	11	5	12	4	22
Segontium	Number	27	27	68	195	67	394	68
	Sooted %	0	0	2	1	0	2	1
	Burnt %	7	0	19	8	21	6	8
Menai Straits	Number	4	0	12	10	4	24	0
	Sooted %	0	—	50	30	0	33	—
	Burnt %	0	—	33	0	25	8	—
Caersws	Number	22	26	18	99	14	212	39
	Sooted %	0	0	11	3	0	9	3
	Burnt %	0	0	22	2	7	3	3

It tends to be the jars followed by the bowls and dishes that are sooted and burnt, whilst the phenomenon is only occasionally noted on flagons and beakers. In the few studies of this phenomenon that have been published, a similar distribution of sooting or burning is reported;[1] and it seems reasonable to conclude that the jar was the principal cooking vessel. Generally the shapes chosen were ovoid with the greatest girth towards the shoulder, and with an everted rim to allow a lid to be securely held during cooking. The recurrent dish and bowl forms that show sooting and burning have straight, slightly outbent sides, occasionally with a small horizontal rim.

One of the very few detailed examinations of sooting has shown there is a significant difference between the heavily sooted rims, and the much less commonly sooted and burnt bases.[2] This would imply that the bodies and bases of the vessels were firmly bedded in the hearth, perhaps in the accumulated ash, with only the upper parts open to direct heat. The shapes of the vessels and this type of heat would be ideal for stewing or slow baking; and the ubiquity of cooking jars on most sites suggests that stewing would have been one of the principal cooking techniques.

Occasionally the pottery suggests other cooking methods associated with particular ethnic or regional groups. About AD 200 the kilns at the legionary fortress at York started to produce vessels which have strong similarities to shapes being made at that time in north Africa.[3] Given that the African emperor Septimius Severus was in residence at York between the years AD 208 to 211, and Africans are known to have been present in the army; it seems reasonable to conclude that these were vessels being made for a north African clientele, with cooking requirements that were not satisfied by the normal range of shapes available. One of the new forms was a bowl with a convex base which was designed to be used over a brazier. This was a type of cooking that is known to have been favoured in north Africa at the time, with the braziers also being made of pottery. Experimental work comparing a stew cooked in a jar on a hearth, and in a casserole on a brazier, has shown that the texture of the latter is much drier than that cooked in a jar.[4] The casseroles were used on other sites in the north of Britain where African soldiers were present, but in York itself did not find favour amongst the civilian population; presumably the

---

[1] Hammerson in Hinton 1988: 247–9; Evans 1993: 105 Table 1. [2] Evans 1995: Table 5.3.
[3] Swan 1992: 8, fig. nos 16–25; Monaghan 1997: 872–3, 999 form BA.
[4] Croom 2001: 44–5.

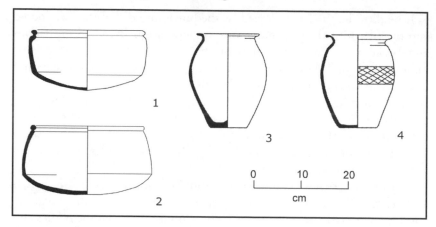

Figure 6.1. Early third-century 'north African' casseroles and cooking jars from York. (After Perrin 1981: fig. 35.452 (2); Perrin 1990: fig. 114.1225 (1); Monaghan 1997: figs. 385.3777, 3789 (3, 4).) Scale 1 : 8.

resulting stew was not found to have the correct texture. They seem to have been a short-lived fashion of a transient ethnic group.

One problem with assuming that these casseroles were used in exactly the same way as in north Africa is that fragments of the braziers have rarely been identified in Britain. It is possible that the braziers, being less well fired than the casseroles, have not survived in a recognisable form;[5] but it is worth considering whether or not it was the size of the vessel that was important. The casseroles come in a range of sizes, but are generally large. Fig. 6.1 shows two typical examples (nos. 1 and 2) compared with typical examples of the cooking jars (nos. 3 and 4) in use amongst the general population of York at the time. The casseroles would have held a greater quantity than the jar, possibly suggesting that what was important was the communal form of dining that they allowed and encouraged. A casserole such as this can be placed centrally amongst a group of diners who can help themselves to the contents. Such an action would not be so easy with the standard cooking jar, where the contents were probably decanted into individual bowls or plates prior to serving.

Another vessel type possibly associated with particular ethnic groups is the tripod bowl, which stands on three feet to lift the base above the direct heat (fig. 6.2). These are never a common part of any pottery assemblage,

[5] Vivienne Swan pers. com.

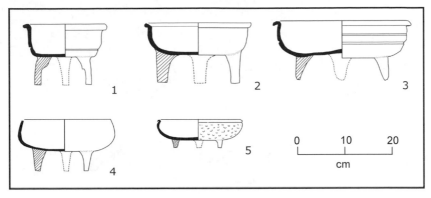

Figure 6.2. Tripod cooking bowls. (After Zienkiewicz 1986: fig. 19 (1); Rush *et al.* 2000: fig. 50 (2); Davies *et al.* 1994: fig. 65 (3); Frere 1972: figs. 106–7 (4–5).) Scale 1 : 8.

but do occur on military and urban sites of the first century.[6] At that time such bowls were the typical cooking pot of the south of France;[7] and where they occur on Romano-British sites it is tempting to see them as providing evidence of the presence of individuals from that region. Certainly at the places they are found, it would not be unusual to have individuals from those areas. There appears to have been sufficient demand in some areas[8] for the form to be made by the local industries, hinting at the cosmopolitan nature of society in some of the larger cities.

Specialised pottery cooking utensils also seem to have developed within sections of the native population apparently without any external prompt-ings from immigrant groups. An interesting example of this is what have been termed 'chapatti discs'. These are flat, thick discs of fired clay with a wide range of diameters from c. 14 cm to nearly half a metre. They are burnt on the underside and have carbonised deposits on the upper side around the edges. The suggestion that these are bake stones for something like a flat bread with or without a topping seems very probable. They have a very limited distribution centred on the Oxfordshire – Warwickshire region, and are noticeably more common on the rural than on the urban sites there. They start to appear in the later first century but appear

[6] Colchester – Symonds and Wade 1999: 470; Verulamium – Wilson in Frere 1972: 282 no. 231, 284 no. 234; London – Davies *et al.* 1994: 75, fig. 65 no. 379, 130 fig. 111 no. 708; Castleford – Rush *et al.* 2000: 109 nos. 135–6; Caerleon – Greep in Zienkiewicz 1986: 60 no. 1.18, fig 19; Malton – Wenham and Heywood 1997: 86 no. 237.

[7] Tuffreau-Libre 1992: 76.

[8] Colchester, London, Malton: see note 6.

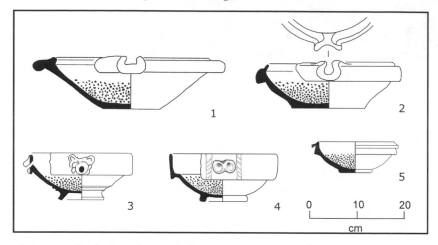

Figure 6.3. A selection of mortaria showing size ranges. 1–2: Cream coarse pottery. 3: samian: 4: colour-coated. 5: Crambeck. (After Miller *et al.* 1986: no. 1.73 (1); Symonds and Wade 1999: figs. 4.13, 4.20 (2, 4); Cool 2004b: fig. 4.127 (3); Monaghan 1997: fig. 377.3399 (5).) Scale 1 : 8.

commonest in the late Roman period.[9] They are absent from Iron Age pottery assemblages in the area, and so are clearly a Roman-period innovation to cook something that only appears to have been appreciated within a small subset of a local community.

In the Classical Roman kitchen envisaged by the recipes of Apicius, mortars were needed to grind a variety of ingredients to produce either a puree that could be poured, or a more solid mass which was then shaped by hand. Amongst the finds from most Romano-British sites there are utensils that seem ideally suited to perform this function. The commonest are coarse pottery mortaria. These are cream-coloured shallow bowls with a pronounced rim, which normally has a wide pouring spout at one point, and grit embedded in the interior surface (Fig. 6.3 nos. 1–2).

Mortaria were also made in samian pottery which was normally only used for tablewares (Fig. 6.3 no. 3). They differ from the cream examples in having a pouring spout that emerges through the upper wall taking the shape of a lion's or bat's head, rather than having an open channel on the rim. It was a very late addition to the range with the commonest type (Dressel 45) emerging about AD 170 amongst the Central Gaulish

[9] Jeremy Evans unpublished, see also Booth *et al.* 2001: 261

products, and continuing to be made in the third century by the East Gaulish industries.[10] There was sufficient demand for the form to be copied by the British colour-coated industries (see Fig. 6.3 no. 4).[11] This production started in the mid-third century, when imports of samian had almost disappeared, and continued well into the fourth. On these, the spouts were not considered to be an essential feature. Sometimes the wall is imperfectly perforated, and in others no spout is present. Indeed, on some there is only a painted representation of a spout.

Nothing like mortaria had been used in Britain prior to the conquest, other than on a very small number of elite sites.[12] The form is very much one that is associated with life after that event. Some were imported from the continent; but industries producing them were rapidly established in Britain, and there was a thriving trade in mortaria throughout the Roman period.[13] A similar pattern may be seen in stone mortars. These were used in much smaller quantities than the pottery ones, but again rapidly started to be made in Britain after the conquest.[14]

Strangely enough, though mortaria tend to occupy a privileged place in pottery studies with reports specially devoted to them, the function they served is rarely considered. Presumably it is taken as being self-evidently for the preparation of food, with the implication that this was being done in a 'Roman' manner.[15] Interestingly, in the early days of mortaria study this equation was doubted, and one suggestion was that the bowls were used in cheese making with the grits forming a rough surface that would provide a reservoir of bacteria to aid the curding of a cream cheese.[16]

At a superficial level, it is very tempting to equate the ubiquity of pottery mortaria in Britain with the adoption of a Roman cuisine. Some helpfully even have graffiti specifically stating that they are mixing bowls (*pelves*) or mortars (*mortaria*).[17] There are good reasons for doubting that the presence of such vessels always implies cooking methods that would have been recognisable to cooks from the Mediterranean heartlands. A variety of uses is suggested when size, distribution and wear characteristics are considered.

Fig. 6.4 compares the internal diameter of over 600 pottery and 50 stone mortars. It makes no claim to be a random sample, but is probably

---

[10] Bird 1993: 8.
[11] Tyers 1996: fig 217 no. 84; Young 1977: 127; Forms 97–100; Fulford 1975: 68 Type 79.
[12] See p. 166.   [13] Tyers 1996: 116, figs. 103–4.   [14] Cool 2005.
[15] See for example Tyers 1996: 116.   [16] Oswald 1943: 46.
[17] RIB II.6 2496.3, 2797.4; RIB II.7 2501.18.

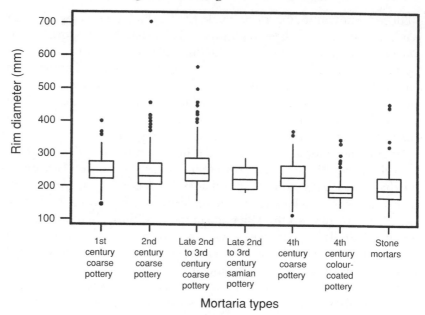

Figure 6.4. Boxplot showing the internal diameters of pottery mortaria and stone mortars by date. (The boxes enclose the inter-quartile range, dots represent outliers.)

representative. The pottery vessels are presented according to typological date and fabric. The coarse pottery mortaria maintain a fairly uniform average size across the centuries, though it is noticeable that there appear to be more small vessels in the late Roman period. Diameters as small as 112 mm and 120 mm have been recorded for some from the late fourth-century Crambeck industries of Yorkshire (see Fig. 6.3 no. 5).[18] The large examples tend to be of the late first to mid-third centuries, and are apparently missing in the late third and fourth centuries. These must have been used in a different way from most mortaria as they are far too heavy to hold, and it has long been suggested that they had some specialised culinary or commercial use.[19] Samian mortaria are similar in size to the average coarse pottery ones, but the colour-coated copies are noticeably smaller. This, together with the evidence of the small fourth-century coarse pottery ones, suggests that by that time, some mortaria were being used for a specialised function.

[18] Monaghan 1997: 937 no. 3398; Evans in Wilson 2002b: 334 no. M60B.
[19] Hartley 1973: 41; Richardson in Miller *et al.* 1986: 110.

Coarse pottery mortaria are far from being an ubiquitous element of material culture across the empire, and Britain appears to stand apart as being an unusually heavy consumer of them.[20] That they were not a vital part of Roman cookery is shown by their rarity in Italy as demonstrated by the fact that a recent exhibition of the evidence of food and flavours at Pompeii did not feel the need to include any examples within the wide range of vessel types on display.[21] This might hint that mortaria are not being used in Britain simply as kitchen utensils to produce Romanised food. This hypothesis is strengthened when the distribution of these vessels is considered. Whilst it is conceivable that a new cuisine might have been adopted in the towns and the more prosperous rural sites of the south of England, it becomes much harder to imagine this happening in the rural, native sites of the north. The people who lived in these appear to have had virtually no use at all for Roman material culture. Yet even here mortaria sherds are found, often from an early date and frequently forming a disproportionately large part of the pottery assemblage.[22]

The best way of establishing what the vessels were used for would be a detailed study combining residue analysis and detailed study of the wear and sooting patterns. So far, mortaria do not seem to have been subject to modern residue analysis, and it is difficult to establish wear patterns in any rigorous way. It can be established that the interiors often show consider-able wear, and that there are consistent indications that the vessels may have been used in cooking as sooting and burning are regularly recorded (see Table 6.1).

The combination of the various strands of the evidence suggests that these bowls may have had a variety of different functions, changing both with time, and with the social group that they were being used in. Within early rural communities there is the distinct possibility that some may not have been used in the kitchen at all. A noticeable phenomenon on rural sites of the first to second centuries is that the inhabitants seem dispro-portionately interested in acquiring large decorated samian and glass bowls which clearly were not being used in cooking.[23] Presumably such bowls served a role in those societies that may have been different to the roles they served in urban or military life. Perhaps on these sites mortaria were regarded simply as large bowls.

It is also seems likely that the bright red mortaria made in samian and other colour-coated pottery may have served a different purpose than the

[20] Hartley 1998: 209.   [21] Stefani 2005.
[22] Cool 2004a: Table 2.   [23] Cool and Baxter 1999: 93.

Table 6.2. *A comparison of the functional categories in selected late second- to third-century samian assemblages.*

Site	Dishes	Bowls	Cups	Mortaria	Quantification
Catterick Bridge	34	51	24	6	Min. nos.
Catterick, Bainesse	117	217	112	9	Min. nos.
Alchester, site B	76	164	138	9	Min. nos.
Alchester, site C	14	27	13	1	Min. nos.
Lincoln, the Park	1269	380	552	62	EVE

coarse pottery cream forms. Samian pottery is a tableware not a kitchen-ware. The low incidence of the form as shown in Table 6.2 suggests it was never used in large numbers. Presumably this was not a form that each individual might require in the same way they needed cups and bowls. The spouts, where present, would have been practical for decanting dry ground powders or liquid, but not a thick puree. Samian mortaria possess grits like the coarse pottery ones. Sometimes grits show evidence of having been worn down, but this is not always the case.[24] It is questionable whether they were always used, or perceived of, in a similar way to the other mortaria. At the third-century cemetery at Brougham, samian mortaria were included as grave goods, but coarse pottery ones were only represented amongst the unstratified deposits assumed to be derived from graveside ceremonies.[25] This suggests the mourners per-ceived them in very different ways. It may be that mortaria began to serve new functions in the later Roman period, perhaps explaining the decrease in size noticeable in some late coarse pottery ones. What these various functions were, will only become clearer when as much attention is devoted to wear patterns as is currently devoted to fabric.

Mortaria have been examined at some length because they provide a cautionary tale of how it can be far too easy to equate a type of vessel with a description in the ancient sources. Once different variants of the vessel are examined together with the information derived from the contexts in which they are found, such an equation becomes much more problematic. Next, we move onto a different type of problem; one where there is a mismatch between our perception of function and the perceptions of those who actually used them.

[24] Dickinson in Monaghan 1997: 947.   [25] Evans in Cool 2004b: 355.

Evaluating the role of metal vessels in cooking is less easy than considering the role of pottery. Partly this is due to survival. Once broken, most pottery vessels are good for nothing more than the rubbish dump. Damaged metal ones, by contrast, can either be mended or recycled. Consequently metal vessel fragments are rare as site finds. Most metal vessels that are recovered whole were deliberately deposited; either as grave goods, or as offerings in religious or magical rites. There is also the problem already alluded to that what may look like cooking vessels to the modern eye, clearly had far different functions as far as their users were concerned. The classic example is the handled open dish or bowl then known as a *trulleum* which has distinct similarities to the modern saucepan. The shallow hemispherical form, often with an elaborate handle terminating in a ram or lion head (see Fig. 6.5 no. 2), was part of a set with a jug.[26] Far from being a cooking implement, these sets were for washing hands; both domestically and in religious ceremonies. They were an integral part of sacrifice, and are often depicted on the sides of altars. An example from Birrens has a ram head *trulleum* carved on one side and the instruments of sacrifice on the other (Fig. 6.5 no. 4). It is also noticeable that the deeper form is often found in clearly religious contexts such as the sacred spring at Bath (Fig. 6.5 no. 1), and so it might be suspected that these too had a part to play in libations where offerings were poured out for the deity. Shallow-handled metal dishes (Fig. 6.5 no. 3) were part of the bathing regime and are sometimes termed bath-saucers.[27] Though some of these vessels could have been put to culinary use, such a function should not be unthinkingly assumed.

Other types of metal vessels do seem to have had a culinary function, but one that seems to have been very specialised. Frying pans with folding handles were in use during the third to fourth centuries.[28] The evidence currently suggests that these were favoured by the civilian population, and predominantly by those living in the countryside. Despite the assumption often made that these would be an ideal piece of military equipment,[29] the contexts of the known examples from Britain suggest that this was not the case, the identification of the only possible example from a military site being doubtful as it comes from an unusually early context.[30] Fragments from them are very rare, and it is reasonable to conclude they were not common. Like the 'chapatti discs' discussed earlier in this chapter, iron

[26] Nuber 1972.   [27] den Boesterd 1956: 13–5; Koster 1997: 84.
[28] Manning 1985: 105; Keevil 1992.   [29] Alcock 2001: 107.
[30] Scott in Evans and Metcalf 1992: 168 no. 32.

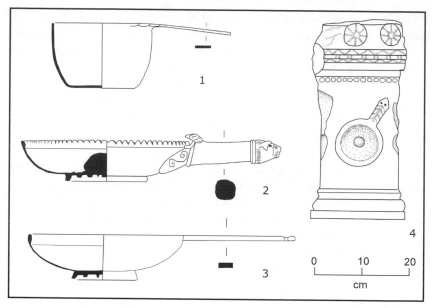

Figure 6.5. Metal vessels used in sacrifice (nos. 1–2) and bathing (no. 3) with altar depicting *trulleum* (no. 4). (After Cunliffe 1988: fig. 8.24 (1); Havis and Brooks 2004: figs. 147–8 (2–3); Keppie and Arnold 1984: pl. 1 (4).) Vessels – Scale 1 : 8.

frying pans were probably designed for a very particular dish favoured by a small subset of the population.

One metal vessel form that seems self-evidently designed for cooking is the cauldron, but even here there are problems with associating it with everyday cooking practices. Cauldrons are known from both late Iron Age and Roman contexts,[31] and their continuing use is also shown by the iron suspension chains. There is a continuity in the development of these running from the late Iron Age through to the later fourth century and beyond.[32] The survival of the cauldrons themselves is often due to the fact that they had been used as containers for votive hoards and were deliberately deposited in lakes and pools. The suspension hooks and chains again also tend to be found because they had been placed in special hoards or as grave goods.[33] Fragmentary parts of both cauldrons and suspension gear are strikingly rare on domestic sites. Even when they do occur, it is noticeable that they often form parts of deposits that were special in some

---

[31] Piggott 1952–53: 13.   [32] Manning 1983.   [33] Manning 1983: 136–42.

way. The pair of cauldron hooks found at Danebury, for example, were clearly part of a structured deposit.[34]

The amount of wear and patching seen on some[35] clearly indicates they had seen practical use as cauldrons, but their pattern of deposition argues against them being everyday, utilitarian items. Whilst in the later Iron Age the scarcity of fragments on domestic sites may reflect nothing more than the fact that metal finds in general tend to be rare then, the same cannot be said for Roman-period ones. In the later Iron Age metal was clearly carefully curated and recycled. In the Roman period, whilst recycling was practised, metal is present in much higher quantities in the archaeological record. If cauldrons and their suspension gear were standard cooking equipment, fragments ought to be more visible in the archaeological record and they are not. They are considerably rarer than those from the various types of metal vessels associated with drinking and dining.[36]

In a fascinating survey of cauldron use reviewing the early medieval Welsh and Irish myths, early Welsh Law and the archaeological incidence of cauldrons, it was noted that cauldrons appear special from the late Bronze Age to the medieval period.[37] The myths clearly relate cauldron use to the realm of the gods and the otherworld, and the contexts in which they are deposited indicate this as well. Cauldrons may well have been used for cooking, but in very particular contexts and situations. The food cooked in them would probably have been special, and may not always have been intended for human consumption.

All the evidence we currently have points to them belonging to the ritual rather than the everyday realm, and their use may have been restricted to very narrow parts of the community. During the Roman period, cauldrons and suspension gear tend to be found in hoards and so it is difficult to know who was using them. Before and after that period, they are found forming part of the grave goods of individuals who were clearly high-ranking members of their communities. In the later Iron Age, for example, a tripod, suspension chain and cauldron was placed in an obviously elite burial at Stanfordbury[38] and a cauldron in another at Baldock.[39] Seven centuries or so later a cauldron with its very long and elaborate suspension chain was found in the Sutton Hoo ship burial.[40] The amount of skill required on the part of the smith to forge the

[34] Cunliffe and Poole 1991: 353 nos. 2.299–300. [35] Piggott 1952–53: 28 no. C.1.
[36] See Table 15.3. [37] Green 1998: 75. [38] Stead 1967: 55.
[39] Stead and Rigby 1986: 55 no. 6.
[40] Bruce-Mitford 1972: 39 figs. 16–7.

elaborate chains, not forgetting the amount of metal needed to make them, would have made cauldrons an excellent vehicle for elite display. Given their association with the otherworld, however, it is probable that they were buried with these individuals not merely as a symbol of conspicuous consumption, but because these people were believed to have a special relationship with that world either as king or priest.

UTENSILS

One of the great advantages the Roman cooks had over their late Iron Age predecessors was that iron became a much more commonly used material, and a wide range of knives and cleavers became available.[41] As we shall see in Chapter 9, this had an effect on butchery practice, but it must undoubtedly have made a cook's life easier to have a range of knives for different purposes; and the ubiquity of knife-blade fragments in site assemblages suggests that these would have been available to all strata of society for much of the Roman period. This may have changed in the later fourth century as there are some grounds for thinking that attitudes towards iron were changing and this may have been because it was becoming scarcer.[42]

Spoons of non-ferrous metals and bone are not uncommon as site finds, but their sizes and their associations strongly suggest that these were items for use in the dining room rather than as kitchen utensils. Metal spoons frequently form parts of services of tableware throughout the Roman period.[43] Spatulas and spoons of wood that would have been ideal cooking utensils are occasionally recovered from damp environments and were probably common.[44] Iron flesh-hooks were often combined with a ladle at the other end. Where these have come from good dated contexts, a later second- to fourth-century date is suggested.[45] They seem relatively common on rural sites and in small towns, especially in the south-east north of the Thames. They are occasionally found on sites with military associations, but appear curiously absent on major urban sites. Again this may suggest they are linked with particular cooking and dining practices.

---

[41] Manning 1985: 108–23.   [42] Cool 2000a: 52.

[43] Painter 2001: 69, fig. 7; Painter 1977a: 30–32.

[44] Padley and Winterbottom in McCarthy 1991(fascicule 3): 205 nos. 783–4.

[45] Carlisle – Padley in McCarthy 1991: fascicule 2, 133 no. 333; Kelvedon – Rodwell 1988: 76 no. 81, fig. 59; Scole – Rogerson 1977: 144 no. 14, fig. 61; Catterick – Mould in Wilson 2002a: 120 no. 45, fig. 290.

SOURCES OF HEAT

It is clear that the principal heat source throughout the Iron Age was the hearth, centrally positioned in the roundhouses. This form of architecture continued to be used well into Roman period in many areas.[46] Hearths were also used even when the architecture takes on a more traditionally Romanised form. In the late-first-century strip buildings at Leadenhall Court, London, for example, it is noticeable that most are supplied with hearths rather than ovens.[47] One reason for this may well have been the perceived danger of having ovens within timber buildings. This is graphically demonstrated at this site, where one building had been provided with an attached room that had an oven which eventually needed to be rebuilt because of destruction by fire.[48] The same fear of fire getting out of control was the impetus for the positioning of the bread ovens in forts. They are built into the backs of ramparts giving space for any fires to be brought under control before they spread.[49]

In some kitchens both hearths and ovens were present, sometimes with hearths at both ground level and on raised platforms. This would have provided a range of heat sources, and the possibility of a wide range of cooking practices.[50] Some of these ovens may have been fairly sophisticated as it has been suggested that a pottery pipe found at Gestingthorpe was part of some form of hood or chimney to remove fumes. Residues suggested olive oil, pork and wine had contributed to the condensates that had been trapped in its sooty linings.[51]

Kitchens where a range of heat sources have been recognised are often part of large houses which were clearly the residences of members of the upper classes; and it has to be questioned to what extent oven cooking would have been practised by all ranks of society. A wood-fired oven is very versatile, providing a range of temperatures as it cools down but it does require a considerable supply of fuel.[52] This was not necessarily cheap or easily available, especially in the towns, as a large part of the country had been deforested by the Roman period.[53] In Colchester, where many domestic buildings have been excavated, it has been noted that most of the ovens are early, possibly hinting of a move to the use of braziers.[54]

---

[46] E.g. Jarrett and Wrathmell 1981: 90 fig 43 – early second century.   [47] See fig. 17.2B.
[48] Milne and Wardle 1996: 40 fig. 41.   [49] Johnson 1983: 200–2.
[50] Colchester – Crummy 1984: 54; Crummy 1992: 101; Caerleon – Zienkiewicz 1993: 52–4.
[51] Evans (John) Elbeih, and Biek in Draper 1985: 99.   [52] Hartley 1954: 39–41.
[53] Dark and Dark 1997: 31.   [54] Crummy 1984: 25.

These would require less fuel but of course would be more limited in their range of products.

Hearths, however, can be very versatile cooking installations. We have already seen how they would be ideal for heating the contents of the cooking jars. With the aid of gridirons; pots can also be raised above the direct heat of the fire;[55] and food can also be baked using the process known to the Romans as *sub testu*. Here the item to be baked is placed on the hearth and a cover, previously heated, is placed over it. The whole ensemble is then buried in hot ash.[56] Its efficiency is demonstrated by the fact that the creation of a miniature oven inside a heat source has survived into the present. Hartley described it as hearthstone cooking, and David suggests a version of it for baking bread in an electric oven.[57] Special covers known as a *clibanus* or *testum* were manufactured in the Roman world. An increasing number have been identified from Britain,[58] but they are still rare – possibly because fragments are being misidentified as tile. Many of the large bowls could have been used in this way, and the flanges often noted on the sooted examples would have been particularly useful in manipulating the hot cover at the end of cooking.

The precise fuel used would probably depend on the type of installation and the area of the country. In addition to wood and charcoal, peat and coal were options in some parts of the country; the latter being exploited rapidly after the conquest and being found on a range of site types throughout the Roman period.[59]

Given the continued popularity of hearths, the virtual absence of firedogs in the Roman period is interesting. These were a feature of late Iron Age elite graves together with other evidence of the important role that feasting played during the funeral ceremonies, and presumably during the life of the deceased.[60] They do not appear to have had any practical use other than holding the logs of the fire together, as they do have any attachments for spit roasting.[61] They are occasionally found in elite burials of the immediate post-conquest period;[62] but thereafter they appear to disappear with the exception of the example from the later second-century deposit at Welshpool.[63]

[55] Manning 1985: 100.   [56] Cubberley *et al.* 1988.
[57] Hartley 1954: 47; David 1977: 303.
[58] Williams and Evans 1991; see also Evans in Wilson 2002b: 201; Compton, Evans, Sell and White in E. Evans 2000: 303–5.
[59] Dearne and Branigan 1995.   [60] Stead 1967: Table 1.
[61] Saunders 1978: 19–20.   [62] Foster in Niblett 1999: 150 no. 13, fig. 58.
[63] Boon 1961: 27 no. 7.

The differing trajectories of cauldrons and their suspension gear and fire dogs during the Roman period is quite informative. Possession of both showed that you could command access to scarce resources of material and craftsmanship. Both had been thought of as important parts of the burial rituals of the late pre-Roman elite in the south-east, sometimes as at Baldock and Standfordbury occurring together in the same grave.[64] The continued use of cauldrons, compared to the disappearance of firedogs, underlines the fact that the former were indeed special. They were part of the ritual life of the people. Firedogs, by contrast, would appear to be a fashion item. Perhaps it was the increased availability of iron that sealed their fate. Once anything ceases to be scarce, elites have a tendency to abandon it and to seek new items whose possession acts as a mark of distinction.[65]

FROM KITCHEN TO DINING ROOM

Throughout much of the Iron Age there do not appear to have been separate categories of cooking and tablewares. The differentiation starts to appear in the south-east in the century or so before the Roman invasion,[66] but it is not until the Roman period that it starts to be more widely seen.

A good place to start to explore what it was thought appropriate to eat and drink out of, is a group of graves of wealthy, native individuals buried in the later first to early second centuries with what appears to be a meal and its serving vessels. In some cases this is made explicit because bones clearly from joints of meat were also included. In one cremation burial at Winchester[67] dated towards the end of the first century, for example, bones from a young pig were found on a shale tray together with an iron knife and a spoon. Graves like this will be discussed in more detail in Chapter 17; here it is sufficient to note that they regularly contain place settings. These consist of a pottery cup and a shallow bowl, both of sizes suitable for each person to have an individual serving. Interestingly, though such graves frequently have place settings for four people, this only extends to the vessels. Other eating implements such as spoons or knives are either absent or present only as single items suggesting it was not seen as vital that everyone had their own. This contrasts with the picture derived from broadly contemporary hoards of silver plate. In that found in the House of the *Menander* at Pompeii, there were sufficient

---

[64] Stead and Rigby 1986: 55–60 nos. 6–8, Stead 1967: 55.
[65] Bourdieu 1986: 247.   [66] See pp. 155–7.   [67] Biddle 1967: 230–45.

spoons for each diner represented by the dishes and cups to have had their own.[68] The rarity of cutlery in these graves would suggest that food was normally eaten with the fingers and with the aid of bread to mop up the juices.

The emphasis on individual servings seen in these graves is supported by the distribution of graffiti cut into pottery vessels. Graffiti of all types occur on vessels including makers' names, indications of how much a vessel contained and occasionally what was in it. On cups, beakers and dishes, personal names indicating individual ownership are by far the dominant type.[69]

A number of studies have shown that the increase in the proportion of the classes of vessels associated with individual place settings (cup, dishes and bowls) in an assemblage and the decline in the proportion of jars can be seen as the defining feature of a Romanised assemblage.[70] The preference for individual settings was not uniform across the country. Detailed study of well-dated assemblages in the north of Britain has shown that in the second century there was a noticeable division between the rural sites which favoured jars, and the military and urban sites where the proportion of dishes and bowls was much higher. This division that can still be seen in the late fourth century, though by that time jar use has risen on other types of sites as well.[71] Something similar can be seen on a group of sites in the Midlands,[72] where the inhabitants of the rural sites are certainly using far more jars than dishes and bowls.

The lower amounts of tablewares on the rural sites would definitely imply that food was being served in a different way. There is always the temptation to suggest that the levels of tablewares on rural sites are depressed because many of them were being made in other materials such as wood that have not survived. There are, however, a considerable number of waterlogged assemblages where organic material survives, and it cannot be said that wooden or leather vessels are at all common in them. A jar-dominated assemblage probably implies that the common dining regime was communal, with everyone helping themselves from a single dish. As already noted, the standard cooking jar is not a very practical vessel to use for this. Wide-mouthed jars would have been more suitable; and it has been observed that the proportion of these in rural assemblages in South and West Yorkshire rises steadily from the late

---

[68] Painter 2001.   [69] Evans 1987: 201.
[70] Millett 1979: 37–9; Evans 1993; Evans in Booth *et al.* 2001: 368–74.
[71] Evans 1993: figs. 7 and 13.   [72] Evans in Booth *et al.* 2001: fig. 7.56.

second century.[73] As the author of that study has noted, pottery reports do not often distinguish between narrow-necked and wide-necked jars. Where this is done, it can be seen that wide-necked jars are generally at a very low level where the bowl – dish category remains high.[74] Exploring the incidence of wide-mouthed jars compared to that of dishes and bowls might well be a very fruitful way of exploring how people ate. As will be discussed in Chapter 16, the difference between eating from a communal pot and having one's own plate is quite a fundamental one.

[73] Leary in Brown *et al.* forthcoming.
[74] Evans in Booth *et al.* 2001: Table 7.31.

CHAPTER 7

The store cupboard

INTRODUCTION

In most kitchens there is a cupboard or shelf where the cook stores basic ingredients for which there is a regular need but which, for various reasons, do not have to be regularly brought in as fresh produce. Most modern British kitchens will have salt, sugar, cooking oil, and possibly a range of proprietary sauces such as tomato ketchup or brown sauce. This chapter looks at this category of food in the Romano-British kitchen.

SALT

Sodium is vital for life as without it cells become dehydrated. As sodium is continually lost through bodily functions such as sweating, it has to replaced by what we eat. People who mainly exist on a carnivorous diet can acquire the sodium they need from meat and blood. People who eat a diet with a higher proportion of plant food need to add salt (sodium chloride) to their diet.[1]

During the late Iron Age and Roman period, salt was needed in large quantities, both as a condiment and to preserve food. It was produced by evaporation. Many salterns were to be found in areas such as the Fenland, and the coasts of Essex, Kent and the southern counties. The manufacturing process involved trapping seawater, which has a salt content of about 3%, in shallow ponds and tanks. As the water gradually evaporated by the action of the sun and wind, a brine was produced. When the salt level had risen sufficiently so that it formed a supersaturated solution (at least 26%), the salt could be made to precipitate by heating the brine. It was placed in large vessels made of briquetage, a type of poorly fired handmade pottery. These were supported on stands and

---

[1] Kurlansky 2002: 9–10.

bonfires lit beneath them. The saltern sites tend to be recognised because of the large quantities of briquetage present. This was a seasonal activity, limited to the months when there was high sunlight, low rainfall and good winds.[2]

Salt could also be produced away from the coast at the brine springs of Cheshire and Worcestershire. These produced brine that was already supersaturated, so no preliminary evaporation was needed. A litre of seawater will yield 0.031 kg salt, whereas the same amount of brine from the Droitwich springs produces 0.294 kg.[3] Briquetage has been found in large quantities on these sites suggesting clay vessels were used, but the Cheshire industry also used lead evaporating pans.[4] Possibly salt would have been another source for the lead poisoning that is sometimes noted in skeletons.[5]

Both the coastal and the inland industries were already well established during the Iron Age, and the trade can traced via the briquetage known as Very Coarse Pottery (VCP) as the salt was clearly moved in the containers it was made in.[6] Even before Britain became part of the empire, salt was being produced in large quantities. The capacities of various brine settling tanks dated to the early first century AD at Droitwich have been calculated, and it is estimated that the smallest found would have produced 1.56 tonnes of salt at a time and the largest 4.17.[7] Seven of these tanks were excavated, and it is very likely that the complex contained more beyond the boundaries of the excavations. Excavated evidence of salt production at Middlewich belongs to the post-conquest period;[8] but given the place was known as *Salinae* in the Roman period,[9] one might suspect a similarly large production centre was already in place by the time the Army arrived in the area.

It is often asserted that salt was an Imperial monopoly, and that this may have meant that access to it was difficult for some parts of the population.[10] However, there is no evidence of how the industry was organised in Britain, and the pattern of widespread, dispersed production is at odds with the model of a commodity held under monopolistic control. It was also very cheap. The Vindolanda tablets appear to record a price of 12 asses for 85 pounds of salt whereas 60.5 pounds of bacon /lard cost 8 *denarii* and 2 *asses*.[11] There were 16 *asses* to the *denarius* so, pound

[2] Bradley 1975: 21 fig. 10; Gurney 1986: 141 fig. 89.   [3] Woodiwiss 1992: 4.
[4] Penney and Shotter 1996; Shotter 2005: 43–5.   [5] See p. 22.
[6] Morris 1994; Nevell 2005.   [7] Woodiwiss 1992: 13.
[8] Bestwick 1975: 67.   [9] Rivett and Smith 1979: 451.
[10] E.g. Jackson and Potter 1996: 688–9; Alcock 2001: 72.
[11] Bowman and Thomas 1996: 306–7.

for pound, bacon was approximately 15 times the price of salt. Again this argues against it being a source of revenue for the state. It is interesting to speculate whether the view of state control that has arisen was unconsciously adopted from the experience of British rule in India. There salt was a state monopoly, effectively policed, and this became an issue around which the Independence movement coalesced.[12]

Unlike the situation in the Iron Age, for much of the Roman period salt generally becomes invisible once it leaves the production sites. There are a few finds of briquetage from sites other than salterns, hinting that salt may occasionally have been transported in the evaporation vessel,[13] but this does not appear to have been usual. It has been suggested that the large storage jars in North Kent shelly ware which are ubiquitous on London sites of the later first and second centuries could have been salt containers, as the area they are coming from had many salterns.[14] Pottery jars would have been an ideal transport medium for salt as they would have kept the contents dry. A very common and widespread cooking ware made in Dorset (BB1) came from an area with many salterns.[15] Perhaps some of the common BB1 jars found all over the country started life as salt packaging. Even if they did not, the very obvious supply routes that they map[16] can be taken as a picture of how salt could have travelled from one end of the province to the other.

FISH SAUCE

Another source of salt in the diet was the condiment known as *garum*. This was a fish sauce made by alternating layers of oily fish, herbs and flavourings, and salt in a vat; and then leaving it in the sun until the contents had fermented and the sauce formed.[17] The end result was a liquid that could be variously called *garum, liquamen,* or *muria;* and a sediment called *allec*. The literary sources tend to use the names of the liquid indiscriminately, so if there was any real difference between them, this has now been lost. Whatever it was called, it was a very pungent seasoning. To modern eyes the large number of Roman recipes that call for it to be used, including sweet confections,[18] are startling. An appreciation of how it would have worked in cooking can be gained from considering how the sauce

[12] Kurlansky 2002: 334–53.   [13] Richardson in Miller *et al.* 1986: 131.2.
[14] Davies *et al.* 1994: 101–2; Miles 1975.   [15] Tyers 1996: 182–6; Farrar 1975.
[16] Allen and Fulford 1996.   [17] Curtis 1991: 6–15.
[18] Apicius. 4.ii.35   a dish of pears cooked in honey and raisin wine.

nahm pla functions in Thai cuisine, as this is made in the same way as *garum*,[19] and can be looked on as its modern equivalent. An authority on Thai cooking describes it thus:

Fish sauce is an unusual condiment: it smells and tastes extremely pungent, yet when combined with other ingredients it melds into the whole, supports other flavours and is unobtrusive.[20]

In the recipes he gives, the food for one individual per meal could require 1 to 2 tablespoons of *nahm pla* (15–30 ml). By chance we have from Vindolanda an account that notes 1.5 *sextarii* (0.8 litres) of *muria* was used in the commanding officer's household on 24 June in the period AD 97 to 103.[21] Given the Thai rate of use, that amount would have seasoned food for between 25 and 50 people. We don't know how many people would have eaten in the *praetorium* that day, but the lower end of the estimate is a possibility given the day was a festival. This document is also useful in that it shows fish sauce may not have been a universal ingredient; but rather something used in food for special days. There is no mention of it for the days on either side of the festival.

The principal source for the fish sauce coming to Britain was the Iberian peninsula.[22] It was shipped in a variety of well-recognised amphora forms which could contain both fish sauce and pickled fish (see fig. 3.1 no. 3).[23] These have been recognised in Iron Age contexts in southern Britain which pre-date the conquest,[24] generally on sites which show evidence of other elite imports from the Roman world. At Braughing, for example, as well as other amphora-borne commodities,[25] there were also glass vessels which are very uncommon before the conquest. It is sometimes suggested that the late Iron Age sites where this Roman material appears in quantity, may have been centres for Roman traders.[26] If that is correct, then the presence of fish-sauce amphorae could not be used as evidence that the local elite inhabitants were altering their cooking practices. The presence of such an amphora in a probable pyre debris deposit at the pre-conquest cemetery at King Harry Lane, Verulamium,[27] however, would seem to suggest that

---

[19] Thompson 2002: 154.   [20] Thompson 2002: 156.
[21] Bowman and Thomas 1994: 153 no. 190.
[22] Curtis 1991: 46–64; Martin-Kilcher 2003: 69–70, footnote 4.
[23] Peacock and Williams 1986: Classes 16–22.
[24] Peacock in Partridge 1981: Table VII; Williams and Peacock 1994: 32.
[25] Williams in Potter and Trow 1988: Table 13.   [26] Potter and Trow 1988: 158–9.
[27] Williams in Stead and Rigby 1989: Table 7 burial 206, fig. 128.

Table 7.1. *A comparison of dated amphora assemblages (+ means present but less than 0.5% of assemblage; − means absent).*

	Date	Oil (%)	Wine (%)	Fish (%)	Other (%)	Total (kg)
Kingsholm	Neronian	42	37	12	9	97.60
Exeter	c. 55–80	61	15	21	3	67.40
Wroxeter	c 57–79	57	19	21	3	88.31
London, Billingsgate	c. 70–150	69	23	7	1	115.8
Wanborough	Mid 1st – mid 2nd C	97	−	3	−	10.67
Carlisle	Late 1st – early 2nd C	100	−	−	−	39.60
Gloucester	2nd C	68	25	−	+	4.76
Wroxeter	2nd C	88	6	4	2	21.36
Bainesse	2nd C	98	2	−	−	34.43
Carlisle	2nd C	98	2	−	−	31.80
South Shields	2nd C	100	+	−	+	31.16
Lincoln	Mid 2nd – mid 3rd C	83	17	−	−	11.31
Alchester	Mid 2nd – mid 3rd C	100	.	−	−	16.03
London, NFW	c. AD 200 – 250	82	18	−	−	30.60
London, Shadwell	3rd C	73	27	−	−	8.07
Caister	3rd and 4th C	62	38	−	−	18.42
Newcastle upon Tyne	3rd and 4th C	82	18	−	−	31.34

such ingredients were reaching the native population, as there is nothing in the deposit to mark the deceased as different in any way from the rest of the community.

The evidence for the consumption of fish sauce and other pickled fish products becomes much more common after the conquest. Table 7.1 shows amphora assemblages derived from dated contexts on a number of civilian and military sites. Fragments from fish sauce amphorae form a sizeable proportion of the early military assemblages (Kingsholm, Exeter and Wroxeter). They are present in civilian urban assemblages but at a lower level (Wanborough, Gloucester and Wroxeter). It is noticeable that they are less regularly part of second century assemblages, and appear to be absent from later ones.

Properly quantified amphora data are still not common, but there is a considerable amount of data which can be examined from the point of view of presence/absence. Table 7.2 shows data such as this, also from dated contexts.

Table 7.2. *The presence (+) / absence (.) of amphora types in dated assemblages.*

Site	Date	Type	Oil	Wine	Fish	Other
Longthorpe	*c.* 45–60	Military	+	+	+	+
Nanstallon	55–80	Military	+	.	.	.
Castleford	71–86	Military	+	+	+	+
York	71–100	Military	+	+	+	+
Segontium	Late 1st – early 2nd C	Military	+	+	+	+
Canterbury	50–80	Urban	+	+	.	.
London	75–90	Urban	+	+	+	.
Dorchester	Late 1st – early 2nd C	Urban	+	+	+	+
Cirencester	Early – mid 2nd C	Urban	+	+	+	.
Chelmsford	Late 1st – mid 2nd C	Urban	+	.	.	.
Towcester	Late 1st – mid 2nd C	Small town	+	.	+	.
Castleford	*c.* 140–180	Vicus	+	+	+	+
Wilcote	2nd C	Roadside	+	+	.	.
Cramond	Later 2nd – early 3rd C	Military	+	.	.	.
Greta Bridge	Later 2nd – late 3rd C	Vicus	+	+	.	.

Again the pattern shows presence at both military and urban civilian sites up to the mid-second century, and thereafter an absence. This absence is a curious one as the Iberian fish-products industry continued to export its products in quantity to other northern provinces into the third century, and in declining quantities it is still recorded in the fourth century.[28] It is always possible that the later ones are being overlooked in amphora assemblages; but the evidence currently suggests that Iberian fish sauce was not being used in either military or civilian contexts by the later second century. It is possible that fish sauce continued to be used, but came from different areas. Brittany, for example, has extensive installations that have been linked to its production in the second and third centuries.[29] There is also some evidence that it was being produced in Britain itself. Deposits of local fish bones plausibly interpreted as the debris from *garum* production have been recovered from a third-century context on the waterfront in London and from an undated deposit in York.[30] Large quantities of sand eels from late Roman waterfront contexts at Lincoln might also have been associated with *garum*

[28] Curtis 1991: 59; Martin-Kilcher 2003: 77–8.   [29] Sanquer and Galliou 1972.
[30] Bateman and Locker 1982; Jones in O'Connor 1988: 126–30.

production[31] Unfortunately these northern industries are not associated with distinctive, durable packaging and so their products cannot be traced on consumer sites.

It is noticeable that fragments from fish sauce amphorae tend to be restricted to military and urban sites. Whether this pattern can be used to suggest that this ingredient did not find favour with the rural population is open to question. As can be seen from Table 3.2, even the smaller of these amphorae contain between 14 and 18 litres. Given the Thai rate of use this is far more than even a large household would have had need of. Decanting into smaller containers must have been standard. A shopping list dated to AD 85–92 found at Vindolanda, for example, requests eight *sextarii* of *muria*,[32] approximately a quarter of one of the smaller amphorae.

Overall, the picture we have of fish sauce in Britain is that its use was far from universal. Even in an elite household like that of Cerialis at Vindolanda, it may have been mainly used on high days and holidays. Urban populations developed a taste for it but not necessarily rural ones; and there is every indication that its use declined by the late second century. Its use in late Roman Britain seems rare.

OLIVE OIL

In the Roman world olive oil was used not just as a cooking ingredient. It was also a vital part of the bathing regime, and was used as the base for perfumes and as fuel for lamps. Fragments of the very distinctive large spherical Spanish olive oil amphorae (see Fig. 3.1 no. 1) start to appear in south-central and south-eastern England, and very occasionally further north, up to fifty years prior to the conquest.[33] In the absence of bath-houses and the appropriate types of lamps in late Iron Age Britain, it may be assumed that it was imported for culinary purposes. This suggests that that in some sectors of native society, cooking practices were changing prior to the conquest. Where it is possible to track the introduction of the different amphora-borne commodities in the Iron Age, it appears that olive oil was adopted before fish sauce.[34]

After the conquest, olive oil amphora fragments are found widely and continue to be found into the third century (see Tables 7.1 and 7.2). At that point it becomes more difficult to establish the level of supply due to

---

[31] Dobney *et al.* 1995: 54. [32] Bowman and Thomas 1994: 278 no. 302.
[33] Williams and Peacock 1983: 266–7; Fitzpatrick 2003: 17, fig. 8.
[34] Peacock in Partridge 1981: Table VII.

changes in the Mediterranean olive oil industry. During the third century the Spanish olive producers, who had dominated the market, were overtaken by producers in north Africa. They marketed their oil in a different type of amphora (see fig. 3.1 no. 4) which, though it held about the same amount as the Spanish globular amphora, was considerably lighter. As can be seen from the figures in Table 3.2, the same volume of oil might be represented by either 10 kg of north African amphorae or 20 kg of Spanish amphorae. If the level of supply had been maintained, the quantities of north African fragments should have been about half that of the Spanish ones. This is not the pattern that is observed. At York 591 kg of Dressel 20 fragments have been found in comparison to only 13.4 kg of north African ones.[35] Even allowing for the fact that the period of when Spanish supply could be expected was slightly longer (York was founded *c.* AD 71); there is a serious mismatch between these figures. Spanish imports didn't cease entirely in the later Roman period but were transported in smaller amphorae.[36] At York these only add another kilogram to the late olive oil amphora assemblage. The pattern seems to be that though the import of olive oil continued, it was at a much lower level.

Various reasons for this have been advanced;[37] but whatever they were, it would have had an impact on cooking practice as much of the oil imported into Britain would have been used in the kitchen. Lamp use declined markedly after the first century in Britain and so the use of oil as a fuel would have been negligible by the second century;[38] and the only non-culinary use was as oil for the baths.

Given the pattern of supply, it could be hypothesised that the greatest penetration into different parts of society could be expected during the second century. Dressel 20 fragments are not uncommon on rural sites during that period; both in the southern lowland,[39] and in northern and western areas where the level of Romanised material culture is generally low.[40] Were these being used for their contents, or were they brought onto the sites empty as very large containers, in the manner that oil drums can get reused for other purposes?[41] It may be significant that glass bottles, common from the later first to the early to mid-third centuries, are often

[35] Williams in Perrin 1990: Table 22; Williams in Monaghan 1997: Table 175.
[36] Carreras Montfort and Williams 2003.
[37] Williams and Carreras 1995: 238–40.   [38] Eckardt 2002: 58.
[39] Williams in Rickett 1995: 98; Waugh in Going and Hunn 1999: 96; Williams in Green 1987: Mf3. C1 Table XXVI.
[40] Jones in Cowell and Philpott 2000: Table 4.3; Evans in Roberts *et al.* 2001: Table 8.
[41] Evans in Longley *et al.* 1998: 213.

the only type of glass vessel present on rural sites.[42] In the very rare circumstances where the contents of these has survived and been analysed, it has been olive oil.[43] Whether or not the use of olive oil spread down into small, marginal rural communities in the second century could only really be answered by a programme of residue analysis on types of pottery used in cooking. Olive oil is one of the foodstuffs that can be detected by lipid analysis. One of the relatively few published analyses which relates to Roman pottery detected oil and albumen in the burnt residue on an early to mid-second-century dish at Chelmsford, possibly indicative of an accident relating to the cooking of a *patina* made with oil and eggs.[44]

SPICES AND FLAVOURINGS

It is not unusual for the recipes in Apicius to call for several different herbs and spices, and to conclude with the injunction 'sprinkle with pepper and serve'. We know from many written sources that a considerable number of different spices were available at the heart of empire.[45] Judging the extent they were in use in Britain is difficult, as many will have been used in a ground form, and so will not be recovered. Another problem is that the routine environmental analysis of waterlogged deposits, which would provide the best information, is a relatively recent phenomenon. Until very recently, for example, the only evidence there was for the use of black pepper in the province consisted of a reference to the purchase of it to the value of 2 *denarii* in one of the Vindolanda writing tablets, and pepper grinders such as those from the late fourth-century Hoxne hoard.[46] Now the extensive environmental sampling undertaken as part of excavations in London in the 1990s has produced examples of mineralised black peppercorns from three sites,[47] So it is to be expected that the pattern presented here will be augmented considerably in the next few years as more environmental reports become available.

Table 7.3 has been prepared to show the presence of various spices in a selection of waterlogged deposits. Those from Castleford, Vindolanda, Ribchester and Leicester come from aggregated samples taken across the sites. The Bearsden sample is from a ditch believed to have received

[42] Cool and Baxter 1999: 84. [43] Stefani 2005: 89 no. 105.

[44] Evans, John in Going 1987: 91; see for example Apicius IV.ii.17. [45] Miller 1969.

[46] Bowman and Thomas 1994: 135 no. 184; Bland and Johns 1993: 25–6.

[47] Gray in Drummond-Murray *et al.* 2002: 246 Table 121. The example from Bath (Durrani 2004) was a misidentification (Peter Davenport *pers. com.*)

Table 7.3. *The presence (+) / absence (.) of various spices in waterlogged deposits.*

	Date	Type	Coriander	Poppy seed	Celery	Dill	Summer savory	Mustard	Fennel
Castleford	Late C1	Military	+	+	+	.	.	+	.
Caerleon	85–100	Military	+	.	.	+	.	.	.
Vindolanda	85–120	Military	+	+	+	+	.	+	.
Ribchester	70–150	Military	+	+	+	+	.	.	.
Bearsden	142–58	Military	+	+	.	.	.	.	.
Leicester	120–200	Urban	+	.	.	.	.	.	.
London	Late C2	Urban	+	+	+	+	.	.	+
York	Late C2–C3	Military	+	+	.	+	+	.	.
Dragonby	C2–C3	Rural	+	.	+	.	+	+	.
Bancroft	C3–C4	Villa	+	.	+	.	+	.	.
South Shields	Early C4	*Vicus*	+	.	+	.	.	.	.

the discharge from the bath-house latrines, and thus represents faecal remains. The London sample comes from a pit filled with kitchen waste; and those from Caerleon, York, Dragonby and South Shields are well fills. The Bancroft sample is particularly interesting as it is a chance accumulation reflecting what was growing in the villa gardens. Though all of the flavourings in the table could be grown in Britain, and are occasionally recorded in prehistoric contexts;[48] they appear to be additions to the diet particularly associated with the Roman period. Coriander is ubiquitous, and has been found in many other analyses from Roman sites. Interestingly, it is a very common ingredient in Apicius, occurring in 18% of the recipes. The next commonest spice in the table, poppy seed, does not occur in the recipes, but was recommended by ancient dieticians as an addition to bread.[49] A cautionary note has to be sounded about automatically assuming all poppy seeds recovered were for culinary use. Those from charred grain assemblages are likely to be weeds of cultivation;[50] but culinary or medicinal use is indicated by mineralised examples from cesspits such as one in the legionary fortress at Colchester.[51] Given the associations, it is likely that those noted in Table 7.3 were culinary as well.

An interesting feature of the table is that summer savory only appears in the later deposits, and is missing from the early military samples. This may be chance, but it also appears to be absent from other early military samples such as at Carlisle,[52] though it does occur in London in a late first-century context.[53] It is possible that it was a later addition to the range of ingredients. It was certainly in use in the Classical Roman kitchen as it occurs in 6% of the recipes in Apicius.

At present, judged against the wealth of spices and flavourings known to have been in use in Roman cuisine, the British evidence is meagre. Lovage for example, a very popular ingredient featuring in a third of the recipes in Apicius, is known only from a reference to it in a shopping list from Vindolanda.[54] The poverty of the British evidence is likely to change in the coming years as the results of more environmental reports are published. Comparing the list of herbs and spices reported so far from the environmental sampling at Vindolanda (see Table 7.3) with the list derived from the writing tablets is instructive, as they show there was a

---

[48] Willcox 1977: 273.   [49] Dioscurides *Materia Medica*: IV.64.
[50] Letts in Smith *et al.* 1997: 268.   [51] Murphy in Crummy 1992: 283.
[52] Goodwin and Huntley in McCarthy 1991: fascicule 1 54–60.
[53] Davis in Milne and Wardle 1996: Table 2.
[54] Bowman and Thomas 1994: 175 no. 204.

much wider range in use there than the interim environmental report so far hints at. The tablets mention anise, caraway, cumin, lovage, mustard seed, thyme and pepper,[55] and only mustard occurs in both the tablets and from the sampling. The environmental list derives from samples taken during the excavations of the 1970s and 1980s and nothing is yet known of what has been recovered during the more recent excavations. When this is finally published it will be fascinating to see how the environmental and written evidence compare.

SWEET THINGS

Honey was the principal sweetener of antiquity, but was also considered a potent drug by ancient medical authorities.[56] Given the bad reputation it now enjoys, it is ironic that the same doctors also considered sugar to be a beneficial medicine.[57] Sugar was a rare and exotic item, but honey was common with much discussion in the ancient literature over which varieties were best. Unfortunately, archaeologically honey is virtually invisible. It had no distinctive, durable packaging, and the hives for the bees would have been made of organic materials that do not survive. We know that at Vindolanda it was brought in large quantities as an account dated to the end of the first century refers to purchasing one or more *modii* of it (a *modius* was 8.6 litres).[58] An equally large quantity is recorded on a sherd from a storage jar found in a second-century pit at Southwark. This has a graffito recording that the contents were 24 *librae* of honey (*c.* 8.4 litres).[59] Two other tablets from Vindolanda mention it apparently in connection with medical supplies.[60] It is also possible that there is evidence of honey, in the form of a concentration of *salix* pollen, from a mid-second-century pit at the Castleford.[61] Other than that, we have little evidence of what must have been a widely available ingredient.

Another sweet ingredient was the syrup made from boiling down grape must.[62] These syrups were given different names (*defrutum, sapa* and *caroenum*) depending on the reduction required for each.[63] Such products were made in Spain and southern Gaul, and shipped in distinctive amphorae.[64] The dates of these overlap, with the Spanish ones dating

---

[55] Bowman and Thomas 1994: 135 no. 184, 175 no. 204; 2003: 40 no. 588, 44 no. 591.
[56] Scarborough 1995: 22 footnote 110.   [57] Discurides *Materia Medica* II. 104.
[58] Bowman and Thomas 1994: 157 no. 191.   [59] RIB II.8 no. 2503.3.
[60] Bowman and Thomas 2003: 44–7 nos. 591–2.
[61] Bastow in Abramson *et al.* 1999: 173.   [62] See p. 22.   [63] Sealey 1985: 63.
[64] Peacock and Williams 1986: Classes 15 and 59.

from the first century BC to the late first century AD[65] whilst the Gallic form continued in use into at least the early second century. Later forms that might have transported the syrups have not been identified.

In Tables 7.1 and 7.2 the *defrutum* amphorae appear as part of the category 'other', as they only ever form a very small part of the amphorae assemblage. It is noticeable that *defrutum* is only represented in the first-century assemblages. In the second-century ones, the category is represented by amphorae that transported fruit. This chronological pattern is also noticeable elsewhere. At Southwark they regularly occur in the first-century assemblages, but are very rare in those of the early to mid-second century.[66] Therefore, though the Gallic sources appear to have continued to export syrups into the second century, the amphora evidence suggests they were not being imported in any quantity to Britain by then. There are some indications that the syrups may have continued to arrive but in different packaging. Olives were often preserved in these syrups and the amphorae transported both the preserved olives and syrups on their own. Though the evidence for the amphorae disappears in the first century, olives continue to be found up to the early fourth century implying a continuing supply, possibly transported in Spanish olive oil amphorae.[67] Given the decline in Spanish olive oil imports, it seems likely that these syrups would have disappeared from the British diet by the third century at the latest. They were always only a minor element of the diet for a small number of people.

[65] Carreras Montfort 2003: 88.
[66] Symonds in Drummond-Murray *et al.* 2002: Tables 44, 49, 54, 57, 61, 65.
[67] Sealey and Tyers 1989: 68–9, see also p. 123.

CHAPTER 8

Staples

INTRODUCTION

A staple food may be defined as something that forms the most important part, or a principal part, of the diet.[1] Judged by the literary sources, cereal foods performed this role in antiquity. Cato specifies the quantity of wheat and bread suitable for a household, and relegates all other food-stuffs to the role of relishes. Vegetius, writing about supplying the army in the field, lists grain together with wine and salt, as the provisions whose shortages should be prevented at all times.[2] Considering the quantities of quernstones found, and the evidence of the charred grain deposits, it seems very likely that the inhabitants of Roman Britain viewed foods derived from grain in a similar way. This chapter explores what those foods might have been, and how they were prepared. It also attempts to explore how the consumption of different grains might have been regarded, as within the Roman world there was a hierarchy of esteem relating to this.

THE GRAINS THEMSELVES

Three different types of wheat are found in the charred grain assemblages of Roman Britain – emmer (*Triticium diococcum*), spelt (*Triticium spelta*) and bread wheat (*Triticium aestivum*). Emmer had been grown in Britain since the Neolithic period. Spelt appears to have been an introduction of the first millennium BC, and was well established by the late Iron Age. Bread wheat, which is less disease resistant, occurs sporadically from the Neolithic period onwards, but it is not until the post-Roman period that it appears to have become a popular crop.[3] The different types needed

---

[1] Davidson 1999: 751.   [2] Cato 56, 58; Vegetius III.3.   [3] Jones 1981: 106–7.

different threshing regimes, and had different cooking properties which were well known to the cookery writers of antiquity.

Emmer and spelt are glume wheats. When threshed the head of the wheat breaks up into separate spikelets where the grain is still enclosed in the glume surrounding it. The spikelets have to be broken up to release the grain. This can be done by heating the spikelets (parching), and then pounding them to release the grain. Bread wheat by contrast is free threshing, with the grain being released from the glume in the initial stage.[4] The glume wheats can also be prepared simply by pounding, though it is harder work.[5] This method might have been preferred if the aim was to make leavened bread, as too intense a heat during parching could destroy the enzymes in the grain necessary if the bread is to rise. Glume wheats can be transported to the point of consumption in separated spikelet form, and the final preparation prior to milling can be done there. The presence of carbonised or mineralised glumes, even when no grains are present, can be a useful indication of the consumption of these types of wheat. At Leicester their consistent presence in an extensive sampling programme showed that spelt wheat was being prepared and consumed in the town throughout the Roman period.[6] Given that bread wheat does not have to be parched, it might be suspected that it is under-represented in the carbonised deposits, and it may have been more widely used than they indicate.

These wheats produce flours of different qualities. To make leavened bread, it is necessary for the grain to contain the insoluble proteins glutenin, gliadin and aglobulin that form gluten when wetted. As one old baking manual describes, the gluten may be thought of as the little balloons that hold the gas formed by yeast, and provide the open texture of leavened bread.[7] Spelt and bread wheat contain these proteins, and will produce a well-risen loaf. Emmer, by contrast, produces bread that does not rise so well. It has a heavy texture, but it does produce better porridge than spelt and bread wheat.[8] Emmer is also better for making cakes, and Cato seems to appreciate this as his recipe for fried honey-soaked dough-nuts (*globi)* calls for emmer.[9] An account from Vindolanda also itemises a variety of wheats by different names, suggesting that the cooks in the *praetorium* appreciated the difference and had need of a variety.[10]

[4] Hillman 1981: fig. 4.   [5] Braun 1995: 36.
[6] Monkton in Connor and Buckley 1999: 353.   [7] Banfield 1937: 7.
[8] Dickson and Dickson 2000: 120.   [9] Cato 79.
[10] Bowman and Thomas 1994: 157 no. 191; Pearce 2002: 934, Table 2.

The other principal grain recovered is barley. This is a free-threshing grain which lacks sufficient of the proteins to form gluten to produce a good loaf. Bread made from it is flat, grey and goes dry quickly, though it can be mixed with wheat to form a better quality loaf.[11] It makes good griddle cakes, and it may have been such a food that formed the last meal of Lindow man.[12] Other grains such as oats and rye are recovered, but they tend to form small parts of the assemblages. It is often open to question as to whether they had been deliberately grown, or were just present as weeds.

CLEANING AND MILLING

Although grain could be stored over a long period, flour could not. Wholemeal flour retains traces of endosperm, so there would have been a need to grind flour on a regular basis.[13] For this reason many consumers would have acquired grain rather than flour or meal, and would have ground it themselves. Cleaning the grain crop was a chore shared by both the producers and the consumers. Depending on whether the grain was free-threshing or not, the crop may have been shipped as clean grain or as spikelets. Certain weed and chaff elements could be removed by sieving, but others had to be picked out by hand as they were of similar size to the grain itself. A vivid example of the consumer having to do this was revealed in a granary at the fort at South Shields, which had been burnt in the late third or early fourth century. The grain being stored was dehusked spelt and bread wheat in approximately equal quantities. The samples from close to the entrance consistently had more glume bases and weed seeds in them than those in the body of the granary. This was plausibly interpreted as soldiers collecting their allocations, and then cleaning them in the better light by the entrance before going back to their barracks. It was noticed that the weed seeds were dominated by corncockle, something that is poisonous to both men and animals, and which needs to be carefully picked out.[14]

In the majority of cases converting the grain to flour or meal would have been done in the home with hand querns. The normal quern of the later Iron Age was the beehive quern. This had a domed upper stone with a narrow feed pipe through which a spindle passed. The spindle lodged

[11] David 1977: 62.   [12] Holden 1995: 79.   [13] Banfield 1937: 19–20.
[14] van der Veen in Bidwell and Speak 1994: 243–58.

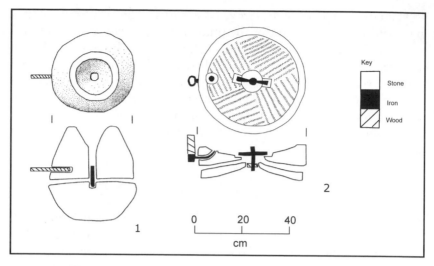

Figure 8.1. Beehive (no. 1) and lava (no. 2) querns. Scale 1 : 16.

in a socket in the lower stone. Handles were normally inserted into a socket in the side, and were inclined or horizontal (Fig. 8.1 no. 1). These were heavy stones. The grain was fed through the feed pipe on the upper stone, and wear patterns suggest they may have been used in an oscillating, back and forth motion.[15] The grain was mashed between the upper and lower stone with a tearing, crushing action.

When the army arrived in Britain it brought with it a much more effective type of hand quern made of lava from the Mayen area of Germany (Fig. 8.1 no. 2) These were disc-shaped with an inclined grinding face between upper and lower stones. The upper stone was held in position by means of a rynd across the base of the feed pipe, through which the spindle passed. This allowed the space between the two faces to be adjusted and ensured that in the area at the edge (the skirt), the two stones fitted together well, important if the meal was to be finely ground.[16] Being made of lava, these stones were much lighter than the beehive querns, and the ability to adjust the space between the stones meant the grain was sheared and ground between the dressed faces rather than crushed. The handle was vertical which would have facilitated a rotary action, though some wear patterns suggest they, too, may sometimes have

[15] Wright in Wilson 2002a: 268.   [16] Welfare in Bidwell 1985: 157.

been used with a back and forth motion.[17] The new, improved, flatter designs were adopted by quarries in Britain, and examples made in British rock types such as the Millstone Grit from the Pennines were appearing by late in the first century AD.[18] These Romano-British flat querns did not signal the automatic decline of the beehive quern. The industry producing the examples made in the very distinctive Hertfordshire Puddingstone seems primarily to be a Romano-British one,[19] and the bases of four beehive querns were found *in situ* in a probably third-century building at the Dalton Parlours villa, showing they were still in use then.[20]

Grinding grain by hand mill is hard work. Ethnographic observation in Algeria has shown that a skilled housewife could produce 3 kg of flour in an hour and a half; often having to regrind the coarsest fraction. This figure is broadly comparable with the rate of 1.8 kg per hour noted in India.[21] In Algeria it was considered to be a long and arduous task which was painful on the shoulders. By good fortune, an account on a writing tablet from Carlisle has survived which provides the allowance of wheat and barley given out to a cavalry unit. Taking these figures we can calculate how long it would have taken to prepare the grain for eating.[22] The allowances appear to cover three-day rations and, as is normal in antiquity, they are expressed by volume. Each *turma* was issued with wheat at a rate of 5 or 6 *modii* a day. The 500-strong unit was divided into 16 *turmae* or squadrons, and depending whether or not the officers rations were included, this would have been for about 30 – 33 men. A litre of sifted spelt flour weighs *c.* 0.45 kg. Working at a conversion of 0.55 litres to one *sextarius*,[23] a *modius* would be *c.* 4 kg. Assuming that the people doing the grinding were as skilled as the Algerian housewives, converting the wheat to flour would have occupied each *turma* 10 to 12 person-hours a day.

Given the time and discomfort involved in hand grinding, it is not surprising that alternatives were sought. A hand quern cannot easily be operated if it is more than c. 0.5 m in diameter, but stones with diameters of 0.6 m or more are found in quernstone assemblages. These were for powered mills, either driven by water, man or animal power. This was an innovation associated with the Roman period, and the development of the flatter rotary querns. Their use seems to be concentrated in urban and

---

[17] Wright in Wilson 2002a: 270.   [18] Welfare in Bidwell 1985: 157.
[19] King 1987: 70.   [20] Tindall in Wrathmell and Nicholson 1990: 43.
[21] Jansen 2001: 209; Alcock 2001: 25.   [22] Tomlin 1998: 36 no. 1.
[23] RIB II.2 no. 2415.56.

military centres and in villas; they do not seem to be much in evidence in the smaller rural settlements.[24] Very occasionally parts of the hour-glass-shaped stones that would have been used in donkey mills are found. Two, made from lava derived from central France, have long been known from London and Corfe Mullen. A third, not made of lava, has recently come to light from the fort at Clyro.[25] Donkey mills such as these were used in commercial bakeries in the Mediterranean area.[26] It is probably of significance that the latest find of such a stone from Britain was found at a military site. As the calculations in the previous paragraph show, considerable amounts of time would have been taken up grinding corn for soldiers' rations, and some form of mechanisation would have been attractive when the troops were in their base camps. Powered mills in other military settings are certainly suggested by large flat stones over 0.6 m with ownership marks specifying which century they belonged to.[27]

Some people would have been lucky enough to be able to buy meal and flour, but for most households milling would have been a lengthy, arduous chore. The lower stones of hand querns have to be securely bedded so that they do not move when the upper stone is rotated. Where quernstones have remained *in situ*, they are bedded into the floor.[28] Naturally a bias to querns in this situation is to be expected from archaeological evidence; but this position might be expected to have been the norm, rather than popular museum reconstructions which have the querns placed at a convenient waist-height on a wooden surface. Both ethnographic and experimental observations point to the bedding of the querns being most effective at ground level,[29] with the operator consequently having to sit or squat alongside. In the light of this, the fact that at the Poundbury cemetery nearly three times more women than men showed modifications to their skeleton associated with squatting, is probably a very good indicator that grinding corn was woman's work.

BREAD OR PORRIDGE?

Depending on the type of quern used, the amount of regrinding, and the amount of sieving, it would have been possible to produce different grades

---

[24] Wright in Wilson 2002a: 280.   [25] Williams-Thorpe and Thorpe 1988: Anon 2002: fig. 17.
[26] E.g. those from Pompeii – Stefani 2005: 67.
[27] RIB II.4 nos. 2449.2, 2449.19, possibly also 2449.3 and 2449.18.
[28] Frere 1972: 78; Tindall in Wrathmell and Nicolson 1990: 43; Price 2000: 99.
[29] See note 21.

of meal as well as finer flour. The traditional early Roman staple had been *puls*, a porridge made with emmer, but from the second century BC this had increasingly been augmented by bread.[30] Given the regular presence of spelt in the carbonised grain deposits, it seems likely that bread was preferred in Britain during the Roman period as well. Apart from the evidence of the digested remains of wholemeal wheat bread in what appears to be an outflow of a mid-second-century latrine at the fort at Bearsden,[31] there is little direct evidence of this, though the information derived from skeletons is suggestive. The wear on the teeth is indicative of a diet where it was necessary to chew most of the food.[32] The teeth often show heavy wear, and there is a lack of oclusal caries consistent with the eating of relatively coarse-grained wholemeal bread. The wear on the teeth comes about not just because of the glassy phytoliths from the grain casing, but also from tiny fragments of stone from the querns. The teeth are in a constant state of eruption to cope with this,[33] and the wear prevents oclusal caries developing. A diet where cereal is consumed in a soft form like porridge does not result in this type of wear.

With wholemeal stone-ground flour, the leaven for the bread would form naturally if it was mixed with water and left. Wild yeasts in the atmosphere combine with the sugars released from the grain to produce a fermentation. If a wooden bread trough was used for the mixing, such as the one found in London,[34] it would be likely to have been impregnated with the yeasts aiding fermentation.[35] Once the initial fermentation had happened, more flour could be added, the dough left to rise again, and then more flour and salt added to build up the final dough which was baked after a final rising. Keeping back a piece of the original dough would enable the baker to start the next batch of bread without undertaking the initial fermentation. This, at least, is the theory: though in practice the procedure may not be found to be quite so simple, as Jeffrey Steingarten's entertaining account shows. Baking bread from scratch in this way is a long-drawn-out affair; five to seven days from initial mixing to finished loaf.[36] The result would depend on the skill of the baker, and

[30] Tchernia 1986: 59; Braun 1995: 37.
[31] Knights *et al.* 1983: 143.
[32] Farwell and Molleson 1993: 182–3.
[33] Roberts and Manchester 1995: 53.
[34] Unpublished. High Street Londinium exhibition 2001, Museum of London.
[35] Hartley 1954: 501.
[36] See Steingarten 1998: 15–27; and David 1977: 296 for a less enthusiastic view.

the degree to which bran had been sifted out of the flour, as bran tends to make bread heavy.

In addition to this type of sourdough bread, yeast may have been derived from brewing beer. Pliny the Elder[37] noted that in Spain and Gaul they used the froth from brewing beer as a leaven, and it resulted in a lighter bread. Given the evidence for beer drinking and making in Roman Britain, it seems probable the British bakers would have been familiar with this more reliable source of leaven. Seventeenth- and eighteenth-century authors noted that the important thing to do when using ale barm was to wash it well by mixing it with water, allowing it to stand and then pouring off the water. This was to remove the bitterness, but they were dealing with hopped bitter beer as opposed to the unhopped ale of the Roman period, so it is not clear whether a similar cleansing period would be needed. If not, then the production of bread would have been much quicker than the process involved with sourdough bread, as Hannah Glass, writing in the mid-eighteenth century, implies ale balm will raise a loaf in two hours.[38]

Not all bread would have been baked in ovens, given the cost implications of the fuel.[39] One form of specialised vessel for baking bread may have been the shallow dishes in Pompeian-Red ware. The name reflects the colour of the vessels, rather than implying that they all originated at Pompeii.[40] These have a red slip internally which extends over the rim and part way down the exterior; this may have served as a non-stick coating. They are regularly found sooted as if they have been on an open hearth,[41] and at Pompeii several have been found with shallow loaves still in them.[42] The dishes come with matching lids which would have covered the contents whilst on the fire. This was a first to early second-century fashion, and the ware tends to be restricted to military sites and major urban centres, suggesting it was a cooking method restricted to a small part of the non-British community. However, there is an intriguing presence of these dishes and lids in pre-conquest contexts at Sheepen, an elite tribal centre close to Colchester.[43] This suggests that as well as ingredients such as oil and wine, cooking practices, and possibly cooks themselves, may have been imported.

---

[37] Pliny, 18.68.   [38] David 1977: 89–99.
[39] See p. 51.   [40] Tyers 1996: 156–9.
[41] Davies *et al.* 1994: 131.   [42] Green 1979: 130.
[43] Hawkes and Hull 1947: 221 Form 17A; Peacock 1977: 158.

WHITE BREAD, BROWN BREAD AND BARLEY CAKES

In societies with a differentiated cuisine, the form in which the staple food is taken often reflects the hierarchy inherent in a class system; and the poorer classes may well strive to emulate the elite. In a society whose staple is bread, the whiteness of the bread is often a matter of concern. White bread needs flour which has been carefully prepared, and sifted to remove as much of the bran as possible. There is much waste involved in preparing a flour like this; and also a great deal of effort. It fulfils all the requirements of being an item for, literally, conspicuous consumption. The rich eat white bread; the masses brown, and aspire to white even though brown bread is a far more nutritious food. The bran, that is carefully sifted out to make white flour, contains not only fibre but also many important fats, minerals and vitamins. The Roman medical writers clearly appreciated this, and recommended bread made from wholemeal flour, an appreciation that was not to be revived until the nineteenth century.[44]

Many different breads are known from the ancient literary sources, and discussions of them clearly consider not just their nutritional value, but also the esteem they are held in.[45] It seems very likely that the differences between white and brown bread with regard to social status would have been appreciated in Roman Britain; but from our current evidence it is difficult to explore this. Skeletal evidence would be useful if the wear state of teeth and their caries rate was compared to the perceived status of the individual as indicated by their grave goods and the nature of the burial. Do people in elite graves show evidence that they might have been eating white bread made with more refined flours? Unfortunately the records of individual skeletons as currently published are rarely detailed enough for this to be possible; but it might be an area to explore in the future.

One area that can be explored is the differences between those who ate wheat bread and those who ate barley bannocks. To Roman eyes wheat ruled supreme; barley was something you fed horses, or used as a punishment ration in the army.[46] In the north of Britain, though, barley appears to have been the preferred grain in civilian contexts;[47] whereas in civilian contexts in the south and Midlands, spelt wheat predominated.[48] There is

[44] White 1995: footnote 7; David 1977: 49. [45] Garnsey 1999: 121; Flemming 2000: 480.
[46] Braun 1995: 33–4; Garnsey 1999: 119–20. [47] Huntley in Wilson 2002a: 443–5.
[48] E.g. Murphy in Leach 1982: 288; Murphy in Crummy 1992: 281; Monkton in Connor and Buckley 1999: 353; Gray in Drummond-Murray *et al.* 2002: 245–6.

not necessarily any ecological reason for this; spelt is a hardy crop resistant to the cold as well as to pests.[49] Barley will not make good bread but it does make good griddle cakes, which are much easier to make and bake than wheat bread. Mixed to either a dough or a batter with skim milk, they can rapidly be cooked on a bake stone on the hearth.[50] There is an obvious visual difference between such griddle cakes and a raised loaf, even if the latter has not risen very much. It would have been obvious to any visitors to the north that the natives were eating a different food and one that, to some, was not thought fit for human consumption. One wonders if it gave rise to similar disdainful sentiments as Dr Johnson's celebrated definition of oats as 'A grain, which in England is generally given to horses, but in Scotland appears to support the people'.

There is a certain amount of evidence that even if this was the initial reaction, barley was preferred as a staple by some elements of the military. In some forts wheat was clearly preferred,[51] but in others barley dominates. In the case of Ribchester this may indicate nothing more than the fact it was a cavalry fort,[52] and large quantities of barley were needed for the horses. Elsewhere barley occurs stored in large quantities where the garrison was an infantry unit, as at Birdoswald.[53] Infantry units would have needed animal feed for officers' mounts, but the quantities do suggest that it may well have been for human consumption. Samples dominated by barley have been recovered from the forts at Newcastle upon Tyne and Catterick[54] at times when the units in the garrison may have been mixed infantry and cavalry. Though these may be reflecting animal feed, it was specifically noted that the grain from Catterick was a fully processed, cleaned crop, and it was doubted that this degree of care would have been exercised if it had been for animal consumption.

Whether the adoption of barley as a staple by certain units was just a case of adopting local food is open to question. It may be that their preference for barley bannocks was connected with the traditional cuisine of the area the unit was raised in. There is good evidence that at Catterick the garrison may have recently arrived from the Danubian territories.[55] At Birdoswald the unit had originally come from the same area. Though it had been long stationed in Britain, there is some evidence that it had kept

---

[49] Jones 1981: 106. [50] David 1977: 535–6.
[51] Knights *et al.* 1983: 143; Nye in Casey *et al.* 1993: 83; van der Veen in Bidwell and Speak 1994: 249.
[52] Huntley and Hillam in Buxton and Howard-Davis 2000: 351.
[53] Huntley in Wilmott 1997: 141–4.
[54] Huntley and Daniell in Snape and Bidwell 2002: 239; Huntley in Wilson 2002a: 439.
[55] Wilson 2002a: 452.

some contacts with its homelands.[56] It should not automatically be assumed that soldiers from such a unit would necessarily have shared the cultural prejudices of a unit raised in Italy.

There is a certain amount of evidence that wheat bread may have been seen as something to adopt in emulation of Roman ways by some elements in native society. On two comparable rural sites in West Yorkshire there were noticeably different wheat to barley ratios. The one with a high wheat to barley ratio was the one that had more pottery finewares, amphora fragments and an imported lava quern.[57] The Dalton Parlours villa in the same county has also produced a high wheat to barley ratio.[58] There are thus grounds for thinking that in this area part of the Roman 'package' that was adopted by the native elite population could have included a change in the form of their staple food. This does not always appear to have been the case,[59] but it does suggest that examining the botanical remains from rural sites against a background of the evidence of the material culture found on them might be a fruitful avenue of research; and cast light on changing attitudes to food.

---

[56] Wilmott 1997: 407.
[57] Swillington Common and Parlington Hollins – Roberts *et al.* 2001: 158–62, 248.
[58] Murray in Wrathmell and Nicholson 1990: Table 27.
[59] See, for example, Longley *et al.* 1998: 243.

CHAPTER 9

Meat

INTRODUCTION

Domesticated animals can be kept for reasons other than to provide food. In addition to meat and milk, cattle (or more specifically oxen) were important beasts of burden; pulling carts and farm machinery. Sheep provide wool in addition to meat and milk; and it is only pigs that are solely raised for meat. Judging from the butchery marks seen on cattle and sheep bones, their role in providing meat was important. Nearly all the meat consumed in late Iron Age and Roman Britain came from cattle, sheep and pigs; and virtually all our information about this comes from the animal bone evidence. Using the animal bones to map consumption patterns is fraught with difficulties, some of which have been outlined in Chapter 2, but certain broad patterns do emerge; and it is clear that the meat eaten by different communities depended on spatial, chronological and social factors.

BEEF, LAMB OR PORK?

The study of animal bone from Romano-British sites only became standard practice in the 1970s; prior to that it was not unusual for them to be ignored and discarded.[1] As the number of such studies grew, it became apparent that the proportions of cattle, sheep and pigs present varied in a systematic way on different types of site. The proportions of cattle and pig bones were higher on the more Romanised sites (military establishments, major towns and villas), and sheep bones formed a larger proportion of the assemblages on the native sites, continuing a pattern that had been dominant in the later Iron Age.[2] The sort of differences may be seen in

---

[1] See for example Meddens in Ellis 2000: 316; Stallibrass in Wilson 2002a: 392.
[2] King 1978; 1999: 178–80.

Table 9.1. *A comparison of later first- to mid-second-century animal bone assemblages (NB: the Castleford fort assemblage is restricted to the later first century).*

Site	Type	Cattle (%)	Sheep (%)	Pig (%)	Total	Quantification method
Castleford	Fort	64	26	10	14155	NISP
Ribchester	Fort	63	25	11	2473	Zones
Castleford	Vicus	59	28	13	3648	NISP
Wroxeter	Urban	53	29	18	1548	NISP
Leicester	Urban	44	39	17	2039	Zones
Wilcote	Roadside rural	38	52	9	3116	Zones

Table 9.2. *The relationship between deadweight and meat yield with the possible implications for bone weights using an example from Colchester.*

	Cattle	Sheep	Pig
Average weight (kg)	363.00	35.00	79.00
Amount wasted (%)	50	45	25
Meat yield (kg)	181.50	19.25	59.25
Amount wasted (kg)	181.50	15.75	19.75
Colchester bone weight (kg)	30.70	4.26	4.69
Colchester bone weight (%)	77	11	12
Meat represented (kg)	30.70	5.21	14.07
Meat (%)	61	10	28

Table 9.1 where a number of assemblages of later first to mid-second-century date are shown. The rural site of Wilcote stands out as the only one where sheep are dominant. The urban sites, though interestingly not the military ones, stand apart with their higher proportion of pigs.

Tables such as this are useful for showing these systematic patterns, but it has to be remembered that the animal bones from different species, no matter how comparably quantified, are not directly equivalent in terms of meat yield. The different sizes of the animals, and the different amounts of waste they generate when butchered, have to be considered. Table 9.2 illustrates this. The first four rows show data derived from a nineteenth-century military manual providing advice to officers in charge of supply.

About half of the carcase of a cow and a sheep are discarded, but only a quarter of that of a pig. Rows three and four show the meat and waste yield. The next four rows explore the implications of this using a second- and third-century assemblage from a city-centre site in Colchester that had been quantified by weight.

It is freely admitted that extrapolating meat yield from bone weight in this way requires the making of some rather large assumptions, not the least of which is that the Romano-British population had the same attitude as a Victorian military officer to the parts of the animal that were edible. It does, however, highlight the fact that merely looking at the proportions of bones is unlikely to reflect the diet adequately. By weight of bone fragments sheep and pig meat look to form about the same amount of the diet at Colchester. Taking waste into consideration, nearly three times the amount of pork than of lamb may have been consumed. Such calculations have to be borne in mind when looking at animal bone assemblages with apparently very low proportions of pig bones. Even on those sites pork and its by-products may have been more commonly consumed than the figures suggest.

We know that eating pork and bacon was a distinctly Roman trait from both the literary sources and the bone assemblages of central Italy. These show a pattern that is dominated by pig with low cattle and sheep levels. The pattern of cattle and pork consumption that marks military and urban sites in Britain is thus not a 'Roman' one, but has much more in common with that of the northern Gaulish and German provinces. It has been plausibly argued by King that what we are seeing is a 'militarisation' rather than a 'Romanisation' of the diet.[3] He suggests that pork may have been thought of as being a high-status food, citing the higher proportion of pig bones in assemblages from legionary forts. Certainly there are some other indications from Britain that seem to support this.

Within the military domain there are several instances where pork consumption can be directly related to senior members of units. At Vindolanda a variety of pork products (pork fat, young pig and ham) are mentioned in the accounts relating to the *praetorium* and the house-hold of the commanding officer. The only other meat products mentioned are venison and a prodigious number of chicken and geese; and certainly the venison would have been an uncommon food.[4] At Caerleon

---

[3] King 1999: 189.
[4] Bowman and Thomas 1994: 153 nos. 190 and 191; 2003, 23 no. 581. See also p. 100.

a similar suite of food is associated with a senior officer's house. There, the replacement of the timber fortress with one built in stone *c.* AD 85–100, sealed a well in a large courtyard house. This had been backfilled with debris including kitchen refuse. Amongst the mammal bone, cattle was in the majority but the number of pig bones was high, and there was also a relatively high presence of game and domestic fowl.[5] In the third-century military cemetery at Brougham, where there was a wide range of animal offerings on the pyre, pork was conspicuous by its rarity. Where it did occur, it was associated with individuals who appeared to be amongst the highest social class buried there.[6]

In civilian contexts the bone evidence associated with the palace at Fishbourne is particularly striking. Pig appears to be the commonest meat animal during the occupation of the palace. The specialist who studied this group argued that because of the different size of the animals, beef would still have been the commonest meat.[7] In the light of the evidence presented in Table 9.2, this conclusion is open to question. Clearly pork was a common meat on the tables of what was one of the royal families of Roman Britain. Finally the evidence from a mid-second-century pit at Bishopsgate in London can be considered. There an animal bone assemblage high in pig bones, together with game and domestic fowl, was found with many pottery food preparation vessels and amphorae.[8] The bone assemblage has distinct similarities to that in the well in the officer's house at Caerleon. Many of the vessels were complete or near complete, and the suspicion has to be that this is an instance of structured deposition. If so, then the food offerings may well have been regarded as special fare.

On many rural sites pig bones remain a relatively small part of the assemblage throughout the period under consideration. Even when pork was regularly being eaten in towns, the rural settlements surrounding them often show much lower levels of consumption.[9] On rural sites with a long continuous history stretching through the late Iron Age to the late Roman period such as Dragonby, a change in the diet can be seen occurring during the Roman period, but it consists of a rise in cattle at the expense of sheep. Pig levels remain consistently low.[10] It is on sites where elements of the native elite were clearly adopting many other new

[5] Hamilton-Dyer in Zienkiewicz 1993: Table 2 well 2.
[6] Bond and Worley in Cool 2004b: 328.   [7] Grant in Cunliffe 1971: 378–9.
[8] Tyers 1984.   [9] Levitan in Down 1989: 260; Reilly in Smith *et al.* 1997: 273.
[10] Harman in May 1996: fig. 8.2.

ways that a taste for pork develops. At the Dalton Parlours villa, for example, pig levels rise from 5% in the contexts associated with the roundhouses to 18% in those associated with the villa.[11]

Even allowing for the fact that the bones may not be accurately mapping meat consumption because of the differing proportion of waste they represent, it does appear that pig meat was not much favoured by most native elements of society. The animal bone evidence is matched by the evidence that is starting to emerge from lipid analysis of pottery. A large programme of analysis of sherds from four Iron Age sites in southern England showed that lipids associated with pork were strikingly absent from them.[12] It is interesting to speculate why pigs were avoided, given that it is such a useful meat animal, fecund and quickly maturing. In a review of animal exploitation in Iron Age Wessex, it was suggested that it may have been for environmental reasons, due to the absence of suitable woodland for them to forage in.[13] Though the lack of this may have been a problem if there had been a desire to keep them in herds, there would have been no reason not to keep them in more confined conditions. The cottage pig, raised by poorer labourers in restricted space to provide both a meat source and some income, has often been a feature of both rural and urban societies.[14] The presence of neonate pig bones in towns such as Lincoln, Silchester and Dorchester[15] suggest that pigs were being bred in towns, presumably in confined conditions. The reasons for the low level of consumption in the Iron Age and the rural Romano-British population must surely lie more in the cultural than the environmental realm. Whether this lay in the area of religious taboo, as in the case of the Jewish and Muslim prohibition on the consumption of pork, or was because the pig was a special animal, only consumed on special days, can only be guessed at. In some cases it might be suspected that the latter was the reason as it is noticeable that pork joints are sometimes included as grave offerings, by communities that are not consuming much of the meat in normal life.[16]

---

[11] Berg in Wrathmell and Nicholson 1990: Tables 13 and 18.
[12] Copley *et al.* 2005: fig. 3.   [13] Maltby 1994: 9.
[14] Malcolmson and Mastoris 1998: 45–65 ; Luard 1986: 150.
[15] Dobney *et al.* 1995: 44; Hamilton-Dyer in Fulford *et al.* 1997: 134; Maltby in Woodward *et al.* 1993: 326.
[16] Maltby in Davies *et al.* 2002: 169.

TOUGH BUT TASTY?

What meat tastes like, and how tough it is, depends on many factors including how old the animal was, the breed it came from, what it lived on and how long it was hung for. Unfortunately archaeological evidence provides little useful information about most of this, though it can normally say how old the beast was.

It is clear that the supply of beef to Romano-British towns was well organised, and that there must have been specialist butchers and slaughtermen involved with this. The evidence comes from large dumps of primary butchers' waste with a high proportion of bones from skulls, shoulder blades and feet. At Lincoln in the later fourth century, sufficient of this sort of debris was available for it to be used as parts of the dumps constructed at the river waterfront when it was being consolidated and extended.[17] Elsewhere, large dumps have been found that seem to reflect the place where the slaughtering and butchery was taking place. Sometimes this was centrally located as at Dorchester and Cirencester, and sometimes it lay just beyond the walls as at Chichester.[18] These primary deposits are a good place to start examining the age of the beef regularly consumed.

Age is generally calculated using the eruption and wear on teeth, and the fusion of the epiphyses at the end of the long bones. This means an estimate of the age distribution can be gained up to the age of four years. After that the beast is mature, and it becomes difficult to know how old it is. A striking feature of the primary butchery waste deposits is that the majority of the beasts were mature, i.e. older than four years. Modern practice in Britain is for prime beef to come from steers aged eighteen to twenty-four months. At this point they are well grown, and the additional cost of feeding them until they are fully mature will not be balanced by the additional yield in meat. The age of the cattle being slaughtered in the Romano-British towns suggests that they had a working life, either to produce milk or to be beasts of burden, prior to being eaten. This would suggest that most beef eaten in the towns would probably have been rather tough, and would probably have needed prolonged cooking to make it tender. It is not surprising that cooking jars, ideal for long slow cooking, are so common.

---

[17] Dobney *et al.* 1995: 10.
[18] Maltby in Woodward *et al.* 1993: 317–21; Maltby in Holbrook 1998: 358–3; Levitan in Down 1989: 245–9.

In modern parlance, veal comes from calves less than six months old. This would have been a much more tender meat, but it is rare to get evidence of it in towns. This may in part be due to problems of survival as immature bones are less well calcified. At Dorchester it was noted that evidence for calves was disproportionately gathered from cesspits where the preservation was good, and it was suggested that calves may have been processed differently to the mature animals.[19] It is noticeable that in the extensive deposits of bones from Wroxeter thought to be secondary waste, (i.e. that from the butcher as he sells on to the customer), evidence of veal was rare despite being derived from pits where preservation was good.[20] There is also clear evidence for the presence of veal calves in urban environments at other periods.[21] So, though depositional conditions may have had some effect, they do not seem sufficient to explain the rarity of calves in towns. It seems reasonable to conclude that veal would have been only an occasional luxury in Romano-British towns.

On rural sites, by contrast, a wider range of ages is recorded. As these will have been the production sites, this is unsurprising; illness and fatalities could be expected, and not all the beasts will have been for human consumption. Occasionally though there is clear evidence for the consumption of veal, as at the roadside settlement at Asthall.[22] Elsewhere there is sometimes a slight amount of evidence for an annual cull of younger beasts.[23] There are thus hints in the evidence that though beef may not have been the preferred meat on rural sites, the quality may have been better there than in the towns.

Distinct breeds of domestic animal are a relatively recent innovation in Britain, associated with the various agricultural improvements of the eighteenth century. The nearest breed to the Celtic Shorthorn type, that was common in the late Iron Age and Romano-British period, is probably the Dexter. This was a product of selective breeding from Irish hill cattle in the eighteenth century. It is currently used as both a dairy cow and for beef production. Other modern breeds that may have some similarities with the Roman beasts are the Kerry and the Welsh Black, both marketed these days as beef cattle. If it is appropriate to extrapolate back from these breeds to Roman cattle, it may be noted that nowadays all these are thought to produce very good tasting meat, which attracts

[19] Maltby in Woodward *et al.* 1993: 320.   [20] Meddens in Ellis 2000: 322.
[21] O'Connor 1988: 86.   [22] Powell, Clark and Searjeantson in Booth 1997: 142.
[23] Harmen in May 1996: 155.

a premium price. So, providing it was cooked with care, the beef could well have been tasty.

Up to now the evidence of the sheep bones has been discussed as if it was unproblematic. The reality is that what is being counted as sheep in most bone reports, are actually bones that could come from sheep *or* goats, as it is difficult in faunal analysis to distinguish between the bones of the two. Where efforts to distinguish between them have been made, sheep are commoner than goats. It is generally considered that in the Iron Age goats were rarely exploited as meat, and the pattern remained fundamentally the same in the Roman period.[24]

Goats were certainly present amongst the herds of Roman Britain, as can be seen from the large numbers available for sacrifice at the temple at Uley.[25] There is also the evidence of the leather to consider. Properly tanned leather was one of the great technical innovations of the Roman period, and an increasing number of assemblages preserved in damp environments have been studied. From these, it is clear that goatskin was often preferred over other leathers for such things as tents.[26] It is possible that these skins were imported, or that they have been wrongly identified and the leather actually comes from particularly hairy sheep;[27] but as it stands, the evidence suggests that the beasts were present in some numbers. Other direct evidence of them comes from tiles. In tile yards, when the tiles were laid out to dry, it wasn't unusual for animals and humans to walk over them leaving an impression on the surface. Where these marks have been studied in detail, goats are sometimes found to be almost as common as sheep.[28]

There is some evidence that goat meat may have been preferred when it was young.[29] Certainly in urban sites such as Colchester, Dorchester and at Southwark, where an attempt has been made to distinguish between sheep and goats, the latter that are identified are overwhelmingly juveniles, of an age where kid would be an appropriate description.[30] Sheep meat by contrast was clearly eaten at all stages of development from suckling lamb to mature mutton. The taste of sheep meat changes and intensifies with the age of the beast. In Victorian times, when the taste of mature mutton was much appreciated, it was derived from animals of three to five years. Modern British tastes now favour lamb of less than one

[24] Maltby 1981: 159–60.
[25] Levitan in Woodward and Leach 1993: 258, 266. Further discussed on pp. 211–13.
[26] Van Driel Murray *et al.* 1993: 56–7.   [27] Van Driel Murray in Cool and Philo 1998: 334.
[28] Cram and Fulford 1979: 205.   [29] Levitan in Woodward and Leach 1993: 301.
[30] Luff 1993, 66; Maltby in Woodward *et al.* 1993: 321 Table 56; Ainsley in Drummond-Murray *et al.* 2002: 266.

year.[31] In many bone assemblages there is evidence that most of the sheep meat eaten was from animals less than two years old. This can be noted both in assemblages from large urban centres,[32] where the beasts will have been deliberately brought in for consumption, as well as at rural settlements, which might be thought of as production centres.[33] This pattern suggests the sheep flocks were being managed with a principal aim being to produce supplies of prime young meat. In most assemblages there is evidence of some animals old enough to be regarded as stronger tasting mutton, and the taste for this may be a feature the later Roman period. Half of the sheep bones in the third-century butchers' waste in the *macellum* at Wroxeter could be regarded as mutton,[34] whilst in a number of urban assemblages where a comparison can be made between the early and later Roman period, an increase in the proportion of older beasts can be noted.[35] Whether this marks a change in taste, as has happened in modern Britain, or whether it reflects an increase in the importance of wool production, and a change in herd management because of this, is an open question.

It has been observed that there was regional and chronological variation in the size of sheep in the Roman period, and this may reflect a mixture of the native small sheep and some introduced larger sheep breeds.[36] The taste of sheep meat across the country will thus not have been uniform, even if the age was comparable. One feature of the meat that may be noted is that it is likely to have been leaner than is normal currently. Modern breeds descended from the types of native sheep that would have dominated in the early first millennium, such as the Welsh Black Mountain and the Soay, are always noted as being a lean meat.

As is to be expected, pigs were generally slaughtered when they were about twelve to eighteen months old and provided prime meat. Given that pigs develop rapidly, the slaughter of a beast before this age is not a rational economic decision. There was a market for suckling pig; and where it is possible to relate this to a particular type of occupation, it is often found to be associated with high-status occupation, and there are

---

[31] Davidson 1999: 441, 525.
[32] Luff 1993: 70; Maltby in Woodward *et al.* 1993: 323–4; Gidney in Connor and Buckley 1999: fig. 164.
[33] Locker in Neal *et al.* 1990: Table 1; Hamshaw-Thomas and Bermingham in Hands 1993: 171; Stallibrass in Jackson and Potter 1996: 592; Powell and Clark in Booth *et al.* 2001: 402.
[34] Meddens in Ellis 2000: 325.
[35] Levitan in Down 1989: 251; Maltby in Woodward *et al.* 1993: 323–4; Dobney *et al.* 1995: 39.
[36] Maltby in Woodward *et al.* 1993: 324.

grounds for thinking it was regarded as a luxury delicacy. At Fishbourne the consumption of this type of meat went up markedly during the palace phase of occupation, compared with what had been consumed before. It is also present in the special deposit at Bishopsgate, London, where several unusual meats were present.[37]

CUTS OF MEAT AND PRESERVATION

One of the notable changes that marks the transition from the Iron Age to the Roman period can be seen in butchery practice. The Iron Age population used knives to prepare the carcase: Roman butchers used cleavers.[38] Cleavers allowed very intensive butchery to be carried out on cattle carcases, maximising the utilisation of the meat. It is clear that this change was not restricted to the military and urban population, but spread to the rural one as well, presumably because of the much greater availability of iron. By the later second century, for example, this technique was not only being used in a major urban centre such as Cirencester,[39] but also in much smaller settlements in the surrounding region.[40]

The fragmentation seen in the cattle bones in the butchers' waste in the *macellum* at Wroxeter provides a good example of the type of butchery that can be expected.[41] Scapulae were especially strongly represented, as well as the pelvis and ribs. Long bones show a considerable amount of fragmentation consistent with extracting the marrow. The type of butchery seen on the scapulae is typical of a pattern often seen on this bone. The central spine was chopped off, and there was trimming and chopping around the glenoid cavity (part of the joint with the forelimb). This sort of trimming would be appropriate if it was intended to salt the shoulder for preservation, as it would allow the brine to penetrate the muscle mass.[42] Shoulders often seem to have been preserved in some way. A frequently observed modification consists of a hole punched through the scapula which has been plausibly interpreted as allowing the shoulder to be hung up so it could be dried or smoked.[43] The scapulae with these holes can also show knife marks, interpreted as the result of cutting the

[37] Grant in Cunliffe 1971: 383; Tyers 1984: 374.   [38] Maltby 1985: 20.
[39] Maltby in Holbrook 1998: 358.
[40] Hanshawe-Thomas and Bermingham in Hands 1993: 174; Powell, Clarke and Searjeantson in Booth 1997: 146.
[41] Meddens in Ellis 2000: 322–4.   [42] Dobney *et al.* 1995: 27.
[43] O'Connor 1988: 83.

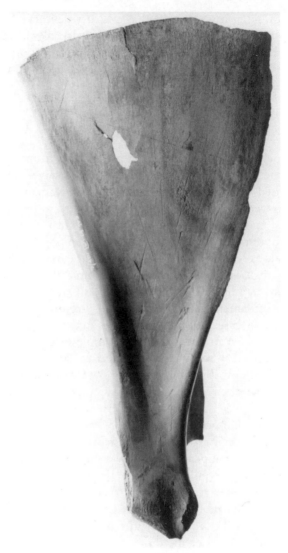

Figure 9.1. Cattle scapula from Castleford showing typical puncture and knife marks from carving suggesting the meat had been preserved on the bone. (Photo: P. Gwilliam, copyright Archaeological Services WYAS – Abramson *et al.* 1999.

dried meat off (fig. 9.1).[44] The scapulae with suspension holes have most frequently been recorded in military contexts,[45] but are also present on urban and rural sites.[46] Smoking and/or air drying would not be a particularly efficient way of preserving shoulders of beef,[47] salting would be better for long-term preservation. It may well be, therefore, that the shoulders were being smoked because the taste of smoked beef was enjoyed; rather than because there was a need to preserve fresh food for later consumption. A taste for tongue is also indicated by the heavy fragmentation of the mandibles.

Fragmentation of long bones is frequently observed, sometimes there are rubbish deposits that consist just of that sort of waste. Some specialists argue that they are the end product of a process that was intended primarily to produce broth or grease, as marrow can be extracted without such intense fragmentation.[48] The ancient world certainly esteemed marrow as a delicacy, and as a useful food in the armoury of a doctor. Dioscurides ranks the marrow of different animals and provides instructions as to how it should be prepared.[49] It seems likely that the opportunity to extract the marrow was taken, even if the fragments were later exploited to make glue. The idea that these bones were being used to make soup or broth in large quantities seems less likely in a Roman context. Making such stocks and broths is very much a phenomenon that arose during the nineteenth century with attempts to relieve the poor.[50]

Sheep and pigs also regularly show butchery marks, but for these smaller beasts it is a case of dividing the carcase up into manageable joints left on the bone, rather than the filleting regularly seen on the cattle carcases.

EATING HORSE – THE GREAT TABOO?

A notable feature of most bone reports is that though horse bones are identified, they very rarely show any signs of dismemberment or butchery. The horse is a large animal and if they had been eaten regularly, the distinctive chop marks of butchery should be present. When marks are seen on the bones, these tend to be knife cuts which can plausibly be

[44] Note 40; Berg in Abramson *et al.* 1999: 233.
[45] Morris in Ward 1988: 25; Hamilton-Dyer in Zienkiewicz 1993: 134; Izard in Wilmott 1997: 369.
[46] Maltby in Woodward *et al.* 1993: 319; Hanshawe-Thomas and Bermingham in Hands 1993: 174.
[47] Davidson 1999: 256, 728.   [48] See Berg in Abramson *et al.* 1999: 235 for discussion.
[49] Dioscurides II.95.   [50] Stokes 1996: 42.

associated with skinning.[51] It is sometimes asserted that horsemeat was being eaten, but the evidence in the form of butchery marks is often not presented in a way that can be independently assessed.[52] That horse was not a regular food item will not surprise a modern British reader, as to most of the population it is not an acceptable meat animal. Our aversion stems to a great degree from a thousand years or more of Christian prohibition, based on the perceived connection with paganism and barbarity. Many other religions also ban the practice.[53] Interestingly, one of the few cases in Roman Britain where the regular consumption of horsemeat can be convincingly shown occurs at a temple site.[54] Whether horse was, or was not, eaten may also have had a ritual or religious basis in Roman Britain. It has been suggested that the early Iron Age coin series from southern Britain show that the horse was viewed as a special animal; possibly associated with ideas of who had authority over the land.[55] If it was indeed looked on in this way, it is easy to see why horsemeat would not normally enter the food chain. Ideas of who owned land might have changed under Roman rule, but changing fundamental cultural beliefs about what could be eaten would not have been so easy.

[51] Berg in Abramson *et al.* 1999: 236.   [52] E.g. Bullock and Allen in Smith *et al.* 1997: 198.
[53] Gade 2000.   [54] Luff in Turner 1999: 206, fig. 132.
[55] Creighton 2000: 22–6.

CHAPTER 10

Dairy products

INTRODUCTION

Dairy products are a problem for archaeology because they leave little direct trace other than residues. Though we know from the literary sources that a range of cheeses and other milk products were consumed and enjoyed in the Mediterranean heartlands,[1] our knowledge of what was available in Britain is fairly minimal. Caesar referred to the tribes of the interior living on milk and meat, but as he also maintained they wore skins,[2] this seems more likely to belong to the realms of describing a generalised barbarian, than to the accurate reporting of eating practice. This chapter will outline what we do know about dairy products in Britain, but given the dearth of information it will be rather short. Given the results starting to emerge from residue analysis of prehistoric pottery,[3] it might be anticipated that a much longer one would be possible were Roman pottery ever to be analysed in a similar way.

MILK

The previous chapter has shown that milk-producing animals in the form of cattle, sheep and goats were present in some numbers in Roman Britain. To what extent they were exploited for milk is unknown. It is clear that in general cattle were not being managed primarily as dairy animals. In a dairy herd, most male calves are surplus to requirements so they are fattened and slaughtered as veal. This can often be seen in post-medieval animal bone assemblages,[4] but is not observable in the Roman ones. Cows could have been milked while suckling their young, though

---

[1] Alcock 2001: 57–60; Dalby 2000: 253.
[2] Caesar V.14. [3] Copley *et al.* 2005.
[4] O'Connor 1988: 86; Luff 1993: 57–8.

the yield would be lower. Modern Dexter cattle are promoted as both house cows, and suckler cows for raising both their own calf and another.[5]

The skeletal evidence would also argue against widespread consumption of cow's milk. Tuberculosis is a disease that is spread from cattle to humans largely by the drinking of infected milk. It is noticeable that in Britain it was a common disease by the seventeenth century,[6] corresponding with the post-medieval rise of dairy herds as seen in the animal bone assemblages. The disease causes changes in the bones, but these are only seen rarely in late Roman skeletons.[7] A possible 3 cases were seen at Poundbury out of a population of over 1,400 burials; while at the East Cemetery in London there were possibly 2 cases out of 550 individuals.[8] These are the individuals that lived long enough with the disease for the skeleton to be affected. Others could have died of it before that happened; but at present the evidence does not suggest tuberculosis was a major problem in late Roman Britain.

The goat is a very likely candidate for having been a dairy animal, given the evidence we have for their presence, and the fact that they did not seem to have been a favoured meat when adult. The kill-off pattern for sheep suggested that in the earlier Roman period they were being bred primarily for their meat. As there appears to be more evidence for mutton in the later Roman period, older beasts may have became more common, possibly with a greater exploitation of sheep milk.

BUTTER AND CHEESE

Raw milk is not necessarily either a pleasant or safe drink in societies without refrigeration. It is better to convert it to butter or cheese to ensure long-term storage. In both cases there is an initial ripening to allow bacteria to sour the milk. Butter is produced from cream that is churned to form an emulsion. The equipment for this is traditionally made of organic materials, thus generally leaving no archaeological trace. It is noticeable that recipes for baked goods in the ancient literary sources call for cheese where modern practice would be to use butter.[9] The same sources indicate butter was considered a salve rather than a foodstuff in the Mediterranean world.[10] How it was regarded in the north is unknown.

---

[5] http://www.dextercattle.co.uk/breed.shtml – last accessed August 2006.
[6] Roberts and Manchester 1995: 136–7.   [7] Stirland and Waldron 1990.
[8] Farwell and Mollesson 1993: 185; Conheeney in Barber and Bowsher 2000: 287.
[9] Leon 1943: 215–6.   [10] E.g. Columella V.12.5.

Given the paucity of evidence for butter, it is really very irritating that the one account or shopping list from Vindolanda that might mention it, is so badly damaged that the reading cannot be secure.[11]

Cheese is made from ripened milk, kept warm during the initial stages to allow the bacteria to grow. Curdling may be encouraged by the addition of an agent like rennet. This separates the curds from the whey. The precise type of cheese produced depends on how the curds are treated. In a soft cheese they may just be drained. In harder cheeses they will be broken up by cutting or shredding to aid drainage. They are then placed in a form that needs to be perforated, as whey will still be draining from the cheese. Once the cheese is stiff enough to be removed from the form, modern practice would be to salt it. It can then be matured, which often involves it being infected by particular organisms to produce a distinctive taste or smell.[12]

Archaeologically, it might be possible to recognise cheese making at two stages; the point where the milk is kept warm initially, and the point at which it is drained and/or formed. Given that the milk has to be heated, a pottery or metal vessel would be expected, rather than one made of wood. Similar durable materials might be used for the strainers and forms, though cloth would have been adequate for the first, and wood for the second. For the heating stage it is worth bearing in mind that mortaria may have been used. The regular observance of sooting on them would be consistent with a vessel kept on or near a hearth; and an irregular interior is also thought to be helpful in the development of curds.[13] What is needed for these vessels is a rigorous programme of wear and lipid analysis.

For the draining and pressing stage, there are pottery vessels that would have been suitable. The strainers are normally wide bowls with perforated bases. A cylindrical form with a perforated base which has internal concentric ridges is also found, and this is normally given the name of cheese press (fig. 10.1). Residue analysis of a strainer bowl at Poundbury did show evidence for milk products,[14] so it seems reasonable to suspect that they could have been used in cheese production.

Like mortaria, strainers and cheese presses are a post-conquest introduction; unlike mortaria they are rare. This can easily be seen by looking at studies that provide a form series, the presses and strainers if present

[11] Bowman and Thomas 1994: 175 no. 204.
[12] Davidson 1999: 159–61.   [13] Oswald 1943: 45–6.
[14] Evans and Card in Green 1987: Table LV; see also fig. 88.36.

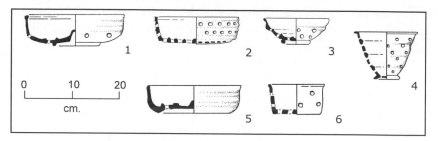

Figure 10.1. Military cheese presses and strainers from Longthorpe and Holt. (After Dannell and Wild 1987: fig. 41 (1, 3–5) and Grimes 1930: fig. 72 (2 and 6).) Scale 1 : 8.

tend to be placed in the miscellaneous category at the end.[15] There is evidence that strainers and presses were introduced by the military. One of the products of the kilns associated with the military works depot outside the fortress at Longthorpe were cheese presses, together with the occasional, rather unusual form of strainer bowl.[16] These kilns are dated to the 50s, and are a very early example of the army producing the vessels it had need of. Production of strainers and presses can also be seen at other military kiln sites such as at Holt, which served the fortress at Chester, and at York.[17] Not all military units seem to have felt the need for such vessels. At Colchester cheese presses tend to be a second-century phenomenon, and there are none associated with the fortress assemblages.[18] It is possible that we are looking at a particular style of cheese making, linked to particular units or regions. Consideration of the various ways British cheeses were traditionally drained, cut and formed shows that cheese makers could have quite precise requirements.[19] It is quite probable that those of antiquity had similar preferences.

The use of presses and strainers clearly moved beyond the military in the civilian population, both urban and rural. They were, for example, a product made in small numbers throughout the life of the South Yorkshire pottery industry.[20] Though some of these products were initially destined for a military market, the late Roman production was essentially destined for the local, native community. They continued to be in demand into the fourth century as cheese presses were made in Crambeck ware.[21]

[15] E.g. Monaghan 1997: 1022; Bell and Evans in Wilson 2002b: 396.
[16] Dannell in Dannell and Wild 1987: 151–3.
[17] Grimes 1930: 168 nos. 206–9; Monaghan 1997: 1022 nos. 4116, 4119, 4120.
[18] Bidwell and Croom in Symonds and Wade 1999: 476 type 199.   [19] Hartley 1954: 486–91.
[20] Buckland *et al.* 1980: 161.   [21] Monaghan 1997: 1022 no. 4118.

Cheeses made using these pottery vessels must always have been a minority, possibly specialist, product. Fragments from a strainer or a cheese press are very distinctive, so their rarity seems to be real and not just the result of them being overlooked during analysis. Most cheese made in Britain would appear to have been made with utensils made of organic materials, presumably continuing traditions established in the Iron Age.

Poultry and eggs

INTRODUCTION

This chapter will explore the consumption of poultry, regarded here as domesticated birds kept in farmyards, and their eggs. With these categories of foodstuff, we return to an area where direct evidence survives. It requires there to have been a systematic sampling programme for that evidence to be recovered in a reliable way, especially in the case of eggshell. These birds, especially domestic fowl, were not only sources of food, they also had a symbolic role in religion. There is some evidence too, that they were more likely to be eaten by certain sectors of the community, than by others. The pattern of their consumption is a very useful tool for exploring Romano-British society, and is likely to become even more valuable as the results of routine sampling become available.

THE BIRDS

The domestic birds kept in Roman Britain were chickens, ducks and geese. In the Mediterranean world during the Roman period, pigeons and doves were deliberately reared as food animals, just as they were to be in Britain during the medieval period.[1] Though these birds appear to have been introduced into Roman Britain, there is little evidence that they were a common food item.[2] The first evidence for the domestic fowl (*Gallus gallus*) in Britain occurs in late Iron Age contexts; and it was deliberately bred for food, cock fighting and religious purposes.[3] The ducks and geese present on Romano-British sites were a mixture of domestic and wild animals.[4] Here no attempt will be made to differentiate between the two.

---

[1] Johnston 2000: 563. [2] Parker 1988: 202.
[3] Maltby 1997: 402; for cock fighting see Luff 1993: 90.
[4] See for example O'Connor 1988: 100 Table 27; Hamilton-Dyer in Zienkiewicz 1993: 135 Table 2.

Table 11.1. *A comparison of the recovery of different types of poultry at selected urban sites.*

	Fowl (%)	Duck (%)	Goose (%)	Total	Quantification method
Colchester Culver St	63.0	30.5	6.5	1578	NISP
Colchester Gilberd	83.5	13.0	3.5	1382	NISP
Dorchester	84.0	15.0	1.0	1572	Fragment
Leicester	85.0	8.0	7.0	428	Zones
Southwark	82.0	18.0	—	462	Weight (g)

Table 11.1 shows the proportions of bones belonging to the three different types of birds on five urban sites which have produced relatively large assemblages. The methods of quantification vary, but the pattern is the same. In all, domestic fowl dominate. Apart from Culver Street, where special circumstances may have applied, ducks and geese are much rarer. This general pattern between the species is the one normally observed, but it is clear that chicken was not regularly eaten on all types of site. In an interesting study, Maltby assessed the contribution of chicken to the diet by looking at the proportions of domestic fowl, sheep and goats in the bone assemblages of a large number of different sites, using NISP measures. He was able to show that there was a noticeable urban – rural divide with the sites with the highest proportion of chicken being the large towns. Chicken was moderately well represented on military and villa sites, but tended to be rare or absent on rural sites.[5] The consumption of chicken could thus be seen as one of the ways in which Roman manners and tastes were adopted in some environments, but not in others.

The sizes of the bones of domestic fowl recovered show that they were of a variety of sizes, and it is possible that some male birds were deliberately castrated to produce large plump capons.[6] Where butchery marks are noted the recurrent pattern is for them to show that the feet and the wing tips were cut off.[7] Very little other carcase modification is recorded, so the assumption would be that these birds were often cooked whole, rather than jointed.

There are some indications that poultry in general may have been a high-status foodstuff. Chicken, ducks and geese were present in the

[5] Maltby 1997.　　[6] Luff 1993: 97; Maltby in Woodward *et al.* 1993: 332.
[7] Maltby in Woodward *et al.* 1993: 331; Hamilton-Dyer in Fulford *et al.* 1997: 133.

Table 11.2. *A comparison of sheep/pig and poultry bone fragments from Culver Street, Colchester and Fishbourne.*

	Date	Sheep/Pig (%)	Poultry (%)	Total
Culver St	60–150	76	24	1782
	150–400	63	37	2075
Fishbourne	Pre-palace	70	30	1173
	Palace	61	39	882

kitchen-waste deposit associated with a senior officer at Caerleon during the late first century.[8] Large quantities of chicken and the occasional goose are recorded on one of the Vindolanda tablets that seems to be an account of poultry consumed in the *praetorium* in the period AD 102–4.[9] It is tantalisingly incomplete, but the implication is that chicken was an acceptable dish even when the governor of the province was dining. Domestic fowl, including capons, and goose bones were also present in the special deposit at Bishopsgate along with other high-status food items.[10]

The way in which poultry was regarded can be explored by looking at groups of bones where the status of the site is known to have changed. In the case of the Culver Street assemblage summarised in Table 11.1, it is noticeable that the high levels of ducks and geese are associated with the mid-second-century occupation and later. At that site there is a rebuilding programme in the early to mid-second century, resulting in more sub- stantial houses, including ones with mosaic floors, being built.[11] It can be suggested that the later occupation on the site may well be of higher status than the earlier occupation. Maltby used the proportions of sheep : goat : domestic fowl to map the differing consumption of chicken. Here a slightly different approach is taken, and the total of the poultry bones is compared to the combined total of pig and sheep (Table 11.2). For the Colchester data the quantification is by NISP. Data from Fishbourne are also included comparing the pre-palace bone with that associated with the palace. The latter is old data published at the beginning of animal bone studies. The pig/sheep numbers approximate to a NISP measurement.

---

[8] Hamilton-Dyer in Zienkiewicz 1993: Table 2.   [9] Bowman and Thomas 2003: 23 no. 581.
[10] Tyers 1984: 374.   [11] Crummy 1992: 31.

The poultry appear to be a raw fragment count. It cannot be stressed too much that such quantification is not ideal. This, though, is the sort of data that is often available. Despite this caveat, the pattern is the same in both cases. The proportion of poultry bone rises with the higher-status occupation. There is a hint here that the consumption of poultry is not just an indicator of the adoption of Roman ways. A high level of consumption may well be an indication of an elite lifestyle. More rigorous quantification of the bone could well be used to explore this.

The consumption of poultry took place not just in a normal domestic context, but also within the setting of a religious experience. Chicken bones, probably indicative of meals consumed during religious ceremonies, have been found at temple sites relating to a variety of religions and these will be examined in more detail later in the book.[12]

It is within the ritual area that poultry may have been consumed, even by those who did not normally favour it. It is noticeable that domestic fowl are often included as grave goods. These may not always have been present as a food item. The cockerel was one of Mercury's attributes, and he was a chthonic deity who accompanied the soul after death.[13] Some of the remains may be sacrifices to the god, in the hope that he would be helpful to the deceased. In others the bird had clearly been eaten before being deposited.

A particularly interesting example of this was found in a rural inhumation cemetery at Foxton.[14] Chicken bones were recovered from a high proportion of the grave fills. They were disarticulated, but those from each individual were found in a compact heap in close contact with the deceased. In the best preserved, most of bones were present, including head and feet. It was suggested that the birds had been cooked, and the flesh stripped from the bones which were then placed either in a small bowl or as a heap. An integral part of the funeral ritual would thus have consisted of eating chicken. As we have seen generally chicken doesn't feature very highly in rural diets. The settlement the dead came from has not been excavated, and so it is not possible to say whether the population of this particular rural settlement did commonly feature chicken in their diet. On some other rural sites it can be shown that chickens feature in the funeral ritual, but were not commonly eaten in the settlement.[15] Eating a

---

[12] See pp. 211–13 and 215.
[13] Toynbee 1971: 286 footnote 94; MacDonald in Clarke 1979: 410.
[14] Moore in Price *et al.* 1997: 148–9.
[15] Maltby in Davies *et al.* 2002: 168–9; Richardson in Rahtz and Watts 2004: 268, 271–2.

chicken dinner for many of the inhabitants of Roman Britain may thus have been an uncommon, and emotionally charged, event.

EGGS

Given the pattern established for the exploitation of the birds, it is not surprising that the evidence for the consumption of eggs mirrors it. In urban environments where there has been a systematic environmental sampling programme, eggshell fragments are frequently reported to be common.[16] Conversely, on rural sites with similar programmes, no egg-shell is recorded.[17] Eggs feature lavishly in the recipes of Apicius, often in the form of a *patina*, an egg custard in which various sweet and savoury fillings could be included.[18] The residues identified on a greyware dish at Chelmsford[19] could well be the remains of such a recipe. In Britain, the distribution of the evidence for eggs suggests such dishes could have been consumed in the larger towns, but would have been unknown across much of the country. Evidence from a writing tablet at Vindolanda dated to AD 85–92, suggests egg cookery on a lavish scale, as one shopping list calls for 'a hundred or two hundred eggs if they are for sale there at a good price'.[20] This was probably for the commanding officer's household, and should not be regarded as typical of all military cooking.

Where it is possible to identify the type of bird that produced the egg, it was normally a hen; though duck and goose egg fragments are occasion-ally found as well. At Leicester there was a little evidence of how some of the eggs may have been cooked. Differential colour changes were consist-ent with baking eggs by piercing the narrow end and placing the blunt end in the embers of a hearth.[21] If this was a common way of cooking eggs, then Martial's epigram about the round-bowled spoon called a *cochleare,* in use during the first and second centuries, may be relevant:

I am convenient for snails, but no less useful for eggs. Do you know why I am rather called a snail spoon?[22]

These spoons have sharply pointed handles which could indeed have been used for piercing the shells. In Britain, the use of these seems to decrease

[16] O'Connor 1988: 99; Murphy in Crummy 1992: 280; Boyer in Connor and Buckley 1999: 329–33.
[17] Smith *et al.* 1997; Turner 1999.   [18] E.g. Apicius IV.2.
[19] John Evans and Going in Going 1987: 91.   [20] Bowman and Thomas 1994: 278 no. 302.
[21] Boyer in Connor and Buckley 1999: 331.   [22] Martial XIV.121.

as you go down the settlement hierarchy,[23] a pattern very similar to that of the consumption of poultry and eggs.

As with the consumption and use of poultry in ritual contexts, eggs also appear to have played a role in this aspect of life. It is not uncommon to find eggs in funerary contexts;[24] but whether the contents were consumed prior to deposition, or whether they were placed there as a symbol of a new life, cannot generally be established.

[23] Cool 2004a.
[24] Wenham 1968: 106 no. 27, 107 nos. 40, 41; Clarke 1979: 27; Grave: 22; Turner 1999: 224.

CHAPTER 12

Fish and shellfish

INTRODUCTION

The people of the ancient Mediterranean world, or at least those who wrote books, had a somewhat ambiguous view of seafood. It was at the same time a dubious foodstuff, and one that had connotations of great luxury, especially in the Roman milieu.[1] There are ongoing debates as to what contribution to the diet fish actually made.[2] In Britain we do not have the wealth of literary sources, but we do have an increasing number of fish bone assemblages, and patterns of consumption are starting to emerge. For fish bones, sampling and flotation are essential. They can be recovered by hand excavation, but the result will be governed by the competence and knowledge of the excavator, and the size of the bone. I well recall in the mid-1970s, when working as a finds supervisor for a big urban excavation, the sudden appearance of cod and ling vertebrae on the finds trays amongst all the normal potsherds and mammal bone. This took place the day after everyone working on the site had listened to a lecture by a highly enthusiastic fish bone specialist. As fish bones go, these are large; but they had rarely appeared in the preceding weeks. It was a classic example of the phenomenon that what goes on the finds tray is what the excavator recognises. Not all digging teams can have the opportunity of being similarly enthused and, even if they are, they would still miss the smaller species. The best evidence will always come from systematic sampling.

FISH

An appreciation of the role of fish in the Romano-British diet can be gained by looking at the assemblages from urban sites. In these,

[1] Purcell 1995; Holland 2003: 183–6.   [2] Summarised in Purcell 1995: 133.

comparisons can be made between the Roman and medieval periods.[3] The regular pattern is for the medieval contexts to produce considerably more bones than the Roman ones. Fish formed an important part of the medieval diet, because of the number of fast days imposed by the Church. For almost half the year, Christians were forbidden to eat meat and substituted fish instead.[4] The urban fish bone assemblages suggest that fish is likely to have formed a far smaller part of the diet in the Roman period.

The species regularly identified are freshwater ones, and those which live in estuarine or inshore waters. Freshwater fishes regularly encountered include eel, roach, salmon and trout. The marine fish often include herring, flat fishes like plaice and flounder, sea bream and grey mullet. Cod is only occasionally noted, reflecting the fact that the development of the deep-sea fisheries post-dated the Roman period. The picture appears to be of a rather casual exploitation of what was to hand. At Dorchester, close to the sea, it is noticeable that marine fish dominate;[5] while at Leicester, an inland town in the Midlands, there is a mixture of marine and freshwater species.[6] Some of these fish may have been preserved rather than fresh. Oily fish spoil quickly, so the presence of herring or mackerel bones at inland sites, such as Leicester, suggests they may have arrived in a preserved form. An amphora found in a Flavian context on the London waterfront had a written label which declared its contents were 'Lucius Tettius Africanus's finest fish sauce from Antinopolis' (modern Antibes).[7] It contained iris and box seeds, and fish-head bones thought to be mackerel. The label specifically says the contents are *liquamen*, so it is possible that some of the oily fish bones arrived as part of fish sauce. The industries that produced fish sauce also produced salted fish;[8] and this might be another way in which these species arrived.

Against this background of low level, sporadic consumption there is a little evidence that fish may have been regarded as a luxury commodity. There are not yet enough adequately sampled sites to say whether consumption patterns differed in town and country; though there are occasional hints that they might have. In the Dorchester area fish bones are recovered from the urban samples, but appear rare or absent from

[3] O'Connor 1988: Table 32; Jones in Hinton 1988: 433; Locker in Crummy 1992: 278; Nicholson in Connor and Buckley 1999: Table 74.
[4] Kurlansky 1998: 24.
[5] Hamilton-Dyer in Woodward *et al.* 1993: Table 67; Hamilton-Dyer in Smith 1993: 80.
[6] Nicholson in Connor and Buckley 1999: Table 74.
[7] RIB II.6 no. 2492.24.   [8] Curtis 1991: 10.

the rural ones.[9] It is noticeable that fish were consumed at rural sites where there are other signs of prestige development, such as the villa at Gorhambury.[10] An intriguing insight is also gained from looking at the associations of certain unusual fish. Though cod is rare, one of the places where it has been recovered is in the pit at Bishopsgate, London, which has been noted several times as containing evidence for luxury foodstuffs. At Colchester, cod bones were found in association with a substantial town house.[11] In another second-century London pit, bones from a sturgeon were found associated with many chicken bones.[12] If the suggestion that a high level of chicken consumption indicates an elite lifestyle is correct, the sturgeon could well have been consumed by someone in the upper echelons of society. As well as being rare, both cod and sturgeon are large, striking in appearance, and very good to eat. Sturgeon in particular has long been thought of as fit for royalty. In 1529 it was an enormous sturgeon, ceremonially accompanied by a fanfare, that formed the first course of a grand banquet given in honour of the marriage of the Duke of Ferrara to the daughter of the King of France.[13] Literary sources make it clear that rare catches were suitable gifts for patrons in the Mediterranean world.[14] There are hints in the associations of these bones that something similar may have been going on in Britain.

There is also one other piece of evidence pointing to fish, or at least seafood, as being something that featured disproportionately in the diets of the elite. At Poundbury, a sample of the bodies from the fourth-century cemetery were studied using stable-isotope analysis. It was shown that those in what might be considered graves belonging to the richer segment of society, i.e. buried in the mausoleums or in lead coffins, had stable-isotope values that could be associated with a marine diet. Their contemporaries buried in wooden coffins showed no detectable marine element in their diet.[15]

SHELLFISH

We move now from an area where, until recently, there has been all too little evidence to one where there is almost too much. On some sites,

---

[9] Hamilton-Dyer in Woodward *et al.* 1993: Table 67; Hamilton-Dyer in Smith 1993: 80; compare Maltby in Davies *et al.* 2002: Table 20; Smith *et al.* 1997.
[10] Locker in Neal *et al.* 1990: 212.　　　[11] Locker in Crummy 1992: 278.
[12] Drummond-Murray *et al.* 2002: 121.　　　[13] Hollingsworth 2004: 22.
[14] Purcell 1995: 143.　　　[15] Richards *et al.* 1998.

oyster shells are so common that they are discarded and little useful information extracted. In the early 1950s the excavator of the fort at Caister-on-Sea noted 'at first the shells were counted until, at an early stage in the digging, the number passed 10,000, when counting was discontinued'.[16] Until recently they were a category of find that was not thought worthy of specialist attention; and even now, many reports are published where they are treated in only a cursory manner, if at all.[17] This is unfortunate, because the pioneering work of Jessica Winder[18] has shown that a wealth of information can be extracted from them.

The oyster beds in England lie along the south coast, and in the Essex – north Kent area. One of Winder's most valuable observations was that it was possible to identify the source of the shells by studying the infestations they show. The worm *Polydura hoplura* is confined to the southern coast. It leaves blisters on the inner edge of the shell, and shells with this sort of infestation must have come from the south coast. The worm *Polydura ciliate,* which leaves bore holes in the shells, prefers the conditions found in the Essex – north Kent beds, though can occur as well on parts of the south coast. Properly studied, the shells will show where the oysters were coming from. Those eaten in Silchester came, unsurprisingly, from the south coast. Those eaten in Leicester had made the much longer journey from the Thames estuary.[19] Whether other beds were exploited to serve the northern market is unknown, but presumably likely. By the early twentieth century, surveys were noting a distinct paucity of oyster beds in the north-east and north-west coasts;[20] but oysters were common in the Forth until the nineteenth century.[21] It is possible that other beds may have existed in the Roman period. It is unfortunate that, though there is a writing tablet from Vindolanda recording the gift of fifty oysters, the place of origin given is otherwise unknown.[22] Oysters can survive in good condition for up to three weeks out of water, providing they are from inter-tidal beds, where they are exposed to the air for part of each day.[23] What they were transported in is unknown, though wooden barrels or pottery jars would be an obvious solution. Clearly, given their widespread distribution, the trade in oysters was well organised.

---

[16] Ellis in Darling and Gurney 1993: 238–9. [17] References suppressed to protect the guilty.
[18] Winder 1992.
[19] Somerville in Fulford *et al.* 1997: 135–9; Monkton in Connor and Buckley 1999: 340.
[20] Winder 1992: 269. [21] Heppell in Holmes 2003: 136.
[22] Bowman and Thomas 1994: 272 no. 299. [23] Winder 1992: 275.

In Italy oysters were deliberately cultivated,[24] but there is no evidence that there was any need to do that in Britain. The oyster beds appear to have been an under- or non-exploited resource prior to the Roman period, and the shells found give every appearance of coming from a natural, unmanaged population.[25] Where the age of oysters from Roman sites has been considered, it can range widely. At Alington Avenue outside Dorchester, they varied from two to eleven years, with the commonest age being five. In the centre of the town the age ranged from one to sixteen.[26] This contrasts with modern managed populations where oysters are harvested at about four years.

After the conquest, many people seem to have developed a taste for them. This does not appear to be a new foodstuff that the native population rejected, as they can be found on rural and roadside sites of no great pretensions, at some distance from the oyster beds.[27] We generally eat them raw today as they are a delicacy; in the historic past when they were abundant, they were frequently cooked.[28] This can be done by simply placing them on the embers of a hearth. If they were cooked in this way, it might account for the fact that, when the shells have been studied in detail, obvious opening marks on the shells, left by knives and other implements, occur on only a minority.[29] Baking them would lead to the shells opening without any force being required.

British oysters were obviously well regarded in the Roman world as there are several mentions of them in the ancient literature; but whether they actually travelled as far as Rome, as one of Juvenal's satires implies, is open to question.[30]

Although oysters were the shellfish of choice, other species are also recovered. In some cases, their presence on a site may not have been because they were being eaten, but because they probably came attached to seaweed that was being used to improve the soil, possibly having previously acted as packing for the oysters.[31] At Colchester the presence of tiny shells, and shells which had obviously been empty for some time when they were collected, was explained in this way.[32] Mussels were

---

[24] Günther 1897.   [25] Winder 1992: 273.
[26] Winder 1992: 151; Winder in Woodward *et al.* 1993: 348.
[27] Everton in Leech 1982: 144; Alvery in May 1996: 171; Hands 1998: 249; Booth *et al.* 2001: Table 9.22.
[28] Davidson 1999: 564.
[29] Alvery in May 1996: 171; Monkton in Connor and Buckley 1999: 341.
[30] Dalby 2000: 284 footnote 59.
[31] I am grateful to Andrew Jones for this suggestion.
[32] Murphy in Crummy 1992: 277.

probably eaten. With some exceptions,[33] they are always in a noticeable minority compared with oysters. In part, this pattern may be the result of differential survival. Oyster shells are robust; mussel shells less so. It was observed at Leicester that mussel shells were only recovered from the sieved samples, whereas oysters were easily collected by hand.[34] The presence of mussels at inland sites, such as Leicester, again attests to the efficiency of the shellfish trade. As with oysters, mussels occur at inland rural sites, both those of some pretensions such as the villa at Shakenoak, and small villages such as Catsgore.[35]

Other types of shellfish occur in much smaller quantities, and some may have arrived as chance inclusions with the other shells. For others, there is evidence of them being eaten in their own right. A group of cockles found in a ditch by the bath-house of the villa at Halstock,[36] can plausibly be interpreted as a tasty snack enjoyed in the context of taking a bath, which often provided the opportunity of snacking on fast food. It is also noticeable that the carpet shell (*Venerupis* sp.) is noted from time to time in shell reports. At Colchester they were clearly being eaten, as they were found as articulated valves.[37] These are a type of clam that has long fallen from favour as a foodstuff in Britain, but on the continent is still considered a delicacy;[38] as they were by ancient Roman writers.[39] One might assume, too, that the fragments of the shells of edible crabs found at York indicated that these were consumed in the city regularly.[40]

The potential of the evidence for the consumption of fish and shellfish is only just starting to reveal itself. As more sites with good sampling programmes are published, a better picture of fish consumption should become available. It is also to be hoped that oyster and other shells will start to attract a little more attention than they currently receive. However, it is worth entering one note of caution. We should not impose our own standards of luxury when exploring Roman consumption patterns, especially in this category of food. It is salutary to realise that oysters, now synonymous with luxury in Britain, were in the Roman period apparently available to a wide range of society. In the Mediterranean world they could be a luxury delicacy[41] but in Roman Britain, with its prolific oyster beds, they may not have had the same resonance. Availability is all. One

---

[33] Zienkiewicz 1986: 220 Table 1. [34] Monkton in Connor and Buckley 1999: 341.
[35] Brodribb *et al.* 1971: 127; Everton in Leech 1982: 144. [36] Winder 1992: 157.
[37] Murphy in Crummy 1992: 277. [38] Davidson 1999: 139.
[39] Dalby 2000: 53. [40] O'Connor 1988: 119; Hall and Kenward 1990: 407.
[41] Dalby 2000: 248.

person's luxury may be another's mundane food. It is useful to remember the poet Edwin Muir's observation on growing up in the Orkneys. He observed that white bread brought at the village shop was a luxury, but that he ate so much crab and lobster as a boy that he had never been able to enjoy them since.[42]

---

[42] Muir 1954: 59.

CHAPTER 13

Game

INTRODUCTION

There are various strands of evidence that suggest hunting might have been a popular pastime in Roman Britain. According to Strabo, writing at the time of the Emperor Augustus, hunting dogs were one of the items exported from late Iron Age Britain.[1] Hunting is mentioned several times in the Vindolanda writing tablets,[2] and hunting imagery is found in a wide range of contexts such as mosaic floors,[3] large pieces of silver plate[4] and pottery hunt cups.[5] This range suggests that scenes from the hunt were attractive to people both at the upper end of the social hierarchy, and those further down it.

This apparent popularity of hunting as a pursuit is puzzling when viewed from the perspective of animal bone assemblages. Unlike modern British practice which has been, in Oscar Wilde's classic definition 'the unspeakable in full pursuit of the uneatable',[6] the species shown being hunted in the Roman scenes – deer, boars and hares – are all edible ones. If these animals were regularly being hunted, it is to be expected that this would be reflected in the animal bone assemblages. Certainly in the medieval period, when hunting was the preserve of the aristocracy and a popular pursuit amongst them, there is a noticeable increase in deer bones on the sites where they lived.[7] On all types of Romano-British sites, by contrast, evidence for game is generally rare and often absent. This chapter will examine the evidence for the consumption of game, and will conclude with a consideration of why there should be this mismatch between the artistic and the real world.

---

[1] Strabo IV.5.2.
[2] Bowman and Thomas 1994: 206; 2003: 47 no. 593, 48 no. 594, 77 no. 615.
[3] Henig 1995: 159, fig. 85.   [4] Johns 1981: pl. VII; Henig 1995: fig. 96.
[5] E.g. Symmonds and Wade 1999: fig. 5.34 no. 129.
[6] *A Woman of No Importance* Act 1.   [7] Grant 1981: 209.

Table 13.1. *A comparison of sheep/pig and deer bones at selected sites (* indicates present but at levels of less than 0.5%).*

Site	Type	Date	Sheep/Pig (%)	Deer (%)	Total	Quantification
Wroxeter	Fort	c. 60–90	96	4	2003	NISP
Castleford	Fort	c. 70–95	99	I	5176	NISP
Colchester	Town	c. 60–150	94	6	1439	NISP
Wroxeter	Town	c. 90–170	99	I	822	NISP
Wilcote	Rural	c. 50–150	100	*	3193	Zones
Leicester	Town	c. 50–250	100	*	2181	Zones
Colchester	Town	c. 150–400+	93	7	1393	NISP
Leicester	Town	c. 250–400+	98	2	1451	Zones
Caister	Fort	c. 200–400+	84	16	1122	NISP
Segontium	Fort	c. 250–400+	89	11	2445	NISP

VENISON, BOAR AND HARE

Inspection of animal bone reports reveals that, when present, the commonest game species is deer, followed by hare and then, very rarely, by wild boar. In order to gain an insight into how much game might have been consumed, Table 13.1 has been prepared, comparing deer bones to those of pigs and sheep. These were selected to represent the domesticated species because so much of the data are expressed as NISP measurements, and there is a need to discount the distorting effect of heavily butchered cattle bone. As ever, using so much NISP data is less than satisfactory, but it does allow the general pattern to emerge. It should be noted that the more reliable zonal method of quantification, used at Leicester and Wilcote, regularly returns very low figures; suggesting the NISP figures are overestimating the proportion of deer. The urban bone assemblages have consistently low levels, with only Colchester showing a proportion above 5%. Even there, it is clear that bones from the game species are proportionately much scarcer than those from poultry (cf. Table 11.2). This low level is often commented on in other urban assemblages as well.[8] It could be argued that such a pattern is to be expected in towns, and that it is sites in rural areas where game would be more common. The only site that falls into this category in Table 13.1 is Wilcote where the number of deer bones is again negligible. As with the urban

[8] Dobney *et al.* 1995: 21; Maltby in Woodward *et al.* 1993: 330–1; Maltby in Holbrook 1998: 368.

sites, this pattern regularly repeats itself in other rural assemblages which it has not been possible to include in Table 13.1.[9]

The military sites show a less consistent pattern, possibly because soldiers, or at least senior officers, included hunting amongst their pastimes. In County Durham the commanding officer of a cavalry unit dedicated an altar to Silvanus after killing a 'wild boar of remarkable fineness which many of his predecessors had been unable to bag'.[10] At Vindolanda, the commanding officer Cerialis wrote to his friend Brocchus, asking for some hunting nets to be sent,[11] and in another note referred to his huntsman.[12] Even if hunting was common around forts, there is often very little evidence that the kill formed more than an occasional addition to the diet. This can be seen in the first-century sites in Table 13.1, which are comparable to contemporary urban assemblages. At other forts, a similar scarcity it often reported.[13] Interesting exceptions to this pattern can be seen in the late Roman military assemblages at Caister on-Sea and Segontium. Why venison should be so much more popular on these sites is not clear. Both lie in relatively marginal positions, and possibly it is reflecting local abundance. Certainly the garrisons at both sites seemed prepared to exploit various unusual foodstuffs, as seal bones were also very occasionally recovered at Segontium; whilst at Caister-on-Sea badgers appear to have been eaten.[14]

In the table all species of deer were grouped together. The larger red deer was the commonest, but roe deer were also present. The fallow deer, a Roman introduction that did not become properly established until the Norman period,[15] was very rare. There are important differences between the three from a culinary point of view. These days, the small roe deer is considered the best to eat.[16] Certainly the cooks in the *praetorium* at Vindolanda made a distinction between the two types of meat, as did the recipes of Apicius.[17] The record of a gourmet dinner given by Julius

---

[9] Locker in Neal *et al.* 1990: Table 18; Berg in Wrathmell and Nicholson 1990: 187; Harman in May 1996: 161; Stallibrass in Jackson and Potter 1996: Table 40; Noddle in Price 2000: 235.

[10] RIB I no. 1041.

[11] Bowman and Thomas 1994: 206. (In the interests of accuracy it should, perhaps, be noted that the word could also mean counterpanes, but the editors of the texts prefer hunting nets, feeling it unlikely that these two would be discussing soft-furnishings.)

[12] Bowman and Thomas 2003: 77 no. 615.

[13] Izard in Wilmott 1997: table 34; Stallibrass in Wilson 2002a: 399–400.

[14] Noddle in Casey *et al.* 1993: Table 6.1; Harman in Darling and Gurney 1993: 226.

[15] Grant 1981: 206.   [16] Drysdale 1983: 119; Davidson 1999: 825.

[17] Bowman and Thomas 1994: 157 no. 191; Apicius VIII. 2 and 3.

Caesar also implies that it was roe deer rather than red deer that was the venison of choice for discerning eaters.[18]

What is clear is that venison, and the other larger game species, were an unusual item in most people's diets. So eating game could well have only taken place in special circumstances. When exploring what these were, it is useful to look at both the associations with other animal bones, and which types of deer were being eaten. Given the epigraphic evidence of a link between senior military officers and hunting, the closed group of kitchen refuse from a senior officer's kitchen within the fortress at Caerleon is a good place to start.[19] It has deer, hare and wild boar bones as well as evidence of pork and poultry consumption. Roe deer bones are more numerous than red deer. These associations suggest very strongly that here game is part of an elite dining regime, favouring the rare and the tasty. A similar set of associations can be seen in the Bishopsgate pit in London,[20] where only roe deer is found. A comparison of two wells infilled with domestic rubbish in the second century in Southwark is also informative. The one with the roe deer bones had proportionately more pork and chicken bones in it than the one that did not have the deer.[21] Again the implication would be that roe deer was a delicacy.

At both Caister-on-Sea and Segontium where venison appeared relatively abundant, it was red deer that was the commonest species; possibly suggesting that at those sites it was consumed because it was available rather than because a large amount of elite dining was going on. This would fit the pattern of opportunistic exploitation of other wild animals at these sites already noted.

WILD BIRDS

One of the difficulties of looking at patterns of game-bird consumption is deciding what was present because it had been caught and eaten; and what was there as a chance death within a human settlement. The choice of which birds to eat is very much culturally conditioned, as a brief reflection on modern attitudes to some of the less commonly identified species will show. Golden plovers and snipe[22] are both now generally considered acceptable and tasty. We would have no problem about considering that

---

[18] Dalby 2000: 248.   [19] Hamilton-Dyer in Zienkiewicz 1993: Table 2 well 2.
[20] Tyers 1984.   [21] Drummond-Murray *et al.* 2002: Table 24.
[22] Parker 1988: Table 1; Gidney in Connor and Buckley 1999: 318 table 66; Maltby in Woodward *et al.* 1993: 333 Table 62; Hamilton-Dyer in Fulford *et al.* 1997: 133.

these were present as items of food. Small passerines are also found.[23] Whether such birds are eaten today, depends on which side of the English Channel you live on. On the continental side, they are considered a delicacy: on the British side, it is culturally unacceptable to eat song birds. On neither side of the Channel is it now considered appropriate to eat buzzards, but a bone from one found at Piercebridge with knife marks, shows that they were being eaten, at least occasionally, in Roman Britain. A list of snares left by one of the garrisons at Vindolanda notes nets for ducks and thrushes and snares for swans as well as a dragnet for fishing, so presumably all of these species were considered edible.[24]

Even if the optimistic view is taken, i.e. that many of the bird bones found in archaeological assemblages are there because the birds had been eaten, it still only reveals a pattern of casual, opportunistic consumption. As with other types of game, many people would never have eaten it. In chapter 11, it was noted that the geese and ducks present on Romano-British sites are often a mixture of wild and domesticated species. It might be questioned though, to what extent the presence of the wild ones indicates wild-fowling, as opposed to the birds themselves appropriating man-made ponds, as may often be seen in public parks today. Setting the ducks and geese to one side, the most commonly encountered wild bird is the raven. These are often found as complete skeletons, sometimes in obviously ritual contexts.[25] The most likely explanation seems to be that these intelligent birds were being kept as pets. Following the raven, the woodcock is the next most commonly encountered species.[26] This is a wader which would have been most likely to have been caught during the winter. It is a bird which today inspires strongly polarised views as to whether it is good eating or not;[27] presumably similar differences of opinion existed in Roman Britain. The bird that is the commonest game bird today, the pheasant, is encountered only rarely,[28] reflecting the fact that then it was a wild bird, whereas today it is commercially bred to provide sport in organised 'shoots'.

One particularly interesting discovery was the remains of at least four cranes in the kitchen waste of the senior officer's household at Caerleon. Crane bones are very occasionally found;[29] but, given the association with

---

[23] Parker 1988: Table 1; Hamilton-Dyer in Fulford *et al.* 1997: 133.
[24] Bowman and Thomas 2003: 47 no. 593.   [25] Parker 1988: 208–9, Table 1.
[26] Parker 1988: Table 1; Cowles in Woodward and Leach 1993: 263; Hamilton-Dyer in Fulford *et al.* 1997: 133; Gidney in Connor and Buckley 1999: Table 66.
[27] Drysdale 1983: 85.   [28] Parker 1988: 202.
[29] Parker 1988: Table 1; Maltby in Woodward *et al.* 1993: 333 Table 62; Dobney *et al.* 1995: 51; Harman in May 1996: 163.

other table delicacies, this is the best evidence we have that they were being eaten. The cook clearly did not know the trick given in Apicius, of cooking the bird with its head on, but clear of the sauce. When cooked the head could be grasped in a hot linen cloth and pulled off, bringing the tough tendons out with it. This would not have been possible at Caerleon as the back of the head had been chopped off.[30]

ART, REALITY AND HUNTING

The picture of game consumption outlined in the previous pages is that it was generally at a low, or non-existent, level but was occasionally associated with high-class dining. If hunting was a popular pastime amongst the elite, it has left little trace in the food remains. Why then the pervasive hunting themes in art? One reason may well be that the mosaic floors and vessels with hunting scenes are not depicting a popular pastime but are allegorical, depicting the quest for understanding. In the floor mosaics hunting scenes are frequent in ones with overtly religious symbolism associated with some of the mystery religions where the worshipper passed from initiation to understanding.[31]

Hunting scenes also occur within religious settings in other media. A scene engraved on a mid-fourth-century glass bowl depicting a rider and hounds driving a hare into a net, is often used to illustrate the popularity of hunting in Roman Britain.[32] It belongs to a group of bowls all engraved in the same way with scenes of the hunt depicting stags and boars, as well as hares.[33] Other bowls from the same workshop depict mythological scenes, and ones from both the Old and New Testaments of the Christians. The bowls, including the hunting ones, often have inscriptions around their rims which include exhortations such as 'life to you and yours' and 'live in God'. These are surely better seen as overtly religious items rather than sporting souvenirs. The boar hunt on the Risley Park silver lanx is accompanied not only by Bacchic scenes around the rim, but also by an inscription on the underside recording its donation to a Christian church.[34] The implications would be that the elite of the fourth century, to which many of these items originally belonged, had a greater interest in their immortal souls, than in the chase.

---

[30] Apicius VI.2,ii; Hamilton-Dyer in Zienkiewicz 1993: 136.
[31] Perring 2003: 105.   [32] E.g. Salway 1993: 415.
[33] Harden 1960.   [34] Johns 1981.

Once the link between depictions of hunting and the sport itself is broken, it becomes less surprising that even at a palace such as Fishbourne, evidence for venison consumption is very slight.[35] Hunting may not have been a popular pastime for the elite. Possibly this may have been because, over much of the country, deer and wild boar were not very numerous because the habitat was not available. In the medieval period, hunting was an aristocratic pastime that needed the deliberate creation, and maintenance, of hunting parks. There is nothing in the landscape that suggests a similar policy was being pursued in Roman Britain. Where game was available, as appears to have been the case in the vicinity of Caister-on-Sea and Segontium, it was being hunted and eaten but within a late military milieu. Within this, what may have been of interest was not so much the meat as the trophies. At various military sites, including Segontium, boars' tusks, either mounted in copper alloy or pierced for suspension, have been found;[36] whilst at a site associated with the *Classis Britannica* in Kent, where hunting was clearly being carried out, one of the finds was an impressive antler from a mature stag.[37] In none of these cases can it be proven that the objects were the result of hunting; the boars' tusks may have been from domestic animals and the antler may have been shed. They do, however, hint at an interest in trophies, and provide a context for hunting.

Finally, one reason for the low levels of game consumption could be cultural, as with the current British aversion to eating song birds. Caesar notes the fact that in the Britain of his day, hares were raised but not eaten.[38] Unfortunately, he does not elaborate on the reason for this, though a religious taboo, or the fact that they were regarded as pets, are possibilities. Both stags and boars feature in Celtic mythology,[39] and this too may have set them aside from the food chain.

If hunting for food wasn't much practised in Britain during the Roman period we are left with Strabo's report that hunting dogs were an export prior to the invasion. There does not seem to have been any major change in consumption patterns between the late Iron Age and the Romano-British period, as evidence for game is as conspicuous by its rarity in the earlier animal bone assemblages[40] as it is in the later ones. There is the

---

[35] Grant in Cunliffe 1971: 378.
[36] Henderson in Bushe-Fox 1949: 141, nos. 173–4; Allason-Jones and McKay 1988: 198, 36 nos. 118–22; Allason-Jones in Casey *et al.* 1993: 202 no. 451.
[37] Harman in Brodribb and Cleere 1988: 273.   [38] Caesar V.12.   [39] Henig 1984: 18–9.
[40] E.g. Wilson in Parrington 1978: 111 Table X; Grant in Cunliffe 1984: 525; Rackham in Heslop 1987: 107; Grant in Cunliffe and Poole 1991: 478.

question of whether Strabo's evidence can be accepted at face value. He also states that the Britons liked to import glass vessels.[41] Evidence for the presence of pre-conquest imports of these is extremely rare, and certainly does not support any major trade in them.[42] Giving him the benefit of the doubt, however, and assuming British hunting dogs were famous enough to be in demand on the continent, what were they being trained to hunt? Perhaps 'the unspeakable in full pursuit of the uneatable' has a longer history in Britain than has hitherto been suspected.

[41] Strabo IV.5.3.
[42] Price 1996; Cool 2003: 139.

CHAPTER 14

Greengrocery

INTRODUCTION

With fruit and vegetables we revert to a type of foodstuff which will only survive in particular conditions, and which will only be found if a sampling programme has been undertaken. Furthermore, there is a distinct bias between the survival of the two categories. Fruit generally has seeds whilst things classed as vegetables generally don't. Seeds which can become mineralised or charred are more likely to be preserved than the leafy parts of vegetables. The latter may survive in exceptional circumstances, such as the cabbage stalk found in a late fourth-century well at Vindolanda;[1] but in general fruits are more visible in the archaeological record than vegetables. Unlike cereals which were routinely processed by heating, fruit and vegetables are not well represented in the charred-plant-remains assemblages. Most direct evidence thus comes from the waterlogged and mineralised remains. Packaging in the form of amphorae also provides evidence of preserved items, but again this favours fruits.

FRUIT

Good places to start the exploration of the fruit consumed are cesspits. Seeds and pips will often pass through the digestive track, and the conditions in cesspits are ideal for mineralisation to take place. Naturally such environments favour fruits with small seeds. Table 14.1 shows what has been identified in a variety of cesspits, together with material from the outfall of a latrine at Bearsden and from the Church Street sewer within the fortress at York.

As can be seen, fig seeds are ubiquitous. Figs were imported as, though fig trees can survive in Britain, the tiny wasp that is needed to fertilise the

---

[1] Birley 1977: 89.

Table 14.1. The incidence of fruit remains in selected cesspits (NB – Bearsden also had evidence for bilberry).

	Date	Type	Fig	Grape	Cherry	Blackberry	Apple/pear	Sloe	Raspberry	Elderberry	Strawberry
Colchester [1]	44–49	Fort	+	.	+	.	.	.	.	+	.
Colchester [2]	44–49	Fort	+	+	.	.	.	.	+	+	.
Gorhambury	43–61	Villa	+	+	.	+	.	+	.	.	.
Southwark	60/1	Town	.	.	.	.	+	.	.	.	.
Carlisle	Late C1	Vicus	+	+	+	+	+	+	.	.	.
Leicester	Mid C1–mid C2	Town	+	.	.	+	+	+	.	.	.
Dorchester [1]	Late C1	Town	+	.	.	+	+	.	.	.	.
Dorchester [2]	By mid C2	Town	+	.	.	+	+	.	.	.	.
Bearsden	142–58	Fort	+	.	.	+	.	.	+	.	+
Stonea	C3	Rural	+	.	.	.	.	.	.	.	.
York	C2–C4	Fort	.	+	.	+	+	+	+	+	+

120

flowers cannot.[2] Figs dry well, and we can assume that it was in this form that they were known in Britain. The presence of figs in a cesspit at Gorhambury is of particular interest. The building it was associated with was possibly pre-conquest. At the latest it was burnt during the Boudican rising, but may have been destroyed earlier. It provides evidence that this exotic fruit was being consumed on a native site very early in the Roman period, and possibly pre-conquest.

Fig seeds are often found elsewhere in waterlogged deposits. Even in the early days of the analysis of such deposits, it was pointed out that they were found regularly in London and elsewhere;[3] and the pattern has continued. There are some grounds for thinking they may have been a regular part of the military diet. In their dried form they would store well and would certainly be useful to a quartermaster in case of shortages. They were common at a large campaigning base at Castleford used during the expansion into the north;[4] and they are regularly recovered from water-logged contexts associated with other military sites.[5] Their presence at both urban and rural sites would suggest they were also a widespread food for the civilian population.

In the Mediterranean world, depending on the variety, figs were both a poor person's staple food and a delicacy for the elite. Cato notes that the bread ration for the chain gang, the lowest type of slave, could be reduced when figs were in season;[6] whilst Roman gourmets delighted in named varieties imported from various islands.[7] Whether such differences were appreciated within Roman Britain is beyond the scope of environmental archaeology to tell us. Fig seeds do sometimes occur in contexts where there is other evidence that the deposits derive from high-class dining activities, such as the kitchen waste associated with a senior officer's house at Caerleon.[8] It is tempting to wonder if these may have been special in some way, as opposed to a more standard issue that might have been consumed by the campaigning army at Castleford.

The other main exotic fruit in Table 14.1 is the grape. Again the presence of them in the Gorhambury pit is important evidence for their consumption by native Britons at an early stage. Though there is now pollen evidence to show that grapes were grown in Britain in at least one

---

[2] Davidson 1999: 297–8; Tyers in Hinton 1988: 448. [3] Willcox 1977: 278–9.
[4] Bastow in Abramson *et al.* 1999: Tables 8–10.
[5] Goodwin and Huntley in McCarthy 1991: Fascicule 1 59, fig. 50B; Huntley and Hillam in Buxton and Howard-Davis 2000: 356 Table 32; Kenward *et al.* 1986: 255 Table 255.
[6] Cato 56. [7] Dalby 2000: 111, 151.
[8] Caseldine and Busby in Zienkiewicz 1993: 137.

vineyard,[9] most will have arrived preserved. The ancient agricultural manuals provide directions for preserving fresh grapes by sealing the cut stalk with boiling pitch and then sealing the bunches in pottery jars.[10] This would have left behind the 'packaging' as an alien component in the pottery assemblage. Given it is absent, it may be assumed grapes arrived as dried raisins. It would appear these were not uncommon in urban and military environments.[11] At York, as well as occurring within the fortress sewer system, they are regularly present in the later second- to third-century contexts at the General Accident site in the *colonia* and in an early to mid-third-century well fill at Bedern in the fort.[12] It may be noted, though, that in this extensively sampled city, it is the seeds of figs that are more regularly encountered. Though they were not reported from the Church Street sewer, they were present at the General Accident site and the Bedern well, as well as in a layer associated with a late first-century warehouse, and in a well at Skeldergate in use during the second to fourth century.[13] Something similar may be noted at Carlisle[14] and possibly also at Southwark[15] where fig seeds tend to be more regularly present in samples than grape seeds are. Admittedly a fig has many more seeds than a grape, but the presence – absence data does hint that grapes may have been rarer than figs.

The other exotic species in Table 14.1 is possibly the cherry, though it is not always possible to distinguish between the fruit produced by the native gean cherry (*Prunus avium*) and the imported sour cherry (*P. cerasus*); and it is clear that both were eaten.[16] The sour cherries may have arrived as preserved fruits, but one exotic fruit which must indicate that the trees themselves were introduced to Britain is the mulberry. The fruits of these must be fully ripe before being eaten and are very easily damaged. They would not have been transported long distances, so the presence of mulberry seeds in Romano-British contexts indicates the deliberate introduction of the trees. The introduction must have taken place in the first century as the seeds have been found in late-first-century contexts in London. Willcox recorded that they were common in

---

[9] Meadows 1996.   [10] Columella XII: 44–5.

[11] Willcox 1977: 279; Goodwin and Huntley in McCarthy 1991: 60; Caseldine and Busby in Zienkiewicz 1993: 137; Bastow in Abramson *et al.* 1999: Table 15, 22; Huntley and Hillam in Buxton and Howard-Davis 2000: 356 Table 32.

[12] Hall and Kenward 1990: 407 Table no. 129a; Kenward *et al.* 1986: 247 Table 76.

[13] Kenward and Williams 1979: Table 12; Hall *et al.* 1980: Table 50.

[14] Goodwin and Huntley in McCarthy 1991: 60.

[15] Tyers in Hinton 1988: 48; Gray in Drummond-Murray *et al.* 2002: tables 116–24.

[16] Willcox 1977: 278; Huntley in McCarthy 2000: 77.

London, and they have been noted at Silchester and Colchester,[17] but they have not often been recorded elsewhere. It is possible they were regarded more as an exotic garden plant than as a regularly planted fruit tree.

The other fruits in Table 14.1 are all native species which regularly occur in other waterlogged deposits, though it is only in the cesspits and sewage deposits that we have certain evidence that they were being eaten. The relative scarcity of apple/pear seeds in the cesspits probably hints that the core wasn't eaten as their seeds often occur in deposits that appear to include kitchen waste.[18] The level of their consumption is hinted at by a shopping list probably relating to the provisioning of the commanding officer's house at Vindolanda during the period AD 85–92. It calls for one hundred apples 'if you can find nice ones'.[19]

Fruits with larger stones are naturally not represented in the cesspit deposits, but the exotic ones which would not grow in Britain were clearly being imported as food. Olives are known from both the stones and the amphorae they were imported in,[20] the latter being primarily a first-century phenomenon in Britain. They are also attested in the Vindolanda tablets. The person doing the shopping for apples was also instructed to buy olives, and presumably they would have been preserved in this way. The list calls for a *modius* (8.6 litres) of olives which would have represented about two thirds of an olive amphora.[21] It is believed that the production of amphorae ceased in the mid-second century, but olive stones continue to be found in later contexts indicating they must have been imported in other forms of packaging. At the General Accident site in York, olives were found throughout the mid-second- to mid-third-century sequence.[22] Olives were clearly being eaten at some point between *c.* AD 160 and 240 in the fortress baths at Caerleon,[23] in the late second and third century in London,[24] in the early to mid-third century at Colchester,[25] and in the third century or possibly the early fourth at the villa at Great Holts Farm, Boreham.[26] The distribution of both the amphorae and the olive stones seems in the main limited to major urban and military sites, and currently there is no secure evidence that importation continued in the fourth century.

---

[17] Willcox 1977: 279 Table 1; Murphy in Crummy 1992: 281.   [18] Willcox 1977: 278.
[19] Bowman and Thomas 1994: 278 no. 302.   [20] See p. 68 and fig. 3.1.6.
[21] Sealey and Tyers 1989: 60.   [22] Hall and Kenward 1990: Table 129a.
[23] Zienkiewicz 1986: 224.   [24] Willcox 1977: 278 Table 1.
[25] Murphy in Crummy 1992: 281. Period 4b infill – p. 76.
[26] Murphy in Germany 2003: 209.

Another exotic fruit with a large stone is the date. Date stones have occasionally been recovered,[27] but most evidence for their importation comes from the packaging. Date amphorae are often called carrot amphorae because of their shape.[28] These disappear about the middle of the second century,[29] and unlike the case of the olives, there are no stones from later contexts to suggest the continued import. There is epigraphic evidence that carrot amphorae also transported other palm fruits. An example from a ditch fill dated to AD 84–5 at Carlisle had the inscription KOYK which indicates the fruit was that of the doum palm (*Hyphaene thebaica*). These are large fruits the size of tennis balls with fibrous tough pulp which is edible if soaked, and tastes like gingerbread or caramel.[30]

The commonest carrot amphora has a small capacity: *c.* 3 litres[31] compared to *c.* 13 litres and 30 litres for olive amphora types (see Fig. 3.1 no. 7). Though the amphorae were small, which might indicate that dates and other palm fruit were delicacies, there is good evidence that they were common in the military diet in the first century. The amphorae from Carlisle come from a military context at a time when the fort there was a major northern base. At the Neronian forts at Exeter and Kingsholm they represent 6% and 7% (by weight) of the amphora assemblage.[32] Date amphorae were well represented in the assemblages belonging to the late first-century forts at Castleford;[33] and present, though in relatively small amounts, in the fortress at Wroxeter.[34]

In urban amphora assemblages they appear much rarer. Occasional sherds are found in London but in quantities too small to warrant tabulating in a study that explored the type of amphora-borne commodities present.[35] Similar patterns appear in other major cities such as Canterbury, Dorchester and Leicester.[36] In the smaller urban centres sherds from these amphorae often appear to be absent, even at places

---

[27] Murphy in Crummy 1984: 40; Caseldine and Busby in Zienkiewicz 1993: 137; Mackinder 2000: 12.
[28] Peacock and Williams 1986: Types 12 and 66.
[29] Sealey 1985: 89.
[30] Caruana 1992: 60 no. 12, 61–2; Tomlin 1992.
[31] Sealey 1985: Table 2.
[32] Holbrook and Bidwell 1991: Table 14; Timby in Hurst 1985: Table 4.
[33] Rush *et al.* 2000: 150 Tables 12–13, 15.
[34] Darling in Webster 2002: Tables 5.15–16.
[35] Symonds in Drummond-Murray *et al.* 2002: Table 102.
[36] Arthur 1986: 253; Williams in Woodward *et al.* 1993: Table 28; Williams in Connor and Buckley 1999: Table 5.

such as Alcester that has seen extensive excavation.[37] Dates appear to have been much rarer in the civilian diet than in the military one. They may have been viewed as a rare delicacy, or alternately an unsuitable food. It is probably no coincidence that the only record of a date stone in a civilian context comes from a most unusual *bustum* burial in London, where it was found as part of a variety of uncommon food items placed on the pyre.[38]

Members of the plum family are not uncommon in waterlogged deposits. Stones of the small native plum, the sloe (*Prunus spinosa*), appear to be the most frequently consumed variety.[39] Their presence in cesspits indicates they were eaten whole, which is an interesting contrast to modern practice. Currently they are considered too astringent to eat in that way, and are used to flavour drinks or to make jam, presumably not an option in Roman Britain in the absence of sugar. The fruits of bullace (*P. insititia*) are larger and less astringent but still not currently thought suitable for eating as fruit. It is not a native species, but is found in contexts as early as the 70s.[40] Plums (*P. domestica*), another non-native species, were clearly being imported at a very early stage of the Roman occupation as one was found in former barracks at Colchester which had been burnt during the Boudican rising of AD 60/1.[41] These could have been imported dried as prunes, or possibly preserved in syrup. A graffito on a globular amphora from Brough on Noe has been read as 'PRVN[A]' (plums) but the reading is disputed.[42]

A most unusual exotic find from London was a peach stone from a first- to second-century context.[43] Peaches would have been an exotic find everywhere in the western empire at that time as the trees only started to be grown in Italy in the first century AD.[44]

Pine nuts from the stone pine are another exotic ingredient that would have been available in Britain; but to what extent they were exploited as a culinary ingredient is hard to judge. They were clearly being used ceremonially as fuel in temples,[45] and many of the records may relate to this type of use. One example where they were regarded as an ingredient, given the associations with other foodstuff, was at the villa at Great Holts Farm, Boreham.[46]

---

[37] Cracknell and Mahany 1994; Cracknell 1996; Booth and Evans 2001.
[38] Mackinder 2000: 12.   [39] Huntley in McCarthy 2000: 77.
[40] Bastow in Abramson *et al.* 1999: Tables 11 and 13.   [41] Murphy in Crummy 1984: 40.
[42] RIB II.6 no. 2493.46.   [43] Willcox 1977: 279 Table 1.
[44] Vaughan and Geissler 1997: 78.   [45] Shepherd 1998: 161.
[46] Murphy in Germany 2003: 212.

NUTS

Nut shells from the native hazel are a common find but not all come from the human food chain. At Carlisle some had clearly been nibbled by small mammals.[47] Hazel nuts have been identified in cesspits and similar deposits;[48] and one of the individuals found at Lindow had clearly been eating raw hazelnuts shortly before his death.[49] The quantities hazel nuts are sometimes found in also indicate they may have been collected and deliberately stored, and this seems to be what was happening in a mid-second-century grain store at Castleford when it burned down.[50]

The other nut most often encountered is the walnut, though it cannot be said to be common.[51] This is not a native species and it is unclear whether the trees themselves were grown in Britain during the Roman period, or whether it was just the nuts that were an occasional import. Almonds have very occasionally been recovered. They were another of the foodstuffs placed on the pyre of the woman buried in the London *bustum* burial which had a variety of unusual offerings.[52] Both their rarity and this unusual context mark almonds out as an exceptional foodstuff.

VEGETABLES

We have one particularly vivid piece of information about vegetable consumption in Roman Britain. It relates to a slave at Vindolanda who considered radishes such a vital part of the Saturnalia festival that he was prepared to spend half a *denarius* on them.[53] Other than that, our knowledge is very sporadic and patchy. Of the different types of vegetables it is the legumes such as beans, peas and lentils that are easiest to recognise archaeologically. In part this is because they are occasionally found as part of charred grain assemblages, where it can be assumed they are accidental contaminants, self-seeding from a neighbouring field or an earlier crop. They are also occasionally recovered in a mineralised form from cesspits.

The Celtic bean had certainly been grown in the south of England during later prehistory, though its introduction into other areas may have

[47] Huntley in McCarthy 2000: 77.   [48] Knights *et al.* 1983: 143.
[49] Holden 1995: 80.
[50] Bastow in Abramson *et al.* 1999: 172.
[51] E.g. Willcox 1977: 279 Table 1.
[52] Giorgi in Mackinder 2000: 66.   [53] Bowman and Thomas 1994: 276 no. 301.

come later.[54] Peas, by contrast, tend to be more commonly found on Roman period sites than ones of the late Iron Age.[55] Other types of pea-like seeds also seem to have been consumed. The contents of a jar preserved by charring, caused by the fire that destroyed the north wing of the palace at Fishbourne, seemed to belong to the *Lathyrus* species which includes the vetchlings.[56]

Lentils are not native to Britain and, though they can be grown here, they are not hardy. When they first started to be identified within Romano-British contexts there was some debate as to whether they were chance contaminants of imported grain.[57] The discovery of quantities in kitchen waste that did not contain grain indicated that they were being eaten as a food in their own right, a conclusion that has since been confirmed by the discovery of an account from Vindolanda dated to the period AD 97–102/3 which mentions them.[58] It is possible that they may have started to be imported prior to the conquest as they have been found in the early cesspit at Gorhambury.[59]

Although legumes of any type are only occasionally recorded, it seems likely they played an important part in the diet. At Vindolanda there are records of them being acquired in large quantities for the *praetorium*. A shopping list of AD 85–92 calls for 2 *modii* (17 litres) of bruised beans, and an account of AD 97–102 records the purchase of at least 5 *modii* (a minimum of 47 litres).[60] Elsewhere in the empire too, beans are recorded as being supplied to the army in large quantities.[61]

The consumption of leafy and root vegetables is the most difficult aspect of the diet to explore. It is also one where equating the names in the literary sources to modern varieties can be most misleading, due to the amount of selective breeding that has taken place since the Roman era. A classic example here is the carrot. Modern museum displays will not infrequently include reconstructions of kitchens with produce, including carrots which are invariably orange.[62] Unfortunately orange carrots are a product of seventeenth-century Dutch horticulturalists.[63] The Roman carrot was white, not unlike an early parsnip, and there are some grounds for thinking that the ancient writers sometimes confused the two.[64] For the record, seeds from parsnips are occasionally

---

[54] Green 1981: 141; van der Veen 1985: 213.
[55] Green 1981: 141.   [56] Greig in Cunliffe 1971: 376.   [57] Halbaek 1964: 162.
[58] Willcox 1977: 279 Table 1; Bowman and Thomas 1994: 175 no. 204.
[59] Neal *et al.* 1990: 28.   [60] Bowman and Thomas 1994: 159 no. 192, 278 no. 302.
[61] Davies 1971: 133.   [62] For example Alcock 2001: colour plates 8 and 25.
[63] Vaughan and Geissler 1997: 184.   [64] Grant 1996: 107 footnote 53.

found in waterlogged deposits, but those from carrots seem much rarer.[65]

Brassica seeds are not uncommon, indicating that leafy vegetables such as cabbage and rape were probably eaten. A particularly useful deposit that indicates such seeds do represent food crops, and are not just casual wild inclusions, comes from the garden of the Bancroft villa where they are found alongside the deliberately cultivated seeds of coriander and summer savory.[66] It is also probable that the leaves of vegetables that would normally today be eaten as root vegetables, such as beet and turnip, were eaten.[67] Traditionally in British cuisine young nettles have been seen as a useful vegetable, given they are available earlier in the spring than many others.[68] It is interesting to note that seeds from both the stinging nettle (*Urtica dioica*) and the small nettle (*U. urens*) were present in some quantity in the cesspit at Stonea suggesting they may have been a food item there as well.[69] The range of the green vegetables exploited may have been wider than it is today.

[65] E.g. Bastow in Abramson *et al.* 1999: Tables 8, 10 and 14.
[66] Peterson and Robinson in Williams and Zepvat 1994: 581.
[67] Monkton in Connor and Buckley 1999: 353.
[68] Hartley 1954: 387.
[69] van der Veen in Jackson and Potter 1996: Table 65.

CHAPTER 15

Drink

INTRODUCTION

Prior to the advent of tea and coffee, much of what was drunk in Britain was alcoholic, and this is likely to have been the case during the Roman period as well. One of the advantages of alcoholic drinks was that they were frequently safer to drink than water. Though Roman engineering associated with water supply is often admired, it does not necessarily follow that a pure and healthy product was being delivered. Ancient writers were well aware of the problems that impure waters could bring. Pliny noted that everyone agreed water was better when boiled.[1] It can also be doubted whether liquid milk formed a regular part of the diet of many in Roman Britain. The cattle herds do not appear to have been managed as dairy animals, and most milk would have been turned into cheese. Prior to modern refrigeration, milk would rapidly sour. There was also the problem that it could be disease-ridden. The modern levels of liquid milk consumption owe more to deliberate state-sponsored advertising campaigns to cope with over-production than to long-established drinking habits.[2]

Of the various different types of beverages consumed, it is wine that leaves most evidence archaeologically, both in the packaging and in the utensils used in its consumption. There is also a certain amount of evidence for the brewing of beer. Other drinks may be suspected, but archaeological evidence for them is very scarce. Writers such as Dioscurides and Pliny list a wide range of wines made from fruit and vegetables other than the grape;[3] but unless the pit at Doncaster with the pips of hundreds of apples is evidence of an apple wine or cider-making episode,[4] evidence for these is missing. It might also be suspected that mead would

---

[1] Pliny XXXI.23.   [2] Vernon 2000: 699.
[3] Dioscorides V, 28–98; Pliny XIV.18–20.
[4] Buckland and Magilton 1986: 198 and 200.

have been consumed, but the evidence for this is even rarer than evidence for honey. Here we will first look at the evidence for the drinks themselves, before considering what drinking vessels are telling us.

The Roman world already had a well-developed wine culture by the time Britain came within its orbit during the later Iron Age. Italy appears to have undergone an expansion in the production and consumption of wine in the second century BC.[5] By the middle of the first century, wines were ranked in order of merit and knowledgeably discussed in a manner that would do credit to modern wine writers. Pliny even appreciated the importance of what in modern parlance would be called the *terroir*, i.e. the interaction of soil, topography and climate.[6]

From the ancient literature it is obvious that there was a wide range of styles available. Some places such as Cos and Rhodes were famous for making a very sweet wine from grapes that had been allowed to dry to concentrate their sweetness.[7] Falernian, one of the *grands crus*, included a style that was very dry.[8] If wines survived the heat of their first summer, they could be regarded as vintage; and there are good grounds for thinking that some wines aged in sealed amphorae may have eventually resembled something like a dry sherry.[9] One of the problems was producing a wine that would not turn to vinegar. The agricultural manuals of antiquity provide detailed instructions about growing vines and making wine, and some of the instructions such as including seawater are very alien to modern vinification practices. It would appear that boiled seawater and other additives were being used as preservatives, and would not necessarily have resulted in an unpleasant salty taste. Experimental work using Columella's instructions found that generally no salt was detected in the tasting.[10]

Although we know that this sophisticated wine making and drinking culture existed in the ancient world, it is difficult to evaluate the extent to which people in Britain partook of it. Though it is possible to establish where the wine might have come from, that does not necessarily imply it was good wine even if it came from an area of a known *grand cru*. Wines from Campania were put into amphorae with a distinctive black sand

[5] Tchernia 1986: 58.
[6] Pliny XIV.viii–ix, see especially viii.70; Tchernia 1986: 350 appendix V.
[7] Tchernia 1986: 105.   [8] Dalby 2000: 48–9.
[9] Tchernia and Brun 1999: 142–5.   [10] Tchernia and Brun 1999: 120–1.

fabric. These would have included not only the Falernian wines, ranked second only to Setinum in esteem, but also those of Pompeii, dismissed by Pliny because they gave him a headache that lasted till noon of the following day.[11] We know that something that purported to be Falernian was present at Colchester and London because there are amphora sherds with painted inscriptions stating this;[12] what we cannot know is whether drinking the contents of other black-sand amphorae would have been a pleasurable experience or one more likely to have given you a hangover.

The Colchester and London fragments suggest there was a market for good wine in Britain. At Vindolanda one account records the acquisition of both a named wine, Massic (a type of Falernian), and quantities of unnamed wine.[13] This would suggest that, at least in the commanding officer's household, different wines were being drunk from choice. Other named wines include Aminean wine, mentioned on a sherd from Caerleon.[14] This is an Italian wine, but it is known the vines were exported, and this particular one would appear to have been Spanish.[15] Sweet wines of unknown provenance are recorded at Mumrills and Exeter,[16] and there is a reference to *mulsum* (a mixture of wine and honey) at Vindolanda.[17]

The earliest wine amphora fragments in Britain are from an Italian type in use during the later second century BC to about the middle of the first century BC.[18] The distribution is limited, being concentrated in Wessex and in the Essex – Hertfordshire area.[19] From the mid-first century BC a wider range of amphora types are noted and it is clear that wine from Catalonia in the north-east part of the Iberian peninsula was also being consumed. Judged by the number of amphora fragments recovered this diversification of supply was not matched by an increase in consumption. If anything the amount of wine imported may have declined.[20] The area of the country which wine reached remained limited to the south. Dragonby in Lincolnshire is one of the most northerly sites with imported pottery prior to AD 43, but there is no evidence of amphora-borne commodities of any type associated with the Iron Age occupation.[21]

In the ancient literature, the Celtic populations outside of the Roman world were notorious for their voracious appetite for wine. It was a trait

<hr />

[11] Pliny XIV.viii. 62 and 70.   [12] Sealey and Davies 1984; RIB II.6 no. 2492.40.
[13] Bowman and Thomas 1994: 153 no. 190.   [14] RIB II.6 no. 2493.12.
[15] Sealey 1985: 83.   [16] RIB II.6 nos. 2493.14 and 2493.16.
[17] Bowman and Thomas 1994: 278 no. 302.
[18] Peacock and Williams 1986: Class 3 (Dressel 1A).
[19] Fitzpatrick 2003: fig. 2.   [20] Fitzpatrick 2003: 13–4.
[21] Willis 1996: 188; Williams in May 1996: 598.

that set them apart as barbarians, for they drank it neat and not mixed with water as civilised persons were supposed to. The amphora evidence paints a much more complex picture. Whilst the quantities imported into southern Gaul from the second century BC do appear very large, the north appears far more abstemious.[22] The amphorae in late Iron Age Britain also suggests wine was not part of most people's lives even in the south. As a rare and uncommon import it may have conferred distinction on the individuals able to obtain and disperse it. The distribution patterns tend to suggest that how this was done varied in different areas. In the south-central area amphora fragments are found overwhelmingly on settlement sites, whereas in the Essex – Hertfordshire area they form an important part of burial rituals.[23] In some elite graves complete amphorae are found, suggesting the consumption of considerable amounts of wine during the funeral ceremonies. The five found in the Welwyn Garden City burial,[24] and the minimum of seventeen at the Lexden tumulus,[25] would have represented approximately 135 and 460 litres of wine respectively. Such funerary feasts are unlikely to have taken place very often. So, though wine consumption may be more archaeologically visible in the Essex – Hertfordshire area because of the burials, opportunities for wine drinking may have been more frequent in the Wessex area.

Wine does not appear to have been imported in quantity until after the conquest. Much of this will have been for the army. From the literary sources it is clear that the rations of a soldier included *posca* and wine; and that strict disciplinarians insisted the troops drank only the former.[26] In the Anglophone literature *posca* is normally translated as sour wine, whereas the Francophone studies see it as vinegar which was diluted with water at a rate of 1:10.[27] The latter interpretation would explain strict generals' preference for it. That the soldiers had access to wine, even when on campaign, can be seen from the amphora fragments from the early forts. Table 7.1 shows the proportion of wine amphorae in a number of dated assemblages. The first three rows were all early forts, and wine amphorae are present in appreciable quantities. The case of the earliest fort at Castleford is particularly useful here. It was a campaigning base for the early expansion into the north during the 70s. The quantification is by minimum numbers, but if translated into quantities of content, 28% of amphora-borne commodities were wine.[28]

[22] Tchernia 1986: 90; Woolf 1998: 179.   [23] Millett 1990: fig. 9.
[24] Stead 1967: 7.   [25] Williams in Niblett 1999: 193.
[26] Roth 1999: 24–5, 38.   [27] Tchernia 1986: 11–13.
[28] Rush *et al.* 2000: Table 18.

Table 15.1. *Wine sources at first-century forts based on amphora weights.*

Site	Date	Gaul (%)	Rhodes (%)	PW10 (%)	Total (kg)
Kingsholm	Mid-60s	4	90	6	22.49
Exeter	c. 55–80	19	24	57	10.13
Wroxeter	c. 57–79	65	25	10	12.42
Inchtuthil	c. 78–84	52	—	48	2.28

One thing that most writers on the Roman army are united about is that the mechanisms of army supply are not understood.[29] There does not appear to have been a central bureaucracy, and it may have been that quartermasters working at a divisional, or even unit, level negotiated the supplies with individual merchants. The supply to first-century forts is certainly varied as can be seen in Table 15.1. Unfortunately the standard wine amphora (PW10) was made in Italy, Gaul and Spain, and attempts are not regularly made to differentiate the fabrics. At Wroxeter, when this was done, it was found the sources included Italy (including Campania), Catalonia, southern Spain and the east Mediterranean.

In addition to the weight data presented in Table 15.1, hints as to the pattern of supply can be gained from other military amphora assemblages less usefully quantified. In the first fort at Castleford occupied between *c.* AD 71–4 and 86 the wine amphorae are either Gallic or PW10, with the former appearing to provide the bulk of the supply (86% of the estimated total capacity).[30] At Blake Street within the fortress at York, Gallic amphora fragments were again in the majority compared to PW10 amphorae in the first two phases of occupation dated to *c.* AD 71–100.[31] At the *scamnum tribunorum* site within the fortress at Caerleon equal quantities of Gallic amphorae and PW10 were estimated for the earliest phase of *c.* AD 75 to 90 – 100.[32] At none of these sites is there any indication that wine from Rhodes was being drunk. The strong presence of wine from Rhodes in the earlier forts may have been because of state action. The island was incorporated into the empire in AD 44 as a punishment for the deaths of some Roman citizens, and confiscation of wine to supply the army is a possibility.[33] Certainly its disappearance from the Flavian forts and the

---

[29] Alston 1995: 112; Roth 1999: 264.
[30] Rush *et al.* 2000: Table 19.
[31] Monaghan 1993: Table 117.
[32] Zienkiewicz 1992: Table 3.
[33] Sealey 1985: 134.

Table 15.2. *Wine sources in London during the first century.*

Date	Gaul (%)	Rhodes (%)	PW10 (%)	Total (kg)
50–60/61	44	21	35	4.68
75–100	62	13	27	22.77

growing dominance of the Gallic sources seems to suggest a reorganisation of supply to the military.

To a certain extent the pattern of supply to those parts of the civilian population that wished to consume wine was similar to the military pattern. Wine was certainly reaching what appears to be the native focus of settlement at Colchester in the Gosbecks and Sheepen area in the period AD 43 to 60–1. The amphora fragments have been calculated to represent a minimum of 21 Rhodian amphorae, 5 Gallic and 44 PW10; the last mentioned coming from Italy and Spain.[34] The pre-Boudican figures for London also show a strong Rhodian presence, but the pattern thereafter seems to deviate from the military pattern as Rhodian wines are still present, though in lower quantities (Table 15.2).

The presence of Rhodian wine amphorae in other urban assemblages of the later-first- and/or earlier second-century assemblages can be also be noted.[35] In general though, by the end of the first century, the majority of the wine that was drunk in Britain came from Gaul. Certainly, where wine amphorae can be identified on rural sites, they tend to be the typical Gallic shape.[36] It is also noticeable that most amphorae made in Britain were of this shape;[37] presumably because, to most people in the country, this was the 'proper' shape for a wine amphora.

A curious feature of wine supply to Britain in the second and third centuries is that while the rest of the country is drinking Gallic wine, the soldiers on the northern frontier were not. Gallic amphorae are seriously under-represented in the assemblages from Hadrian's Wall; and it has been suggested, on the assumption that wine of some form would have been drunk, that it came from the Rhineland and was shipped in barrels.[38]

[34] Sealey 1985: Table 1, 7.
[35] Clark in Connor and Buckley 1999: 116; Williams in Woodward *et al.* 1993: Table 28.
[36] Wallace and Turner-Walker in Clarke 1998: Table 11; Williams in Hands 1998: 226; Neal 1974: 231 no. 217.
[37] Symonds 2003.
[38] Bidwell 1985: 182; Croom and Bidwell in Casey and Hoffmann 1998: 178.

Soldiers in contemporary forts in Yorkshire, by contrast, did have access to Gallic wine. As Evans has noted,[39] this implies the Yorkshire forts and the Wall forts were being supplied by different quartermasters. Given this is a regional pattern, this might imply wine supply was coordinated at that time at a divisional level. It opens up the possibility that, by tracing the boundary between those forts with Gallic amphorae and those where they are under-represented, it might be possible to explore the command structure in the north.

The wine supply to the northern forts continues to show differences from that of the rest of the country in the later Roman period. A distinctive form of black-sand amphora from Campania with an almond-shaped rim forms a substantial part of the mid-third to mid-fourth-century amphora assemblages of forts such as South Shields, Newcastle upon Tyne and Wallsend;[40] and in both military and civilian assemblages at York.[41] These amphorae are occasionally found in purely civilian contexts in the north,[42] but are rare elsewhere. In the south, wine from Gaul continues to dominate in the third century, both on military sites such as the Saxon shore fort at Caister-on-Sea and in civilian assemblages such as those from London.[43]

Gallic amphorae cease production in the third century, and with their disappearance we cease to be able to map wine consumption over much of the country. The degree to which wine was shipped to Britain in barrels throughout the period is the great unknowable feature of the wine trade. The manufacture of Romano-British amphorae for transhipment seems to be a first-century phenomenon, but barrels made of silver fir were being reused in third- and fourth-century contexts, and these presumably indicate the continuing import of Gallic wine in large quantities. It is salutary to reflect that at Droitwich five large barrels were found reused in mid-third to mid-fourth-century contexts.[44] They were comparable in size to the Silchester barrels for which capacities of approximately 900 litres have been calculated.[45] Nothing in the pottery report for this site hints at the presence of any amphora-borne commodity; but, unless these barrels were being brought empty over long distances for reuse, considerable amounts of wine were being drunk somewhere in the area.

---

[39] Evans in Wilson 2002b: 482.
[40] Bidwell and Speak 1994: Table 8.9: Williams in Snape and Bidwell 2002: 150–1.
[41] Williams in Perrin 1990: 345, Tables 23, 27, 30, 31, 32.
[42] Evans in Neal 1996: 71.
[43] Darling and Gurney 1993: Table 29; Miller *et al.* 1986: fig. 76 Phases 4 and 5; Lakin *et al.* 2002: Tables 7 and 9.
[44] Crone in Woodiwiss 1992: 111, Table 7.   [45] RIB II.4, page 1.

The evidence for wine production in Britain is sparse, but the discovery of a vineyard at Wollaston in the Nene valley in the mid-1990s finally established beyond doubt that wine was made in the province. Excavations there uncovered shallow ditches spaced at 5 m intervals, each ditch being lined on either side by post-holes with traces of root balls of plants at 1.5 m intervals. Pollen recovered from the ditches established that the plants had been vines trained onto the wooden supports along the edges of the trench. Over 6 km of these ditches were found, and it is estimated that there would have been at least 4,000 separate vines which could have produced over 10,000 litres of wine.[46] Taking into consideration similar trenches in the area, it is estimated that a figure of 30,000 litres might be more realistic.[47] Though this might seem a great deal, in reality it would have been a very modest amount compared to the volumes produced and shipped in the Mediterranean where a single cargo could amount to more than three times that amount.[48] In addition to the vineyard evidence, it is also clear that amphorae were being manufactured by Romano-British potters, primarily in the first century.[49] Whether these represent the packaging for small-scale production such as that at Woolaston, or are for the distribution of wine originally shipped in large barrels, is unclear. How the Woolaston wine was shipped is unknown. The Nene Valley had a large pottery industry, but none of its products have been identified as being likely amphorae.

On rural native sites it is much more common to find fragments of olive oil amphorae than ones from wine amphorae, but the wine-barrel problem means that it is difficult to be certain that this means no wine was being consumed. It could be of course that wine was coming onto the sites transported in different containers. Another way of tracing wine consumption is to look not at the packaging but at the utensils that were used when drinking it. Within a Romano-British milieu, these show a rather surprising pattern.

Drinking wine in a Roman manner involved mixing it with water, which could be either hot or cold. There were a range of utensils involved in this including jugs for holding the wine and water, large bucket-shaped vessels for mixing, and ladles for decanting the mixture. A unique sarcophagus from Simpelfeld in the Netherlands provides a snapshot of what such a set might have looked like in the later second to third century. The interior of it had been carved to represent an elegant lady reclining on a

[46] Meadows 1996.   [47] Brown and Meadows 2000: 492.
[48] Sealey 1985: 126.   [49] Symonds 2003.

Figure 15.1. Detail of the Simpelfeld sarcophagus showing the wine service. Top row glass cups, mixing buckets centrally, water and wine jugs bottom. (Photo: M. J. Baxter.)

couch along one side, and along all the others her household goods were set out. On the wall facing her, a shelving unit is depicted. On the lowest level there are two jugs, above these are two handled buckets, and above those are three cups, probably made of glass given their shapes (Fig. 15.1). The jugs include a distinctive type with a beaked spout and a narrow-necked funnel-rimmed one. The beaked jug belongs to a family of jugs made from sheet bronze and iron that have hinged lids. Limescale deposits inside them make it clear they were regularly used for heating water.[50] The Simpelfeld sarcophagus makes it clear they were part of wine-drinking sets.

One of the problems with studying metal vessels is that, because they were large, they would generally have been recycled at the end of their

---

[50] Koster 1997: 30.

useful lives. Fragments from them are much less common in ordinary site assemblages than fragments of pottery and glass vessels, because of different rubbish-disposal practices. Fortunately various of the metal vessels used in serving wine were made from multiple component parts and individual pieces do occur with some regularity. A picture of where they were being used can be built up from these.

For the water jugs, the hinged lids must often have broken and been discarded from the numbers found. The lids themselves commonly had separately made and distinctive knobs inserted into them to aid opening. These too are found in site assemblages, as are the handles. The mixing buckets can be identified from the escutcheons and mounts which were soldered onto the body to hold the handles. The large basins used for hand washing in polite dining regimes also had separately made handles.[51] (See fig. 15.2).

A survey of the finds assemblages of nearly 400 separate excavations is presented in Table 15.3. The types of sites have been divided into broad categories. The military category includes not just forts but the *vici* and *canabae* in their vicinity. The small-town category includes both walled small towns and more straggling roadside settlements. An attempt has been made to distinguish between those rural sites which seemed to have some pretensions to a 'Roman' lifestyle (villas) and those which seem better described as basic farmsteads or villages (rural). As can be seen, less than half of the excavations produced fragments of metal vessels of any type. The number of sites producing fragments of saucepan-shaped *trullea*, water-jug and bucket fittings associated with serving wine, and fittings from the basins and handled dishes used for hand washing are shown in columns 3 to 7.

Saucepans, as probably befits a multi-purpose vessel,[52] were the most frequently encountered type, but water jugs were common finds as well. Both they and the bucket fittings occur all the way down the settlement hierarchy, which is not the pattern seen for the hand-washing equipment. Admittedly they are not common on the rural sites with only 2% of that category of site producing any evidence of them, compared with 8% of the military sites, 18% of the towns, 3% of the villas and 9% of the small towns; but the mere fact that they can be recognised on rural sites does suggest wine was being consumed on at least some of them and in a 'Roman' manner.

It is always possible that the water jugs were being used to heat water for other purposes, but it is difficult to see what else the buckets would

---

[51] Tassinari 1993: 232.   [52] See p. 47.

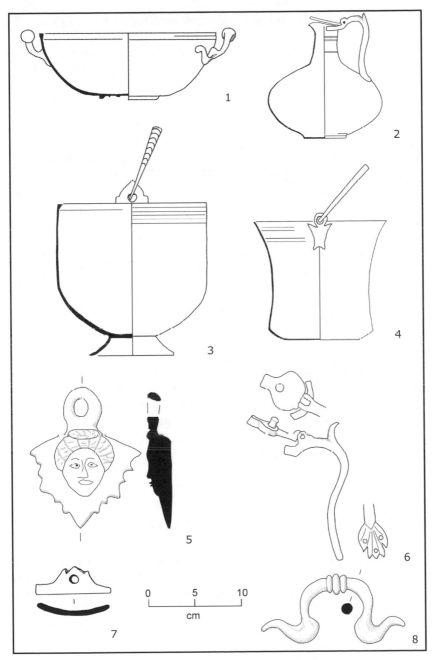

Figure 15.2. Metal vessels used for hand washing (no. 1) and the wine service (nos. 2–4) (scale 1 : 6). Nos. 5 and 7 are typical bucket fittings (scale 1 : 2). No. 6 is a water-jug handle and no. 8 a basin handle (scale 1 : 4). Scale bar correct for 1 : 4. (After McCarthy 1991: fig. 78 (5); P. Crummy 1992: fig. 15.5 (6); Frere 1972: fig. 40 (7); N. Crummy 1983: fig. 76 (8). Nos. 1–4 based on originals in Tassinari 1993 and den Boesterd 1956.)

Table 15.3. *Incidence of metal vessels on different types of site.*

Site type	Site total	With vessels	Saucepan	Water jug	Bucket fittings	Basin fittings	Handled dish
Military	126	59	26	10	9	5	3
Town	74	34	5	13	5	6	1
Small town	46	14	1	4	1	2	2
Villa	34	14	1	1	1	2	—
Rural	81	13	2	2	3	—	—
Religious	17	5	1	—	1	—	—
Total	384	148	36	30	20	15	6

have been used for. The escutcheons and handle attachments are generally soldered to the body of the vessel with a lead alloy that would melt at relatively low temperatures, so it would have been impractical to use them for any cooking purpose. There is also some other evidence that might support of the use of the water jugs as part of the wine service in the countryside. At Whitton in south Glamorgan there was not only the lid from a jug, but the terminal from a wine ladle.[53] Though there was no evidence in the form of amphorae that wine was being drunk there, these vessel fragments strongly suggest it was. Sheepen appears to have been the focus of native settlement at Colchester in the pre-Boudican period. Not only were large quantities of wine being drunk, but it was being consumed in a 'Roman' way, as fragments from a minimum of three water jugs were recovered.[54] In fact the whole dining experience may occasionally have been in the Roman fashion as two basin handles were also recovered.[55]

BEER

My fellow soldiers have no beer. Please order some to be sent. (Masclus to Cerialis at Vindolanda[56])

The ancient sources often mention beer as something brewed by the Celtic tribes, and there is also a reference to it in Diocletian's price edict where Celtic beer is priced at twice the cost of Egyptian beer, and half the

---

[53] Webster in Jarrett and Wrathmell 1981: 182 no. 50 and 51.
[54] Hawkes and Hull 1947: 332 nos. 12–14 and 17.
[55] Hawkes and Hull 1947: 332 nos. 15–16.
[56] Bowman and Thomas 2003: 84 no. 628.

cost of ordinary wine.[57] The basic ingredient was malted grain, i.e. grain that has been allowed to sprout to a point where the starch has been converted to a soluble sugar. The germination is then halted by the application of gentle heat, and the resulting malt ground. When it is mixed with water, the sugars are dissolved out into the liquid, which can then be fermented into an alcoholic drink by yeast. In many beer-making cultures, special yeasts have been developed over the years, but wild yeast in the atmosphere will also produce this effect. The modern Belgian lambic beers, for example, are fermented by wild yeasts.

What would the beer that Masclus's fellow soldiers wanted have tasted like? It would certainly have differed in one way from that of modern Britain, and very possibly in a second. It would have been unhopped as hops only started to be used in European beer-making in the twelfth century. Some writers still regarded them as an alien adulterant to British beer in the seventeenth century.[58] Hops add a certain bitterness to the beer, but more importantly they act as a preservative. The beer of Roman Britain could more accurately be described as ale, and would not have had a very long shelf life. Secondly, it seems very likely that, at least in the south of the country, it was not barley that formed the base of the beer, but wheat. Spelt wheat is the principal grain in all the charred-grain assemblages that can plausibly be interpreted as the result of a malting process.[59] This is unfortunate for those scholars who like to reconstruct the political history of Britain between the invasions of Caesar and Claudius from the coins and the scant historical references. The head of barley on the reverse of some coins cannot have been symbolising beer. This rather spoils the story that different tribes, by choosing barley or vine leaves on their coins, were showing pro- and anti-Roman sympathies.[60]

An eminent modern beer writer has described wheat as producing 'a distinctive, fruity tartness', and resulting in a pale, hazy yellow beer.[61] Modern brewers prefer barley because it has a higher proportion of fermentable sugars, the husk on the grain acts as a natural filter, and the taste of wheat and hops do not combine well. That at least some early brewers realised the advantage of barley in beer is suggested by a deposit of malt found at Colchester in a Boudican context. This had a combination

---

[57] Pliny XIV.29; Graser 1940: 322.
[58] P. Clarke 1983: 3; Drummond and Wilbraham 1957: 114.
[59] E.g. van der Veen 1991: 312; Letts in Smith *et al.* 1997: 268; Robinson in Houlston 1999: 149; Murphy in Bedwin and Bedwin 1999: 21; Alvey and Smith in Sparey-Green 2002: 300–7; Fryer in Bales 2004: 49–54.
[60] Frere 1987: 31. [61] Protz 1995: 8.

of spelt and barley in the ratio of 10:1.[62] Other Boudican grain deposits consisted of virtually pure spelt with only the occasional grain of barley, suggesting that the malt was being deliberately manipulated to give a special taste. In the north, given that barley was the staple grain, it might be suspected that beer was brewed from barley. The taste and colour of the beer may have been another way in which the north and the south varied, though at present we lack the debris from malting in the north that would allow us to explore this.

Until relatively modern times, two sorts of beer were produced. Strong ale was produced by the initial fermentation; then small beer, which was only weakly alcoholic, could be produced by pouring more water over the wort. Both types would have made a valuable contribution to the diet, as it has been calculated that even small beer would had the equivalent of 150–200 calories a pint. It is probable that beer was drunk by all sectors of Romano-British society, and that it was looked on as healthy for all ages as home-brewed beer was until moderately recently.[63] Certainly at Vindolanda, it is not just the common soldiers who request beer. Quite large amounts are recorded as coming into, or being dispersed from, the commanding officer's house. In one account which relates to a seven day period in June, Celtic beer is noted on four of the days. For one of the days where there is no reference, there are missing entries; and the final day has only one entry and the note that the 'lords' were away. The quantities of beer are noted in three cases as 2 *modii*, 3 *modii* and between 3 and 4 *modii*. Substituting 2 *modii* for the missing quantity, this account suggests a household consumption of at least 90 litres for the week.[64] Another account that may have been associated with the occupation of centurions' quarters records the acquisition of beer in containers that held 100 pints.[65] Given the whole garrison with servants and dependents would have been well over 500 individuals, a considerable amount of time and energy must have been invested in brewing. It is not surprising that at Vindolanda there were individuals who could be described as both maltsters (*braciarius*) and brewers (*ceruesarius*) as both would have been full-time jobs.[66]

Given the short shelf life of unhopped beer, brewing is likely to have taken place on all sorts of sites, but it is the sort of process that does not

---

[62] Murphy in Crummy 1992: 282.   [63] Drummond and Wilbraham 1957: 114.
[64] Bowman and Thomas 1994: 153 no. 190; conversion following RIB II.2, 58.
[65] Bowman and Thomas 1994: 145 no. 186.
[66] Bowman and Thomas 1994: 131 no. 182; 2003: no. 102.

leave archaeological traces. Brewing tubs are likely to have been of wood, and when made it could have been stored in wooden barrels as was done until recently. The malting process itself can be identified on a small number of sites, of which features excavated at Fordington Bottom, to the west of Dorchester are a good example. There a working area in a late Roman settlement consisted of a yard surface, an H-shaped corn dryer and a pit that had been provided with mortared flint walls faced with *opus signinum* to produce a watertight cistern. Samples from the final use of the cistern and dryer showed that malting had been taking place using primarily spelt wheat with an admixture of 5–6% barley.[67] The whole ensemble can plausibly be interpreted as a maltings with the initial steeping taking place in the cistern, the stone yard surface possibly providing a sprouting area, and the corn drier turning the sprouted grain to malt. The malt may have been for consumption on the farm itself, but its location less than 2 km from the centre of the Roman town would have made it possible to transport either malt or beer to the town for sale.

Though corn driers are occasionally found in the earlier Roman period, they are predominantly a third- and fourth-century phenomenon concentrated in southern and eastern England. The charred grain assemblages show that they were used for a variety of purposes including malting.[68] The development of corn driers may have had an impact on beer production as they probably allowed malt to be produced more effectively. Whether this resulted in more beer being brewed is an open question.

SPICED AND INFUSED DRINKS

The taste for spiced wine in the Roman period is well documented. Not only were spices and aromatics added during the vinification process, but recipes for strongly spiced aperitifs also exist.[69] Though it is sometimes asserted that strainers would form part of the utensils used to serve wine, evidence of this is curiously sparse in the heartlands of the Empire by the first century AD. There are no strainers in the elegant silver drinking service depicted in the tomb of Gaius Vestorius Priscus who died in AD 70 at Pompeii, though all the other vessel types that might be expected are present.[70] The author of the standard work on gold and silver plate felt it was remarkable that 'very few silver strainers have been found at Pompeii

[67] Barnes in Smith *et al.* 1997: 217; Letts in Smith *et al.* 1997: 267–70.
[68] van der Veen 1991.   [69] Pliny XIV.xxiv 124–8; Dalby 2000: 245–6.
[70] Stefani 2005: 48 top.

and Herculaneum' and went on to conclude that perhaps by then wine was strained in the kitchen using bronze vessels.[71] Such a conclusion became harder to uphold after the publication of a monumental work cataloguing the extant bronze vessels from Pompeii which showed that strainers formed a very small part of the overall bronze-vessel assemblage.[72] So if the wine was being infused with spices, any straining that was needed would perhaps have been most commonly done using an item such as a sieve made from cloth, like the linen strainer referred to by Pliny as a device for reducing the strength of wine.[73] It is also probable that the host or drinker would not have been called upon to strain the drink at the point of consumption. The recipes Apicius gives for spiced and perfumed wine are for large quantities, made over a number of days and presumably 'bottled' for later consumption.[74]

Long-handled metal strainers and their matching bowls (fig. 15.3 no. 3) seem much more a feature of the areas beyond the frontiers of the empire by the first century.[75] A similar pattern is noticeable in their distribution within Britain. They have been found far beyond the frontiers of the province, at Glenshee and Helmsdale,[76] but are rare within it. The distinctive handles used on both the strainers and bowls were uncommon in the assemblages used as the data set for Table 15.3. They were only recorded at five sites compared to the thirty seven that have produced saucepan handles. Symmetrical flanged strainers are even rarer and again have a predominantly Highland distribution.[77]

The evidence both from Britain and elsewhere does not support the idea that these strainers were a major part of the wine service, and in at least some places they may have been used for the preparation of some other type of infused drink. Helmsdale is far to the north in the Highlands, a long way from any regular supplies of wine; while a grave excavated early in the twentieth century in Denmark, contained a long-handled strainer and bowl, with residues from a drink made with rye and flavoured with cranberry, bilberry, whortleberry and box-myrtle leaves.[78] So it seems more likely that the strainers are reflecting a taste for an infused beer.

Various other types of vessels also indicate a liking for infused beverages. Spouted strainer bowls have been found in late Iron Age and early Roman contexts in south-eastern England (Fig. 15.3 nos. 1–2). Copper-alloy

---

[71] Strong 1966: 144–5.   [72] Tassinari 1993: 69 type K3000.

[73] Pliny XIV.xxviii.138; see Sealey in Brown 1999: 122–3 for further discussion of this point.

[74] Apicius I. 1 and 4.   [75] Koster 1997: 46.

[76] Curle 1932: 386 no. 64, 392 no. 79.   [77] Tomalin 1989.

[78] Cited by Curle 1932: 307.

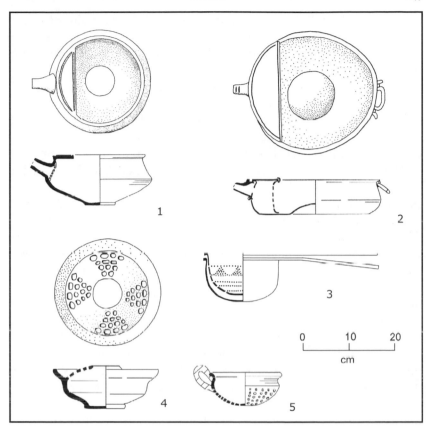

Figure 15.3. Strainers used for infused drinks. (After Niblet 1985: Mf fig. 33 (no. 1); Stead 1967: fig. 12 (no. 2); den Boesterd 1956: pl. III (no. 3); Grimes 1930: figs. 72–3 (nos. 4–5).) scale 1 : 8.

examples have come from a rich burial at Welwyn of the later first century BC, one of the conquest period graves at Stanway, a late-first-century AD burial at Wheathamstead and various domestic sites in Bedfordshire, Suffolk and Norfolk.[79] Pottery versions are quite common in pre-Boudican contexts at Sheepen outside Colchester and are also known in London.[80] In general the distribution is in eastern England, north of the Thames and

[79] Stead 1967: 24; Crummy 1997: 67; Anon 2004: 33; Sealey in Brown 1999: 121; Sealey in Bales 2004: 30–1.

[80] Hawkes and Hull 1947: 273–5 figs. 50 no. 8 and 57 no. 12; Niblett 1985: fig. 33. Marsh 1978: 181 Type 46.

south of the Wash.[81] The Stanway bowl contained the remains of worm-wood which would have produced a very bitter drink. There is a recipe in Apicius that uses wine and wormwood to produce a Roman absinth;[82] but, as Paul Sealey has pointed out, fragments of these bowls are found on sites with no evidence of wine consumption, and so there is the distinct possi-bility that they were used to make an infused beer.[83] Whether it was always infused with wormwood is open to question. The Stanway grave also contained surgical instruments and an amphora of fish sauce, so the contents of the bowl may have been medicinal rather than enjoyable.

There are various other pottery vessels that could have been used as strainers for infused drinks, though they always very rare. In the case of the open bowls with perforations in their lower sides and bases, it is possible that they were multi-functional utensils as they could have functioned like a modern colander (fig. 15.3 no. 5). In the case of the utensil long-termed 'wine-coolers', the association with the preparation of an infused drink seems secure. These are bowls with an integral lid that rises from the interior of the wall to a central narrow aperture (fig. 15.3 no. 4). The narrowness of the aperture means that it could only have been used with liquids, and the lid has many small perforations so that it could have functioned as a strainer. These vessels have been the subject of a detailed study by Scott Martin.[84] He has shown that they occur primarily on urban and military sites and were produced in the later first- to early second-century period. They are widely spread through the province, but often give the impression of being special commissions, and were clearly not in the regular repertoire of any of the larger pottery industries. It is suggested that they functioned by having the liquid and infusing ingredi-ents introduced through the central aperture which was then stoppered with a bung. The ingredients would be left to infuse and then the liquid drained off by tipping the bowl to allow it to flow through the perfor-ations. The resulting drink seems very likely to have been alcoholic because the perforations on an example from Germany spell out a drinking slogan in a suitably incoherent form,[85] but whether what was being spiced was wine, beer or mead is unknown.

Both the strainer bowls and the wine coolers have a fairly limited period when they were in use, and were not common. The strainer bowls appear most popular amongst the native population in East Anglia during

[81] Sealey in Brown 1999: 121.   [82] Apicius I.3.
[83] Sealey in Bales 2004: 30. See also Sealey in Brown 1999: 122–4 for an extended consideration of this.
[84] Unpublished.   [85] Marsh 1978: 181.

the late first century BC and first century AD. The wine-coolers were favoured by some elements of the military and urban communities during the later first to early second centuries. and may reflect a passing taste for a style of drink that originated in the Rhineland. The rarity in Britain of both these styles of vessels and the metal strainers, suggests that the taste for infused and/or spiced drinks was never widespread within the province. Had it been, it seems very likely that the prolific Romano-British pottery industries would regularly have featured utensils to cater for it, but they never did.

PINTS AND HALF PINTS

The type of glasses people drink out of can tell you much about the drinking habits of the community they live in. The British have long consumed beer in pint (c. 0.6 l) or half-pint quantities. With the rise of wine drinking, the standard glass offered in a public house is now 175 ml or 250 ml. Across the Channel in much of western Europe, the standard beer glass comes in 0.2 l and 0.4 l sizes, and you are more likely to receive a glass of wine in a 125 ml size.[86] The difference in glass sizes provides an immediate insight into the different drinking cultures. Differences that in Britain lead our political and medical establishment to berate us for overindulgence, and on the continent mean that in some areas there is an equation between being British and being a drunken yob. Archaeology struggles to recreate the intricacies of drinking practice and rituals in all their nuances, but some insights can be gained by looking at the vessels it was consumed from.

Tall pottery vessels, often made in finer fabrics, have long been known as beakers. Some of the beakers can have a very large capacity raising the question of whether they were all drinking vessels. Fortunately this can be examined via a group made in the Moselle valley in the third century which very conveniently have drinking mottos written on them (fig. 15.4). These say such things as 'Drink', 'Serve unmixed wine', 'Mix for me', 'Wine gives strength' and 'Spare the water'; as well as more general good wishes such as 'Good luck to the user' and 'Be happy'.[87] Even when the mottos don't explicitly refer to wine or drink, they are frequently decorated with vine

---

[86] Observations by the author over many enjoyable years. The continental figures do not apply in resorts frequented by many British tourists where litre glasses can often be observed.

[87] RIB II.6 89–97; Tyers 1996: 138–40; Steures 2002.

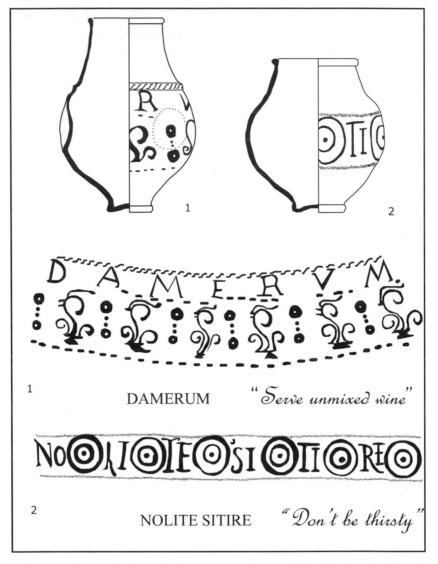

Figure 15.4. Pottery beakers with drinking mottos from Verulamium (no. 1) and York (no. 2). (After Frere 1972: fig. 133; RCHME York: pl. 35.) Scale approximately 1 : 4.

leaves or bunches of grapes. Their association with wine drinking thus seems well established. Fig. 15.5 plots the rim diameter against the height of a number of these beakers from British sites together with broadly

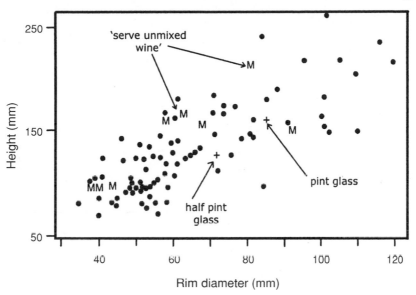

Figure 15.5. Plot of the size of late second- to third-century pottery beakers. Beakers with mottos relating to drinking indicated by 'M', standard 'straight' pint and half-pint glasses given for comparison.

contemporary beakers of late second- and third-century date, and a standard modern pint and half-pint glass for comparison. As can be seen, the motto beakers are found throughout the size range seen for the other beakers, suggesting it is safe to consider that beakers are drinking vessels, or at least vessels associated with drinking.

Pottery cups and glass drinking vessels are at the lower end of the capacity of the beakers. Pottery cups are a regular feature in first- and second-century assemblages, but become scarcer in the third century as samian pottery ceases to be imported. The native fineware industries, whose products replaced the samian products, made beakers not cups. Interestingly from the late second century onwards there is a noticeable increase in the number of glass cups found. A cylindrical colourless form starts to be found on many sites of that date, often in quite large numbers.[88] By the fourth century, vessel glass assemblages are dominated by drinking-vessel fragments,[89] again indicating high levels of use on many sites. Small capacity vessels would thus appear to continue to be

[88] Cool and Price 1995: 82–5.   [89] Cool and Baxter 1999: 88–9.

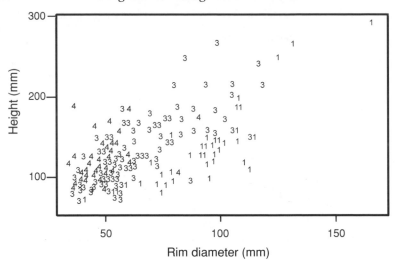

Figure 15.6. Comparison of the sizes of first (1), third (3) and fourth (4) century pottery beakers.

available throughout the Romano-British period, though increasingly made of glass from the late second century.

Fig. 15.6 compares the beakers plotted in fig. 15.5 with those from first- and fourth-century contexts. Whilst the early group includes some that are as large as the late second- and third-century ones, the fourth-century group generally lacks the medium to large ones. This suggests that the way in which drink was consumed may have changed by the fourth century. There are various options to explain this. It could be that the larger beakers were used for a particular type of drink that went out of fashion. The motto beakers though show that both large and small beakers were associated with wine drinking. It could be that some of the larger ones were used as mixing bowls for wine and water, and other vessels were used for this in the fourth century. This type of use seems at odds with the mottos, where even large examples admonish their users to fill them with unmixed wine or to spare the water; though admittedly these could just be a joke intended to entertain a drinking party. One from Verulamium with the motto 'Serve unmixed wine' (fig. 15.4 no. 1) would have held well over 800 ml (*c.* 1.5 pints).[90] The two other possibilities are that the larger

90 RIB II.6 no. 2498.4; capacity based on Steures 2002: fig. 3.

beakers were communal vessels which were shared amongst several drinkers, or that some individuals drank truly prodigious amounts. The different sizes and materials of the vessels associated with drinking, together with the hints that there may have been changes with time, suggests that it could be profitable to look in more detail at the types associated with particular well-dated episodes to see if any additional light can be shed on drinking rituals. An attempt will be made to do this in Chapters 16 to 19.

CHAPTER 16

The end of independence

INTRODUCTION

Up to now we have been exploring the different foods and drinks one by one. The next four chapters examine patterns of eating and drinking chronologically. They look at what particular communities' preferences were, and how these change with both time and place.

We start with the late Iron Age. It is not possible to draw a boundary between prehistoric and Roman Britain at a particular date. In the south-east of England some communities were adopting what looks like a 'Romanised' lifestyle a century or more preceding the formal invasion. So much so that it has been argued that the south-east could be regarded as occupied by a series of client kingdoms between Caesar's raids and the Claudian invasion.[1] Elsewhere much of the population carried on their lives after AD 43 happily oblivious to the fact that they were now part of the Roman empire. In many sites in Gloucestershire, for example, noticeable changes in the way people dressed and the things they used are not detectable until the second century.[2]

This chapter explores some of the variety in eating practice that can be detected in the century or so prior to the conventional date of the conquest. As a convenient shorthand, areas will be referred to by the *civitas* names they were to become known as during the Roman period, even though these were probably administration entities that emerged in the Roman period, and do not necessarily reflect the tribal names or boundaries of the later Iron Age.

When looking at late Iron Age communities, we are faced with a major problem concerning chronology. Pottery in large parts of the country is not a helpful chronological indicator.[3] The advent of intensive radiocarbon

[1] Creighton 2000.   [2] Cool in Miles *et al.* forthcoming.
[3] See Willis 2002 for discussion.

dating programmes has often shown that sites were occupied for much longer than would have been suspected from their sparse finds assemblages.[4] So, though an attempt will be made to concentrate on the last century BC and the earlier first century AD, in some areas this is impossible and a broader period of up to half a millennium has to be considered.

POTS AND PANS IN THE LATE IRON AGE KITCHEN

Pottery was central to the preparation and serving of food in many parts of Roman Britain. This does not appear to have been the case in many parts of the country during the Iron Age, a state of affairs that has interesting implications for cooking practice. Simplified greatly, in the later Iron Age the area to the south and east of the Severn – Humber line used pottery whilst to the north and west it is much rarer and in some areas absent. It is always possible that in these aceramic areas more pottery might have been used but has just not survived. Some northern Iron Age vessels are very crudely made and poorly fired; so much so that in some cases they can easily fragment after only gentle handling or even, it sometimes feels to anyone unfortunate enough to have to deal with them, simply by being looked at.[5] The prognosis for such pottery surviving in large quantities is small. Equally its use as a cooking pot is also unlikely as fabrics such as those would be unlikely to survive the thermal shock associated with heating for very long. It seems reasonable to conclude that whatever cooking method was favoured in these areas did not rely on the use of pottery.

During the later centuries of the first millennium BC, well-defined regional styles of vessels developed in the pottery-using areas but the range of forms in use was limited, consisting mainly of jars and deep bowls.[6] Both were used as cooking vessels judged by the sooting and carbonised deposits recorded on them, though there may have been regional preferences. At a settlement at Abingdon occupied throughout the later Iron Age, virtually all of the sooted vessels which could be assigned to a form were jars, despite the overall jar – bowl assemblage having a ratio of 60 : 40.[7] At the broadly contemporary northern site at Thorpe Thewles over a

---

[4] E.g. Roberts *et al.* 2001: 249.
[5] For example Cool 1982: 93 Type I; Type II puts up a little more resistance.
[6] Cunliffe 2005: figs. A:15–30. [7] De Roche in Parrington 1978: 42–65 Table IV.

quarter of the predominantly jar assemblage had cooking residues.[8] At Danebury, by contrast, both jars and bowls were sooted, including finely decorated examples.[9] Despite this, it can be questioned to what extent the use of any type of pottery vessel was central to the cooking process even on pottery-using sites. On those with relatively large late Iron Age pottery assemblages, the actual amount of pottery found is often small in comparison to what will be found later on Roman period ones. As a very crude measure, the c. 8,000 Iron Age sherds from Abingdon can be compared to the 11,400 from the Roman road-side settlement at Asthall in the same area (c. 26 km apart).[10] Both were settlement sites of no great pretensions probably occupied for broadly similar lengths of time. The disparity does not appear too great until the area excavated is considered. In the case of the Iron Age site this was 5,100 m², whereas for the Roman site it was only c. 900 m². At Asthall 90% of the assemblage, judged by the most reliable measure the EVE, consisted of jars, reflecting the large number that will be used and thrown away if they form a regular part of the cooking regime. No Iron Age site appears to match the rate of jar use seen on many Roman period sites, even if allowances are made for the fact that some may have been so poorly made that they have not survived.

An analysis of over 250 Iron Age sherds from southern England has shown that a high proportion with detectable lipids were associated with the processing of dairy products (ranging from 39% to 71% of those with lipids).[11] The authors conclude that this shows that dairy products were 'an extremely important commodity during the period'.[12] This conclusion is questionable because pottery is not that common. What the analysis does suggest is that, within the later Iron Age communities that used them, pottery vessels might have had quite a specific culinary role rather than being used for a wide range of ones as they were to be later.

How then was food cooked? The popular image is of a cauldron suspended over a central hearth, but the evidence points to cauldron use being restricted to a small part of society, probably for special magical or religious purposes.[13] So, if lots of people were not using either pottery vessels or metal cauldrons to cook with, what were they using? The honest answer is that we don't know. In earlier prehistory there was a tradition of cooking food in troughs of boiling water that had been heated by hot stones (pot-boilers). Experimentally this has been shown to be

---

[8] Swain in Heslop 1987: 63.
[9] Brown in Cunliffe and Poole 1991: 286 Table 67.
[10] Parrington 1978; Booth 1997.
[11] Copley *et al.* 2005: 489.
[12] Copley *et al.* 2005: 493.
[13] See p. 49.

quite an efficient way of cooking,[14] but if it was a widespread cooking method it might be expected that large numbers of heat-affected pebbles would be present on later prehistoric sites. Though this is indeed the case on some such as at Dinorben where they were described as 'abundant' and 'numerous',[15] many other site reports make no specific mention of them.

TABLEWARES IN LATE IRON AGE SOCIETY

Most later Iron Age pottery assemblages lack tablewares such as shallow bowls, dishes, bottles and jugs. If these were required, it has to be assumed that they were made in other materials such as wood and leather though there is little evidence of this, even in sites where there is good organic preservation. From the late second century BC some potters in southern Britain started using the wheel to make vessels, giving them the ability to produce different shapes. The implications of why the wheel was introduced into Britain so late compared with areas across the Channel has rarely been commented on,[16] but clearly it has important implications for eating and drinking as a whole range of new shapes such as closed flagon or bottle forms became much more simple to produce. Previously there does not appear to have been the need for a differentiated suite of cooking and eating vessels. Where sooting and limescale have been studied, fineware and finely decorated vessels that might be assumed to have been tablewares are just as likely to show evidence of being cooking vessels as more superficially utilitarian ones.

In many places the introduction of the wheel does not appear to have radically changed the range of shapes being made. In others, new shapes did start to be made. Some parts of those societies were clearly developing a need for them, suggesting dining practices were changing. Towards the end of the first century BC these new vessels include shallow platters and dishes, cups, pedestal beakers, large capacity beakers and flagons (see fig. 16.1). Some of these vessels were imports from Gaul and the Rhineland, primarily from the *terra nigra* and *terra rubra* industries of north Gaul,[17] but others are local imitations.[18] Shape cannot automatically be used to identify function, but in the case of the beakers, cups and platters it does seem very likely that they were tablewares. The imported

---

[14] Alcock 2001: 102.   [15] Gardner and Savoury 1964: 179; Savoury 1971: 55.
[16] Hill 2002: 151.   [17] Tyres 1996: 161–6.
[18] Pollard 1988: 31; Symmonds and Wade 1999: 212.

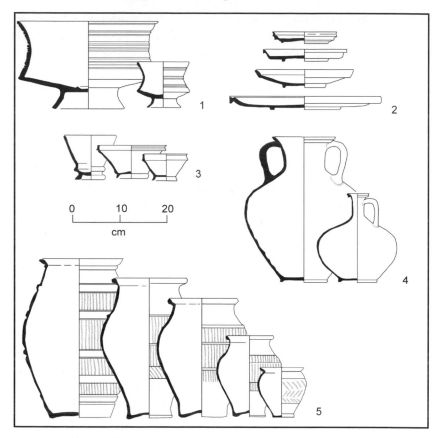

Figure 16.1. Pottery tablewares found in the King Harry Lane cemetery showing the range of sizes of tazze (1), platters (2), cups (3), flagons (4) and beakers (5). (After Stead and Rigby 1989). Scale 1 : 8.

examples are carefully made, frequently thin-walled vessels with carefully fired slips and burnished surfaces producing glossy vessels in a range of red to orange and black to grey colours. Some independent evidence of their use comes from graves where the platters have been recorded as containing animal bone, suggesting their role was to serve food.[19]

The core area where such vessels were popular prior to the Roman conquest is the Kent – Essex – Hertfordshire area where both platters and beakers were being produced by local industries. Further north and west

[19] E.g. Stead and Rigby 1989: 302 no. 111.

the take up of the new suite of vessels was variable, and often did not take place until well after the conquest. Although it is well-established that Caesar's conquest of Gaul resulted in an increase in cross-Channel contacts and trade between Britain and the continent, this alone cannot explain this inrush of new forms and their imitations; nor why some areas adopted them and some did not.

What we are seeing in the core south-eastern area is a major change in eating and drinking habits. This has occasionally been doubted. It has been pointed out that the metal vessels found in elite graves are those associated with sacrifice and not wine drinking, and so should be seen as a 'do it yourself Roman ritual kit'.[20] In part this is true, but the jug and handled bowl set were used in both sacrifice and polite dining. The notion that these sets are being acquired simply for sacrifice overlooks the scale of the change in the pottery assemblage. That is reminiscent of the boom in tea drinking in the eighteenth century, the rituals of which required not only the tea services for serving and drinking the beverage, but also pots in different materials for brewing it, canisters for keeping it in and teaspoons for stirring it. Different tea services were kept for green and bohea tea.[21] It was not until after the Commutation Act of 1784 that the price fell. Even before this, though initially the preserve of the rich, people of quite modest social standing aspired to it. The case of Nicholas Peacock, a farmer and land agent in County Limerick, and his wife Catherine who came from gentleman-farmer stock, is instructive.[22] His accounts relate to the 1740s and 1750s both before and after the marriage. This couple was positioned quite a distance down the social scale; indeed before his marriage the vessels in the house were made of wood and the cutlery of base metal. After the marriage the consumption of tea becomes necessary, and the accounts tell of the purchase of the tea itself, the teacups and even silver spoons.

In the late Iron Age context the range of new vessels is presumably associated with the rituals surrounding both new items of food and drink, for which there is contemporary evidence from the amphora assemblages, and new ways of consuming established items. The well-documented growth in tea drinking provides a useful model against which to explore this change in late Iron Age society. When first introduced it was the preserve of the rich, and the 'correct' vessels to drink it from were imported Chinese porcelain tea bowls. Local ceramic industries such as

[20] Creighton 2000: 201.   [21] Barnard 2004: 128–9.
[22] Barnard 2004: 107–8, 131, 135–6.

that of Josiah Wedgewood soon began to make the tea-wares necessary for its polite consumption, even when it was still an expensive, highly taxed commodity. As their manufacture spread, they evolved into new forms that took them away from the Chinese originals, for example, larger handled cups rather than small bowls. Early in the nineteenth century a new meal, teatime, evolved. This could either be the elegant and dainty afternoon tea favoured by the upper classes or the high tea with more substantial food offerings enjoyed by those who had to work for their living.[23] By the nineteenth century tea was the national British drink but, as is often the way of commodities that go from being the preserve of the elite to being available to all, attitudes to it have changed. So much so that when today a senior politician states that it is his beverage of choice, suspicions arise that he is trying to manipulate his image to appear an ordinary man of the people, for tea-drinking would not be expected for a person of his class.[24]

Alas, archaeology does not enable us to reconstruct such a richly textured account; but the evidence we do have allows us to see if something similar was happening in the late Iron Age. We could expect that sites where a high proportion of the new vessel forms were actually imported would be the elite sites. The extent to which the new food and drink items were adopted by the rest of society should be reflected in both the number of the new forms that are found further down the settlement hierarchy, and the ratio of imported to native versions. With time, elite sites might be expected to move on to a different type of assemblage as some other commodity took on the role of being a mark of elite distinction. The next section explores whether this is indeed what happens.

NEW FASHIONS IN HERTFORDSHIRE

We are fortunate that a group of sites of varying status belonging to the final half century or so before the Roman conquest have been excavated in the Hertfordshire region. They provide data against which the model proposed above can be tested. The first is the settlement in the Braughing – Puckeridge area. This lay at the boundary of the Catuvellaunian and Trinovantian *civitas* areas. Its precise status, whether it was a royal centre or not, has been the subject of much discussion.[25] What is clear is that people of the

[23] Davidson 1999: 6 and 380–1.   [24] Burkeman 2005.
[25] Summarised in Potter and Trow 1988: 156–8; see also Creighton 2000: 205.

highest social status lived there. It is, for example, one of only two sites of this date in the entire country where imported glass vessels have regularly been found.[26] Two sites excavated within the complex are particularly useful: the Skeleton Green excavations[27] and those alongside the later Ermine Street.[28] In both cases the main focus of activity was in the last decades of the first century BC and the first quarter of the first century AD. At Skeleton Green, buildings, pits and wells were recovered, while at the Ermine Street site pits but no buildings were found.

The second site is at Gorhambury which lies to the north of Verulamium which at this point was a tribal centre for the grouping that was to become known as the Trinovantes.[29] Here a set of enclosures and buildings were recovered. Occupation appears contemporary with that at the Braughing sites but continued into the Roman period when the site eventually developed into a masonry villa. During the late Iron Age the objects found provide no hints that this was the residence of part of the tribal elite, and its inhabitants were probably someway down the social hierarchy compared to those at Braughing.

The Braughing sites were excavated in 1971–2, that at Gorhambury in the 1970s and early 1980s, and this has some influence on the nature of the data that can be extracted from the published sources. On the whole the pottery was not quantified in any of the ways that would allow direct comparison between sites. The only measure in common is the minimum number which is far from ideal. By using it we can acquire a broad picture, but a more accurate one would come from the use of EVEs. The date of the excavations also make it unlikely that the phenomenon of structured deposition[30] would have been recognised, either during the digs themselves or later during analysis of the results. In at least one case at Gorhambury, the description of the pottery from a lower ditch fill as consisting of 'semi-complete vessels'[31] strongly suggests that it was taking place. Given that much of the pottery used here derives primarily from the pit fills, there is the distinct possibility that it may have been biased by special choices. This cannot be explored further here, but in future a comparison of the vessel types chosen to be part of structured deposits with those in contemporary use might provide further insights into how they were perceived and used.

---

[26] Charlesworth in Partridge 1981: 72 no. 18, 119 nos. 1–3; Price and Cool in Potter and Trow 1988: 81 nos. 1–5.
[27] Partridge 1981.   [28] Potter and Trow 1988.   [29] Neal *et al.* 1990.
[30] See discussion p. 13.   [31] Parminter in Neal *et al.* 1990: 178 context 105.

In addition to the settlement sites, various burial sites provide data. The most important for our purposes are two at Verulamium – the King Harry Lane cemetery[32] and the Folly Lane burial[33] – and one at Welwyn Garden City.[34] King Harry Lane is a cremation cemetery where a wide cross section of the community were buried, judged by the age and sex profiles of the deceased. Ignoring the intermittent use of the area as a cemetery later in the Roman period, the excavators favoured a date range of *c.* AD 1 to 60 for its period of use based on the ceramic evidence. The dating of the numerous brooches found has caused Mackreth to challenge this.[35] He would place its use slightly earlier, starting *c.* 15 BC and running on to *c.* AD 40. What is certain is that this was the burial place of a predominantly pre-conquest population, though possibly not of those of highest rank. The Folly Lane burial and that at Welwyn Garden City were clearly those of high-ranking members of the tribe. At Folly Lane a complex series of ceremonies surrounded the cremation and burial of an adult in about AD 55. The date of the Welwyn Garden City burial is uncertain. It contains a pair of imported platters dated to *c.* 30 BC[36] but lacks the wider range of Gallo-Belgic wares seen at the end of the century.

The pottery from the Braughing sites, excluding mortarias and amphorae, has been quantified in Table 16.1 according to shape and whether the vessels were imported or made locally. Whether an item was imported or not would have been visually very obvious to its users. The continental potters achieved much greater control of the firing conditions than the native potters did, so the colour of the imports was much more uniform than that of the native vessels which had more variegated surfaces. The top five categories (platters, cups, beakers, flagons and tazze) can be regarded as new tableware forms. At Skeleton Green they make up make up over half the assemblage and of that nearly 80% are imported. At the Ermine Street site, the tablewares make up 44% of the assemblage. It is not possible to assign all the flagons to either the local or imported category from the published information, but if they are ignored, then 72% of the tablewares were imported. These figures can be compared to those from Gorhambury (Table 16.2). There tablewares form less than a quarter of the assemblage and less than a third of those are imported. Despite the inadequacies of the quantification method, the evidence would suggest that the new patterns of consumption were not limited to the elite, but

---

[32] Stead and Rigby 1989.   [33] Niblett 1999.
[34] Stead 1967.   [35] Mackreth in Jackson and Potter 1996: 318.
[36] Fitzpatrick and Timby 2002: 163.

Table 16.1. *Pottery vessels from the Braughing excavations by source (minimum numbers).*

	Skeleton Green				Ermine Street			
Form	Italian	Gallic	Local	Total	Italian	Gallic	Local	Total
Platters	10	55	20	85	4	37	17	58
Cups	7	16	—	23	3	22	—	25
Beakers	—	43	16	59	—	41	25	66
Flagons	—	7	2	9	—	?	?	15
Tazze	—	2	—	2	—	2	—	2
Jars	—	28	41	69		3	65	68
Storage jars	—	—	18	18	—	—	34	34
Bowls	—	—	40	40	—	—	40	40
Lids			15	15		—	39	39
Total	17	151	152	320	7	105	220	347

Table 16.2. *Pottery vessels from Gorhambury by source (minimum numbers).*

Form	Italian	Gallic	Local	Total
Platters	—	2	3	5
Cups	1	—	1	2
Beakers	—	1	4	5
Flagons	—	—	1	1
Tazze	—	—	—	0
Jars	—	—	27	27
Storage jars	—	—	3	3
Bowls	—	—	12	12
Lids	—	—	1	1
Total	1	3	52	56

were adopted lower down the social scale just as in the case of tea-drinking.

An interesting feature of the tablewares at the sites is the presence or absence of tazze (bowls on high feet – fig. 16.1 no. 1). They are a rare but consistent presence at Braughing but absent at Gorhambury. In the slightly earlier elite burial at Welwyn Garden City, three of the thirty-six pottery vessels are tazze. Two other elite burials in the same tradition

Table 16.3. *Tableware forms in formal burials at the King Harry Lane cemetery.*

Phase	Date	Platter	Beaker	Cup	Pedestal cup	Tazza	Flagon	Total
1	1–40	27	55	9	4	5	15	115
2	35–55	34	41	7	3	—	17	102
3	40–60	32	81	9	—	—	14	136
?	—	—	14	—	—	—	—	14
Total		93	191	25	7	5	46	367
Urn		—	121	—	—	1	17	140
Accessory		93	70	25	7	4	29	227

found at Welwyn also contained pottery tazze.[37] There may be hints here that different strata of society adopted different aspects of the new table services and these can be explored at the King Harry Lane cemetery.

In the King Harry Lane report, 472 burial features are recorded for the Iron Age cemetery. A small number are inhumations but most reflect cremation burial activity. The descriptions of the features make it clear that not all of them are formal burials; there are also deposits of pyre debris and other types of deposits of the type that is normal in a cremation cemetery.[38] In what follows, only the deposits that are clearly urned cremation burials or formal cremation deposits with grave goods are considered. In the tables, the dating given for the phases follows that presented by the excavators.

Table 16.3 shows that of all the new open tableware forms, tazze are the least popular in the cemetery and restricted to the first phase. Their rarity is even more pronounced than the figures show as one example had been reworked in antiquity to turn it into a low platter. Of the four deposited as tazze, two came from burials with three vessels, one was part of an assemblage of seven vessels and the fourth came from the grave with the most vessels found (ten). In phase 1 more than two thirds of the formal burials only had one or two vessels so, if status can be equated with the number of vessels in a grave, tazze are associated with the higher-status graves. This is also suggested in the case of the burials with seven and ten vessels as each had a high proportion of imports in it. Tazze were thus an

---

[37] Smith 1912: 3.   [38] McKinley 2000.

Table 16.4. *Incidence of cups in the graves at King Harry Lane.*

	Number of pottery vessels in grave									
	1	2	3	4	5	6	7	8	9	10
Total	214	80	32	18	6	3	3	—	2	1
With cups	1	1	3	4	1	3	2	—	2	1
Percentage	<1	1	9	22	17	100	67	—	100	100

early part of the service, possibly confined to the highest society. Their role in the new patterns of consumption was obviously not found to be vital as these patterns spread to other parts of the community.

The King Harry Lane evidence suggests that the role of the cup (fig. 16.1 no. 3) was also changing. Overall the ratio of platter : beaker : cup amongst the accessory vessels in the cemetery was very similar to that seen at Braughing, but when the distribution and types of cups are considered, again there are suggestions that they were restricted to the more wealthy members of the community. Over 80% of the cups in the formal burials are imports and, as can be seen in Table 16.4, they are overwhelmingly concentrated in graves with large numbers of vessels in which there was often more than one cup. The evidence would be consistent with a divergence in what was considered an appropriate part of the service in different parts of society; with an increasing number of people considering that beakers were central to drinking rituals, but with the elite considering cups were essential too.

The Folly Lane complex provides further insight into the ways in which the different vessels were used and possibly regarded. There were obviously very elaborate ceremonials surrounding the funeral held there in c. AD 55. A funerary chamber was constructed possibly for the display of the body before it was cremated. Some of the pyre debris was placed in the funerary chamber which was then deliberately dismantled and buried. Amongst this debris were fragments of pottery vessels that had presumably been used in the ceremonies surrounding the display and burning of the body. Some showed clear signs of having been on the pyre. Overwhelmingly, this pottery consists of tablewares and the remains of a minimum of thirty-five platters and ten cups, but only one beaker, were recovered.[39] If this can be regarded as a representative sample of the vessels used during

---

[39] Niblett 1999: 182–93.

the funerary feasts, then again it is suggesting that cups were preferred, or seen as appropriate, for those of the highest rank.

The patterns of use for the different vessels suggest that not only were new habits of dining emerging in large parts of the community, but that there may well have been subtle differences between those practised by the leaders and those down the social scale. The next section explores what these habits might have been.

NEW PLATES, NEW CUISINE?

Given the amphora evidence of wine imports during the first century BC, there is a temptation to associate the tableware services with wine consumption. Some of the tribal chiefs of the middle first century BC were certainly buried with grave goods that suggest a knowledge of polite drinking rituals in the Roman world. One of the Welwyn burials not only had a wine amphora but also a large bronze bowl of the type used for hand washing during dining,[40] and it is likely that the large cylindrical bronze bowl from the Welwyn Garden City burial served a similar purpose.[41] As we have seen, however, the new table service extends down the social hierarchy, and it does not appear to be the preserve merely of the elite. Were it to be associated regularly with wine drinking, it could be expected that far more evidence for wine amphorae would be recovered, but it is not until after the Roman conquest that wine appears to have been imported into the country in any quantity.

The capacity of the beakers would also suggest that they were not habitually used for wine (see fig. 16.1 no. 5 for range). Fig. 16.2 shows the beakers used as accessory vessels from the King Harry Lane cemetery together with the third-century motto beakers from fig. 15.5. As can be seen, the beakers from the King Harry Lane site tend to have a much larger capacity than the motto beakers which themselves included some of the larger beakers plotted in fig. 15.5. Considerable amounts of wine, even if diluted, would have been needed to fill a King Harry Lane beaker. Given their size, beer would be a much more appropriate drink to put in them; and even then, given the size of many larger ones, they were possibly vessels for communal rather than individual use.

As Tables 16.1–16.3 make clear, the serving of food had as important a role, possibly a more important one, than the drinking vessels. Platters are

---

[40] Smith 1912: 3 first vault no. 3, fig. 11; see also p. 138.
[41] Stead 1967: 26, fig. 14.

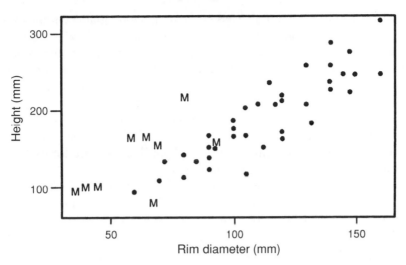

Figure 16.2. Sizes of beakers used as accessory vessels at the King Harry Lane cemetery compared to the size of motto beakers (M).

the commonest vessel type at each settlement site and equally are the most numerous type of accessory vessel at King Harry Lane. At that site, the platters range in size from 130 mm to 320 mm diameter with half of the examples lying between 170 mm to 215 mm (see fig. 16.1 no. 2). This is about the size of a small modern dinner plate and it would be reasonable to assume that it was used for serving individual portions. In one of the very few discussions of what the significance of this pottery might have been, as opposed to the minutiae of its typology, Hill has pointed out that platters like this allow food to be presented in a very different way than is possible in a bowl.[42] Bowls are ideal for gravy-rich stews where all the ingredients are mixed in the cooking process. Plates allow different foodstuffs to be presented individually, with the possibly of saucing the individual elements differently. This sort of cooking means more work for the cook; a stew normally needs less time and attention than several different dishes that only come together as a whole at the point of serving. Plates also allow more attention to be paid to the visual presentation of the food, and the possibility of individuals picking and choosing which elements of the meal they will eat.

---

[42] Hill 2002: 149.

Plates are very useful if a society develops a differentiated cuisine of the type discussed in Chapter 5. One of the requirements for that is access to a range of different ingredients, and the late Iron Age certainly saw an increase in the range of foodstuffs available. As well as the amphora-borne commodities such as olive oil and salted fish products, the domestic fowl first appears in Britain at this point. Other exotic ingredients are suggested by finds such as the distinctive mica-dusted jars which were being imported from the central Loire area of Gaul.[43] There would have been little point in importing this fundamentally utilitarian form for itself, and a role as packaging seems much more likely.

Some of these new ingredients definitely imply new and more careful ways of cooking. A chicken can be stewed in much the same way as the types of meat available before, but the use of fish sauce in an unpractised way can lead to quite disastrous results. It could be argued that the presence of fish sauce amphorae in elite Welwyn-style burials such as Mount Bures and Snailwell, each of which had three examples,[44] was just a matter of elite display and it does not imply that the contents were necessarily regarded as cooking ingredients. Such an argument becomes doubtful when only fragments are found in a probable pyre debris deposit at King Harry Lane;[45] and it certainly does not hold in the case of the broken fragments on settlement sites. These can be found not only at sites such as Braughing,[46] but also at the Sheepen site outside Colchester in pre-conquest contexts.[47] Such finds imply the contents were being used, presumably as a culinary ingredient. Other changes in cooking practice are suggested by the presence of early mortaria at the elite sites at Braughing and Sheepen in pre-conquest deposits.[48] As discussed in Chapter 6, there are strong reasons to suspect that in some places in Britain the popularity of the mortaria *cannot* be taken as an indication of the adoption of a Romanised cuisine.[49] In this case, given that the mortaria are present as part of what might be thought of as a package of ingredients and tablewares, it does seem reasonable to view them as indicative of new cooking practices.

[43] Tyers in Partridge, 1981: 102; Tyers 1996: 142–3.
[44] Stead 1967: 53; Tyers 1996: 52; Lethbridge 1953: 25, pl IV.
[45] Stead and Rigby 1989: 326 no. 206.1.
[46] Williams in Partridge 1981: 202; Williams in Potter and Trow 1988: Table 13.
[47] Hawkes and Hull 1947: 252 Form 185.
[48] Hartley in Partridge 1981: 198 nos. 16 and 17; Hawkes and Hull 1947: 254 Forms 191A and B.
[49] See pp. 45–6.

Table 16.5. *Associations of the principal types of tablewares at the King Harry Lane Cemetery. (infants are aged 0 to 5, immature are 5–18).*

	Infant	Immature	Male	Female	Adult
Platter	3	8	21	4	35
Beaker	1	6	13	3	20
Cup	1	3	2	2	10
Flagon	—	12	11	5	14
Total identified	10	20	59	21	156

An intriguing question arises as to what part of society developed these skills. Hill has suggested that the additional time needed in preparation might have led to a greater separation between the cooks and the consumers; and has wondered, rather provocatively, whether this might have been a women/children versus men division.[50] Whilst it might traditionally be felt that woman's place is in the kitchen, the associations of the different vessel types in the King Harry Lane cemetery provides no support for the theory that men were the primary beneficiaries of the new meals.

Table 16.5 shows the associations of the four principal types of tablewares in those graves where it is possible to age and sex the individuals buried in them. The cases where more than one individual is present in a grave are omitted, and the bottom line shows the total number of aged and/or sexed individuals in each category. As can be seen, all the forms are fairly evenly spread amongst all the different types of individuals when the total number in each category are considered. By comparing the number of male and female graves with platters with the numbers without, it can be shown that there is no statistically significant difference between them.[51] Whoever was doing the cooking in the community that buried its dead at King Harry Lane, all ages and sexes appear to have been considered equally in need of the vessels that would ensure a good meal in the next world.

Taken as a whole, the evidence points to quite fundamental changes in cooking and dining practices in the south-east during the century preceding the Roman conquest amongst the Trinovantes, the Catuvellauni and probably part of the Cantii of Kent. There is every sign that a differentiated cuisine was developing. The mere availability of foreign imports was not sufficient to trigger such a change elsewhere; so the interesting question is,

[50] Hill 2002: 150. [51] For methodology see Cool and Baxter 2005.

why here? The answer must surely lie within the internal dynamics of these communities. At the time as the eating changes are taking place, the same people develop the need to bury their elite dead with spectacular funerals consuming large amounts of resources. Dining and drinking parties may well have been another arena in which the standing of the household was displayed; and there are distinct hints in the record that it may have been judged by presentation and taste as much as by quantity.

MEANWHILE ELSEWHERE

The area of England that has been considered in detail in the previous two sections always tends to dominate any consideration of late Iron Age Britain because it is so visible archaeologically. Not only are large ceramic assemblages not uncommon; but spectacular burials are found from time to time and a form of historical narrative can be pieced together from the ancient sources and the native coinage. Then as now the south-east does not give a representative picture of what was going on in Britain as a whole. It is interesting to look as a comparison at the lands of the Durotriges in the Dorset area, where there is evidence for the importation of exotic foodstuffs in the late Iron Age, but no evidence for the wide-spread development of a differentiated cuisine.

Hengistbury Head, probably at the border of the territories of the Durotriges and their neighbours the Atrebates, has produced important evidence for the import of amphora-borne commodities in the first half of the first century BC.[52] The commonest appears to have been wine, but olive oil and fish sauce are also present. The site is believed to have been an import point rather than a settled community and the distribution of early wine amphorae in an arc of sites around it in Dorset and Hampshire would seem to confirm this.[53] Alongside the amphorae at Hengistbury Head there are also other pottery imports from the continent in the form of jars and bowls from Armorica, but these are not found much beyond the immediate hinterland of the site.[54] With the turmoil brought about in Gaul by Caesar's campaigns, the trade route leading into Hengistbury Head was obviously disrupted, but later wine amphora finds continue to be found in the region, suggesting that not all links had been severed.[55]

[52] Tyers 1996: 50 Table 12. [53] Fitzpatrick 2003: Fig. 2.
[54] Fitzpatrick and Timby 2002: 162–3. [55] Fitzpatrick and Timby 2002: 162.

The Durotrigian potters did start to use the wheel, and there is evidence that by the end of the Iron Age in this area, pottery production was a centralised rather than a domestic industry. The forms produced continued to be based on traditions stemming from the middle Iron Age and were primarily bowls and jars.[56] Some new forms such as tazze and handled tankards did appear, but the platter and beaker forms are missing from the range. The Durotrigians obviously also felt no need to acquire these from the Gallo-Belgic industries when these products started to pour into the country further to the east. It is clearly not the case that the potters would have been unable to produce shallow forms allowing food to be displayed had there been a demand. When the army provided one after the conquest, a range of shallow dishes and bowls were produced by this industry.[57]

Everything suggests that despite the early exposure to exotic ingredients, this had no impact on cooking practice or patterns of dining. The only changes that might perhaps be detected are in drinking vessels. The appearance of the pottery tankards is broadly contemporary with the first appearance of those made of wood with copper-alloy fittings, whose earliest examples occur in one of the Welwyn graves discussed above, and in a broadly contemporary one at Aylesford in Kent.[58] The use of the wood and copper-alloy tankards runs well into the Roman period and they have a scattered distribution, but there are two distinct concentrations; one in the Hertfordshire – Essex – Suffolk area and one in the Dorset – Somerset one.[59] The latter can be seen as part of marked regional interest in this vessel form as it was to become a very common product of the later Severn Valley pottery industry.[60]

That the Durotrigian potters were making the tankard form in the late Iron Age shows that their customers had a use for it, and that the vessels they needed were starting to diversify; but compared with the changes seen in the south-east, this diversification seems minimal. Durotrigian society was very different to that of the Trinovantes and Catuvellauni. There was a continued preference for using hillforts. Equally, though there was a well-developed tradition for inhuming the dead, the community obviously did not feel the need for spectacular elite burials. The lack of interest in diversifying their cuisine may well have been part of this attitude to life.

---

[56] Brown in Sharples 1991: 198–203.   [57] Sharples 1991: 108 Type 33.
[58] Corcoran 1952; Smith 1912: 21 fig. 21; Evans 1892: 357.
[59] MacGregor, M. 1976: Map 19; more are now known but the pattern is not broadly changed.
[60] Tyers 1996: 197.

A similar picture emerges further north. The east Midlands was a pottery-using area throughout the first millennium BC with what has been described as a ceramic industry of 'daunting diversity' during the final century before the conquest.[61] This diversity continued to be played out within the traditional jar and bowl assemblage. In this area imports of other forms are very rare,[62] and there is very little diversification of the form repertoire. At Dragonby in north Lincolnshire it is possible to study quite an extensive sequence of pottery use running from the later Iron Age to the later Roman period. Such diversification that takes place centres on the drinking-vessel element with local imitations of the beaker forms appearing to replace smaller capacity cups in the early to mid-first century AD.[63] Platters and dishes do not become visible until after the conquest.

Moving north into the territory of the Brigantes, we enter a society that seems to have had little use for pottery. In the West Yorkshire area Dalton Parlours has a sequence of enclosures and roundhouses and a long occupation dated by radiocarbon to the second half of the first millennium BC. It also has one of the larger pottery assemblages for the area but this amounts to only some forty vessels in total, primarily jars.[64] Other sites in the area occupied over a similarly long period have often produced no pottery whatsoever,[65] or only a single vessel that has all the hallmarks of being placed as a special structured deposit.[66] On such sites the only evidence for eating practices is often the quern and charred grain assemblage, as soil conditions frequently mean that not even animal bone survives. What they were eating and how they cooked it, is a matter of guesswork.

CONCLUSIONS

What are these patterns telling us? The reason why the continental commodities themselves and the pottery tablewares that aided their consumption are *not* found in many areas of Britain in the later Iron Age is sometimes discussed in terms of those areas being actively prevented from acquiring them, perhaps by tribes further south controlling the trade networks.[67] This is presumably based on the assumption that

---

[61] Knight 2002: 136.   [62] Willis 1996: 185–91, figs 2–3.
[63] Elsdon in May 1996: 415 Type 11.
[64] Sumpter in Wrathmell and Nicholson 1990: 130.
[65] Burgess in Roberts *et al.* (eds.) 2001: 72–83.
[66] Evans in Roberts *et al.* (eds.) 2001: 158 no. 22.
[67] Willis 1996: 191.

naturally everyone will have wanted these things. Perhaps a better way of looking at this is that there wasn't the demand for them. It would be wrong to think that these communities could not acquire exotic imports. They are found occasionally in even quite small settlements. The excavation of roundhouses and enclosures in the vicinity of the Ferrybridge henge in West Yorkshire, dated to the early to mid-first century AD, produced not only a Gallo-Belgic eggshell beaker and an imported Alésia brooch, but also a grape pip.[68] Further north at Stanwick which was clearly a major tribal centre, the imports include a black obsidian cup.[69] Even within Italy this would have been a sign of great luxury, and it was probably one of the most expensive imported items in the whole country.

The reason why imports from the Roman world are not more visible in large parts of the country probably lies more in the social than the political realm. In many communities there appears to have been neither the desire to experiment with a new cuisine, nor internal pressures that could have led to its adoption. It would probably be unwise to cast this within the models of active or passive resistance to 'Romanisation' that have become popular,[70] though of course it would be possible to do so. More likely we come back to the fish sauce problem. Exotic ingredients are only desirable if you know how to cook with them properly. Today when supermarkets bring us delicacies from all around the world, and bookshops and television screens provide instant instruction on how to prepare them, it is easy to forget this. Yet, less than forty years ago when my father was a greengrocer in a small rural town, attempts to introduce new items failed because people did not know what to do with them. The avocado pear was a case in point. One elderly couple was perfectly happy to try them, but reported back later that they didn't think much of the experience. Questioning established that they had eaten them as you would a dessert pear, and had naturally found them wanting. In the face of innate conservatism in matters of food, what is truly interesting is probably not why most of the country saw no reason to change well-established eating and drinking habits in the late Iron Age; but why parts of the south-east did.

---

[68] Roberts 2005: 135 no. 17, 155 no. 6, 184.   [69] Cool and Price 1995: 14.
[70] For example Mattingly (ed.) 1997.

CHAPTER 17

A brand-new province

INTRODUCTION

There can be no doubt that whatever influence the Roman state had in southern Britain before the Claudian conquest, it was only after it that the major impact of being formally part of the Roman world started to be seen. People and goods poured into the new province. Soldiers, administrators, traders and craftsmen arrived as did items that virtually no Briton would have seen before, such as glass vessels. New patterns of eating and drinking were introduced, but it would be wrong to see a simple Roman – native dichotomy developing. There was no more a single Roman way of doing things, any more than there was a single native way. In this chapter, five case studies relating to the first to second centuries are presented to show some of the patterns. They do not represent all of the ways of life being practised at this time, but they do give a taste of the diversity that emerges from the archaeological record.

SOLDIERS AND SETTLERS AT COLCHESTER

Colchester (fig. 17.1) provides a good place to start exploring practices introduced by the Roman forces. In the late Iron Age an important tribal centre existed there in the Sheepen – Gosbecks area, and it was the place where Claudius came to take official possession of the new province. A fortress was built to the east of the native centre by the Twentieth Legion and following its redeployments to the west of Britain in AD 49, the site became the first colony to be established in the province. The colonists were, no doubt, drawn from the soldiers of the invasion army due to be discharged. It was clearly intended to be the capital of the new province but it was burnt to the ground in AD 60/1 during the Boudican rising.[1]

---

[1] For general account see Crummy 1997: 9–84; see also Tacitus *Annales* XII.32; XIV. 29–39.

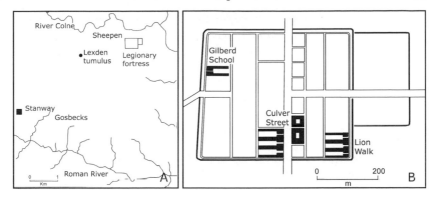

Figure 17.1. Colchester: location of different areas (A) and location of the excavated sites within the fortress (B). (After P. Crummy 1997.)

The fortress and *colonia* lie beneath the modern town. Excavations in advance of the redevelopment of large parts of the centre in the 1970s and 1980s provided a wealth of evidence. Being built on a previously un-occupied site and then destroyed sixteen years later means that Colchester provides an almost unparalleled opportunity to see how the soldiers and colonists lived. All the material from the excavations has been published, though not always in strictly comparable ways. Within the sites it was variously possible to assign some phases to the fortress occupation before the legion departed in AD 49, and others to that and an initial phase of the *Colonia* thought to end about AD 55. Elsewhere the stratigraphy does not make it possible to separate the occupation within the AD 44 to AD 60/1 period, but the pre-Boudican deposits are always distinct from the occupation that came afterwards when *colonia Victricensis* was refounded.

The production of the *Colchester Archaeological Reports* was a remark-able achievement by what has always been one of the smaller professional units.[2] There are minor problems with assessing the evidence because of when the excavations took place. For those conducted in the 1970s there is less environmental evidence than would be normal now; but sieving did take place on many sites and has produced some useful results. A more fundamental problem concerns the pottery. From the published

[2] Sites and environmental evidence – Crummy 1984; 1992 and Crummy *et al.* 1993. Small finds – Crummy 1983 and Crummy 1992. Animal bone – Luff 1993. Glass vessels – Cool and Price 1995. Pottery – Symonds and Wade 1999.

Table 17.1. *Proportions of the principal domesticates at Colchester in contexts dated to AD 49–60/1.*

	End date	Cattle (%)	Sheep (%)	Pig (%)	Total weight (kg)
Culver Street A	60/1	64	10	23	4.058
Culver Street E	49	72	10	13	7.291
Culver Street E (2)	60/1	72	8	14	50.902
Gilberd School A (1)	49	69	14	13	12.310
Gilberd School A (2)	60/1	61	14	16	21.029
Gilberd School A (3)	60/1	62	12	15	25.153

material it is impossible to reconstruct pottery assemblages that would have been associated with particular areas of the fort and city. This is particularly unfortunate, as the site reports occasionally indicate very distinctive suites of vessels were present in particular areas. Here a general picture can be presented with occasional detailed snapshots relating to particular groups of people at particular times. There can be no doubt that a much more richly textured understanding would result if the pottery was subject to reanalysis.

As is clear from Table 17.1, beef was the principal meat consumed by both the soldiers and colonists. Taking into consideration the differential waste associated with sheep and pig carcases (see Table 9.2), it is likely that pork and ham products were consumed in greater quantities than lamb and mutton. The bones of domestic fowl occur regularly in contexts of this date, and it is clear that eggs were also being eaten.[3] Most of the meat consumed came from domesticated species, suggesting hunting and snaring played a negligible role in this community. Evidence for venison is so rare as to be almost non-existent on most sites; and it is also noticeable that geese and duck bones were much rarer than those of domestic fowl.

The Boudican conflagration provided ideal conditions for the preservation of cleaned grain in stores awaiting consumption. It is clear, both from grain stores and debris close to cooking hearths, that the preferred grain for bread-making was spelt wheat. Emmer is found less commonly

---

[3] Luff 1993: Table 5.1; Murphy in Crummy 1992: 280.

Table 17.2. *Amphora-borne commodities in Colchester AD 44–60/1 by weight kg (* = amphorae made in Britain).*

Contents	Source	To AD 55	To AD 60/1	Total
Wine	Italy/Spain	7.159	35.492	42.651
Wine	France	2.689	7.505	10.194
Wine	Rhodes	4.809	5.938	10.747
Wine	Crete	0.050	0.469	0.519
Wine	Unknown	0.235	2.826	3.061
Wine	Britain*	—	7.474	7.474
Subtotal (wine)		14.942	59.704	74.646
Defrutum	Spain	1.595	6.167	7.762
Olives	France	1.131	8.592	9.723
Fruits	Italy	—	3.045	3.045
Dates	Unknown	—	0.029	0.029
Fish products	Spain	12.158	18.184	30.342
Olive Oil	Spain	42.903	215.823	258.726
Unknown		0.100	2.270	2.370
Total		72.829	313.814	383.616

but fully cleaned samples were found on two sites indicating that a range of flours would have been available for different types of baking.[4]

The presence of exotic fruits is indicated by both the evidence of amphorae (see Table 17.2) and by mineralised and carbonised remains. Carbonised dates were found in a Boudican destruction context at Lion Walk. Judged by the quantities of the relevant amphora fragments found, they are likely to have been a rare delicacy.[5] Dried fruit may have been imported in greater quantities. Mineralised grape and fig seeds were present in two latrines belonging to the military phase, alongside seeds of locally available fruits such as elderberry, raspberry and cherry.

These latrines also produced bones indicating the consumption of fish. The species included mackerel and herring though naturally much was not identifiable to species. Generally fish remains were not very common even on the sites where quite extensive sieving was carried out,[6] and it seems that fresh fish was not often consumed. Fish sauce and salted fish products were popular ingredients judged by the amphora evidence (Table 17.2), and it might be suspected the remains in the latrines came

[4] Murphy in Crummy 1984: 105, 108, 110; Murphy in Crummy 1992: 281–2, 330.
[5] Murphy in Crummy 1984: 40.   [6] Locker in Crummy 1992: 278.

Table 17.3. *Pottery-vessel forms from Colchester AD 44–60/1 (quantified by EVEs).*

Form	To AD 55	To AD 60/1	Total
Flagon	17.14	42.60	59.74
Cooking jar	14.63	35.49	50.12
Beaker	7.90	27.89	35.79
Bowl	8.37	21.45	29.82
Storage jar	3.44	20.64	24.08
Lid	4.29	19.14	23.43
Dish	3.31	10.97	14.28
Jar	2.90	9.76	12.66
Cup	5.30	3.94	9.24
Mortarium	2.06	5.84	7.90
Constricted-neck jar	1.13	5.33	6.46
Cooking dish	1.06	4.98	6.04
Handled jar	3.14	1.32	4.46
Cheese press	—	0.11	0.11
Total	74.67	209.46	284.13

from eating these, rather than fresh fish. Certainly the species identified are oily ones of the type used to make salted fish products. An interesting feature of the amphora assemblage is that while the proportion of wine amphorae stays approximately level at 16–17% in both the military contexts and those of the later *colonia*, that of the fish products plummets from 14% to 5%. Either tastes were changing or perhaps the colonists found them too expensive when they no longer had their salaries as soldiers. Certainly the figures would suggest that it was a much less common part of the diet in the years immediately prior to the Boudican rising than it had been earlier.

It is clear from the wine amphorae present that both the soldiers and the colonists had access to a range of different wines. The brewing of wheat beer is attested by a deposit of malt carbonised in AD 60/1.[7] If we can equate large-capacity drinking vessels with beer and smaller capacity ones with the consumption of wine, then there are hints of an intriguing difference in consumption patterns. Table 17.3 shows the different forms of pottery vessels present. In it bowls, dishes and cups are under-represented

---

[7] Murphy in Crummy 1992: 282.

as samian vessels were not quantified in the report. This is a particular problem for estimating how many small-capacity cups were used, as those in samian pottery were likely to have been very common. In the 1970 excavations at Sheepen, for example, approximately 350 fragments of samian vessels were recovered from precisely contemporary contexts, and of these half came from cups.[8] All that can be said from Table 17.3 is that beakers were one of the commonest forms, and cups are present but in unknown quantities. Twice as many samian cups as those in all other fabrics would have to be present to bring them up to comparable levels with the beakers.

An exceptional number of cups were found in one of the military latrines. A minimum of twelve Italian eggshell examples and at least two similar cups in other wares were present, whilst a third is associated with the house.[9] The only other pottery catalogued as coming from the deposit were fragments of a large decorated samian bowl,[10] though this of course does not rule out the possibility that other uncatalogued items were also found. It can be stated categorically that no glass vessels were found in the latrine.

The latrine was part of a large courtyard house facing onto the *principia* across the *via principalis* and would have been the home of one of the senior officers in the legion. One can only speculate on why so many cups were found in this deposit. Was it the result of one particularly riotous party, or did particular individuals make a habit of retiring to this multi-seater facility with cups of wine for quiet contemplation? What the evidence does point to is that wine was probably the drink of choice of the officers who lived there. Within the sites at Colchester, Culver Street where this latrine was found can be regarded as a high-status area during the fortress period. Not only were parts of tribunes' houses excavated, but there were also the centurial quarters of the First Cohort of the legion. On two other sites, Lion Walk and the Gilberd School, parts of barrack blocks were recovered, and these areas may be thought of as lower-status ones. The possibility exists that it might be possible to map differences in the drinking preferences of the officers and the men by looking at the assemblages from these fortress-period contexts. The way the pottery has been published means that it is impossible to establish the beaker and cup proportions at particular sites, but some progress can be made with the glass vessels.

[8] Dannell in Niblett 1985: MF2 D3–D11.
[9] Symmonds and Wade 1999: 227 no. 43, 242 nos. 1–3 and 4, 259 no. 85, 444 no. 37.
[10] Dannell in Symmonds and Wade 1999: 30 no. 459.

Table 17.4. *Glass-vessel forms from Colchester AD 44–60/1 (quantified by EVEs).*

Type	To AD 49	To AD 55	To AD 60/1	Total
Large bowl	2.40	3.20	8.00	13.60
Cup	—	1.00	4.60	5.60
Jug	0.42	0.98	2.80	4.20
Jug/flask	0.80	0.20	2.60	3.60
Beaker	—	0.40	2.80	3.20
Bowl (other)	—	1.20	2.00	3.20
Bottle	0.28	0.42	1.54	2.24
Cantharus	—	—	0.60	0.60
Jar	—	0.17	0.38	0.55
Amphorisk	—	—	0.28	0.28
Total	3.90	7.57	25.60	37.07

As can be seen from Table 17.4, the glass from the pre-Boudican contexts is dominated by large bowls. These are primarily of the pillar moulded form and all have the sort of rim which would allow them to be large drinking vessels, as opposed to other forms of bowls where the rim formation would make this impossible. Smaller-capacity cups and beakers also occur, but do not appear to become very common until the later part of the period. When the distribution of these forms is looked at across the military contexts, the large bowls dominate the assemblages from the men's barracks at Lion Walk and the Gilberd School but are surprisingly rare on the high-status site at Culver Street. If the pillar moulded bowls were used as drinking vessels then, taken with the evidence of the cups from the tribune's latrines, it hints at a difference between the drinking habits of the officers and men. This might be a wine – beer difference or an individual cup – communal bowl one. It would be a fruitful area to explore within pottery assemblages in the future.

Another difference in drinking habits is suggested by the absence of spouted strainer bowls from the city-centre sites. These large bowls are found in a variety of primarily native contexts both before and after the conquest in this area.[11] Whatever the precise drink was that they were used to make, the soldiers and colonists don't appear to have developed the taste for it.

---

[11] See pp. 144–6, fig. 15.3 nos. 1–2.

The pottery vessels cast useful light on cooking practices. As can be seen in Table 17.3, cooking jars are very numerous. It is likely that they were the commonest form present, as the flagon total may be inflated by the fact that flagon rims tend to break as complete or substantially complete circuits. The shallow dishes and lids with non-stick surfaces (Pompeian-Red ware and the like), occur in some numbers and as far as can be judged from the catalogued examples, across all the sites. Given that mortaria are always regarded as the Roman kitchen utensil *par excellence*, the relatively small amount recovered is interesting. It could be argued that this is because mortaria were used communally and might not often be broken, unlike individual drinking vessels which would be needed in large quantities and be subject to high levels of breakage. The same considerations would apply equally to storage jars, yet they are far more numerous. The figures appear to be telling us that mortaria were not regarded as essential in all kitchens. This again throws into stark relief the popularity that the mortaria was gaining amongst some sections of the British population. If this most Roman of communities did not see the form as truly essential, why was it found to be so useful elsewhere?

It is worth asking, though, whether or not this is a 'Roman' community. The legionary soldiers and the colonists would indeed have been Roman citizens but it would be a mistake to think that should be automatically equated with an Italian ethnicity. It is known that the first six governors of the new province were Italian as were the known legionary commanders.[12] Given the army command structure at the time, there are likely to have been Italians amongst the lower-ranking legionary officers and the commanders of the auxiliary units. It has been estimated that twenty years or so before the conquest in 43 approximately half the men being recruited came from outside of Italy, especially from Spain and Gallia Narbensis, and it would have been these individuals who would have supplied the pool of retiring soldiers.[13] Three of the legions, including the Twentieth that was to be stationed at Colchester, came from bases in the Rhineland while the fourth came from the Danubian garrison in Pannonia and men from these areas are to be expected too. Amongst the auxiliary units there were Batavians from the mouth of the Rhine and units from Thrace.[14] Thus the bulk of the population of pre-Boudican Colchester is likely to have had a much wider range of ethnic affiliations than simply an Italian one. They may have thought of themselves as

[12] Birley 1979: 39; Webster 1980: 90–2.
[13] Millett 1999: 195.   [14] Webster 1980: 85–7.

'Roman', but their tastes in food and drink may have been very different from those of a contemporary Italian.

This seems to be borne out by several features of the early Colchester data. It was beef not pork that was the preferred meat. This is a German preference, not an Italian one.[15] If the men did indeed prefer beer, then this too might reflect ethnic preferences. After all, fifty years later at Vindolanda, Batavian troops were complaining that they had run out of beer, not wine.[16] As far as drinking goes, it may be that the lower ranks of the legion had more in common with the native population than they did with their officers. This can only be speculation at present, but could be tested by further work on the pottery from the excavations.

LONDON LIFE

It is hard for a modern British audience to conceive of a time when London did not dominate national life, but that was the situation when the first colony at Colchester was thriving. London had not been a centre of native occupation prior to the conquest as Colchester had been. At the time of its destruction during the Boudican rising in AD 60/1, Tacitus described it as not being a Roman colony but rather a centre for traders and merchandise.[17] Its precise status, both then and later, is unclear; but after the Roman authorities had defeated Boudicca's forces and regained control of the province, it was clearly a boom town and probably the seat of provincial government.

The excavations at Leadenhall Court in London provide a most useful snapshot of life in London as this new city became established. Not only can deposits relating to relatively short-lived periods of occupation be identified; but the site has been published in an exemplary manner, so properly quantified data can be extracted to build up a detailed picture.[18]

The site lies in the heart of the developing city. Prior to about AD 70 the area was still rural, occupied first by a small cemetery and then by a farmstead. Recognisable urban land-use started about AD 70. Occupation continued for about fifteen years and then the area became a building site for the erection of the city's forum and basilica. It is with the urban occupation of c. AD 70–85 that we are concerned here (site Period 3). The site was occupied by a large multi-roomed building, strip buildings, outhouses and middens (Fig. 17.2). The outhouses at the back of the

---

[15] King 1999: 189.   [16] Bowman and Thomas 2003: 84 no. 628.
[17] Tacitus *Annales* XIV.33.   [18] Milne and Wardle 1996.

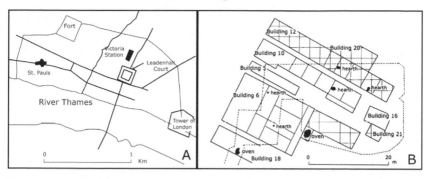

Figure 17.2. Leadenhall Court, London. Location of the site at the north-west of the later *forum and basilica* (A). Main excavation area (within dotted lane) showing structures of site Period 3. Cross-hatched structures relate to latest developments (B). (After Milne and Wardle 1996: figs. 10–11.)

properties seemed to have served a variety of purposes. One was alongside a latrine pit and so may have been a room for ablutions. They may also have acted as storerooms as the highest concentration of amphorae were noted in them. Hearths and ovens were associated with the strip buildings and multi-roomed building rather than the outhouses, so it can be surmised that the kitchens were in the main buildings. Given the relatively small amount of occupation on the site prior to this phase of occupation, residuality is only a minor problem. What was found associated with the Period 3 contexts should, on the whole, reflect what was used and consumed on the site.

The inhabitants consumed a considerable amount of pork as well as beef. The division between the meat of the three main domesticated species is 49% cattle, 35% pork and only 16% lamb.[19] Numerous chickens were also eaten, but the contribution of any other type of meat was negligible. The charred plant remains were too few to be able to judge what the preferred grain was. Both spelt wheat and barley were present. What is clear is that the final cleaning of grain for consumption took place on the site, and it was ground there using imported lava querns. The inhabitants had access to imported foodstuffs such as lentils and figs, but the range of spices and flavourings revealed by the waterlogged remains is meagre. Only poppy seed and an unusually early occurrence of summer savory represent this area of foodstuffs. The inhabitants were heavy users

[19] Based on West in Milne and Wardle 1996: Table 6, the meat yields would be beef 8.785 kg, pork 6.357 kg, lamb 2.786 kg. See Table 9.2 and Appendix for calculations.

Table 17.5. *Pottery and glass vessels associated with Phase 3 contexts at Leadenhall Court, London (EVE data).*

Building number	Large building B6	Strip building 10 and 12	Outhouses 14 and 16	Total
Pottery beaker	2.93	3.45	4.00	10.38
Pottery cup	1.22	2.76	5.57	9.55
Glass drinking vessel	—	2.40	2.20	4.60
Pottery flagon	3.90	5.17	9.43	18.5
Glass jug	0.28	0.28	0.84	1.40
Pottery bowl	2.69	5.52	6.55	14.76
Pottery dish	1.71	1.38	5.39	8.48
Glass bowl	0.40	0.80	1.20	2.40
Pottery jar	7.31	10.34	13.27	30.92
Pottery lid	0.73	2.41	2.70	5.84
Mortarium	1.46	1.72	0.89	4.07
Glass bottle	—	0.70	0.14	0.84
Total	22.63	36.93	52.18	111.74

of olive oil as 84% of the amphora assemblage[20] consisted of olive oil amphora sherds. They also had a marked taste for *garum* and other fish products (6% of the sherds). Wine (9% of the sherds) came from a range of sources including Gaul, Rhodes and elsewhere in the Mediterranean. Sherds from the distinctive amphorae that shipped olives and dates indicate that these too were occasional delicacies.

The pottery and glass vessels being used are summarised in Table 17.5. It would appear that smaller-capacity drinking vessels (pottery cups and glass drinking vessels) were marginally preferred overall to the larger-capacity beakers. Bowls were also marginally preferred to the shallower dish and platter forms but sufficient of each are present for a variety of stews and drier dishes to be served. The ratio of glass drinking vessels to glass bowls (pillar moulded variety) shows a noticeable difference to the pattern seen in pre-Boudican Colchester. There the bowls dominated the glass assemblage and were especially common in the barrack areas. The inhabitants of Leadenhall Court appear to have had less interest in acquiring them, even though they were still common at this time.

---

[20] Quantified by weight.

Amongst the kitchen wares jars dominate, and again mortaria have low figures. They are the least common of the pottery forms and make up only 4% of the assemblage. They are even less common than glass drinking vessels. Some cooks may have been using stone mortars instead of pottery ones, as fragments of a Purbeck-marble mortar were found in a context belonging to this phase. Some use was made of non-stick Pompeian-Red ware vessels, but the quantity of fragments made in these fabrics suggests such use would have been the exception rather than the rule. Fragments of glass bottles are rare. This may be due to the date of the site as they do not become common until the end of the first century, though it is noticeable that they are much commoner in contemporary military assemblages (see next section).

Other utensils are rare. No knife blades or handles were associated with contexts of this date, though a single round-bowled spoon was recovered from a Period 3 latrine.

In general the finds from this site do not indicate that the inhabitants were particularly wealthy. Even the more elaborate multi-roomed building had only poor-quality painted wall plaster. Some of the buildings had tiled roofs but most would probably have been thatched. The inhabitants should probably be regarded as of the middling sort: rich enough to acquire the latest fashionable colourless glassware and to have efficient lava querns, but not of such status to have well-built and decorated homes. What the ethnicity of the people living here was is unknown. Their preferred meats fall into the immigrant rather than native consumption pattern and they obviously were happy to consume other imported foodstuffs such as lentils. As already noted, the precise status of London during the period under consideration here is unclear, but it seems likely that it was primarily populated by an immigrant community.[21] The consumption patterns seen at Leadenhall Court could be taken to be those of not particularly wealthy, civilian immigrants.

LIFE ON CAMPAIGN

The period under consideration at Leadenhall Court was the time when northern Britain was absorbed into the province. Up to about AD 70 the border had lain in the Midlands. To the north had lain the lands of the Brigantes. Their queen Cartimandua was probably a client of Rome, but

[21] See, for example, Millett 1996.

she fell from power in AD 69. The reasons that Tacitus gives for this are the stuff of historical romance.[22] Indeed it is surprising that the story hasn't been adapted as a best-selling historical saga with associated television series. Whether or not the reason her husband took control of the territory was really as a result of her setting him aside and taking his standard bearer as her consort, or whether there was some other reason, the result was the same. The Roman authorities now appeared to be faced with a hostile power on their northern border. At the same time a new dynasty, the Flavians, came to be in power in Rome. The new emperor Vespasian had seen military service in Britain as one of the legionary commanders in the Claudian invasion force, and possibly this influenced what happened next. The decision was taken to absorb the rest of Britain into the province. During the next fifteen years or so the army advanced to the north, sweeping through northern England, southern Scotland and on into the Scottish Highlands.[23] Tacitus says this was the period when Britain was conquered and then immediately thrown away.[24] His view was undoubtedly coloured by the fact that his father-in-law Agricola had been the final governor of Britain involved in this expansion; and it was his conquests in Scotland that had been abandoned when the frontier was settled on the Tyne – Solway line by the end of the century.

During the period of the Flavian advance, the garrison of Britain consisted of four legions with a nominal strength of 20,000 men and an equivalent number of auxiliary troops. The redeployment of the army resulted in many new forts being established. Some were temporary, some saw intensive occupation for a short period before the army moved on, while the sites of others became towns which are still occupied today, such as Carlisle and York. Castleford in West Yorkshire provides a very good place to look at how a campaigning army provisioned itself. Urban occupation there is relatively recent, and in many places the Roman deposits are relatively undisturbed. A series of excavations took place between 1974 and 1985 and the results appeared in three monographs between 1998 and 2000,[25] though much of the specialist work was completed between five and ten years before the volumes appeared. This leads to some problems when attempting to extract data for a synthetic approach. The quantification of the pottery, for example, is somewhat

---

[22] Tacitus *The Histories* III.45.
[23] Frere 1987: 81–104 is still a good general account though some details are now clearly incorrect.
[24] Tacitus *Annales* I.2.
[25] Cool and Philo 1998; Abramson *et al.* 1999; Rush *et al.* 2000.

idiosyncratic reflecting the fact that the report was written at a time when different types of quantification were being experimented with. On the whole the data are clearly presented, and some sites had the great advantage of having waterlogged deposits which preserved an important sequence of organic remains. The only noticeable absence appears to be any report on the bird or fish bones.

The army arrived sometime during the governorship of Petilius Cerialis (AD 71–73/4). There was then intense occupation until about AD 95. This occupation is normally described in terms of two separate forts with their associated civilian settlements (*vici*). The first of these is dated to the period up to about AD 86/7. During that period the same area was often occupied by a succession of different buildings and the layout does not conform to the normal internal organisation of a fort. Nor have any defences been identified. This is in contrast to the second fort belonging to the period of the mid-80s to the mid-90s where the line of the defences can be suggested, and the layout of the buildings conforms a little more to what is normally expected of a fort. There are some grounds for thinking that what is described as the first fort and *vicus* was in fact one of a series of different base camps for a large campaigning force, intermittently occupied. In what follows we shall be looking at the evidence derived from this first phase of occupation, before the second fort and *vicus* were established. Precisely which units would have been in the garrison is unknown. Various aspects of the finds recovered suggests the force may have been mixed, with both legionary and auxiliary troops being present.

The mammal bone was the subject of a very detailed study quantified by fragment count, diagnostic zones and minimum numbers. Judged by all measures and in all the separately studied groups the order of frequency of the three main meat animals is cattle, sheep and then pig. Table 17.6 shows the division between these in two groups. One is derived primarily from slaughter waste incorporated into levelling and make-up layers (Tr15IV/15V/18). The other group is derived from a waterlogged midden in Trench 14 and is a mixed group of both slaughter and cooking waste.

By any measure, beef was the main meat consumed. An attempt has been made to quantify the lamb and pork intake using the average weights provided in Table 9.2 and the minimum numbers. These show that pork may have been commoner in the diet than the other measures suggest, but it would not have been as common as it was in the diet of the people in Colchester and London. The reason for that is probably because the units garrisoned at Castleford were living off the land. It is noticeable that the

Table 17.6. *Animal bone from the principal domesticates from selected Fort I contexts at Castleford.*

	Quantities	Trench 15/18	Trench 14
Cattle	Fragment count (NISP)	1,638	1,727
	Zone count	552	1,057
	Minimum number	79	61
	Notional meat (kg)	18,157	11,072
Sheep	Fragment count (NISP)	755	999
	Zone count	(?)	789
	Minimum number	69	55
	Notional meat (kg)	1,328	1,089
Pig	Fragment count (NISP)	301	416
	Zone count	(?)	371
	Minimum number	20	18
	Notional meat (kg)	1,185	1,067

age range of the cattle at this time is much broader than was to be the case for the cattle consumed in Fort II.[26] The soldiers might well have been seizing what they could find with little concern for maintaining the viability of the herd. The butchery patterns seen on even low-meat-yielding parts such as cattle mandibles show that the butchers of Fort I were anxious to maximise the amount of meat acquired from each carcase. The Fort I midden on Site 14 is also the only place in all of Castleford where cattle scapulae have been found with the typical knife marks and punched holes indicative of preserving by salting or drying.[27] Everything points to the meat supply having to be eked out. The soldiers might have preferred to eat pork and ham, but what was more easily available was lamb and mutton. Interestingly, despite the obvious need to maximise the meat supply, hunting does not appear to have been seen as a way of doing this as game was very rare.

The problems with the meat supply could have come about because the supply chain for fresh produce was erratic. A similar pattern of living off the land is revealed in the charred grain assemblages where barley is the dominant grain in the assemblages associated with the early fort whereas wheat is dominant by the second century.[28] Barley would have been what

[26] Abramson *et al.* 1999: 228 Table 39.
[27] For the butchery see Abramson *et al.* 1999: 233; see also p. 89 and fig. 9.1.
[28] Bastow in Abramson *et al.* 1999: Tables 17, 19 and 20.

was locally available in bulk. There does not appear to have been as great a problem with staples that could be stockpiled, though there appears to have been an emphasis on commodities regarded as essential. Amphorae show the presence of olive oil, wine, fish sauce and other fish products.

The fragments have been quantified by minimum numbers which is not ideal, but the minimum amounts they would have carried can be calculated.[29] The Phase I fort contexts and the contemporary contexts in the area that was to become the *vicus* in Period 2, produced fragments of sufficient amphorae to have transported *c.* 9,600 litres of goods. This will be only a small sample of what was imported, but probably broadly reflects the proportions coming into the fort. 77% would have been olive oil, 20% wine, nearly all of which was from Gaul, and 3% would have been preserved fish products. These were obviously regarded as essential. Other amphora-born commodities were not and are only represented by a carrot amphora that would have contained dates. This is in interesting contrast to the amphora from earlier military assemblages such as at Kingsholm and Exeter where amphorae transporting preserved fruit, olives, fruit syrups etc. accounted for 9% and 5% of the assemblages.[30] The rarity of exotic fruits in the diet of the soldiers is well demonstrated by comparing the number of fig seeds from the waterlogged midden in Trench 14 with the number recovered from mid-second-century water-logged pits on Site 10 in the *vicus* area. In the 8.4 kg of the midden that was sampled for environmental analysis, there were only 18 fig seeds in total. This compares to just under 4,000 seeds from a 1kg sample from one of the pits.[31]

Acquiring products from the vicinity also extended to utensils as can be seen in the quern assemblage.[32] Fragments from imported lava quern-stones are present in the Fort I contexts but the local beehive querns are well represented too. All of the flat rotary querns from the early contexts for which a diameter can be calculated are of the size suitable for hand mills. There is no evidence of mechanisation even though the numbers in the garrison would probably have been large.

The pottery and glass vessel assemblages are summarised in Tables 17.7 and 17.8. Amongst the pottery vessels, jars and flagons dominate as they did at Leadenhall Court, but here there are almost twice as many cups as there are beakers. Whether this reflects different drinking habits from the

---

[29] Rush *et al.* 2000: Tables 18 and 19.   [30] See Table 7.1.
[31] Bastow in Abramson *et al.* 1999: Tables 8–12, 15.
[32] Buckley and Major in Cool and Philo 1998: 241–7.

Table 17.7. *Pottery vessels from Fort I contexts at Castleford (minimum numbers).*

Form	Number	Percentage
Cup	143	4.3
Beaker	77	2.3
Dish	262	7.8
Bowl	295	8.8
Lid	53	1.6
Flagon	733	21.8
Jar	1,719	51.2
Mortarium	71	2.1
Cheese press	3	—
Total	3,356	

Table 17.8. *Glass vessels from Fort I and the Phase I vicus area at Castleford (EVE data).*

Form	Fort area	*Vicus* area	Total
Drinking vessel	2.40	0.20	2.60
Pillar moulded bowl	2.00	1.20	3.20
Other bowl	0.40	—	0.40
Jar	0.19	—	0.19
Jug	0.42	0.42	0.84
Bottle	2.24	0.28	2.52
Total	7.65	2.10	9.75

civilian population in London is open to question. Military sites tend to have large quantities of samian pottery supplying what might be considered the personal tablewares (dishes, bowls and cups). The samian industry produced cups rather than beakers so the preference for cups may just be reflecting what was easily available. What is less easy to explain is that again the pillar moulded glass bowl form is dominating the glass-vessel assemblage as it did in the barrack areas at Colchester. Pillar moulded bowls frequently dominate first-century military assemblages, and whatever their purpose, they were obviously ones that had an appeal for the military. Conversely, glass drinking vessels were much less used at Castleford than they had been at Leadenhall Court.

Mortaria were obviously in little demand, and the cooks also appear not to have used the non-slip Pompeian-Red ware platters for cooking.[33] Amongst the utensils, small round-bowled spoons were very popular as no less than five of the twelve examples found were stratified in contexts associated with the earliest occupation.[34] Knives and cleavers, by contrast, were much less common, though this possibly reflects the fact that iron was not well preserved here.

What is interesting about the Castleford data is what was regarded as essential by this 'Roman' community. Adequate supplies of olive oil were essential, probably because of the range of purposes it served. A certain amount of wine was important too, but relishes like fish sauce could, on the whole, be done without. They would eat whatever varieties of meat and grain were locally available, but they would probably cook and serve them by their normal procedures. Certainly the number of bowls and dishes indicate the need for deeper vessels presumably for the more liquid dishes (soups, stews, porridge), as well as shallower ones for drier foods. The number of spoons also suggests a different way of eating than that which would have been practised in the surrounding native sites.

COUNTRY LIFE

Rural sites rarely provide the precision of dating that has been possible for the urban and military sites just considered, and longer timespans have to be considered. To provide examples of consumption patterns amongst the native populations, two rural agricultural sites have been selected. The first is in Gloucestershire at Claydon Pike to the east of Cirencester, excavated between 1979 and 1983. Some post-excavation work was carried out in the 1980s, the bulk of the analysis was completed in the past few years.[35] The second is Orton Hall Farm on the fen edge in Cambridgeshire. This was dug in the early 1970s with final publication in 1996.[36]

The dates of the excavations means that there were no systematic sampling programmes. Perversely, the delays in publication have been useful as, though the quantification methods used are variable, some useful figures can be extracted. This would probably not have been the case had they been published soon after they were dug. Both sites have the advantage that it is possible to separate out the earlier occupation from

---

[33] Rush *et al.* 2000: 93 type 26, Tables 21–2.
[34] Cool and Philo 1998: 94 nos. 449–53, 455–7, 459–61; also Greep in the same: 277 no. 138.
[35] Miles *et al.* forthcoming.   [36] Mackreth 1996.

Table 17.9. *Animal bone from the principal domesticates from Period 2 contexts at Claydon Pike and Period 1 contexts at Orton Hall Farm.*

		Claydon Pike	Orton Hall Farm
Cattle	Fragment count (NISP)	964	712
	Minimum numbers	12	—
	Notional meat (kg)	2,178	—
Sheep	Fragment count (NISP)	722	1,160
	Minimum numbers	22	—
	Notional meat (kg)	424	—
Pig	Fragment count (NISP)	173	48
	Minimum numbers	8	—
	Notional meat (kg)	474	—

that belonging to the late Roman period. In the case of Claydon Pike, occupation started early in the first century prior to the conquest. Phase 2 relates to the occupation from the early first to the early second century, prior to a major reorganisation of the landscape which seems to have been associated with a much more Romanised lifestyle. At Orton Hill Farm, occupation started about the middle of the first century AD and the first period of occupation extended to about AD 175 when again there was a major reorganisation of the site with the establishment of rectilinear buildings where before there had been roundhouses.

The bone from the three main meat animals are shown in Table 17.9. The quantification methods are not ideal, but it will be realised that there are striking differences when compared with the proportions of bones recorded from Colchester, London and Castleford. At Orton Hall Farm, for the first time the numbers of sheep bone fragments are in a clear majority. On rural sites such as these, it could be questioned whether all animal bone represents food waste in the way it must do on an urban site. The other functions of cattle and sheep in providing traction, dairy produce and wool may have been as important. At Claydon Pike it was noted that, during Phase 2, the sheep tended to be slaughtered earlier than they were to be later on the site. At the age of one to two years they would have been prime young meat animals, suggesting they were being produced primarily for meat rather than wool or milk. The butchery marks on the cattle bones also indicate they were being processed for meat. Given this, a notional meat yield for the minimum numbers of beasts at Claydon Pike has been calculated using the average weights provided in Table 9.2. As ever, these should be read with health warnings, but it does

make clear that even when fragment-count and minimum-number measures are large for sheep, the amount of meat they are contributing may be
low. Even allowing for this, the figures for Orton Hall Farm suggest that
sheep meat featured more on the menu there than pork.

One thing that these two rural sites do share with the military and urban
sites already discussed is an avoidance of game. In both cases evidence of
deer consists merely of antler fragments and thus does not indicate venison
was being eaten. There are two fragments of hare bones from Orton Hall
Farm, but at Claydon Pike hare bones do not appear until later in the
sequence. Whether this avoidance was cultural, or simply means there was
not the game in the vicinity to be exploited is unknown; but the absence on
a wide range of sites shows that not eating game was the rule rather than the
exception. Other sources of animal protein were provided by poultry. At
both sites domestic fowl, ducks and geese are present, with domestic fowl
being the commonest type represented.[37] At Orton Hall Farm, oysters were
also eaten, even though the site was 50 km from the sea.[38]

The presence of the oysters is a useful reminder that rural sites were not
necessarily isolated. They could acquire foodstuffs and other items from
outside if they were required. At Orton Hall Farm a lava quern was
acquired at this time, which must have been a great boon for whoever had
to grind the corn.[39] The presence or absence of things is thus partially a
matter of choice on the part of the inhabitants as well, of course, as of the
vagaries of archaeological discovery. At Orton Hall Farm lava querns and
oysters were found useful, but amphora-borne commodities appear to be
absent. The converse was true at Claydon Pike where a small number of
amphora sherds suggest some olive oil and fish sauce was reaching the site.[40]

As can be seen in Table 17.10, the pottery assemblages from these two
sites are strikingly different to those from the urban and military sites. In
both cases it is dominated by jars, and the tablewares are much less
common than they were in the assemblages discussed earlier in this
chapter. Taking beakers, cups, dishes, bowls and flagons as tablewares,
at Leadenhall Court they made up 60% of the assemblage (see Table
17.5). At Claydon Pike they contribute only 16%. At Orton Hall Farm
they represent 19% of the coarse pottery assemblage. The overall figure is
higher but cannot be calculated because, unlike at Claydon Pike, the
samian pottery has not been usefully quantified by EVEs. Even if every

[37] Harman in Mackreth 1996: 218–9; Sykes in Miles *et al.* forthcoming.
[38] King, J. in Mackreth 1996: Mf 8; B13 Table 80.   [39] Mackreth 1996: Mf 8: B12 sf11321.
[40] Williams in Miles *et al.* forthcoming.

Table 17.10. *Pottery vessels from Period 2 contexts at Claydon Pike and Period 1 contexts at Orton Hall Farm.*

| | Claydon Pike | Orton Hall Farm | |
	All pottery (EVE)	Coarse pottery (EVE)	Samian (fragment)
Beaker	0.40	1.73	—
Cup	0.75	—	5
Flagon	0.44	6.61	—
Tankard	0.93	—	—
Bowl	4.69	1.34	12
Dish	0.62	1.69	46
Lid	0.09	1.34	—
Jar	36.2	47.06	—
Mortaria	0.09	0.25	—
Total	44.20	60.02	63

one of the samian fragments identified was a rim sherd though, it is highly unlikely that the tableware figure would come anywhere close to the level seen at Leadenhall Court. It is clear that the tableware forms were not so important to the inhabitants of these rural sites as they were to the inhabitants of the urban and military ones. This is reflected in the glass-vessel assemblages from the sites too. These are meagre in the extreme, consisting at both solely of a single fragment of a glass drinking vessel.

An interesting difference does start to emerge if the figures from the two sites are compared. Though the tableware levels are reduced in comparison to those of urban and military sites, the inhabitants of Orton Hall Farm assemblage did seem to show a greater interest in them than the people at Claydon Pike did. The latter primarily wanted bowls, the former appear to have had a greater use for flagons and shallow dishes. This may well be reflecting the different parts of the country the sites are in. Orton Hall Farm lies on the edge of the area where a diversified range of forms was available in the late Iron Age. Claydon Pike lies in an area where diversification did not happen, and from the look of the first- to early second-century pottery assemblage on the site, the inhabitants continued to find little use for a wider range of forms even when they became more widely available. So while these are both comparable rural sites with similar ingredients available, the way they were being prepared was probably different. Bowls continued to suffice for the people of Claydon Pike. The dining regime at Orton Hall Farm obviously required more diversity.

POLITE DINING

A group of late first- and second-century graves in the south-east and south-central part of Britain allows an insight to be gained into dining practices. Their location, often in rural settings or outside towns with little evidence of major immigrant communities, strongly suggests that these are the graves of native Britons. They frequently contain suites of vessels that appear to be place settings and evidence for food in the form of animal bones from joints of meat. Some also contain other suites of equipment relating to activities such as a visit to the baths or writing. Not all elements are present in all the burials, and localised traditions have been identified amongst them.[41] They do give a very good picture, though, of how some elements of the native elite were aspiring to live, and what was thought necessary for a good life. The combinations of vessels found provide some of the best indications we have of what these people were eating and drinking out of, and how some of the vessels may have been used.

Though excavated nearly two hundred years ago, the cemetery at the Bartlow Hills in Essex is a good place to start exploring this phenomenon. These were cremation burials placed below barrows in the second century. Most of the material was long since destroyed in a fire, but the accounts published in *Archaeologia* between 1834 and 1842 allow the groups to be reconstructed and, in some cases, dated.[42] Generally elite burials like these are found only as single examples or as pairs, but at Bartlow there are six examples which can be compared. The groups are summarised in Table 17.11.

The graves clearly demonstrate various different aspects of what it was to be 'Roman'. The first barrow dug (1834/1) provides a good example of a group designed for dining. It consists of two jugs (glass and pottery), four samian cup-and-dish sets, two pottery beakers and a glass bottle. The group dug in 1836 focuses on other aspects of a 'Roman' life. There is equipment for the baths (strigils, an enamelled flask for oil, and a glass unguent bottle), a folding iron stool of the type used by magistrates and senior military officers,[43] a jug and *trulleum* set and a lamp. This combination of jug and *trulleum* is the one associated with washing hands before making a sacrifice.[44] The recorded positions of the four from the Bartlow

---

[41] E.g. Millett 1987.
[42] Gage 1834, 1836, 1840; Gage Rokewode 1842. I am most grateful to Miss Brenda Dickinson for providing the dates of the samian stamps described therein.
[43] Jessup 1954: 22–8.   [44] See p. 47.

Table 17.11. *The grave goods from the Bartlow burials (* = contained chicken bones).*

	1834/I	1842	1840	1834/II	1834/III	1836
Samian date	100–25	160–90	150–80	—	—	—
Coin date	—	—	—	117+	—	—
Samian cup	4	2	1	—	—	—
Samian dish	4	1	1*	—	—	—
Glass drinking vessel	—	1	1	1	—	—
Pottery beaker	2	4	1	—	—	1
Wooden tankard	—	—	—	1	—	—
Pottery flagon	1	—	—	—	—	—
Glass jug	1	—	—	—	—	—
Glass bottle	1	—	2	1	2	1
Water jug	—	—	—	—	—	1
Lamp	1	1	1	—	1	1
Jug and *trulleum* set	—	1	1	—	1	1
Glass flask	—	1	—	—	—	1
Ointment pot	—	—	—	—	—	1
Strigil	—	—	—	—	—	1
Chair	—	—	—	—	—	1

cemetery make it very clear that they were indeed seen as a set. In each case they were found together with the jug placed in or on the *trulleum*, and it is tempting to see them as representing the ability to sacrifice in the 'correct' manner. The goods with the individual in 1836 could be seen as demonstrating authority, proper relationship with the gods and appropriate hygiene. It seems reasonable to conclude that the graves with place settings were also regarded as 'correct' for a 'Roman' life.

A cremation burial from Stansted, dated to the early to mid-second century, makes it even easier to identify these different aspects of the Roman life, given the way in which the grave goods were laid out (see fig. 17.3).[45] Centrally the cremated remains had been placed on a pewter tray. To the left of this was equipment for sacrifice (a jug and *trulleum* set) and bathing (a bath saucer). A large copper-alloy basin with a samian dish placed internally was also on the left side. To the right was equipment for dining (seven small samian bowls and dishes of varying sizes, one samian cup, one copper-alloy pedestal cup, a glass flask and a two-handled

---

[45] Havis and Brooks 2004: 217–27.

copper-alloy amphorisk). Beyond the bottom edge of the tray there were three groups of items. These were, from left to right: a carrot amphora and a pottery beaker, a pillar moulded glass bowl and a glass drinking vessel, and a joint of pork with a bone-handled knife.

It is tempting to see this last group of material as the remains of food. This is certainly true of the amphora, which would have contained dried dates and other palm fruit, and the joint of pork. There are noticeable gaps in the layout of the grave goods in this area which is curious given the crowding seen in the tablewares on the right of the tray. The pork joint had been placed directly onto the base of the chest, and so other solid foodstuffs that have not survived could have been placed similarly in the gaps. If there was food to the left and right in this area, this would open up interesting questions about the role of the pottery beaker, positioned with the amphora. Perhaps it was acting as a serving vessel of some form.

Generally, within these graves, cup forms far outnumber beakers. Where both are recovered, and the position of the vessels has been carefully recorded, the beakers and the cups are not placed together. This can be seen in the late first-century Burial 2 at Victoria Road, Winchester (see fig. 17.4).[46] The main focus was a shale tray on which had been placed a large dish and cup, both of samian, bones from two joints of pork with each group having its own knife, and a single copper-alloy spoon. To one side were three samian cups and two jugs (one copper-alloy jug and one glass). Extending to the end of the grave from the tray were three samian dishes. One had another dish inverted over it, the other two each had a pair of samian cups placed in them. At the end of the grave there was a large pottery flagon and a pottery beaker placed on either side of the row of dishes. The beaker was thus placed at almost the maximum distance possible from the jug and cup group. It is possible it was for the consumption of whatever was in the large flagon, but the position away from the main focus of the tablewares possibly suggests that, as at Stansted, it could be viewed as a food container.

There is no doubt that the samian dishes can be regarded as vessels for eating out of, as bones from meat are sometimes found in them. The deliberate covering of one at Grange Road also suggests that when it went into the grave it contained something that needed to be protected. Where multiple sets of dishes are recovered, there is often a single larger one suggesting a serving dish from which individual portions were taken. At

---

[46] Biddle 1967: 230–45.

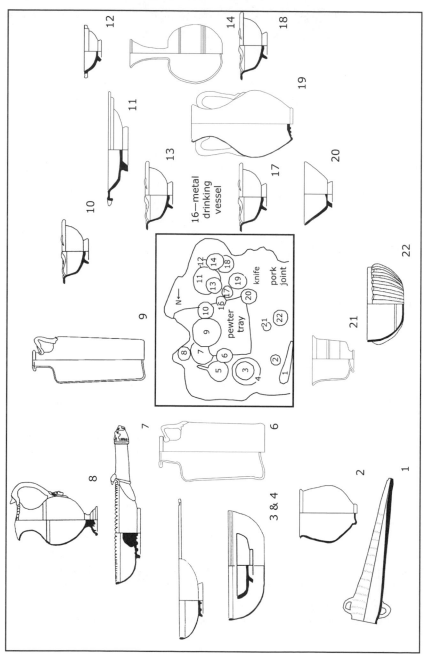

Figure 17.3. Cremation Burial 25 at Stansted. Scale of vessels 1 : 8 apart from nos. 1, 6 and 9 (1 : 16). (Based on Havis and Brooks 2004: figs. 145–52.)

Figure 17.4. Burial 2 at Grange Road, Winchester. (Courtesy of the Winchester Excavation Committee.)

Grange Road the largest dish was placed on the platter alongside the meat joints suggesting that perhaps it also contained food when placed in the grave.

The role of the vessels generally called cups is more equivocal. In some cases the interpretation of them as drinking vessels seems very reasonable. The grouping of the cups and jugs at Grange Road suggests that all were concerned with drinking, but it is noticeable in that grave that whereas there are four individual-sized dishes, there are eight cups. All are the same form though two are noticeably smaller. The separation of the cups into a group with the jugs and another group of four, including the small ones, with the dishes suggest they may have been serving two functions even though they were the same shape. Certainly the goods accompanying a contemporary grave at Verulamium excavated in 1989 suggest this.[47] The interim publications available unfortunately do not describe the internal

---

[47] Frere 1991: 259–60, pl. xxvi; Anon 1990: 413–5.

layout. Amongst the finds, however, there are clearly four identical place settings in samian pottery, each consisting of a shallow dish with one large and one small cup.

Whilst it is always possible that the different sizes were needed for different drinks, it is equally possible that many of the samian 'cups' actually functioned as individual bowls for food. This would certainly have been the case at Stansted. Four of the small samian dishes there are of a type traditionally termed a cup (Dragendorff Form 35), but given they have a wide out-turned rim with relief decoration in the form of barbotine leaves, they are very unlikely to have functioned as drinking vessels. They are much more likely to have been vessels for eating from. This might explain the wear marks seen internally on some cups and thought to have been brought about by stirring.[48] Even if some of the 'cups' in the graves were in fact bowls, what is clear is that the drinking vessels preferred were small-capacity ones.

Some of the graves make it very clear that two containers were considered necessary for whatever liquid was being served, suggesting this may indeed have been wine that needed to be mixed with water. The forms of the containers though are very varied. At Bartlow 1834/I and Grange Road, jugs were used made of pottery and glass, and of glass and copper alloy respectively. At Stansted this part of the service was supplied by a glass flask and a copper-alloy amphorisk. Elsewhere it has to be suspected that glass bottles were being used. At both Bartlow 1840 and the grave excavated at Verulamium in 1989, a pair of glass bottles were present and there were no other candidates for any liquid container.

Two other interesting features emerge from the graves with dining equipment. One is the presence in the graves of joints of pork. Given the scarcity of pork on native sites normally, this too would appear to be yet another way in which the deceased were being marked out as adopting Roman ways. It is clear, however, that the Roman 'package' was not being bought wholesale in its entirety. In these graves utensils such as knives and spoons are rare. Even when they occur in graves where there would appear to be multiple place settings, they occur in numbers that suggest that it was not thought important that everyone should have their own. This is not the pattern that would be suspected from sets of silver plate from the heart of the empire.[49] It is also not the pattern that emerges from the soldiers at Castleford or from the soldiers and settlers at Colchester where

---

[48] Biddulph 2005.   [49] See p. 53.

spoons were found with some regularity on the pre-Boudican sites.[50] The native elite might have been prepared to accept many aspects of 'being Roman', but changing table manners and the actual act of conveying the food to the mouth may have been one step too far.

CONCLUSIONS

This examination of the eating habits in five broadly contemporary communities has shown how varied they were. Major differences can be observed between the immigrants and the natives, but equally there are differences within these communities. The inhabitants of Leadenhall Court and Castleford were eating different things and probably drinking in different ways. If the people living at Claydon Pike had been invited to dinner in the households of the native elite buried at Winchester and Bartlow, they would probably have thought both the food and the way it was served strange and alien. Equally though, they would probably have been just as uncomfortable dining at Orton Hall Farm.

The studies also show that the way in which the results of excavations are analysed and reported can have important consequences when we try to look at the wider, rather than site-specific, picture. How much more nuanced this chapter could have been if assemblages of the same type of thing had been quantified uniformly!

[50] Crummy 1983: 69 no. 2008; Crummy, N. in Crummy, P. 1992: 156 no. 535, 215 no. 124.

CHAPTER 18

Coming of age

INTRODUCTION

The previous chapter showed some of the different patterns of eating and drinking that can be identified during the first to second centuries. This chapter continues the story into the later second and third centuries, by which time much of Britain had been part of the empire for a century or more. It is during this period that the impact of belonging to this wider world can start to be seen more regularly on the rural sites where many of the native British population would have continued to live. Here we will explore first how the habits of the native population were changing, before going on to look at the evidence from particular types of activities being engaged in by both native and immigrant communities.

LEICESTER: A BRITISH TOWN

The lifestyles of the two urban communities described in the previous chapter were those of immigrants. The excavations at Causeway Lane, Leicester, provide an opportunity to look at how the British adapted to town life. Leicester (*Ratae Corieltavorum*) was the *civitas* capital of the Corieltavi. It had been a tribal centre prior to the conquest but did not acquire the formal trappings of a city such as a planned street layout and a forum until the second century.[1] Causeway Lane is situated in the north-west of the town, and the remains recovered included structures facing onto the road and backyards with rubbish pits and wells. It was excavated in 1991 with an extensive sampling and sieving programme which yielded good environmental evidence. The publication is of very high quality with well-quantified find assemblages.[2] Here we will concentrate on the

---

[1] Wacher 1995: 343–5.   [2] Connor and Buckley 1999.

evidence of the Phase 3 contexts, dating from the middle second to early third centuries.

Looking at the type of meat consumed is complicated during this phase because, in addition to food waste, the bone and horn debris from a tannery was deposited as the infill of a ditch. Ignoring this material, the division between the species is 50% cattle, 34% sheep and 16% pigs (based on a zonal count).[3] Allowing for the varying quantities of meat the species can provide, this probably reflects a primarily beef diet with approximately equal amounts of pork and lamb as alternatives. Compared with the quantities recovered from the late-first- to mid-second-century contexts on the site, there is an increase in the number of pig bones compared to those from sheep. Possibly this reflects an increasing acceptance of pig-meat products.

As ever, evidence of game consumption was very slight, and the principal type of poultry represented was the domestic fowl. The number of eggshell fragments recovered suggest that the consumption of hens' eggs was common, occasionally augmented by goose eggs.[4] The remains of fish were rare both at this period and during the rest of the Roman period. This was especially noticeable because occupation continued into the medieval period, and the much higher consumption of fish then is immediately apparent from the figures recorded.[5] It is possible that some of the small amount of fish consumed came in the form of salted fish products as the species list includes herring and mackerel. Unfortunately the amphora report does not differentiate the types recovered by phase, but in general those associated with *salaison* industries are poorly represented. They form only just over 1% by weight of the entire assemblage.[6] The population of Leicester, or at least the part of it living at Causeway Lane, do not appear to have developed a taste for fish, either salted or fresh.

The amphora assemblage in general shows that both olive oil and wine from a range of sources was reaching the site. The quantity of olive oil amphora fragments (*c.* 124 kg) looks impressive until they are put into context. The area of the site excavated was 1,875 m^2 and the figure represents the numbers recovered from at least a century or possibly two, depending on how late olive oil continued to arrive at the site. By contrast, at Leadenhall Court with its immigrant population, 107 kg of

[3] Gidney in Connor and Buckley 1999: Table 65 (total zones 2279).
[4] Gidney in Connor and Buckley 1999: Table 66; Boyer in Connor and Buckley 1999: 329–33.
[5] Nicholson in Connor and Buckley 1999: Table 74.
[6] Williams in Connor and Buckley 1999: Table 5.

olive oil amphora fragments were recovered from an excavation of less than half the size (*c.* 890 m²) and representing a time period of slightly under fifty years.[7] This pattern can be seen within other *civitas* capitals as well. The 1988 excavations at County Hall, Dorchester were approximately the same size as the Leadenhall Court ones, but only produced a total of 13.2 kg of olive oil amphora fragments.[8] It is always possible that people were acquiring their oil and wine in smaller quantities and bringing it home in other containers but, judged by the amphora evidence, the Britons who lived in towns appear to have used less olive oil and drunk wine much less commonly than those where the population was primarily of immigrant stock.

A process of change is apparent in the types of vessels being used. Those made of pottery and glass vessels are summarised according to the principal forms in Table 18.1. This shows that the proportion of jars in the assemblage falls after the mid-second century. In part this may be because there was a need for more tablewares, but it may also be because in Phase 3 Black Burnished ware (BB1) vessels started to be available. These were specialised cooking wares made in Dorset which were available not only as jars, but also as shallow dishes. The rise in the proportion of dishes from Phase 2 to Phase 5 reflects the increasing number of these that were in use. This hints that there may have been a diversification of cooking practices taking place, away from a primarily jar-based technique. Another change appears to be the greater need for mortaria in the later period compared to low levels of use in the earlier phases.

Some change might also be underway in the drinking-vessel assemblage. At Causeway Lane, pottery beakers always outnumbered pottery cups, but it is possible that the use of smaller-capacity drinking vessels was actually increasing as time progressed. The glass-vessel assemblage is small, but a marked increase of glass cups is apparent from the late second century onwards.

A broadening of the culinary horizons can certainly be seen in the Causeway Lane assemblage. The inhabitants might not have liked fish, but they were prepared to try lentils, flavour their dishes with coriander,[9] eat more pork and possibly bake as well as stew. It was not a 'Roman' lifestyle that was emerging, but it was certainly different from what was going on in much of the countryside.

[7] See p. 182; amphora data from Groves in Milne and Wardle 1996: Tables 7–9.
[8] Williams in Smith 1993: Table 15.
[9] Monckton in Connor and Buckley 1999: 353.

Table 18.1. *Principal pottery and glass-vessel types from contexts of Phases 2, 3 and 5 at Causeway Lane, Leicester (* indicates residual in this phase. PMB = pillar moulded bowl).*

		2		3		5	
		Late 1st to mid-2nd century		Mid-2nd to early 3rd century		Late 2nd to mid-4th century	
Phase		EVE	%	EVE	%	EVE	%
Pottery	Cup	7.26	6	4.33	8	8.56	5
	Beaker	11.57	10	8.98	16	23.21	13
	Flagon	7.94	7	4.53	8	18.65	10
	Bowl	17.03	14	7.88	14	23.92	13
	Dish	12.16	10	6.99	13	28.80	16
	Lid	2.66	2	2.16	4	2.88	2
	Jar	59.89	49	18.05	33	63.82	35
	Mortarium	2.61	2	1.76	3	10.50	6
	Total	*121.12*		*54.68*		*180.34*	
Glass	Drinking	0.20	—	0.80	—	2.00	—
	PMB	0.60	—	—		0.40*	—
	Bowl	0.40	—	—	—	0.20*	—
	Jug	0.42	—	0.14	—	0.84	—
	Jar	0.57	—	—		—	—
	Bottle	0.42	—	0.70	—	0.20	—
	Total	*2.61*	—	*1.64*	—	*3.64*	—

THE COUNTRYSIDE REVISITED

In the previous chapter the evidence from Claydon Pike for the first to early second century was examined. At some point during the first half of the second century, the site saw a major reorganisation of the landscape with rectilinear buildings and enclosures replacing everything that had gone before. The main aisled building had a tiled roof and painted walls internally. The change in the landscape was associated with major changes in lifestyle. People started to wear hob-nailed shoes, women started to wear their hair in Roman styles using hairpins. Furnishings were augmented by some luxurious items like a metal oil lamp. This phase of occupation (site Phase 3) lasted until the late third century, and the material associated with it can be used to see whether all these changes were matched by changes in eating and drinking.

The site at Parlington Hollins in West Yorkshire provides a useful comparison to Claydon Pike. Approximately one quarter of a hectare was

Table 18.2. *Principal pottery and glass-vessel types from Claydon Pike (Phase 3) and Parlington Hollins. Figures in brackets for Claydon Pike are the percentages of the forms present in Phase 2 as shown in Table 17.9 (*note the flagon category covers flagons at Claydon Pike and constricted neck jars which served a similar purpose at Parlington Hollins).*

		Claydon Pike		Parlington Hollins	
		EVE	%	EVE	%
Pottery	Beaker	3.6	2 (1)	0.16	2
	Cup	4.6	3 (2)	0.12	2
	Flagon*	3.4	2 (1)	0.74	10
	Tankard	3.9	3 (2)	—	—
	Bowl	17.3	11 (11)	0.40	6
	Dish	7.3	5 (1)	0.55	8
	Lid	2.1	1(<1)	—	—
	Jar	110.3	70 (82)	4.48	62
	Mortarium	4.4	3(<1)	0.77	11
	Total	*156.9*	—	*7.22*	—
Glass	Cup/Beaker	1.80	—	—	—
	Bowl	0.40	—	—	—
	Jug	1.42	—	—	—
	Flask	0.40	—	—	—
	Jar	0.36	—	—	—
	Bottle	1.12	—	—	—
	Total	*5.50*	—	—	—

dug in the mid-1990s in advance of road construction.[10] Being a recent excavation it had all the benefits of environmental sampling, but this generally only provides information about the grain consumed as bone does not survive well. This site also underwent a major transformation in the second century when rectilinear enclosures were laid out. There was at least one rectilinear building in the vicinity, judged by the roof tiles recovered, and it continued in occupation to the end of the third century.

It is instructive to look at the pottery and glass vessels first as the evidence from these is directly comparable, in a way that the animal bone is not. The assemblage from the Phase 3 contexts at Claydon Pike and the complete assemblage from Parlington Hollins is summarised in Table 18.2. The most notable feature is how small the assemblage from the West Yorkshire site is, despite the large area excavated. This, it has to be

[10] Holbrey and Burgess in Roberts *et al.* 2001: 83–105.

Table 18.3. *Animal bone from the principal domesticates from Period 3 contexts at Claydon Pike and Roman contexts at Parlington Hollins.*

	Claydon Pike		Parlington Hollins	
	NISP	%	NISP	%
Cattle	941	53	70	19
Sheep	682	38	289	77
Pig	168	9	15	4
Total	1,791	—	374	—

realised, is one of the more prolific sites in the area! This part of the country had not habitually used pottery during the later Iron Age. Figures such as these suggest that even people like those who lived here who did change some aspects of their life, continued to find little use for pottery vessels, even in the third century. Judged from the sooting on the vessels, dishes were being used to cook with as well as jars. Quite what the relatively large numbers of mortaria were being used for is unknown, but it seems highly unlikely that here they were being used in the Classical manner envisioned in Apicius's recipes. One is recorded as being burnt around the rim so use in some cooking, as opposed to preparation, process might be suspected. At Claydon Pike, pottery vessels were more central to cooking and eating. The second to third centuries saw a slightly increased demand for pottery tablewares and a variety of glass-vessel types became acceptable. A copper-alloy water jug probably also belongs to this phase of occupation. On the whole, however, the vessel assemblage continued to be dominated by jars, and does not show the type of diversity seen on contemporary urban sites.

Approximately equal quantities of mammal bone were found at Parlington Hollins and in the main domestic area at Claydon Pike (6345 and 6672 fragments respectively), but the poor preservation meant that only 9% could be identified to species at the former site, whereas 29% could be at the latter. This means that the Parlington Hollins data will probably under-represent young beasts and pigs whose bones are known not to survive well in adverse conditions. Even allowing for this, the data presented in Table 18.3 would suggest that sheep meat featured more strongly in the diet at Parlington Hollins than it did at Claydon Pike.

At Claydon Pike the overall distribution between the species remained much the same as it had been in Phase 2, but an interesting pattern arose when the distribution of the species across the site was considered. It was noticed that pig and domestic-fowl bones accounted for 60% of those associated with the main aisled building. In one well fill of this period, fowl and pig bones were also associated with a small amount of bone from roe deer and hare, which was otherwise very rare. It was thought that this might represent the debris from a single high-status meal. These observations open up two interesting possibilities. One is that different elements of the people living on the site were favouring different diets. The other is that, for special occasions, the meats selected were perceived to be of higher status. The combination seen in the well is very reminiscent of the debris from the senior officers' kitchen at Caerleon.[11] They will not have eaten like that all the time, but for a feast a more 'Romanised' cuisine was seen as appropriate. Perhaps it was at such occasions that the lamp and the water jug for the wine service were brought out. The amphorae suggest olive oil and Campanian wine were reaching the site during this phase. The quantities were small, so perhaps these too were special-occasion commodities. Certainly, for the lamp to have functioned, oil would have been needed, reminding us that not all olive oil was used for cooking.

One thing that both sites have in common is that in both cases the principal grain was wheat (emmer and spelt).[12] This is unexceptional at Claydon Pike, but barley would normally be expected in West Yorkshire. The choice of grain might be one additional way in which the inhabitants of Parlington Hollins marked themselves out from their neighbours.

These two sites demonstrate that rural Britain continued to be different from urban Britain, but equally there was no one rural way of life. The inhabitants of both these sites aspired towards things Roman as is demonstrated by the tiled roofs, but this did not result in the same way of doing things. Regional differences of habits continue to play a very important role; and the mere availability of new types of goods and consumables in an area does not mean that all communities will adopt them. The inhabitants of Parlington Hollins may have been regarded as dangerously modern by their neighbours who, because they found no use for much Romanised material culture, will have continued to live in an

---

[11] See p. 83.
[12] Young and Richardson in Roberts *et al.* 2001: 221 Table 44; Straker, Jones and Perry in Miles *et al.* forthcoming.

essentially late Iron Age way. This, of course, makes them relatively invisible to archaeology in this area.[13]

One intriguing feature of the data from both these sites relates to the question raised in Chapter 5 of whether or not a differentiated cuisine, with all the cultural stratification that implies, can be discerned within Roman Britain. Whilst one might expect to observe it in obviously Romanised sites, these two native rural sites also appear to be showing different facets of what might be expected of such a cuisine. The inhabitants of Parlington Hollins were definitely differentiating themselves in many ways, including what they were eating, from their neighbours, whilst at Claydon Pike the choice of what has regularly featured as elite dining ingredients for a special meal, suggests an awareness that different food was appropriate for different occasions.

AN OUTING TO THE BATHS

There is some evidence that certain places were associated with particular eating habits. The next two sections explore two of these cases. A visit to the baths in the Roman period was not just about getting clean. The larger ones provided opportunities to take exercise, get beauty and health treatment and to generally enjoy oneself. Seneca's letter complaining about the noise emanating from a public bath-house describes the type of people involved and, interestingly for our purposes, notes the cries of pastry cooks, sausage sellers, confectioners and other hawkers of refreshments.[14] Drains in bath-houses often provided traps for the detritus of activities carried out in them. Analysis of these assemblages show that the finds are precisely the sort that would be expected from the known activities that went on in the baths. Fragments from glass flasks used to hold the oil needed for cleaning the skin are numerous; whilst amongst the small finds the types of personal ornaments are precisely those most likely to be kept on when people aren't wearing many clothes. Many women lost the pins they were using to fasten their hair, whilst the steam clearly loosened the adhesive that held intaglios in finger-rings and many were washed away.[15] Given the evidence of these finds, it is reasonable to suppose that any evidence for food and drink in the drains will relate directly to what was being consumed during visits to the baths.

[13] See p. 170.
[14] *Epistulae Morales* 56 – quoted in Zienkiewicz 1986: 17.
[15] Cool *et al.* 1995: Table 138, 1642; Cool and Baxter 1999: 81, fig. 4.

In Britain the best place to study bath-house activity centres on the baths in the legionary fortress at Caerleon.[16] There a 28 m stretch of the drain from the *frigidarium* was found with its vaulted stone roof intact. The baths had been built in the 70s and silts and rubbish in the drain had built up to the early second century when the drain had been remodelled and enlarged. This had involved laying a new stone floor on those silts and replacing the roof at a higher level. Silt then continued to accumulate until *c.* AD 230 when the baths went out of use. Drain Group 1 material was sealed below the remodelled floor, and securely relates only to activities in the bath-house. Drain Group 4 material is from above the new floor and is dated to *c.* AD 160 – 230. It relates primarily to activities in the bath-house, but there is some evidence that unrelated rubbish was washed in after disuse and when the baths were being decommissioned in the later third century.

The excavations were completed in 1981 and a sieving programme retrieved the bones from small animals. Unfortunately the conditions in the drain had not resulted in any waterlogged or mineralised plant remains. This gap in the evidence can be plugged by reference to what was found in a sewer associated with the Church Street bath-house in the fortress at York. This was excavated in 1972–3, a time when a group of specialists in York were pioneering methods of acquiring environmental evidence, and one of the earliest in-depth environmental reports resulted from the excavations. The sewer is neither as well dated nor as undisturbed as the Caerleon drain deposit, but it does contain a similar range of small finds and glass vessels and will have been reflecting similar activities.[17]

The bone from the Caerleon drain makes it clear that food vendors specialised in finger food.[18] This can best be seen in the remains from Drain Group 1 which is dominated by chicken and sheep bones, the latter consisting in the main of rib and vertebra fragments indicative of the consumption of lamb or mutton chops. These often had knife cuts but they were also well chewed, a good indication of being held whilst eaten. Evidence for pork is much less common but again is indicative of snack food in the form of chops and trotters. Cuts like these continued to be consumed judged by the deposits accumulating during the later second to

---

[16] Zienkiewicz 1986.
[17] Site – Whitwell 1976; small finds – MacGregor, A. 1976; environmental evidence – Buckland 1976.
[18] O'Connor in Zienkiewicz 1986: 226–30.

third century, but during that time there was an increase in debris from the main meat-bearing bones. In part this might be due to contamination, but it could also indicate a growing taste for meat sliced off the bone.

Other snack foods available included shellfish. Mussels were consumed throughout the use of the baths, but oysters became more popular later on.[19] Mussel and oyster shells were also recovered from the York sewer with the latter being commonest.[20] There is some tantalisingly ambiguous evidence of the consumption of other seafood snacks at York. The remains of a number of immature fish of species typical of a riverine habitat close to tidal influences were recovered.[21] The specialist that studied them suggested these were young fish washed into the sewer when the River Ouse was in flood, and then trapped there; though he considered it interesting that the commonest species, the smelt, had penetrated that far inland. An alternative interpretation might be that these were the Roman equivalent of whitebait – a dish of very young small fish served deep-fried and eaten whole.[22] There is no record of such a dish being eaten in the Roman period, but it would fit the picture of fast food snacks that emerges from the animal bone and seashell deposits.

Drain deposits such as these are not the places where large amphora fragments are likely to accumulate, but the availability of amphora-shipped delicacies is indicated by the recovery of an olive stone at Caerleon and grape pips at York.[23] Seneca's reference to pastry cooks and confectionaries are a timely reminder that many items of food tend to be invisible archaeologically, though perhaps the seeds from strawberries, raspberries and blackberries found at York might hint of their presence. This might be the debris of raw fruit, but all would make good tarts. Equally, though the poppy seeds found there might have had a medicinal purpose as doctors were known to practise in baths, they could also have been the debris from seed-encrusted cakes and buns.[24]

The heat of the baths and the taking of exercise, not to mention the consumption of all the snacks, would undoubtedly have given people a thirst. The number of beaker fragments recovered in the drain deposits at Caerleon certainly underlines the fact that liquid was being consumed there.[25] What was in them, unfortunately, is unknown.

[19] Zienkiewicz 1986: 222 Table 1.   [20] Rackham in Buckland 1976: Table 5.
[21] Wheeler in Buckland 1976: 33–4.   [22] Davidson 1999: 846.
[23] Zienkiewicz 1986: 224; Greig in Buckland 1976: 24.
[24] Greig in Buckland 1976: Table 2.   [25] Greep in Zienkiewicz 1986: fig. 14.

The picture presented of the baths as a place to indulge in fast food snacks has been derived from two military bath-houses because they are the two sites with the best-preserved drain deposits. It is likely that similar practices went on in public bath-houses in the towns, and even sometimes in domestic baths. The taste for a saucer of shell fish to nibble whilst relaxing after a bath was certainly not restricted to the legionaries and their families. It can also be seen at the Halstock villa in Dorset, where a group of forty-seven cockles were found in the ditch outside the bath-house, reminiscent of the debris of a single snack.[26] It is possible that the type of food eaten at bath-houses might have cut across normal consumption patterns, because in the public bath-houses you would have been buying it in. The preference for lamb or mutton chops at the Caerleon bath-house, for example, is not one seen in the contemporary barracks where people cooked for themselves.

WORSHIPPING MERCURY AND MITHRAS

The role of food and drink within religious ceremonies varied according to the deity being worshipped. In some a communal meal was central, in others there is more ambiguity as to what happened to the sacrificed animals. Here the rites surrounding two known gods will be explored; one with a large temple complex at Uley in rural Gloucestershire who probably attracted predominantly native worshippers, the other outside the fort of Carrawburgh on Hadrian's Wall with a military congregation.

Part of the temple complex at Uley was excavated between 1977 and 1979.[27] Religious activity on the hilltop started early in the first century AD, possibly focusing on a sacred grove, and involving the construction of palisades and a timber shrine. In the second century a masonry Romano-Celtic temple was built surrounded by other masonry buildings, presumably for the use of the priesthood and worshippers. This continued in use with various modifications until the early fifth century, by which time all the buildings had been demolished. During the Roman period the god being worshipped was clearly Mercury. The variety of epigraphic evidence makes it clear that though the worshippers expressed themselves using Latin, none had the *tria nomina* of the Roman citizen. Their names were either Celtic or derived from Roman *cognomina*,[28] and it seems likely that this was a British congregation.

---

[26] Winder 1992: 157.   [27] Woodward and Leach 1993.
[28] Tomlin in Woodward and Leach 1993: 117.

One of the most remarkable features of the discoveries at Uley was the animal bone assemblage consisting of nearly a quarter of a million fragments. These overwhelmingly belonged to sheep or goats. Most unusually on a British site, many goats could be identified and, apart from the earliest phase of religious activity, they outnumbered sheep. Similarly the numbers of domestic fowl after the initial phase were very high. Given that the goat and the cock are attributes of Mercury, it seems very reasonable to conclude that the unusual composition of the animal bone assemblage is the direct result of these two animals being sacrificed. The report on this material by Bruce Levitan is exemplary, and the reader is warmly recommended to consult it in its entirety.[29] Here I will concentrate on the evidence associated with the second and third centuries (site Phase 4), as it is possible to map patterns that cast light on how sacrificial beasts were regarded.

In Phase 4 parts of three buildings were excavated in addition to the temple itself (see fig. 18.1), and animal bones were associated with two of them; Structure X to the north and Structure IV to the south. These are summarised in Table 18.4.

As can be seen, there were differences between the two groups. That from Structure IV was overwhelmingly dominated by ovicaprids, and amongst them goats were in the majority. Structure X had a more mixed range of animals and a more equal division between the sheep and goats. When other aspects of the bones were considered, it could be seen that the differences between the two went further. A feature of the ovicaprine bones from Uley, much commented on in the report, was the very low level of butchery marks seen on them. This was much lower than is normally seen in a domestic assemblage. The assemblages from the structures showed markedly different rates. In Structure IV less than 1% of the bones had evidence of butchery. In Structure X, by contrast, 8% showed butchery. Different parts of the carcase dominated in the different structures as well. In Structure IV skulls and lower-limb bones were much more numerous than they were in Structure X.

The evidence of the more mixed species, the butchery marks and the types of bones present suggests that Structure X may represent the debris from animals that were being eaten. The remains in Structure IV in contrast suggest either that the animals were not being eaten or, if they were, they were being cooked in a different way. Spit-roasting whole would be a

---

[29] Levitan in Woodward and Leach 1993: 257–301.

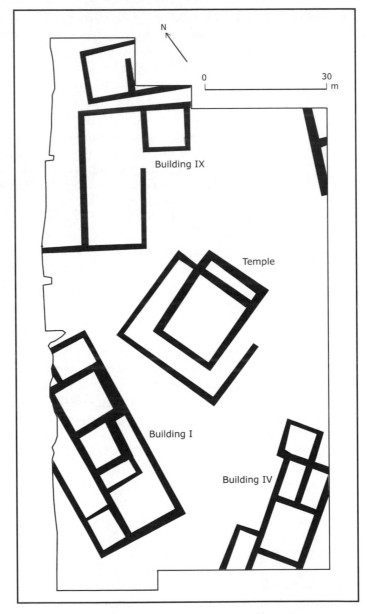

Figure 18.1. The Uley temple complex. (After Woodward and Leach 1993.) Structure X lay below the later Building IX.

Table 18.4. *Animal bones from Phase 4 contexts at Uley (number of identified bones).*

	Building IV		Building X	
	Number	%	Number	%
Sheep/goat	960	72	73	13
Cattle	22	2	103	19
Pig	24	2	103	19
Domestic fowl	322	24	273	49
Total	1,328	100	552	100
Sheep : goat ratio	95 : 204		59 : 54	

possibility. A difference in function between the two buildings is also hinted at in the pottery report. Though the data are not presented in a way that can be properly examined, it is noted in passing that Structure IV has relatively little pottery, whilst Structure X is one of the buildings with an essentially domestic assemblage.[30] This too might suggest that cooking and eating was being carried out in Structure X but not in Structure IV.

Where it could be established, the age and sex of the bones from Structure IV would support the idea that these were sacrificial animals. The ovicaprids were predominantly young and male. The ages of the domestic fowl were more mixed, but again males were in the majority. The evidence from these two structures points to sacrificial animals being regarded in a different light from ones it was permissible to eat. If they were eaten, they would certainly have been cooked differently. The presence of goats in Structure X makes it clear that goat meat and domestic fowl were not excluded from ordinary meal preparation, so it must have been something special about these particular animals that set them apart.

Whilst feasting may well have played a part in the festivals held at Uley in the summer, there is no evidence that it played a central part in the worship of the god in the same way that it did in the worship of Mithras. He was a saviour god whose adherents looked to a life after death and were initiated into various grades of the mysteries. It is known that a meal was an important part of the gatherings because early Christian writers inveighed against it as a devilish imitation of their own ritual meals.[31]

---

[30] Woodward and Leach 1993: 245, 248.   [31] Clauss 2000: 108–13.

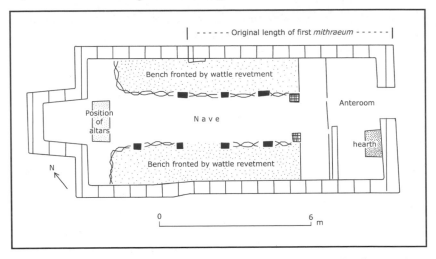

Figure 18.2. The *mithraeum* at Carrawburgh. (After Richmond and Gillam 1951.)

In Britain his worshippers were overwhelmingly drawn from the Roman army.[32]

He was worshipped in *mithraea* and these were of a very distinctive form with benches down either side which would have allowed the worshippers to recline whilst eating. The best-preserved temple in Britain was that found outside the fort of Carrawburgh. It was discovered in 1949 when a dry summer meant that the peat that had engulfed it shrank to reveal the tops of altars still *in situ*. It was dug by the leading Romano-British archaeologist of those days and published with admirable promptness,[33] but of course this was a considerable time before the development of environmental archaeology. The waterlogged conditions of the site would have been an ideal environment for the preservation of plant remains, but this was an opportunity lost. The animal bones do provide an insight into the meals consumed there.[34]

The *mithraeum* was built and used in the third century and underwent various alterations whilst always maintaining the same basic plan (fig. 18.2). It would have attracted senior members of the garrison to worship there as all three altars recovered were dedicated by the commanding officers of the unit.[35] The congregation can never have been very

[32] Henig 1984: 97–109. [33] Richmond and Gillam 1951.
[34] Fraser in Richmond and Gillam 1951: 89–90. [35] RIB nos. 1544–6.

large as the building is small measuring only *c.* 4.9 by 6.7 metres internally in its first phase, though later extended to an internal length of 11 metres. Meals appear to have been cooked in the building. A hearth was present in the anteroom from the enlargement onwards and sooted cooking vessels are associated with the structure from the earliest phase. Animal bones were associated with various phases of the second and third *mithraea.* In the first and third phases of Mithraeum II, the animal bone from the anteroom where the food may have been prepared suggests primarily a liking for pork and some lamb. Beef is much rarer. It is noticeable that all the animals represented were young. A broadly similar pattern was found amongst the bones found incorporated into the floor levels of the nave. In the third phase and in the floor of the final *mithraeum* they came from pigs and sheep. In both cases pig bones were most numerous and again the beasts were generally juvenile. In the second phase, bones of domestic fowl were recovered from the nave floor.

A similar picture of the selection of domestic fowl together with young pigs and sheep as suitable for Mithraic feasts emerges from the study of the copious remains deposited in pits outside the *mithraeum* at Tienen in Belgium, thought to have arisen from a single very large event in the mid-third century.[36] There, only cocks appeared to have been consumed, possibly because of the association of cockerels with the dawn, and of Mithras with the sun. The sex of the domestic fowl on the nave floor at the Carrawburgh *mithraeum* is not commented on, but bones from cocks were present there incorporated into the wattle revetments which fronted the benches.[37]

Just as the choice of meats was different from that which would normally have been consumed within the fortress, so too was the pottery assemblage. It was dominated by pottery beakers to a much greater extent than is normal from military sites in the third century.[38] This evidence of the drinking activities that went on as part of the worship of Mithras is also evident in the pottery assemblage from the contemporary *mithraeum* at the fort at Rudchester where beakers were numerous.[39]

What becomes apparent from looking at the animal bones associated with the worship of two very different gods by two entirely different communities, is that there may have been something in common. Food for the god, or food eaten in the company of the god, appears to be different from that eaten under normal circumstances. The animal for

---

[36] Lentacker *et al.* 2004. [37] Platt in Richmond and Gillam 1951: 91.
[38] Evans 1993: 114 Appendix 1. [39] Gillam and MacIvor 1954: 216.

sacrifice and/or consumption varied according to the deity, but the unifying factor was that juvenile or sub-adult animals were preferred. This is true not just at these two sites, but at other temple sites where the animal bones have been examined in detail such as at Harlow and Chelmsford.[40] A variety of reasons could be suggested for this. Perhaps they tasted better and were regarded as delicacies; perhaps if you were offering something to a god it wasn't worth expending the resources to raise the beast to adulthood. Another possibility may be that the animal needed to be unblemished to be a suitable offering, and young beasts provided the best opportunity of this. In the case of the Uley beasts, it was certainly noted that they were fit and healthy.[41]

It would be interesting to pursue the age and state of health of the animals from temple sites, but currently there is relatively little data available.[42] If animals for the gods did have to be unblemished, then it would open up an interesting vista on how the population of Roman Britain regarded their world. It is unlikely that such a belief would have existed in isolation, and not have been part of an outlook that encompassed other aspects of life. Douglas has shown how the rules laid down in Leviticus on how Jews should live their lives, including all the dietary prohibitions, stemmed from the belief that things had to be complete. The injunction that animals for sacrifice had to be unblemished was just one part of this.[43] Plainly the population of Roman Britain was not Jewish, and even if they too thought sacrificial animals had to be unblemished, it need not have meant that they had such strict dietary and other rules. It would, though, suggest that concepts of purity and taboo were active, and might go some way to explaining why certain things like game were so rarely eaten.

FOOD AND DRINK FOR THE DEAD AT BROUGHAM

The cemetery at Brougham provides an opportunity to examine what elements of food and drink were though necessary for different parts of a military community in the third century. The site was excavated in 1966 and 1967 in advance of road building, but the archive was not analysed

---

[40] Legge and Dorrington in France and Gobel 1985: 127; Luff in Turner 1999: Table 142 (Phase IV data).
[41] Levitan in Woodward and Leach 1993: 301.
[42] Subsequent to writing this a very useful survey of just such data has been published – King 2005.
[43] Douglas 1966: 42–58.

and published for nearly forty years.[44] The date of the excavation means that no sampling procedures were in place to acquire the carbonised plant remains that were undoubtedly present. There were also problems in that some elements of the archive had gone missing in the time between excavation and analysis. The data are flawed, but the analysis has revealed that what remains are internally consistent and tell quite a remarkable story.

The cemetery lies outside the fort and was in use during the period *c.* AD 220 to 300. Both this and the military equipment found in the burials and other deposits indicate that it was soldiers and their families that were buried there. The unit in garrison was a *numerus,* a cavalry unit recruited from the tribes on the empire's border. Various strands of evidence from the cemetery itself including epigraphy, the types of objects found and some burial practices strongly suggest that this unit came from territory bordering the Danubian provinces centred on modern-day Hungary. There can be no doubt that this was an immigrant community, but it would probably have been regarded as alien not just by the local British community, but also by the soldiers in the neighbouring forts.

The burial rite was cremation and the deceased were given items at two stages of the funeral. There were pyre goods burnt with the body and vessels placed with the burnt remains in the formal burial. By looking at the associations between the age and sex of the deceased, and the goods that were associated with them, it was found that different items were thought appropriate for different people.

With regard to food items, one of the most interesting observations is who had joints of meat placed on their pyres. The burnt animal bones could be divided into two categories; those where sufficient fragments from a range of the different parts of the skeleton survived to suggest the entire animal had been placed on the pyre, and those where the fragments were limited to a particular part such as a leg, which suggested that they had come from a joint. The whole carcases included three horses, one cow, two sheep and one dog. As neither horses nor dogs are normally regarded as meat sources, it seems likely that the animals burnt entire may have served a purpose other than food provision, such as sacrifice. Attention will focus here on the associations of the meat joints. These are summarised in Table 18.5 for those deposits which contained the remains of a single individual who could be aged.

---

[44] Cool 2004b; animal bone – Bond and Worley in Cool 2004b: 311–31.

Table 18.5. *The pyre good meat-bone associations for burials at Brougham.*

	Sheep	Bird	Cattle	Pig	Total deposits
Adult	9	3	2	—	73
Male	7	3	—	1	24
Female	4	7	2	—	27
Immature	2	—	—	—	23
Infant	—	1	—	—	15
Total	22	14	4	1	162

The first surprising feature of this table is the dominance of sheep. Elsewhere in the area, beef was the main meat in urban and military contexts. This can be seen from the bone assemblages associated with a building occupied in the second to third century in Carlisle, some 35 km to the north, and that associated with third- to mid-fourth-century granaries in the fort at Birdoswald, a further 25 km along Hadrian's Wall. Both were dominated by cattle bone, ovicaprid bones were much scarcer, while pig bones were present at the military site but absent in the small urban assemblage.[45] The Brougham community, however, felt sheep meat was the most appropriate thing to place on the pyre. Pork was surprisingly rare. There is evidence of it on one pyre and in one burial where an unburnt shoulder of pork was placed on a dish in the grave. In both cases the association was with an adult male of high status. The bird bones were mainly from small domestic fowl, though goose was also present. Whether they were placed on the pyre as food, or were there for a ritual purpose,[46] is unclear.

The second striking feature of Table 18.5 is the rarity of any evidence for meat on the pyres of people younger than eighteen. A domestic fowl was present on the pyre of an infant, but this could have been present as a sacrifice. Two immature individuals (five–eighteen years) had joints of sheep meat but otherwise this category of individuals had no meat remains despite being well represented in the cemetery. It can be shown using statistical significance tests that this pattern would not have come about by chance.[47] In this community meat, or at least meat on the bone, was not considered an appropriate pyre good for young people. It is here

[45] Rackham in McCarthy 1990: Table 30 Period 9; Izard in Wilmott 1997: Table 33.
[46] See p. 101.   [47] Baxter in Cool 2004b: 469.

that the absence of any environmental remains is particularly to be lamented as it might be that vegetable-based foods such as fruit and grain were thought appropriate for the young people.

Some interesting attitudes to vessels also emerge, of which two have direct relevance to eating and drinking practices. In this community, glass drinking vessels were seen as the preserve of adult males and were placed in their graves. Several adult females had large copper-alloy buckets of the type used to mix wine.[48] Though it seems dreadfully stereotypical to suggest it, the data would support the view that it was woman's work to prepare alcoholic beverages, and man's role to drink them. In the previous chapter the role of samian cups was questioned, and it was suggested that they were probably also used as serving bowls. This seems unequivocal at Brougham where samian cups are only ever found in graves where the individual is younger than eight. Where it was possible to age the children closely, one was two to three years and another three to four. It would seem much more likely in these circumstances that they should be regarded as feeding dishes for toddlers rather than drinking vessels.

The evidence from Brougham is difficult to interpret at present because it is unclear to what extent the attitudes expressed in their burial rites are specific to this community or were more widely shared. The evidence at present would suggest they may be very community-specific, as certainly their burial ritual appears very unlike that practised at the same time by the garrison who occupied the fort to the south.[49] Some attitudes seem to be more widely shared such as the association of pork with high rank, but whether the taste for lamb was driven by ethnicity or funerary ritual is unknown. What the analysis did show was that various vessel types were regarded as age and gender specific. Analysis of more cemetery assemblages, where there is good information about the age and sex of the deceased, might prove to be very informative about dining practice.

CONCLUSIONS

The cases presented in this chapter have shown that deep-seated regional differences persisted well into Roman period and that even in the third century Britain was far from sharing a common cuisine or attitude to food. They have also shown that different events, be they secular or religious, could cut across normal eating habits providing people with

[48] See page 136 and fig. 15.2 no. 3.   [49] Lambert 1996.

the opportunity to taste different foods. Comparing the food associated with these 'special events' with that consumed by the community normally has the potential to cast light on wider attitudes to the world. Why, for example, is there a regular association of the consumption of young animals with religious events? Was it just that they were tastier, or did the gods demand unblemished beasts, and more widely perhaps, unblemished behaviour by their worshippers in certain matters?

CHAPTER 19

A different world

INTRODUCTION

The third century had been a difficult time for many parts of the empire. A succession of short-lived emperors had fought for control. There was pressure around its borders as barbarian tribes clamoured to be admitted, with incursions into areas where everyone had thought themselves safe for centuries. Britain had been peripheral to much of this turmoil, though Saxon raiding of the east and southern coasts was a problem. The political chaos of the third century was brought under a semblance of control by the reforms of Diocletian who came to power in AD 284. The empire that emerged from these in the fourth century was a very different place than that of the empire of the first and second centuries.

In continental scholarship there is a tradition of studying the world of late antiquity as a period that extends from the late third century into the seventh century. On this side of the Channel there is not this tradition as Roman Britain was long thought to end in AD 410 after the army had left Britain in AD 407.[1] What happened then is a very big question. It sometimes seems that there are as many answers as there are authors prepared to write books and papers on the end of Roman Britain, and they are legion. People tend to divide into two camps. There are those that consider the Roman way of life ended in the early fifth century, and what came after is somebody else's problem as it is certainly nothing to do with Roman Britain. Then there are those that think life continued and evolved, and that the AD 410 divide is an artificial construct. I belong to the latter tendency, and the reader should be aware that some of what they are now going to read would be disputed by those who take the other view.[2]

---

[1] For brief summary see Frere 1987: 357–8.   [2] See, for example, Esmonde Cleary 2000: 91.

Traditionally, major changes are attributed to the early fifth century including the sudden collapse of the pottery industries.[3] If that was indeed the case, it would have had major implications on how people cooked and ate. Pottery had become central to these processes even in many areas which had been aceramic prior to the Roman invasion. Understanding what happened to the vessel assemblages at the end of the fourth century is so central to the topic of this book, that much of this chapter will be taken up by a consideration of it, following a section on the dating problems we are faced with. Sites where we can study the eating habits of a community at the end of the fourth century, without the patterns being blurred by problems of residuality and redeposition, are rare, but the opportunity will be taken to explore one where this can be done. Finally the possible impact of Christianity on the diet of the population will be considered.

DATING PROBLEMS

As was outlined in Chapter 1, the foundations underpinning our ability to date most contexts derives from coinage. The understanding of the dates of pottery types depends on repeated associations in independently dated contexts and their stratigraphic relationships. Occasionally the dating is provided by dendrochronology or even, very rarely, by writing tablets where the date has been considerately included; but in essence pottery provides the backbone of dating.

Coinage was supplied by the state for two purposes: to pay the army and to provide a medium by which people could pay taxes. Gold and silver coins went to the army as pay, and returned to the state as taxes. Copper-alloy coinage was the small change that oiled the wheels of this circulation. With the withdrawal of the army in AD 407 there would have been no point in supplying either type of coinage to Britain. Site finds make it clear that the supply must have generally ceased in the AD 395–402 period, because coinage issued after that date is rare. This reflects the fact that the production of the western mints was much reduced after that date, and coins later than AD 402 are uncommon everywhere.[4] In some areas the supply seems to cease even before that. In the north-east, for example, it has been noted that coinage after AD 388 is rare.[5]

---

[3] Millett 1990: 225–6.   [4] Guest 2005: 28.   [5] Brigstock 2000: 35.

The consequence of this is that there is no independent yardstick against which to measure the date of a context or a new pottery type. Coins only ever provide a *terminus post quem,* and may often give too early a date but the dating of pottery and other types of items does not rely on a single coin; it will be a composite of many associations. These will highlight the anomolous early coins. From the end of the fourth century, this is no longer possible as no new coinage enters the coin pool. That the existing coinage continued to circulate, and presumably be used in transactions well into the fifth century, is suggested by at least two factors. The copper-alloy coinage of Theodosius (AD 375–95) often shows considerable wear,[6] and the edges of silver *siliquae* were carefully clipped to maintain the appearance of the coin whilst acquiring new bullion, to make new coins that imitated the existing ones.[7] So, contexts and associations that appear respectably late fourth century might well be several decades later. With this in mind we shall now explore vessel use in the fourth to fifth century.

VESSELS IN THE FOURTH CENTURY AND LATER

The best way to start to explore what sort of vessels people felt the need of is to compare assemblages of this period with those of the earlier centuries. Glass vessels show the changes that occurred particularly clearly. Table 19.1 shows dated assemblages that have been quantified according to form. Flasks and unguent bottles are not considered here as there is good evidence that many would have been connected with toilet regimes rather than being associated with eating and drinking.

In this table cups, bowls and jugs may be considered as tablewares whilst jars and bottles were more likely to have been used as containers. As can be seen, there are changes in the fourth-century assemblages. Jar forms are absent and the bottles form a lower proportion of the assemblage than they did earlier. Large tables of data like this can be a daunting prospect to interpret, and what the figures are telling us becomes much more obvious when the plots resulting from a correspondence analysis (CA) of the data are inspected (fig. 19.1). This is a very useful technique for dealing with this type of data, and for more details about it the reader is referred to the references given below.[8] Here all that is needed

---

[6] Brigstock 2000: 35. [7] Guest 2005: 110–5.
[8] Treatments designed for archaeologists are Baxter 1994: 100–39; Shennan 1997: 308–41 and Baxter 2003: 136–46. See also Cool and Baxter 1999; 2002.

Table 19.1. *Glass-vessel assemblages of various dates (see column 1 for approximate date ranges) quantified according to form (EVE measures). The labelling used in fig.19.1 is shown italicised in brackets in Column 1.*

Sitez	Cup	Bowl	Jug	Jar	Bottle	Total
London 75–90 *(1)*	7.60	4.20	3.64	0.20	2.52	18.16
Gloucester 71–100 *(1)*	3.40	2.40	1.40	0.36	4.55	12.11
Castleford 70–100 *(1)*	9.20	5.60	3.00	1.80	5.75	25.35
Carlisle 71–105 *(1)*	2.80	5.40	1.26	0.38	7.28	17.12
Chester 75–120 *(1)*	4.00	3.52	1.54	0.69	3.78	13.53
York 71–120 *(1)*	6.40	6.00	0.84	1.44	3.08	17.76
Colchester 65–150 *(1)*	9.20	5.60	3.00	1.80	5.75	25.35
Dorchester 75–150 *(1)*	3.60	1.20	1.42	1.43	2.52	10.17
Wroxeter 80–150 *(1)*	5.20	2.13	2.70	0.57	4.48	15.08
Verulamium 150–60 *(2)*	5.00	1.20	1.10	0.34	2.53	10.17
Pentre Farm 120–200 *(2)*	5.80	1.40	0.49	0	1.96	9.65
Catterick 150–250 *(2)*	5.40	0.54	0.56	0.20	3.64	10.34
Lincoln 160–230 *(2)*	4.20	0.40	1.37	0.40	2.31	8.68
York 175–250 *(2)*	4.20	1.40	1.12	0.36	2.31	9.39
York 160–280 *(2)*	7.20	0	0.28	0.34	1.68	9.50
Caister 300–400+ *(4)*	25.80	0.80	0.70	0	1.84	29.14
Colchester 300–400+ *(4)*	9.20	3.20	1.44	0	0.61	14.45
Dorchester 300–400+ *(4)*	5.00	2.80	0.84	0	1.36	10.00
Stanwick 300–400+ *(4)*	8.73	1.80	1.47	0	1.45	13.45
Towcester 300–400+ *(4)*	9.40	0	1.18	0	1.27	11.85
Winchester 300–400+ *(4)*	10.20	2.00	1.26	0	1.56	15.02
Wroxeter 300–400+ *(4)*	24.20	2.60	4.13	0	2.32	33.25
York 300–400+ *(4)*	10.00	3.00	0.70	0	0.98	14.68

is to explain that the technique produces, amongst other things, two plots, one describing the rows, the other the columns which can be shown separately or superimposed. The row plot shows the assemblages that have relatively similar proportions of forms in the same area of the plot. The column plot shows the relationship of the forms according to the proportions found in the different assemblages. The plots should be read in relation to the origin (the point where the axes cross). A group of sites in one area of the assemblage (row) plot will generally have a more than usually high proportion of the forms which are plotted in the same position, relative to the origin, on the form (column) plot.

Fig. 19.1 shows that the compositions of the assemblages change markedly with time. The first- to second-century assemblages are much more varied than the fourth-century ones, having a higher proportion of the container forms. The fourth-century assemblages are dominated by drinking vessels

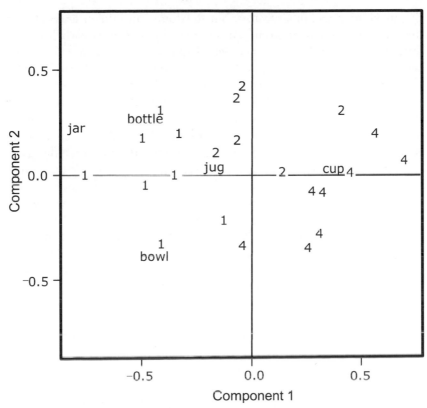

Figure 19.1. Correspondence analysis plot showing the change of glass-vessel assemblage compositions with time. (Date from Table 19.1: for explanation, see text.)

almost to the exclusion of everything else. It is clear that, by the fourth century in Britain, glass was regarded primarily as a medium appropriate to drink out of. Even glass flasks for toiletries become much less common. The interesting feature of fig. 19.1 is that the move towards glass being used primarily for drinking vessels starts early. The second- to third-century assemblages are positioned between the early and late ones, and at least one of these (York AD 160–280) has an assemblage very similar to a fourth-century one presumably reflecting the higher proportion of third-century material in it.

The study from which these assemblages have been extracted was able to show that the types of vessels in use also varied according to the type of site, its location and other factors, but the dominant influence was always the period it was derived from.[9] At different times people clearly had very different uses for glass vessels, and what happens in the later fourth to fifth century can clearly be seen as a continuum of this. It is possible to isolate a number of assemblages that appear to date to the very late fourth century and into the fifth century.[10] What can be seen in them is that the closed forms such as jugs and bottles become even scarcer than they were earlier in the century, and the concentration of forms that could be drunk out of is even more pronounced. In the light of this, the fact that the glass industries of the south-east of England were producing a very distinctive form of glass beaker in the later fifth and sixth centuries comes as no surprise.[11] This is normally seen as an Anglo-Saxon form, but were we in Britain to embrace the concept of the late antique, it would be seen as the natural development of the late Roman industries. Certainly the 'Anglo-Saxon' use of glass in the fifth and sixth centuries continues the pattern that had been developing in Britain from the third century, rather than that seen in the continental 'homelands'. It has been noted by the leading expert in the field that whereas bottles were a fairly common type in France and the Rhineland during the fifth and sixth centuries, they were not at all popular in England.[12] Viewed from the Roman side of the great divide of AD 410, this too comes as no surprise.

Why was there this change? The evidence at Brougham indicated that glass drinking vessels were reserved for adult males.[13] The association of glass drinking vessels and the elite is also seen beyond the frontiers of the province. In the later second and third centuries it is glass drinking cups rather than any other sort of glass vessel that are occasionally found on elite sites in the Highlands of Scotland, on the Shetland and Orkney Islands and even at Tara in Ireland.[14] Drinking out of glass may have served as a mark of distinction in the later Roman period in some communities. Perhaps what was important was the display element. The colour of the drink would be clearly visible, and might even have been enhanced by the glass. Fourth-century glass was a greenish colourless shade with many tiny bubbles, and vessels were thin-walled. The overall effect would have been a glass that shimmered, catching any light.

From the point of view of someone familiar with the patterns of use of glass vessels from the Roman to Anglo-Saxon periods, the normal model

[9] Cool and Baxter 1999. [10] Cool 1995: 13.
[11] Kempston beakers – see Evison 2000: 62. [12] Evison 2000: 65.
[13] See p. 219. [14] Cool 2003: 142.

of the sudden collapse of the pottery industries in the early fifth century has always appeared curious. Did people really suddenly stop cooking and eating in the manner that had been habitual to them for generations? What sort of cataclysmic event could have triggered such an abrupt change? As discussed in earlier chapters, in some areas it took a century or more for people to change their habits in response to the greater availability of things that followed the conquest, and some never did. When the model of the transition from the Roman to the Anglo-Saxon world was one of marauding invaders raping and killing most people who they came into contact with and enslaving the others, the collapse of the pottery industries was explicable. Most people would not subscribe to such a model now, so where does the explanation lie? Some people have argued that the disappearance of the industries is because they were embedded in a monetised economy with the skill concentrated amongst a relatively small group of people. With the cessation of coinage use, they could no longer survive, and pots ceased to be made.[15] Pots to cook in, however, are not so many optional fripperies to be easily discarded. Whole new skills would have to be learnt. Did the change really happen so abruptly?

It is worth exploring whether the changes in pottery use had its origins at a much earlier period, as with the glass. There are hints that this may have been the case, as it has long been observed that the second half of the fourth century sees a decrease in the overall number of different pottery forms in use.[16] This can be seen very well when the pottery from York is examined. Occupation started there in the early 70s and continued well into the fifth century at least. Many excavations have been carried out both in the fort and *colonia* and the pottery from them is available in an estimable study.[17] As part of this a set of ceramic phases was developed together with a type series. Table 19.2 is derived from this and includes all the forms that had sufficient examples to allow a date range to be assigned to them. Samian pottery and mortaria were treated as special cases and cannot be tabulated in the same way and so are excluded. With the exception of the samian vessels, it probably includes all the main types that the inhabitants had a use for. It was explicitly commented that 'the overall number of mortaria used in York was very low',[18] so the absence of mortaria from the table is not important. They can be imagined as having a small but consistent presence throughout the period. The absence of

---

[15] Evans, J. 2000: 41.   [16] Fulford 1979: 121.
[17] Monaghan 1997.   [18] Monaghan 1997: 931.

Table 19.2. *The principal pottery vessel forms in use in Roman York*
excluding those made in samian pottery and mortaria.

Date	Beaker	Cup	Flagon	Platter	Dish	Bowl	Jar	Lid	Total
1A – 71–100	1	1	4	1	—	2	4	—	13
1B – 100–120	4	1	3	—	—	4	4	1	17
2A – 120–60	4	1	4	2	3	7	4	3	28
2B – 160–200	7	3	6	3	4	6	10	4	43
3A – 200–225	9	2	4	1	3	3	7	2	31
3B – 225–80	7	2	1	1	4	2	6	—	23
4A – 280–360	2	—	2	—	3	1	7	—	15
4B – 360–410	1	—	2	1	3	5	5	—	17
4C – 410+	—	—	—	—	1	—	2	—	3
Total	35	10	26	9	21	30	49	10	190

samian vessels distorts the picture more. Were they to be included the
numbers for the cup, platter, dish and bowl categories would have been
increased by a small number in all ceramic phases up to about Ceramic
Phase 3A.

The widest range of forms available was in the second and early third
centuries. The figures for Ceramic Phase 2A are possibly lower than might
be expected, as this period was a very quiet one at York with much of the
garrison away. The decline in the range of forms available starts in the
third century and, had it been possible to include the samian forms in the
table, the decline would have been even more noticeable. It is not just that
there would have been less choice within forms. Some, like lids and cups,
just disappear, whilst others such as flagons and platters become much
rarer. The disappearance of cups may be because glass was increasingly
favoured for small-capacity drinking vessels,[19] but the decline in other
types is not compensated by similar vessels in other materials. Glass and
small-find assemblages, for example, do not show any balancing increase
in fragments from jugs.

A correspondence analysis of the table (Fig. 19.2) again shows that the
assemblage composition is very dependent on the period. One feature of
CA is that it is possible sometimes to use it to recover chronological
pattern, as the points frequently occur in a horseshoe pattern that can be
read in order.[20] On the plot, the known chronological order is almost

---

[19] See p. 149.   [20] Baxter 1994: 118–23; 2003: 137–8.

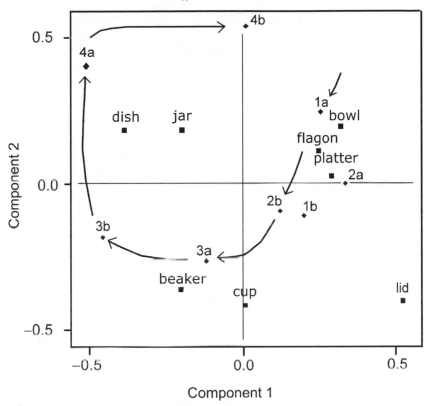

Figure 19.2. Correspondence analysis plot showing the changes in pottery vessels available at York with time. Note the phases plotting in sequence shown by the arrowed line. (Data from Table 19.2.)

precisely picked up by the changing proportions of the different forms present. Only the positions of the points for Ceramic Phases 1B and 2A are inverted. A comparison of the two plots makes it clear that whereas the early periods are characterised by tableware forms, the later ones are characterised by jars and dishes, and so are cooking orientated. As with the glass, change in the fifth century does not come suddenly to an unchanging suite of vessels, but could be looked on as having its origins much earlier.

The precise pattern of change is not the same in all areas,[21] but it is not just in the north that jars increasingly dominate the pottery assemblages

---

[21] Compare Evans 1993 and Millett 1979.

towards the end of the fourth century. At the Great Holts Farm villa near Chelmsford, a number of pottery assemblages of very late fourth- to fifth-century date were recovered.[22] In these (measured by EVEs) 60% of the assemblage consisted of jars followed by 24% dishes, 9% bowls and just over 1% mortaria. Beakers and flagons made up a mere 6% of the assemblage. It could be argued that this is a continuation of the rural patterns discussed in Chapters 17 and 18 where rural sites often seem to have a less varied and smaller tableware range. Finding late fourth-century urban assemblages where residuality is not a problem is difficult, but where it can be done a similar pattern often emerges. The case of Wroxeter will be discussed below, but the black earth deposits of the late fourth and fifth centuries at Canterbury also have a pottery assemblage where well over half of the, admittedly small, assemblage consists of jars with the rest divided between dishes and bowls.[23]

What is also noticeable is that the fourth century sees a reappearance of various handmade potting traditions in a variety of areas where wheel-made pottery had long been dominant. This can be observed both in the south and the north.[24] These handmade industries concentrated on cooking wares. The demise of the large industries that made the tablewares might have come about because there was no longer the demand for them, and that demand may have been in decline for some considerable time before the fifth century, as ways of serving food and drink changed.

Another factor that may possibly have been important is the appearance of the pottery. The large regional industries that came to dominate fourth-century pottery supply specialised in colour-coated wares often of glossy black or red shades.[25] These and other industries also produced white wares decorated by red painting. It is just possible that these were no longer to people's taste. This might seem a rather frivolous reason for the demise of these industries, but it might have been a contributory factor. A feature of very late fourth- to fifth-century small-find assemblages is a fascination with certain colours, and a deliberate seeking out of objects made of them.[26] Indeed I have often advised people, not entirely in jest, that if they want to find fifth century sites, they should look for ones where there are an unusually high preponderance of green, orange and

[22] Martin in Germany 2003: figs. 85–8.   [23] Pollard in Blockley *et al.* 1995: Table 16.
[24] Pollard 1988: 143, 151; Tyers 1996: 191–2; Monaghan 1997: 867.
[25] New Forest, Oxfordshire and the Nene Valley – see Tyers 1996.
[26] Cool 2000a: 54.

black objects. If this change of taste is affecting items such as jewellery, gaming equipment and textile equipment, why not pottery?

If we want to discover what happens at the end of the fourth century, a greater openness to looking at the pottery associated with sequences that clearly date from the fourth century into the sixth century would probably pay useful dividends. Normally this tends to be written off as clearly residual, occasionally with the grudging admission that if people had curated it carefully, it could still have been in use for a few decades into the fifth century. A sequence at the temple at Bath is a good example of this where there was clearly a tension between the excavators' view that occupation was continuing into the sixth century, and the pottery specialists' view that it ended in the early fifth century.[27] If all the later assemblages are fundamentally residual fourth-century material, then logically they should resemble an assemblage of that date appropriate for the type of site and region they are found in. In the case of small finds this is clearly not the case. The assemblages that can definitely be dated to the end of the fourth century and beyond can be shown to be very different to those of the early to mid-fourth century, despite being composed of 'fourth century' material.[28] Could the same be true of the pottery?

The Baths Basilica complex at Wroxeter ought to provide the ideal testing ground for exploring this. Over a thirty-five-year period starting in 1955, major campaigns of excavations were carried out that provide a sequence that stretches from the mid-first century to the seventh century. The two teams that carried out the work had very different priorities and interests, and this resulted in very different styles of excavation and publication. Despite three substantial monographs having been published reporting on the work, it is not easy to establish what the sequence of the material culture was over the period.[29] The team that concentrated their attention on the very late Roman to sub-Roman period took the view that as most of the very substantial amount of material recovered was from make-up layers, it did not relate to the occupation of the site. It was published in a summary form and resources concentrated on the structural narrative.[30] Whilst it is no doubt admirable that we have 2.5 kg of loose plans with the monograph itemising, it seems, the position of every cobble; it has meant that what is probably a key assemblage for understanding the fifth and sixth century languishes in an English Heritage store in dire need of a major research project to rescue it.

---

[27] Summarised in Tyers 1996: 79.   [28] Cool 2000a.
[29] Barker *et al.* 1997: Ellis 2000; Webster 2002.   [30] Barker *et al.* 1997: 12.

Even with the sadly curtailed data available in the publications, it is possible to show that the pottery should probably not be dismissed as residual make-up material of no interest. It may not be directly related to the Baths Basilica, but it does suggest that pottery was continuing to be used in Wroxeter a century or more after the proposed end of the Roman pottery industries. The late and sub-Roman occupation on the site was assigned a set of lettered Phases. Phase W extends from the late fourth century (post AD 367) to the end of the fifth century. Phase X was dated from the end of the fifth century to the mid-sixth century, Phase Y belonged to the mid-sixth century and Phase Z related to the great rebuilding seen on the site of the mid-sixth to the seventh century. Here Phases X and Y are treated as a single phase as they overlap. The pottery assemblages associated with these phases can also be compared to groups of pottery recovered from the other excavations on the site. These consist of the material used to infill the swimming pool (*natatio*) in the period *c.* AD 210–30, material deposited during the third century in the court-yard, and two groups from the portico. One of these dates to the early to mid-fourth century, the other contains very late fourth material. No suggestion was made that this indicated sustained occupation well into the fifth century, but the suspicion has to be that this is a very late group, contemporary with the material from Phase W in the other excavations. The pottery from these deposits is summarised in Table 19.3.

If the very late assemblages are just the redeposition of earlier material, then they should show no great difference in functional composition to the groups that definitely were deposited during the third and fourth centuries. As can be seen from the table, this is not the case. Flagons decrease with time, and jars increase. A correspondence analysis of the data (Fig. 19.3) shows clearly that there is a difference between the functional profiles of the third- and fourth-century assemblages and those of the late assemblages. The ordering of the groups along the first axis picks up the proposed chronology very closely. The earlier groups are characterised by the tablewares, the later by the cooking wares. This looks very much like the pattern that might be expected if the pottery was being derived from rubbish sources resulting from active use of the pottery in the fifth and sixth centuries, rather than just redeposition from earlier sources. Indeed it would be very difficult to explain the marked increase in riveted pottery seen in Phase Y (mid-sixth century)[31] other than by

---

[31] Barker *et al.* 1997: 218 Table 16.

Table 19.3. *Pottery from late Roman and sub-Roman contexts at the Baths Basilica, Wroxeter (EVEs).*

Phase	Date	Dish (%)	Bowl (%)	Jar (%)	Flagon (%)	Beaker (%)	Mortaria (%)	Total (EVE)
Natatio	210–30	11.5	23.8	29.8	20.8	9.9	4.3	84.6
Courtyard	3rd century	15.2	19.9	43.0	9.7	8.2	4.3	71.9
PorticoE	4th century	9.4	21.2	42.5	12.4	9.7	4.3	63.6
PorticoL	375+	7.2	24.6	53.8	4.3	3.5	6.7	97.6
W	367–500	11.4	19.3	54.3	4.3	8.0	2.6	126.8
X/Y	500–550	11.9	20.6	51.5	1.2	7.7	7.2	204.3
Z	550–700	12.8	21.4	50.6	2.4	6.1	6.7	314.8

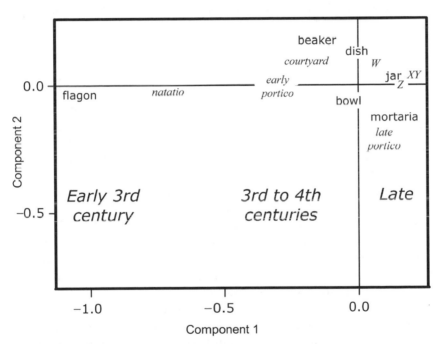

Figure 19.3. Correspondence analysis plot showing the changes in pottery-vessel assemblages at Wroxeter with time. (Data from Table 19.3.)

suggesting pottery was still an essential part of people's lives up to that point, and that it was only then that there started to be pressure on supplies that required careful repair and curation of existing vessels.

This data set, and the conclusions drawn from it, could be criticised on various grounds if one had a mind to. Given that it is derived from two different excavations, it might be that there were different collection and discard regimes in place. The fact that the broadly contemporary assemblages from the late Portico and Phase W plot on the same side of the graph suggests this may not be a major problem. It might be argued that various taphonomic processes were at work in the redeposited material favouring the more substantial vessels, the cooking wares, at the expense of the more thin-walled tablewares. The progressive decline of the flagons would seem to argue against this. Flagon rims are substantial and often break retaining the whole circumference which, when an assemblage is quantified by EVEs, can lead to an overestimate of the flagons in the assemblage in comparison to other forms. It could be expected that they would remain a substantial component in any redeposited group. As the pottery data currently exists, it does seem that there would have to be a great deal of special pleading to argue against continuing use well into the sub-Roman period.

The evidence suggests that the fourth and fifth centuries (and beyond), did see major changes in the way people served food, but possibly not so great a change in the cooking methods. Jar use seems to continue. We know that in Cornwall, potters serenely continued making the local Gabbroic pottery with its emphasis on cooking forms well into the post-Roman period.[32] There seems the distinct likelihood that other local industries specialising in cooking wares could also have survived for longer than is normally realised. After all, how do you date a form that functions well and has no need to develop typologically? Without the independent cross-checking that coinage can provide, it could as easily be late fifth century as earlier. Though it is true that many people in the fourth century would have purchased the products of the big industries working in Oxford, the Nene Valley etc., it should not be forgotten that more local industries continued to have a role to play. At Wroxeter itself, it has been calculated that 20% of the late Roman assemblage was locally produced with a further 14% of unknown origin that could equally have included local material.[33] Potting skills may not have been so centralised within the big industries as is sometimes assumed.

The change in how food and drink were being served is a fascinating one, but currently we do not have the data to explore what was happening

---

[32] Quinnell 2004: 109–11.   [33] Timby in Ellis 2000: Table 4.28.

in the very late assemblages. Tables 19.2 and 19.3 suggest an adoption of a jar – bowl assemblage, but were the bowls part of cooking equipment, for serving individual portions or for serving communal ones? A far greater emphasis on quantifying form, size, patterns of wear and colour of late Roman pottery would allow us to explore this in the future in much greater detail than is currently possible.

GUARDING THE NORTH YORKSHIRE COAST

The signal stations along the Yorkshire and Humberside coast date to the very end of the Roman period. These were tall masonry towers set within a courtyard defined by a wall and ditch. It is thought they were built as watchtowers to act as lookouts for pirate raiding and thus had a military function, though some have argued that they might have been strong places of refuge for the local inhabitants when the raiders came. The finds from them make it clear that both sexes were present, and generally they have a much more domestic rather than military flavour. The stations were certainly built and occupied in the later fourth century. When occupation commenced is a matter of some debate but the most likely date is in the last quarter of the century. How long they continued in occupation is also a matter of debate. If they were military establishments, then presumably not beyond the first decade of the fifth century. If they were places of refuge then a longer timespan would be possible.[34]

Their location makes them very susceptible to coastal erosion, and in the early 1990s the remaining part of the station at Filey was excavated because of this. Though a relatively small excavation, the full environmental sampling programme provides a very interesting snapshot of very late fourth- to fifth-century occupation.[35]

Given the patterns of vessel use discussed in the previous section it will come as no surprise that the relatively small pottery assemblage (23.41 EVEs, 29.24 kg) is dominated by jars. Measured by EVEs they make up 88% of the assemblage, followed by bowls (7.2%), flagons (3.3%) and dishes (1.7%). Drinking vessels are rare, represented by only ten sherds from pottery beakers and one fragment of a glass example. The jars were clearly used both as cooking vessels and water carriers. The sooting patterns make it clear that lids were used whilst cooking, though none were found in the pottery assemblage, possibly because they were made of wood. The rarity of anything to eat

---

[34] For general discussion see Ottaway 2001: 188–90; Wilson 1989.   [35] Ottaway 2001.

food out of in the assemblage might also suggest that wooden bowls were being favoured. An interesting feature is the strong presence (17% by weight) of what are described as very late handmade wares, primarily used to make jars but also the occasional dish and flagon. These are in addition to the other late fourth-century handmade calcite-gritted wares that make up nearly two thirds (by weight) of the assemblage. There are three different fabrics for this late material, which again might serve to suggest that potting skills might not have been as rare at the beginning of the fifth century as is sometimes suggested.[36]

The meat eaten came overwhelmingly from cattle, sheep and pigs.[37] The various measures of quantification when translated into meat weight suggested that there was no one dominant meat species. The bones present show that the meat was being supplied as dressed joints, and possibly in the case of the pigs and sheep in the form of cured hams. Several of the sheep scapulae show the hook damage typical of hanging up joints for curing.[38]

Game, as ever, played a minor role, though the presence of deer scapulae did indicate that venison was consumed. The amount of wild-bird bones recovered outnumbered those of the domestic fowl, but in part this probably reflected the natural deaths of seabirds on this cliff-top site, as opposed to them being elements in the food chain. Such birds were occasionally eaten as one guillemot definitely, and one cormorant possibly, showed cut marks from butchery. The amount of evidence for wild species being consumed is not large, but given the size of the assemblage (small) and given the normal pattern of game exploitation (vanishingly small), it looks more substantial than is often observed. Interestingly, this is a pattern that can be seen in other late military establishments in what might be thought of as marginal areas.[39] Does this indicate that there was stress on the supply chain, or that the possible taboos around eating game were losing their power? The provision of dressed carcases at Filey would suggest that the former was not the case.

With a military community there is always the possibility of individuals being present who do not share the dominant view of what can and cannot be eaten. The increase in game consumed at these sites might be reflecting the fact that some individuals did not share the same ethnicity

---

[36] Monaghan in Ottaway 2001: 140–47, for glass see also 130 no. 26.
[37] The discussion of the environmental evidence is derived from Dobney, Large, Carrott, Hall, Issitt and Large in Ottaway 2001: 148–82.
[38] See p. 89.   [39] See p. 113 Table 13.1

as their fellows. Equally though, the breaking down of taboos might be a factor. There are occasionally hints that more venison was consumed in the very late to sub-Roman period than was the case earlier. At Wroxeter red and roe deer were identified in all the very late phases and were most numerous in the mid-sixth- to seventh-century Phase Z. The total numbers were not large, but the occurrences seem more numerous than those recovered from contexts dating to the first to fourth centuries.[40] Caution has to be exercised in interpreting the figures as it is known that the animal bone from the early contexts was only selectively studied, contexts representing only 22% of the amount studied from the later ones. The earlier contexts produced 18 deer bones, the later 138. If the later contexts had produced deer bones at the same rate as the earlier ones, a figure of about 80 might have been expected. The pattern of a possible increase in game is not always observed. The late fourth- to early sixth-century occupation at Bath continues to show very low levels of venison consumption.[41] Though the picture is not uniform, there are sufficient hints in the record to suggest that investigating the exploitation of wild animals might be a useful way to explore the fifth century.

One dislike that the inhabitants of Filey shared with the inhabitants of much of the rest of the population relates to fish. Despite the sampling regime in place, fish were rare. A total of only sixty measured by NISP which may be compared to the figures for chicken which were eighty four. The amount consumed is even smaller when it is realised that some of the fish bones probably arrived through the action of seabirds roosting in the tower. If ever confirmation was needed that the Romano-British population did not have much of a taste for fish, this is the site that provides it. They lived by a sea full of fish for the taking and the sampling programme would have retrieved the bones had they been there in any quantity, and they were not. Shellfish were more acceptable though again not found in large quantities. Ones that could have been exploited locally and which were relatively numerous were limpets, winkles and mussels. The presence of three oyster shells is of some importance. These would not have been available locally and indicate that even at this very late date the oyster trade was still thriving.

Also of interest is the fact that amongst the charred grain assemblage, spelt wheat appears to be as common as barley, though neither is particularly

---

[40] Compare Armour-Chelu in Barker *et al.* 1997: 358–9 Table 47 with Meddens in Ellis 2000: 328, Table 4.3.

[41] Grant in Cunliffe and Davenport 1985: Mf 3/D2–4, Table 7.

common in the samples. Given that barley tends to be the dominant grain in the north, the presence of the spelt wheat together with the amount of pork and game eaten, might be marking out different eating habits. Whether they were different because of the very late date of the assemblage or because of the people who lived there is, at present, an open question. What is needed is the analysis of other very late assemblages to a similar high level as has been done for Filey. It would be of immense interest to know what the environmental evidence from the Wellington Row site in York is telling us. This was a very large excavation carried out in 1987–91 in the *colonia* area of the city, with the full panoply of sampling for which the archaeologists at York are famous. Only the pottery has been studied and published, but that makes it clear that occupation was going on well into the fifth century.[42] Publication of the site would provide a northern reference assemblage against which evidence such as that of Filey could be compared.

EATING AND CHRISTIANITY

We know that there was an organised Christian community in Britain in the fourth century, if not earlier. British bishops are recorded as attending both the Council of Arles in AD 314 and that of Ariminum in AD 359.[43] There is also an ever growing *corpus* of material with explicitly Christian symbols on it including the mid-fourth-century Water Newton treasure which seems to be the earliest group of Christian silver from the empire.[44] That group is comparatively modest in comparison to other finds of precious metal with Christian symbols such as those from Mildenhall and Hoxne.[45] Such finds, together with the evidence of places like the Lullingstone house church and the explicitly Christian mosaics at Hinton St Mary,[46] suggest that during the fourth century the religion was drawing adherents from the wealthy elite of the province as well as more humble members of the community. It was a time when the doctrines of the Church were still being fought over by rival sects, and it is clear that the British congregation was actively involved in these debates. Pelagius, whose works were declared heretical in AD 418, was British; and there were still many who followed his teachings rather than the orthodox Catholic ones in AD 429.[47] Against this background, it is worth

---

[42] Monaghan 1997: 1108–23.   [43] Frere 1987: 321–2.
[44] Painter 1977a.   [45] Painter 1977b; Bland and Johns 1993.
[46] Salway 1993: pls. facing 256 and 448.
[47] Salway 1993: 320–2.

considering what the growing influence of this religion would have been on the eating habits of the fourth century and later population.

During the millennia after the Roman period in Britain, the Catholic Church developed a vice-like control over the eating habits of its members with nearly half the year declared a fast.[48] The formalisation of this regime came later than the period with which we are concerned, but the Christian emphasis on fasting and the ascetic life had already started. Its development can be traced from the end of the second century, but the most rigorous propaganda for it came with Christianity's rise to power.[49] As the prospect of actual martyrdom receded after the Edict of Milan in 313, certain individuals looked around for other ways to distinguish themselves as part of the Christian elite, and asceticism was one way of doing this. There were always people who argued against this, pointing out that it was the sins of the body that were to be hated, not the body itself; but by the fourth century there were strong voices that 'demanded that the unresurrected living body, especially the female body, was to be hated and mortified'.[50]

It would be naive to think that a congregation that actively partook in the debates raging in the Church would not have been aware of these currents of thought, and there is a small amount of evidence that suggests it did have an effect on some people. One of the curious features of the demographic pattern of the Poundbury cemetery has always been the disproportionate number of young girls buried there. It is worth quoting what the report says about this:

At most ages from about seven years, girls greatly outnumbered the boys. The disproportion was especially marked between thirteen and fifteen when there were nearly four times as many girls as boys. While this ratio continues into the early twenties, the explanation cannot rest simply with death associated with childbearing, but must lie with the treatment accorded girls from an early age.[51]

The cause of death could not be ascertained, and the author went on to suggest that this treatment might have been the result of females being held in less esteem, and having less access to food and health care.

Given that it has been argued that the main cemeteries at Poundbury show many of the features to be expected in a Christian cemetery,[52] an alternative explanation might lie in the religious arena. It is appropriate here to point out that the identification of which cemeteries

---

[48] See p. 105.   [49] Grimm 1996: see especially 192–7.   [50] Grimm 1996: 178.
[51] Molleson in Farwell and Molleson 1993: 180.
[52] Woodward in Farwell and Molleson 1993: 236–7.

are and are not Christian in fourth century Roman-Britain is almost as contentious an area as what happens in the fifth century. The evidence for Christians at Poundbury though is very strong as one of the mausoleums was painted with a scene that includes the explicitly Christian symbol of the *Chi-Rho*.[53]

Within the western world, women seem particularly prone to take control of their lives by fasting. The comparison between medieval female fasting saints and modern anorexics has often been made,[54] and from at least the thirteenth century onwards there are records of holy Christian women choosing to fast to death. At that point the Church disapproved of such a course of action, but in the world of late antiquity there were some Church leaders who would appear to have thought this a good idea. Jerome in the fourth century was providing instructions for the preservation of virginity in women that 'bear a more than chance resemblance to the conditions that give rise to and are involved in anorexia nervosa'.[55] It is noticeable that his instructions for men are more moderate. The suggestion that the unusually high number of young female deaths might be the response to Christian teaching may not be as far-fetched as it might seem, as other aspects of this teaching do appear to be reflected in the material-culture record. The early Church Fathers were obsessed with what females did with their hair, and this may be the reason why the hairpin evidence indicates major changes in hair-dressing styles towards the end of the fourth century in Britain.[56]

Possibly by coincidence there is also evidence of nutritional stress seen in an individual buried at Shepton Mallet in the fourth century accompanied by a silver amulet with the *crux monogrammatica* motif.[57] This was a popular Christian symbol in the fourth century, and would seem to be strong evidence that the individual was Christian. The individual was an adult male probably of middle age. Not only did his teeth show enamel hypoplasia and his skull show cribra orbitalia, but he also had periostitis on his leg. The first two conditions can be interpreted as the result of nutritional stress in childhood, the last the same condition in adulthood.[58] He may just have been a particularly unfortunate individual, but then again he may have been from a particularly devout family.

It is clear from the tone of various of the early Church Fathers' writings on fasting that not everyone was convinced that this was the road to

[53] Green in Farwell and Molleson 1993: 135–9.   [54] Counihan 1999: 93–112.
[55] Grimm 1996: 170–1.   [56] Cool 2000b.
[57] For grave see Leach and Evans 2001: 35; for the amulet Johns in Leech and Evans 2001: 257–60; for the skeleton Pinter-Bellows in Leech and Evans 2001: 279, 281.
[58] See pp. 23–4 for a discussion of these conditions.

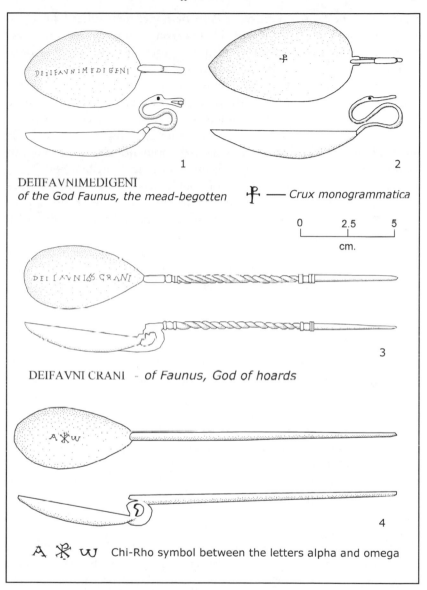

DEIIFAVNIMEDIGENI
of the God Faunus, the mead-begotten

Crux monogrammatica

DEIFAVNI CRANI — *of Faunus, God of hoards*

A ☧ ⍵   Chi-Rho symbol between the letters alpha and omega

Figure 19.4. Fourth-century silver spoons used in both pagan (nos. 1 and 3) and Christian (nos. 2 and 4) worship. (After Johns and Potter 1983: nos. 56 and 74 (1 and 3); Johns and Potter 1985, no. 5 (2); Painter 1977a: 31 no. 11). Scale 1 : 2.

salvation in the fourth century. It is to be hoped that other Christians' experiences were more enjoyable. There is some evidence that food may have been as integral a part of worship for some Christian congregations as it was for their pagan contemporaries. The building thought to be a church at Butt Road, Colchester may provide some, though again the identification is contentious with some reviewers of the report happy to accept this interpretation and others not.[59] It was associated with an exceptional amount of chicken bones and immature pig bones, the classic meats of high-status feasting as has often been noted throughout this book.[60] Spoons also seem to be common to both Christian and pagan worship. Precisely the same types of spoons have religious inscriptions and symbols relating to both Christianity and devotion to other gods (see Fig. 19.4). Quite how these were used is unclear, but the ones with the short bird handles have bowls that are larger than the modern tablespoon and could be used for taking small quantities of presumably alcoholic beverages. Possibly the way some congregations celebrated was much the same whatever god was being worshipped.

CONCLUSIONS

It will be clear from the foregoing that there is a great deal we do not know about culinary habits at the end of the Roman period, however defined. What is clear is that things were changing but that this was not a sudden event, it had its roots a century or more earlier. Changes in what sort of vessels were wanted and how they were regarded start to become apparent in the third century. This did not happen in isolation. It is in the third century as well that we see the decline in the desire for amphora-borne commodities such as oil, whilst fish sauce may have gone even earlier.[61] It is in the third century that the nature of mortaria changes.[62] Tastes were altering in more ways than one. The late fourth and fifth centuries are often looked on as some sort of archaeological black hole. From a culinary point of view they don't look like that. New factors such as Christianity undoubtedly came into the equation, but they were acting on cultural changes that were already in play. A more rigorous attitude to fourth century assemblages and 'residual' material, might well enable us to tease out what those were.

[59] Compare for example Millett in *Archaeological Journal* 152 (1995) pp. 452–3 with Struck in *Britannia* 28 (1997) 498.
[60] Crummy *et al.* 1993: 178–80.   [61] See pp. 62–3.   [62] See p. 43.

CHAPTER 20

Digestif

What has emerged from our explorations of the foodways of Roman Britain?

The first thing is the range of eating habits and preferences in the different regions and how they altered through time. That this is so should surely not surprise us. Even today in a homogenised and globalised world, the different regions of Britain still retain local traditions and preferences. The Staffordshire oatcake is an entirely different beast to the traditional Scottish one. I have looked long and hard for something similar to Wiltshire lardy cakes in the various parts of Britain I have lived in since childhood, but to no avail. My partner remembers, with advantage, the season puddings his Yorkshire-bred mother would make to accompany roast chicken, but has never found their like elsewhere. These are just memories belonging to the second half of the twentieth century. The regional diversity of British cooking before that is well documented in such works as Dorothy Hartley's *Food in England*, which also shows the changes going on over the centuries before the impact of the Industrial Revolution changed British society so fundamentally. It should be expected that there would be differences observable in Roman Britain given that it covers a large geographical area and half a millennium of time. Equally we have seen that there was no one 'Roman' cuisine amongst the people who came to Britain after the conquest. Why should there be? They came from various areas of the empire with their own particular tastes and prejudices. Differences are to be expected.

It is worth bearing this in mind when considering the nature of Roman Britain more widely. There is a tendency to regard it as a single entity or at best a series of dichotomies – Roman–native, urban–rural, military–civilian. The reality was much more complex, and any consideration needs to include its regional and chronological diversity.

Allowing for this, it does seem reasonable to say that for the inhabitants of many parts of Britain, their culinary horizons would have expanded during the period under consideration. We could observe this starting to happen in the century or so before the conquest in parts of the south-east. In some areas the effects can only be seen a century or more after the conquest whilst in others many people wished to have nothing to do with new outlandish tastes and ways of eating. There are also signs that a differentiated cuisine of the type discussed in Chapter 5 was developing in places. Certainly some meats regularly seem to indicate elite dining, often appearing on sites that show a greater openness to a wider type of table-wares, a different choice of grain as a staple, etc.

Regularly observed patterns such as the combination of elite meats raise interesting questions about the nature of the Romano-British population. Why were chicken, pork and game seen as special? Various foods seem regularly to be distinguished by their absence or rarity. Did people not eat fish because they didn't like it? Is game so rare because the habitat for the animals was not available? Or in both cases are there more fundamental reasons that lie in the area of taboo? Young animals seem regularly to be a feature of temple assemblages. Is this because they were unblemished, and if so, what does this tell us about the relationship of the people with their gods? At present we are in the position of being able to identify patterns and ask questions, but not necessarily answer them. What is needed is for the patterns to be checked against new data sets to see if they do indeed recur regularly, and then for their other associations to be explored.

Methodologically these explorations have shown that though there is a great deal of good work going on in the excavation and analysis of sites, there is also work that falls short of best practice. The observant reader will have realised that from time to time I have been rather irritated by what I have found. I have seen good specialist work thoughtlessly consigned to the archive because the person writing the report does not know how to use it. I have seen similar work published but its implications totally ignored by the overall author when writing their discussions of the site. I have frequently thought that many people seem to have no idea what to do with all this information commissioned and produced at great expense. Equally, I have seen specialists so involved with their own area that their reports stand in splendid isolation, not integrated with the rest of the material and presented in such a way that it is impossible for anyone else to integrate them. Archaeology is expensive and to see resources squandered in any of these ways makes me not just irritated but really very angry. It ought to have the same effect on everyone. Yet, I have lost count of the number of reviews of excavation monographs I have read which end with a brief coda along the lines of 'there are lots of specialist reports but space does not allow me to comment on them'. These reports will often occupy half the book or more! It is not enough that they are there. They need to be integrated with each other and the stratigraphy, and if this is not done, it should be commented on. Only in this way will good practice drive out bad.

I would like to think that we excavate sites because we are curious about the past and the people who lived in it, rather than to keep us in employment and fill museum stores with boxes of finds. Various excavations have been referred to repeatedly in this book. That is because the authors of the reports have been curious and have used the data as a pathway into the past. As a result they have discovered much more from their data. These reports are a joy to read, not something that can be said about the majority of excavation reports. It is my hope that with time this attitude will become the rule rather than the exception. I could think of no better prospect than that in ten years time someone else will be writing a book exploring food and drink in Roman Britain because new data, thoughtfully produced, has rendered this one hopelessly out of date.

Appendix : data sources for tables

Table 3.1.   Bainesse – Evans, J. in Wilson 2002b: Table 12 (excluding prehistoric pottery); Leicester – Clark in Connor and Buckley 1999: Tables 9, 12, 15, 22, 23, 28; Lincoln – Darling in Colyer *et al.* 1999: 52 and Table 32; Alchester – Booth *et al.* 2001: Appendix 4; Kingscote – Timby 1998: Table 7; Ivy Chimneys – Turner-Walker and Wallace in Turner 1999: Table 17; Asthall – Booth 1997: 133–4; Chignal – Wallace and Turner-Walker in Clarke 1998: Table 11.

Table 3.2.   Capacity derived from Tyers 1996: 87–104; weight range derived from Peacock and Williams 1986: Table 1; and Martin-Kilchner 1994: 354.

Table 4.1.   London East – Conheeney in Barber and Bowsher 2000, 286; Cirencester – Wells in McWhirr *et al.* 1982: Table 50; Dunstable – Jones and Horne in Matthews 1981: 39; Poundbury – Molleson in Farwell and Molleson 1993: Table 28; Alington Avenue – Waldron in Davies *et al.* 2002: Table 29; Maiden Castle Road – Rogers in Smith *et al.* 1997: Table 33; Colchester – Pinter-Bellows in Crummy *et al.* 1993: Table 2.22; Bradley Hill – Everton in Leech 1981: Table 8.

Table 4.2.   London East – Conheeney in Barber and Bowsher 2000: 285–6; Cirencester – Wells in McWhirr *et al.* 1982: Table 70, 150, 186; Dunstable – Jones and Horne in Matthews 1981: Table 6; Chignall – Stirland in Clarke 1998: 119–22; Poundbury – Molleson in Farwell and Molleson 1993: 183, 185; Alington Avenue – Waldron in Davies *et al.* 2002: 152–3; Colchester – Pinter-Bellows in Crummy *et al.* 1993: 79, 88; Alchester – Boyle in Booth *et al.* 2001: Table 8.2–3.

Table 4.3. Numbers of individuals taken from Molleson and Farwell 1993: Table 50.

Table 6.1. Baldock – Stead and Rigby 1986: 297–378; Dalton Parlours – Sumpter in Wrathmell and Nicholson 1990: 135–46; West Yorkshire – Evans, J. in Roberts *et al.* 2001: 153–76; Warrington – Webster in Hinchliffe *et al.* 1992: 124–50; Segontium – Webster in Casey *et al.* 1993: 250–309; Menai Straits – Longley *et al.* 1998: 220–6; Caersws – Webster in Britnell 1989: 80–124.

Table 6.2. Catterick Bridge – Evans, J. in Wilson 2002b: Tables 41– 2; Catterick Bainesse – Evans, J. in Wilson 2002b: Tables 18–19; Alchester Site B – Dickinson in Booth *et al.* 2001: Table 7.10; Alchester Site C – Dickinson in Booth *et al.* 2001: Table 7.11; Lincoln – Bird in Colyer *et al.* 1999: Table 29.

Table 7.1. Kingsholm – Timby in Hurst 1985: Table 4; Exeter – Holbrook and Bidwell 1991: 14; 1992: Table 6; Wroxeter – Darling in Webster 2002: Table 5.15; London, Billingsgate – Green in Jones, 1980: 40–5; Wanborough – Keay in Anderson *et al.* 2001: Table 13; Carlisle – Taylor in McCarthy 1990: Tables 17 and 20; Gloucester – Timby in Hurst and Pitts 1986: Table 4 – Contexts A3.1. A4.2, A4.4; Wroxeter – Faiers in Ellis 2000: Table 4.22; Bainesse – Evans, J. in Wilson 2002b: Table 12 Phases 3–6; Carlisle – Taylor in McCarthy 1990: Table 23 – Building 8; South Shields – Bidwell and Speak 1994: Table 8.9 – Phases 3–5; Lincoln – Darling in Colyer *et al.* 1999: Table 33; Alchester – Booth *et al.* 2001: Appendix 4; London, New Fresh Wharf – Miller *et al.* 1986: fig. 76 Phases 4 and 5; London Shadwell – Lakin *et al.* 2002: Tables 7 and 9; Caister – Darling and Gurney 1993: Table 29; Newcastle Upon Tyne – Williams in Snape and Bidwell 2002: Table 15.7.

Table 7.2. Longthorpe – Wilson in Frere 1974: 97; Peacock in Dannell and Wild 1987: Table VI; Nanstallon – Fox and Ravenhall 1972: 104 nos. 17–19; Castleford (fort) – Rush *et al.* 2000: Table 12; York – Monaghan 1993: Table 117 Periods 1 and 2; Segontium – Casey *et al.* 1993: 77; Canterbury – Green in Blockley *et al.* 1995: 638; London – Groves in Milne and Wardle 1996: 131; Dorchester – Williams in Woodward *et al.*

1993: Table 28 Period 6; Cirencester – Cooper in Holbrook 1998: Tables 20–21; Chelmsford – Going 1987: Table 9 ceramic phases 2–3; Towcester – Brown and Woodfield 1983: 77; Castleford (*vicus*) – Rush *et al.* 2000: Table 19; Wilcote – Hands 1993: 156; Williams in Hands 1998: 226; Cramond – Maxwell in Rae and Rae 1974: 206; Williams in Holmes 2003: 47; Greta Bridge – Croom and Bidwell in Casey and Hoffmann 1998: 178.

Table 7.3. Castleford – Bastow in Abramson *et al.* 1999: Tables 8–13; Caerleon – Caseldine and Busby in Zienkiewicz 1993: 137; Vindolanda – Seaward in van Driel Murray *et al.* 1993: 105–107; Ribchester – Huntley in Buxton and Howard-Davis 2000: Table 32; Bearsden – Knights *et al.* 1983; Leicester – Monkton in Connor and Buckley 1999: 347 Phase 3; London – Willcox 1977: Table 1 – St Thomas Street; York – Kenward *et al.* 1986: Table 76; Dragonby – van der Veen in May 1996: Table 9.3; Bancroft – Peterson and Robinson in Williams and Zepvat 1994: 581; South Shields – van der Veen in Bidwell and Speak 1994: 260.

Table 9.1. Castleford – Berg in Abramson *et al.* 1999: Fort Tables 26 and 27, *vicus* Table 30 Phases 2 and 3; Ribchester – Stallibrass and Nicholson in Buxton and Howard-Davis 2000: Table 48 Phase 1–4; Wroxeter – Meddens in Ellis 2000: Table 4.30 Period 1 and 2; Leicester – Gidney in Connor and Buckley 1999: Table 66, Phases 2a–h, k, l, 3a, b, e. Wilcote – Hamshaw-Thomas and Bermingham in Hands 1993: Tables 8 and 9.

Table 9.2. The data in rows one and two are derived from Goldsworthy 1996: 292 Table 4. The Colchester bone weight data is derived from Luff 1993: Table 3.5a, Assemblages BKCJ3, CULA2, CULG4, GBSA7.
The calculation is as follows:

$$\text{Cattle:} \left(\frac{\text{bone weight}}{2} \right) \times 2.$$

$$\text{Sheep:} \left(\frac{\text{bone weight} \times 2.222}{100} \right) \times 55.$$

$$\text{Pig:} \left(\frac{\text{bone weight} \times 4}{100} \right) \times 75.$$

Table 11.1.   Colchester – Luff 1993: Table 5.1; Dorchester – Maltby in Woodward *et al.* 1993: 62 (Periods 5–10); Leicester – Gidney in Connor and Buckley 1999: Table 66; Southwark – Ainsley in Drummond *et al.* 2002: Table 125 (London Bridge).

Table 11.2.   Colchester – Luff 1993: Table 3.1 and 5.1; Fishbourne – Grant in Cunliffe 1971: 378 Table I, Eastham in Cunliffe 1971: 389. For comparability to the mammal-bone table, pre-palace deposits include the Period 2 construction assemblage.

Table 13.1.   Wroxeter (fort) – Noddle in Webster 2002: Table 7.1; Castleford – Berg in Abramson *et al.* 1999: Table 30 Phase I and II; Colchester – Luff 1993: Table 3.1 – Culver Street 2 and 3; Wroxeter (town) Meddens in Ellis 2000: Table 4.30 Periods 1 and 2; Wilcote – Hamshaw-Thomas and Bermingham in Hands 1993: Table 6; Leicester – Gidney in Connor and Buckley 1999: Table 66; Caister – Harman in Darling and Gurney 1993: Table 40; Segontium – Noddle in Casey *et al.* 1993: Table 6.1.

Table 14.1.   Colchester – Murphy in Crummy 1992: 50 Table 8.14; [1] Pit C138, [2] Pit EF900. Gorhambury – Wainright in Neal *et al.* 1990: 28, 218. Southwark – Gray in Drummond-Murray *et al.* 2002: 244 OA14 {222}. Carlisle – McCarthy 2000: 21. Leicester – Monkton in Connor and Buckley 1999, Table 84 sample 775. Dorchester – Ede in Smith 1993: 73 MF 8–10; [1]Pit 27, [2]Pit 13. Bearsden – Knights *et al.* 1983. Stonea – van der Veen in Jackson and Potter 1996: Table 65; York – Greig in Buckland 1976: Table 2.

Table 15.1.   Kingsholm – Timby in Hurst 1985: Table 8 (the Dressel 28/30 have been attributed to Gaul following Holbrook and Bidwell 1991: 215). Exeter – Holbrook and Bidwell 1991: Table 14; 1992: Table 6. Wroxeter – Darling in Webster 2002: Table 5.15; Inchtuthil – Darling in Pitts and St Joseph 1985: Table XXIV.

Table 15.2.   Data from Davies *et al.* 1994: Appendix 5 Ceramic phases 1A and 2.

Table 15.3.   The data set scanned is unfortunately too large for the references to be published here.

Table 16.1.   Skeleton Green – Partridge 1981. Key Groups F52, F9, F23, F24, Ditch 1 F60, F50, F39 Ditch 2, F1, G22 Layers 7 and 9. Ermine Street – Witherington and Trow in Potter and Trow 1988: Tables 14–16 with additional information taken from the Arretine report (Hartley in Potter and Trow 1988: 94–6) and that on the Gallic imports (Rigby in Potter and Trow 1988: 110–14).

Table 16.2.   Parminter in Neal *et al.* 1990, Tables 10–13. The Arretine cup was unstratified but can be dated to the pre-conquest period – Dannell in Neal *et al.* 1996: 198.

Table 16.3.   Stead and Rigby 1989: Appendix 6. Formal burials belonging to Phases 1–3 and unphased. Tables based on the following deposits: 2, 3, 9–21, 23–7, 29–32, 34, 35, 37–40, 42–5, 47–50, 52–3, 55–9, 61, 66–77, 79–82, 84–6, 89–93, 95–9, 101, 102, 104, 106–12, 115, 117, 118, 120, 121, 123–5, 127–31, 133–44, 146–54, 156–89, 191–3, 196–205, 207, 208, 210–8, 221–4, 227, 229–42, 244, 248, 249, 251, 252, 255–60, 262–5, 267, 268, 270, 273–6, 278–83, 287–9, 293, 294, 296–303, 305, 307, 309–12, 314–17, 321, 322, 324, 325, 327, 328, 334–41, 343–76, 378–82, 384–91, 393, 395, 397–401, 408, 410, 412–17, 420–7, 434–41, 445, 447–50, 454–7, 449–65, 467, 469, 471, 472.

Table 16.4.   Data set as Table 16.3.

Table 16.5.   Data set as Table 16.3.

Table 17.1.   Luff 1993: Table 3.5a. The Cattle total is a combination of COW and OXO, the sheep a combination of S/G and SMA – see Luff 1993: 24 for justification.

Table 17.2.   Symmonds and Wade 1999: Tables 3.2, 3.4 and 3.6.

Table 17.3   Symmonds and Wade 1999: Tables 4.2, 4.4, 5.2, 5.9, 5.11, 5.14, 5.16, 5.18, 5.20, 5.25, 5.30, 5.36, 6.3, 6.6, 6.14, 6.16, 6.20, 6.26, 6.30, 6.32. PEG groups 3 and 4.

Table 17.4.   Data taken from Cool and Price 1995: quantified by the methodology outlined in Cool and Baxter 1999.

Table 17.5.   Pottery data taken from Groves in Milne and Wardle 1996: Tables 11 and 13. Glass data taken from Shepherd in Milne and Wardle 1996: 104–14 quantified by the methodology outlined in Cool and Baxter 1999.

Table 17.6.   Data from Abramson *et al.* 1999: Tables 26, 36–8 (zone measures are missing for the sheep and pigs from Trenches 15/18 in tables 37 and 38). The notional meat measures are calculated using the minimum numbers of individuals and the average meat weights provided in Table 8.2.

Table 17.7.   Data from Rush *et al.* 2000: Tables 2–4, 8–10, 21, 27.

Table 17.8.   Data from Cool and Price in Cool and Philo 1998: 152–78 quantified by the methodology outlined in Cool and Baxter 1999.

Table 17.9.   Data from Sykes in Miles *et al.* forthcoming and King, J. in Mackreth 1996: Mf 8: B13 Table 80.

Table 17.10.   Data from Green and Booth in Miles *et al.* forthcoming and Perrin in Mackreth 1996: Tables 13–16 using EVE data provided in Mf 11: E12-3.

Table 17.11.   Gage 1834, 1836, 1840; Gage Rokewode 1842. Vessels used to contain the cremated bone have been omitted.

Table 18.1.   Pottery data from Clarke in Connor and Buckley 1999: Tables 12, 15 and 23. Glass data from Davies in Connor and Buckley 1999: 287–92 quantified by the methodology outlined in Cool and Baxter 1999.

Table 18.2.   Data from Sykes in Miles *et al.* forthcoming; Cool in Miles *et al.* forthcoming; Evans in Roberts *et al.* 2001: 163–9.

Table 18.3.   Data from Sykes in Miles *et al.* forthcoming and Richardson in Roberts *et al.* 2001: Table 39.

Table 18.4.   Data from Levitan in Woodward and Leach 1993: Table 15. The quantification method used is number of identified bones. This counted epiphyses and non-repeatable characteristics for other skeletal parts. The aim was to avoid over-counting individual bones that may have been broken into several pieces. For discussion see Levitan in Woodward and Leach 1993: 258.

Table 18.5.   Data from Bond and Worley in Cool 2004b: Tables 7.18–20, 17.22. Deposits where only teeth were included have been excluded. Adults are individuals over the age of 18 who it is not possible to sex. The Male and Female categories are adults who it is possible to sex. Infants are aged 5 or less, immature individuals are aged between 5 and 18. Total deposit data from Cool 2004b: Table 6.9.

Table 19.1.   Data from Cool and Baxter 1999: Tables 1 and 2.

Table 19.2.   Data from Monaghan 1997: 977–1020.

Table 19.3.   Data from Symmonds in Barker *et al.* 1997: unnumbered tables on pp. 294–308 and Timby in Ellis 2000: Table 4.24. Material assigned to a bowl – jar category has been divided equally between jars and bowls. The beaker category includes cups for earlier assemblages.

References

ABBREVIATIONS

AY   Archaeology of York (published by the Council for British Archaeology).

BAR BS   British Archaeological Report, British Series.

BAR IS   British Archaeological Report, International Series.

CAR   Colchester Archaeological Reports.

CBARR   Research Reports of the Council for British Archaeology.

EAA   East Anglian Archaeology.

RCHM   An Inventory of the Historical Monuments of the city of York.

York   Volume I *Eburacum* Roman York (London: Royal Commission on Historical Monuments England, 1962).

RIB   Collingwood, R. G. and Wright, R. P., 1965, *Roman Inscriptions of Britain*, Volume I. *Inscriptions on Stone*, (Oxford: Oxford University Press).

RIB II.1–8   Collingwood, R. G. and Wright, R. P., *The Roman Inscriptions of Britain Volume II. Instrumentum Domesticum (personal belongings and the like). Fascicules 1 to 8*, Frere, S. S. and Tomlin, R. S. O. (eds.) (Stroud: Alan Sutton, 1990–5).

ANCIENT SOURCES

Apicius *De Re Coquinaria* (Philip Reclam edition with German translation by R. Maier, 1991).

Caesar *De Bello Gallico* (Penguin edition. English translation by S. A. Handford, 1951).

Cato *De Agricultura* (Prospect Books edition with English translation by A. Dalby, 1998).

Columella *De Re Rustica* (Loeb edition with English translation by E. S. Forster, and E. H. Heffner, revised edition 1968).

Dioscorides *Materia Medica* (Gunther, R. T. (ed), 1959. *The Greek Herbal of Dioscurides illustrated by a Byzantine AD 512, English edition by John Goodyer AD 1655* (New York reprint of 1933 publication)).

Martial *Epigrams* (Loeb edition with English translation by D. R. Shackleton Bailey, 1993).

Pliny *Natural History* (Loeb edition with English translation by various authors, 1938–63).

Tacitus *The Annals of Imperial Rome* (Penguin edition. English translation by K. Wellesley, revised editon 1971).

The Histories (Penguin edition. English translation by M. Grant, revised edition 1975).

Strabo *The Geographies* (Loeb edition with English translation by H. L. Jones, 1917–32).

Vegetius *Epitoma Rei Militaris* (Liverpool University Press edition with English translation by N. P. Milner, 2nd revised edition 1996).

MODERN WORKS

(Note: Where the actual year of a journal publication differs from the stated year for the volume, the reference is given in the form: author, actual year with the stated year given in brackets after the volume number.)

Abramson, P., Berg, D. S. and Fossick, M. R. 1999. *Roman Castleford. Excavations 1974–85 Volume II: the Structural and Environmental Evidence.* Wakefield: West Yorkshire Archaeological Services.

Alcock, J. 2001. *Food in Roman Britain.* Stroud: Tempus.

Allason-Jones, L. and McKay, B. 1988. *Coventina's Well.* Chesters: Trustees of the Clayton Collection.

Allen, J. R. L. and Fulford, M. G. 1996. 'The distribution of south-east Dorset black burnished category 1 pottery in south-west Britain'. *Britannia* 27: 223–81.

Alston, R. 1995. *Soldier and Society in Roman Egypt.* London: Routledge.

Anderson, A. S., Wacher, J. S. and Fitzpatrick, A. P. 2001. *The Romano-British 'Small Town' at Wanborough, Wiltshire.* London: Roman Society.

Anon. 1990. 'Verulamium', *Current Archaeology* 120: 410–17.

2002. *Portable Antiquities Annual Report 2000–2001.* London: Dept. Culture, Media and Sport.

2004. *Treasure Annual Report 2002.* London: Dept. Culture, Media and Sport.

Arthur, P. 1986. 'Roman amphorae from Canterbury'. *Britannia* 17: 239–58.

Bales, E. 2004. *A Roman Maltings at Beck Row, Mildenhall, Suffolk.* EAA Occasional Papers 20: Ipswich.

Banfield, W. T. 1937. *'Manna' A comprehensive treatise on bread manufacture.* London: MacLaren and Sons Ltd.

Barber, B. and Bowsher, D. 2000. *The Eastern Cemetery of Roman London Excavations 1983–1990.* London: Museum of London Archaeological Service.

Barker, P., White, R., Pretty, K., Bird, H. and Corbishley, M. 1997. *The Baths Basilica Wroxeter: Excavations 1966–90.* London: English Heritage.

Barnard, T. 2004. *Making the Grand Figure.* New Haven: Yale University Press.

Bateman, N. and Locker, A. 1982. 'The sauce of the Thames'. *The London Archaeologist* 4.8: 204–7.

Baxter, M. J. 1994. *Exploratory Multivariate Analysis in Archaeology.* Edinburgh: Edinburgh University Press.

2003. *Statistics in Archaeology.* London: Edward Arnold.

Bedwin, M. and Bedwin, O. 1999. *A Roman Malt House: Excavations at Stebbings Green, Essex 1988.* EAA Occasional Paper 6: Chelmsford.

Bestwick, J. D. 1975. 'Romano-British inland salting at Middlewich (Salinae), Cheshire', in De Brisay and Evans (eds.), pp.66–70.

Biddle, M. 1967. 'Two Flavian burials from Grange Road, Winchester', *Antiquaries Journal* 47: 224–50.

Biddulph, E. 2005. 'Samian wear'. *Current Archaeology* 196: 191–3.

Bidwell, P. T. 1985. *The Roman Fort of Vindolanda at Chesterholm, Northumberland.* London: English Heritage.

Bidwell, P. and Speak, S. 1994. *Excavations at South Shields Roman Fort Volume I.* Newcastle upon Tyne: Society of Antiquaries of Newcastle upon Tyne.

Bird, J. 1993. '3rd-century samian ware in Britain'. *Journal of Roman Pottery Studies* 6: 1–14.

Bird, J., Hassall, M. and Sheldon, H. (eds.) 1996. *Interpreting Roman London.* Oxford: Oxbow Books.

Birley, A. 1979. *The People of Roman Britain.* London: B.T. Batsford.

Birley, R. 1977. *Vindolanda.* London: Thames and Hudson.

Bland, R. and Johns, C. 1993. *The Hoxne Treasure.* London: British Museum Press.

Blockley, K., Blockley, M., Blockley, P., Frere, S. and Stow, S. 1995. *Excavations in the Marlowe Car Park and surrounding areas.* Canterbury: Canterbury Archaeological Trust.

Boon, G. C. 1961. 'Roman antiquities at Welshpool'. *Antiquaries Journal* 88: 13–31.

Booth, P. 1997. *Asthall, Oxfordshire: Excavations in a Roman 'Small Town'.* Oxford: Oxford Archaeological Unit.

Booth, P. and Evans, J. 2001. *Roman Alcester: Northern Extramural Area.* CBARR 127: York.

Booth, P., Evans, J. and Hiller, J. 2001. *Excavations in the Extramural Settlement of Roman Alchester, Oxfordshire, 1991.* Oxford: Oxford Archaeology.

Borgard, P. and Cavalier, M. 2003. 'The Lipari origin of the Richborough 527'. *Journal of Roman Pottery Studies* 10: 96–106.

Bouby, I. and Marinval, P. 2004. 'Fruits and seeds from Roman cremations in Limagne (Massif Central) and the spatial variability of plant offerings in France', *Journal of Archaeological Science* 31: 77–86.

Bourdieu, P. 1986. *Distinction.* London: Routledge.

Bowman, A. K. 1993. *Life and Letters on the Roman Frontier.* London: British Museum Press.

Bowman, A. K. and Thomas, J. D. 1994. *The Vindolanda Writing Tablets (Tabulae Vindolandenses II).* London: British Museum Press.

1996. 'New writing tablets from Vindolanda'. *Britannia* 27: 299–328.

2003. *The Vindolanda Writing Tablets (Tabulae Vindolandenses III)*. London: British Museum Press.

Bradley, R. 1975. 'Salt and settlement in the Hampshire Sussex Borderland' in De Brisay and Evans (eds.), pp.20–5.

Braun, T. 1995. 'Barley cakes and emmer bread' in Wilkins *et al.* (eds.), pp.25–37.

Braund, D. and Wilkins, J. (eds.) 2000. *Athenaeus and his World*. Exeter: University of Exeter Press.

Brigstock, R. J. 2000. 'Coin supply in the North in the late Roman period' in Wilmott and Wilson (eds.), pp.33–7.

Brillat-Savarin, J. E. 1826. *The Physiology of Taste*. New York: Liveright 1926.

Britnell, J. 1989. *Caersws Vicus, Powys: Excavations at the Old Primary School*. BAR BS 205: Oxford.

Brodribb, A. C. C., Hands, A. R. and Walker, D. R. 1971. *Excavations at Shakenoak Farm, near Wilcote, Oxfordshire 2*. Oxford: privately printed.

Brodribb, G. and Cleere, H. 1988. 'The *Classis Britannica* bath-house at Beauport Park, East Sussex', *Britannia* 19: 217–74.

Brown, A. E. and Woodfield, C. 1983. 'Excavations at Towcester, Northamptonshire: the Alchester Road Suburb'. *Northamptonshire Archaeology* 118: 43–140.

Brown, A. G. and Meadows, I. 2000. 'Roman vineyards in Britain: finds from the Nene Valley and new research'. *Antiquity* 74: 491–2.

Brown, F., Boyle, A., Howard-Davis, C. H. and Lupton, A. forthcoming. *A Road Through Time: Archaeological Investigations along the route of the A1(M) Darrington to Dishforth Road Scheme*.

Brown, N. R. 1999. *The Archaeology of Ardleigh, Essex, Excavations 1955–1980*. EAA 90: Chelmsford.

Brothwell, D. R. and Pollard, A. M. 2001. *Handbook of Archaeological Sciences*. Chichester: Wiley.

Bruce Mitford, R. 1972. *The Sutton Hoo Ship Burial: a Handbook*. London: British Museum Press.

Buckland, P. C. 1976. *The Environmental Evidence from the Church Street Roman Sewer System*. AY 14/1: London.

Buckland, P. C. and Magilton, J. R. 1986. *The Archaeology of Doncaster. Volume 1: The Roman Civil Settlement*. BAR BS 148: Oxford.

Buckland, P. C., Magilton, J. R. and Dolby, M. J. 1980. 'The Roman pottery industries of south Yorkshire: a review' *Britannia* 11: 145–64.

Burkeman, O. 2005. 'When the PM came to call'. *The Guardian G2 Supplement* 26 January 2005.

Bushe-Fox, J. P. 1949. *Fourth Report on the Excavations of the Roman Fort at Richborough, Kent*. Oxford: Society of Antiquaries of London.

Buxton, K. and Howard-Davis, C. 2000. *Bremetenacum: Excavations at Roman Ribchester 1980, 1989–1990*. Lancaster: Lancaster University Archaeological Unit.

Carreras Montfort, C. 2003. 'Haltern 70: a review'. *Journal of Roman Pottery Studies* 10: 85–91.

Carreras Montfort, C. and Williams, D. 2003. 'Spanish olive oil trade in late Roman Britain: Dressel 23 amphorae from Winchester'. *Journal of Roman Pottery Studies* 10: 64–8.

Caruana, I. D. 1992. 'Carlisle: excavation of a section of the annexe ditch of the first Flavian fort, 1990'. *Britannia* 23: 45–109.

Casey, P. J., Davies, J. L. and Evans, J. 1993. *Excavations at Segontium (Caernarfon) Roman Fort, 1975–1979*. CBARR 90: London.

Casey, P. J. and Hoffmann, B. 1998. 'Rescue excavations in the vicus of the fort at Greta Bridge, Co. Durham, 1972–4'. *Britannia* 29: 111–83.

Clark, P. 1983. *The English Alehouse: a Social History 1200–1830*. London: Longman.

Clarke, C. P. 1998. *Excavations to the south of Chignall Roman Villa, Essex 1977–81*. EAA 83: Chelmsford.

Clarke, G. 1979. *The Roman Cemetery at Lankhills*. Oxford: Clarendon Press.

Clauss, M. 2000. *The Roman Cult of Mithras*. (Translated by R. Gordon). Edinburgh: Edinburgh University Press.

Colyer, C., Gilmour, B. J. J. and Jones, M. J. 1999. *The Defences of the Lower City*. CBARR 114: York

Connor, A. and Buckley, R. 1999. *Roman and Medieval Occupation in Causeway Lane, Leicester*. Leicester: University of Leicester Archaeological Service.

Cool, H. E. M. 1982. 'The artefact record: some possibilities', in Harden, D. W. (ed.), *Later Prehistoric Settlement in South-east Scotland*. Edinburgh: Dept. of Archaeology, University of Edinburgh, pp.92–100.

1995. 'Glass vessels of the fourth and early fifth century in Roman Britain', in Foy, D. (ed.), *Le Verre de l'Antiquité tardive et du Haut Moyen Age*. Cergy-Pontoise: Musée Archéologique Départemental du Val d'Oise, pp.11–23.

2000a. 'The parts left over: material culture into the fifth century', in Wilmott and Wilson (eds.), pp.47–65.

2000b. 'Hairstyles and lifestyles', *Roman Finds Group Newsletter* 19: 3–6.

2003. 'Local production and trade in glass vessels in the British Isles in the first to seventh centuries AD', in Foy, D. and Nenna M.-D. (eds.), *Échanges et commerce du verre dans le monde antique*. Montagnac: Éditions Monique Mergoil, pp.139–45.

2004a. 'Some notes on spoons and mortaria' in Croxford, B., Eckardt, H., Meake, J. and Weekes, J. (eds.), *TRAC 2003: Proceedings of the Thirteenth Annual Theoretical Roman Archaeology Conference Leicester 2003*. Oxford: Oxbow Books, pp.28–35

2004b. *The Roman Cemetery at Brougham, Cumbria: Excavations 1966–1967*. London: Roman Society.

2005. 'Roman stone mortars – a preliminary survey'. *Journal of Roman Pottery Studies* 12: 54–8.

Cool, H. E. M. and Baxter, M. J. 1999. 'Peeling the onion; an approach to comparing vessel glass assemblages'. *Journal of Roman Archaeology* 12: 72–100.

2002. 'Exploring Romano-British finds assemblages'. *Oxford Journal of Archaeology* 21: 365–80.

2005. 'Cemeteries and significance tests'. *Journal of Roman Archaeology* 18: 397–404.

Cool, H. E. M., Lloyd-Morgan, G. and Hooley, A. D. 1995. *Finds from the Fortress*. AY 17/10: York.

Cool, H. E. M. and Philo, C. (eds.) 1998. *Roman Castleford. Excavations 1974–85 Volume I: the Small Finds*. Wakefield: West Yorkshire Archaeological Services.

Cool, H. E. M. and Price, J. 1995. *Roman Vessel Glass from Excavations in Colchester 1971–85*. CAR 8: Colchester.

Copley, M. S., Berstan, R., Dudd, S. N., Straker, V., Payne, S. and Evershed, R. P. 2005. 'Dairying in Antiquity. I. Evidence from absorbed lipid residues dating to the British Iron Age'. *Journal of Archaeological Science* 32: 485–503.

Corcoran, J. X. W. P. 1952. 'Tankards and tankard handles of the British Early Iron Age'. *Proc. Prehistoric Society* 18: 85–101.

Counihan, C. M. 1999. *The Anthropology of Food and Body*. London: Routledge.

Cowell, R. W. and Philpott, R. A. 2000. *Prehistoric, Romano-British and Medieval Settlement in Lowland North-West England*. Liverpool: National Museums and Galleries on Merseyside.

Coy, J. 1989. 'The provision of fowls and fish for towns', in Serjeantson and Waldron (eds.), pp.25–40.

Cracknell, S. (ed.) 1996. *Roman Alcester: Defences and Defended Area*. CBARR 106: York.

Cracknell, S. and Mahany, C. (eds.) 1994. *Roman Alcester: Southern Extramural Area*. CBARR 97: York.

Cram, L. and Fulford, M. 1979. 'Silchester tile making – the faunal environment', in McWhirr, A. (ed.), *Roman Brick and Tile. Studies in Manufacture, Distribution and Use in the Western Empire*. BAR IS 68: Oxford, pp.201–9.

Creighton, J. 2000. *Coins and Power in Late Iron Age Britain*. Cambridge: Cambridge University Press.

Croom, A. T. 2001. 'Experiments in Roman military cooking methods'. *The Arbeia Journal 6–7* (1997–98): 34–47.

Crummy, N. 1983, *The Roman Small Finds from Excavations in Colchester 1971–9*. CAR 2: Colchester.

Crummy, N., Crummy, P. and Crossan, C. 1993. *Excavations of Roman and later Cemeteries, Churches and Monastic Sites in Colchester, 1971–88*. CAR 9: Colchester.

Crummy, P. 1984. *Excavations at Lion Walk, Balkerne Lane, and Middleborough, Colchester, Essex*. CAR 3: Colchester.

1992. *Excavations at Culver Street, the Gilberd School, and other sites in Colchester 1971–85*. CAR 6: Colchester.

1997. *City of Victory*. Colchester: Colchester Archaeological Trust.

Cubberley, A. L., Lloyd, J. A. and Roberts, P. C. 1988. 'Testa and clibani: the baking covers of classical Italy', *Papers of the British School at Rome* 56: 98–120.

Cunliffe, B. 1971. *Excavations at Fishbourne 1961–1969. Volume II: The Finds*. Leeds: Society of Antiquaries of London.

1984. *Danebury: an Iron Age Hillfort in Hampshire. Volume II. The Excavations 1969–1978: the Finds.* CBARR 52: London.

Cunliffe, B. (ed.) 1988. *The Temple of Sulis Minerva at Bath. Volume II. The Finds from the Sacred Spring.* Oxford: Oxford University Committee for Archaeology.

Cunliffe, B. 2005. *Iron Age Communities in Britain.* London: Routledge 4th edition.

Cunliffe, B. and Davenport, P. 1985. *The Temple of Sulis Minerva at Bath. Volume I. the Site.* Oxford: Oxford University Committee for Archaeology.

Cunliffe, B. and Poole, C. 1991. *Danebury: an Iron Age Hillfort in Hampshire. Volume V: the Excavations 1979–1988: the Finds* CBARR 73b: London.

Curle, J. 1932. 'An inventory of objects of Roman and provincial origin found on sites in Scotland not definitely associated with Roman constructions', *Proc. Soc. Antiquaries Scotland* 66: 277–397.

Curtis, R. I. 1991. *Garum and Salsamata.* Leiden: E. J. Brill.

Dalby, A. 1996. *Siren Feasts.* London: Routledge.

2000. *Empire of Pleasures.* London: Routledge.

Dalby, A., and Granger, S. 1996. *The Classical Cookbook.* London: British Museum Press.

Dannell, G. B. and Wild, J. P. 1987. *Longthorpe II: the Military Works-depot: an Episode in Landscape History.* London: Roman Society.

Dark, K. and Dark, P. 1997. *The Landscape of Roman Britain.* Stroud: Tempus.

Darling, M. J. and Gurney, D. 1993. *Caister-on-Sea. Excavations by Charles Green, 1951–55.* EAA 60: Dereham.

David, E. 1977. *English Bread and Yeast Cookery.* Harmondsworth: Penguin 1979 edition.

Davidson, A. 1999. *The Oxford Companion to Food.* Oxford: Oxford University Press.

Davies, B., Richardson, B. and Tomber, R. 1994. *A Dated Corpus of Early Roman Pottery from the City of London.* CBARR 98. York.

Davies, R. W. 1971. 'The Roman military diet'. *Britannia* 2: 122–42.

Davies, S. M., Bellamy, P. S., Heaton, M. J. and Woodward, P. J. 2002. *Excavations at Alington Avenue, Fordington, Dorchester, Dorset, 1984–87.* Dorchester: Dorset Natural History and Archaeological Society.

Dearne, M. J. and Branigan, K. 1995. 'The use of coal in Roman Britain'. *Antiquaries Journal* 75: 71–105.

De Brisay, K. W. and Evans, K. A. (eds.) 1975. *Salt: the Study of an Ancient Industry.* Colchester: Colchester Archaeological Group.

den Boesterd, M. H. P. 1956. *Description of the Collections in the Rijksmuseum G.M. Kam at Nijmegen V: The Bronze Vessels.* Nijmegen: Dept. of Education Arts and Sciences.

Dickson, C. and Dickson, J. H. 2000. *Plants and People in Ancient Scotland.* Stroud: Tempus.

Dobney, K. M., Jaques, S. D. and Irving, B. G. 1995. *Of Butchers and Breeds. Report on Vertebrate Remains from Various Sites in the City of Lincoln.* Lincoln: City of Lincoln Archaeology Unit.

Douglas, M. 1966. *Purity and Danger*. London: Routledge.

Down, A. 1989. *Chichester Excavations 6*. Chichester: Phillimore.

Draper, J. 1985. *Excavations by Mr H. P. Cooper on the Roman Site at Hill Farm, Gestingthorpe, Essex* EAA 25: Chelmsford.

Drummond, J. C. and Wilbraham, A. 1957. *The Englishman's Food*. London: Pimlico. 1991 reprint of revised edition.

Drummond-Murray, J., Thompson, P. and Cowan, C. 2002. *Settlement in Roman Southwark*. London: Museum of London Archaeological Service.

Drysdale, J. 1983. *Classic Game Cookery*. London: MacMillan.

Durrani, N. 2004. 'Luxury Bath'. *Current Archaeology* 195: 105.

Eckardt, H. 2002. *Illuminating Roman Britain*. Montagnac: Éditions Monique Mergoil.

Edwards, J. 1984. *The Roman Cookery of Apicius*. London: Rider.

Ellis, P. (ed.) 2000. *The Roman Baths and Macellum at Wroxeter*. London: English Heritage.

Esmonde Cleary, S. 2000. 'Summing up', in Wilmott and Wilson (eds.), pp.89–94.

Evans, A. J. 1892. 'On a Late Celtic urn-field at Aylesford, Kent'. *Archaeologia* 52: 316–81.

Evans, D. R. and Metcalf, V. M. 1992. *Roman Gates Caerleon*. Oxford: Oxbow Books.

Evans, E. 2000. *The Caerleon Canabae: Excavations in the Civil Settlement 1984–90*. London: Roman Society.

Evans, J. 1987. 'Graffiti and the evidence of literacy and pottery use in Roman Britain'. *Archaeological Journal* 144: 191–204.

    1993. 'Pottery function and finewares in the Roman north'. *Journal of Roman Pottery Studies* 6: 95–118.

    1995. 'Later Iron Age and 'native' pottery in the north-east', in Vyner, B. (ed.) *Moorland Monuments: Studies in the Archaeology of north-east Yorkshire in honour of Raymond Hayes and Don Spratt*. CBARR 101: York, pp.46–68.

    2000. 'The end of Roman pottery in the north', in Wilmott and Wilson (eds.), pp.39–41.

Evershed, R. P., Dudd, S. N., Lockheart, M. J. and Jim, S. 2001. 'Lipids in Archaeology', in Brothwell and Pollard (eds.), pp.331–49.

Evison, V. I. 2000. 'Glass vessels in England AD 400–1100' in Price, J. (ed.), *Glass in Britain and Ireland AD 350–1100*. British Museum Occasional Paper 127: London, pp.47–104.

Farrar, R. A. H. 1975. 'Prehistoric and Roman saltworks in Dorset' in De Brisay and Evans (eds.), pp.14–20.

Farwell, D. E. and Molleson, T. I. 1993. *Poundbury Volume II: the Cemeteries*. Dorchester: Dorset Natural History and Archaeological Society.

Fitzpatrick, A. P. 2003. 'Roman amphorae in Iron Age Britain'. *Journal of Roman Pottery Studies* 10: 10–25.

Fitzpatrick, A. P. and Morris, E. L. (eds.) 1994. *The Iron Age in Wessex: Recent Work*. Salisbury: Trust for Wessex Archaeology.

Fitzpatrick, A. P. and Timby, J. 2002. 'Roman pottery in Iron Age Britain', in Woodward and Hill (eds.), pp.161–72.

Flemming, R. 2000. 'The physicians at the feast. The place of knowledge at Athenaeus' dinner-table' in Braund and Wilkins (eds.), pp.476–82.

Fox, A. and Ravenhall, W. 1972. 'The Roman fort at Nanstallon, Cornwall'. *Britannia* 3: 56–111.

France, N. E. and Gobel, B. M. 1985. *The Romano-British Temple at Harlow.* Gloucester: Alan Sutting Publishing.

Frere, S. S. 1972. *Verulamium Excavations Volume I.* Oxford: Society of Antiquaries of London.

1974. 'The Roman fortress at Longthorpe'. *Britannia* 5: 1–129.

1987. *Britannia.* London: Routledge. 3rd revised edition.

1991. 'Roman Britain in 1990: sites explored'. *Britannia* 22: 222–92.

Fulford, M. 1975. *New Forest Roman Pottery* BAR BS 17: Oxford.

1979. 'Pottery production and trade at the end of Roman Britain: the case against continuity', in Casey, P. (ed.) *The End of Roman Britain* BAR BS 71: Oxford, pp 120–32.

2001. 'Links with the past: pervasive 'ritual' behaviour in Roman Britain'. *Britannia* 32: 199–218.

Fulford, M., Rippon, S., Ford, S., Timby, J. and Williams, B. 1997. 'Silchester: excavations at the north gate, on the north walls, and in the northern suburbs 1988 and 1991–3'. *Britannia* 28: 87–168.

Gade, D. W. 2000. 'Horse' in Kiple and Ornelas (eds.), pp.542–5.

Gage, J. 1834: 'A plan of barrows called the Bartlow Hills, in the parish of Ashdon, in Essex, with an account of Roman sepulchral relics recently discovered in the lesser barrows'. *Archaeologia* 25: 1–23.

1836: 'The recent discovery of Roman sepulchral relics in one of the greater barrows at Bartlow, in the parish of Ashdon, in Essex'. *Archaeologia* 26: 300–17.

1840: 'An account of further discoveries of Roman sepulchral relics in one of the Bartlow Hills'. *Archaeologia* 28: 1–6.

Gage Rokewode, J. 1842: 'An account of the final excavations made at the Bartlow Hills'. *Archaeologia* 29: 1–4.

Gardner, W. and Savory, H. N. 1964. *Dinorben.* Cardiff: National Museum of Wales.

Garnsey, P. 1999. *Food and Society in Classical Antiquity.* Cambridge: Cambridge University Press.

Germany, M. 2003. *Excavations at Great Holts Farm, Boreham, Essex, 1992–94.* EAA 105: Chelmsford.

Gillam, J. P. and MacIvor, I. 1954. 'The temple of Mithras at Rudchester'. *Archaeologia Aeliana* 4th series 32: 176–219.

Going, C. J. 1987. *The Mansio and other Sites in the South-Eastern Sector of Caesaromagus: the Roman Pottery.* CBARR 62: London.

Going, C. J. and Hunn, J. R. 1999. *Excavations at Boxfield Farm, Chells, Stevenage, Hertfordshire.* Hertford: Hertfordshire Archaeological Trust.

Goldsworthy, A. K. 1998. *The Roman Army At War, 100 BC – 200 AD*. Oxford: Clarendon Press.

Goody, J. 1982. *Cooking Cuisine and Class*. Cambridge: Cambridge University Press.

Gowers, E. 1993. *The Loaded Table*. Oxford: Clarendon Press.

Gozzini Giacosa, I. 1992. *A Taste of Ancient Rome*. (translated by Anna Herklotz). Chicago: University of Chicago Press.

Grant, A. 1981. 'The significance of deer remains at occupation sites of the Iron Age to Anglo-Saxon periods', in Jones and Dimbleby (eds.), pp.205–13.

Grant, M. 1996. *Antithimus: On the Observance of Food*. (Totnes: Prospect Books.)

Graser, E. R. 1940. 'The Edict of Diocletian on maximum prices' in Frank, T. *An Economic Survey of Ancient Rome. Volume V: Rome and Italy of the Empire*. Baltimore: John Hopkins Press, pp.305–421.

Green, C. S. 1987. *Excavations at Poundbury. Volume I: the Settlements*. Dorchester: Dorset Natural History and Archaeological Society.

Green, F. J. 1981. 'Iron Age, Roman and Saxon crops: the archaeological evidence from Wessex', in Jones and Dimbleby (eds.), pp.129–53.

Green, K. 1979. *Report on the Excavations at Usk 1965–1976. The Pre-Flavian Fine Wares*. Cardiff: University of Wales Press.

Green, M. J. 1998. 'Vessels of death: sacred cauldrons in archaeology and myth', *Antiquaries Journal* 78: 63–84.

Greig, J. 1982. 'Garderobes, sewers, cesspits and latrines', *Current Archaeology* 85: 49–52.

Grimes, W. F. 1930. *Holt Denbighshire* Y Cymmrodor 41: London.

Grimm, V. E. 1996. *From Fasting to Feasting: the Evolution of a Sin*. London: Routledge.

Guest, P. S. W. 2005. *The Late Roman Gold and Silver Coins from the Hoxne Treasure*. London: British Museum Press.

Günther, R. T. 1897. 'The oyster culture of the ancient Romans', *Journal Marine Biological Assoc.* 4: 360–5.

Gurney, D. 1986. *Settlement, Religion and Industry on the Roman Fen-edge, Norfolk* EAA 31: Dereham.

Halbaek, H. 1964. 'The Isca grain, a Roman plant introduction in Britain' *New Phytologist* 63: 158–164.

Hall, A. R. and Kenward, H. K. 1990. *Environmental Evidence from the Colonia*. AY 14/6: London.

Hall, A. R., Kenward, H. K. and Williams, D. 1980. *Environmental Evidence from Roman Deposits in Skeldergate*. AY 14/3: London.

Hands, A. R. 1993. *The Romano-British Roadside Settlement at Wilcote, Oxfordshire I Excavations 1990–92*. BAR BS 232: Oxford.

   1998. *The Romano-British Roadside Settlement at Wilcote, Oxfordshire II Excavations 1993–96*. BAR BS 265: Oxford.

Harden, D. B. 1960. 'The Wint Hill hunting bowl and related glasses'. *Journal of Glass Studies* 2: 45–81.

Hartley, D. 1954. *Food in England*. London: Little, Brown. 1999 reprint.

Hartley, K. F. 1973. 'The marketing and distribution of mortaria', in Detsicas, A. (ed.), *Current Research in Romano-British Coarse Pottery*. CBARR 10: London, pp.39–51.

Hartley, K. 1998. 'The incidence of stamped mortaria in the Roman Empire, with special reference to imports to Britain', in Bird, J. (ed.), *Form and Fabric*. Oxford: Oxbow Books, pp.199–217.

Hassall, M. W. C. and Tomlin, R. S. O. 1986. 'Roman Britain in 1985 II: Inscriptions'. *Britannia* 17: 428–54.

Havis, R. and Brooks, H. 2004. *Excavations at Stansted Airport, 1986–91. Volume 1: Prehistoric and Romano-British*. EAA 107: Chelmsford.

Hawkes, C. F. C. and Hull, M. R. 1947. *Camulodunum. First Report on the Excavations at Colchester 1930–1939*. Oxford: Society of Antiquaries of London.

Henig, M. 1984. *Religion in Roman Britain*. London: BT Batsford.
1995. *The Art of Roman Britain*. London: BT Batsford.

Heslop, D. H. 1987. *The Excavation of an Iron Age Settlement at Thorpe Thewles, Cleveland, 1980–1982*. CBARR 65: London.

Hill, J. D. 1989. 'Re-thinking the Iron Age', *Scottish Archaeological Review* 6: 16–24.
2002. 'Just about the potter's wheel? Using, making and depositing Middle and Later Iron Age pots in East Anglia', in Woodward and Hill (eds.), pp.143–60.

Hillman, G. 1981. 'Reconstruction crop husbandry practices from charred remains of crops', in Mercer, R. (ed.) *Farming Practice in British Prehistory*. Edinburgh: Edinburgh University Press, pp.123–62.

Hinchliffe, J., Williams, J. H. and Williams, F. 1992. *Roman Warrington: Excavations at Wilderspool 1966–9 and 1976*. Manchester: Department of Archaeology, Manchester University.

Hingley, R. 2000. *Roman Officers and English Gentlemen*. London: Routledge.

Hinton, P. (ed.) 1988. *Excavations in Southwark 1973–76 Lambeth 1973–79*. London: London and Middlesex and Surrey Archaeological Societies.

Hodder, I. 1982. *Symbols in Action*. Cambridge: Cambridge University Press.

Holbrook, N. (ed.) 1998. *Cirencester: the Roman Town Defences, Public Buildings and Shops*. Cirencester: Cotswold Archaeological Trust.

Holbrook, N. and Bidwell, P. T. 1991. *Roman Finds from Exeter*. Exeter: Exeter City Council and University of Exeter.
1992. 'Roman pottery from Exeter 1980–1990'. *Journal of Roman Pottery Studies* 5: 35–80.

Holden, T. G. 1995. 'The last meals of the Lindow bog men', in Turner, R. C. and Scaife, R. G. (eds.) *New Discoveries and Perspectives*. London: British Museum Press, pp.76–82.

Holland, T. 2003. *Rubicon*. London: Little, Brown.

Hollingsworth, M. 2004. *The Cardinal's Hat*. London: Profile Books.

Holmes, N. 2003. *Excavations of Roman Sites at Cramond Edinburgh*. Edinburgh: Society of Antiquaries of Scotland.

Houlston, M. 1999. 'Excavations at the Mount Roman villa, Maidstone, 1994'. *Archaeologia Cantiana* 109: 71–172.

Huntley, J. P. 2000. 'Late Roman transition in the north: the palynological evidence', in Wilmott and Wilson (eds.), pp.67–71.

Hurst, H. R. 1985. *Kingsholm*. Cambridge: Gloucester Archaeological Publications.

Hurst, H. R. and Pitts, L. F. 1986. *Gloucester, the Roman and Later Defences.* Cambridge: Gloucester Archaeological Publications.

Jackson, R. P. J. and Potter, T. W. 1996. *Excavations at Stonea, Cambridgeshire 1980–85.* London: British Museum Press.

James, S. 2003. 'Writing the legions: the development and future of Roman military studies in Britain'. *Archaeological Journal* 159 (2002): 1–58.

Jansen, W. 2001. 'French bread and Algerian wine: conflicting identities in French Algeria' in Scholliers, P. (ed.), *Food, Drink and Identity* (Oxford: Berg), pp.195–218.

Jarrett, M. G. and Wrathmell, S. 1981. *Whitton: an Iron Age and Roman Farmstead in South Glamorgan.* Cardiff: University of Wales Press.

Jessup, R. F. 1954. 'Excavation of a Roman Barrow at Holborough, Snodland'. *Archaeologia Cantiana* 68: 1–61.

Johns, C. M. 1981. 'The Risley silver lanx: a lost antiquity from Roman Britain'. *Antiquaries Journal* 61: 53–72.

Johns, C. M. and Potter, T. W. 1983. *The Thetford Treasure.* London: British Museum Publications.

   1985. 'The Canterbury late Roman treasure'. *Antiquaries Journal* 65: 321–52.

Johnson, A. P. 1983. *Roman Forts.* London: A. & C. Black.

Johnston, R. F. 2000. 'Pigeons', in Kiple and Ornelas (eds.), pp.561–4.

Jones, D. M. (ed.), 1980. *Excavations at Billingsgate Buildings 'Triangle', Lower Thames Street, London, 1974.* London: London and Middlesex Archaeological Society.

Jones, M. 1981. 'The developments of crop husbandry', in Jones and Dimbleby (eds.), pp.95–127.

Jones, M. and Dimbleby, G. 1981. *The Environment of Man. The Iron Age to the Anglo-Saxon Period.* BAR BS 87: Oxford.

Keevil, G. D. 1992. 'A frying pan from Great Lea, Binfield, Berkshire'. *Britannia* 22: 231–33.

Kenward, H. K., Hall, A. R. and Jones, A. K. G. 1986. *Environmental Evidence from a Roman Well and Anglian Pits in the Legionary Fortress.* AY 14/5: London.

Kenward, H. K. and Williams, D. 1979. *Biological Evidence from the Roman Warehouses in Coney Street.* AY 14/2: London.

Keppie, L. J. F. and Arnold, B. J. 1984. *Corpus Signorum Imperii Romani. Great Britain Volume I Fascicule 4 Scotland.* Oxford: Oxford University Press.

King, A. 1978. 'A comparative survey of bone assemblages from Roman sites in Britain', *Institute of Archaeology Bulletin* 15: 207–32.

   1999. 'Meat diet in the Roman world: a regional inter-site comparison'. *Journal of Roman Archaeology* 12: 168–202.

2005. 'Animal remains from temples in Roman Britain'. *Britannia* 36: 329–69.

King, D. 1987. 'Petrology, dating and distribution of querns and millstones. The results of research in Bedfordshire, Buckinghamshire, Hertfordshire and Middlesex'. *Bulletin of the Institute of Archaeology* 23 (1986): 65–126.

Kiple, K. F. and Ornelas, K. C. (eds.), 2000. *The Cambridge World History of Food.* Cambridge: Cambridge University Press.

Knight, D. 2002. 'A regional ceramic sequence: pottery of the first millennium BC between the Humber and the Nene', in Woodward and Hill (eds.), pp.119–42.

Knights, B. A., Dickson, C. A., Dickson, J. H. and Breeze, D. J. 1983. 'Evidence concerning the Roman military diet at Bearsden, Scotland, in the 2nd century AD'. *Journal of Archaeological Science* 10: 139–52.

Koster, A. 1997. *Description of the Collections in the Provincial Museum G. M. Kam at Nijmegen 13: The Bronze Vessels 2. Acquisitions 1954–1996 (including vessels of pewter and iron).* Nijmegen: Provincie Gelderlan.

Kurlansky, M. 1998. *Cod.* London: Jonathan Cape.

2002. *Salt: a World History.* London: Jonathan Cape.

Lakin, D., Seeley, F., Bird, J., Rielly, K. and Ainsley, C. 2002. *The Roman Tower at Shadwell, London: a Reappraisal.* London: Museum of London Archaeological Service.

Lambert, J. 1996. *Transect through Time. The Archaeological Landscape of the Shell North-Western Ethylene Pipeline.* Lancaster: Lancaster University Archaeological Unit.

Leach, P. 1982. *Ilchester. Volume 1: Excavations 1974–5.* Bristol: Western Archaeological Trust.

Leach, P. and Evans, C. J. 2001. *Fosse Lane, Shepton Mallet 1990.* London: Roman Society.

Leech, R. 1981. 'The excavation of a Romano-British Farmstead and Cemetery on Bradley Hill, Somerton, Somerset'. *Britannia* 12: 177–252.

1982. *Excavations at Catsgore 1970–1973.* Bristol: Western Archaeological Trust.

Lentacker, A., Ervynck, A. and Van Neer, W. 2004. 'The symbolic meaning of the cock: the animal remains from the *mithraeum* at Tienen', in Martens, M. and De Boe, G. (eds.), *Roman Mithraism: the Evidence of the Small Finds.* Brussels: Instituut voor het Archeologisch Patrimonium, pp.57–80.

Leon, E. F. 1943. 'Cato's cakes'. *The Classical Journal* 38: 213–21.

Lethbridge, T. C. 1953. 'Burial of an Iron Age warrior at Snailwell'. *Proc. Cambridge Antiquarian Society* 46 (1952): 25–37.

Longley, D., Johnstone, N. and Evans, J. 1998. 'Excavations on two farms of the Romano-British period at Bryn Eryr and Bush Farm, Gwynedd'. *Britannia* 29: 185–246.

Luard, E. 1986. *European Peasant Cookery.* London: Corgi edition 1988.

Luff, R. 1993. *Animal Bones from Excavations in Colchester, 1971–85.* CAR 12: Colchester.

Mackreth, D. F. 1996. *Orton Hall Farm: a Roman and Early Anglo-Saxon Farmstead.* EAA 76: Manchester.

McCarthy, M. R. 1990. *A Roman, Anglian and Medieval site at Blackfriars Street, Carlisle Excavations 1977–9*. Kendall: Cumberland and Westmorland Antiquarian and Archaeological Society.

1991. *Roman Waterlogged Remains and Later Features at Castle St., Carlisle*. Kendal: Cumberland and Westmorland Antiquarian and Archaeological Society.

2000. *Roman and Medieval Carlisle: the Southern Lanes*. Carlisle: Dept of Archaeological Sciences, University of Bradford.

MacGregor, A. 1976. *Finds from a Roman Sewer System and an Adjacent Building in Church Street*. AY 17/1: London.

MacGregor, M. 1976. *Early Celtic Art in North Britain*. Leicester: Leicester University Press.

MacKinder, A. 2000. *A Romano-British Cemetery on Watling Street*. London: Museum of London Archaeological Service.

McKinley, J. I. 2000. 'Phoenix rising: aspects of cremation in Roman Britain', in Pearce *et al.* pp.38–44.

McWhirr, A., Viner, L. and Wells, C. 1982. *Romano-British Cemeteries at Cirencester*. Cirencester: Cirencester Excavation Committee.

Malcolmson, R. and Mastoris, S. 1998. *The English Pig*. London: Hambledon Press.

Maltby, M. 1981. 'Iron Age, Romano-British and Anglo-Saxon animal husbandry – a review of the faunal evidence', in Jones and Dimbleby, pp.155–203.

1985. 'Assessing variations in Iron Age and Roman butchery practices: the need for quantification', in Fieller, N. R. J., Gilbertson, D. D. and Ralph, N. G. A. (eds.), *Paleaobiological investigations: research design methods and data analysis*. BAR IS 266 : Oxford, pp.19–30.

1994. 'Animal exploitation in Iron Age Wessex', in Fitzpatrick and Morris (eds.), pp.9–10.

1997. 'Domestic fowl on Romano-British sites: inter-site comparisons of abundance'. *International Journal of Osteoarchaeology* 7: 402–14.

Manning, W. H. 1983. 'The cauldron chain of Iron Age and Roman Britain', in Hartley, B. and Wacher, J. (eds.), *Rome and her Northern Provinces*. Gloucester: Alan Sutton, pp.132–54.

1985. *Catalogue of the Romano-British Iron Tools, Fittings and Weapons in the British Museum*. London: British Museum Press.

Marsh, G. D. 1978. 'Early second century fine wares in the London area', in Arthur, P. R. and Marsh, G. D. (eds.), *Early Fine Wares in Roman Britain*. BAR BS 57: Oxford, pp.119–223.

Martin-Kilcher, S. 1994. *Die römischen Amphoren aus Augst und Kaiseraugst: ein Beitrag zur römischen Handels- und Kulturgeschichte. 2: die Amphoren für Wein, Fischsauce, Süfrücte (Gruppen 2–24) und Gesamtaswertung*. Basel: Römermuseum Augst.

2003. 'Fish-sauce amphorae from the Iberian peninsula: the forms and observations on trade with the north-west provinces'. *Journal of Roman Pottery Studies* 10: 69–84.

Matthews, C. L. 1981. *A Romano-British inhumation cemetery at Dunstable* (=*Bedfordshire Archaeological Journal 15*).

Mattingly, D. J. (ed.) 1997. *Dialogues in Roman Imperialism* Journal of Roman Archaeology Supplementary Series 23: Portsmouth, Rhode Island.

May, J. 1996. *Dragonby*. Oxford: Oxbow Books.

Mays, S. 1998. *The Archaeology of Human Bones*. London: Routledge.

Meadows, I. 1996. 'Wollaston: The Nene Valley, a British Moselle?' *Current Archaeology* 150: 212–5.

Merrifield, R. 1987. *The Archaeology of Ritual and Magic*. London: BT Batsford.

Miles, A. 1975. 'Salt-panning in Romano-British Kent', in De Brisay and Evans (eds.), pp.26–31.

Miles, D., Palmer, S., Smith, A. and Edgeley Long, G. forthcoming. *Iron Age and Roman settlement in the Upper Thames Valley: excavations at Claydon Pike and other sites within the Cotswold Water Park*. Oxford: Oxford Archaeology.

Miller, J. I. 1969. *The Spice Trade of the Roman Empire*. Oxford: Clarendon Press.

Miller, L., Schofield, J. and Rhodes, M. 1986. *The Roman Quay at St Magnus House, London*. London: London and Middlesex Archaeological Society.

Millett, M. 1979. 'An approach to the functional interpretation of pottery', in Millett, M. (ed.) *Pottery and the Archaeologist*. London: Institute of Archaeology, pp.35–47.

    1987. 'An early Roman burial tradition in central southern England'. *Oxford Journal of Archaeology* 6: 63–8.

    1990. *The Romanization of Britain*. Cambridge: Cambridge University Press.

    1999. '*Coloniae* and Romano-British studies' in Hurst, H. (ed.) *The Coloniae of Roman Britain: New Studies and a Review*. Portsmouth Rhode Island: Journal of Roman Archaeology Supplementary Series 36, pp.191–6.

    1996. 'Characterising Roman London' in Bird *et al.* (eds.), pp.33–7.

Milne, G. and Wardle, A. 1996. 'Early Roman development at Leadenhall Court, London and related research'. *Trans. London and Middlesex Archaeological Soc.*, 44 (1993): 23–169.

Monaghan, J. 1993. *Roman Pottery from the Fortress*. AY 16/7: York.

    1997. *Roman Pottery from York*. AY 16/8: York.

Moreno Garcia, M., Orton C. R. and Rackham, D. J. 1996. 'A new statistical tool for comparing animal bone assemblages'. *Journal of Archaeological Science* 23: 437–53.

Morris, E. 1994. 'Production and distribution of pottery and salt in Iron Age Britain: a review'. *Proc. Prehistoric Soc.* 60: 371–94.

Muir, E. 1954. *An Autobiography*. London: Methuen revised edition.

Neal, D. S. 1974. *The Excavation of the Roman Villa in Gadebridge Park, Hemel Hempstead 1963–8*. London: Society of Antiquaries of London.

    1996. *Excavations on the Roman Villa at Beadlam, Yorkshire*. Leeds: Yorkshire Archaeological Society.

Neal, D. S., Wardle, A. and Hunn, J. 1990. *Excavation of the Iron Age, Roman and Medieval Settlement at Gorhambury, St. Albans*. London: English Heritage.

Nevell, M. 2005. 'Salt making in Cheshire: the Iron Age Background', in Nevell and Fielding (eds.), pp.9–14.

Nevell, M. and Fielding, A. P. (eds.) 2005. *Brine on Britannia.* (= *Archaeology North West* 7 (Issue 17 for 2004–2005).

Niblett, R. 1985. *Sheepen: an Early Roman Industrial Site at Camulodunum.* CBARR 57: London.

1999. *The Excavation of a Ceremonial Site at Folly Lane, Verulamium.* London: Roman Society.

Nuber, H-U. 1972. 'Kanne und Griffschale. Ihr Gebrauch im täglichen Leben und die Beigabe in Gräbern der römischen Kaiserzeit', *Bericht der Römisch-germanischen Kommission* 53: 1–232.

O'Connor, T. 1988. *Bones from the General Accident site, Tanner Row.* AY 15/2: London.

1989. '"What shall we have for dinner?" Food remains from urban sites', in Serjeantson and Waldron (eds), pp.13–23.

2000. *The Archaeology of Animal Bones.* Stroud: Sutton Publishing.

2001. 'Animal bone quantification', in Brothwell and Pollard (eds.), pp.703–10.

Orton, C. 1993. 'How many pots make five? An historical review of pottery quantification'. *Archaeometry* 35: 169–84.

1996. 'Dem dry bones' in Bird *et al.* (eds.), pp.199–208.

Oswald, F. 1943. 'The mortaria of Margidunum and their development from AD 50 to 400'. *Antiquaries Journal* 22: 45–63.

Ottaway, P. 2001. 'Excavations on the site of the Roman signal station at Carr Naze, Filey, 1993–94'. *Archaeological Journal* 157 (2000): 79–199.

Painter, K. S. 1977a. *The Mildenhall Treasure.* London: British Museum Press.

1977b. *The Water Newton Early Christian Silver.* London: British Museum Press.

2001. *The Insula of the Menander at Pompeii. Volume IV: the Silver Treasure.* Oxford: Clarendon Press.

Parker, A. J. 1988. 'The birds of Roman Britain'. *Oxford Journal of Archaeology* 7: 197–226.

Parrington, M. 1978. *The Excavation of an Iron Age Settlement, Bronze Age Ring-ditches and Roman Features at Ashville Trading Estate, Abingdon, (Oxfordshire), 1974–76.* CBARR 28: London.

Partridge, C. 1981. *Skeleton Green, a Late Iron Age and Romano-British site.* London: Roman Society.

Peacock, D. P. S. 1977. 'Pompeian red ware' in Peacock, D. P. S. (ed.), *Pottery and Early Commerce. Characterization and Trade in Roman and Later Ceramics.* London: Academic Press, pp.147–62.

Peacock, D. P. S. and Williams, D. F. 1986. *Amphorae and the Roman Economy.* London: Longman.

Pearce, J. 2002. 'Food as substance and symbol in the Roman army: a case study from Vindolanda', in Freeman, P., Bennett, J., Fiema, Z. T. and Hoffmann, B. (eds.), *Limes XVIII. Proceedings for the XVIIIth International Congress of Roman Studies held in Amman, Jordan (September 2000).* BAR IS 1084: Oxford, pp.931–44.

Pearce, J., Millett, M. and Struck, M. (eds.) 2000. *Burial, Society and Context in the Roman World.* Oxford: Oxbow Books.

Penney, S. and Shotter, D. C. A. 1996. 'An inscribed Roman salt-pan from Shavinton, Cheshire'. *Britannia* 27: 360–5.

Perrin, J. R. 1981. *Roman Pottery from the Colonia: Skeldergate and Bishophill.* AY 16/2: London.

1990. *Roman Pottery from the Colonia 2: General Accident and Rougier Street.* AY 16/4: London.

Perring, D. 2003. '"Gnosticism" in fourth-century Britain: the Frampton mosaics reconsidered'. *Britannia* 34: 97–127.

Philpott, R. 1991. *Burial Practices in Roman Britain.* BAR BS 219: Oxford.

Piggott, S. 1952–53. 'Three metal-work hoards of the Roman period from southern Scotland'. *Proc. Soc. Antiquaries of Scotland* 87: 1–50.

Pitts, L. and St Joseph, J. K. 1985. *Inchtuthil: the Roman Legionary Fortress Excavations 1952–65.* London: Roman Society.

Pollard, R. J. 1988. *The Roman Pottery of Kent.* Maidstone: Kent Archaeological Society.

Porter, R. and Rousseau, G. S. 1998. *Gout: the Patrician Malady.* New Haven: Yale University Press.

Potter, T. W. and Trow, S. D. 1988. *Puckeridge-Braughing, Hertfordshire: the Ermine Street Excavations 1971–72* (= *Hertfordshire Archaeology* 10).

Price, E. 2000. *Frocester. Volume 1: the Site.* Stonehouse: Gloucester and District Archaeological Research Group.

Price, J. 1996. 'A ribbed bowl from a late Iron Age burial at Hertford Heath, Hertfordshire', *Annales du 13e Congrès de l'Association Internationale pour l'Histoire du Verre.* Lochem: AIHV, pp.47–54.

Price, J., Brooks, I. P. and Maynard, D. J. 1997. *The Archaeology of the St. Neots to Duxford Gas Pipeline.* BAR BS 255: Oxford.

Protz, R. 1995. *The Ultimate Encyclopaedia of Beer.* London: Carlton Books.

Purcell, N. 1995. 'Eating Fish: the paradoxes of seafood', in Wilkins *et al.* (eds.), pp.132–49.

Quinnell, H. 2004. *Trethurgy.* Truro: Cornwall County Council.

Rae, A. and Rae, V. 1974. 'The Roman fort at Cramond, Edinburgh, excavations 1954–1966'. *Britannia* 5: 163–224.

Rahtz, P. and Watts, L. 2004. *Wharram. A Study of Settlement on the Yorkshire Wolds, IX. The North Manor Area and North-west Enclosure.* York: York University Archaeological Publications.

Richards, M. P., Hedges, R. E. M., Molleson, T. I. and Vogel, J. C. 1998. 'Stable isotope analysis reveals variations in human diet at the Poundbury Camp cemetery site'. *Journal of Archaeological Science* 25: 1247–52.

Richmond, I. A. and Gillam, J. P. 1951. 'The temple of Mithras at Carrawburgh'. *Archaeologia Aeliana* Series 4 29: 1–92.

Rickett, R. 1995. *The Anglo-Saxon Cemetery at Spong Hill, North Elmham, Part VII: the Iron Age, Roman and early Saxon settlement.* EAA 73: Dereham.

Rivet, A. L. F. and Smith, C. 1979. *The Place-names of Roman Britain.* London: BT Batsford.

Roberts, C. and Manchester, K. 1995. *The Archaeology of Disease.* Stroud: Sutton Publishing 2nd edition.

Roberts, I. (ed.), 2005. *Ferrybridge Henge: the Ritual Landscape.* Wakefield: West Yorkshire Archaeological Services.

Roberts, I., Burgess, A. and Berg, D. 2001. *A New Link to the Past. The Archaeological Landscape of the M1-A1 Link Road.* Wakefield: West Yorkshire Archaeological Services.

Rodwell, K. 1988. *The Prehistoric and Roman Settlement at Kelvedon, Essex.* CBARR 63: London.

Rogerson, A. 1977. 'Excavations at Scole, 1973'. EAA 5: 97–224.

Roth, J. P. 1999. *The Logistics of the Roman Army at War (264 BC – AD 235).* Leiden: Brill.

Rule, M. and Monaghan, J. 1993. *A Gallo-Roman Trading Vessel from Guernsey.* Guernsey: Guernsey Museum.

Rush, P., Dickinson, B., Hartley, B. and Hartley, K. F. 2000. *Roman Castleford. Excavations 1974–85 Volume III: the Pottery.* Wakefield: West Yorkshire Archaeological Services.

Salway, P. 1993. *The Oxford Illustrated History of Roman Britain.* Oxford: Oxford University Press.

Sanquer, R. and Galliou, P. 1972. 'Garum, sel et salaisons en Armorique Gallo-Romaine', *Gallia* 30: 199–223.

Saunders, C. 1978. 'The iron firedog from Welwyn, Hertfordshire, reconsidered'. *Hertfordshire Archaeology* 5 (1977): 13–21.

Savory, H. N. 1971. *Excavations at Dinorben, 1965–9.* Cardiff: National Museum of Wales.

Scarborough, J. 1995. 'The opium poppy in Hellenistic and Roman medicine' in Porter, R. and Teich, M. (eds.) *Drugs and Narcotics in History.* Cambridge: Cambridge University Press, pp.4–23.

Sealey, P. R. 1985. *Amphoras from the 1970 Excavations at Colchester Sheepen.* BAR BS 142: Oxford.

Sealey, P. R. and Davies, G. M. R. 1984. 'Falernian wine at Roman Colchester'. *Britannia* 15: 250–4.

Sealey, P. R. and Tyers, P. A. 1989. 'Olives from Roman Spain: a unique amphora find in British waters'. *Antiquaries Journal* 69: 53–72.

Serjeantson, D. and Waldron, T. (eds.), 1989. *Diet and Craft in Towns.* BAR BS 199: Oxford.

Sharples, N. F. 1991. *Maiden Castle: Excavation and Field Survey 1985–6.* London: English Heritage.

Shennan, S. 1997. *Quantifying Archaeology.* Edinburgh: Edinburgh University Press. 2nd edition.

Shepherd, J. 1998. *The Temple of Mithras London.* London: English Heritage.

Shotter, D. 2005. 'Salt proprietors in Cheshire. Realities and possibilities', in Nevell and Fielding (eds.), pp.41–6.

Smith, R. A. 1912. 'On Late-Celtic antiquities discovered at Welwyn, Herts'. *Archaeologia* 63: 1–30.

Smith, R. J. C. 1993. *Excavations at County Hall, Dorchester, Dorset, 1988*. Salisbury: Wessex Archaeology.

Smith, R. J. C., Healy, F., Allen, M. J., Morris, E. L., Barnes, I. and Woodward, P. J. 1997. *Excavations along the Route of the Dorchester By-pass, Dorset, 1986–8*. Salisbury: Wessex Archaeology.

Snape, M. and Bidwell, P. 2002. 'Excavation at Castle Garth. Newcastle upon Tyne, 1976–92 and 1995–6: the Excavation of the Roman fort'. *Archaeologia Aeliana 5th Series* 31: 1–249.

Sparey-Green, C. 2002. *Excavations on the south-eastern Defences and Extramural Settlement of Little Chester, Derby* (= *Derbyshire Archaeological Journal* 122).

Stead, I. M. 1967. 'A La Tène Burial at Welwyn Garden City'. *Archaeologia* 101: 1–62.

Stead, I. M. and Rigby, V. 1986. *Baldock. The Excavation of a Roman and pre-Roman Settlement, 1968–72*. London: Roman Society.

    1989. *Verulamium. The King Harry Lane Site*. London: English Heritage.

Stefani, G. (ed.) 2005. *Cibi e Sapori a Pompei e Dintorni*. Pompei: Soprendenza Archeologica di Pompei.

Steingarten, J. 1998. *The Man who ate Everything*. London: Headline Book Publishing.

Steures, D. C. 2002. 'Late Roman thirst: how dark coloured drinking sets from Trier were used'. *Bulletin Antieke Beschaving* 77: 175–9.

Stirland, A. and Waldron, T. 1990. 'The earliest cases of tuberculosis in Britain'. *Journal of Archaeological Science* 17: 221–30.

Stokes, P. 1996. 'Debris from Roman butchery: a new interpretation'. *Petits Propos Culinaire* 52: 38–47.

Strong, D. E. 1966. *Greek and Roman Gold and Silver Plate*. London: Methuen.

Symonds, R. P. 2003. 'Romano-British amphorae'. *Journal of Roman Pottery Studies* 10: 50–9.

Symonds, R. P. and Wade, S. 1999. *Roman Pottery from Excavations in Colchester, 1971–86*. Colchester: CAR 10: Colchester.

Swan, V. G. 1992. 'Legion VI and its men: African legionaries in Britain'. *Journal of Roman Pottery Studies* 5: 1–33.

Tassinari, S. 1993. *Il Vasellame Bronzeo di Pompei*. Rome: 'L'Erma' di Bretschneider.

Tchernia, A. 1986. *Le Vin de l'Italie Romaine*. Rome: École Française de Rome.

Tchernia, A. and Brun, J.-P. 1999. *Le Vin Romain Antique*. Grenoble: Glénat.

Thompson, D. 2002. *Thai Food*. London: Pavilion Books.

Timby, J. R. 1998. *Excavations at Kingscote and Wycomb, Gloucestershire*. Cirencester: Cotswold Archaeology.

Tomalin, D. 1989. 'A Roman symmetrical flanged bronze strainer found in Surrey and its counterparts in Highland Britain'. *Surrey Archaeological Collections* 79: 53–65.

Tomlin, R. S. O. 1992. 'The Roman 'carrot' amphora and its Egyptian provenance'. *Journal Egyptian Archaeology* 78: 307–12.

1996. 'A five-acre wood in Roman Kent' in Bird *et al.* (eds.), pp.209–15.

1998. 'Roman manuscripts from Carlisle: the ink-written tablets', *Britannia* 29: 31–84.

Toynbee, J. M. C. 1971. *Death and Burial in the Roman World.* Baltimore: Johns Hopkins. 1996 reprint.

Tuffreau-Libre, M. 1992. *La Céramique Commune Gallo-Romaine dans le Nord de la France.* Paris: Errance.

Turner, R. 1999. *Excavations of an Iron Age settlement and Roman Religious Complex at Ivy Chimneys, Witham, Essex 1978–83.* EAA 88: Chelmsford.

Tyers, P. 1984. 'An assemblage of Roman ceramics from London'. *The London Archaeologist* 4.14: 367–74.

1996. *Roman Pottery in Britain.* London: Routledge.

van der Veen, M. 1985. 'Evidence for crop plants from north-east England: an interim overview with discussion of new results' in Fieller, N. R. J., Gilbertson, D. D. and Ralph, N. G. A. (eds.) *Palaeobiological Investigation Research Design; Methods and Data Analysis* Oxford: BAR IS 266, pp.197–219.

1991. 'Charred grain assemblages from Roman-period corn driers in Britain'. *Archaeological Journal* 146 (1989): 302–19.

van Driel Murray, C., Wild, J. P., Seaward, M. and Hillam, J. 1993. *Preliminary Reports on the Leather, Textiles, Environmental Evidence and Dendrochronology.* Hexham: Roman Army Museum Publications.

Vaughan, J. G. and Geissler, C. A. 1997. *The New Oxford Book of Food Plants.* Oxford: Oxford University Press.

Vernon, K. 2000. 'Milk and dairy products' in Kiple and Ornelas (eds.), pp.692–702.

Wacher, J. 1995. *The Towns of Roman Britain.* London: BT Batsford, revised edition.

Waldron, T. 1989. 'The effects of urbanisation on human health' in Serjeantson and Waldron (eds.), pp.55–73.

Ward, S. 1988. *Excavations at Chester. 12 Watergate Street 1985: Roman Headquarters Building to Medieval Row.* Chester: Chester City Council.

Webster, G. 1980. *The Roman Invasion of Britain.* London: BT Batsford.

2002. *The Legionary Fortress at Wroxeter.* London: English Heritage.

Wenham, L. P. 1968. *The Romano-British Cemetery at Trentholme Drive, York.* London: HMSO.

Wenham, L. P. and Heywood, B. 1997. *The 1968 to 1970 Excavations in the Vicus at Malton, North Yorkshire.* Leeds: Yorkshire Archaeological Society.

White, K. D. 1995. 'Cereals, bread and milling in the Roman world' in Wilkins *et al.* (eds.), pp.38–43.

Whitwell, J. B. 1976. *The Church Street Sewer and an Adjacent Building.* AY3/1: London.

Wilkins, J., Harvey, D. and Dobson, M. 1995. *Food in Antiquity.* Exeter: University of Exeter Press.

Willcox, G. H. 1977. 'Exotic plants from Roman waterlogged sites in London'. *Journal of Archaeological Science* 4: 269–82.

Williams, D. and Carreras, C. 1995. 'North African amphorae in Roman Britain: a re-appraisal'. *Britannia* 26: 231–52.

Williams, D. and Evans, J. 1991. 'A fragment from a probable Roman *Clibanus* from Catterick, North Yorkshire'. *Journal of Roman Pottery Studies* 4: 51–3.

Williams, D. F. and Peacock, D. P. S. 1983. 'The importation of olive oil into Iron Age and Roman Britain' in Blázquez Martínez, J. M. and Remesal Rodríguez, J. (eds.) *Produccion y comercio del aceite en la Antiquedad 2°congreso internacional.* Madrid: Universidad Computense, pp.263–80.

1994. 'Roman amphorae in Iron Age Wessex' in Fitzpatrick and Morris (eds.), pp.29–32.

Williams, R. J. and Zepvat, R. J. 1994. *Bancroft: a late Bronze Age/Iron Age Settlement, Roman Villa and Temple Complex.* Aylesbury: Buckinghamshire Archaeological Society.

Williams-Thorpe, O. and Thorpe, R. S. 1988. 'The provenance of donkey mills from Roman Britain'. *Archaeometry* 30: 275–89.

Willis, S. 1996. 'The Romanization of pottery assemblages in the east and north-east of England during the 1st century AD. a comparative analysis'. *Britannia* 27: 179–221.

2002. 'A date with the past: late Bronze and Iron Age pottery and chronology', in Woodward and Hill (eds.), pp.4–21.

Wilmott, T. 1997. *Birdoswald.* London: English Heritage.

Wilmott, T and Wilson, P. (eds.), 2000. *The Late Roman Transition in the North.* BAR BS 299: Oxford.

Wilson, P. R. 1989. 'Aspects of the Yorkshire signal stations', in Maxfield, V. A. and Dobson, M. J. (eds.), *Roman Frontier Studies 1989. Proceedings 15th International Congress of Roman Frontier Studies.* Exeter: Exeter University Press, pp.142–7.

2002a. Cataractonium *Roman Catterick and its Hinterland. Excavations and Research, 1958–1997. Part II.* CBARR 128: York.

2002b. Cataractonium *Roman Catterick and its Hinterland. Excavations and Research, 1958–1997. Part I.* CBARR 129: York.

Winder, J. M. 1992. A Study in the Variation of Oyster Shells from Archaeological Sites and a Discussion of Oyster Exploitation. PhD thesis, University of Southampton.

Woodiwiss, S. (ed.) 1992. *Iron Age and Roman salt production and the medieval town of Droitwich: Excavations at the Old Bowling Green and Friar Street.* CBARR 81: London.

Woodward, A. and Hill, J. D. (eds.), 2002. *Prehistoric Britain: the Ceramic Basis.* Oxford: Prehistoric Ceramics Research Group.

Woodward, A. and Leach, P. 1993 *The Uley Shrines. Excavation of a Ritual Complex on West Hill, Uley, Gloucestershire: 1977–9.* London: English Heritage.

Woodward, P. J., Davies, S. M. and Graham, A. H. 1993. *Excavations at the Old Methodist Chapel and Greyhound Yard, Dorchester, 1981–1984.* Dorchester: Dorset Natural History and Archaeological Society.

Woolf, G. 1998. *Becoming Roman.* Cambridge: Cambridge University Press.

Wrathmell, S. and Nicholson, A. (eds.), 1990. *Dalton Parlours: Iron Age Settlement and Roman Villa.* Wakefield: West Yorkshire Archaeological Service.

Young, C. J. 1977. *The Roman Pottery Industry of the Oxford Region.* Oxford: BAR BS 43.

Zienkiewicz, J. D. 1986. *The Legionary Fortress Baths at Caerleon: II the Finds.* Cardiff: National Museum of Wales.

1992. 'Pottery from excavations on the site of the Roman Legionary Museum, Caerleon 1983–5'. *Journal of Roman Pottery Studies* 5: 81–109.

1993. 'Excavations in the *Scamnum Tribunorum* at Caerleon: the Legionary Museum Site, 1983–5'. *Britannia* 24: 27–140.

Index

(NB. British place names given without county affiliations are unitary authorities).

Moving Towards the Virtual Workplace

Moving Towards the Virtual Workplace

Managerial and Societal Perspectives on Telework

Viviane Illegems

*Department of Business Economics and Strategic Management,
Vrije Universiteit Brussel, Belgium*

Alain Verbeke

*Templeton College, University of Oxford, UK
Haskayne School of Business, University of Culgary, Canada*

PARK LEARNING CENTRE
UNIVERSITY OF GLOUCESTERSHIRE
PO Box 220, The Park, Cheltenham, GL50 2QF
Tel: (01242) 532721

Edward Elgar
Cheltenham, UK • Northampton, MA, USA

© Viviane Illegems and Alain Verbeke 2003

All rights reserved. No part of this publication may be reproduced, stored in a retrieval system or transmitted in any form or by any means, electronic, mechanical or photocopying, recording, or otherwise without the prior permission of the publisher.

Published by
Edward Elgar Publishing Limited
Glensanda House
Montpellier Parade
Cheltenham
Glos GL50 1UA
UK ·

Edward Elgar Publishing, Inc.
136 West Street
Suite 202
Northampton
Massachusetts 01060
USA

A catalogue record for this book
is available from the British Library

Library of Congress Cataloguing in Publication Data

Illegems, Viviane, 1973-
  Moving towards the virtual workplace : managerial and societal perspectives on telework / Viviane Illegems, Alain Verbeke.
    p. cm.
  Includes bibliographical references and index.
  1. Telecommuting. 2. Telecommuting—Management. 3. Telecommuting—Social aspects. I. Verbeke, Alain. II. Title.

HD2336.3.I44 2004
331.25—dc21

2003049261

ISBN 1 84376 504 7

Printed and bound in Great Britain by MPG Books Ltd, Bodmin, Cornwall

CONTENTS

FIGURES

TABLES

ACKNOWLEDGMENTS

The research reported in this book was supported by the Fund for Scientific Research-Flanders (Fonds voor Wetenschappelijk Onderzoek-Vlaanderen) and the Scientific Services of the Belgian Prime Minister's Office (Federale diensten voor Wetenschappelijke, Technologische en Culturele Aangelegenheden van de Eerste Minister). The generous financial support from both foundations is gratefully acknowledged.

Chapter 3 and Chapter 4 draw upon an earlier article published in the journal *Technological Forecasting and Social Change*, and excerpts are included here with permission from Elsevier Science. We would like to thank Elsevier Science for their cooperation in this matter.

Many individuals supported the completion of this book. We should like to thank especially Professor Rosette S'Jegers, our colleague at the Vrije Universiteit Brussel. Her comments on earlier versions of the book greatly improved the final product. We would also like to express our gratitude to Dr Brad Abernathy, who edited the entire volume and turned a rather impenetrable manuscript into a readable text. The competent and patient editorial staff at Edward Elgar, especially Ms Francine Sullivan, were instrumental to the initial manuscript's transformation into the present book.

The empirical part of our research could not have been completed without the valuable input of 83 human resources managers and 261 employees of Brussels-based companies, who participated in our surveys.

Finally, we should like to thank our families and friends for their on-going support of our efforts to complete this monograph.

1. INTRODUCTION

The simple act of work-related travel has negative consequences that many of us never think about. Work-related travel takes time and consumes energy. It also causes air pollution, noise pollution, traffic congestion and road accidents. For some employees, work-related travel causes tensions between family life and work. And, since the terrorist attacks in the United States on 11 September 2001, work-related air travel is considered less safe than before.

Telework - the substitution of telecommunication technology for any work-related travel - can alleviate many of these problems (the European term 'telework' is broader than the American term 'telecommuting': telecommuting is a subset of telework, because telecommuting involves only the substitution for the daily commute to and from work).

From a public policy perspective, telework is unlike most other policy tools used to manage work-related travel (such as road pricing). Telework involves a partial or total substitution of the commuting trip, not just a shift of time or mode. Furthermore, telework implementation does not require high public expenditure. Telework can create new job opportunities for groups formerly excluded from the labour markets (for example, people with disabilities and parents with young children or elderly dependants), and it can help alleviate geographic skill shortages. Telework can help in both rural and urban areas. On the one hand, rural areas implement telework as a tool for economic development. Urban areas, on the other hand, generally implement telework to reduce road congestion and air pollution.

Employers implement telework because it can reduce costs and increase productivity, and because employees often perceive it as a benefit.

For their part, employees generally choose telework because it increases flexibility and reduces commuting stress. For some employees, telework is the only way to join the workforce.

This book asks the following questions:

1. What are the advantages and disadvantages of telework, for employers, employees and society at large?
2. Where should policy-makers and employers attempt to implement telework? (Which sectors of the economy? Which jobs? Which employees?)
3. What is the most effective way to implement telework?
4. What policy tools are most appropriate for supporting telework implementation?

The core of this book includes the following five Chapters. In Chapter 2, we try to give the reader an in-depth understanding of both the macro-level, societal **problems** associated with work-related travel (air pollution, noise pollution, traffic congestion, road accidents, etc.) and the tool we propose as an important part of the **solution**: telework. Chapter 2

1. presents a conceptual framework for evaluating policy tools, which can serve a variety of societal and micro-level purposes simultaneously;
2. establishes the societal need for some sort of policy tool to complement road pricing in managing private transport's externalities;
3. introduces and defines 'telework.'

In Chapter 3, we use the general conceptual framework from Chapter 2 and take a closer look at telework's problems of **procedural effectiveness** - i.e., the psychological, sociological and institutional impediments that interfere with telework implementation at the managerial level. To that end, we present a telework-specific conceptual framework that models the implementation of telework. This conceptual framework identifies **target group implementation potential** as the key element determining telework adoption. The target group implementation potential is affected itself by a large number of environmental and individual-level parameters.[1] In our conceptual framework, the decision to implement telework is affected by various factors, each of which we examine in detail:

1. three **environmental** components: the technological, institutional and organizational environments, and
2. the **individual-level** features of the particular employee.

We then apply this conceptual framework to the city of Brussels (the capital of Belgium and the European Union). Drawing on a detailed transport survey of both employers and employees, we identify which employers and employees are most likely to adopt telework, and why.

In Chapter 4, we empirically apply the **environmental** components of our conceptual framework to the city of Brussels. Using data from a survey of 83 organizations in Brussels, we answer a number of managerially relevant questions, such as:

1. What kinds of organizations are likely to have already implemented telework, or to implement it in the future?
2. From the employer's point of view, what are the advantages and disadvantages of telework, and how do employers rate those advantages and disadvantages?
3. In what ways do employers with telework experience perceive telework's advantages and disadvantages differently from employers without telework experience?
4. From the employer's perspective, what public policy tools would most effectively promote telework?

In Chapter 5, we empirically apply the **individual-level** components of our conceptual framework to the city of Brussels, examining the advantages and disadvantages of telework from the employee's point of view. Using data from a survey of 261 employees, we answer such questions as:

1. What kinds of individuals are likely to be teleworking now, or to become teleworkers in the future?
2. From the employee's point of view, what are the advantages and disadvantages of telework, and how do employees rate those advantages and disadvantages?
3. In what ways do employees with telework experience perceive telework's advantages and disadvantages differently from employees without telework experience?

In Chapter 6, we again adopt a societal perspective and attempt to quantify some of the monetary savings of adopting telework. Specifically, we quantify the monetary impact of telework on road transport externalities (e.g., air pollution, noise pollution, traffic congestion), again using the example of Brussels.

We have written this book for three core groups of readers. First, anyone who is an employee in a large organization may be interested in the introduction to telework in Chapters 2 and 3, as well as Chapter 5's survey of Brussels employees. Second, employers will likely be interested in that material, plus Chapter 4's survey of Brussels employers and that chapter's discussion of how and where to best implement telework and empirically measure its effects at the company level. Third, policy-makers and transport economists will likely be interested in all of the above, plus Chapter 6's technical material on empirically assessing the details of telework's impact as an externality-reducing policy tool. The discussion at the end of Chapter 4 about the public policy tools most appropriate for supporting telework implementation may also be of interest to this audience. This book's information about the current number of teleworkers and the growth patterns of telework is relevant to a wide variety of policy-makers. The way that traditional patterns of office-based employment are breaking down and being replaced by remote work forms will influence regional development policy, transport policy, environmental policy, urban planning policy and labour policy. [2]

We have assumed that the reader has a basic understanding of economics and statistics, but we have tried to make the material as understandable as possible for those readers who do not. All material requiring a prior understanding of economics or statistics has been placed in the Appendices.

NOTES

---

[1]   In this respect, we think our model improves on the models of researchers (Mahmassani et al. 1993, Bernardino et al. 1992, Mokhtarian and Salomon 1994; 1997) who assess only individual-level parameters. Our model also improves on the models of researchers (such as Kugelmass 1995, Nilles 1998 and Jackson and van der Wielen 1998) who have investigated the impact of environmental parameters.

[2]   Huws et al. (1999).

2. A SOCIETAL PERSPECTIVE ON TELEWORK

2.1 INTRODUCTION

In this chapter, we briefly discuss a number of macro-level, societal problems caused by the ever-increasing demand for mobility (air pollution, noise pollution, traffic congestion, road accidents, etc.) and the tool we propose in this book as an important part of the solution: telework. Telework is defined here as the substitution of telecommunication technology for work-related travel.

Generally speaking, economists refer to problems like air pollution, noise pollution, traffic congestion and road accidents as 'externalities' (or 'external effects'), and we will begin by defining that important concept. To manage private transport's externalities and other costs, many mainstream transport economists propose government-imposed road pricing - a direct charge on road usage - as the best policy tool. Therefore, we must first show that road pricing, on its own, has problems significant enough to merit looking at other policy tools, including tools that are adopted primarily at the micro-level. In order to explain why we feel that road pricing must be at least complemented by telework, we will present a new conceptual framework for the assessment of policy tools. Within the context of our framework, road pricing may be very effective from a theoretical perspective, but it also has several significant weaknesses that arise from the realities of its implementation.

Once we have shown that road pricing is insufficient to solve the various societal problems caused by the growing demand for mobility, we will examine telework as another policy tool to manage the externalities of work-related travel. We will give a detailed definition of telework and then discuss its advantages and disadvantages.

In summary, this chapter

- presents a conceptual framework for evaluating policy tools, from a societal perspective,
- establishes the need for other policy tools to complement road pricing in managing private transport's externalities, and
- defines 'telework.'

2.2 EXTERNALITIES

The concept of 'externality' is fundamental in economics, but no consensus has been reached yet on either its exact definition, or the appropriate interpretation of its definition.[1]

Nonetheless, there is much agreement on the general characteristics of externalities, which permits us to use the following composite definition. For our purposes, externalities exist when:

1. the behaviour of one or more persons influences a third party,
2. the person influencing the third party may be unaware of this influence (or at least of this influence's exact magnitude),
3. this influence represents a 'spill-over' effect, i.e., an unintended but unavoidable by-product of a primary, intended activity,
4. this spill-over effect occurs outside the market (i.e., there is no price for it that would result from a particular structure of supply and demand),
5. the third party cannot exert influence on the activity it is affected by,
6. the influence has an effect on the welfare position of the third party through its utility function or production function,
7. the third party receives no compensation or does not have to pay for the effect it bears, and
8. this effect results in a divergence between the social and private costs (and benefits) associated with the primary activity.

A driver polluting the air that a third party breathes is a classic example of an externality.

Externalities constitute an important form of market failure. They are the reason that the first-best (as opposed to 'second-best'), neo-classical outcomes prevailing in perfect markets cannot be reached in real life. In a first-best world, the price mechanism alone is conducive to obtaining a socially optimal resource allocation (Pareto efficiency).

Although transport systems are necessary to achieve economic welfare and can facilitate economic growth, they clearly produce large externalities. Because this book focuses on telework, we will limit our discussion of externalities to the effects of private transport on road externalities (primarily accident, environmental and congestion costs), because the main impact of telework is in this area.

Figure 2.1 shows the costs associated with road transport, including the external costs.

Costs to the road user
• vehicle • fuel • travelling time • own risk assumption (including the assessment of possible personal material damage, loss of life, pain and suffering and own loss of production)

Costs to the infrastructure provider
• investments • maintenance • traffic operations and surveillance

External costs		
Accident costs[2]	Environmental costs (environmental costs can have a local as well as a global effect,[3] and they may include costs inflicted upon the current generation as well as upon future generations)	Congestion costs
• material damage (not for the road user himself/herself) • loss of production (not for the road user himself/herself) • loss of life (not for the road user himself/herself) • pain and suffering (not for the road user himself/herself) • police and rescue services and the administration of justice • medical care and rehabilitation	• air pollution • water pollution • soil pollution • noise pollution • pollution caused by production and disposal of vehicles • barrier effects in communities • visual annoyance • severance effects in ecosystems • use of public space for parking	• time lost due to congested roadways (not for the road user himself/herself) • time lost due to congested parking areas (not for the road user himself/herself)

Source: compiled by the authors, based upon Kågeson, 1993

Figure 2.1 Costs of road transport

When calculating external costs and how best to reduce them, one should, where possible, use the marginal external costs, not the average external costs. 'Marginal external costs,' in the context of this book, reflect the change in the total external costs produced by an additional vehicle-kilometre. In other words, the marginal external costs are the costs of an additional vehicle-kilometre, above and beyond the status quo. The difference between marginal and average external costs can be very large. Importantly, marginal external costs can be much higher than average external costs. For example, when a road carries 10 percent of its planned capacity, the last 1 percent of traffic produces more per-vehicle congestion costs than the rest of the traffic does.

This point about marginal external costs is important because, in theory, the most efficient way to reduce the total external costs is to 'charge' the marginal external costs to the road user generating the cost. Accordingly, many mainstream transport economists propose to manage externalities by using government-imposed road pricing, which involves a direct charge on road usage. Implementation of road pricing in a way consistent with economics textbook models requires continuous monitoring of the traffic conditions on all segments of the road network and would need to take into account the features of each vehicle on the road.[4] Only with that information could one determine the correct tax, which would be the marginal cost associated with the marginal change in traffic caused by that type of vehicle in that situation.

From a purely theoretical perspective, such a system would indeed go a long way to reducing externalities. Unfortunately, implementing an ideal road pricing system of this type is technically difficult-to-impossible. For that reason, a uniform tax is often suggested as a second-best policy tool. With a uniform tax, every vehicle pays the same amount of tax, regardless of the real external costs generated by the vehicle (in practice, it is feasible to differentiate this tax according to the vehicle category, e.g., in terms of size, and the time slot within which the road is used).

We feel that road pricing (in either its pure textbook forms or its more practical second-best forms) has significant problems at the level of procedural effectiveness. That is, implementing road pricing faces significant psychological, sociological and institutional impediments. Because of those impediments, road pricing is an insufficient policy tool for managing the externalities of private road transport, and therefore supplementary tools like telework are needed. In order to back up that conclusion, we will now briefly present our conceptual framework for assessing policy tools.

2.3 OUR CONCEPTUAL FRAMEWORK FOR ASSESSING POLICY TOOLS

It is our view that, from a societal perspective, those policy tools should be selected by decision -makers that contribute most to 'real effectiveness'; this is actual goal achievement in practice. When we use the term policy tool, this may include a wide variety of purposeful actions undertaken either at the macro-level or micro-level, and guided by either public agencies or by other economic actors in society, including business firms. However, if a 'policy tool' is adopted primarily at the micro-level by individuals and firms, without direct government intervention being the main driver, the positive impact on macro-level externalities may itself be an unintended by-product of micro-level goal pursuit. The role of government is then simply to fine-tune the macro-level context so as to maximize the adoption of the benevolent micro-level practice.

In our conceptual framework, real effectiveness is a function of both potential effectiveness and procedural effectiveness. We will look first at potential effectiveness.

The potential effectiveness of a policy tool can be determined by a strictly technical evaluation. For each type of road externality, a number of policy tools can be used to solve the problem. The policy tool with the lowest relative cost for a particular expected level of goal achievement (in terms of contribution to reducing a road externality) or the highest goal achievement for a given level of costs is the one with the highest potential effectiveness.[5] Obviously, assessing the potential effectiveness of a policy tool depends on correctly understanding the causes of the problem and the effects of the proposed solutions.

All too often, the potential effectiveness of a policy tool is rated in a static fashion; the policy analyst assumes that, with the exception of the implementation of the proposed policy tool, everything else stays the same.[6] Specifically, potential effectiveness is assessed assuming the status quo in the distribution of entitlements and rights. Looking at potential effectiveness alone may therefore lead to the early elimination of more innovative but higher change-inducing policy tools.[7]

We feel that policy-makers should neither eliminate nor implement policy tools solely on the basis of potential effectiveness. Procedural effectiveness is also important.

Procedural effectiveness looks at the realities of both the choice and implementation of policy tools. Specifically, procedural effectiveness looks at the psychological, sociological and institutional impediments that interfere with successful policy implementation. Procedural effectiveness is a huge and complex topic; for our purposes, we will focus on the following three themes.

1. **The behavioral constraints facing the decision-makers and the actors involved in the administrative implementation system.** Decisions are made and implemented in a context of bounded rationality (incorrect beliefs or beliefs based on incomplete information) and, often, opportunism (selfish motivations).[8]
2. **The values of the target group.** Often, success depends on the positive motivation and voluntary collaboration of the target group.
3. **The capabilities of the administrative system and the target group.** The administrative system and target group must be able to implement in practice what they are supposed to do.

We will start with the first theme and the problem of bounded rationality (incorrect beliefs or beliefs based on incomplete information).[9] In order to predict the exact impact of a policy tool, policy-makers need detailed knowledge of the link between a particular action and the desired result. This includes correct information about the potential effectiveness of alternative policy tools and about possible interactions between various policy tools. The challenge of gathering and processing correct information on the potential effectiveness of a policy tool is itself a problem of procedural effectiveness.[10] Furthermore, developing a policy tool requires bargaining, negotiation and compromise between the government/administration and those affected by the policy tool, namely firms and individuals. During this process, all effects associated with the implementation of a policy tool as perceived by the different actors should, ideally, be taken into account. However, because gathering information can be costly, decision-makers must implement policies based on an incomplete understanding of these sorts of details. We would draw attention to the fact that this often includes an incomplete appreciation of the legitimacy of the policy tool as perceived by the different actors involved.[11]

Like bounded rationality, opportunism (selfish motivations) can significantly influence a policy tool's procedural effectiveness. Policy-makers may select a policy tool that allows them to pursue their own goals rather than societal ones. For instance, a policy tool with high public visibility may be the preferred choice of politicians, because it enables them to gain votes. Furthermore, opportunistic behaviour can also be found among bureaucrats in public agencies. For example, if the public administration has flexibility in implementing a policy tool, then opportunistic behaviour can lead to insufficient enforcement, low attention and little investment of resources from the administration. Finally, policy-makers usually rely on a public agency to prepare an agenda, to provide information and finally to implement the decision made by policy-makers. However, this agency may pursue its own goals rather than societal ones. The solution to this problem is to introduce incentives so bureaucrats acting rationally in their own self-interest also act in the interest of society.[12]

Our second theme has to do with the values of the target group and the concept of legitimacy. In a nutshell, policy-makers and their tools have legitimacy if the values upheld by the policy-makers are the same as the ones held by dominant or key groups in society.[13] These groups in society can readily differ from policy-makers with respect to values such as equity, distributional issues, property rights, ethics and broader economic stabilization concerns.[14]

For example, consider the issue of equity. The equity problem can be described as the problem of dividing the financial burden associated with the implementation of a policy tool fairly among the actors involved. In general, the 'polluter must pay' principle could be followed, and the financial burden could be placed on the actor causing a road externality rather than the actors suffering from it or on society as a whole. Alternatively, the 'rich must pay' principle could be followed, and the financial burden could be placed on those who can afford to pay it. While this second principle may not be desirable from an economic point of view, if it reflects the public's values, then policy-makers in the real world need to consider it.

Illegitimacy is an important consequence of perceived opportunism. For example, the public's negative opinion of the state's intervention is often closely linked to the ineffectiveness of the state's policy tools. This ineffectiveness often arises because the politicians who choose a policy tool neglect to investigate its ultimate real effectiveness. Driven by opportunistic behaviour, some politicians are more concerned with maintaining and gaining power than with effective problem solving, and the public often recognizes this.[15]

Obviously, the public is more likely to consider a policy tool legitimate if it thinks that this tool has been chosen using a fair procedure.[16] Individuals who think that a policy tool has been chosen using a fair procedure are more likely to consider the tool legitimate, even if it results in negative outcomes for them personally.

Moving on to our third theme, we note that the effective implementation of a policy tool, in a context of bounded rationality and opportunism, may be largely dependent on the administrative implementation potential present. Do the actors responsible for the administrative implementation of a tool actually have the capacity to implement the policy tool? When selecting a policy tool, consideration should be given to the skill level of those actors, required to effectively implement the policy tool.[17] Furthermore, the 'jurisdiction' of the policy-maker should also be taken into account. A policy tool with high potential effectiveness may not be feasible for a particular decision-maker to implement, because implementation of that policy tool is possible only at another level of decision-making.[18]

Finally, the target group implementation potential needs to be considered. At the level of the firm or the individual, what are the psychological, sociological, financial and technological impediments to implementing a specific policy? Furthermore, negative spill-over effects (like the undermining of an industry's competitive position vis-à-vis international rivals due to higher costs) can seriously reduce a policy tool's procedural effectiveness.[19] A policy tool should also be flexible enough to allow target groups (e.g., firms) to react to economic changes, such as changes in technology, tastes and resource use.[20]

Now that we have briefly described the elements of our analysis of real effectiveness, we can present our conceptual framework of real effectiveness in pictorial form. As shown in Figure 2.2, real effectiveness requires that policy tools combine both a high potential effectiveness and a high procedural effectiveness with respect to economizing on the behavioral constraints of bounded rationality and opportunism, as well as capitalizing on legitimacy, administrative implementation potential and target group implementation potential.[21]

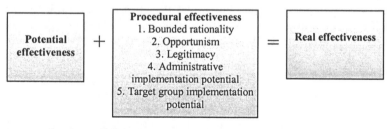

Source: authors' compilation

Figure 2.2   Elements relevant to the assessment of policy tools

We will now use this conceptual framework to assess road pricing, one of the most common solutions proposed to manage road transport externalities.[22] As was noted earlier, road pricing is proposed in relatively pure, textbook forms and also in more practical, second-best forms.[23] The relatively pure forms are technically difficult-to-impossible to implement, and therefore outrageously expensive, at best. Furthermore, in its relatively pure forms, road pricing has a low procedural effectiveness because almost no bureaucracy could have the administrative implementation potential required for a task of such enormous complexity. For precisely those reasons, many transport economists turn to a uniform tax as a second-best policy. Under a uniform tax, every vehicle pays the same amount of tax, regardless of the real external costs generated by the vehicle. This solves the administrative implementation problem but introduces two legitimacy problems. First, the taxation level does not reflect actual external costs. The tool will therefore be perceived unfair by some, because it is mistargeted. Second, the taxation level does not reflect each actor's ability to pay. The tool will therefore be viewed as unfair by some because it is distributively unjust. (Of course, this second problem could be solved in principle by introducing redistribution measures.) As a means of influencing traffic patterns, road pricing can also have target group implementation problems unless there is an extensive public transport network available as a transport option.[24] If no alternatives are available, the volume of travel will probably remain unchanged.[25]

Road pricing, like every policy tool, has strengths and weaknesses. The best policy is often a mix of policy tools, whereby some tools minimize - or compensate for - the negative effects of other tools, in order to maximize the total, net positive effects obtained in practice.[26] For example, the weaknesses of road pricing could be alleviated by introducing telework (we shall discuss this concept extensively below) as a valid policy alternative. At the same time, road pricing could then contribute to minimizing the negative effects of telework through discouraging new traffic induced by telework. For example, the implementation of road pricing would discourage other members of a teleworker's household from using the car newly available to them as a result of the telework activity.

2.4 REASONS FOR PROMOTING TELEWORK

Let us look closer at the reasons for promoting telework. As common sense would predict, commuters make up a large proportion of vehicle traffic. Commuting traffic represents 30 to 40 percent of all vehicle-kilometres travelled in urban areas.[27] In Dutch cities this percentage increases to 70 percent of the traffic flow during peak hours.[28] Unlike many other policy tools, telework involves a partial or total substitution of the commuting trip, not just a shift of time or mode.

Furthermore, telework does not require high public expenditures. In most industrialized countries, the current level of information and communication technology is sufficient to allow enhanced telework implementation. Furthermore, compared to other transport policy tools, telework requires relatively low expenditures from the target groups. The costs are borne primarily by the companies implementing telework, and these costs are often at least compensated by benefits such as enhanced productivity and flexibility, as we shall see in later chapters of this book.

Telework has the additional advantage that it tries to change travel behaviour by offering employers and employees an additional travel choice, namely virtual travel. By contrast, most transport policy tools try to change travel behaviour by reducing the choices offered. For instance, road pricing tries to change travel behaviour by increasing the private cost of a private motorized trip. Put very simply, telework can be viewed as a carrot rather than a stick.

In addition to addressing road externalities, telework helps with a variety of economic, social and ecological objectives.[29] For example, it creates new job opportunities for groups formerly excluded from the labour markets. Throughout this book, we will not only assess telework's potential as an externality-reducing policy tool, but we will also devote substantial attention to these other effects.

Interestingly, policy-makers in the United States and Europe have pursued telework for slightly different reasons. As has just been said, telework can help with several distinct public policy goals; here, we will mention only three. First, telework can reduce the volume of commuting travel, thereby reducing road transport externalities. Second, telework can create new job opportunities for groups formerly excluded from the labour markets. Third, telework can facilitate more flexible working practices. United States policy-makers have issued legislation in order to promote telework primarily within the context of the first public policy area. In Europe, by contrast, the focus has been primarily on the second and third public policy areas.[30] Rural communities in Europe are especially interested in telework as a tool for economic development.[31]

Not only policy-makers are interested in telework. Employers are interested as well, because it can reduce costs and increase productivity, and because employees often perceive it as a benefit.[32] (Chapter 4 will discuss telework's advantages and disadvantages from the employer's perspective.)

Employees are interested in telework because it increases flexibility and reduces commuting stress. Furthermore, telework is sometimes the only way to join the workforce. (Chapter 5 will discuss telework's advantages and disadvantages from the employee's perspective.)

Obviously, telework has some dangers, which will also be addressed in the following chapters.[33] These dangers include:

- atomization of the workforce,
- exploitation of vulnerable groups of workers,

- increased polarisation between core workers (those with relatively secure, good-paying jobs) and peripheral workers (those with insecure, low-paying jobs),
- negative impacts on family life,
- erosion of vocational training structures,
- social isolation,
- increasing precariousness of employment,
- the facilitation and tacit encouragement of poor employment and management practices (such as neglect of workers' health and safety, piece-rate systems and lack of integration into a corporate culture),
- the transfer to peripheral regions of only the most low-skilled and repetitive types of work, and
- a growing mismatch between labour markets and benefit systems, resulting in a variety of unemployment traps and poverty traps - as well as a growth in the underground economy.

2.5 TELEWORK AND OUR CONCEPTUAL FRAMEWORK

Of all the elements of our conceptual framework (Figure 2.2), we will focus in this book primarily on **telework's target group implementation potential**, because that is where most telework adoption problems can be expected to arise in practice. The other components of Figure 2.2 are less critical to successful telework adoption.

Legitimacy is rarely a key issue, because, although telework can have negative consequences in particular cases (as we will discuss in detail in Chapter 4 and Chapter 5), telework is introduced in most organizations as an additional, voluntary option. One exception is the case whereby the nature of the work itself requires mobility (e.g., the work performed by a travelling salesman), but here the employee has chosen this type of work him/herself in the first place. Regulatory agencies so far have not imposed telework on either employers or employees. All current teleworkers surveyed in this study (Chapter 5) expressed their intent to continue adopting this work mode in the future, hence suggesting that telework is indeed performed on a voluntary basis. Furthermore, there is significant societal consensus in favour of telework's many economic, social and ecological benefits.

Similarly, **administrative implementation potential** is not a key barrier either, because telework is generally something that employers and employees do for themselves, without the need for direct government involvement. Even if governments do get involved to the point of distributing subsidies and running pilot projects, telework still does not require the ongoing, sophisticated control and monitoring mechanisms needed to implement many other types of policy tools. Telework is thus a public policy tool only to the extent that public agencies can provide a context and incentives that promote telework adoption by individuals and organizations.

In our opinion, the most significant barrier to telework implementation is simply whether the target group, consisting of employers and employees, will choose to adopt the practice. For that reason, Chapter 4 and Chapter 5 will focus in detail on the managerial issue of telework's target group implementation potential. These chapters address the question, 'Under what situations will employers and employees choose to implement telework?' In these chapters, we will identify from a managerial perspective the conditions necessary for both employers (Chapter 4) and employees (Chapter 5) to choose to implement telework. The book focuses on telework adoption in general. It does not investigate in depth the issue of telework frequency (i.e., the number of days per week that specific employees engage in telework) because sound empirical data on frequency are rare. Hence, any data included in this book on telework frequency are either based on the extant literature or on the surveys we conducted. In addition, we do not explicitly address telework drop-out rates, as our surveys indicated that, after a successful trial period, drop-out seldom occurs. The possibility of drop-out is therefore assumed not to affect the maximum adoption rate of telework discussed in Chapter 6. However, the dropping-out issue is briefly discussed in Chapter 3 (section 3.6).

Chapter 6 shifts back from the managerial perspective to the broader societal view, and addresses telework's potential effectiveness in terms of reducing road transport externalities. It asks the hypothetical question, 'If employers and employees do implement telework, what will the impact be on road transport externalities?'

In other words, assuming that any problems of procedural effectiveness, as discussed in Chapter 4 and Chapter 5, are solved, we can then focus on potential effectiveness in Chapter 6, since this will now approximate real effectiveness. The choices of individual employers and employees in favour of telework, constitute a precondition to attaining the adoption levels required for this practice to have any significant impact on road transport externalities. We think it is one of the particular contributions of this book that it examines telework's costs and benefits from both a managerial and societal perspective.

2.6 HISTORICAL REASONS FOR PROMOTING TELEWORK

As we have said, there are various reasons to adopt telework, and those reasons becomes even clearer when we look at how the arguments for telework have changed through time. The first real interest in telework, in the early 1970s, was provoked by three factors. First, the price of computers had fallen, making home computing a feasible option. Second, it became obvious that telecommunications and data processing would blend into one integrated system. Third, the first international oil crisis focussed attention on the waste of energy in private and public transport systems. Against that backdrop, telework was promoted as a way to save energy by substituting electronic communication for physical transportation.[34]

Over the next few years, various futurist publications appeared, envisioning a positive future in which telework would become the dominant organizational form of work. The best known is the vision of Alvin Toffler. Toffler (1980) envisioned that in the future, most workers would again work from their own house or cottage, as they had before the Industrial Revolution and its centralization of physical and human capital. Because the new types of jobs performed at home would require electronic communication technology, he renamed the home the 'electronic cottage.' According to Toffler, the most powerful force driving this mass telework implementation would be the economic trade-off between transportation and telecommunication. Social factors such as long commuting times and an orientation towards the family unit would also enhance telework implementation. At the same time as Toffler put forward his optimistic vision, various pessimistic visions of the future were formulated, envisioning telework as a tool bringing isolation, atomization and exploitation.[35]

Also at this time, several research projects examined the actual use and future potential of telework. These projects understood that telework would have consequences far beyond its effects on physical commuting. These projects investigated issues such as:

- telework's implications for organizational structure and job design,
- public attitudes toward telework,
- the extent to which telework could satisfy the employment needs of people with disabilities, and
- telework's impact on the general social goal of equal opportunities for all workers.[36]

Ever since those research projects, the full scope of telework has been fairly well understood, and the differences between telework proponents have been mainly differences of emphasis. In the 1980s, the emphasis was on telework as a flexible work arrangement through which family demands could be balanced, geographic skill shortages addressed and economic peripheries integrated with core areas. In the 1990s, the emphasis was generally on workplace design and facility management; telework was viewed as a way to manage work time and work space in order to increase productivity and effectiveness.[37] Now, at the start of the twenty-first-century, a stakeholder approach is often adopted, with an analysis of the full spectrum of effects telework can have on a variety of actors: the teleworkers themselves and their families, the organizations that employ them, the government and society at large.

2.7 THE DEFINITION OF 'TELEWORK'

What, exactly, do we mean by 'telework'? While the general concept - the substitution of telecommunication technology for work-related travel - is clear, the time has come for us to address some questions of detail. First of all, telework is not quite the same thing as (the American term) telecommuting. Even though the two terms are often considered synonyms, there is a slight difference: telecommuting is a subset of telework, because telecommuting involves only the substitution for the daily commute to and from work.[38]

The many definitions of telework in the academic and professional literature differ according to the following five major variables. For each of the following variables, our definition is broad and inclusive.

1.   **The amount and proportion of time spent off the employer's premises.** Some definitions include only full-time telework. Our definition includes part-time telework, even when combined with traditional commuting.

2.   **The location of the work.** Some definitions include only work carried out in the worker's own home. Our definition includes work carried out using the home as a base, work done in certain premises near the home, but not mobile work performed on clients' premises. In that last case, it is mostly the nature of the work itself that imposes professional activities to be conducted outside the office environment, and there is no choice to be made by employees or employers on the location of the work.

3.   **The contractual relationship with the employer.** With our definition, a teleworker can be self-employed, an employee, the director of an independent business, an agent working on commission or even a volunteer. However, our empirical research is limited to employees.

4.   **The nature of the technology used.** Some definitions include only those workers who operate with computers and are connected on-line with their employer or client.[39] Our definition includes any use of telecommunication technology.

5.   **The nature of the relationship with the employer.** Some definitions of telework include only workers who are employed on a full-time basis or primarily by a single employer.[40] Our definition includes part-time workers, as well as people who work for several employers. However, our surveys focused on full-time and part-time workers, employed by a single employer.

Teleworkers come in the following six types (this book focuses on the first four types):[41]

1.   **Employee who works at a satellite office.** This type of employee works within the physical boundaries of the organization but outside of the central and/or branch offices. The difference between a satellite office and a traditional office is that all of the satellite office's employees work there because they live closer to that facility than to their conventional office, regardless of what their jobs are.[42] Offshore satellite offices are set up overseas in order to use the high skills and low wages available overseas. Telecommunication technology is used in order to maintain contact with the central or branch office.

2.   **Employee who works at a telework centre.** This type of employee works at a location situated in a residential area and owned by a third party that rents the facilities to various organizations. A rural telework centre in Europe is called a telecottage; a telework centre serving only a neighbourhood is called a neighbourhood telework centre. In Europe, the first telework centres were established in island communities, such as Gotland and Majorca, in order to attract work from the nearest mainland. The same reasoning also led to the establishing of telework centres in Hawaii (United States) and Kyushu Island (Japan). Even Ireland, a very large island, has successfully created additional employment using telework centres.[43] Telework centres are complex to implement on a large scale because they require a great deal of cooperation among different stakeholders involved.

3. **Electronic homeworker.** This type of employee works for a substantial part of the working day at home on a regular basis. The worker is equipped with telecommunication technology that permits continuous interaction with the employer.
4. **Traditional homeworker.** This type of employee works for a substantial part of the working day at home on a regular basis but uses telecommunication technology only to transmit the results of her/his work.
5. **Nomadic worker.** This type of employee works at various sites in response to changing business needs and uses telecommunication technology to interact with her/his employer, thereby avoiding (at least some) visits to the main office. This type is not viewed as a teleworker in our study, because of the absence of location choice by the worker.
6. **Professional networker.** This type of worker is self-employed and uses telecommunication technology to deliver her/his services to more than one customer.

Although satellite offices require facilities planning and administration, we feel that nonetheless they are particularly attractive, for several reasons. First, they significantly reduce commuting. Second, they provide environments like those of traditional offices (including a secure building space and a professional image). Third, they typically cost less per square foot of office space, due to their location. Fourth, they can provide social and professional interaction, avoiding the social isolation often cited as a disadvantage of telework at home. Fifth, they provide space for workers who do not have the needed space at home. Sixth, they preserve the boundary between work and home environments, for those who wish to have such a boundary.

Telework centres have similar advantages, plus the additional advantages of the ability to share facilities, the ability to have smaller offices and the relief from building ownership worries. On the other hand, these additional advantages come at the cost of less control over the office space.[44]

We define telework as **work from home, a satellite office, a telework centre or any other workstation outside of the main office for at least one day per workweek. Some sort of telecommunication technology is used to substitute for work-related travel, but it need not be continuous, on-line communication.** We recognize that telework in satellite offices and telework centres does not fully eliminate the commuting trip. However, with these practices, the length of the commuting trips is significantly reduced, and the trips generally take place within the local transportation network rather than the inter-regional network.[45]

When generalizing about telework, one must keep in mind the different types of telework. Homework is sufficiently different from work at a telework centre that, when assessing the impacts of the two practices, different variables may be relevant, or the same variables but with different weights.[46] In practice, most empirical studies to date have reported results for homework only. Unless specified differently, the results of extant studies reported in this book always refer to telework performed at home. Our own empirical research, however, includes both homework and work in telework centres.

Telework programmes can differ in flexibility. Some telework programmes are very rigid and allow telework only on predetermined days, while others are flexible in the sense that an employee is required to be in the office only one or two days per workweek, or needs to be accessible by telephone or computer only at certain times.

Telework can be either formal or informal. Informal telework can be defined as ad hoc telework, which is often a local arrangement between an employee and her/his supervisor. Formal telework, on the other hand, takes place on a regular basis and is introduced as part of the organization's human resources policy.[47] Formal arrangements have the advantage of reflecting the organization's commitment to institutionalize this work option, while informal arrangements usually have the advantage of flexibility in design.

2.8 MEASURING TELEWORK

The total volume of telework is measured using the variables of **penetration level** and **frequency**.

1. **Penetration level.** This is the percentage of workers who telework in the active workforce (the active workforce includes only those employees who are currently employed).
2. **Frequency.** This is the number of days per week, on average, that teleworkers (here, meaning 'people who do any telework at all') telework. Prior studies suggest that employees prefer part-time telework over full-time telework,[48] and the frequency of telework reflects this. A weighted average across various studies worldwide[49] suggests a current average frequency of 1.2 days per workweek.

2.9 TELEWORK IN THE EU, JAPAN AND THE UNITED STATES

It is enlightening to compare telework in the EU, Japan and the United States. In the three regions, telework takes different forms and has different penetration levels. Making this comparison and understanding these differences gives us insight into some of the factors that can affect successful telework implementation.

In the United States, most current telework is home-based, because this is easy to organize and relatively inexpensive.[50] In the EU, also, telework is often done on a full-time basis at home.[51] In Japan, however, only a limited number of people actually work at home. These are primarily professionals whose work can be done relatively autonomously. The most common form of telework found in Japan entails working in a local neighbourhood telework centre or in a satellite office. This is primarily because living spaces in Japan tend to be small. Furthermore, compared to other industrialized countries, Japan has a higher proportion of traditional marriages (one-earner households), and the home is still largely viewed as the domain of the woman.[52]

At present, no accurate statistical data is available on the number of teleworkers in the EU, Japan and the United States. (In order to gather reliable statistical data about the penetration level of telework, we feel that standard questions on this should be added to population censuses and labour surveys. Today this is done only in the UK.) There are estimates, however, and some widely-known recent estimates[53] are shown in Table 2.1.

Table 2.1   Penetration levels of telework in the EU, Japan and the United States

	Penetration level of telework as percentage of the workforce
The European Union (formal + informal arrangements)	3.10%
The European Union (formal arrangements)	0.80%
Japan (formal arrangements)	1.05%
The United States of America (formal + informal arrangements)	10.56%

Sources: EU: European Commission, 1998; Japan: Sato and Spinks, 1998 and United States: Nilles, 1999

None of the sources used to construct Table 2.1 provides a clear definition of the types of telework included. Note that the figure for the United States reflects both formal and informal arrangements, while the Japanese figure reflects only formal arrangements. For the EU, separate estimates exist for formal arrangements only, and for the combination of formal and informal arrangements. These results show that many current telework arrangements are informal and thus difficult to assess. Japan and the EU have approximately the same penetration level; the United States has a much higher penetration level.

Although different estimates and findings regarding the penetration level of telework worldwide are available, all findings appear to confirm that home-based telework is most prevalent in the Anglo-Saxon and Nordic countries and in high-tech Singapore, but relatively low in Japan and in the rest of Europe. (For details of telework worldwide, see Huws et al., 1999. For details of telework in Europe, and a country-by-country comparison of barriers and drivers to telework implementation, see Appendix 1.)

The differences in penetration level can be explained by a wide range of economic, social, cultural, regulatory and technological variables. Table 2.2 presents some variables that could explain why the penetration level of telework is higher in the United States than in Japan and the EU. The investments in information technology, the number of computers per hundred white-collar workers and the per capita spending power after adjustment for the basic costs of living are much higher in the United States than in Japan or the EU. Furthermore, the number of inhabitants per square kilometre and the perceived cost of a computer are much lower in the United States than in Japan or the EU (although the number of inhabitants per square kilometre is misleading in the case of the United States, because 76 percent of the population lives in densely populated urban areas[54]).

Government involvement, while not as easy to quantify, also explains the different penetration levels. Until recently, telework implementation in Japan was primarily the initiative of the private sector. In the United States, however, the government has taken a leading role in both promoting and implementing telework.[55] For example, in the United States telework implementation received a major push through a number of air quality regulations. These laws specifically mentioned telework as an alternative for travelling to work.[56] In the EU, government involvement in telework implementation is mostly limited to the expression of some form of commitment, and the issuing of regulations that reduce existing barriers to telework.[57]

Table 2.2 Differences in variables positively correlated with telework implementation

	IT per capita in Euro	PCs/100 white collar workers	Popula-tion per km²	Per capita spending power after adjustment for basic cost of living	Perceived relative cost of a PC
USA	1075	105	28	100	100
Japan	745	24	331	82	122
EU	445	54	176	70.4	145.2

Sources: IT per capita and PCs/100 white collar workers: EITO, 1999; Population per km², Per capita spending power and Perceived relative cost of a PC: European Commission, 1998.

Organizational and cultural barriers are also different in the EU, Japan and the United States. Within organizations, the most important barrier in the United States and the EU is managers' fear that they will lose control over their workers and more specifically over their work.[58] In Japan, other organizational elements are slowing down the implementation of telework. Formal job definitions and regular performance evaluations are rare, so teleworkers are harder to manage.[59] Furthermore, Japanese business culture favours group interests over the interest of the individual, and telework is perceived as benefiting primarily the individual. In addition, face-to-face interaction is highly valued in Japan. Also, the worker characteristics of independence and personal initiative - two characteristics of a successful teleworker - are not highly valued in Japan.

2.10   CONCLUSION

In this chapter, we have argued that, among the tools used to manage private transport's externalities, road pricing implementation faces significant problems in terms of achieving procedural effectiveness. Therefore, it needs to be at least complemented by other policy tools such as telework. We have defined telework as work from home, a satellite office, a telework centre or any other work station outside of the main office for at least one day per workweek. Some sort of telecommunication technology is used to substitute for work-related travel, but it need not be continuous, on-line communication.

We have outlined the various forms that telework can take, and we have provided a brief overview of telework worldwide.

In the next chapter, we will present a conceptual framework specifically for telework implementation, and we will begin to discuss the procedural effectiveness issues associated with telework adoption.

NOTES

1   We have drawn our definition from the definitions of Pigou (1932), Bator (1958), Buchanan and Stubblebine (1962), Stalmans (1974), Heller and Starrett (1976), Baumol and Oates (1988), Pearce and Turner (1990), Doneschansker (1995) and Verhoef (1997).

2   The social costs related to road accidents are not all external costs. When a road user decides to make a trip, she/he takes into account certain risks which consequently are private costs. Hence, only the costs inflicted upon other road users are external costs, as well as certain costs not taken into consideration when deciding whether or not to make a trip.

3   Environmental impacts can be local in the sense that the environmental impact occurs only near major transport infrastructure corridors or modes (for instance, noise pollution, visual intrusion and the emission of lead and carbon monoxides). There are, however, also transboundary effects which can influence the broader environment even at a considerable distance from the transport activity itself (for instance, acid rain as the result of the emission of NO_x). Finally, the impact can also be global if the transport influences the global ecosystem on a planetary scale (for instance, global warming through the emission of CO_2) (Button, 1994).

4   May and Nash (1998).

5   Howlett and Ramesh (1993) and Bohm and Russell (1985).

6   Bohm and Russell (1985).

7   Hickerson (1987).

8   As Elmore has pointed out, decisions concerning the use of policy tools are usually made in a context of uncertainty, multiple interests, competition and limited time (Elmore, 1987).

9   We use 'bounded rationality' to include decision-makers' inability to distinguish between relevant and irrelevant information (Milliken, 1987).

10   See Verbeke and Coeck (1995).

11   Verbeke and Coeck (1995).

12   March and Olsen (1986).

13   Barker (1994).

14   Elkin and Cook (1985) and Bohm and Russell (1985).

15   This will change only if effective problem solving becomes a condition for being politically successful (Mayntz, 1983).

16   The perception of procedural fairness can be enhanced by offering an adequate and sincere explanation (Greenberg, 1990) or through consulting all involved parties in the decision-making process (Greenberg, 1987). When the outcome of a policy is ensured through threats or coercive instruments, the policy is usually judged to be unfair; if mediation is used, the policy is usually judged to be fair (Greenberg, 1990). Interestingly, people are more concerned with the fairness of a procedure if it leads to negative outcomes (Greenberg, 1990). The acceptance of policies and the implementation process is enhanced if information

is generously shared and everyone involved is aware of the capabilities and constraints of the other actors (Feick, 1992).

[17] This factor may explain why an administration tends to favour instruments with which it is familiar (Linder and Peters, 1989).

[18] Mayntz (1983).

[19] Verbeke and Coeck (1995).

[20] Bohm and Russell (1985).

[21] Even if there is high potential and procedural effectiveness, there is no absolute guarantee that specific policy goals will actually be achieved, because of environmental uncertainty problems such as unpredictable technological change. Ignorance of the future is arguably a dynamic bounded rationality problem, but we classify environmental uncertainty as distinct from bounded rationality because it is so different from traditional examples of bounded rationality, such as incorrectly predicting human behaviour or inadequately processing all relevant, presently available information.

[22] Of course, road pricing is only one of many available policy tools. These policy tools are likely to vary in terms of the effects they generate (direct vs. indirect), as well as in their power to change behaviour (positive vs. negative, and strong vs. weak) (Mayntz, 1983). Transport policy tools that cope with road externalities can also be divided into supply-side policy tools (such as infrastructural policies, telematics policies and technology policies) and demand-side policy tools (such as parking fees, fuel taxes, road pricing, area licenses, traffic calming and speed limits) (Verhoef, 1997). In the academic literature, other classifications can also be found.

[23] The reader interested in the details of road pricing is referred to May and Nash (1998) and Jones and Hervik (1992).

[24] May and Nash (1998) and Jones and Hervik (1992).

[25] Giuliano (1992).

[26] Coeck (1993).

[27] Gray et al. (1994).

[28] van Reisen (1997).

[29] Sampath et al. (1991).

[30] Gillespie et al. (1995).

[31] Handy and Mokhtarian (1995).

[32] The telecommunications industry and the computer industry, of course, also perceive telework as an important new market opportunity (Handy and Mokhtarian, 1995).

[33] Huws (1994).

[34] Qvortrup (1992), Olson (1988), Huws et al. (1993) and Jackson and van der Wielen (1998).

[35] Huws et al. (1993).

[36] Huws et al. (1993).

[37] Jackson and van der Wielen (1998).

[38] Nilles (1988), in 1973, was the first researcher to define and investigate the concept of telecommuting. Since then, many more terms have been used to express basically the same concept: 'telework,' 'televillages,' 'telecottages,' 'flexiplace,' 'remote work office,' 'dispersed working,' 'virtual office,' 'hoteling' and 'the elusive office.' See Yap and Tng (1990), Gray et al (1994), Eldid and Minoli (1995), Huws et al. (1993), Huws (1993), Huws (1994) and Kugelmass (1995). Contrary to what many believe, the prefix 'tele' in 'telework' is a Greek word for 'far off' or 'distance' and does not refer to the use of telecommunications. See NUTEK (1997), Mokhtarian (1991a) and Chapman et al. (1995).

[39] See Huws et al. (1999) and Qvortrup (1998).

[40] See Huws (1994) and Huws (1993).

[41] See Huws (1993), Huws (1994), Gray et al. (1994), Gareis and Korte (1999), Empirica (1985), Holti and Stern (1987), Korte (1988), Olson (1982), Olson (1988), Stanworth and Stanworth (1991), Kugelmass (1995) Huws (1996) and McGrath and Houlihan (1998). Note that we do not include the employee who works on the traditional site but is electronically connected to other employees working on the same site or on the site of a supplier, customer or partner. Even though this practice is sometimes called 'organizational telework,' it does not fall within our definition.

[42] Nilles (1998).

[43] Gray et al. (1994).

[44] See Nilles (1998), Kugelmass (1995), Aichholzer (1998), Mokhtarian (1991a) and Bagley and Mokhtarian (1997).

[45] Handy and Mokhtarian (1995).

[46] Bagley and Mokhtarian (1997).

[47] Gray et al. (1994).

[48] Yap and Tng (1990).

[49] For the United States, Rathbone (1992) reports an average frequency of 1.8 days per workweek, while Handy and Mokhtarian (1996a) report a frequency of 1.2 days per workweek. For Singapore, Olszewiski and Lam (1996) estimate the frequency at 2 days per workweek. Lyons et al. (1998) estimate the frequency of telework in the UK at between 1.4 and 1.7 days per workweek. For the Netherlands, the frequency has been estimated at between 1 and 1.5 days per workweek (van Reisen, 1997). Handy and Moktharian (1995) surveyed the literature and found that frequency levels range from 0.8 days per workweek up to 3 days per workweek (Handy and Mokhtarian, 1994).

[50] Mokhtarian and Sato (1994) and Nilles (1998).

[51] European Commission (1998).

[52] Mokhtarian and Sato (1994).

[53] The most widely-known recent estimates of telework volume are a recent survey conducted by the satellite Office Association of Japan (1997), the findings of Jack Nilles (1999) and the ETD estimates (European Commission, 1998).

[54] Huws et al. (1999).

[55] Sato and Spinks (1998).

[56] Sampath et al. (1991).

[57] The Netherlands and Sweden are exceptions; there, governments actively implement telework pilot projects. However, in most European countries private initiatives are the main driver for current telework implementation (European Commission 1998).

[58] European Commission (1998).

[59] Mokhtarian and Sato (1994), Konno (1999) and Spinks (1991).

3. A MANAGERIAL PERSPECTIVE ON TELEWORK ADOPTION: TARGET GROUP IMPLEMENTATION[1]

3.1 INTRODUCTION

In 1971, AT&T predicted that by 1990 all Americans would be working from home.[2] In the late 1970s and 1980s, telework was seen as the work arrangement of the future, and many experts predicted large-scale implementation of telework by the early 1990s.[3] On the demand side, the 1980s also saw large numbers of employees express their interest in telework: 9 percent of all employees in the Federal Republic of Germany were interested, 11 percent in Italy, 14 percent in France and an amazing 23 percent in the United Kingdom.[4]

Yet no telework boom occurred. This is surprising, because recent developments in ICT (information and communication technology) have reduced the coordination and control costs associated with the geographic decentralization of the work force, especially in large service organizations. For a variety of reasons, the centralization of staff in a single office is no longer necessarily the most efficient way to organize economic activity.

So why hasn't telework taken off? The answer is complicated, and this chapter will be at best only a partial answer. Answering the question requires a close look at telework's procedural effectiveness - the various impediments that interfere with telework implementation. To that end, we will present a conceptual framework that specifically models the individual implementation of telework. Ultimately, the target group implementation potential discussed in Chapter 2 is determined by the willingness of individuals to adopt telework. In our conceptual framework, the individual decision to implement telework is affected by the technological, institutional and organizational environments, as well as by characteristics of the individual employee. A close look at these four factors will yield insight into telework's past, present and future.

3.2   OUR CONCEPTUAL FRAMEWORK FOR THE IMPLEMENTATION OF TELEWORK

Several researchers have used individual choice models to explain the adoption of telework,[5] using either the stated preference approach or the revealed preference approach. Although the decision to adopt telework may be an individual's decision, it is usually made in a complex environment that influences the individual. For this book, therefore, we combine individual choice models with an analysis of the relevant environmental parameters (the concept of environment used here, is seen from the individual employee's perspective, and therefore also includes the employee's organization).[6] Our conceptual framework for the implementation of telework, Figure 3.1, gives an overview of all the elements that may influence the individual's decision process related to telework.[7]

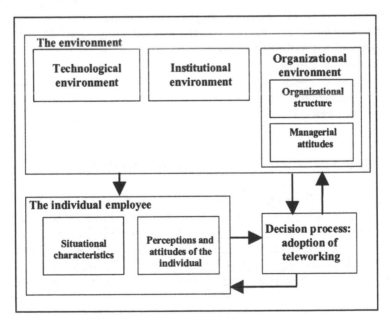

Source: Bernardino et al., 1992

Figure 3.1   Conceptual framework for modelling telework implementation

Let us look first at the top of Figure 3.1. The organization will offer telework as an option only if a minimum set of technological, institutional and organizational requirements is fulfilled. The 'technological' environment reflects the ICT available both to the organization itself and to the employees working for the organization. The 'institutional' environment includes both government regulations and labour union policies. Finally, the 'organizational' environment refers to the employer, especially the employer's organizational structure and managerial attitudes. Once the minimum set of requirements related to these three environments is fulfilled, as described further in this chapter, the likelihood that the organization will offer telework increases substantially. In other words, the target group implementation potential is affected by environmental parameters. These parameters include the organization's effects on the individual's telework options. If multiple individuals react to these options in a particular way, for example by massively selecting telework, this behaviour may itself alter the environmental context, such as prevailing labour laws, but we have not included that last possibility in Figure 3.1, where we focus on the parameters affecting the single employee's decision-making process.

From the individual's point of view, her/his decision to telework will depend not only on the technological, institutional and organizational environment, but also on her/his own situation, perceptions and attitudes. The adoption of telework may then in turn change the individual's initial perceptions and attitudes.

As Figure 3.1 suggests, the decision to implement telework is influenced by a very large number of drivers and barriers. We will start by looking closer at the technological environment.

3.3   THE TECHNOLOGICAL ENVIRONMENT

By definition, teleworkers use technology to communicate and to stay in touch with the organization. It is important to keep in mind, however, that many teleworkers also use technology to do their work at the remote location. We recognize that employees who perform traditional homework with low skill requirements (e.g., routine administrative tasks) may not need any additional ICT at the remote location; employees like these can accomplish a substantial amount of telework effectively with only a telephone, paper and pencil.[8] Knowledge workers, however, typically need ICT in order to do their work. Composing a growing share of the labour force, knowledge workers usually perform highly-skilled jobs in a technologically-enhanced environment. Their main input is information, not physical materials or components.[9]

Knowledge workers generally work with computers, and the technological advancements in computers have been nothing short of extraordinary. The reduction in data communications costs - and the huge improvements in computing speed and power - have made personal computers vastly more affordable and accessible. This, in turn, has made telework much more feasible.[10] Specifically, small, portable computers ('laptops') have had especially large implications for the implementation of part-time telework. Most models of these computers fit easily in a briefcase, allowing employees to work wherever they want. These fast, dependable, portable and user-friendly devices make it easier for organizations to, in effect, extend their communication networks inside their employees' homes.[11]

In addition to personal computers, the rise of e-mail has been another driver of telework implementation. E-mail reliability has increased significantly in recent years, and employees have learned how best to use electronic communication in order to transmit the same message as with conventional communication tools such as the telephone.

The growing network of telephone lines and ISDN (Integrated Services Digital Network) connections is another driver, because telework generally requires fast data transmission. With their enormous capacity, ISDN connections allow quick and efficient data transfer. ISDN connections are used almost exclusively in the business environment.

Almost every industrialized country now has the ICT capacity needed for widespread telework implementation.[12] Some exceptions exist: for example, in some southern European countries the national ICT network is not yet sufficiently extensive to allow the widespread implementation of telework. Although organizations in these countries face no pure technological barriers to implementing telework, the organizations naturally still face major financial barriers. In fact, for an individual organization, from a strategic management perspective, the real barrier to telework may not be the lack of technology but the financial cost of that technology. For example, in some industrialized countries it is still relatively expensive to obtain basic ICT such as an effective intranet at the organization level.[13]

When we talk about 'the technological environment,' a distinction must be made between two elements.

1. **The technological environment that surrounds the organization** consists of the technological options from which the organization can choose.

2. **The technological environment that surrounds the individual employee** consists of the technological options that the organization has already chosen, and from which the potential teleworker can choose.

Up to this point, we have been talking very broadly about the first element: the technological environment external to the organization. In this sense, with the caveats already mentioned, the technological environment is practically unlimited, and it is a telework driver in most industrialized countries. We will now turn to the second element, namely the technological environment faced by the individual, and briefly address the technological choices that an organization should make in order to increase the chances of successful telework implementation.

A good place for an organization to start is by considering each teleworker's present and anticipated future communication requirements, based on that teleworker's functions. Today's technology allows teleworkers to communicate in the following three ways.

1. To **receive and send data**, the technological options include telephone modems for low-speed data over a traditional network, packet data networks for higher-speed, bulk data (not in real time) and the digital ISDN network for real-time data and mobile data networks.
2. To simply **keep in touch**, the technological options include telephones, audio conferencing, pagers, voice mailboxes, cell phones, fax machines and e-mail.
3. To **share information**, the technological options include electronic bulletin boards, groupware or computer-supported cooperative working, remote access to databases, wide area networks and bridges for local area networks.[14]

When selecting telework equipment, the organization should take into account:

1. **Quality of service.** This is a function of, among other things, the service's speed and user-friendliness. Quality of service also includes the service provider's ability to guarantee the nominal bandwidth specified, and the range of bandwidth supported.
2. **Availability of service.** This is a function of the number of POPs (points of presence) that support the service, the level of vendor support and the availability overseas.
3. **Transport and interface standards.**
4. **Price.** The system price includes not only the price of the equipment but also all recurring and non-recurring charges. One of the major

components of price is the number of access lines required to support the necessary range of applications.

5. **Communications security.**
6. **Reliability.** This includes the system's ability to function during power outages, and the reliability of any telephone operations required to support the service.[15]

At this point, some readers may be asking, 'What computing and telecommunication system does the **typical** teleworker need?' Although this book is trying to illustrate the variety of telework, an answer to this common question will help some readers imagine what telework would look like in their own organization. The typical teleworker has a personal computer, a basic telephone or cellular phone and a modem. A fax machine and a copy machine may be available to the typical teleworker, but this is no absolute requirement. She/he also has e-mail, access to databases and perhaps even large file transfer and data conferencing applications (data conferencing applications are applications in which illustrations, text-based specifications and graphics are viewed on the computer screens of all the participants). Finally, she/he has the network connection required to support her/his communication needs. The network connection can either be narrowband (<1.5 Mbps (megabits per second)), wideband (1.5–45 Mbps) or broadband (>45 Mbps). The first solution is appropriate for home workers; the higher-speed connections are more appropriate for centre-based telework. In the central office, one of the computers in the office LAN (local area network) typically acts as a telecommunication server which is connected to a WAN (wide area network) such as the ISDN network or even the POTS (plain old telephone system).[16]

We will conclude this section on the technological environment by reiterating our point, illustrated above in Figure 3.1, that the technological environment is only one factor affecting telework implementation. **The challenge regarding telework implementation lies on the demand side, not the supply side.** On the supply side, the technology is available. But that only makes telework a feasible option.[17] On the demand side, managers must be willing to rethink the way employees work and implement the necessary strategic organizational change.[18] And, just as importantly, employees must perceive that telework will benefit them in economic or quality-of-life terms.[19] We will now look at the next component of our conceptual framework: the institutional environment.

3.4 THE INSTITUTIONAL ENVIRONMENT

A country's welfare system influences the penetration and characteristics of telework in that country.[20] Let us look at four types of welfare system and their influence on telework.

1.　In a free market regime (for example, the UK, the United States, Canada, Australia and Ireland), there is a laissez-faire attitude to labour markets, weak regulation, informal agreements and low levels of collective negotiation. Flexibility in the labour market tends to be external to the firm, where conventional market forces prevail. The average worker spends a relatively short time in any given job, so the mutual commitment between employers and employees is relatively weak. Moreover, the penalties for changing jobs are relatively low. In this regime, it is easy for employers and employees to experiment with new forms of work such as telework, often on an ad hoc basis.

2.　In a regulated labour market regime (for example, Belgium, Germany, France, Italy and Austria), labour contracts are tightly regulated, with legal restrictions on the conditions of employment and social protection. There is strong social dialogue, and a high level of collective bargaining. Employees are hired and fired reluctantly, and the mutual commitment between employers and employees is relatively strong. Flexibility in the labour market tends to be found only at the level of individual firms, involving practices such as jobs involving multiple skills, multiple tasks and flexible work hours. In such an environment, the cost of leaving secure, permanent full-time employment is high. In this regime, a new form of work such as telework will therefore be regarded with considerable suspicion by the work force; telework cannot be implemented in an informal and ad hoc way. It needs to be introduced together with appropriate regulation. While this process can be slow and cumbersome, eventually it may result in better protection of workers' rights.

3.　A social democratic regime (found, for example, in the Nordic countries) is much like a regulated labour market regime. There is strong social dialogue, and trade unions play a major role. Here too, flexibility in the labour market tends to be found only at the level of individual firms. However, because many benefits are universally available regardless of occupation, workers can move from job to job without losing crucial benefits. As a result, it is easier to implement telework in a social democratic regime than in a regulated labour market regime.

4.   Countries with a 'Mediterranean' regime (for example, Spain, Portugal and Greece) have a large 'informal sector', a comparatively undeveloped welfare system, and a relatively high proportion of the population employed in agriculture or other forms of self-employment. Collective bargaining is strong, but only in the formal sector. In the formal sector, the same elements are relevant as in the regulated labour market regime. In the informal sector, telework may exist but is unlikely to be documented or insured.[21]

Besides the drastic step of changing their welfare systems, what can governments do to facilitate telework implementation? For one thing, governments must be agile. As the speed of ICT innovation increases, it becomes more likely that, at least in some countries, institutions such as governments will lag behind technology. For example, in many countries, labour laws discriminate against teleworkers vis-à-vis conventional workers, and this creates a formidable obstacle to telework implementation. Governments must move quickly to stay up-to-date with other relevant issues as well, such as ownership, access and distribution of digital information, privacy, security and copyrights.[22]

Governments can facilitate telework implementation by promoting it directly, and/or by creating an adequate legal framework (employment-related regulations and indirectly-related regulations such as zoning and taxation).

In the EU, the first approach - government promotion - is generally limited to the expression of some form of moral commitment to the practice of telework. The Netherlands and Sweden are exceptions; there, governments play an active role in telework pilot projects.

The second approach - creating an adequate legal framework - is just as important as promotion, if not more important. As labour markets are deregulated, many forms of work protection, which have traditionally been embodied in national statutory provisions are being challenged. Governments must adapt the regulatory framework in order to ensure that teleworkers are adequately protected, without creating rigidities that make it difficult for labour markets to operate flexibly. In order to do this, the most satisfactory solution may be to establish the basic principles in laws and leave the implementation details to discretionary guidelines.[23]

Current laws often create substantial institutional barriers to telework. For instance, current Swedish laws entitle union representatives to visit teleworkers in their telework environment at the employer's expense. Eliminating barriers like these can stimulate telework. In Denmark, for example, telework was stimulated when a new law made a home computer supplied by an employer to an employee exempt from taxation as long as the computer was used for work-related tasks. The Netherlands introduced a similar law, allowing employers to pay a limited tax-free sum to compensate employed teleworkers for their costs related to telework.[24] The efforts in Denmark and the Netherlands to eliminate institutional barriers have resulted in the highest telework penetration levels in the EU.

Sometimes laws not directly related to telework can also prevent telework implementation. Residential zoning ordinances are a good example. Originally written in order to preserve the exclusive character of residential neighbourhoods and exclude occupations that would interfere with that character, these ordinances are sometimes written so broadly that they can be interpreted to exclude certain types of remote work.[25]

Generally speaking, current labour laws are not the best frameworks for encouraging telework implementation. Current laws are almost always based on conventional assumptions regarding workspace, time and action, and telework is unconventional with respect to all three elements. The telework workspace is not the conventional workplace. Furthermore, telework, if implemented part-time, even involves multiple workplaces. Telework's work time is often less well-defined and less separated from the employee's social time. Telework also challenges conventional assumptions regarding work action, because telework requires multiple competencies, including mastering technology-related skills and effectively managing one's own work processes.[26]

3.5 THE ORGANIZATIONAL ENVIRONMENT

As we said earlier, the challenge regarding telework implementation lies on the demand side, not the supply side. Hence, it is critical to understand the business challenges that organizations face, and the possible role of telework in answering these challenges.[27] A complete understanding of telework requires that we examine telework from the organization's point of view.

Although telework is sometimes implemented to reduce costs, many companies implement telework because it gives them a competitive edge,[28] or in order to motivate and retain workers.[29] When telework is used to facilitate outsourcing, it can also increase a company's adaptability and flexibility. Outsourcing or subcontracting of the non-strategic and often capital-intensive part of the value chain is common in today's fast-changing, competitive global markets. Outsourcing can give organizations better control over their non-strategic or low-skilled labour. In today's globally integrated economy, the erosion of national barriers makes available world-class capabilities in other countries. Telework allows companies to outsource outside of their immediate region.

Within a company, telework can result from either top-down or bottom-up pressures. In the case of top-down pressures, management takes the initiative to implement telework in order to achieve cost savings and other benefits. In the case of bottom-up pressures, on the other hand, employees take the initiative and try to persuade management to implement telework.[30] These two scenarios tend to involve different workers and different management motivations. In the top-down scenario, management is typically trying to use technology to increase automation, reduce the skill level needed, and improve control over the labour process. This sort of telework implementation especially affects closely-supervised workers with low skills and little power within the organization. In the bottom-up scenario, on the other hand, management is typically trying to create a more creative and relaxed work environment and to motivate and retain its highly-skilled workers.[31]

In the rest of this section, we will isolate and discuss the factors in the organizational environment that increase the chances of successful telework implementation.

Without question, telework is more likely to be successful if it contributes to the organization's strategic goals[32] and is consistent with the organization's overall strategic direction.[33]

Does telework have greater success in large companies or small ones? There is no clear answer. Large companies that are strongly hierarchical and 'Tayloristic' are highly efficient when faced with steadily-expanding markets. However, today's organizations typically face uncertain and rapidly-changing markets. In order to cope with such an environment, organizations must be flexible, and large, centrally organized units are rarely flexible. A dynamic environment requires smaller units, which can react quicker to changing external conditions.[34] This reasoning suggests that large centralized organizations are likely to introduce telework in order to increase organizational flexibility.[35] Furthermore, large organizations have longer vacancy durations than small organizations, and they recruit from a larger geographic area, making it more likely that they will use telework to fill vacancies.[36] One study of 12 European countries concludes that the likelihood of adopting telework increases with the size of the organization.[37]

On the other hand, a study of telework in Finland concludes just the opposite: the larger the organization, the less likely it is to use telework.[38] Telework may be easier to implement in small organizations because employees are more familiar with each other. Furthermore, the work output of employees working in small organizations is easier to identify than that of employees working in large organizations.[39] It has been suggested also that telework is easier to implement in smaller organizations because they tend to be more dynamic and non-hierarchical, especially those organizations active in the information business.[40]

Clearly, the relationship between size of organization and likelihood of successfully implementing telework is not simple; more data is needed. Perhaps the proper conclusion to draw is that of Huws (1993), who concluded that very large and very small companies are the ones most likely to implement telework.

A culture of electronic communication (e.g., employee familiarity with voicemail and e-mail) is clearly a telework driver.[41]

A flat and flexible organizational structure with minimal bureaucratic rules is another telework driver.[42] It is easier to implement telework in a dynamic and non-hierarchical organization than in a highly structured and hierarchical organization.[43]

Knowledge jobs are more conducive to telework than other kinds of jobs. Therefore, sectors with a higher proportion of knowledge jobs have a higher proportion of telework; the service and public sectors have a high proportion of teleworkers.[44] Table 3.1 gives an overview of the sectoral distribution of UK teleworkers. Telework can be found in all sectors, but 'Banking, finance & insurance' - a sector with a high percentage of knowledge workers (as well as less skilled, clerical workers, whose main tasks consist of processing, in a routine way, large volumes of information) - has a disproportionately high number of teleworkers.

Table 3.1   Sectoral distribution of UK teleworkers

Sector	% of total work force	% of teleworkers
Agriculture and fishing	2	2
Energy and water	1	1
Manufacturing	19	14
Construction	7	11
Distribution, hotels & restaurants	20	10
Transport & communication	7	4
Banking, finance & insurance etc.	**15**	**34**
Public administration, education & health	24	14
Other services	6	9
Total services	71	72

Source: Huws et al., 1999

This sectoral factor often helps explain why the penetration level of telework is higher in certain regions. For instance, in the UK the penetration level of telework is higher in London, the South East and East Anglia partly because, in those regions, the service and public sectors are responsible for most of the employment.[45]

As one would expect, telework achieves higher penetration if the organization is located in an area with high population density and/or high land value, or in an area where traffic is congested and commuting times are long.[46]

Office automation within the organization is another telework driver. Office automation is the application of integrated computer, communication and office product technologies and social science knowledge to support the activities and functions within an office.[47] By permitting more effective management and control of office workers, office automation facilitates flexible, innovative decentralized approaches to the organization of work, such as telework.[48] Furthermore, office automation helps to implement telework by linking and integrating the organization's different information systems. Finally, office automation can also help alleviate managers' concerns about how teleworkers allocate their time outside a traditional office setting and may thereby reduce managers' unwillingness to manage teleworkers.[49]

Besides office automation, another managerial technique that can influence telework implementation is BPR (Business Process Re-engineering). With BPR, process-oriented lines replace functional ones. Organizations that have applied such techniques are more customer-driven and often have flatter, more flexible structures that have outsourced non-core activities. Other key features of BPR are:

1. a shift from simple tasks to multi-dimensional work,
2. a performance focus on output, not presence,
3. employee empowerment,
4. location independence and
5. greater use of IT and telecommunications systems.

Because of these features, the application of BPR techniques may be a telework driver.[50]

For telework to be successful, the organization's managers must be willing to take on new tasks. Workers who are not present at the conventional workplace cannot be managed and supported in traditional ways. To manage teleworkers, special attention must be devoted to:

1. coordinating, controlling and motivating the teleworkers,
2. organizing their availability,
3. facilitating their communication with non-teleworkers,

4.   keeping the teleworkers informed,
5.   preventing the 'out of sight, out of mind' syndrome and
6.   preserving the corporate culture.[51]

Successful telework often requires a change in management style, as well. Face-to-face interactions and direct supervision must be replaced by coordination based on mutual trust.[52] Managers can no longer rely on 'showing up' as a measurement of efficiency; managers must use another criterion, such as output.[53] If managers feel they need to be in full control over the working process in their department, this could prove to be a major organizational barrier, because telework implementation shifts some responsibility from the manager to the teleworker. If managers measure their status by the number of employees literally surrounding them, then this will be a major barrier to telework implementation. Finally, if employees are evaluated on the basis of their punctuality, sociability and appearance rather than the quality of their work, this will be yet another barrier.[54]

The radicalness of the management skills required should not be overstated, however. Similar remote management skills have long been required for managers of branch office directors, supervisors of field workers and employees of consulting organizations.

Largely because of its effects on management, an attempt to implement telework can benefit an organization's structure. In order to implement telework successfully, management must:

1.   treat work as a system, not just a location,
2.   pay more attention to communication patterns and effective communication,
3.   establish well-defined goals and performance-monitoring procedures,
4.   use more effective information which enhances the quality and speed of decision-making and
5.   reassess operating style (for example, the formality of interaction, the political atmosphere and the degree of managerial control).[55]

Within each organization, telework will make more sense for some corporate functions than for others. According to Porter (1985), the activities within any firm can be divided into two major groups, namely primary activities (inbound logistics, outbound logistics, marketing, sales and operations) and support activities (upper management, human resources management, procurement and technology development).[56] Figure 3.2 shows which of these activities are often suited for telework.

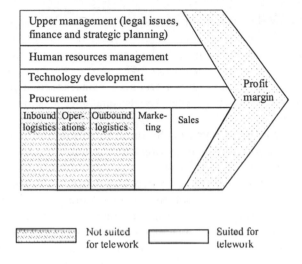

Upper management (legal issues, finance and strategic planning)				
Human resources management				
Technology development				
Procurement				
Inbound logistics	Oper-ations	Outbound logistics	Marke-ting	Sales

Profit margin

Not suited for telework   Suited for telework

Source: Eldid and Minoli, 1995

Figure 3.2 Potential teleworkers and their position in Porter's value chain

The only employees who must be in the corporate office full-time are employees performing operations functions (e.g., manufacturing, quality control) or functions in outbound or inbound logistics (e.g., inventory control).

As one would expect, organizations that make telework mandatory will be less successful than organizations that make it voluntary. Telework also will be more successful if the employee is given adequate opportunities to interact socially and professionally with co-workers. Social and professional isolation constitute, in fact, one of the major causes of dissatisfaction among teleworkers.[57] The employee's desire for social and professional interaction can often be satisfied by making the telework arrangement part-time, as we will discuss below.

Now that we have looked at the technological, institutional and organizational environments surrounding the telework implementation decision, it is time to look at the final component of our conceptual framework: the individual employee.

3.6 THE INDIVIDUAL EMPLOYEE

In the following discussion of the individual employee, we will first discuss the employee's situational characteristics (specifically, the employee's job characteristics, commuting characteristics and socio-demographic characteristics), and then we will discuss the employee's perceptions and attitudes.

One study that investigated why employees stopped working in a telework centre found that the most important reason for dropping out was job-related (for example, changing position within the organization, leaving the organization, technological difficulties, and/or high costs).[58] The second most important reason for dropping out was the negative attitude of the supervisor and/or employer. This study concluded that employees usually stop working in telework centres because of external circumstances, not because of dissatisfaction with the telework work arrangement itself.[59] Another study identified three main elements influencing withdrawal from a telework arrangement:

1. the need for a community (social interaction),
2. compulsion (when personal needs outside of work make telework necessary), and
3. comfort (the support the telework arrangement gets from management).[60]

Individuals with a high need for community are more likely to withdraw from a telework arrangement, while individuals with high levels of compulsion and comfort are less likely to withdraw. With respect to comfort, it is important that managers truly support the telework arrangement and do not just tolerate it.

3.6.1 SITUATIONAL CHARACTERISTICS OF THE INDIVIDUAL

3.6.1.1 Job characteristics
Certain job characteristics correlate with successful telework. As has been said, telework is well suited for both knowledge workers and unskilled workers.[61] Tasks that are location-dependent, poorly defined, demand face-to-face contact or do not require intense individual effort are not suitable for telework.[62] Tasks which include a substantial creative element requiring complex communication through face-to-face contact with other employees, are generally not suitable for telework either. On the other hand, tasks that are

location-independent, well-defined or routine are generally suitable for telework.[63]

It is useful to think in terms of tasks rather than jobs. Jobs often consist of a variety of tasks, some of which are suitable for telework. Where this is the case, part-time telework may be appropriate. For example, if an employee with a need for face-to-face communication can bundle that communication into periodic scheduled visits with her/his co-workers, that employee can be a part-time teleworker. Part-time telework avoids many of the problems associated with telework (such as social and professional isolation), while preserving many of the benefits (such as increased productivity, improved staff retention and increased job satisfaction).

The self-employed are particularly interested in telework, and a high proportion of teleworkers are self-employed.[64] Many self-employed teleworkers were once conventional workers employed by the same organization in a traditional capacity.

A high percentage of teleworkers today perform clerical jobs,[65] but a strong presence of clerical jobs in an organization simultaneously acts as a barrier to further growth of this practice.[66] This negative effect seems to arise because clerical workers lack general job control and functional suitability; furthermore, management often doubts that clerical workers can be productive when away from the office.[67] A large clerical labour force in an organization is a barrier to telework implementation, while a high number of knowledge workers is a driver to telework implementation.[68] Interestingly, there seems to be a significant split within the category of clerical workers. Only a small percentage of receptionists and secretarial workers perceive their job as suited for telework, but a large percentage of data processing employees indicate that their job is suited for telework.[69] It seems that only a small proportion of the total clerical labour force has jobs suited for telework and that the employees in the majority of those jobs suited for telework are already teleworking today.

Managers are more likely than other employees to adopt telework.[70] Generally speaking, managers enjoy high levels of autonomy and are trusted by their supervisors to do their jobs well. Managers tend to have more autonomy than their staff and may themselves already have been managed remotely to some degree.[71] However, managers tend to have a strong preference for face-to-face contact, so managerial telework is almost always only part-time.

The following occupation classes have a disproportionate share of teleworkers:

1.   managers and administrators,

2.   professional occupations, and
3.   associate professional and technical occupations.

Table 3.2, an overview of the occupational distribution of UK teleworkers, shows this unbalanced representation.

Table 3.2   Occupational distribution of UK teleworkers

Occupational category	% of total work force	% of teleworkers
Managers and administrators	16	26
Professional occupations	10	23
Associate professional & technical occupations	10	18
Clerical, secretarial occupations	15	9
Craft and related occupations	12	12
Personal, protective occupations	11	1
Sales occupations	8	8
Plant and machine operatives	9	1
Other occupations	8	1

Source: Huws et al., 1999

Appendix 2 lists occupations suited for telework. Note that most occupations are suited for part-time telework, not full-time telework.[72]

3.6.1.2 Commuting characteristics

Besides the characteristics of the job itself, the commute required to perform that job is also relevant to the employee's decision whether or not to telework. As one would expect, interest in electronic homework is usually highest in small towns and suburban regions around big cities with low levels of public transportation. The level of interest is lower in the big cities themselves. The time spent commuting seems to play a major role in determining attitudes toward electronic homework: the interest in electronic homework in suburban regions increases with the size of the city surrounded. Commuting distance may also be a factor driving telework, although the data is not as clear as for commuting time.[73]

In the future, the commuting trip may become more expensive (as a result of increasing road pricing and parking pricing) and/or take longer (as a result of higher congestion). These factors would be telework drivers.

Although the effect of commuting stress on productivity has not yet been recognized, it is possible that many workers need to recover from getting to work for at least the first half-hour of the day. If the impact of commuting stress on productivity is established, that will also drive telework implementation.[74]

3.6.1.3 Socio-demographic characteristics

3.6.1.3.1 Household complexity

The more complex the employee's household, the greater the employee's desire for flexibility, and hence the greater the employee's desire for telework. 'Household complexity' is a function of the size of the household, the number of household members who need special care,[75] and the employee's capacity to manage non-work requirements. This last factor is especially important these days, as two-income families and single-parent families tend to be the standard, and as the proportion of working women with small children has increased.[76] Furthermore, as the baby boom population moves on to retirement age, the number of households with elder-care responsibilities will increase. Employees with high household complexity value flexibility because it helps them satisfy both work and non-work requirements. This sort of flexibility is especially valued by women with children under six years old; telework can give these women the flexibility to handle child-related illnesses and other emergencies.[77]

Caring for children (or the elderly) and working at home cannot be literally combined at the same time. If child-care facilities were needed to go out to work, they will also be needed to work at home. Most teleworkers with little children have child-care arrangements. Telework is useful because it allows employees to arrange work hours around family commitments; it does not allow employees to literally fulfill both work and family commitments at the same time.[78]

3.6.1.3.2 Housing conditions

The adoption of electronic homework on a regular basis becomes easier if all or part of a room is set aside for home office functions and it is possible to work undisturbed in that space, without interruption from other household members.[79] Hence, individuals living in small houses or apartments will be less likely to adopt telework due to spatial constraints.[80]

3.6.1.3.3 Gender

Gender has often been put forward as a key determinant of the telework choice. However, the situation is complicated. There are no simple generalizations about which gender has a more positive attitude towards telework.[81] Women more than men choose to telework in order to maintain their flexibility to schedule child and elderly care.[82] This is obviously related to the fact that women still bear a disproportionate share of the household responsibilities. Women more than men are attracted to telework as a solution for employees who need to work while permanently or temporarily unable to access the work place.[83] Men more than women are attracted to telework as a way to get more work done. In many countries, men are disproportionately over-represented in the telework work force. In the UK, 68 percent of all teleworkers are men;[84] in Finland, 75 percent of all teleworkers are men;[85] in Sweden, 62 percent of teleworkers are men.[86] It seems that men are more likely to telework part-time, while women are more likely to telework full-time.[87] In Sweden, for example, most male teleworkers telework part-time, while most female teleworkers telework full-time.[88] This is consistent with the finding that women have a stronger preference than men for full-time telework.[89]

This gender preference regarding the adoption of telework is due to more than just the above reasons; it is also partly due to the difference between men's and women's typical occupations. Today, most women are employed in low-skilled jobs with poor working conditions, while most men are employed in highly-skilled jobs with very good working conditions. Women are over-represented in clerical/secretarial occupations, while highly-skilled men are over-represented in technical/managerial/professional occupations.[90] Research indicates that if occupational differences are eliminated, men and women exhibit the same preference pattern.[91]

3.6.1.3.4   Wage

Teleworkers' wages vary considerably,[92] but, on average, teleworkers earn more than non-teleworkers, due to a combination of factors. First, employees with higher incomes are more likely to have the necessary spare room to organize a workplace in their home.[93] Second, jobs suited for telework may be, on average, higher-paying than jobs not suited for telework.[94] However, this general conclusion should not obfuscate the fact that, at present, we still find many clerical workers engaged in telework and performing routine tasks.

3.6.1.3.5   Education

Like wages, teleworkers' education also varies considerably, but, on average, teleworkers have more education than non-teleworkers,[95] likely due to the same two factors as in the previous paragraph. More-educated employees are more likely to have the necessary room at home, and jobs suited for telework may, on average, require higher education than jobs not suited for telework.[96]

3.6.1.3.6   Age

Generally speaking, the acceptance of telework decreases with employee age. In Italy, Germany, the UK and France, for example, the acceptance of electronic homework decreases rapidly with employee age.[97] This relationship holds for the United States, as well.[98] One explanation is that the youngest age group is the most familiar with information technology. Another explanation is that each age group includes both single or childless people, who may prefer to stay in the conventional work environment in order to maximize social contacts, as well as people who may prefer to stay at home to spend more time with their families. In the age category 30 - 39, the latter group of people is larger than the former, which would help explain that group's stronger positive attitude toward the adoption of telework.[99]

In some countries, though, the opposite relationship holds, and younger workers are less likely to telework. In Sweden, for example, one third of all teleworkers are in the 40 - 49 age group. The next largest group is the 50 - 59 age group; the 30 - 39 age group comes in third. These findings can be explained by the fact that individuals in the older age groups have already established themselves in the labour market and in many cases do not seek further career advancements. Employees in the older age groups have more of the resources (experience, clients or capital) needed for homeworking. Although individuals in the younger age groups may be more familiar with ICT technology and more open to change, they have a greater need for promotion.[100] Finally, employees in the older age groups have often been with the same organization longer, so employers may have more certainty about their loyalty to the organization.[101]

Let us now move from discussing the individual's situational characteristics (job characteristics, commuting characteristics and socio-demographic characteristics) to discuss the individual's beliefs and attitudes. At the most general level, a particular individual's attitude toward telework is determined by that individual's beliefs about the outcomes of the actual implementation of telework and the values of these outcomes for that individual. Those beliefs and values can be analyzed using the following categories.

3.6.2 PERCEPTIONS AND ATTITUDES OF THE EMPLOYEE

Lifestyle preferences reflect an individual's very long-term preferences. A person's lifestyle is determined by three major life decisions: participation in the labour force, formation of a household and orientation toward leisure. These major choices provide the basis for smaller decisions, including the decision to adopt telework. Hence, parameters related to work or career, family and leisure will influence the adoption of telework.

The individual's actual adoption of telework is also closely linked to the subjective norm that exists about telework. The subjective norm concerns the individual's normative beliefs about what supervisors and co-workers think should be done, and the individual's motivation to comply with their wishes.[102] For this reason, as we have said before, the attitudes of the employer and management are crucial to the adoption of telework.

3.6.2.1 Personal attitudes
Some employees will simply never make good teleworkers, no matter what their employment situation may be. In order to be a good teleworker, an individual needs to be self-disciplined, well-organized in time management, dedicated, able to work on her/his own, self-confident, able to communicate well, flexible, trustworthy, and able to get along well with clients and colleagues; good teleworkers also need to have (or be able to learn) the necessary ICT-specific skills.[103]

3.6.2.2 Awareness/misunderstanding of telework
Individuals who have a negative misperception about telework are unlikely to consider it as an option. Although many people have heard the term 'telework,' few understand what it really involves. The image of telework is sometimes rather negative due to several false perceptions of the practice.

1. Many people think telework implies unskilled, low-paid office work, through either a full-time contract or a freelance relationship. A common image is that of a mother with young children, isolated from the working office community, engaged in monotonous word processing.
2. Many people think that telework means working at home. This is the most common form of telework, but telecentres and satellite offices are at least as feasible as homework when not taking into account cost constraints.
3. Some people think that telework is just for computer programmers and other data processing jobs. However, this is not the job criterion that should be used. A much more sensible criterion is whether or not an employee has a number of tasks that are location-independent for at least one fifth of her/his working hours.
4. Many people assume that telework means being away from the office full-time. If this were the case, the majority of jobs would be unsuitable for telework. **Full-time telework is generally not advisable.** Teleworkers need to come into the office on a regular basis to attend

meetings, make presentations and socialize with co-workers, even if their job profile would, theoretically, allow full-time telework.

These myths or misunderstandings are major barriers to the adoption of telework. If the misunderstanding is severe and negative enough, it can act as a binding constraint. However, moderate levels of misunderstanding will simply increase or decrease the likelihood of adopting telework.

3.6.2.3 Risk aversion
Risk-averse employees are less likely to try telework. Telework is a relatively new working form not yet commonly implemented in organizations. For that reason, risk-averse employees will tend to perceive telework as a high-risk undertaking with an unknown effect on their employment potential.

3.6.2.4 Satisfaction with life
Interestingly, individuals who are generally satisfied with their lives are more willing to adopt telework. The explanation for this correlation may be that general satisfaction with life is linked to the control an individual has over her/his work.[104]

3.6.2.5 Dissatisfaction with non-telework arrangement
As one would expect, dissatisfaction with a current non-telework arrangement (for example, dissatisfaction with the low amount of quality time currently spent with one's family) drives telework adoption. Telework allows employees to rearrange their working hours to better suit their multiple interests.

3.7 CONCLUSION

Like the automobile, the internet and intranet will change society. These technologies will allow us to move from physically-oriented to non-physically-oriented communication structures, in which spatial and temporal boundaries will be significantly reduced.[105] Most industrialized countries are evolving from a culture based on physical contacts to a virtual society where goods and services are accessible without the need for face-to-face interaction. For instance, electronic inventory management and procurement systems are widely adopted in organizations, and electronic money transfers, distance learning, home banking and teleshopping are increasingly used by average individuals.

Telework is part of this evolution toward a virtual society. The virtual workplace should therefore be viewed not as a societal feature that requires enforcement, but rather as the natural result of an evolution towards a virtual society.

However, we should be realistic about the future scope of telework. In order to realistically assess the future potential of telework, the conceptual framework outlined in this chapter needs to be taken into account. This chapter's conceptual framework has identified the target group implementation potential as critical to telework adoption. The target group implementation potential is itself determined by a number of environmental and individual-level parameters. In the next chapter, the relevance of the environmental parameters affecting the target group implementation potential will be empirically evaluated for the Brussels business environment. Then, in Chapter 5, the relevance of the individual-level parameters also identified in this chapter will be empirically evaluated for Brussels employees.

NOTES

[1]   This chapter builds upon the article: V. Illegems, A. Verbeke and R. S'Jegers, (2001), 'The Organizational Context of Teleworking Implementation', *Technological Forecasting and Social Change*, **68**, 275 - 91. Excerpts from this article were reprinted with permission from Elsevier Science.

[2]   Qvortrup (1998), Sturesson (1998) and Korte and Wynne (1996).

[3]   Mokhtarian and Salomon (1996a), Gillespie et al. (1995), Huws (1993), Jackson and van der Wielen (1998), Reichwald and Möslein (1999), Qvortrup (1992), Korte (1988), Köhler et al. (1988a) and Steinle (1988).

[4]   Empirica (1985).

[5]   Mahmassani et al. (1993), Bernardino et al. (1992), Mokhtarian and Salomon (1994), Mokhtarian and Salomon (1996a), Mokhtarian and Salomon (1996b) and Mokhtarian and Salomon (1997).

[6]   The environmental parameters are emphasized by Kugelmass (1995), Nilles (1998), Limburg (1998) and Huws (1993), and applied to the Brussels context by Illegems et al. (1999, 2000 and 2001).

[7]   Typically, the decision process has two tiers: the individual first decides whether or not to telework and then decides the frequency with which to telework. In some cases, of course, the adoption of telework and the determination of the frequency are not distinct decisions - namely, when the latter decision is an integral part of the former.

[8]   Nilles (1998).

[9]   For this reason, knowledge workers themselves do not need to be physically centralized; only the information does. Current ICT technology makes this relatively easy. For this reason, knowledge workers often make ideal teleworkers. We will discuss this further in the sections on the organizational environment and the employee's situational characteristics.

[10] Teo et al. (1998), Huws et al. (1999), Gordon (1988) and Bernardino et al. (1992).

[11] The wide range of other sophisticated new communication and computerized equipment available at decreasing cost is another major driver to telework implementation.

[12] Weijers and Weijers (1988).

[13] Fortunately, the current liberalization of the telecommunications market increases competition and reduces the cost of telework.

[14] Gray et al. (1994).

[15] Eldid and Minoli (1995).

[16] Nilles (1998) and Cross and Raizman (1986).

[17] Agres et al. (1998), Steinle (1988), Olson (1988), Gordon (1988) and Olson (1982).

[18] Gray (1997).

[19] Gurstein (1991).

[20] Huws et al. (1999).

[21] Ibid.

[22] Privacy protection is especially relevant for telework. Employers need to supervise their teleworking employees, but the teleworker's privacy must be respected (de Vries 1988).

[23] Huws (1994).

[24] European Commission (1998).

[25] Cross and Raizman (1986).

[26] Valenduc and Vendramin (1999). For these reasons, the Belgian law on homework therefore argues that detailed rules should be established at the sectoral level (SERV 1999).

[27] Gray (1997).

[28] Kondo (1999).

[29] As we will discuss further below, telework can have the spill-over effect of benefiting the company's organizational structure.

[30] Gordon (1988) and Huws (1993).

[31] Tomaskovic-Devey and Risman (1993), Bernardino et al. (1992), Olson (1982) and Kraut (1989).

[32] Reichwald and Möslein (1999) and Stanworth and Stanworth (1991).

[33] Gray (1997).

[34] Steinle (1988).

[35] Evidence provided by Empirica (1985) suggests that in larger organizations employees are more interested in electronic homework (Huws et al. 1993).

[36] van Ommeren (1998).

[37] van Ommeren (1998).

[38] Zamindar (1995). Although Finland was included in the van Ommeren study, 50 percent of the total sample was collected in the UK, Denmark and Sweden. Tomaskovic-Devey and Risman (1993) found that large organizations were less likely to adopt telework unless employee retention was a major issue, in which case the organization was likely to adopt telework.

[39] Luukinen et al. (1996).

[40] Apgar IV (1998).

[41] Huws et al. (1999). Media use is largely determined by the attitude of co-workers, as well as management, organizational and group norms and interaction patterns at the workplace. Hence, in an organization favouring electronic communication, the individual employee is more inclined to favour electronic communication (Shin et al. 1999) and consequently facilitate the adoption of telework.

[42] Huws et al. (1999).

[43] Apgar IV (1998).

44   van Ommeren (1998) and Huws (1993).
45   Huws (1993).
46   Huws (1993).
47   Huws et al. (1993).
48   Olson (1982).
49   Watad and DiSanzo (2000).
50   DG XIII-B (1995).
51   Bergum (1998). Some managers fear that telework will involve significantly more work for
     them in terms of preparing work assignments and monitoring progress (Olson, 1988).
52   NUTEK (1997).
53   However, if telework is implemented on a part-time basis only, these requirements should
     not be exaggerated (Bergum 1998).
54   Cross and Raizman (1986).
55   Bush (1990).
56   It is worth noting that planning and implementing telework requires the involvement of
     human resources management, upper management and technology development. HRM
     departments calculate the costs and benefits of telework and then plan the programmes,
     determine the number of participants (as well as the functions and departments that can
     participate), and finally select the individuals. Upper management is involved because it
     needs to approve the plans suggested by the HRM department. The technology development
     department is contacted by the HRM department in order to see whether technological
     difficulties can be overcome (Eldid and Minoli, 1995).
57   This fact has been noted repeatedly in the literature. For a discussion, see Bélanger (1999).
58   Varma et al. (1998).
59   Employees quitting telework arrangements often indicate the desire to begin telework again
     when the circumstances permit.
60   Fireman (1998).
61   Telework by unskilled labour will cause some unskilled jobs to disappear in certain areas
     because the jobs can be performed cheaper in Third World countries or in less-developed
     rural areas in the industrialized world (Qvortrup, 1992).
62   Bush (1990).
63   Nilles (1997).
64   Empirica (1985), Huws (1993), Olson (1988), Huws (1988), Handy and Mokhtarian (1995)
     and Kraut (1989).
65   Huws (1993) and Stanworth and Stanworth (1991).
66   Mannering and Mokhtarian (1995).
67   Mannering and Mokhtarian (1995).
68   Tomaskovic-Devey and Risman (1993).
69   Mahmassani et al. (1993).
70   Mokhtarian and Salomon (1996b).
71   Mokhtarian et al. (1998).
72   Lists of occupations suited for telework are bound to become obsolete as ICT opens up new
     choices in terms of who does what type of work, where, when and how (Huws et al. 1999).
73   Sullivan et al. (1993), Mokhtarian and Salomon (1996a), Handy and Mokhtarian (1994) and
     Mahmassani et al. (1993).
74   Olson (1988).
75   Mannering and Mokhtarian (1995).
76   Olson (1988), Handy and Mokhtarian (1994) and Handy and Mokhtarian (1996b).
77   Mannering and Mokhtarian (1995), Mokhtarian and Salomon (1996b), Kraut (1989) and
     Holti and Stern (1987). Other research findings indicate that the presence of children under

the age of 16 has a positive influence on the adoption of telework. See Mahmassani et al. (1993) and Bernardino et al. (1992).

[78] Gray et al. (1994) and Kraut (1989).

[79] Mannering and Mokhtarian (1995) and Huws et al. (1999).

[80] Gurstein (1991).

[81] Empirica (1985).

[82] Mokhtarian et al. (1998) and Moktharian and Salomon (1996a).

[83] Mokhtarian and Salomon (1997) and Kraut (1989).

[84] Huws et al. (1999).

[85] Luukinen (1996).

[86] Engström and Johanson (1998).

[87] Huws (1994).

[88] Engström and Johanson (1998).

[89] Huws et al. (1999).

[90] Chapman et al. (1995).

[91] Huws (1996).

[92] Huws et al. (1993). For example, see Luukinen (1996) for data on Finland.

[93] Van Neerven (1991), Mannering and Mokhtarian (1995) and Bagley and Mokhtarian (1997).

[94] Handy and Mokhtarian (1994).

[95] See Luukinen (1996) for data on Finland, and Engström and Johanson (1998) for data on Sweden.

[96] A high education level increases the likelihood of the availability of a comfortable home office, thus leading to a preference for home-based telework over centre-based telework (telework centre workspaces are generally perceived to be inferior to home offices) (Bagley and Mokhtarian, 1997).

[97] Empirica (1985), discussed in Huws et al. (1993).

[98] Mokhtarian and Salomon (1996a).

[99] Huws et al. (1993).

[100] Engström and Johanson (1998).

[101] Kraut (1989).

[102] Yap and Tng (1990).

[103] Kinsman (1987), Huws et al. (1999) and Nilles (1998).

[104] Mannering and Mokhtarian (1995).

[105] Agres et al. (1998).

4. A MANAGERIAL PERSPECTIVE ON TELEWORK ADOPTION: PARAMETERS AFFECTING THE EMPLOYER'S VIEW[1]

4.1 INTRODUCTION

This chapter describes in more detail and empirically assesses the environmental components of last chapter's conceptual framework (i.e., the technological, institutional and organizational environments surrounding the decision to implement telework by the target group). Our analysis builds upon the empirical findings of a survey we conducted among a large number of human resources managers of large firms in Brussels.

In this chapter, we address the following questions:

1. What kinds of organizations are likely to have already implemented telework, or to implement it in the future?
2. From the employer's point of view, what are the advantages and disadvantages of telework, and how do employers rate those advantages and disadvantages?
3. In what ways do employers with telework experience perceive telework's advantages and disadvantages differently from employers without telework experience?
4. In what ways do employers planning to implement telework perceive its advantages and disadvantages differently from employers not planning to implement telework?
5. From the employer's perspective, what policy tools would most effectively promote telework?

4.2 ENVIRONMENTAL BARRIERS AND DRIVERS IN THE BRUSSELS BUSINESS ENVIRONMENT

Human resources managers of 230 companies in Brussels were asked to complete a questionnaire regarding telework. We defined telework in the survey as work from home, a satellite office, a telework centre or any other workstation outside of the main office for at least one day per workweek. Some sort of telecommunication technology is used to substitute for work-related travel, but it need not be continuous, on-line communication. These organizations were selected on the basis of two criteria:

1. The organization had to have at least 90 employees in Belgium.
2. It had to have an office or production facility in Brussels.[2]

Of those companies, 83 completed and returned the questionnaire. At the time of the questionnaire, 19 of the 83 organizations had already implemented telework; all 19 expressed the desire to implement telework on a larger scale in the future. Twenty other organizations suggested they would start implementing telework in the near future.

To analyse the questionnaire data, we used both revealed preferences (preferences revealed by a factual situation, in this case whether the organization has or has not implemented telework) and stated preferences (preferences indicated by a statement, in this case whether the organization states it intends to implement telework in the future). Stated preference analysis has been criticized on the grounds that the presentation of a hypothetical choice lacks realism. Furthermore, an individual's stated preferences (in this case representing the organization's preferences) may not correspond closely to her or his actual preferences. Nonetheless, we chose to include stated preference analysis for a number of reasons. First, the number of firms presently adopting telework is relatively small. Second, the questionnaire explicitly highlights both the advantages and disadvantages of telework, in order to generate a more realistic hypothetical choice for those firms that have not yet adopted telework. Third, relatively high levels of familiarity with the concept of telework suggest that respondents are capable of evaluating their decision in terms of quite realistic comparisons. (Of course, some errors will remain in this regard, as individuals may respond based on hearsay or vague information rather than on accurate knowledge.) Finally, some research concludes that stated preference analysis provides a reasonable account of an individual's current choices.[3]

We looked at many economic sectors[4] and a wide range of organizations.[5] The parameters studied represent environmental elements from the perspective of the employee that may be conducive or detrimental to telework adoption. For each environmental characteristic included in the survey, we formulate hypotheses regarding its likely impact on the current and future adoption of telework. We construct hypotheses that allow both stated and revealed preference analysis. First, we compare organizations intending to implement telework in the future (this category includes organizations that have already implemented telework) with organizations not intending to do so: this is the stated preference analysis. With each hypothesis, we try to assess whether organizations that share a particular characteristic (e.g., being active in a knowledge-based sector) have a different propensity to engage in future telework adoption (in terms of intent), as compared to organizations that do not share this characteristic (in this case, these are organizations active in other sectors than knowledge-based ones). Then, we compare organizations that have already implemented telework with organizations that have not yet done so: this is the revealed preference analysis. Here, with each hypothesis, we try to assess whether organizations that share a particular characteristic (e.g., being active in a knowledge-based sector) have a different propensity to engage in current telework adoption, as compared to organizations that do not share this characteristic (in this case, these are organizations active in other sectors than knowledge-based ones). These comparisons are made based on a χ^2-analysis in the case of a dichotomous variable. However, in cases whereby the comparison is performed for a continuous variable, a t-test is used. If the calculated p-value is lower than or equal to 0.05, then the hypothesis is accepted with a confidence level of 95 percent. If the calculated p-value is lower than or equal to 0.1, then the hypothesis is accepted with a confidence level of 90 percent.

4.2.1 AWARENESS OF THE CONCEPT OF TELEWORK

The literature suggests that if organizations have no in-depth knowledge of the concept of telework, this acts as a (dichotomous) constraint and essentially precludes telework from being chosen as a possible work arrangement.[6]

Hypothesis 1a: If an organization has no in-depth knowledge of the concept of telework, it is less likely to intend implementing telework in the future.

Hypothesis 1b: If an organization has no in-depth knowledge of the concept of telework, the organization is less likely to have implemented telework already.

Our empirical findings support both hypotheses. Organizations that have not been faced explicitly with the concept are less willing to implement telework in the future (hypothesis a) and also are less likely to have implemented it already (hypothesis b). (hypothesis 1a: 2 groups: 21.3 percent versus 80.6 percent,[7] χ^2, p = 0.000) (hypothesis 1b: 2 groups: 0 percent versus 52.8 percent, χ^2, p = 0.000)

4.2.2 CORE COMPETENCIES

As indicated earlier, knowledge workers perform many tasks suited for telework. This suggests the hypothesis that sectors where knowledge is a key asset may represent a good environment in which to implement telework.

Hypothesis 2a: If an organization is active in a knowledge-based sector, it is more likely to intend implementing telework in the future.

Hypothesis 2b: If an organization is active in a knowledge-based sector, the organization is more likely to have implemented telework.

These hypotheses were confirmed. (hypothesis 2a: 2 groups: 63 percent versus 27 percent, χ^2, p = 0.001) (hypothesis 2b: 2 groups: 34.8 percent versus 8.1 percent, χ^2, p = 0.004)

4.2.3 INTERNAL ORGANIZATION

4.2.3.1 Electronic communication
Electronic communication has eliminated boundaries of space and time, making an increasing number of tasks location-independent. Hence, one might expect that organizations where electronic communication prevails would be more inclined to implement telework.

Hypothesis 3a: If there is electronic communication within an organization, it is more likely to intend implementing telework in the future.

Hypothesis 3b: If there is electronic communication within an organization, the organization is more likely to have implemented telework.

Both hypotheses were confirmed. (hypothesis 3a: 2 groups: 53.5 percent versus 8.3 percent, χ^2, p = 0.004) (hypothesis 3b: 2 groups: 26.8 percent versus 0 percent, χ^2, p = 0.041)

4.2.3.2 LANs (Local Area Networks)

LANs can be easily connected to WANs (Wide Area Networks). If the conventional office has a LAN, remote workers can easily access files there.

Hypothesis 4a: If a LAN is accessible to the majority of the employees, it is more likely to intend implementing telework in the future.

Hypothesis 4b: If a LAN is accessible to the majority of the employees, the organization is more likely to have implemented telework.

Both hypotheses were confirmed. (hypothesis 4a: 2 groups: 53.7 percent versus 18.8 percent, χ^2, p = 0.012) (hypothesis 4b: 2 groups: 26.9 percent versus 6.3 percent, χ^2, p = 0.078)

4.2.3.3 Dominant coordination and control mechanism

In order to organize business effectively, organizations require coordination and control mechanisms. According to Mintzberg (1981), there are six main categories of coordination and control mechanisms:

1. mutual adjustment,
2. direct supervision,
3. standardization of work,
4. standardization of outputs,
5. standardization of skills, and
6. standardization of norms.

In any organization, one of these modes usually dominates. As indicated earlier, direct supervision is not an appropriate mechanism to manage teleworkers; the more output-oriented modes are better.

Hypothesis 5a: If the coordination and control within an organization is output-oriented, it is more likely to intend implementing telework in the future.

Hypothesis 5b: If the coordination and control within an organization is output-oriented, the organization is more likely to have implemented telework.

Hypothesis 6a: If the coordination and control in an organization is primarily based on direct supervision, it is less likely to intend implementing telework in the future.

Hypothesis 6b: If the coordination and control in an organization is primarily based on direct supervision, the organization is less likely to have implemented telework.

The correlations found as a result of testing hypothesis 5 (hypothesis 5a: 5 groups: 92.9 percent versus 44.4 percent versus 36.4 percent versus 38.9 percent versus 31.8 percent,[8] χ^2, p = 0.005) (hypothesis 5b: 2 groups: 43.8 percent versus 5 percent, χ^2, p = 0.000) and hypothesis 6 (hypothesis 6a: 2 groups: 61.8 percent versus 30.6 percent, χ^2, p = 0.009) (hypothesis 6b: 2 groups: 41.2 percent versus 8.3 percent, χ^2, p = 0.001) were significant. No significant results were found for the other coordination and control mechanisms.

4.2.3.4 Information processes
Internal information flows largely determine organizational decision-making. These information flows may be sequential or reciprocal, strongly focused on routine or non-routine decision-making, and focused on teamwork or not.

Hypothesis 7a: If sequential internal information flows are dominant, it is more likely to intend implementing telework in the future.

Hypothesis 7b: If sequential internal information flows are dominant, the organization is more likely to have implemented telework.

Hypothesis 8a: If internal information flows are strongly focused on non-routine decision-making, it is more likely to intend implementing telework in the future.

Hypothesis 8b: If internal information flows are strongly focused on non-routine decision-making, the organization is more likely to have implemented telework.

Hypothesis 9a: If internal information flows that result from teamwork are dominant, it is less likely to intend implementing telework in the future.

Hypothesis 9b: If internal information flows that result from teamwork are dominant, the organization is less likely to have implemented telework.

The empirical findings suggest that hypothesis 7 is significant, but – surprisingly - the relationship appears negative rather than positive. (hypothesis 7a: 3 groups: 26.1 percent versus 46.7 percent versus 63.3

percent,[9] χ^2, p = 0.027) (hypothesis 7b: 2 groups: 8.7 percent versus 28.3 percent, χ^2, p = 0.057) The reason for this could be that most knowledge workers function in a context of reciprocal information processes, rather than sequential ones. The relationship put forward in hypothesis 8, namely that a strong focus on non-routine decision-making drives telework implementation, is supported by the data. (hypothesis 8a: 2 groups: 59.5 percent versus 34.1 percent, χ^2, p = 0.021) (hypothesis 8b: 2 groups: 33.3 percent versus 12.2 percent, χ^2, p = 0.022) In contrast, the presumed negative impact of teamwork on telework implementation was not confirmed. On the contrary, as teamwork becomes more important to an organization, telework implementation becomes more likely. (hypothesis 9a: 3 groups: 25 percent versus 37 percent versus 59.1 percent,[10] χ^2, p = 0.05) (hypothesis 9b: 2 groups: 10.3 percent versus 34.1 percent, χ^2, p = 0.01) Here again, the underlying factor may be that potential teleworkers are mainly knowledge workers. These workers mostly work in teams and can effectively communicate electronically.

4.2.3.5 Flexible work hours
Flexible work hours allow organizations to adjust more smoothly to the global nature of business. They also allow employees to organize their work according to their personal preferences. One would expect that experience with flexible work hours would increase the propensity to implement other innovative work arrangements.

Hypothesis 10a: If an organization has experience with flexible work hours, it is less likely to intend implementing telework in the future.

Hypothesis 10b: If an organization has experience with flexible work hours, it is more likely to have implemented telework.

The empirical results confirm these correlations. (hypothesis 10a: 2 groups: 58.3 percent versus 17.4 percent, χ^2, p = 0.001) (hypothesis 10b: 2 groups: 31.7 percent versus 0 percent, χ^2, p = 0.002)

4.2.3.6 Degree of autonomy
The hypothesis that local subsidiaries of a foreign multinational enterprise would not implement telework because of a lack of intra-organizational power was not confirmed. Although some local subsidiaries did report they would not implement telework because their request had been refused by the head office, other subsidiaries reported just the opposite.

4.2.4 HUMAN RESOURCES ISSUES

4.2.4.1 Number of employees
Implementing telework on a regular basis in medium-sized and large organizations requires adjustments in the way work is organized, and this rethinking of the work process requires substantial resources. This suggests that telework may be more feasible in larger organizations.

Hypothesis 11a: The greater the number of employees that work in an organization, the more likely its intent to implement telework in the future.

Hypothesis 11b: The greater the number of employees that work in a organization, the more likely that it has implemented telework.

A significant correlation was found for this hypothesis. (hypothesis 11a: t-test, p = 0.046) (hypothesis 11b: t-test, p = 0.057)

4.2.4.2 Category of employees
Because knowledge workers are mainly white-collar workers, one might expect that organizations where blue-collar workers dominate the work force would not implement telework, whereas organizations with a majority of white-collar workers would be more willing or likely to implement telework.

Hypothesis 12a: If most employees in an organization are blue-collar workers, it is less likely to intend implementing telework in the future.

Hypothesis 12b: If most employees in an organization are blue-collar workers, the organization is less likely to have implemented telework.

Hypothesis 13a: If most employees in an organization are white-collar workers, it is more likely to intend implementing telework in the future.

Hypothesis 13b: If most employees in an organization are white-collar workers, the organization is more likely to have implemented telework

Hypothesis 12 was confirmed. (hypothesis 12a: 2 groups: 22.2 percent versus 58.9 percent, χ^2, p = 0.002) (hypothesis 12b: 2 groups: 11.1 percent versus 28.6 percent, χ^2, p = 0.076) Hypothesis 13 required special treatment, because the concept of 'white-collar workers' is not used in Belgium. Instead, 'kaderleden' (members of the managerial team) and 'bedienden' (white-collar workers that are not part of the managerial team) constitute the two components of this part of the work force. Hence, hypothesis 13 was tested twice, once for 'kaderleden' and once for 'bedienden.' Hypothesis 13a was confirmed, whereas hypothesis 13b was not. (hypothesis 13a: 'kaderleden': 2 groups: 56.6 percent versus 30 percent, χ^2, p = 0.02 and 'bedienden': 2 groups: 55.8 percent versus 32.3 percent, χ^2, p = 0.038)

4.2.4.3 Work arrangement
As an extension of the hypothesis on flexible working hours, it could be assumed that companies with a work force largely composed of employees with a temporary contract would be more likely or willing to introduce telework.

Hypothesis 14a: If a substantial part of the employees of an organization have temporary contracts, it is more likely to intend implementing telework in the future.

Hypothesis 14b: If a substantial part of the employees of an organization have temporary contracts, the organization is more likely to have implemented telework.

No significant result was found for hypothesis 14a. Surprisingly, the relationship in hypothesis 14b appears negative rather than positive. That is, organizations are less likely to have implemented telework if a substantial part of their employees have temporary contracts. (hypothesis 14b: 2 groups: 13.6 percent versus 33.3 percent, χ^2, p = 0.033) One possible explanation is that employers are more likely to let senior employees telework because they have proven themselves loyal.[11] Expressed in more general terms, organizations may be likely to introduce telework arrangements only if the employees are well 'socialized' - and such socialization is less likely to occur in the case of workers with temporary contracts. However, this result is not supported by the stated preference results (hypothesis 14a). The main reason for this is probably that most organizations willing to implement telework in the future will tend to do this as a motivational tool for highly-skilled workers with long-term contracts, so that the presence of employees with short-term contracts will no longer be relevant to the telework decision-making process.

4.2.4.4 Outsourcing
As mentioned earlier, outsourcing of the non-strategic and often capital-intensive part of the value chain is now increasingly required because firms in many industries are faced with stronger competition from flexible, cost-effective rivals at the international level. Outsourcing represents the outcome of firm-level decision-making processes that systematically seek to redefine

the boundaries between the firm and its environment, and to reassess the firm's 'administrative heritage.' In such a context, new innovations can flourish and one would expect that telework implementation, as a new way to organize work efficiently, would also be considered more seriously.

Hypothesis 15a: If outsourcing is used for a number of non-strategic and capital-intensive parts of the value chain in an organization, it is more likely to intend implementing telework in the future.

Hypothesis 15b: If outsourcing is used for a number of non-strategic and capital-intensive parts of the value chain in an organization, the organization is more likely to have implemented telework.

These hypotheses were confirmed. (hypothesis 15a: 2 groups: 66.7 percent versus 42.6 percent, χ^2, p = 0.092) (hypothesis 15b: 2 groups: 53.3 percent versus 16.2 percent, χ^2, p = 0.002) To the extent that higher outsourcing can be viewed as a proxy for firm-level flexibility in the face of strong rivalry and innovation in industry, it also appears to be associated with telework adoption. This result suggests that the choice to adopt telework is not a stand-alone decision, but one of perhaps several responses to improve firm efficiency and effectiveness when environmental forces impose a 'reengineering mentality' on companies.

4.2.4.5 Education level
A high employee education level may be viewed as a proxy for the skill level required in an organization and may therefore also be relevant to telework implementation.

Hypothesis 16a: If most employees in an organization have a high education level, it is more likely to intend implementing telework in the future.

Hypothesis 16b: If most employees in an organization have a high education level, the organization is more likely to have implemented telework.

Both hypotheses were confirmed. (hypothesis 16a: 2 groups: 55.1 percent versus 35.3 percent, χ^2, p = 0.075) (hypothesis 16b: 2 groups: 30.6 percent versus 11.8 percent, χ^2, p = 0.044)

4.2.4.6 Characteristics of the commuter trip
Between 1985 and 1995, the average road-traffic density in Brussels increased by 21 percent. This suggests that the tension between mobility

demand and infrastructure supply has also risen. Furthermore, the congestion has become particularly bad around the Brussels ring-road as well as on the access roads to the city business district. Organizations with the majority of their employees coming from inside the Brussels region would consequently be expected to have fewer problems with late arrivals and early departures of employees due to traffic congestion than organizations with a majority of employees coming from other regions.

Hypothesis 17a: If most employees in an organization perform an intra-regional commuting trip, it is less likely to intend implementing telework in the future.

Hypothesis 17b: If most employees in an organization perform an intra-regional commuting trip, the organization is less likely to have implemented telework.

Hypothesis 17a was confirmed, but no significant result was found for hypothesis 17b. (hypothesis 17a: 2 groups: 34.1 percent versus 61.5 percent, χ^2, p = 0.012) This result suggests that congestion issues faced by employees may not have been a key reason for firms to adopt telework in the past, but will become more critical in the future.

4.2.4.7 Traffic conditions

The highest levels of telework are found in cities with more than 500,000 inhabitants. In addition, organizations active in a knowledge-based sector, and that have a higher propensity to implement telework, tend to be located in large cities. Also, large cities are usually at the core of the geographical regions with the most severe road congestion problems.[12] As mentioned above, road congestion has risen dramatically in recent years in the Brussels central business district. Organizations located in that area are therefore more likely to have problems related to road congestion, such as early departures and late arrivals of staff. For that reason, these organizations may be more willing or likely to implement telework.

Hypothesis 18a: If an organization is located in a congested area, it is more likely to intend implementing telework in the future.

Hypothesis 18b: If an organization is located in a congested area, the organization is more likely to have implemented telework.

Hypothesis 18a was confirmed. (2 groups: 55.8 percent versus 37.5 percent,[13] χ^2, p = 0.095). No significant result was found for hypothesis 18b.

This parallels the results found immediately above, for hypotheses 17a and 17b, and suggests that, in the future, the problems related to congestion may become a more important telework driver.

4.3 ADVANTAGES AND DISADVANTAGES FROM THE EMPLOYERS' POINT OF VIEW

Telework becomes a possible work option only if the employer or management perceives that the benefits associated with telework implementation outweigh the costs. To obtain insight into the managerial perceptions of the advantages and disadvantages of telework, the human resources managers were asked to assess 13 potential advantages and 13 potential disadvantages, previously identified in the literature on telework.[14]

A quantitative analysis of the costs and benefits of telework implementation is not an easy task. This is partly due to methodological problems, such as the lack of academic and managerial consensus on the relevant benefits and costs of telework implementation, but also partly due to the absence of relevant quantitative data.[15] Furthermore, most effects resulting from telework implementation are medium term and qualitative in nature. Hence, when assessing a monetary value for the different effects of telework implementation, these qualitative effects are systematically overlooked. Many employers implement telework to obtain a long-term sustainable strengthening of their human resources base, but conventional analysis of financial effects would largely neglect this effect. Furthermore, efficiency analyses often overlook network effects. Often, only costs and benefits related to the teleworkers themselves are assessed and not the overall impacts; the latter would also include direct and indirect effects resulting from relationship changes between teleworkers and conventional workers.[16] For these reasons, proper evaluation of telework requires evaluation tools that encompass criteria for which it is not possible to obtain an expression in monetary terms.

Despite these difficulties, several researchers have attempted to quantify the costs and benefits of telework.[17] Figure 4.1 breaks down the savings to the employer, as calculated in one study on this subject.

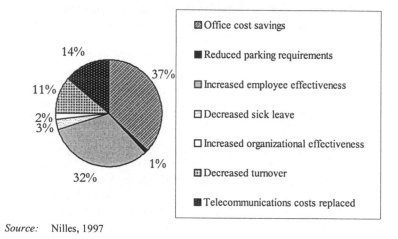

Source: Nilles, 1997

Figure 4.1 Employer savings due to telework implementation

When implementing a telework pilot programme, one should not assess the costs and benefits immediately. The benefits reported in the first two months after introducing a telework pilot programme can be overoptimistic, because the volunteers may be delighted with the opportunity to telework and this will be reflected in higher work performance and generally improved job satisfaction. Only when the novelty wears off and employees have accustomed themselves to the new work circumstances will the true costs and benefits of telework be revealed.[18]

4.3.1 POTENTIAL ADVANTAGES OF TELEWORK IMPLEMENTATION FROM THE EMPLOYER'S POINT OF VIEW

Thirteen potential advantages were selected based on an in-depth study of the current literature. After giving an overview of these potential advantages, we will assess them empirically using the results of our survey.

4.3.1.1 Improved flexibility

The introduction of telework can be seen as part of an overall strategy towards 'flexibilization' of both the labour force and the broader organization. Telework can help in periods of organizational transformation and in periods of workload fluctuation; it can also help with outsourcing non-organization-specific jobs.[19] Market fluctuations can also make an organization unsure of its long-range requirements. Telework implementation often allows better control over building space, support facilities and costly equipment, especially during periods of business expansion or when customers are geographically very dispersed.[20]

4.3.1.2 Improved productivity

An increase in productivity is often reported as an advantage of telework. This advantage is obviously of great interest to organizations. Telework enhances productivity because it reduces interruptions, provides an attractive environment for work requiring high levels of concentration, reduces time spent commuting, and reduces incidental absence.

Telework also allows employees to work at their peak hours of efficiency.[21] It has been suggested that the adoption of telework allows employees to better match their working hours with their biological clocks. Some people work best early in the morning; others are more productive in the middle of the night. Telework allows people to work at their own personal peak period.[22]

Another suggested explanation is that teleworkers tend to underestimate the amount of time they actually work because they feel guilty or inadequate.[23] Also, part of the explanation is surely that teleworkers work during the time they used to spend commuting; regardless of whether they have become more productive per hour, they have increased the number of hours they work. Telework programmes can also improve work quality and increase the speed of an organization's communication and decision-making processes, enhancing its general overall productivity.[24] For instance, telework implementation usually leads to enhanced data sharing and use of intranets. This, in turn, may then streamline interdepartmental work and improve the management of outsourced services and partnerships.[25] Intangible benefits, such as more responsible and conscientious scheduling, production of better documentation and better planning and organization of available time, also enhance the overall performance.[26]

The increase in telework productivity is difficult to measure precisely, but researchers estimate that telework increases productivity by 15 - 25 percent.[27]

That being said, however, one must consider the possibility that the productivity enhancements reported by some telework projects may be partially due to the Hawthorne effect. That is, some of the productivity increase may be the result of the attention the teleworkers get, because they are working in a new way.[28] In addition, teleworkers are de facto shielded from having to perform 'little' office jobs, which are typically not formally measured as part of their productive efforts but reflect services provided to peers or managers higher up in the hierarchy. Such jobs are typically 'allocated' to employees on the basis of geographic proximity in the conventional office (e.g., 'Would you mind reading and commenting on this important report?'). Employers implementing telework programmes should keep in mind that the increase in productivity is highest if a teleworker works from home only a few days per week. This suggests that the first tasks done remotely are those needing a high degree of concentration. If an employee teleworks full-time - a practice we do not generally recommend - the teleworker also does tasks at home that would be performed in the same way at the conventional office, with no increase in productivity. Telework's productivity advantage is also perceived by individual employees, as we will see in Chapter 5.

4.3.1.3   Improved customer service

Telework allows organizations to offer extended customer service by remaining open longer hours. For instance, 24-hour service can be offered more easily using telework, because many employees are reluctant to come to the conventional office in the middle of the night. Although this advantage is not now a main driver for organizations to implement telework, it may become one in the future as more and more two-earner families and single-parent families discover the time-saving possibilities of catalogue shopping, especially when ordering is as easy as a toll-free telephone call.[29] Another explanation for the improvement in customer service is that people who do not work in a conventional office setting can devote less time and energy to typical office routines and more to customers. Furthermore, customer service can also be enhanced by increased use of electronic communication; customers can reach employees more quickly and receive more direct and personal attention.[30]

4.3.1.4   Reduction in absenteeism

Telework may reduce absenteeism due to sickness; it almost certainly reduces absenteeism due to other causes.[31] Telework changes the definition of 'too sick to work.' Certain illnesses are no longer a barrier to work because the need to commute is effectively eliminated, face-to-face interaction with colleagues is no longer required, and the work need not be performed during the conventional office day.[32] Telework's increased autonomy and time flexibility will usually improve health, but stress caused by social isolation, computer problems, and a negative impact on family relationships will usually decrease health. Telework's effect on absenteeism due to other causes is more clearly positive. Many unplanned absences are due to family-care emergencies, minor illnesses and personal appointments that must be scheduled during the day.[33] Furthermore, telework reduces work stress, so teleworkers will therefore take fewer 'mental health days' than conventional workers.

4.3.1.5 Optimal human resources management (improved retention of qualified staff, enhanced recruiting potential, reduction of staff turnover and reduction of staff redundancy)

Telework has been used by employers to attract qualified applicants and to make themselves more attractive than other employers. Telework is generally seen as a good management tool to hire and retain skilled employees.[34] It is particularly effective at retaining valued employees when operations are expanded and space constraints develop, or when the conventional office is relocated.[35] Telework implementation also enhances recruiting potential by enabling organizations to recruit specialized personnel who prefer to work near their homes and enjoy doing so part-time or during unusual hours. Telework can also open up new labour markets (such as the disabled and some individuals with young children or elderly dependants). Today, these sources remain largely untapped.[36] Telework implementation can also help reduce staff redundancy. Non-strategic employees can be employed as freelancers, thereby reducing their costs to the organization.

4.3.1.6 Solution for the lack of adequate office space

Telework can be a solution when there is insufficient office space of the right size and cost.

4.3.1.7 Gains in office space

When telework is implemented, a number of tasks are no longer carried out at costly centralized locations, but rather at less costly facilities or in the employees' homes. Today, the cost savings associated with gains in office space are not a major driver for organizations. However, as the percentage of the work force that adopts telework increases and the implications in terms of gains in office space become significant, management will consciously take telework into account when planning long-range facilities.[37] Of course, a gain in office space is not a necessary result of the adoption of telework. If an organization has a few teleworkers but maintains the same building, the costs related to office space will not change. However, if a substantial number of employees start teleworking, the organization could reduce its office space, particularly if the organization introduces a system of office sharing.[38]

4.3.1.8 Positive influence on the image of the organization

Telework implementation may bring the organization positive publicity if the public is informed that the organization implements an 'enlightened' work style.[39] Telework is widely viewed as an 'enlightened' work form because it is seen as ecologically sensitive and socially responsible (because it allows the organization to hire disabled persons and gives workers more flexibility to combine family and work responsibilities).[40]

4.3.1.9 Improved possibilities for child care and care for the elderly

As telework implementation increases the flexibility to adjust working time to family needs, it allows employees to care more effectively for elderly people and/or children. These benefits of time flexibility are also relevant to individual employees, as we will see in Chapter 5.

4.3.1.10 Improved job opportunities for disabled persons

Physically disabled persons and other persons who find it difficult to commute have often been viewed as a group that would benefit from telework. Telework facilitates the integration of disabled persons because it allows them to work in the environment best equipped to accommodate their personal needs. However, it has also been suggested that telework is not necessarily always favourable to all disabled persons. If telework keeps them out of the main office environment, it may socially isolate them further.[41]

In addressing this question, we would emphasize the fact that disabled persons are not a homogenous group. The needs of disabled persons vary enormously depending largely on the type of disability. For many disabled persons, the prime motive to work is not economic but social - they want social interaction with their co-workers. Many disabled persons want to make a visible contribution to society. Because homework is hidden from the majority of society, these aims would not be fulfilled through telework. Finally, it must also be noted that many disabled persons have no work experience and therefore have no experience with the work routines needed to plan a work day.[42] We conclude, therefore, that telework is likely to help those disabled persons with restricted mobility for whom the alternative to telework is unemployment.[43] To the extent that telework is a necessary condition for employers seriously to consider such disabled persons as potential employees, it is important to assess managerial perceptions on this issue. This potential advantage of telework is obviously also perceived by individual employees, as we will see in Chapter 5.

4.3.2 EMPIRICAL ASSESSMENT OF THE ADVANTAGES OF TELEWORK IMPLEMENTATION FROM THE EMPLOYER'S POINT OF VIEW

Now that we have looked at telework's potential advantages, we will assess those advantages empirically.

The comparison of the perception of advantages is constructed using both revealed and stated preferences. First, we compare organizations that have already implemented telework with organizations that have not yet done so (revealed preference). Then, we compare organizations willing to implement telework in the future with organizations not willing to do so (stated preference).

4.3.2.1 Comparison of the perception of advantages between human resources managers of organizations that have implemented telework and organizations that have not yet implemented telework

All the human resources managers rated 11 of the 13 proposed advantages in the same way. Eleven of the 13 potential advantages were considered actual advantages, namely: (1) improved flexibility; (2) improved productivity; (3) improved retention of qualified staff; (4) reduction in absenteeism; (5) enhanced recruiting potential; (6) reduction of staff turnover; (7) solution for the lack of adequate office space; (8) gains in office space; (9) positive influence on the image of the organization; (10) improved possibilities for child care and care for the elderly and (11) improved job opportunities for disabled persons. However, (1) improved flexibility, (2) improved productivity and (3) improved retention of qualified staff were rated more positively by human resources managers of organizations that have already implemented telework. Improved customer service and reduction in staff redundancy were not considered actual advantages by either group (Table 4.1a).

4.3.2.2 Comparison of the perception of advantages between human resources managers of organizations willing to implement telework in the future and organizations not willing to implement telework in the future

Again, all the human resources managers rated the same 11 out of 13 potential advantages as actual advantages. However, in this case besides (1) improved flexibility, (2) improved productivity and (3) improved retaining of qualified staff, also (4) a positive influence on the organization image was rated more positively by human resources managers of organizations willing to implement telework in the future (Table 4.1b).

Table 4.1a *Advantages of telework implementation (present telework situation)*

	GROUP 1: Telework has been implemented	GROUP 2: Telework has not been implemented	Significance of the difference in perception of the advantage between group 1 and group 2
ADVANTAGE			
Improved flexibility	yes[+]	yes	significant t-test, p = 0.012
Improved productivity	yes[+]	yes	significant t-test, p = 0.021
Improved customer service	no	no	not significant
Improved retention of qualified staff	yes[+]	yes	significant t-test, p = 0.077
Reduction in absenteeism	yes	yes	not significant
Enhanced recruiting potential	yes	yes	not significant
Reduction of staff turnover	yes	yes	not significant
Reduction in staff redundancy	no	no	not significant
Solution for the lack of adequate office space	yes	yes	not significant
Gains in office space	yes	yes	not significant
Positive influence on the image of the organization	Yes	yes	not significant
Improved possibilities for child care and care for the elderly	yes	yes	not significant
Improved job opportunities for disabled persons	yes	yes	not significant

Note: yes[+] = a more positive yes

Source: authors' own calculations

Table 4.1b   Advantages of telework implementation (future telework situation)

	GROUP 1: Telework will be implemented in the future	GROUP 2: Telework will not be implemented in the future	Significance of the difference in perception of the advantage between group 1 and group 2
ADVANTAGE			
Improved flexibility	yes[+]	yes	significant t-test, p = 0.005
Improved productivity	yes[+]	yes	significant t-test, p = 0.017
Improved customer service	no	no	not significant
Improved retention of qualified staff	yes[+]	yes	significant t-test, p = 0.080
Reduction in absenteeism	yes	yes	not significant
Enhanced recruiting potential	yes	yes	not significant
Reduction of staff turnover	yes	yes	not significant
Reduction in staff redundancy	no	no	not significant
Solution for the lack of adequate office space	yes	yes	not significant
Gains in office space	yes	yes	not significant
Positive influence on the image of the organization	yes[+]	yes	significant t-test, p = 0.082
Improved possibilities for child care and care for the elderly	yes	yes	not significant
Improved job opportunities for disabled persons	yes	yes	not significant

Note: yes[+] = a more positive yes

source: authors' own calculations

4.3.3 POTENTIAL DISADVANTAGES OF TELEWORK IMPLEMENTATION FROM THE EMPLOYER'S POINT OF VIEW

The introduction of telework is also likely to be associated with a number of disadvantages. Thirteen potential disadvantages of telework were hypothesised, namely: (1) social isolation; (2) less promotion possibilities for teleworkers; (3) more work hours for teleworkers; (4) negative influence on the business environment; (5) less loyal employees; (6) opposition of trade unions; (7) hinders face-to-face interaction; (8) hinders training; (9) hinders teamwork; (10) hinders the security of internal data; (11) hinders the fulfilment of health regulations; (12) requires costly investments; and (13) unclear labour legislation. After giving an overview of these potential disadvantages, we will assess them empirically using the results of our survey.

4.3.3.1 Increased social isolation
Telework reduces the social interactions at the conventional workplace, and this could lead to social isolation, which may be bad for the employees' long-term commitment to the organization. The magnitude of this effect is, however, greatly reduced if telework is implemented on a part-time basis or if telework takes place in a satellite office or telework centre. The problem of social isolation is also relevant at the level of individual employees, as we will see in Chapter 5.

4.3.3.2 Reduction of promotion possibilities for teleworkers
A major concern is the influence of telework on the teleworker's career. 'Out of sight' may imply 'out of mind.'[44] The adoption of telework may result in fewer promotion possibilities for competent individuals if the organization uses subjective rather than objective evaluations of employees' performance. However, if performance standards are set and applied equally to teleworkers and conventional workers, this reduces significantly the risk of excluding eligible teleworkers from promotions. Furthermore, teleworkers must continue to have regular meetings with their supervisors and managers.[45]

4.3.3.3 Increase in the number of working hours
In theory, conventional workers and teleworkers should both perform the same number of working hours. However, the 'working hours' of conventional workers usually include interruptions by colleagues, social interactions and breaks, while teleworkers tend to deduct such events from their reported working hours. As previously noted, it is also possible that employees who start teleworking convert some or all of their commuting time into working time and therefore work more hours.[46]

Although a higher number of work hours performed may be viewed as an advantage to any organization in the short run, it may also lead to resentment by teleworkers in the long run and may thereby create agency problems inside the organization.

4.3.3.4 Negative influence on organizational culture

A unified organizational culture shared by all employees, which influences all day-to-day actions, is one of the main characteristics of successful organizations.[47] Maintaining a unified organizational culture becomes more difficult if a large percentage of the employees work at remote locations.[48] If the teleworkers have already worked for the organization for a considerable length of time, this problem is significantly reduced, since these employees are likely to have internalized the 'correct way of doing things.'[49] However, if new employees start teleworking right away, socialization may not have occurred.[50] Fortunately, implementing telework on a part-time basis significantly reduces this problem. Even if telework is implemented on a full-time basis, the core values and goals can still be transmitted to teleworkers, for instance through regular electronic newsletters. Some evidence suggests that maintaining the corporate culture is not an issue when implementing telework to the extent that management actively promotes and supports this culture among all employees, including the teleworkers.[51]

4.3.3.5 Reduced employee loyalty

A loss of loyalty is another disadvantage often cited as a consequence of implementing telework. However, no good statistical evidence on this subject exists. Some results indicate that teleworkers are less loyal than conventional workers, but when the same ranks in the employee hierarchy are compared, no significant differences can be found. This indicates that loyalty is a function of rank, and telework itself does not affect loyalty at all.[52] Organizations often select teleworkers internally in order to avoid the perceived loyalty problem; often, an employee is given the option to telework only after she/he has proven to be loyal.[53]

4.3.3.6 Opposition of trade unions

Trade unions often have mixed feelings about telework, because in the past homework has involved exploitation. For instance, the International Labour Organization, in their 258th session in 1993,[54] defined 'homeworkers' as mostly women who work long hours for less than the minimum wage, are isolated and are not protected by current labour laws. Some unions see telework as a step backwards to the twenty-first century equivalent of nineteenth-century cottage industry, undermining pay levels, job security, quality of work, child-care services and occupational health and safety standards, while increasing part-time employment and social isolation.[55] Traditionally, unions have vehemently opposed legal arrangements under which the most vulnerable segments of the work force get even weaker and lose the protections of collective work legislation and the social security system.[56] Another important factor lying behind union opposition is the fear that telework implementation would make union activity more difficult.[57]

Recently, however, trade unions have modified their resistance to telework.[58] Trade unions now oppose only certain forms of decentralization. Unions do not object to telework for highly-skilled workers who have a high level of bargaining power.[59]

The Danish Trade Unions, for example, are not opposed to telework in general, but they have formulated a number of guidelines related to this practice:[60]

1. Telework implementation should be voluntary and reversible.
2. Individual agreements should be made within the framework set out by collective bargaining agreements. The agreements should respect prevailing wage levels and work conditions.
3. Teleworkers should have the same access to career opportunities as their colleagues.
4. Teleworkers should have the same access to job training and courses as their colleagues.
5. The introduction of telework should not be used to introduce flexible employment models such as freelance work. No conversion of status from employee to subcontractor should occur.
6. Teleworkers should be given the ability to maintain sufficient contacts with their colleagues and their trade union.
7. There should be clear rules for data protection and privacy. Clear rules should be established in order to prevent information misuse such as, for instance, electronic access to the employee's personal information.

The same issues have also been raised by unions in the United States and the UK. Additional guidelines proposed by these stakeholder groups include: (1) that teleworkers should spend at least two days a week at the conventional office, (2) that the employer supplies proper equipment and furniture or reimburses the employee for the purchase of such items, and (3) that only existing staff should be recruited to become teleworkers.[61]

4.3.3.7 Hinders face-to-face contact

On average, an office worker spends about 65 percent of her/his time in interpersonal communication, of which 32 percent is face-to-face, and the majority of this is with the immediate work group.[62] During these face-to-face meetings, individuals lay the foundations for trust and the creation of shared values and expectations. Furthermore, individuals behave differently face-to-face than when they interact from a distance. Technology makes it possible to transmit only explicit and quantifiable information, but this is not the only type of information used in face-to-face communication. Routine and regular information can easily be handled through ICT, but face-to-face communication is the best way to communicate high-quality information.[63] When part-time telework is implemented, critical high-quality information can still be communicated face-to-face, but this can not be done spontaneously. That being said, however, one should keep in mind that a lot of face-to-face interaction occurs simply because of spatial proximity and habit; often, the message could have been transmitted just as well through ICT.[64] Furthermore, there are some indications that people can, to a certain extent, build and maintain social relationships using only computer-mediated communication.[65] This disadvantage of telework is also acknowledged by individual employees, as we shall see in Chapter 5.

A side effect of the potential difficulties related to face-to-face communication is that extra costs and resources are necessary in order to supervise remote workers. However, problems with supervision tend to diminish over time as better communication systems are put in place.[66]

4.3.3.8 Hinders training

Telework may hinder training in the sense that traditional, informal on-the-job training methods are harder to maintain. When experienced staff are teleworking, they may no longer be available at the conventional workplace. Hence tacit learning becomes more difficult.[67] Furthermore, teleworkers' skills may rapidly become obsolete if no new training is provided after they start teleworking. Telework requires more formal and explicit training (instead of on-the-job-training), and this training should be accessible in the form of stand-alone modules.[68] Training requirements will also differ depending on whether teleworkers are recruited internally or externally. Teleworkers recruited internally are likely to have already received substantial on-the-job-training and may require only additional training to keep their skills up-to-date. However, teleworkers recruited externally will still need the same type of initial training that conventional staff receive when entering the employing organization. Such initial training should include the provision of general information on the organization and its core values. It should also convey specific information on the benefits and facilities open to the particular job category, and on the role of the department/hierarchy and the key people who will support/work with the new teleworkers.

Teleworkers also require training related to their specific work form. This training should include guidance on: (1) where and how to set up a home office; (2) planning for security, safety and ergonomics in the home office; (3) setting up optimal schedules and work plans; (4) dealing with family, friends and neighbours; (5) focusing on the work product; (6) staying in touch with clients and colleagues; and (6) managing their career from a distance. Some of these topics (such as where and how to set up a home office) may be less critical for teleworkers operating in satellite offices and telework centres. Individuals other than the teleworkers may also need training. Sometimes the manager and even the family members of teleworkers may benefit from a training programme (the provision of training to family members is politically sensitive, however, because it could be perceived as an intrusion into the employees' private lives). Managers may require training in areas such as: (1) managing by results, rather than by observation; (2) fine-tuning skills for setting performance standards; (3) giving ongoing performance feedback; (4) keeping teleworkers connected with the office-related social and information networks; (5) career planning guidance for teleworkers; and (6) early problem detection. Most of these skills could also benefit on-site managers; however, on-site managers often do not need as much expertise in areas such as being able formally to determine performance expectations, to track progress and to provide appropriate feedback, due to the 'luxury' of frequent and close contacts with on-site employees.[69]

4.3.3.9 Hinders teamwork

Two somewhat outdated ideas support the perception that telework makes teamwork more difficult. The first idea is that if people are not working at the same place, they are not truly working together. However, partly as a result of electronic communication, many geographically dispersed work teams currently share common goals and jointly contribute to results. The second idea is that good teamwork requires high-quality, personal interaction. While there is some truth to this, only a fraction of what team members produce requires this kind of interaction.[70] Coordination problems such as scheduling meetings can be solved by distributing the regular work schedule of each telework team member to the co-teamworkers, and by allowing telephone calls to the teleworkers' remote work locations.[71] Furthermore, software known as 'groupware' is available specifically to support groups working together as teams. Zamindar (1995) makes the interesting point that teamwork may even act as a catalyst for telework adoption, in two ways. First, teamwork may help to overcome potential teleworkers' fears about social isolation. Second, work within teams is often organized with a strong focus on specific tasks to be performed by each individual, rather than on these individuals' more general, assigned roles in the organization. Telework is ideally suited to deal with such work decomposition, which may require individual employees to extend the scope of their professional activities beyond their formal job description.

That being said, however, there is no denying that electronic communication can replace only some face-to-face communication. Research has made it clear that ICT cannot replace all face-to-face interactions. Electronic communication like e-mail is not the best way to communicate complex messages, nor is it appropriate for communication that needs rapid feedback, because it is asynchronous. Hence, e-mail may be suitable for exchanging information, but not for negotiations or discussions.[72]

4.3.3.10 Hinders the security of internal data

The fear of unauthorized access to vital organization information is another barrier to telework implementation. Two possible forms of intrusion exist: industrial espionage and intrusion by employees. At first glance, one might think that the latter is independent of telework. However, if an organization implements telework in such a way that teleworkers become self-employed contractors, their loyalty to the organization may well diminish, and hence the risk of intrusion by freelance teleworkers may be higher than the risk of intrusion by conventional employees.[73] However, this problem can be avoided if the employees are not turned into self-employed freelancers and enough actions are taken to maintain the loyalty of the employees. Furthermore, an organization active in the internet age can no longer keep all of its access devices behind well-protected physical barriers. Today, sales and field representatives often already have remote access to central information databases. Implementing telework is just the next step in remote access.

Besides unauthorised access, other threats also exist, namely (1) theft of data; (2) theft of equipment; (3) loss of data integrity and (4) loss of processing facilities.[74] To avoid these threats, different means can be used, such as (1) physical and environmental security; (2) identification and authentication; (3) access control; (4) software and data security; (5) communication and data-exchange security; (6) security management; and (7) accountability and audit.[75]

4.3.3.11 Hinders the fulfilment of health regulations

Employers have a general obligation to provide a safe and healthy environment and to aim for continuous improvement, reducing or eliminating risks, and providing information and training to employees.[76] When individuals telework from home, it may be especially difficult for the employer to ensure that health and safety requirements are met. In order to ensure that the equipment, work environment and facilities are safe, regular pre-arranged visits by the manager responsible for safety are advisable. [77]

4.3.3.12 Requires costly investments

The technology that employees require in order to telework depends on their type of job. Generally, the primary rule of hardware requirements is that a teleworker needs whatever he or she used in the conventional office, plus a telecommunication capability. Telework certainly leads to additional investment expenditures and increases communication costs (although research indicates that this increase is much lower than the savings in transportation costs).[78]

If the employer tries to reduce its costs by asking employees to bear the costs of telework, employee interest in telework drops significantly.[79] In one study, when employees were asked to consider adopting telework several days per week, 86.1 percent expressed their willingness to do so if their salary increased and no personal costs were incurred. This percentage dropped to 66 percent if the employee kept the same salary and incurred no additional costs. A further drop to 38 percent occurred if the employee had to pay for the additional telephone line, and to 29 percent if the employee had to buy her/his own personal computer.[80]

4.3.3.13 Faces unclear labour legislation

The full range of labour legislation for conventional workers available today is not applicable to tele-homeworkers.[81] If the teleworker has the status of a self-employed individual, the conventional rules for the self-employed prevail. However, if the teleworker has an employee - employer agreement, only part of the conventional labour legislation applies.[82] In addition, the labour legislation for conventional workers will not cover all issues of importance to teleworkers.[83] This lack of transparency regarding applicable labour legislation creates uncertainty for firms and the danger of labour disputes and lawsuits.

4.3.4 EMPIRICAL ASSESSMENT OF THE DISADVANTAGES OF TELEWORK IMPLEMENTATION FROM THE EMPLOYER'S POINT OF VIEW

Now that we have looked at telework's disadvantages from a theoretical perspective, we will assess those disadvantages empirically.

As with our earlier discussion of advantages, our comparison of the perception of disadvantages is constructed using both revealed and stated preferences. First, we compare organizations that have already implemented telework with organizations that have not yet done so (revealed preference). Second, we compare organizations intending to implement telework in the future with organizations not intending to do so (stated preference).

4.3.4.1 Comparison of perceived disadvantages by human resources managers of organizations that have implemented telework and organizations that have not yet implemented telework

The human resources managers of organizations that have already implemented telework identified only seven of the potential disadvantages discussed above as real disadvantages, namely: (1) social isolation; (2) hinders face-to-face interaction; (3) hinders teamwork; (4) hinders the security of internal data; (5) hinders the fulfilment of health regulations; (6) requires costly investments; and (7) faces unclear labour regulations. In contrast, the human resources managers of companies that have not yet implemented telework identified nine of the potential disadvantages as real disadvantages, namely: (1) social isolation; (2) less promotion possibilities; (3) negative influence on the business environment; (4) opposition of trade unions; (5) hinders face-to-face interaction; (6) hinders teamwork; (7) hinders the security of internal data; (8) hinders the fulfilment of health regulations; and (9) unclear labour legislation.

It is interesting to observe that 'social isolation' and 'hinders teamwork' were not considered to be as serious by human resources managers of organizations that have actually implemented telework. No human resources managers expected a drop in employee loyalty. The issue of unclear labour regulations was identified as a disadvantage only by human resources managers of organizations that have already adopted telework. This implies that only those organizations actually understand the full complexity of current labour regulations. Another interesting difference is that only human resources managers of organizations that have already implemented telework perceive the disadvantage of costly investments. This suggests that the investments required to implement telework do not constitute a major barrier to the adoption of the practice, since the required resource allocation is largely underestimated (see Table 4.2a.).

4.3.4.2   Comparison of the perceived disadvantages by human resources managers of organizations intending to implement telework in the future and organizations not intending to implement telework in the future

Both groups identified the same disadvantages, with the exception of the possible problem of internal data security. Here, organizations intending to implement telework in the future are more convinced that it is a problem (see Table 4.2b).

Table 4.2a   *Disadvantages of telework implementation (present telework situation)*

	GROUP 1: Telework has been implemented	GROUP 2: Telework has not been implemented	Significance of the difference in perception of the disadvantage between group 1 and group 2
DISADVANTAGE			
Increased social isolation	yes	yes[+]	significant t-test, p = 0.088
Reduction in promotion possibilities	no	yes	significant t-test p = 0.004
Increase in work hours	no	no	not significant
Negative influence on the organizational culture	no	yes	significant t-test p = 0.012
Reduced employee loyalty	no[+]	no	significant t-test p = 0.017
Opposition of trade unions	no	yes	significant t-test p = 0.013
Hinders face-to-face interaction	yes	yes	not significant
Hinders training	no	no	not significant
Hinders teamwork	yes	yes[+]	significant t-test, p = 0.096
Hinders the security of internal data	yes	yes	not significant
Hinders the fulfilment of health regulations	yes	yes	not significant
Requires costly investments	yes	no	significant t-test p = 0.019
Faces unclear labour legislation	yes[+]	yes	significant t-test p = 0.079

Notes:
yes[+] = a more convinced yes
no[+] = a more convinced no

Source: authors' own calculations

Table 4.2b   Disadvantages of telework implementation (future telework situation)

	GROUP 1: Telework will be implemented in the future	GROUP 2: Telework will not be implemented in the future	Significance of the difference in perception of the disadvantage between group 1 and group 2
DISADVANTAGE			
Increased social isolation	yes	yes	not significant
Reduction of promotion possibilities	no	no	not significant
Increase in work hours	no	no	not significant
Negative influence on the organizational culture	yes	yes	not significant
Reduced employee loyalty	no	no	not significant
Opposition of trade unions	no	no	not significant
Hinders face-to-face interaction	yes	yes	not significant
Hinders training	no	no	not significant
Hinders teamwork	yes	yes	not significant
Hinders the security of internal data	yes$^+$	yes	significant t-test, p = 0.085
Hinders the fulfilment of health regulations	yes	yes	not significant
Requires costly investments	yes	yes	not significant
Faces unclear labour legislation	yes	yes	not significant

Note: yes$^+$ = a more convinced yes

Source: authors' own calculations

Earlier in this chapter, we saw that human resources managers of companies that have implemented telework attribute the same **advantages** to telework as do human resources managers of companies that have not adopted this practice (both groups perceived eleven advantages in Table 4.1a). Human resources managers with telework experience, however, identify a lower number of **disadvantages** (seven versus nine in Table 4.2a). They do not view the potential problems of 'social isolation,' 'reduction in employee loyalty' and 'hinders teamwork' as relevant in practice. **Human resources managers of companies that have not yet implemented telework thus appear to have other perceptions about the disadvantages of telework**.

Similar research outcomes were found by Lam et al. (1995) for Singapore. These findings suggest that some of the problems related to telework implementation as perceived by those currently not engaged in telework are in fact less serious than expected.

4.4 CHOICE MODEL OF THE ADOPTION OF TELEWORK BY EMPLOYERS

In Appendix 3 and Appendix 4, we use our empirical data to produce a model to predict which employers are most likely (a) to have implemented telework already, and (b) to adopt this practice in the future. Using the revealed preference data, we generate a model that describes the main determinants of present telework adoption, namely: **(1) awareness of the concept of telework; (2) the presence of a coordination and control mechanism which is output-oriented; (3) experience with flexible work hours; (4) activities in a knowledge-based sector; (5) experience with outsourcing; (6) a factor highly correlated with a variable related to the opposition of trade unions and a variable related to clear labour regulations.** Using the stated preference data, we generate a model that suggests that **future telework adoption will be primarily influenced by the following variables: (1) awareness of the concept of telework; (2) experience with flexible work hours; and (3) the availability of electronic communication.** Readers interested in the statistical analysis are referred to those Appendices.

Note that experience with outsourcing is a current telework driver, but not a future telework driver. By contrast, the availability of electronic communication is a future telework driver but not a current one. This is further evidence that current telework is often driven by cost savings (because outsourcing is often used to improve cost control over non-strategic or low-skilled jobs), while future telework will often be directed at highly-skilled workers.

4.5 EFFECTIVENESS OF POLICY TOOLS TO SUPPORT TELEWORK IMPLEMENTATION

We assessed the expected effectiveness of three policy tools, taking into account the possibility that managers of organizations that have already implemented telework may have different views than managers of organizations that have not yet adopted this practice (Table 4.3a). The first policy tool suggested to the human resources managers was the introduction of road pricing, which would increase the cost of using private road transport. Both groups of human resources managers stated that such a measure would not enhance telework implementation. However, the human resources managers of organizations that suffer most from road congestion stated that telework implementation would be enhanced by the introduction of road pricing (2 groups: 61.1 percent versus 29.4 percent, χ^2, p = 0.060).

Both groups also stated that granting subsidies[84] and distributing information on best practices would likely enhance telework adoption. According to the human resources managers, the widespread distribution of information on 'best telework practices' in large and well-known companies is the most efficient way to stimulate telework implementation.

Similar results were obtained when we compared the answers given by the human resources managers of organizations that intend to adopt the practice in the future versus those that will not (Table 4.3b).

Table 4.3a   The expected effectiveness of policy tools to promote telework implementation (present telework situation)

	GROUP 1: Telework has been implemented	GROUP 2: Telework has not been implemented	Significance of the difference in perception of the disadvantage between group 1 and group 2
Implementing a policy tool, such as road pricing, that makes private road transport more expensive to use	no influence	no influence	not significant
The awarding of a financial subsidy	positive	positive	not significant
Distribution of information about best practices	positive	positive	not significant

Source: authors' own calculations

Table 4.3b   The expected effectiveness of policy tools to promote telework implementation (future telework situation)

	GROUP 1: Telework will be implemented in the future	GROUP 2: Telework will not be implemented in the future	Significance of the difference in perception of the disadvantage between group 1 and group 2
Implementing a policy tool, such as road pricing, that makes private road transport more expensive to use	no influence	no influence	not significant
The awarding of a financial subsidy	positive	positive	not significant
Distribution of information about best practices	positive	positive	not significant

Source: authors' own calculations

4.6 CONCLUSION

Our survey conducted among 83 organizations in Brussels led to a number of insights into the environmental drivers of - and barriers to - telework implementation. Our data suggests that, at present, the adoption of telework in an organization is mainly determined by the following parameters: (1) awareness of the concept of telework; (2) the presence of a coordination and control mechanism which is output-oriented; (3) experience with flexible work hours; (4) activities in a knowledge-based sector; (5) experience with outsourcing; (6) a factor highly correlated with a variable related to the opposition of trade unions and a variable related to perceived clear labour regulations. Furthermore, our data suggests that future telework adoption may be primarily influenced by the following variables: (1) awareness of the concept of telework; (2) experience with flexible work hours; and (3) the availability of electronic communication.

We made two further observations in this chapter. First, human resources managers of companies that have not yet implemented telework appear to have a more pessimistic view about telework's disadvantages. Second, the human resources managers think that the most effective public policy tool to promote telework is the diffusion of information on 'best practices.' We note that this policy tool seems particularly appropriate, given that a large part of the problem is a possible misperception of telework's disadvantages.

In the next chapter, we will look at the remaining part of our conceptual framework for telework implementation: the individual-level component. We will describe that component in more detail and then apply it empirically.

NOTES

[1] This chapter builds upon the article: V. Illegems et al. (2001), 'The organizational context of teleworking implementation', *Technological Forecasting and Social Change*, **68**, 275 - 91. Excerpts from this article were reprinted with permission from Elsevier Science.

[2] These 230 companies were selected using stratified random sampling. With this method, the relevant population is first divided into a number of sub-groups, according to the industrial sector in which each organization is active. If the sample had been based on a random selection, the likelihood of inclusion of organizations active in the various relevant industries (sectors with a high number of service jobs) would have been very low (De Pelsmacker and Van Kenhove, 1994).

[3] Comparing revealed preference and stated preference data, Wardman (1988) concluded that, overall, stated preference analysis provided a reasonable account of individuals' current choices.

4 Compare with other studies, such as Bélanger (1999) and Teo et al. (1998), which investigated employees' attitudes towards telework implementation in only one sector, namely the IT sector.

5 Compare with other studies, such as Mokhtarian et al. (1998), which investigated employees within a single organization. Although we tried to have a representative image of business in Brussels, there may be sampling bias (i.e., the population sample may not be representative of the work force), as well as self-selection response bias (i.e., there may be a significant difference between the people returning the survey and those who did not return the survey).

6 Mokhtarian and Salomon (1997).

7 In other words, 21.3 percent of the respondents that were unaware of (or poorly-informed about) the concept of telework (prior to our questionnaire) may implement telework in the future while 80.6 percent of the respondents that were already aware of (or well-informed about) the concept of telework may implement telework in the future.

8 Among respondents that indicated that the use of output-oriented control and coordination as the most important coordination and control method, 92.9 percent may implement telework in the future. The other numbers represent the percentage of organizations that indicated that output-oriented control and coordination is the second most important method, the third most important method, the fourth most important method and the least important method, respectively, that may implement telework in the future.

9 Among respondents that indicated that sequential information flows constitute the most important flow type, 26.1 percent may implement telework in the future. The other numbers give the percentage of respondents that indicated sequential information flows as the second most important type of flow and the least important type of flow, respectively, that may implement telework in the future.

10 Among respondents that indicated teamwork as the most important type of information flow, 59.1 percent may implement telework in the future. The other numbers give the percentage of respondents that indicated teamwork as the second most important type of flow and as the least important type of flow, respectively, that may implement telework in the future.

11 Kinsman (1987).

12 Korte and Wynne (1996).

13 55.8 percent of the respondents that are located in areas that have problems with road congestion (Brussels postal zones 1000, 1030, 1040, 1050, 1060 and 1210) may implement telework in the future. The other number gives the percentage of respondents that is located in other postal zones that may implement telework in the future.

14 For more on the advantages and disadvantages of telework, see Moon (1998), Huws (1993), Nilles (1997), Nilles (1998), Kugelmass (1995), Teo et al. (1998), Weijers et al. (1992), Bélanger (1999), Reichwald and Möslein (1999), Gray et al. (1994), Kinsman (1987), Harman and Bordow (1998), Lam et al. (1995), Bush (1990), Mahmassani et al. (1993) and Duxbury et al. (1987).

15 Weijers et al. (1992).

16 Gareis (1998).

17 For every employee adopting telework one or two days per workweek, it has been estimated that the employer could save between $6,000 and $12,000 annually (Nilles 1997). A similar figure of $8,000 per year is presented by Eldid and Minoli (1995).

18 Gray et al. (1994).

19 Weijers and Weijers (1988).

20 Cross and Raizman (1986).

[21] Because it is very difficult to measure productivity itself, the perceived increase or decrease in productivity is often used instead. See Bélanger (1999), Cross and Raizman (1986), Kugelmass (1995) and Huws et al. (1993).

[22] Gordon (1988) and Huws et al. (1993).

[23] Huws et al. (1993).

[24] Cross and Raizman (1986).

[25] Huws (1998).

[26] Olson (1982).

[27] Kinsman (1987) found that teleworkers reported a productivity increase of 20 - 50 percent, while Yanabu (1999) found productivity increases of 10 - 30 percent. Cross and Raizman (1986) report that teleworkers are on average 20 percent more productive than their colleagues at the conventional workplace (Bush, 1990). Rathbone (1992) reports an increase in productivity of 15 - 20 percent and Kraut (1989) reports an increase of 15 - 25 percent.

[28] Huws et al. (1993) and Stanworth and Stanworth (1991).

[29] Gordon (1988).

[30] Apgar IV (1998).

[31] Steward (1999) found that teleworkers had less illness-related absenteeism.

[32] Steward (1999).

[33] Kugelmass (1995).

[34] Teo et al. (1998), Olson (1988) and Gordon (1988).

[35] Cross and Raizman (1986) and Apgar IV (1998).

[36] Stanworth and Stanworth (1991).

[37] Gordon (1988).

[38] On the other hand, if the organization allows telework in the form of working at satellite offices and telework centres, the cost for office space could increase due to a loss of economies of scale.

[39] Olson (1988).

[40] On the other hand, telework may have a negative impact on the image of the organization if it creates the impression that clients deal with an 'invisible' work force (Salomon, 1994).

[41] Gordon (1988).

[42] Huws (1996).

[43] Büssing (1998).

[44] Nilles (1998).

[45] When analysing the relationship between telework and (opportunities for) promotions at work, one should bear in mind that some teleworkers purposely forego promotions in order to retain positions that do not require full-time presence at the conventional office (Kugelmass, 1995).

[46] Olson (1988) and Gordon (1988).

[47] Stanworth and Stanworth (1991).

[48] Kondo (1999).

[49] Stanworth and Stanworth (1991) and Gainey et al. (1999).

[50] Kondo (1999).

[51] Kondo (1999) and Gray et al. (1994).

[52] Kugelmass (1995).

[53] Huws et al. (1993).

[54] ILO (1995).

[55] Qvortrup (1992) and Stanworth and Stanworth (1991).

[56] Kubicek and Fischer (1988) and Holti and Stern (1987).

[57] Korte and Wynne (1996).

[58] Qvortrup (1992) and Korte and Wynne (1996).

59   Stanworth and Stanworth (1991).
60   Qvortrup (1999).
61   Gray et al. (1994).
62   Fireman (1998).
63   Bergum (1998) and Bush (1990).
64   Gareis (1998).
65   Alvehus and Lindström (1998).
66   Stanworth and Stanworth (1991).
67   Huws (1998).
68   Huws (1996).
69   Gray et al. (1994).
70   Ibid.
71   Kugelmass (1995).
72   Shin et al. (1999).
73   Holti and Stern (1987).
74   Gray et al. (1994).
75   Ibid. and Nilles (1998).
76   Stanworth and Stanworth (1991).
77   Gray et al. (1994). The Belgian ARAB rules ('Algemeen Reglement van de Arbeidsbescherming' or general standards of labour protection) are specific on this issue. If there is an employee - employer relation, the employer should evaluate the risks related to the safety and health of the employee, including the design of the workplace. The employer should take the necessary measures to prevent diseases. The employer should also make sure that the employee can cope with the relevant safety and health issues and that the dwelling is a suitable work environment. In order to repect this requirement, the employer needs to control the installation of the relevant electronic circuits and to verify the required certificates regarding the cleaning of chimneys and heating systems. The employer should also take into account all regulations regarding fire prevention, fire extinguishers, ventilation, noise prevention and safety of equipment. In this Belgian context, a prior investigation of the home work environment should be conducted by the head of the organization's 'safety and hygiene committee,' as well as by the organization's medical doctor and in collaboration with the employee (Imbrechts, 1995). Inspections of the work environment should also be possible by the employer, as well as by the safety and hygiene committee (ced.samson, 1998). (Organizations with more than 50 employees have a legal obligation to create a safety and hygiene committee, which has equal employee/employer representation. The main objective of this committee is to act as a safeguard in the context of safety and health issues in the workplace.) See Bernardino et al. (1992).
78   SERV (1999).
79   Mahmassani et al. (1993).
80   Ibid. In principle, telework programmes may prescribe that the employee or the employer should provide the equipment and pay for the operating costs, or that such costs should be shared between the two parties. In Belgium, the Belgian law of 6 December 1996 regarding homework prescribes that the employer should bear these costs.
81   Köhler et al. (1988a) and Köhler et al. (1988b).
82   de Vries (1988).
83   The Belgian law of 6 December 1996 regarding homeworkers who have an employee - employer relation prescribes how a number of issues should be handled. Employees must not do dangerous work at home (Belgisch Staatsblad, 24-12-1996). The same provision prohibiting work at home that endangers health and morality can also be found in other

countries like Denmark and the Netherlands (de Vries, 1988). The Belgian law also stipulates that the employer must provide the necessary equipment. If an employee works only part of her/his working hours at home, then only the work done at home falls under this law. With every employee who becomes a homeworker (part-time or full-time), the employer needs to make an individual agreement that includes at least the workplace chosen, a short description of the work, the agreed work roster or the minimum volume of work. The agreement should also explicitly determine the allowance for costs related to homework. If nothing is stipulated in the individual contract, the law prescribes that the employer should pay the employee 10 percent of her/his wage and that this sum should be increased if the employee can document that her/his costs are higher (Belgisch staatsblad, 24-12-1996).

[84] Gordon (1988) has identified four types of financial subsidies that could enhance telework adoption:

1. Income tax credits for employers who reduce the number of employees commuting to the conventional office.
2. Income tax credits/reimbursements for start-up and training costs for employers setting up satellite offices in economically depressed regions.
3. Real estate incentives and/or more favourable zoning rules for employers that are planning to 'underbuild' their new facilities (i.e., planning less office space than needed for the current number of employees).
4. Real estate incentives for employers or developers willing to create telework centres by converting unused buildings.

5. A MANAGERIAL PERSPECTIVE ON TELEWORK: PARAMETERS AFFECTING THE EMPLOYEE'S VIEW

5.1 INTRODUCTION

The adoption of telework is ultimately an individual decision. For a telework initiative to be successful, it is not enough that the **employer** decides that the company benefits outweigh the company costs, as discussed in the last chapter. The **employee** must also decide that the personal benefits outweigh the personal costs. This chapter will look at that decision, describing in more detail and empirically assessing the individual-level component of Chapter 3's conceptual framework on target group implementation. Our analysis builds upon the empirical findings of a survey we conducted among a large number of employees working in Brussels.

   In this chapter, we address the following questions:

1. What kinds of individuals are likely to become teleworkers?
2. From the employee's point of view, what are the advantages and disadvantages of telework, and how do employees rate those advantages and disadvantages?
3. In what ways do employees with telework experience perceive telework's advantages and disadvantages differently from employees without telework experience?
4. In what ways do potential teleworkers (i.e., those willing to telework should the opportunity arise, including current teleworkers) perceive telework's advantages and disadvantages differently from those employees not willing to telework?

5.   In what ways do potential regular teleworkers (i.e., those willing to telework at least once a workweek should the opportunity arise, including employees currently teleworking at least once a workweek) perceive its advantages and disadvantages differently from those employees not willing to become regular teleworkers?

5.2   INDIVIDUAL-LEVEL BARRIERS AND DRIVERS AMONG EMPLOYEES EMPLOYED IN BRUSSELS

A total of 261 employees from 16 different organizations in Brussels were asked to complete a questionnaire regarding telework. As was the case in Chapter 4, we defined telework in the survey as work from home, a satellite office, a telework centre or any other workstation outside of the main office for at least one day per workweek. Some sort of telecommunication technology is used to substitute for work-related travel, but it need not be continuous, on-line communication. These 16 organizations were selected based on their willingness to cooperate with our project. We included organizations intending to implement telework in the future, as well as organizations not intending to do so. Within each organization, we included current teleworkers (if present), employees who do not currently telework but who expressed their interest in teleworking in the future, and employees unwilling to telework.

The vast majority of the sample did not currently telework, so we used both stated-preference and revealed-preference analysis. The former helps us predict future adoption rates of telework, whereas the latter helps us understand the present situation.

Our sample consisted of 131 men and 130 women, ranging in age from 21 to 62.[1] Of the 261 employees in the sample, 54 were already teleworking, 165 individuals stated their willingness to telework on a regular basis in the future (current teleworkers as well as employees willing to adopt telework), and 23 stated they were willing to telework occasionally. Like many earlier studies, our study found that those interested in telework greatly prefer home-based, part-time telework.[2] Overall, 82.4 percent of the potential regular teleworkers preferred to telework at home.[3]

Because employees make little distinction between low and moderate frequencies of telework,[4] we used the following three frequency categories:

*   no telework,
*   'occasional' telework (less than once a workweek), and

- 'regular' telework (at least once a workweek). This category thus includes what is sometimes called 'low' and 'moderate' frequencies.

For each individual-level characteristic included in the survey, we formulate hypotheses regarding its likely impact on the current and future adoption of telework. First, we compare current teleworkers with non-teleworkers (revealed preferences). Then, we compare potential teleworkers with employees not willing to telework (largely stated preferences). Finally, we compare potential regular teleworkers with employees not willing to become regular teleworkers (largely stated preferences).

These comparisons are made based on a χ^2-analysis in the case of a dichotomous variable, similar to the approach adopted in Chapter 4. However, if the comparison is done for a continuous variable, a t-test is used. If the calculated p-value is lower than or equal to 0.05, then the hypothesis is accepted with a confidence interval of 95 percent. If the calculated p-value is 0.1, then the hypothesis is accepted with a confidence interval of 90 percent.

5.2.1 JOB CHARACTERISTICS

5.2.1.1 Location independence
Employees with location-independent jobs can work wherever they want. Hence, one would expect that they would be particularly interested in telework. This reasoning leads to the following three hypotheses.

Hypothesis 1a: If an employee has a location-independent job, she/he is more likely to be a teleworker.

Hypothesis 1b: If an employee has a location-independent job, it is more likely she/he is willing to be a teleworker in the future.

Hypothesis 1c: If an employee has a location-independent job, it is more likely she/he is willing to be a regular teleworker in the future.

Hypotheses 1b and 1c were confirmed. (hypothesis 1b: 2 groups: 78.4 percent versus 41.9 percent,[5] χ^2, p = 0.000) (hypothesis 1c: 2 groups: 78.8 percent versus 44.7 percent, χ^2, p = 0.000). These results suggest that location-independent workers may telework more in the future than they do now.

5.2.1.2 Face-to-face interaction with customers
Hypothesis 2a: If an employee has a job that requires face-to-face interaction with customers, she/he is less likely to be a teleworker.

Hypothesis 2b: If an employee has a job that requires face-to-face interaction with customers, it is less likely she/he is willing to be a teleworker in the future.

Hypothesis 2c: If an employee has a job that requires face-to-face interaction with customers, it is less likely she/he is willing to be a regular teleworker in the future.

Interestingly, these hypotheses were not confirmed. This suggests that, even though a job requires face-to-face interaction with customers, typically part of the job can still be done remotely.

5.2.1.3 Face-to-face contact with other employees
Telework hinders face-to-face contact with other employees. Thus, one would expect that employees requiring face-to-face contact with other employees would be less interested in telework.

Hypothesis 3a: If an employee needs face-to-face contact with other employees, she/he is less likely to be a teleworker.

Hypothesis 3b: If an employee needs face-to-face contact with other employees, it is less likely she/he is willing to be a teleworker in the future.

Hypothesis 3c: If an employee needs face-to-face contact with other employees, it is less likely she/he is willing to be a regular teleworker in the future.

These hypotheses were confirmed. (hypothesis 3a: 2 groups: 15 percent versus 26.4 percent, χ^2, p = 0.024) (hypothesis 3b: 2 groups: 65.4 percent versus 78.4 percent, χ^2, p = 0.021) (hypothesis 3c: 2 groups: 67.2 percent versus 77.8 percent, χ^2, p = 0.078)

5.2.1.4 Taking work home
One would expect that a habit of taking work home would create familiarity with working from home, and thus lead to a greater acceptance of telework (especially given that homework is the form of telework preferred by 82.4 percent of the potential regular teleworkers).

Hypothesis 4a: If an employee already takes work home, she/he is more likely to be a teleworker.

Hypothesis 4b: If an employee already takes work home, it is more likely she/he is willing to be a teleworker in the future.

Hypothesis 4c: If an employee already takes work home, it is more likely she/he is willing to be a regular teleworker in the future.

These hypotheses were confirmed (hypothesis 4a: 2 groups: 32.6 percent versus 8.9 percent, χ^2, p = 0.000) (hypothesis 4b: 2 groups: 80.7 percent versus 62.9 percent, χ^2, p = 0.001) (hypothesis 4c: 2 groups: 83.1 percent versus 61.5 percent, χ^2, p = 0.000)

5.2.1.5 Supervisory role
On the one hand, some research suggests that supervisors are not suited for telework because they must be physically present at the conventional workplace in order to manage their supervisees.[6] On the other hand, supervisors have many of the characteristics needed to become good teleworkers. Based on the first point of view, we formulated the following hypotheses.

Hypothesis 5a: If an employee is a supervisor, she/he is less likely to be a teleworker.

Hypothesis 5b: If an employee is a supervisor, it less likely she/he is willing to be a teleworker in the future

Hypothesis 5c: If an employee is a supervisor, it is less likely she/he is willing to be a regular teleworker in the future.

Only hypothesis 5a gave a statistically significant result. However, it was the exact opposite of the result we expected. (hypothesis 5a: 2 groups: 28.9 percent versus 17.8 percent, χ^2, p = 0.046) These results indicate that supervisors today are viewed as good candidates for telework adoption. In the future, as more people adopt telework, the need for a physical, supervisory presence in the main office may become more important in some cases.

5.2.1.6 Work arrangement

One might expect that part-time workers would be particularly inclined to adopt telework, because employers who hire part-time workers - and employees who choose to be part-time workers - typically value flexibility.

Hypothesis 6a: If an employee is a part-time worker, she/he is more likely to be a teleworker.

Hypothesis 6b: If an employee is a part-time worker, it is more likely she/he is willing to be a teleworker in the future.

Hypothesis 6c: If an employee is a part-time worker, it is more likely she/he is willing to be a regular teleworker in the future.

These hypotheses, however, were not confirmed, indicating that full-time employees are as likely as part-time employees to engage in telework.

5.2.1.7 Flexible work hours

An employee with flexible working hours already has some experience in managing her/his own work schedule. Hence, one would expect that such an employee - as well as the employee's supervisor - would view the employee as a likely candidate for telework.

Hypothesis 7a: If an employee has experience with flexible working hours, she/he is more likely to be a teleworker.

Hypothesis 7b: If an employee has experience with flexible working hours, it is more likely she/he is willing to be a teleworker in the future.

Hypothesis 7c: If an employee has experience with flexible working hours, it is more likely she/he is willing to be a regular teleworker in the future.

These hypotheses were confirmed. (hypothesis 7a: 2 groups: 23.4 percent versus 11.1 percent, χ^2, p = 0.048) (hypothesis 7b: 2 groups: 77.1 percent versus 53.7 percent, χ^2, p = 0.001) (hypothesis 7c: 2 groups: 77.7 percent versus 54.2 percent, χ^2, p = 0.001)

5.2.1.8 Communication requirements

E-mail, an internet connection and a modem are standard equipment for highly-skilled knowledge workers. Since this type of worker will probably constitute the majority of future teleworkers, we hypothesized it is more likely that employees with these communication requirements would be willing to telework in the future. Many current teleworkers, however, may still be low-skilled workers who, in the past, have been asked to telework in order to reduce costs. These teleworkers typically do not require e-mail, an internet connection and a modem, so we hypothesized that employees with sophisticated ICT requirements would be less likely to be current teleworkers (although Chapter 4 did indicate the importance, at present, of being active in a knowledge-based sector and having a highly skilled workforce as characteristics of organizations adopting or contemplating the adoption of telework).

Typically, a fax is needed only in the context of secretarial duties. Because this type of employee is often location-dependent, we hypothesized that it is less likely for employees needing a fax in order to perform their duties, to be current or future teleworkers.

Hypothesis 8a: If an employee's job requires that she/he has an internet connection, it is less likely that she/he is a teleworker.

Hypothesis 8b: If an employee's job requires that she/he has an internet connection, it is more likely that she/he is willing to be a teleworker in the future.

Hypothesis 8c: If an employee's job requires that she/he has an internet connection, it is more likely that she/he is willing to be a regular teleworker in the future.

Hypothesis 9a: If an employee's job requires that she/he has a modem, it is less likely that she/he is a teleworker.

Hypothesis 9b: If an employee's job requires that she/he has a modem, it is more likely that she/he is willing to be a teleworker in the future.

Hypothesis 9c: If an employee's job requires that she/he has a modem, it is more likely that she/he is willing to be a regular teleworker in the future.

Hypothesis 10a: If an employee's job requires that she/he has e-mail, it is less likely that she/he is a teleworker.

Hypothesis 10b: If an employee's job requires that she/he has e-mail, it is more likely that she/he is willing to be a teleworker in the future.

Hypothesis 10c: If an employee's job requires that she/he has e-mail, it is more likely that she/he is willing to be a regular teleworker in the future.

Hypothesis 11a: If an employee's job requires that she/he has a fax, it is less likely that she/he is a teleworker.

Hypothesis 11b: If an employee's job requires that she/he has a fax, it is less likely that she/he is willing to be a teleworker in the future.

Hypothesis 11c: If an employee's job requires that she/he has a fax, it is less likely that she/he is willing to be a regular teleworker in the future.

Hypotheses 8b, 8c, 9b and 9c were confirmed, implying that the need for this type of communication infrastructure does not affect the adoption of telework today, but may in the future. (hypothesis 8b: 2 groups: 77.4 percent versus 64.9 percent, χ^2, p = 0.029) (hypothesis 8c: 2 groups: 79.3 percent versus 63.3 percent, χ^2, p = 0.009) (hypothesis 9b: 2 groups: 76.6 percent versus 54.5 percent, χ^2, p = 0.003) (hypothesis 9c: 2 groups: 77.5 percent versus 54.1 percent, χ^2, p = 0.003) No significant results were obtained for the hypotheses constructed around the job requirement of e-mail. All hypotheses constructed around the job requirement of a fax were significant. (hypothesis 11a: 2 groups: 13 percent versus 33.7 percent, χ^2, p = 0.000) (hypothesis 11b: 2 groups: 67.5 percent versus 80.8 percent, χ^2, p = 0.019) (hypothesis 11c: 2 groups: 67.4 percent versus 83.1 percent, χ^2, p = 0.009) This strongly suggests that jobs requiring faxes are more likely to include many location-dependent tasks, requiring the employee to be physically present at the office.

5.2.1.9 Occupation

Clerical and managerial occupations are widely considered to be suited for telework. The first group consists of low-skilled workers performing relatively simple information handling, easily adaptable to telework. Opinions differ, however, regarding managers' suitability for telework. On the one hand, they seem well-suited for telework, because they have experience in unbundling, scheduling and prioritizing complex work packages and they have the required self-discipline to work remotely. On the other hand, they need to manage people, and they often cannot do this remotely. However, if telework is adopted on a part-time basis, the magnitude of this latter problem is reduced.

Hypothesis 12a: If an employee has a clerical occupation, she/he is more likely to be a teleworker.

Hypothesis 12b: If an employee has a clerical occupation, it is more likely she/he is willing to be a teleworker in the future.

Hypothesis 12c: If an employee has a clerical occupation, it is more likely she/he is willing to be a regular teleworker in the future.

Hypothesis 13a: If an employee is a manager, she/he is more likely to be a teleworker.

Hypothesis 13b: If an employee is a manager, it is more likely she/he is willing to be a teleworker in the future.

Hypothesis 13c: If an employee is a manager, it is more likely she/he is willing to be a regular teleworker in the future.

The empirical results were significant for the hypotheses regarding clerical occupations, but the results were precisely the opposite of what we expected. (hypothesis 12a: 2 groups: 11.4 percent versus 26 percent, χ^2, p = 0.006) (hypothesis 12b: 2 groups: 60.2 percent versus 78 percent, χ^2, p = 0.002) (hypothesis 12c: 2 groups: 57.1 percent versus 80.7 percent, χ^2, p = 0.000) There seem to be two types of clerical occupations: location-dependent ones such as receptionists, and location-independent ones such as data entry personnel. In our sample, there may have been a dominance of clerical workers with location-dependent work. Of our three hypotheses regarding managers, only hypotheses 13b and 13c were confirmed. (hypothesis 13b: 2 groups: 88.5 percent versus 67 percent, χ^2, p = 0.001) (hypothesis 13c: 2 groups: 90.6 percent versus 67.2 percent, χ^2, p = 0.001) This supports our general conclusion that future teleworkers may generally be highly-skilled and have substantial managerial duties.

5.2.1.10 Coordination and control mechanism
As discussed in the previous chapter, direct supervision is rarely the best way to manage teleworkers. Management by objectives is usually more appropriate. This can be achieved in practice either by implementing management by output, or by considering the employee's educational level to be a sufficient guarantee for strong job performance with respect to the employee's pre-set objectives.

Hypothesis 14a: If an employee is managed by direct supervision, she/he is less likely to be a teleworker.

Hypothesis 14b: If an employee is managed by direct supervision, it is less likely she/he is willing to be a teleworker in the future.

Hypothesis 14c: If an employee is managed by direct supervision, it is less likely she/he is willing to be a regular teleworker in the future.

Hypothesis 15a: If an employee is managed by output, she/he is more likely to be a teleworker.

Hypothesis 15b: If an employee is managed by output, it is more likely she/he is willing to be a teleworker in the future.

Hypothesis 15c: If an employee is managed by output, it is more likely she/he is willing to be a regular teleworker in the future.

Hypothesis 16a: If the educational level of the employee is seen to guarantee job performance, the employee is more likely to be a teleworker.

Hypothesis 16b: If the educational level of the employee is seen to guarantee job performance, it is more likely she/he is willing to be a teleworker in the future.

Hypothesis 16c: If the educational level of the employee is seen to guarantee job performance, it is more likely she/he is willing to be a regular teleworker in the future.

The empirical results confirm the hypotheses regarding direct supervision. (hypothesis 14a: 2 groups: 4.8 percent versus 22.5 percent, χ^2, p = 0.056) (hypothesis 14b: 2 groups: 42.9 percent versus 74.6 percent, χ^2, p = 0.002) (hypothesis 14c: 2 groups: 36.8 percent versus 76 percent, χ^2, p = 0.000) With respect to management by output, only the hypothesis regarding current teleworkers was significant. (hypothesis 15a: 2 groups: 32.9 percent versus 16.5 percent, χ^2, p = 0.004) With respect to the significance of educational level, only the hypotheses regarding future teleworkers were significant. (hypothesis 16b: 2 groups: 88.4 percent versus 68.8 percent, χ^2, p = 0.009) (hypothesis 16c: 2 groups: 86.8 percent versus 69.8 percent, χ^2, p = 0.032)

5.2.1.11 Workaholism
Workaholics may prefer telework because it allows them to increase their productivity.[7] We used two parameters as rough proxies for workaholism: total working hours and unpaid overtime.

Hypothesis 17a: The more hours an employee works, the more likely that she/he is a teleworker.

Hypothesis 17b: The more hours an employee works, the more likely that she/he is willing to be a teleworker in the future.

Hypothesis 17c: The more hours an employee works, the more likely that she/he is willing to be a regular teleworker in the future.

Hypothesis 18a: The more unpaid overtime an employee works, the more likely she/he is a teleworker.

Hypothesis 18b: The more unpaid overtime an employee works, the more likely she/he is willing to be a teleworker in the future.

Hypothesis 18c: The more unpaid overtime an employee works, the more likely she/he is willing to be a regular teleworker in the future.

The empirical results indicated that workaholics are more likely or willing to be teleworkers, both today and in the future. (hypothesis 17a: t-test, $p = 0.013$) (hypothesis 17c: t-test, $p = 0.008$) (hypothesis 18a: t-test, $p = 0.075$) (hypothesis 18c: t-test, $p = 0.021$)

5.2.1.12 Teamwork
Good teamwork requires that everyone in the team shares ideas and can draw upon the resources of the entire team. Thus, one might expect that individuals functioning in teams would be less likely to adopt telework.

Hypothesis 19a: If the employee is a team member, she/he is less likely to be a teleworker.

Hypothesis 19b: If the employee is a team member, it is less likely she/he is willing to be a teleworker in the future.

Hypothesis 19c: If the employee is a team member, it is less likely she/he is willing to be a regular teleworker in the future.

No significant results were found for these hypotheses. This is an interesting result, as it suggests that the presence of weak or strong group dynamics has little impact on telework choices.

5.2.1.13 Routine and non-routine decision-making

Employees who are involved in non-routine decision-making enjoy a greater autonomy and consequently also enjoy greater trust from their managers.[8] Hence, one would expect that these employees would be more likely to prefer telework than employees involved in routine decision-making.

Hypothesis 20a: The more important routine decision-making is in the employee's job, the less likely that she/he is a teleworker.

Hypothesis 20b: The more important routine decision-making is in the employee's job, the less likely that she/he is willing to be a teleworker in the future.

Hypothesis 20c: The more important routine decision-making is in the employee's job, the less likely that she/he is willing to be a regular teleworker in the future.

Hypothesis 21a: The more important non-routine decision-making is in the employee's job, the more likely that she/he is a teleworker.

Hypothesis 21b: The more important non-routine decision-making is in the employee's job, the more likely that she/he is willing to be a teleworker in the future.

Hypothesis 21c: The more important non-routine decision-making is in the employee's job, the more likely that she/he is willing to be a regular teleworker in the future.

These hypotheses were all confirmed. (hypothesis 20a: t-test, $p = 0.010$) (hypothesis 20b: t-test, $p = 0.003$) (hypothesis 20c: t-test, $p = 0.002$) (hypothesis 21a: t-test, $p = 0.010$) (hypothesis 21b: t-test, $p = 0.001$) (hypothesis 21c: t-test, $p = 0.002$)

5.2.1.14 Ad hoc meetings

Because ad hoc meetings are (by definition) unscheduled, teleworkers can have difficulty attending such meetings. This suggests that workers who must attend ad hoc meetings may be less likely to be teleworkers.

Hypothesis 22a: The more an employee needs to attend ad hoc meetings, the less likely it is that she/he is a teleworker.

Hypothesis 22b: The more an employee needs to attend ad hoc meetings, the less likely it is that she/he is willing to be a teleworker in the future.

Hypothesis 22c: The more an employee needs to attend ad hoc meetings, the less likely it is that she/he is willing to be a regular teleworker in the future.

The empirical results were significant only for the future-oriented hypotheses. The correlation found, however, was the opposite of the one expected. Perhaps telework is a proxy for readiness to be flexible regarding work arrangements, which may imply that potential teleworkers can more readily accommodate, at least in their minds, the requirement to be present at non-scheduled events. (hypothesis 22b: t-test, p = 0.037) (hypothesis 22c: t-test, p = 0.010)

5.2.2 COMMUTING CHARACTERISTICS

Telework is particularly attractive for employees with stressful commutes. Several parameters can give an indication of commuting stress, including the employee's commuting distance and the commuting time length (morning and evening).

5.2.2.1 Commuting distance
Hypothesis 23a: The longer an employee's commuting distance, the more likely that she/he is a teleworker.

Hypothesis 23b: The longer an employee's commuting distance, the more likely that she/he is willing to be a teleworker in the future.

Hypothesis 23c: The longer an employee's commuting distance, the more likely that she/he is willing to be a regular teleworker in the future.

These hypotheses were confirmed. (hypothesis 23a: t-test, p = 0.047) (hypothesis 23b: t-test, p = 0.001) (hypothesis 23c: t-test, p = 0.000)

5.2.2.2 Duration of the morning commute
Hypothesis 24a: The longer the duration of an employee's morning commute, the more likely that she/he is a teleworker.

Hypothesis 24b: The longer the duration of an employee's morning commute, the more likely that she/he is willing to be a teleworker in the future.

Hypothesis 24c: The longer the duration of an employee's morning commute, the more likely that she/he is willing to be a regular teleworker in the future.

Only the hypotheses regarding future telework were confirmed. (hypothesis 24b: t-test, $p = 0.001$) (hypothesis 24c: t-test, $p = 0.000$) This likely indicates that the duration of the morning commute is not yet very important in the decision to telework, but may become more important in the future.

5.2.2.3 Duration of the evening commute
Hypothesis 25a: The longer the duration of an employee's evening commute, the more likely that she/he is a teleworker.

Hypothesis 25b: The longer the duration of an employee's evening commute, the more likely that she/he is willing to be a teleworker in the future.

Hypothesis 25c: The longer the duration of an employee's evening commute, the more likely that she/he is willing to be a regular teleworker in the future.

As with the morning commute, only the hypotheses regarding future telework were confirmed. (hypothesis 25b: t-test, $p = 0.008$) (hypothesis 25c: t-test, $p = 0.002$) Hence, we reach a similar conclusion: it appears that the duration of the evening commute is not yet very important in the decision to telework but may become more important in the future.

5.2.3 THE ROLE OF THE CAR IN THE WORKER'S ACTIVITIES

5.2.3.1 Use of a car during working hours
If an employee is not supposed to be in the office all the time anyway - perhaps because customers need to be visited during working hours - then the psychological step of adopting telework becomes much smaller: neither the manager nor the employee's peers then expect a permanent presence in the office during conventional working hours.

Hypothesis 26a: If an employee uses a car during working hours, she/he is more likely to be a teleworker.

Hypothesis 26b: If an employee uses a car during working hours, it is more likely she/he is willing to be a teleworker in the future.

Hypothesis 26c: If an employee uses a car during working hours, it is more likely she/he is willing to be a regular teleworker in the future.

The empirical results confirmed these hypotheses. (hypothesis 26a: 2 groups: 36.2 percent versus 10.7 percent, χ^2, p = 0.000) (hypothesis 26b: 2 groups: 84.8 percent versus 63.8 percent, χ^2, p = 0.000) (hypothesis 26c: 2 groups: 87 percent versus 63.4 percent, χ^2, p = 0.000)

5.2.3.2 Use of a company car

If an employee is given a company car, this indicates that the employer trusts the employee, regardless of the employee's actual need for such a car or the fact that it may lead to taxation benefits as compared to an equivalent raise in salary. The presence of such trust may also be critical to telework adoption. Furthermore, such an employee is less likely to use public transport for her/his commuting trip. Hence the validation of the impact of usage of a company car is also critical for the transport implications described in Chapter 6.

Hypothesis 27a: If an employee uses a company car, she/he is more likely to be a teleworker.

Hypothesis 27b: If an employee uses a company car, it is more likely she/he is willing to be a teleworker in the future.

Hypothesis 27c: If an employee uses a company car, it is more likely she/he is willing to be a regular teleworker in the future.

The empirical results confirmed all the above hypotheses (hypothesis 27a: 2 groups: 46.2 percent versus 15.1 percent, χ^2, p = 0.000) (hypothesis 27b: 2 groups: 88.5 percent versus 68.3 percent, χ^2, p = 0.004) (hypothesis 27c: 2 groups: 91.3 percent versus 68.4 percent, χ^2, p = 0.002)

5.2.4 SOCIO-DEMOGRAPHIC CHARACTERISTICS

5.2.4.1 Gender

It is not yet clear which gender is more attracted to telework. Some studies suggest that women are more attracted to telework, because it gives them increased flexibility to schedule their household responsibilities. However, other studies conclude that men are more attracted to telework, because men today tend to work in more highly-skilled and more location-independent jobs suited for telework. In addition, they may define themselves more in terms of their work content, whereas women attach more importance to personal contacts and close working relationships. We formulated hypotheses that suggested that men would be more attracted to telework.

Hypothesis 28a: Male employees are more likely to be teleworkers.

Hypothesis 28b: It is more likely that male employess are willing to be teleworkers in the future.

Hypothesis 28c: It is more likely that male employees are willing to be regular teleworkers in the future.

The empirical results confirmed all the above hypotheses. (hypothesis 28a: 2 groups: 26.7 percent versus 15.4 percent, χ^2, p = 0.025) (hypothesis 28b: 2 groups: 80.9 percent versus 63.1 percent, χ^2, p = 0.001) (hypothesis 28c: 2 groups: 81.3 percent versus 64.3 percent, χ^2, p = 0.004)

5.2.4.2 Age
With respect to age and the propensity to telework, studies have produced different results. Some researchers conclude that the acceptance of electronic homework decreases with age among the older workforce.[9] However, other researchers conclude that one-third of all teleworkers are in the (relatively old) 40 - 49 age group.[10] We formulated the following hypotheses.

Hypothesis 29a: The older an employee is, the less likely that she/he is a teleworker.

Hypothesis 29b: The older an employee is, the less likely that she/he is willing to be a teleworker in the future.

Hypothesis 29c: The older an employee is, the less likely that she/he is willing to be a regular teleworker in the future.

We found no statistically significant results related to age.

5.2.4.3 Housing conditions
Since homework is generally the most preferred kind of telework, one would expect that employees with office space at home would be particularly interested in telework.

Hypothesis 30a: If an employee has office space at home, she/he is more likely to be a teleworker.

Hypothesis 30b: If an employee has office space at home, it is more likely she/he is willing to be a teleworker in the future.

Hypothesis 30c: If an employee has office space at home, it is more likely she/he is willing to be a regular teleworker in the future.

These hypotheses were all confirmed. (hypothesis 30a: 2 groups: 25.1 percent versus 10.4 percent, χ^2, p = 0.007) (hypothesis 30b: 2 groups: 76.5 percent versus 61.0 percent, χ^2, p = 0.011) (hypothesis 30c: 2 groups: 77.2 percent versus 61.8 percent, χ^2, p = 0.017)

5.2.4.4 Educational level

Broadly speaking, there are currently two main types of teleworkers: highly-skilled and low-skilled. Although both types are well-represented in the telework population today, evidence from this study and others suggests that, in the future, most teleworkers may be highly-skilled workers. We therefore expect that a high educational level would correlate with future telework adoption, but not with current telework adoption.

Hypothesis 31a: If an employee has a high educational level, she/he is more likely to be a teleworker.

Hypothesis 31b: If an employee has a high educational level, it is more likely she/he is willing to be a teleworker in the future.

Hypothesis 31c: If an employee has a high educational level, it is more likely she/he is willing to be a regular teleworker in the future.

As expected, hypothesis 31a was neither confirmed nor disconfirmed. This is consistent with the fact that there are currently large numbers of both highly-skilled and low-skilled teleworkers. As expected, the hypotheses linking future telework to high education levels were both confirmed. (hypothesis 31b: 2 groups: 84.1 percent versus 64.1 percent, χ^2, p = 0.000) (hypothesis 31c: 2 groups: 86.7 percent versus 64 percent, χ^2, p = 0.000)

5.2.4.5 Wage

One would expect employees with a higher income to be more interested in telework, largely because homework is the preferred form of telework and high-income employees would be more likely to have the means to organize a workplace at home.

Hypothesis 32a: The higher the income of the employee, the more likely that she/he is a teleworker.

Hypothesis 32b: The higher the income of the employee, the more likely that she/he is willing to be a teleworker in the future.

Hypothesis 32c: The higher the income of the employee, the more likely that she/he is willing to be a regular teleworker in the future.

These hypotheses were confirmed. (hypothesis 32a: 3 groups: 41 percent versus 19.1 percent versus 15.6 percent,[11] χ^2, p = 0.007) (hypothesis 32b: 3 groups: 87.2 percent versus 76.3 percent versus 53.3 percent, χ^2, p = 0.001) (hypothesis 32c: 3 groups: 88.2 percent versus 78.1 percent versus 53.7 percent, χ^2, p = 0.001)

5.2.4.6 Household complexity
If a household is large or has children under three, managing the household is complex and employee flexibility is important to satisfy family needs.[12]

Hypothesis 33a: The larger an employee's household, the more likely she/he is a teleworker.

Hypothesis 33b: The larger an employee's household, the more likely she/he is willing to be a teleworker in the future.

Hypothesis 33c: The larger an employee's household, the more likely she/he is willing to be a regular teleworker in the future.

Hypothesis 34a: If an employee has children under three, she/he is more likely to be a teleworker.

Hypothesis 34b: If an employee has children under three, it is more likely she/he is willing to be a teleworker in the future.

Hypothesis 34c: If an employee has children under three, it is more likely she/he is willing to be a regular teleworker in the future.

No significant results were found for the hypotheses regarding household size. Of the hypotheses regarding the presence of children under three, only 34a - the hypothesis comparing current teleworkers with non-teleworkers - was significant. (hypothesis 34a: 2 groups: 32.4 percent versus 19.4 percent, χ^2, p = 0.072) Although parents of young children want flexibility now while their children are young, perhaps they expect that flexibility may be less important in the future, partly because their children will have grown up.

5.2.5 PERCEPTIONS AND ATTITUDES

5.2.5.1 Awareness
If an employee has little knowledge of the telework concept, she/he will not even consider it.[13]

Hypothesis 35a: If an employee has no familiarity with the concept of telework, she/he is less likely to be a teleworker.

Hypothesis 35b: If an employee has no familiarity with the concept of telework, it is less likely she/he is willing to be a teleworker in the future.

Hypothesis 35c: If an employee has no familiarity with the concept of telework, it is less likely she/he is willing to be a regular teleworker in the future.

These hypotheses were confirmed. (hypothesis 35a: 2 groups: 0 percent versus 23.5 percent, χ^2, p = 0.005) (hypothesis 35b: 2 groups: 34.6 percent versus 76.5 percent, χ^2, p = 0.000) (hypothesis 35c: 2 groups: 27.3 percent versus 77.6 percent, χ^2, p = 0.000)

5.2.5.2 Considered telework as a personal option
Employees who have never considered telework as an option of personal choice are less likely to adopt it.

Hypothesis 36a: If an employee has never considered telework as an option of personal choice, she/he is less likely to be a teleworker.

Hypothesis 36b: If an employee has never considered telework as an option of personal choice, it is less likely she/he is willing to be a teleworker in the future.

Hypothesis 36c: If an employee has never considered telework as an option of personal choice, it is less likely she/he is willing to be a regular teleworker in the future.

The empirical results confirmed these hypotheses. (hypothesis 36a: 2 groups: 2.6 percent versus 35.6 percent, χ^2, p = 0.000)[14] (hypothesis 36b: 2 groups: 50 percent versus 89.7 percent, χ^2, p = 0.000) (hypothesis 36c: 2 groups: 47.3 percent versus 89.7 percent, χ^2, p = 0.000)

5.2.5.3 Employer's normative beliefs

The attitudes of the employing organization in general and the direct supervisor in particular will strongly influence an employee's behaviour and attitudes.

Hypothesis 37a: If the employer has a positive attitude towards telework, it is more likely that the employee is a teleworker.

Hypothesis 37b: If the employer has a positive attitude towards telework, it is more likely that the employee is willing to be a teleworker in the future.

Hypothesis 37c: If the employer has a positive attitude towards telework, it is more likely that the employee is willing to be a regular teleworker in the future.

Hypothesis 38a: If the direct supervisor has a positive attitude towards telework, it is more likely that the employee is a teleworker.

Hypothesis 38b: If the direct supervisor has a positive attitude towards telework, it is more likely that the employee is willing to be a teleworker in the future.

Hypothesis 38c: If the direct supervisor has a positive attitude towards telework, it is more likely that the employee is willing to be a regular teleworker in the future.

All these hypotheses were confirmed. (hypothesis 37a: 2 groups: 42.6 percent versus 6 percent, χ^2, p = 0.000) (hypothesis 37b: 2 groups: 88.9 percent versus 60.3 percent, χ^2, p = 0.000) (hypothesis 37c: 2 groups: 88.9 percent versus 60.3 percent, χ^2, p = 0.000) (hypothesis 38a: 2 groups: 45.3 percent versus 4.7 percent, χ^2, p = 0.000) (hypothesis 38b: 2 groups: 89.6 percent versus 60.4 percent, χ^2, p = 0.000) (hypothesis 38c: 2 groups: 89.8 percent versus 60.2 percent, χ^2, p = 0.000)

Up to this point, we have looked at the relationship between telework adoption and the objective characteristics of the employee and her/his situation. We will conclude this section by moving from objective to subjective individual-level factors, in order to examine the final element of our telework-specific conceptual framework (see chapter 3, Figure 3.1). To that end, we will now examine the relationship between telework adoption and ten employee beliefs (perceptions) and attitudes.

5.2.5.4 Belief regarding the stressfulness of the commute

One would expect that employees who consider their commutes to be stressful would be more interested in telework.

Hypothesis 39a: The more stressful the commute is (as perceived by the employee), the more likely that the employee is a teleworker.

Hypothesis 39b: The more stressful the commute is (as perceived by the employee), the more likely that the employee is willing to be a teleworker in the future.

Hypothesis 39c: The more stressful the commute is (as perceived by the employee), the more likely that the employee is willing to be a regular teleworker in the future.

These hypotheses were confirmed. (hypothesis 39a: t-test, p = 0.003) (hypothesis 39b: t-test, p = 0.002) (hypothesis 39c: t-test, p = 0.001)

5.2.5.5 Belief related to the ability of the commute to allow the employee to make a distinction between family and professional life

Hypothesis 40a: The stronger the employee's belief that the commute allows him/her to make a distinction between family and professional life, the less likely that she/he is a teleworker.

Hypothesis 40b: The stronger the employee's belief that the commute allows him/her to make a distinction between family and professional life, the less likely that she/he is willing to be a teleworker in the future.

Hypothesis 40c: The stronger the employee's belief that the commute allows him/her to make a distinction between family and professional life, the less likely that she/he is willing to be a regular teleworker in the future.

Only the hypotheses regarding future telework were confirmed. (hypothesis 40b: t-test, p = 0.019) (hypothesis 40c: t-test, p = 0.035) Hence, an employee's belief that the commute allows him/her to make a distinction between family and profession life plays no significant role in explaining the current adoption of telework.

5.2.5.6 Belief that the commute has a negative impact on society

As mentioned elsewhere in this book, commuting to work has negative impacts on society (for example, commuting has an impact on energy consumption, air pollution, noise pollution, traffic congestion and road accidents). This suggests the following hypotheses.

Hypothesis 41a: The stronger the employee's belief that the commuting trip has a negative impact on society, the more likely that she/he is a teleworker.

Hypothesis 41b: The stronger the employee's belief that the commuting trip has a negative impact on society, the more likely that she/he is willing to be a teleworker in the future.

Hypothesis 41c: The stronger the employee's belief that the commuting trip has a negative impact on society, the more likely that she/he is willing to be a regular teleworker in the future.

All these hypotheses were confirmed. (hypothesis 41a: t-test, $p = 0.002$) (hypothesis 41b: t-test, $p = 0.001$) (hypothesis 41c: t-test, $p = 0.000$)

5.2.5.7 Belief regarding the importance of face-to-face contact with the direct supervisor

Hypothesis 42a: The stronger the employee's belief that face-to-face contact with the direct supervisor is important, the less likely that the employee is a teleworker.

Hypothesis 42b: The stronger the employee's belief that face-to-face contact with the direct supervisor is important, the less likely that the employee is willing to be a teleworker in the future.

Hypothesis 42c: The stronger the employee's belief that face-to-face contact with the direct supervisor is important, the less likely that the employee is willing to be a regular teleworker in the future.

Only the hypotheses related to future telework were confirmed. (hypothesis 42b: t-test, $p = 0.002$) (hypothesis 42c: t-test, $p = 0.001$) This suggests that an employee's belief regarding the importance of face-to-face contact with the direct supervisor plays no significant role in explaining the current adoption of telework. The non-significant result for current teleworkers may be explained by the fact that current teleworkers realize part-time teleworking still permits them to have the necessary face-to-face contact whereas this insight may be lacking among the potential teleworkers.

5.2.5.8 Belief regarding the importance of face-to-face contact with other employees

Hypothesis 43a: The stronger the employee's belief that face-to-face contact with other employees is important, the less likely that the employee is a teleworker.

Hypothesis 43b: The stronger the employee's belief that face-to-face contact with other employees is important, the less likely that the employee is willing to be a teleworker in the future.

Hypothesis 43c: The stronger the employee's belief that face-to-face contact with other employees is important, the less likely that the employee is willing to be a regular teleworker in the future.

Again, only the hypotheses regarding future telework were confirmed. (hypothesis 43b: t-test, $p = 0.001$) (hypothesis 43c: t-test, $p = 0.004$) This suggests that an employee's belief regarding the importance of face-to-face contact with other employees plays no significant role in explaining the current adoption of telework. The non-significant result for current teleworkers may be explained by the fact that current teleworkers realize part-time teleworking still permits them to have the necessary face-to-face contact, whereas future, potential teleworkers may lack this insight.

5.2.5.9 Belief regarding the importance of the office atmosphere

If the employee derives benefits from functioning in a formal office setting, because of the 'atmosphere' prevailing in this setting, telework becomes less likely.

Hypothesis 44a: The stronger the employee's belief that the office atmosphere is important, the less likely that she/he is a teleworker.

Hypothesis 44b: The stronger the employee's belief that the office atmosphere is important, the less likely that she/he is willing to be a teleworker in the future.

Hypothesis 44c: The stronger the employee's belief that the office atmosphere is important, the less likely that she/he is willing to be a regular teleworker in the future.

Again, only the hypotheses related to future telework were confirmed. (hypothesis 44b: t-test, $p = 0.002$) (hypothesis 44c: t-test, $p = 0.001$) The employee's belief in this regard appears to play no significant role in explaining the current adoption of telework.

5.2.5.10 Belief regarding the importance of working without interruptions from colleagues

Hypothesis 45a: The more important it is to work without interruptions from colleagues (as perceived by the employee), the more likely that the employee is a teleworker.

Hypothesis 45b: The more important it is to work without interruptions from colleagues (as perceived by the employee), the more likely that the employee is willing to be a teleworker in the future.

Hypothesis 45c: The more important it is to work without interruptions from colleagues (as perceived by the employee), the more likely that the employee is willing to be a regular teleworker in the future.

These hypotheses were confirmed. (hypothesis 45a: t-test, $p = 0.036$) (hypothesis 45b: t-test, $p = 0.003$) (hypothesis 45c: t-test, $p = 0.027$)

5.2.5.11 Belief regarding the importance of working without interruptions from family

Hypothesis 46a: The more important it is to work without interruptions from family (as perceived by the employee), the less likely that the employee is a teleworker.

Hypothesis 46b: The more important it is to work without interruptions from family (as perceived by the employee), the less likely that the employee is willing to be a teleworker in the future.

Hypothesis 46c: The more important it is to work without interruptions from family (as perceived by the employee), the less likely that the employee is willing to be a regular teleworker in the future.

The empirical results confirmed none of these hypotheses.

5.2.5.12 Belief regarding the importance of the distinction between family and professional life

Hypothesis 47a: The more important the distinction between family and professional life is (as perceived by the employee), the less likely that the employee is a teleworker.

Hypothesis 47b: The more important the distinction between family and professional life is (as perceived by the employee), the less likely that the employee is willing to be a teleworker in the future.

Hypothesis 47c: The more important the distinction between family and professional life is (as perceived by the employee), the less likely that the employee is willing to be a regular teleworker in the future.

These hypotheses were also confirmed. (hypothesis 47a: t-test, $p = 0.004$) (hypothesis 47b: t-test, $p = 0.000$) (hypothesis 47c: t-test, $p = 0.000$)

5.2.5.13 Belief regarding the importance of the availability of the organization's restaurant

Hypothesis 48a: The more important the availability of the organization's restaurant is (as perceived by the employee), the less likely that the employee is a teleworker.

Hypothesis 48b: The more important the availability of the organization's restaurant is (as perceived by the employee), the less likely that the employee is willing to be a teleworker in the future.

Hypothesis 48c: The more important the availability of the organization's restaurant is (as perceived by the employee), the less likely that the employee is willing to be a regular teleworker in the future.

Our empirical results confirmed none of these hypotheses.

5.3 ADVANTAGES AND DISADVANTAGES FROM THE EMPLOYEE'S POINT OF VIEW

An employee considering telework faces a complex set of advantages and disadvantages. The employee's own personality and particular life situation will affect the relative weights assigned to those advantages and disadvantages. For instance, the flexibility to schedule work around child care arrangements is not relevant for an employee without children.[15] The advantages and disadvantages of telework will also depend on the type of telework (centre-based versus homework). For example, centre-based telework is perceived to be better with respect to social interaction, while homework is perceived to be better with respect to integrating work and private life.

5.3.1 POTENTIAL ADVANTAGES AND DISADVANTAGES OF TELEWORK IMPLEMENTATION FROM THE EMPLOYEE'S POINT OF VIEW

Based on an in-depth study of the current literature, 33 advantages and disadvantages were identified and presented to the surveyed employees.[16] In this section, we will list the potential advantages and disadvantages we identified and comment on them where appropriate. In the next section, we will assess them empirically using the results of our survey.

5.3.1.1 Flexibility
(Potential advantages: more flexibility, easier to access banks and public services, more flexibility in arranging personal free time, more flexibility to schedule work.)

The first category of potential advantages, 'flexibility,' is often suggested as a major advantage of telework. However, there is little evidence that employees actually change their working hours when they become teleworkers.[17] Furthermore, some supervisors expect their supervisees to continue to work during conventional hours.

5.3.1.2 Work
(Potential disadvantages: less in touch with the organization, more problems with the direct supervisor, fewer promotion possibilities, more self-discipline required, abuse by employer, abuse by employee. Potential advantages: more work done, stronger orientation of control and coordination toward output, less work-related stress, possibility of more accurate work evaluation, possibility of increased autonomy.)

Employees fear that lack of face-to-face communication and visibility to management will lead to fewer promotion possibilities.[18] However, this fear may be ill-founded; the relationship between career development and telework has not yet been examined sufficiently to warrant a definitive conclusion.[19] This issue is certainly less of a problem if telework is adopted on a part-time basis. For women on maternity leave, telework can even help their career, by preserving career continuity and allowing them to keep their skills up-to-date during the leave.[20]

Telework requires self-discipline in order to separate work from leisure time; teleworkers cannot rely on formal time schedules or the presence of a supervisor to get their work done.[21] A lack of self-discipline is therefore a constraint to the adoption of telework.[22] In extreme cases, lack of teleworker self-discipline can lead to overeating and alcoholism, especially if the teleworker works from home.[23]

Telework can also lead to abuse by employers. For example, some teleworkers perceive telework as a one-sided special favour to accommodate their personal needs, and consequently accept inferior work arrangements.[24] In exchange for the flexibility of telework, some employers stop giving extra pay for overtime.[25] Some employers force the teleworker to become self-employed. This makes teleworkers a much more flexible work force, because they can be laid off much easier, and they must take their own measures to deal with sickness and holidays.[26] Some employers may even reduce wages, although the evidence for this practice is unclear. As with conventional workers, teleworkers' pay varies widely. Kraut (1989) in an older study concludes that, overall, homeworkers working full-time receive 70 percent of the income of conventional workers in general. For the component of current teleworkers consisting of low-skilled workers, this result can be partly explained by the lower bargaining power of low-skilled workers and the fact that employers implement telework for this type of worker in order to reduce costs.

Generally speaking, teleworkers get more work done than non-teleworkers - up to 60 percent more than conventional workers.[27] Teleworkers face fewer interruptions, they are de facto shielded from having to perform 'little' office jobs, they tend to work longer hours than their colleagues at the conventional office,[28] and, unlike their colleagues at the conventional office, they usually do not count their social interaction time as 'work.'[29]

While on this issue of teleworkers getting more work done, it is worth pointing out that this tendency can reach extreme proportions: telework may increase the risk of workaholism. Highly-skilled employees with high job responsibilities (a type of employee likely to adopt telework) are used to working uncompensated overtime at home. Telework schemes will be particularly attractive to employees who are comfortable working alone (and are thus at a higher risk of workaholism). Male teleworkers with limited social interests have an especially high risk of becoming workaholics. However, it should be kept in mind that workaholism does not necessarily lead to stress, sickness or even unhappiness. All things considered, workaholics may be better off teleworking because telework reduces their commuting stress and allows them to more flexibly integrate their work and family life.[30]

Telework has the potential to increase general job satisfaction. If telework programmes are voluntary, it can be safely assumed that the teleworker prefers telework over conventional work. On average, homeworkers are at least as satisfied with their working conditions as office-based workers.[31]

Interestingly, dissatisfaction with work or life in general is seldom observed in studies of teleworkers.[32]

Telework can either increase or decrease work-related stress. If the work-related stress is simply a result of a negative social or physical environment in the conventional office, then the adoption of telework can reduce this type of stress.[33] Two other commonly-discussed types of work-related stress also affected by telework are activity conflict and activity ambiguity. Activity conflict results from simultaneous conflicting or incompatible demands or expectations from different sources, while activity ambiguity results from a lack of necessary information regarding important aspects of performance and expectations. Telework will generally decrease activity conflict, because teleworkers are expected to perform a more narrowly defined set of activities, and that in itself reduces the possibility of conflicting expectations. Furthermore, as the lines of communications become more formal, the teleworker is less likely to face conflicting demands from two or more supervisors. On the other hand, in some cases, telework will increase work-related stress. For example, a teleworker performing a boundary function may face demands from external parties (e.g., clients) that conflict with demands from her/his own organization. In this case, telework can make the stress from activity conflict worse, by reducing contact with the employing organization. This can cause the teleworker to lose touch with the interests and norms of her/his own organization and may increase confrontation and friction with peers and supervisors. Furthermore, telework will usually increase stress for individuals with jobs consisting of unclearly specified sets of activities (high ambiguity). Whereas conventional employees receive both formal and informal information regarding performance and expectations, teleworkers do not receive that part of the information that comes only from informal office contact.[34]

It is often claimed that telework increases employee autonomy and independence. Certainly, the teleworker's greater control over work hours and work patterns enhances her/his autonomy. However, many white collar workers today already experience a high degree of autonomy with respect to their work hours and work patterns, so it is unlikely that the adoption of telework will further enhance the autonomy of these highly-skilled workers. Furthermore, one should not assume that telework will enhance autonomy for low-skilled workers either, because the home environment may be more demanding and offer less freedom than the workplace (for instance, employees with child care responsibilities).[35]

5.3.1.3 Work environment

(Potential disadvantages: less equipment available, higher personal operational costs, negative influence on the organizational culture. Potential advantages: more working space, less need to dress 'appropriately.')

Teleworkers may have access to less equipment than conventional workers. For instance, a teleworker working at home is unlikely to have a photocopier.

However, the teleworker's home workspace may be larger, more pleasant, and often more conducive to concentration. Many teleworkers who leave (currently popular) 'open concept' offices greatly appreciate a home workplace with less noise, fewer interruptions and more privacy. On the other hand, a home workspace may not be as ergonomic as a conventional one.[36]

5.3.1.4 Family

(Potential advantages: more personal free time, more free time with family and friends.)

It is unclear whether telework allows the teleworker to truly spend **more** time with family or to engage in **more** leisure activities. Telework's real impact in this area lies in allowing teleworkers to determine **when** they will spend time with their family and **when** they will engage in leisure activities.[37]

5.3.1.5 Social and professional interaction

(Potential disadvantages: social isolation, less possibility for social interaction, less possibility for professional interaction.)

Social isolation, the subjective feeling of 'being alone,' is one of the major psychological problems faced by teleworkers.[38] Most people need human contact, and there is no perfect substitute for the stimulation, immediate feedback and fun of exchanging ideas face-to-face with other people.[39] However, the workplace is not the only place that alleviates the feeling of being alone. Interaction with family and friends can also help alleviate this feeling. Furthermore, the disposition to have the feeling of 'being alone' very much depends on the individual's personality.[40] Here, it should also be pointed out that some employees may actually desire a degree of social isolation. The research of Di Nicola and Parrotto (1998) indicates that, although workers considering telework request a large number of technological devices in order to facilitate communication with their colleagues, they also request a certain amount of isolation in order to properly perform certain tasks. And, as has been said before, social isolation is much less of an issue for a part-time teleworker.

Another frequently cited disadvantage of telework implementation is the constraint telework puts on social (non-job related) and professional (job-related) interaction. Most employees have a need to socialize with fellow workers.[41] This is especially an issue for high-frequency teleworkers, and for those with routine duties, who often attain little satisfaction from the job itself. Such interaction is less of an issue in managerial and highly-skilled jobs, where satisfaction is primarily obtained through the job itself.[42]

5.3.1.6 Employer or employee relocation

(Potential advantages: a solution if the employer relocates, a solution if the employee moves.)

Largely location-independent, a teleworker has more flexibility to stay in her/his current job if the employer relocates or the employee moves.[43]

5.3.1.7 Home environment

(Potential disadvantages: more distractions from other people, more conflict situations with other household members, more difficult to make a distinction between professional life and family life.)

If family and friends do not accept that the teleworker is at home to work, they may distract the teleworker. This problem can be particularly severe if the teleworker is always accessible due to a lack of spatial separation (e.g., if there is no spatially distinct home office). Hence, low-skilled teleworkers are more likely to encounter these distractions, since they are less likely to have the resources to create a spatially distinct home office.[44] This is not a problem with centre-based telework.[45]

Telework can cause family conflict if the availability of the necessary ICT equipment tempts teleworkers to use it in a way that decreases the amount of time previously spent with the family.[46] Conflict can also arise within 'single earner' families, if the person staying at home and taking care of domestic responsibilities feels that her/his territory is being invaded when the income-earner starts working out of the home.[47] Finally, conflict can also arise if space at home needs to be used for more than one purpose.[48]

The distinction between family and professional life is psychologically important, and this distinction needs to be addressed when implementing telework. Traditionally, the workplace has been seen as the domain of work, while the home has been seen as the domain of non-work. These two different environments not only require different behaviours, they also allow the individual to express different aspects of her/his personality. The majority of the work force has different spaces for work and leisure; the teleworker who works from home does not. These teleworkers cannot use the commuting trip to 'get into work mode' in the morning, to 'unwind' in the afternoon,[49] or to 'shift gears' between work and leisure.[50] The elimination of the buffer between work and family life may transfer stress from the work sphere to the private sphere.[51] According to Mirchandani (1999), many homeworkers use rituals to preserve the distinction between professional and family life. Homeworkers create their own spatial boundaries (a room or a designated area dedicated as an office), or their own temporal, behavioural or psychological boundaries (e.g., regular work schedules, or dressing differently when working versus relaxing).

5.3.2 EMPIRICAL ASSESSMENT OF ADVANTAGES AND DISADVANTAGES PERCEIVED BY EMPLOYEES

Now that we have looked at telework's potential advantages and disadvantages, we will assess those advantages and disadvantages empirically.

In our survey, we asked our sample of 261 employees to rate the above potential advantages and disadvantages. In their opinion, what are the actual advantages and disadvantages of telework, and how important are those advantages and disadvantages? We examine below whether different groups of respondents have different perceptions. First, we compare current teleworkers with non-teleworkers (revealed preference). Then, we compare potential teleworkers (i.e., those willing to telework should the opportunity arise, including the current teleworkers who indicated they would like to remain teleworkers in the future) with employees not willing to telework (stated preference). Finally, we compare potential regular teleworkers (i.e., those willing to telework at least once a workweek should the opportunity arise, including the employees currently teleworking at least once a workweek who indicated they would like to remain teleworkers in the future) with those employees not willing to become regular teleworkers (stated preference).

These differences will reveal some of the sociological, psychological and institutional barriers that prevent people from adopting (or even considering) telework.

5.3.2.1 A comparison of the perception of telework's disadvantages between current teleworkers and non-teleworkers

As shown in Table 5.1a, non-teleworkers rate seven of the 16 potential disadvantages as real disadvantages, namely: (1) less in touch with the organization; (2) fewer promotion possibilities; (3) more self-discipline required; (4) higher personal operational costs; (5) social isolation; (6) less possibility for social interaction; and (7) less possibility for professional interaction. Current teleworkers, on the other hand, rate only four of the 16 potential disadvantages as real disadvantages, namely (1) less in touch with the organization; (2) higher personal operational costs; (3) less possibility for social interaction; and (4) less possibility for professional interaction. It is remarkable that current teleworkers do not perceive 'social isolation' and 'fewer promotion possibilities' - two potential disadvantages often perceived as major barriers to telework implementation - as real disadvantages. Compared to current teleworkers, non-teleworkers are more convinced that teleworkers are less in touch with the organization. Current teleworkers, on the other hand, are more convinced than non-teleworkers that (1) abuse by employer; (2) abuse by employee; (3) negative influence on the organizational culture; and (4) more communication problems with the direct supervisor are not disadvantages, while they are more convinced that higher personal operational costs constitute a disadvantage of telework.

5.3.2.2 A comparison of the perception of telework's disadvantages between potential future teleworkers (including current teleworkers) and employees not willing to telework

Table 5.1b shows that employees not willing to telework perceive 11 of the 16 potential disadvantages as real disadvantages. Furthermore, employees not willing to adopt telework feel more strongly than potential future teleworkers that four are disadvantages, namely (1) less in touch with the organization; (2) social isolation; (3) less possibility for social interaction; and (4) less possibility for professional interaction. Potential future teleworkers are more convinced that the possibility of more problems with the direct supervisor is not actually an issue.

Comparing Table 5.1b with Table 5.1a shows that:

- Potential future teleworkers as a group, perceive one disadvantage that current teleworkers do not: social isolation.
- Employees not willing to telework perceive four disadvantages that current non-teleworkers do not: (1) less equipment available; (2) negative influence on the organizational culture; (3) more communication problems with the direct supervisor; and (4) more difficult to make a distinction between professional and family life.

5.3.2.3 A comparison of the perception of telework's disadvantages between potential, future regular teleworkers (including current regular teleworkers) and employees not willing to become regular teleworkers

This comparison, shown in Table 5.1c, is almost identical to the comparison in Table 5.1b.

Table 5.1a   Individual-level disadvantages of the adoption of telework (a comparison of current teleworkers and non-teleworkers)

DISADVANTAGE	GROUP 1: Tele-workers	GROUP 2: Non-tele-workers	Significance of the difference in perception of the disadvantage between group 1 and group 2
Work			
1. Less in touch with the organization	yes	yes[+]	significant t-test, p = 0.012
2. More problems with the direct supervisor	no	no	not significant
3. Fewer promotion possibilities	no	yes	significant t-test, p = 0.026
4. More self-discipline required	yes	yes	significant t-test, p = 0.060
5. Abuse by employer	no[+]	no	significant t-test, p = 0.026
6. Abuse by employee	no[+]	no	significant t-test, p = 0.001
Work environment			
7. Less equipment available	no	no	not significant
8. Higher personal operational costs	yes[+]	yes	significant t-test, p = 0.066
9. Negative influence on the organizational culture	no[+]	no	significant t-test, p = 0.002
Social and professional interaction			
10. Social isolation	no	yes	significant t-test, p = 0.002
11. Less possibility for social interaction	yes	yes	not significant
12. Less possibility for professional interaction	yes	yes	not significant
13. More communication problems with the direct supervisor	no[+]	no	significant t-test, p = 0.099
Home environment			
14. More distractions from other people	no	no	not significant
15. More conflict situations with other household members	no	no	not significant
16. More difficult to make a distinction between professional life and family life	no	no	not significant

Notes :
yes[+] = a more convinced yes
no[+] = a more convinced no

Source: own calculations

Table 5.1b   Individual-level disadvantages of the adoption of telework (a comparison of potential future teleworkers with employees not willing to telework)

DISADVANTAGE	GROUP 1: Willing to telework	GROUP 2: Not willing to telework	Significance of the difference in perception of the disadvantage between group 1 and group 2
Work			
1. Less in touch with the organization	yes	yes[+]	significant t-test, p = 0.061
2. More problems with the direct supervisor	no[+]	no	significant t-test, p = 0.032
3. Fewer promotion possibilities	no	yes	significant t-test, p = 0.078
4. More self-discipline required	yes	yes	not significant
5. Abuse by employer	no	no	not significant
6. Abuse by employee	no	no	not significant
Work environment			
7. Less equipment available	no	yes	significant t-test, p = 0.001
8. Higher personal operational costs	yes	yes	not significant
9. Negative influence on the organizational culture	no	yes	significant t-test, p = 0.000
Social and professional interaction			
10. Social isolation	yes	yes[+]	significant t-test, p = 0.000
11. Less possibility for social interaction	yes	yes[+]	significant t-test, p = 0.089
12. Less possibility for professional interaction	yes	yes[+]	significant t-test, p = 0.052
13. More communication problems with the direct supervisor	no	yes	significant t-test, p = 0.000
Home environment			
14. More distractions from other people	no	no	not significant
15. More conflict situations with other household members	no	no	not significant
16. More difficult to make a distinction between professional life and family life	no	yes	significant t-test, p = 0.022

Notes:
yes[+] = a more convinced yes
no[+] = a more convinced no

Source: own calculations

Table 5.1c *Individual-level disadvantages of the adoption of telework (a comparison of potential, future regular teleworkers with employees not willing to become regular teleworkers)*

DISADVANTAGE	GROUP 1: Willing to become regular tele-workers	GROUP 2: Not willing to become regular tele-workers	Significance of the difference in perception of the disadvantage between group 1 and group 2
Work			
1. Less in touch with the organization	yes	yes[+]	significant t-test, p = 0.033
2. More problems with the direct supervisor	no[+]	no	significant t-test, p = 0.025
3. Fewer promotion possibilities	no	yes	significant t-test, p = 0.061
4. More self-discipline required	yes	yes[+]	significant t-test, p = 0.095
5. Abuse by employer	no	no	not significant
6. Abuse by employee	no	no	not significant
Work environment			
7. Less equipment available	no	yes	significant t-test, p = 0.000
8. Higher personal operational costs	yes	yes	not significant
9. Negative influence on the organizational culture	no	yes	significant t-test, p = 0.000
Social and professional interaction			
10. Social isolation	yes	yes[+]	significant t-test, p = 0.000
11. Less possibility for social interaction	yes	yes'	significant t-test, p = 0.052
12. Less possibility for professional interaction	yes	yes[+]	not significant t-test, p = 0.049
13. More communication problems with the direct supervisor	no	yes	significant t-test, p = 0.000
Home environment			
14. More distractions from other people	no[+]	no	significant t-test, p = 0.059
15. More conflict situations with other household members	no	no	not significant
16. More difficult to make a distinction between prof. life and family life	no	yes	significant t-test, p = 0.013

Notes:
yes[+] = a more convinced yes
no[+] = a more convinced no

Source: own calculations

5.3.2.4 A comparison of the perception of telework's advantages between current teleworkers and non-teleworkers

Of the 17 potential advantages, only 'more working space' and 'possibility of more accurate work evaluation' are not perceived as advantages by either current teleworkers or current non-teleworkers (Table 5.2a). The 15 other potential advantages were perceived by both groups as real advantages. Current teleworkers are more convinced than non-teleworkers that six are advantages, namely (1) more work done; (2) more flexibility to adjust work schedule; (3) easier to access banks and public services; (4) a solution if the employer relocates; (5) a solution if the employee moves; and (6) more ecologically responsible behaviour.

5.3.2.5 A comparison of the perception of telework's advantages between potential future teleworkers (including current teleworkers) and employees not willing to telework

As shown in Table 5.2b, potential teleworkers feel that 15 of the 17 potential advantages are indeed real advantages. The only exceptions are 'more working space' and 'possibility of more correct work evaluation'. Employees not willing to telework do not recognize the following as advantages: (1) more work done; (2) more working space; (3) a solution if the employer relocates; and (4) a solution if the employee moves. Potential future teleworkers are more convinced than employees not willing to telework that the following are real advantages: (1) stronger orientation of control and coordination toward output; (2) less work-related stress; (3) easier to contact banks; and public services and (4) more ecologically responsible behaviour. Employees not willing to telework are even more convinced than potential future teleworkers that 'more working space' does not constitute an advantage of telework.

5.3.2.6 A comparison of the perception of telework's advantages between potential future regular teleworkers (including current regular teleworkers) and employees not willing to become regular teleworkers

This comparison, shown in Table 5.2c, is almost identical to the comparison in Table 5.2b.

Table 5.2a   Individual-level advantages of the adoption of telework (a comparison of current teleworkers and non-teleworkers)

ADVANTAGE	GROUP 1: Tele-work ers	GROUP 2: Non-tele-work ers	Significance of the difference in perception of the advantage between group 1 and group 2
Work			
1. More work done	yes[+]	yes	significant t-test, p = 0.000
2. Stronger orientation of control and coordination toward output	yes	yes	not significant
3. Less work-related stress	yes	yes	not significant
4. More flexibility to adjust work schedule	yes[+]	yes	significant t-test, p = 0.009
5. Possibility of more accurate work evaluation	no	no	not significant
6. Possibility to perform daily activities more independently	yes	yes	not significant
Work environment			
7. More working space	no	no	not significant
8. Less need to dress 'appropriately'	yes	yes	not significant
Flexibility			
9. More flexibility	yes	yes	not significant
10. Easier to contact banks and public services	yes[+]	yes	significant t-test, p = 0.049
11. More flexibility in arranging personal free time	yes	yes	not significant
Family			
12. More free time with family and friends	yes	yes	not significant
13. More personal free time	yes	yes	not significant
Relocation			
14. A solution if the employer relocates	yes[+]	yes	significant t-test, p = 0.002
15. A solution if the employee moves	yes[+]	yes	significant t-test, p = 0.000
More ecologically responsible behaviour	yes[+]	yes	significant t-test, p = 0.052
Able to work more effectively if permanently or temporarily disabled	yes	yes	not significant

Note: yes[+] = a more convinced yes

Source: own calculations

Table 5.2b   Individual-level advantages of the adoption of telework (a comparison of potential future teleworkers with employees not willing to telework)

ADVANTAGE	GROUP 1: Willing to telework	GROUP 2: Not willing to telework	Significance of the difference in perception of the advantage between group 1 and group 2
Work			
1. More work done	yes	no	significant t-test, p = 0.000
2. Stronger orientation of control and coordination toward output	yes[+]	yes	significant t-test, p = 0.013
3. Less work-related stress	yes[+]	yes	significant t-test, p = 0.017
4. More flexibility to adjust work schedule	yes	yes	not significant
5. Possibility of more accurate work evaluation	no	no	not significant
6. Possibility to perform daily activities more independently	yes	yes	not significant
Work environment			
7. More working space	no	no[+]	significant t-test, p = 0.009
8. Less need to dress 'appropriately'	yes	yes	not significant
Flexibility			
9. More flexibility	yes	yes	not significant
10. Easier to contact banks and public services	yes[+]	yes	significant t-test, p = 0.078
11. More flexibility in arranging personal free time	yes	yes	not significant
Family			
12. More free time with family and friends	yes	yes	not significant
13. More personal free time	yes	yes	not significant
Relocation			
14. A solution if the employer relocates	yes	no	significant t-test, p = 0.000
15. A solution if the employee moves	yes	no	significant t-test, p = 0.000
More ecologically responsible behaviour	yes[+]	yes	significant t-test, p = 0.017
Able to work more effectively if permanently or temporarily disabled	yes	yes	not significant

Notes:
yes[+] = a more convinced yes
no[+] = a more convinced no

Source: own calculations

Table 5.2c   *Individual-level advantages of the adoption of telework (a comparison of potential, future regular teleworkers with employees not willing to become regular teleworkers)*

ADVANTAGE	GROUP 1: Willing to become regular teleworkers	GROUP 2: Not willing to become regular teleworkers	Significance of the difference in perception of the advantage between group 1 and group 2
Work			
1. More work done	yes	no	significant t-test, p = 0.000
2. Stronger orientation of control and coordination toward output	yes⁺	yes	significant t-test, p = 0.012
3. Less work-related stress	yes⁺	yes	significant t-test, p = 0.007
4. More flexibility to adjust work schedule	yes⁺	yes	significant t-test, p = 0.050
5. Possibility of more accurate work evaluation	no	no	not significant
6. Possibility to perform daily activities more independently	yes⁺	yes	significant t-test, p = 0.097
Work environment			
7. More working space	no	no⁺	significant t-test, p = 0.005
8. Less need to dress 'appropriately'	yes	yes	not significant
Flexibility			
9. More flexibility	yes	yes	not significant
10. Easier to contact banks and public services	yes⁺	yes	significant t-test, p = 0.098
11. More flexibility in arranging pers. free time	yes	yes	not significant
Family			
12. More free time with family and friends	yes	yes	not significant
13. More personal free time	yes	yes	not significant
Relocation			
14. A solution if the employer relocates	yes	no	significant t-test, p = 0.000
15. A solution if the employee moves	yes	no	significant t-test, p = 0.000
More ecologically responsible behaviour	yes⁺	yes	significant t-test, p = 0.007
Able to work more effectively if permanently or temporarily disabled	yes	yes	not significant

Notes:
yes⁺ = a more convinced yes
no⁺ = a more convinced no

Source: own calculations

There is an interesting parallel with Chapter 4's survey results: among both employers and employees, those with telework experience perceive roughly the same advantages - but fewer disadvantages - as those without telework experience. Table 5.2a shows that teleworkers and non-teleworkers generally agree about telework's advantages. Teleworkers, however, identify a lower number of disadvantages (four versus seven in Table 5.1a) and identify 'less in touch with the organization' as less of a problem. Because teleworkers have a more realistic picture of telework's advantages and disadvantages, based on their personal experience, non-teleworkers appear to have an overly-pessimistic view of the disadvantages of telework.

5.4 CHOICE MODEL OF THE ADOPTION OF TELEWORK BY EMPLOYEES

In Appendix 5, Appendix 6 and Appendix 7, we use our empirical data to produce a model to predict which employees are most likely to (a) be teleworking already, and (b) be willing to telework in the future. Using the revealed preference data, we generate a model that describes the main determinants of present telework adoption, namely: **(1) the use of a car during work hours; (2) the availability of a company car; (3) the consideration of the personal implications of telework as an available option; (4) holding a clerical function; (5) a positive attitude of the direct supervisor regarding telework; (6) experience with taking work home; (7) a factor highly correlated with a variable reflecting whether telework is perceived as a solution if the employer were to relocate and a variable reflecting whether telework is perceived as a solution if the employee were to move; and (8) a factor highly correlated with a variable reflecting whether teleworkers are socially isolated, a variable reflecting whether telework has a negative influence on the culture within an organization and a variable reflecting whether teleworkers are less in touch with the organization.** Using the stated preference data, we generate a model that suggests that future telework adoption may be primarily influenced by the following variables: **(1) the use of a car during work hours; (2) the consideration of the personal implications of telework as an available option; (3) holding a managerial function; (4) a factor highly correlated with a variable reflecting whether telework is perceived as a solution if the employer were to relocate and a variable reflecting whether telework is perceived as a solution if the employee were to move; (5) a factor highly correlated with a variable reflecting whether teleworkers are socially isolated, a variable reflecting whether telework** has a negative influence on the culture within an organization and a variable reflecting whether teleworkers are less in touch with the organization; and (6) a factor highly correlated with a variable reflecting whether face-to-face contact with the direct supervisor is important, a variable reflecting whether face-to-face contact with other employees is important and a variable reflecting whether the atmosphere in the office is important. Readers interested in the statistical analysis are referred to those Appendices.

Note that holding a managerial function is a future telework driver, but not a current telework driver. This is further evidence that future telework may often be directed at highly-skilled workers.

5.5 CONCLUSION

Our survey of 261 employees in Brussels led to a number of insights into the various individual-level drivers of - and barriers to - telework implementation. Immediately above, we have noted the parameters that we feel mainly determine present and future telework adoption. In this chapter, we also observed that, while teleworkers and non-teleworkers generally agree about the **advantages** of telework, non-teleworkers appear to have an overly-pessimistic view of its **disadvantages**.

In the next chapter, we will examine some of the consequences for society if employers and employees implement telework in significant numbers.

NOTES

[1]　More specifically, our survey was completed by 42 people in their twenties, 94 people in their thirties, 93 people in their forties, 29 people in their fifties and one person in her/his sixties.

[2]　See Korte and Wynne (1996) for data on Germany, France, the UK, Italy and Spain.

[3]　As with our survey of human resources managers, there may be sampling bias and self-selection response bias.

[4]　Mannering and Mokhtarian (1995).

[5]　In other words, 78.4 percent of the respondents with location-independent jobs indicated that they were willing to become teleworkers in the future; 41.9 percent of the respondents without location-independent jobs indicated that they were willing to become teleworkers in the future.

[6]　Bélanger (1999) and Yap and Tng (1990).

[7]   Mokhtarian and Salomon (1996b).
[8]   Bush (1990).
[9]   Mokhtarian and Salomon (1986a).
[10] Enström and Johanson (1998).
[11] 41 percent of the current teleworkers earning more than 50,000 Euro/yr. The other numbers are for current teleworkers earning between 25,000 and 50,000 Euro/yr and those earning less than 25,000 Euro/yr, respectively.
[12] Mannering and Mokhtarian (1995).
[13] The knowledge of telework was measured by a question regarding the familiarity with the telework definition, adopted in our survey..
[14] In other words, 2.6 percent of the respondents that have never considered telework as a personal choice option indicated they were teleworkers; 35.6 percent of the respondents that had considered this practice as a personal choice option, indicated that they were teleworkers. The former percentage, which for our sample is higher than zero, suggests that a few teleworkers are involved in a top-down telework implementation practice, whereby telework was imposed by management.
[15] Managerial, professional and technical occupations report the greatest positive benefits (Stanworth and Stanworth, 1991).
[16] Yap and Tng (1990), Mokhtarian et al. (1998), Mirchandani (1999), Nilles (1997), Gray et al. (1994), Kinsman (1987), Eldid and Minoli (1995), Harman and Bordow (1998), Olszewiski and Mokhtarian (1994), and Duxbury et al. (1987).
[17] Steward (1999).
[18] Mokhtarian et al. (1998), Huws et al. (1993), Salomon and Salomon (1984), and Stanworth and Stanworth (1991). See also Duxbury et al. (1987).
[19] Bergum (1998).
[20] Stanworth and Stanworth (1991).
[21] Huws et al. (1993), Mokhtarian and Salomon (1997), Bagley and Mokhtarian (1997), Bush (1990), and Mokhtarian and Salomon (1994).
[22] Mannering and Mokhtarian (1995) and Salomon (1994).
[23] Bush (1990).
[24] Fireman (1998) and Stanworth and Stanworth (1991).
[25] Stanworth and Stanworth (1991).
[26] Holti and Stern (1987).
[27] Cross and Raizman (1986).
[28] Gurstein (1991).
[29] Mirchandani (1998).
[30] Kugelmass (1995).
[31] Kraut (1989). However, the adoption of telework may also reduce the availability of peer group support. If this cannot be replaced by support from out-of-work sources (because only peers can understand the problem), this can reduce job satisfaction (Shamir and Salomon, 1985).
[32] Chapman et al. (1995).
[33] Gurstein (1991).
[34] Generally speaking, telework would be expected to increase an employee's quality of life. By 'quality of life,' we include quality of life both at work and away from work. These are, of course, interdependent (Büssing, 1998). Several features of telework are relevant here, the major factors being increased concentration and focus while working, increased control over work, and increased flexibility (especially increased flexibility to combine work and family life). That being said, telework sometimes decreases quality of life; the blending of work and private life can lead to stress and activity conflicts. See Büssing (1998) and Kraut (1989).

[35] Shamir and Salomon (1985).
[36] Büssing (1998).
[37] Ibid.
[38] Stanworth and Stanworth (1991).
[39] Cross and Raizman (1986).
[40] Huws et al. (1993).
[41] Cross and Raizman (1986) and Olson (1988).
[42] Mokhtarian et al. (1998) and Salomon and Salomon (1984).
[43] Cross and Raizman (1986).
[44] Gurstein (1991).
[45] Bagley and Mokhtarian (1997).
[46] Olson (1988)
[47] Stanworth and Stanworth (1991).
[48] Köhler et al. (1988a).
[49] Mirchandani (1999).
[50] Salomon and Salomon (1984).
[51] Shamir and Salomon (1985).

6. A SOCIETAL PERSPECTIVE ON TELEWORK: THE ALLEVIATION OF ROAD TRANSPORT EXTERNALITIES

6.1 INTRODUCTION

Telework implementation as a policy tool is usually analysed at two levels. Macro-level or societal analysis looks at the costs and benefits of telework for society at large; micro-level or managerial analysis looks at the costs and benefits for a single organization and its employees. This book assumes that those two levels of analysis are related and are both important. In the past two chapters, we have analysed telework from a managerial perspective, in an attempt to better understand the drivers and barriers of employers' and employees' implementation decisions. In this chapter, we will study telework from a societal perspective. If employers and employees decide to adopt telework, what will the impact be on society? From a macro-level point of view, the previous two micro-level chapters dealt with telework's procedural effectiveness (specifically, its target group implementation potential) as a precondition to attaining the adoption levels required for telework to have any significant impacts on road congestion and other road transport externalities.

This chapter will quantify telework's potential effectiveness at alleviating road congestion and other road transport externalities. It will measure the maximum societal impact achievable if the necessary conditions of procedural effectiveness are fulfilled, especially in terms of high target group implementation potential. We will first investigate the theoretical impact of telework on travel behaviour, energy consumption and air pollution, and then we will study the example of Brussels.

6.2 TELEWORK'S THEORETICAL IMPACT ON TRAVEL BEHAVIOUR

Many current mobility problems result from the urbanization of rural areas. At the intra-city level, many cities consist of a number of concentric zones. In the centre is the central business district with retail stores and offices. The next concentric zone often contains deteriorating older manufacturing plants and warehouses. This is then followed by a zone of older, high-density residential areas that are often declining into slums. The outermost zone consists of newer housing developments. In these newer housing developments, there is a 'jobs - housing imbalance,'[1] and, as a result of the concentric zone layout, the distance between these homes and the workplace is often high. Thus, individuals living in the outermost zones of the city who need to commute to the city centre must travel a long distance within a large city. Hence, the distance between the residence and the workplace may be high for many, highly-skilled metropolitan workers, and this contributes to the transportation problem. Simultaneously, at the inter-city level, there is a trend away from the dominant traditional commuting patterns of 'centre-to-centre' and 'periphery-to-centre' towards a new pattern of 'suburban zone to suburban zone.' This trend also contributes to transportation problems, since urban mass transit systems are designed primarily to transport people to the city centre.[2] In some cases, this trend can also be observed at the intra-city level; although this alleviates commuting to the city centre, it aggravates congestion on the ring roads around the city, as individuals commute between (often distant) suburban areas of the same city.

The effect of ICT on travel is complex. ICT has two types of effects on travel: substitution effects and complementarity effects. With a substitution effect, one system replaces particular functions of another system. In the case of telework, a particular use of ICT will sometimes replace a particular trip.

There are two types of complementarity effects. In the first type, one system causes an increase in the efficiency of another system. For example, the use of ICT will lead to better organizational coordination, which will make some travel unnecessary. In the second type of complementarity, increased use of one system causes increased use of the complementary system. Instead of simply reducing trips, ICT use will also generate trips, as we will see later in this chapter.[3]

In order to assess the impact of telework on travel, energy use and air quality, the ideal evaluation methodology would involve travel diary surveys before and after the start of a telework programme in order to assess the changes that occur.[4] Multiple 'after-surveys' would be even better, since they would yield information about how changes evolve over time.[5] The diary should collect information about the travel mode, the trip destination (hence giving an indication of the trip distance), the time of day and the travel time. Ideally, a seven-day diary should be used, to get information about telework days, non-telework workdays, and non-workdays. This would allow researchers to assess not only the shift of trips between telework workdays and non-telework workdays but also between weekdays and weekends. The survey should include not only the teleworker, but also each household member with a driver's licence. This lets researchers identify changes in trip responsibilities among household members, thereby generating a more complete picture of the use of household vehicles. Finally, a control group of non-teleworkers and all their household members with driver's licences should be surveyed, in order to capture the effects of changes that affect everyone, such as changes in oil prices or changes in traffic policies.[6]

Only a few studies of telework's impact on travel, energy use and air quality incorporate elements of such an optimal evaluation. Furthermore, the majority of these studies were conducted between 1986 and 1992.[7] Only the ENTRANCE study, the ERICSSON study and the Vrije Universiteit Brussel (VUB) study are of a more recent vintage. This chapter will focus on the VUB study. An overview of the most relevant studies is given in Table 6.1.

Table 6.1 An overview of studies examining the impact of telework implementation on travel, energy use and air quality

Study	Sample size (teleworkers who completed all surveys)	Travel diary survey	Before survey	After survey	Type of trips	Household members	Control group
State of California Pilot Study (USA) (homeworkers) 1987 - 1990	73	Yes 3 days	Yes	Yes (1)	All	Yes	Yes
Puget Sound Study (USA) (homeworkers/workers in telecentres) 1990 - 1991	63	Yes 2 days	Yes	Yes (2)	All	Yes	Yes
Netherlands Study: experiment 1 (homeworkers)	30	Yes 7 days	Yes	Yes (4)	All	Yes	No
Netherlands Study: experiment 2 (homeworkers)	30	Yes 7 days	Yes	Yes (3)	All	Yes	No
ENTRANCE-Southampton study (UK) (homeworkers) 1998	24	Yes 7 days	Yes	Yes (1)	All	Yes	No
Arizona AT&T (USA)	99	No	Implicitly derived	Implicitly derived	Commuting trip (CT)	No	No
Bell Atlantic studies (USA)	50	No	Implicitly derived	Implicitly derived	Commuting trip	No	No

Table 6.1   An overview of studies examining the impact of telework implementation on travel, energy use and air quality

Study	Sample size	Travel diary survey	Before survey	After survey	Type of trips	Household members	Control group
Sweden time-use data study (1990 - 1991) (homeworkers)	82	No	No	No	Travel in general implicitly derived	No	Yes
Southern California Association Governments (SCAG) (USA)	18	No	Implicitly derived	Implicitly derived	Commuting trip + indications of non-work travel of teleworkers during telework days	No	No
Canada time-use data study (1992) (homeworkers)	392	No	No	No	Travel in general implicitly derived	No	Yes
The ERICSSON study (Sweden) (2000)	140 teleworkers (97 regular teleworkers)	No	Implicitly derived	Implicitly derived	All implicitly derived	No	No
The Residential Area-Based Offices (RABO) project-USA (only telecentre users)	24	Yes 3 days	Yes	Yes (1)	All	No	Yes
The Los Angeles insurance firm study (only teleworkers in satellite centres) 1973	108	No	No	No	Commuting trips + non-work trips of teleworkers	No	No

Table 6.1   An overview of studies examining the impact of telework implementation on travel, energy use and air quality

Study	Sample size	Travel diary survey	Before survey	After survey	Type of trips	Household members	Control group
VUB-Brussels study (Belgium) – current teleworkers (homeworkers + teleworkers in telecentres)	54	No	Implicitly derived	Implicitly derived	Commuting trip + indications of non-work travel of teleworkers during telework days + indications of travel of household members during telework days	No	Yes
VUB-Brussels study (Belgium) – potential regular teleworkers (homeworkers + teleworkers in telecentres)	165	No	Implicitly derived	Implicitly derived	Idem VUB-Brussels study (Belgium) – current teleworkers	No	Yes

Sources : Adapted from Mokhtarian et al., 1995, Hamer et al., 1991 (The Netherlands study: experiment 1), Hamer et al., 1992 (The Netherlands study: experiment 1 & The Netherlands study: experiment 2), Pendyala et al., 1991, Kitamura et al., 1990 (The State of California study), Kitamura et al., 1991 (The State of California study), Lyons et al., 1998 (The ENTRANCE Southampton study), Skåmedal, 2000 (The ERICSSON study), Nilles, 1988 (The Los Angeles insurance firm study), Michelson et al., 1999 (Canada time-use data study & Sweden time-use data study) and Balepur et al., 1998 (The RABO project).

Stepping back and looking at longer time periods, we can see that telework implementation on a large scale will have short-term, medium-term and long-term impacts, as shown in Figure 6.1 and discussed in more detail below.

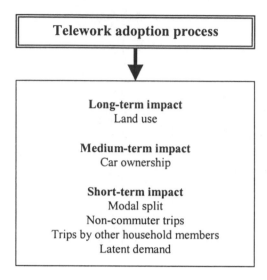

Source: Sullivan et al., 1993

Figure 6.1   The impact of telework implementation on travel

6.2.1 SUBSTITUTION EFFECTS

When the purpose of a trip is merely to exchange information, ICT can often substitute for the trip.[8] Two prime candidates for substitution are commuting and work-related travel other than commuting.[9]

6.2.1.1   Commuting trips
In urban areas, 30 to 40 percent of all vehicle-kilometres travelled are commuting trips.[10] One would therefore expect that telework would alleviate congestion.[11]

However, experience shows that the congestion is relieved only temporarily.[12] Latent demand (i.e., new demand resulting from telework adoption) arises and moderates the achieved reductions in congestion levels. We will address latent demand below; for the moment we will ignore it.

Assuming a status quo for all other trips, the reduction in the teleworkers' commuting trips will produce a decrease in the total number of trips generated by teleworkers. Consequently, road congestion during peak hours will be alleviated. During peak hours, even a small reduction in traffic can reduce congestion significantly.[13]

The effect on passenger traffic flows is different with centre-based and satellite-based telework. In these cases, the commuting trip becomes shorter and at least some commuting trips move out of the busiest road sections during peak times. Furthermore, non-motorized modes of travel (such as bicycling or walking) become more realistic options, due to the shorter commuting distances involved.[14]

As one would expect, empirical data shows that telework reduces teleworkers' commuting trips. For instance, an analysis of telework adoption in the Bergen and Oslo areas revealed a potential travel reduction of between 3 percent and 6 percent, assuming a 20 percent telework penetration level.[15] An analysis for the United States predicted a reduction in vehicle trips of 5.4 percent during peak hours if 32 percent of the workforce were to telework 1.8 days per workweek.[16] Although not based on surveys, these estimates are in line with the empirical findings of two Dutch experiments. The first Dutch experiment revealed that if a sample of workers starts teleworking approximately once a workweek, the number of trips made by that sample on a particular day decreases by 19 percent during peak hours. The second Dutch experiment found a decrease of 11 percent.[17]

Table 6.2   Impact of telework implementation on trips made by teleworkers

Total impact of telework implementation (1.2 days per workweek) on number of trips made by the teleworkers in the population on a particular day	The Netherlands study: experiment 1	The Netherlands study: experiment 2
General	-17%	-10%
Peak hours	-19%	-11%
Off-peak hours	-15%	-10%
Weekday	-18%	-13%
Weekend	-13%	0%

Sources: Hamer et al., 1991 (The Netherlands study: experiment 1) and Hamer et al., 1992 (The Netherlands study: experiment 1 & The Netherlands study: experiment 2)

Table 6.3 shows the reduction in commuter vehicle-kilometres per telework occasion, according to several studies.[18]

Table 6.3   Savings in commuter vehicle-kilometres per telework occasion

Study	Average distance of round-trip commute (kilometres)	Percentage drive-alone	Commuter vehicle-kilometres saved/ telework occasion
State of California Pilot Study (USA)	62.4	81%	50.54
Puget Sound Study (USA)	57.6	63%	36.29
ENTRANCE-Southampton study (UK)	48	95.8%	45.98
Arizona AT&T (USA)	49.76	74%	36.82
Bell Atlantic studies (USA)	64		
San Diego studies (USA)	62.08	79%	49.04
Southern California Association Governments (SCAG) (USA)	67.2	67%	45.02
VUB-Brussels study (Belgium) – current teleworkers	85.6	59%	50.5
VUB-Brussels study (Belgium) – potential regular teleworkers	82	52%	42.64

Source: Adapted from Mokhtarian et al., 1995 and Lyons et al., 1998

On average, teleworkers have substantially longer commutes than other workers in the same region.[19] Thus, when someone chooses to telework, it probably won't be an average commuter getting off the road; it will probably be a 'long distance commuter.' This factor helps explain telework's high impact on travel reduction.

Like previous surveys, our survey revealed that potential teleworkers in Brussels interested in teleworking one or more days per week have longer commutes than conventional workers, with respect to both distance and time. The average Brussels commuter has a one-way commuting distance of 26.9 kilometres; potential teleworkers have a one-way commuting distance of 41 kilometres.[20] The average one-way commuting time is 48 minutes;[21] for potential teleworkers, it is 57.47 minutes during the morning peak and 54.72 minutes during the evening peak, according to our survey.

However, simple dislike of long commutes is not the only explanation for the correlation between long commutes and interest in telework. The average commuting trip increases with the employee's hierarchical position in an organization. For instance, the commuting trip of an executive is 1.8 times longer of that of a clerical worker.[22] This factor must also be considered.

6.2.1.2 Work-related travel other than commuting

About 10 percent of intra-city road traffic is associated with business activities other than commuting to work.[23] Because this type of travel often occurs for the purpose of face-to-face social communication, ICT does not substitute for it as well as ICT substitutes for commuting travel. Nonetheless, increased use of e-mail, other electronic messaging and teleconferencing can substitute for some work-related travel.

Teleconferencing looks particularly promising in this regard. Instead of travelling to the same location, each teleconferencing participant travels to one of two or more dispersed sites. Often, the dispersed site is the participant's own workplace, so the total travel cost is zero. Teleconferencing can be audio-only, audio-visual or computer-based.

One study of the United States suggests that 34 percent of (non-commuting) business travel could be replaced by audio-only conferencing and an additional 10 percent could be replaced by video-conferencing; the remaining 56 percent of business travel cannot be replaced.[24] Generally speaking, travel is less expensive than telephone conferencing or video-conferencing when the number of participants is low and the length of the meeting is long.[25] Travel is also less expensive when the number of locations involved is large, unless the distance between the locations is also large.[26] When the distance between locations is so large as to require air travel, safety becomes an additional relevant concern for some employees, especially in light of the terrorist attacks in the United States on 11 September 2001. These attacks have led many firms to reconsider the costs and benefits of their employees' air travel.

6.2.2 MODAL SPLIT

Even ignoring the problem of latent demand, it is clear that not all telework will reduce vehicle-kilometres travelled by car. If telework substitutes for a train or bus journey, or a journey as a passenger, there will be no reduction in vehicle-kilometres travelled by car. In those cases, there will be no direct impact on either the environment or traffic flows.[27] Furthermore, when someone substitutes telework for public transport, public transport services will lose revenue. A complete assessment of telework's impact therefore requires an examination of the potential teleworkers' modal split (i.e., their use of various transport modes - car, train, bus, subway, bicycle, etc. - when commuting) before they started teleworking. Capturing such data is difficult, since teleworkers in informal programmes are hard to locate, and even organizations with formal telework programmes rarely keep such records.[28]

The evidence about potential teleworkers' modal split is not entirely clear. On the one hand, potential teleworkers are primarily information workers, with an increasing proportion of highly skilled knowledge workers, and we know that information workers commute by car more than non-information workers do.[29] Furthermore, in the State of California study, the control group of non-teleworkers used public transport more often than the teleworkers did.[30] There are also indications that teleworkers' households tend to be more car-dependent.[31]   For these reasons, one could conclude that potential teleworkers are more car-dependent than the average worker.

Our survey of employees working in Brussels shows that 52 percent of the employees willing to telework regularly, drove to work alone. This number is in line with the national survey conducted by the National Institute of Statistics in Belgium (1991), which reported that 54.7 percent of the general workforce drives to work alone.

We therefore conclude that the evidence about potential teleworkers' modal split suggests that teleworkers use their cars to commute at a rate equal to or slightly higher than that of the general workforce. This implies that telework could indeed have a substantial impact in terms of congestion reduction.

However, it has been suggested that partial-day telework can have a negative effect on modal split, because the commuting trip is then made during off-peak hours, when there is less public transport available. In that case, there is a high probability of a modal shift from public transport to car usage.[32]

It has also been suggested that telework may lead to the demise of carpool initiatives.[33] If a potential teleworker previously carpooled to work with another person, the carpool initiative might end if one of the participants started teleworking. As a result, each employee would drive alone to the conventional office, including the teleworker on non-telework days.[34] However, the empirical results suggest that this does not actually happen. For instance, the San Diego study found that carpool initiatives did not stop when their members started teleworking, although there were changes in carpooling frequency. The ERICSSON study confirmed that telework implementation does not influence carpool initiatives.[35]

6.2.3 NON-COMMUTER TRIPS

Telework changes trip composition. Between 25 and 50 percent of all trips are 'linked.'[36] Often, workers incorporate non-work trips (e.g., shopping trips, trips to drop off children at school or personal business trips) into their travel behaviour. When the commuting trip is replaced by a virtual one or reduced partially, this leads to a reduction in trip chaining.[37] Telework changes the spatial distribution of the destinations of non-commuting trips: typically, the trip destinations become more concentrated around the home location and less around the work location. This redistribution of trips toward the local street network shifts traffic onto the local network, which is usually beneficial from an overall road externality impact perspective.[38] Furthermore, due to the shorter distance, the employee may opt for non-motorized modes or public transport for these trips.[39] Even if teleworkers continue to use cars for these trips, to the extent that the teleworkers can now schedule these trips outside of peak hours, traffic congestion will be smoothed. Of course, child-care schedules and employers' expectations to maintain conventional work hours can restrict this flexibility,[40] in which case the trips may have to continue to take place during peak hours.

Several empirical studies suggest that teleworkers actually perform fewer non-commuting trips than conventional workers.[41] However, Mokhtarian et al. (1995) have noted three methodological reasons why these empirical studies might erroneously report a decline in non-commuting trips. First, participation in a telework programme whose main objective is to determine telework's impact on travel may condition the participants to reduce their travel. Second, there may be intentional 'cheating,' especially if the participants know that the pilot project is trying to determine telework's potential as a trip reduction measure. Here, respondents may deliberately under-report their number of trips, especially the ones made during work hours. Finally, the apparent reduction may also be the consequence of participant fatigue, leading to an under-reporting of the number of trips made. We conclude that the impact on non-commuting trips appears to be marginal; the main effect of telework seems to be on the commuting trip itself.[42]

6.2.4 OTHER HOUSEHOLD MEMBERS

If there are as many drivers as cars in a household, the ability to telework may eliminate the need for an additional car. Consequently, this could lead to changes in vehicle ownership in the medium-term.[43] In the short-term, when an individual who used to commute by car starts teleworking, the car becomes available to other household members, and this may generate additional trips, particularly in households with fewer cars than drivers.[44]

Our empirical study of employees employed in Brussels reveals that, in 14.1 percent of the cases, the commuting trip of a potential regular teleworker could theoretically simply be replaced by a commuting trip of another working member of the household (who previously did not have access to a car).[45] In 15.2 percent of the cases, there was a possibility that the adoption of regular telework would lead to non-commuting trips by other household members.

However, in several other studies, telework did not appear to cause additional trips by other household members. This suggests that predictions are difficult in this area, and that new studies should carefully assess car use by other household members.[46]

6.2.5 CAR OWNERSHIP

Neither the State of California study, the San Diego study, nor the ERICSSON studies provided any evidence that telework implementation acts as an incentive to eliminate a household car.[47]

6.2.6 TRAVEL-GENERATING EFFECTS

Telework may not only substitute for travel, it may also generate travel, in several ways. Telecommunication applications increase access to information about outside activities and possibilities for interaction. Hence, telecommunications may create the desire to participate in such activities and interactions, and thereby generate travel.[48]

6.2.6.1 Short run: latent demand

Furthermore, as teleworkers leave the roads, other workers will, to some extent, take their place. In the case of mobility demand, the travel time elasticity of demand is often higher than the price elasticity of demand. Since telework by definition reduces the number of commuter trips, the traffic flow during peak hours will temporarily become less congested. However, this initial improvement in traffic flow will then be moderated when a number of new road users perceive the lowered congestion and start using the roads during peak hours.[49] Research based on earlier experiences regarding the effect of latent demand when other policies were introduced (but not based on empirical data) indicates that approximately half of the potential reduction in vehicle-kilometres achieved through telework will be replaced by new traffic.[50]

6.2.6.2 Long run: residential relocation

As the number of commuter trips decreases due to part-time or full-time telework, the distance between the conventional workplace and the residence becomes less important. Since a relocation of the workplace is one of the four most important reasons to relocate the residence,[51] telework could theoretically be a factor causing the teleworker to move to a new residence farther away from the conventional workplace. This outcome becomes more likely if the former residence was chosen as the result of weighing convenient commutes against undesirable intrinsic residential characteristics. Such a move would increase the length of the commuting trip on non-telework days, thus generating additional travel on those days.[52] At this point in time, no empirical data is available to support this hypothesis, however (partly because most evaluation studies to date have been short-term).[53] The results of the State of California project indicate that 6 percent of the teleworkers involved considered moving further away from work after the two-year period. However, of those 6 percent only 28 percent reported that the ability to telework played a significant role, and there was no significant difference between the actual moves of the teleworkers and the control group.[54] This result is confirmed by the results of the ERICSSON study. Although 3 percent of the sample stated that they had plans to move further away from their conventional workplace, the moves did not actually take place.[55]

One must be careful to distinguish cause and effect here. As we have said, early adopters of telework are often people with long commuting distances. Presumably, telework seemed particularly attractive in part because of the long distance between the residence and the conventional workplace. Our suggestion in the previous paragraph - that increased residential dispersion is not a consequence of telework adoption - is consistent with our conclusion earlier in this book, that the present dispersed location of residences is a major driver for the adoption of telework.[56]

6.3 TELEWORK'S THEORETICAL IMPACT ON ENERGY CONSUMPTION

Transport accounts for a substantial part of total energy end use. Despite fuel efficiency improvements, only small further improvements are envisioned.[57] Hence, if telework is an effective substitute for travel, it could significantly contribute to energy conservation.[58]

According to various estimates, the total energy cost of transportation in the United States represents 23.8 to 25.2 percent of gross national energy use.[59] Furthermore, commuting accounts for 15 percent of the United States' transportation energy consumption. Therefore, although telework is not the most direct measure for saving energy, its effect on energy consumption could be significant.

At high penetration levels, the effects would be very substantial. If ICT led to the substitution of travel wherever reasonably possible, total energy consumption would fall by 1 to 3 percent.[60] If 50 percent of the workforce started teleworking 85 percent of the work time at home or in a telework centre, the amount of fuel used for commuting in the United States would be reduced by 43 percent.[61] Of course, lower penetration levels would bring lower payoffs: it has been estimated that the adoption of telework by 1 percent of the workforce would reduce energy consumption by approximately 0.06 percent, not taking into account the effects of latent demand.[62]

Reduced cooling and heating costs at the (now smaller) conventional office would produce additional energy savings. However, savings in office energy would probably be relatively small, given that the use of heating, air conditioning and lights would not decline by much if only a small number of employees are teleworking.[63] Furthermore, any savings at the conventional office would be partially offset by increased costs of heating and cooling at the teleworkers' homes (where facilities are often less efficient),[64] and the energy costs of the telecommunication systems.

Various methods have been used to assess the savings in energy consumption per telework occasion due to the elimination of the commuting trip. These methods are illustrated in Table 6.4.[65] It should be noted that only the third study takes into account a lower fuel efficiency for the remaining distances covered by car after the introduction of telework, due to a higher number of short, non-linked trips.

Table 6.4   Impact of telework implementation on energy use for travel

	Average fuel efficiency	Average reduction in energy use (in litres) due to a telework occasion (with correction for vehicle-kilometres)
Method 1: Average fuel efficiency multiplied by the average number of kilometres saved by not performing a commuting trip		
Arizona AT&T study	11 km/l (researchers did not elaborate on how this figure was determined)	3.4 l
Puget Sound study	10.6 km/l (researchers did not elaborate on how this figure was determined)	3.4 l
Method 2: Average of the self-reported fuel efficiency multiplied by the self-reported savings in commuting		
SCAG study	10.1 km/l	5.3 l
Method 3: Fuel savings estimated based on the results of air quality models		
State of California study EMFAC 7E Air quality model	7.6 km/l (after introduction of telework) 7.9 km/l (before introduction of telework)	8.3 l

Source: adapted from Mokhtarian et al., 1995

Three studies have estimated the increased use of energy in the home due to telework, as shown in Table 6.5. Based on these findings, the extra energy used at home will offset between 11 and 25 percent of the travel energy savings.[66]

Table 6.5   Impact of telework implementation on energy use in the home

	Home energy increase in kilowatt-hours (kwh)/ telework occasion)
Puget Sound study Method: the researchers did not elaborate on the method used	+5.5 kwh
SCAG study Method: energy use is estimated based on hours of use of different appliances (e.g. heating, air conditioning, computers)	+7.9 kwh
State of California study Method: comparison of monthly energy bill of teleworkers and non-teleworkers (in order to translate this cost into kilowatt-hours, the average cost for one kilowatt-hour in the investigated area was used)	+20.5 kwh

Source: adapted from Mokhtarian et al., 1995

We conclude that, even taking into consideration increased energy use in the home, telework still reduces overall energy use. We view the State of California study as the most scientifically rigourous, because it uses the most scientifically 'grounded' methods to estimate both the reduction in gas consumption and the offsetting increase in energy use at the teleworker's home. It results in the highest net energy savings (Table 6.6), but that result is partially explained by the fact that the teleworkers in that study had by far the highest average commuting distance. Consequently, average net energy savings for teleworkers in general may be much lower.

Table 6.6   Impact of telework implementation on energy use

	Travel energy reduction (in kwh/ telework occasion)	Home energy increase (in kwh/ telework occasion)	Net energy savings/telework occasion
Puget Sound study	33 kwh	5.5 kwh	27.5 kwh
SCAG study	51.4 kwh	7.9 kwh	43.5 kwh
State of California study	80.6 kwh	20.5 kwh	60.1 kwh

Source: adapted from Mokhtarian et al., 1995. The energy savings due to savings in commuting vehicle-kilometres in kilowatt-hours (kwh) were obtained by assuming 9.7 kwh per litre

6.4 TELEWORK'S THEORETICAL IMPACT ON AIR POLLUTION

Telework reduces the number of daily commuter trips, thereby reducing the total emissions caused by vehicle activity.[67] The impact of a particular penetration level of telework on air quality depends on a number of parameters such as: distance travelled by car, number of cold starts,[68] number of hot starts, speed, type of vehicle and ambient temperature.

1.   *Distance travelled by car* or vehicle-kilometres: the greater the distance travelled by car, the greater the total emission volumes will be.
2.   *Number of cold starts and number of hot starts*: when a vehicle with a warmed-up engine is started, it produces a lower emission of pollutants than a vehicle with a cold engine. Therefore, if teleworking causes people to make more unlinked trips, this might actually increase pollution.[69]
3.   *Speed*: a U-shaped relationship exists between speed and emission levels. Up to around 80 - 96 kilometres per hour, the emission of pollutants decreases as the speed increases. Above 80 - 96 kilometres per hour, the emission of pollutants increases as speed increases. In addition, multiple accelerations and decelerations during a trip increase the emission of pollutants. Stop-and-go travel (in traffic jams, for example) is particularly bad with respect to certain pollutants.[70]
4.   *Type of vehicle*: the emission of pollutants caused by vehicle activity varies with the type of vehicle. For instance a catalytic converter lowers the emission of pollutants.

5.   *Ambient temperature*: the emissions generated by a cold start are highly
     correlated with the temperature of the surrounding air at that time. Cold
     starts caused by a trip to work early in the morning or late at night
     produce higher emissions than cold starts during regular daytime hours.
     Telework reduces such early and late night commuter trips.[71]

Road transport is the primary cause of the emission of nitrogen oxides
(NO_x), volatile organic compounds (VOC), carbon monoxide (CO) and
particulate matter with a diameter of less than 10 microns (PM10). Road
transport also contributes to the emission of sulphur dioxide (SO_2),
tropospheric O_3 (ozone) and carbon dioxide (CO_2). Tropospheric O_3 is a
secondary pollutant caused by the emission of VOC and NO_x. VOC and
PM10 can cause cancer. NO_x, O_3, SO_2 and CO_2 may cause respiratory
infections, chronic obstructive pulmonary diseases and asthma. O_3 also has a
negative effect on the growth of vegetation. SO_2 is a soured component that
affects buildings as well as soil and water.[72]

It is important to note that telework could have one negative effect on air
pollution. The amount of emissions produced is closely linked to the travel
pattern. Since telework implementation could reduce trip chaining, this might
result in more cold starts and shorter trips, producing higher levels of
emissions for each kilometre travelled.[73]

In reality, however, the State of California study found a different overall
result. This study estimates the total impact of telework on air quality by
using air quality models and data from travel diaries regarding number of
trips, cold and hot starts, average speed and vehicle-kilometres travelled
before and after telework implementation. According to this study, the
adoption of telework decreases the emission of VOC by 2.72
grams/eliminated kilometre (in spite of the higher fuel consumption per
remaining kilometre travelled by car, as noted above).

So far, the State of California study and the Puget Sound study are the only
two rigorous studies to estimate telework's impact on emissions.[74] The air
quality models used (EMFAC 7E and BURDEN 7E) in the State of
California Study have estimated a reduction in volatile organic compounds
(VOC) of 1.1 grams/eliminated kilometre, a reduction in NO_X of 0.9
gram/eliminated kilometre and a reduction in CO of 9 grams/ eliminated
kilometre.[75] Furthermore, the teleworkers in the State of California study
performed 60 percent fewer cold starts on telework days.[76]

The Puget Sound air quality models led to the conclusion that, because
teleworkers make 30 percent fewer trips, travel 63 percent fewer vehicle-
kilometres and perform 44 percent fewer cold starts on telework days,
teleworking substantially reduces the emissions of VOC, CO, NO_X and PM

(Table 6.7).[77] No conclusions were drawn for the emission of sulphur oxides (SO_X) or lead, because the small population involved in this study did not generate measurable amounts of these pollutants. The emission of PM and NO_X, which is primarily related to running-exhaust, decreased due to the reduction in vehicle-kilometres travelled. The reduction in cold starts, of which the largest reductions were in the morning, contributed mainly to the reductions in the emissions of VOC and CO.

Table 6.7   *Impact of telework implementation on the emission of several pollutants*

Reductions in emission of a particular pollutant measured in grams per telework occasion on a particular day	State of California study	Puget Sound study
VOC	70.2	25.96
NO_X	62	27.32
CO	581.2	204.15
PM	-	6.92

Sources: State of California study: Mokhtarian et al., 1995 and Puget Sound study: Henderson et al., 1996

6.5 THE IMPLICATIONS FOR BRUSSELS OF TELEWORK ADOPTION

In the remaining pages of this book, we will use the above conclusions regarding telework's impact on travel behaviour, energy consumption and air pollution to quantify the total monetary savings that would be caused by increased implementation of telework in Brussels. We will examine telework's monetary impact on road congestion, air pollution, noise pollution and road accidents, as well as the monetary savings related to energy savings. Note that our analysis does not include telework's positive impact in other macro-level areas, such as:

- workforce satisfaction,
- workforce productivity, and
- aggregate new job opportunities for groups formerly excluded from the labour markets (e.g., disabled people, parents with young children, and people in rural areas).

We conclude that, in the medium-run, the total savings due to increased telework implementation could realistically range between 240.4 million and 524.8 million Euro per year.

We will start by estimating the impact of telework implementation on the number of commuting trips to/from Brussels.

6.5.1 IMPACT OF TELEWORK IMPLEMENTATION ON THE NUMBER OF COMMUTING TRIPS TO/FROM BRUSSELS

6.5.1.1 Model of Olszewski and Lam

The method developed by Olszewski and Lam (1996) can be used to estimate the reduction in motorized round-trip commutes and vehicle round-trip commutes caused by a specific penetration level and frequency of telework. This method considers only work-related trips and assumes that the modal split for potential teleworkers is identical to the modal split for other employees. The analysis requires the following steps :

1. determination of the total number of daily motorized round-trip commutes for Brussels,
2. determination of the total number of daily vehicle round-trip commutes for Brussels, and
3. determination of the daily reduction in the number of trips caused by telework implementation in Brussels.

These three steps are described in more detail below.

6.5.1.1.1   Determination of the number of daily motorized round-trip commutes (M)

The total number of daily motorized round-trip commutes, including both private and public motorized trips, is given by formula 6.1:

$$M = B \; x \; t \qquad\qquad (6.1)$$

B = the workforce,
t = the average number of motorized round-trip commutes per employee per day.

The coefficient t is lower than one because absences on account of illness, leave and strikes need to be taken into account. In addition, employees who bicycle or walk to work or who are self-employed (in which case they usually work where they live) should not be included in the analysis. The first step in the calculation of the t-coefficient consists of determining the correction for illness, leave and strikes. We use data for Belgium and assume that the same data applies to Brussels. If we assume an average of 22 work days per month, a Belgian employee would then work 264 days a year. However, every Belgian employee is entitled to at least 22 vacation days and 11 public holidays, for a total of 33 days of leave per year. On average, a Belgian employee is sick 7.7 days per year.[78] According to the 'Statistisch jaarboek van België' (Nationaal Instituut voor de Statistiek, 1994), a total of 153,706 strike days were registered for the Belgian workforce, or 0.004 days per employee. This suggests that on average an employee does not work 264 days a year but rather 223.3 days a year (264 - 33 - 7.7 - 0.004); this results in a t-coefficient of 0.8458.

Next, we remove the self-employed. In Brussels, 17.08 percent of workers are self-employed. Finally, we must take into account that 5.8 percent of the trips of the active Brussels workforce are on foot rather than motorized.[79] All of these corrections result in a final t-coefficient of 0.66 for Brussels ($t_{Brussels} = 0.66$). There are 628,736 workers in Brussels ($B_{Brussels} = 628,736$). Thus the total number of daily motorized round-trip commutes in Brussels is 414,966 ($M_{Brussels} = 414,966$).

6.5.1.1.2 Determination of the number of daily vehicle round-trip commutes (V)

The number of daily vehicle round-trip commutes includes only those motorized round-trip commutes that involve a private vehicle. This number is also corrected for car-pooling (formula 6.2).

$$V = (B \times t \times p) / O = (M \times p) / O \qquad (6.2)$$

p = the number of trips performed using a private car, expressed as a percentage of the total number of motorized trips,
O = the average vehicle occupation.

For 69.57 percent of the commuting traffic in Brussels, a private car is used ($p_{Brussels} = 0.6957$).[80] The average vehicle occupation in Brussels is 1.27 persons per vehicle ($O_{Brussels} = 1.27$).[81] Therefore the number of daily vehicle round-trip commutes is 227,316 ($V_{Brussels} = 227,316$).

6.5.1.1.3   Determination of the reduction in trips caused by telework implementation

First the reduction in the number of motorized round-trip commutes is determined (M_r) (formula 6.3).

$$M_r = M \times a \times f \qquad\qquad (6.3)$$

Then the reduction in the number of vehicle round-trip commutes is computed (V_r) (formula 6.4).

$$V_r = V \times a \times f \qquad\qquad (6.4)$$

a = the penetration level of telework
f = the average frequency with which one teleworks, in the context of a five-day workweek.

As of the year 2000, when the empirical part of our study was conducted, the penetration level of telework in Brussels was estimated at 4.8 percent. This percentage resulted from an extrapolation to the year 2000 of the 3.97 percent that was found for 1996 in an earlier part of our study (see Appendix 8). According to the European Commission (1999), the penetration level of telework at around 2000 was 6.2 percent. To take the European Commission's estimate into account, we created two scenarios, using the two different estimates of current penetration levels.

Then, to determine a medium-term estimate of telework penetration, we used data from our survey of Brussels-based human resources managers, which suggested a maximum medium-range penetration level of 21.5 percent of the workforce (see Appendix 9). So, for our two scenarios, we assumed that the medium-range additional penetration would be 16.7 percent (21.5 percent - 4.8 percent) and 15.3 percent (21.5 percent - 6.2 percent), respectively.

We also created additional scenarios to investigate the potential long-term implications of telework. Assuming that 50 percent of the workforce consists of information workers, with a growing component of highly skilled knowledge workers, and that 80 percent of those workers are potential teleworkers, we estimated that the maximum penetration of telework could be as high as 40 percent.[82] To take that estimate into account, we constructed two extra scenarios with additional penetration levels of 35.2 percent (40 percent - 4.8 percent) and 33.8 percent (40 percent - 6.2 percent). Finally, we added another two scenarios to reflect the fact that the percentage of information workers (including highly skilled knowledge workers) in

Brussels (77 percent) is much higher than in the rest of Belgium[83]. Hence, following the same reasoning as above, the maximum penetration level of telework in Brussels would be 62 percent (80 percent of 77 percent). This produced scenarios with additional penetration levels of 57.2 percent (62 percent - 4.8 percent) and 55.8 percent (62 percent - 6.2 percent). Although those figures may appear unrealistically high at present, it should be taken into account that these calculations were performed for an urban area with a very high and growing percentage of knowledge workers.

Based on the arguments presented in Appendix 8, we estimate that the frequency of telework in the Brussels-Capital Region is 1.5 days per workweek (in the context of a five-day workweek). This figure is consistent with the average frequency observed in several empirical studies regarding telework. Drawing on the results of our survey of human resources managers, we also investigated the effects of a future telework frequency of 3 days per workweek (again, in the context of a five-day workweek).

The daily reductions in motorized round-trip commutes and vehicle round-trip commutes are presented in Table 6.8a and Table 6.8b. If telework reaches a significant level, the impact on traffic externalities will also be significant. In Table 6.8a, we see that, according to the model used, a penetration level of telework of 4.8 percent and a frequency of 1.5 days per workweek would reduce the number of commuter trips by 1.4 percent, or 3,273 vehicle round-trip commutes per day.

A penetration level of 57.2 percent and a frequency of 1.5 days per workweek would reduce commuter trips by 17.2 percent, or 39,007 vehicle round-trip commutes per day.

Table 6.8a Reduction in trips caused by telework implementation in Brussels
based on a frequency of telework of 1.5 days per workweek

	Frequency of 1.5 days per workweek							
Penetration level of telework as a percentage of Brussels workforce	4.8%	6.2%	15.3%	16.7%	33.8%	35.2%	55.8%	57.2%
Reduction in motorized round-trip commutes (M_r) per day	5,976	7,718	19,047	20,790	42,078	43,820	69,465	71,208
Reduction in vehicle round-trip commutes (V_r) per day	3,273	4,228	10,434	11,389	23,050	24,005	38,053	39,007
Reduction in motorized round-trip commutes, expressed as a percentage of the total number of motorized round-trip commutes per day	1.4%	1.9%	4.6%	5%	10%	10.6%	16.7%	17.2%
Reduction in the vehicle round-trip commutes, expressed as a percentage of the total number of vehicle round-trip commutes per day	1.4%	1.9%	4.6%	5%	10%	10.6%	16.7%	17.2%

Source: authors' own calculations

Table 6.8b shows that, according to the model used, a penetration level of 4.8 percent and a frequency of 3 days per workweek would reduce the number of commuter trips by 2.9 percent per day, or 6,547 vehicle round-trip commutes per day. A penetration level of 57.2 percent and a frequency of 3 days per workweek would reduce commuter trips by 34.3 percent, or 78,015 vehicle round-trip commutes per day.

Table 6.8b Reduction in trips caused by telework implementation in Brussels based on a frequency of telework of 3 days per workweek

	Frequency of 3 days per workweek							
Penetration level of telework as a percentage of Brussels workforce	4.8%	6.2%	15.3%	16.7%	33.8%	35.2%	55.8%	57.2%
Reduction in motorized round-trip commutes (M_r) per day	11,951	15,437	38,094	41,580	84,155	87,641	138,931	142,416
Reduction in vehicle round-trip commutes (V_r) per day	6,547	8,456	20,868	22,777	46,100	48,009	76,105	78,015
Reduction in motorized round-trip commutes, expressed as a percentage of the total number of motorized round-trip commutes per day	2.9%	3.7%	9.2%	10%	20.3%	21.1%	33.5%	34.3%
Reduction in the vehicle round-trip commutes, expressed as a percentage of the total number of vehicle round-trip commutes per day	2.9%	3.7%	9.2%	10%	20.3%	21.1%	33.5%	34.3%

Source: authors' own calculations

6.5.1.2 Model of Mokhtarian

A similar theoretical model has been developed by Mokhtarian (1998). Her model, however, also incorporates the possibility that not everybody who is able to telework will actually have a preference to adopt this practice. In addition, even a preference to adopt the practice does not necessarily lead to actual adoption.[84] Furthermore, this model also incorporates possible travel-generating effects.

In the first step, the model determines the maximum expected number of teleworkers on a particular workday (T) (formula 6.5).

$$T = E \times A \times W \times C \times F \qquad (6.5)$$

E = the average number of people employed in a certain geographic area and time frame,

A = the proportion of the workforce that is able to telework,

W = the proportion of the workforce able to telework that is willing to telework,

C = the proportion of the workforce able and willing to telework that actually chooses to telework,

F = the average frequency of telework expressed as a fraction of a five-day workweek.

In order to assess E, the active Brussels workforce is multiplied by a coefficient. This coefficient is lower than one because of working days lost on account of illness, leave and strikes; self-employed individuals and those working at home are also taken into account (E = 440 932).

In order to assess A, we first use the two numbers from the previous model, namely additional penetration levels of 16.7 percent (21.5 percent - 4.8 percent) (A_1 = 0.167) and 15.3 percent (21.5 percent - 6.2 percent) (A_2 = 0.153).

However, barriers such as manager unwillingness and a lack of knowledge about telework can be eliminated over time. It can even be argued that office automation will eventually even further increase the number of jobs suited for telework. Therefore, as an indication of the maximum number of teleworkers in the far future, we can use the percentage of information workers (including highly skilled knowledge workers) in Brussels. After subtracting the number of current teleworkers, this yields two other values for A (A_3 = 0.558 and A_4 = 0.572).

When estimating W, Mokhtarian (1998) suggests that, based on empirical data, this percentage may be as high as 88 percent. We find a similar result when analysing the survey conducted among employees: 92 percent of the employees able to telework were also willing to telework (W_1 = 0.92). However, Mokhtarian (1998) points out that, due to selection bias in studies with our type of methodology, this figure may be too high. People who do not want to telework are less likely to return a survey related to telework. Hence, Mokhtarian (1998) concludes that it is more likely that this figure is, in reality, close to 50 percent (W_2 = 0.5).

In some situations, constraints are not powerful enough to eliminate a preference for telework, but they may be sufficient to prevent the person from actually choosing telework (for example, the absence of a separate office space at home may be an insufficient constraint to eliminate the preference for telework but could prevent the person from actually choosing telework).[85]

For this reason, C comes into play; we use the estimate of Mokhtarian (1998), namely 76 percent (C = 0.76).

For current telework frequency, we use 1.5 days per workweek ($F_1 = 0.3$). Based on the suggestions of the surveyed human resources managers, we also include a plausible frequency of 3 days per workweek ($F_2 = 0.6$).

Table 6.9 shows the number of teleworkers in Brussels on any particular day according to the different scenarios resulting from the above assumptions. In the most pessimistic scenario, there will be 7,691 teleworkers per day; in the most optimistic scenario, there will be 105,808.

Table 6.9 Estimates of the maximum teleworkers on a particular day (T) based on previous assumptions

$T_1 = E \times A_1 \times W_1 \times C \times F_1$	15,446
$T_2 = E \times A_2 \times W_1 \times C \times F_1$	14,151
$T_3 = E \times A_3 \times W_1 \times C \times F_1$	51,609
$T_4 = E \times A_4 \times W_1 \times C \times F_1$	52,904
$T_5 = E \times A_1 \times W_2 \times C \times F_1$	8,394
$T_6 = E \times A_2 \times W_2 \times C \times F_1$	7,691
$T_7 = E \times A_3 \times W_2 \times C \times F_1$	28,049
$T_8 = E \times A_4 \times W_2 \times C \times F_1$	28,752
$T_9 = E \times A_1 \times W_1 \times C \times F_2$	30,892
$T_{10} = E \times A_2 \times W_1 \times C \times F_2$	28,302
$T_{11} = E \times A_3 \times W_1 \times C \times F_2$	103,219
$T_{12} = E \times A_4 \times W_1 \times C \times F_2$	105,808
$T_{13} = E \times A_1 \times W_2 \times C \times F_2$	15,418
$T_{14} = E \times A_2 \times W_2 \times C \times F_2$	15,381
$T_{15} = E \times A_3 \times W_2 \times C \times F_2$	56,097
$T_{16} = E \times A_4 \times W_2 \times C \times F_2$	57,505

Source: authors' own calculations

In a second step, the model estimates the impact on transportation by assessing the net reduction in vehicle-kilometres travelled (VN). Here, a conceptual approach is followed that is very similar to the one of Olszewski and Lam (1996). However, in addition, the travel-generating effects of telework are also considered (formula 6.6).

$$VN = V - (N + R + L) \times V \qquad (6.6)$$

V = the total expected commuter vehicle-kilometres eliminated on any given weekday (see formula 6.7),

N = the expected increase in travel due to non-work trip generation, expressed as a fraction of the reduction in vehicle-kilometres traveled,

R = the expected increase in travel due to longer commute distance as a result of residential relocation, expressed as a fraction of the reduction in vehicle-kilometres travelled,

L = the expected increase in travel due to latent demand, expressed as a fraction of the reduction in vehicle-kilometres travelled.

$$V = T \, x \, \alpha \, x \, D \qquad\qquad (6.7)$$

α = the proportion of telework occasions that eliminate a vehicle commuter trip,

D = the average round-trip commuter distance in drive-alone vehicle-kilometres of individual teleworkers on any particular day.

When estimating V, one has to take into account only the proportion of the vehicle-kilometres travelled alone. Hence, α will be less than one after eliminating the person-kilometres travelled by soft modes and public transport and correcting for carpooling, taking into account the same estimates as used in the Olszewski and Lam model ($\alpha = 0.55 = 0.7/1.27$). When estimating D, one has to take into account that, so far, most empirical studies have concluded that teleworkers face longer than average commuting trips. However, if the teleworkers use telecentres or satellite offices, only part of the commuter vehicle-kilometres is eliminated - roughly 65 percent.[86]
This leads us to formula 6.8:

$$V = \beta_1 \, x \, T \, x \, \alpha \, x \, D + \beta_2 \, x \, T \, x \, \alpha \, x \, 0.65 \, x \, D \qquad (6.8)$$

β_1 = the percentage of homeworkers in the total telework population (regular teleworkers). Based on the results of the employee survey, this is estimated at 82.4 percent,

β_2 = the percentage of centre-based teleworkers in the total telework population. Based on the results of the employee survey, this is estimated at 17.6 percent,

D = the average one-way commuter distance. In the survey of potential teleworkers, this distance is 41 kilometres; hence a round-trip commute is 82 kilometres. For the telecentre users, the reduction of 65 percent suggested by other researchers is used.

When estimating the increase in non-commuter travel (N), one must note that no empirical evidence confirms this hypothetical increase. On the contrary, evidence seems to point in the opposite direction. Hence, we assume that N equals zero. Similarly, no evidence supports an increase in travel due to residential relocation. Hence, we assume that R is also zero.

At this point, no empirical evidence exists regarding the impact of latent demand (L) on travel savings due to telework. However, a number of researchers have suggested that approximately half of the potential reduction in vehicle-kilometres will be replaced by new traffic.[87] Hence L is estimated at 0.5.

Table 6.10 gives an overview of the reduction in vehicle-kilometres per day, for the different scenarios. Table 6.10a assumes a telework frequency of 1.5 days per week, whereas Table 6.10b assumes a frequency of 3 days per week.

Table 6.10a Reduction in vehicle-kilometres due to various levels of telework (frequency of telework of 1.5 days per workweek)

	Reduction in kilometres on any particular day due to various levels of telework	Reduction in kilometres on any particular day due to various levels of telework, taking into account latent demand, non-commuter travel and residential relocation
Average frequency of 1.5 days per workweek		
$VN_1 = (\beta_1 x T_1 x \alpha x D + \beta_2 x T_1 x\ \alpha x 0.65 x D)$ $- 0.5\ (\beta_1 x T_1 x \alpha x D + \beta_2 x T_1 x \alpha x 0.65 x D)$	653,703km	326,852 km
$VN_2 = (\beta_1 x T_2 x \alpha x D + \beta_2 x T_2 x\ \alpha x 0.65 x D)$ $- 0.5\ (\beta_1 x T_2 x \alpha x D + \beta_2 x T_2 x \alpha x 0.65 x D)$	598,896km	299,448km
$VN_3 = (\beta_1 x T_3 x \alpha x D + \beta_2 x T_3 x \alpha x 0.65 x D)$ $- 0.5\ (\beta_1 x T_3 x \alpha x D + \beta_2 x T_3 x \alpha x 0.65 x D)$	2,184,188km	1,092,099km
$VN_4 = (\beta_1 x T_4 x \alpha x D + \beta_2 x T_4 x \alpha x 0.65 x D)$ $- 0.5\ (\beta_1 x T_4 x \alpha x D + \beta_2 x T_4 x \alpha x 0.65 x D)$	2,238,995km	1,119,497km
$VN_5 = (\beta_1 x T_5 x \alpha x D + \beta_2 x T_5 x \alpha x 0.65 x D)$ $- 0.5\ (\beta_1 x T_5 x \alpha x D + \beta_2 x T_5 x \alpha x 0.65 x D)$	355,250km	177,625km
$VN6 = (\beta 1 x T6 x \alpha x D +$ $\beta 2 x T6 x \alpha x 0.65 x D) - 0.5\ (\beta 1 x T6 x \alpha x D +$ $\beta 2 x T6 x \alpha x 0.65 x D)$	325,497km	162,749km
$VN7 = (\beta 1 x T7 x \alpha x D +$ $\beta 2 x T7 x \alpha x 0.65 x D) - 0.5\ (\beta 1 x T7 x \alpha x D +$ $\beta 2 x T7 x \alpha x 0.65 x D)$	1,187,085km	593,543km
$VN8 = (\beta 1 x T8 x \alpha x D +$ $\beta 2 x T8 x \alpha x 0.65 x D) - 0.5\ (\beta 1 x T8 x \alpha x D +$ $\beta 2 x T8 x \alpha x 0.65 x D)$	1,216,838km	608,419km

Source: authors' assessment

Table 6.10b   *Reduction in vehicle-kilometres due to various levels of telework (frequency of telework of 3 days per workweek)*

	Reduction in kilometres on any particular day due to various levels of telework	Reduction in kilometres on any particular day due to various levels of telework, taking into account latent demand, non-commuter travel and residential relocation
Average frequency of 3 days per workweek		
VN9 − (β1xT9xαxD + β2xT9xαx0.65xD) − 0.5 (β1xT9xαxD + β2xT9xαx0.65xD)	1,307,406km	653,703km
VN10 = (β1xT10xαxD + β2xT10xαx0.65xD) − 0.5 (β1xT10xαxD + β2xT10xαx0.65xD)	1,197,793km	598,896km
VN11 − (β1xT11xαxD + β2xT11xαx0.65xD) − 0.5 (β1xT11xαxD + β2xT11xαx0.65xD)	4,368,418km	2,184,209km
VN12 = (β1xT12xαxD + β2xT12xαx0.65xD) − 0.5 (β1xT12xαxD + β2xT12xαx0.65xD)	4,477,989km	2,238,995km
VN13 = (β1xT13xαxD + β2xT13x αx0.65xD) − 0.5 (β1xT13xαxD + β2xT13xαx0.65xD)	652,518km	326,259km
VN14 = (β1xT14xαxD + β2xT14x αx0.65xD) − 0.5 (β1xT14xαxD + β2xT14xαx0.65xD)	650,952km	325,476km
VN15 = (β1xT15xαxD + β2xT15xαx0.65xD) − 0.5 (β1xT15xαxD + β2xT15xαx0.65xD)	2,374,128km	1,187,064km
VN16 = (β1xT16xαxD + β2xT16xαx0.65xD) − 0.5 (β1xT16xαxD + β2xT16xαx0.65xD)	2,433,717km	1,216,859km

Source: authors' assessment

6.5.1.3   Monetary savings in external costs related to road congestion
for Brussels

Of the two models described above, we prefer Mokhtarian's. It takes into account that not everybody able to telework will actually be willing to adopt the practice, and not everybody who is able and willing to telework will ultimately choose to telework. This is an interesting feature of the model, as it tries to internalize some aspects of procedural effectiveness and bring these elements into the realm of the strictly technical analysis. The outcomes of the model will thus to some extent be lower than those that would be calculated if behavioral complexities were assumed away. Furthermore, Mokhtarian's model takes into account latent demand, residential relocations and non-commuting travel, and it differentiates between the impact of homework and work in telecentres. Therefore, it is the model we will use to assess telework's impact on road congestion.

To estimate the monetary savings in external costs related to road congestion due to a particular level and frequency of telework, we use formula 6.9:

$$MC = VN \times C \qquad\qquad (6.9)$$

MC= monetary savings in external costs related to road congestion due to a particular level and frequency of telework,

VN= savings in vehicle-kilometres due to a particular penetration level and frequency of telework. We looked at the scenarios with a 15.3 percent and 16.7 percent additional penetration level and high weight coefficient for willingness to telework (W = 0.92),

C = marginal external cost of road congestion per vehicle-kilometre. We use the assessment of Mayeres et al. (1997) (59 BEF/km ≈ 1.46 Euro/km).

Table 6.11 gives an overview of the monetary savings in external road congestion costs for different penetration levels and frequencies of telework. In the medium run (2010), the savings could range between 195.3 million and 426.4 million Euro per year.

Table 6.11 Monetary savings in external costs related to road congestion
due to a particular penetration level and frequency of telework

	Reduction in vehicle-kilometres per day	Monetary savings related to road congestion per day in Euro	Monetary savings related to road congestion per year in million Euro
Frequency of 1.5 days per workweek			
Penetration level of 15.3%	598,896	875,928	195.3
Penetration level of 16.7%	653,703	956,088	213.2
Frequency of 3 days per workweek			
Penetration level of 15.3%	1,197,793	1,751,858	390.7
Penetration level of 16.7%	1,307,406	1,912,175	426.4

Source: authors' own calculations

6.5.2 IMPACT OF TELEWORK IMPLEMENTATION ON ENERGY USAGE FOR COMMUTERS TO/FROM BRUSSELS

To estimate the reduction in energy usage per day and per year, we looked at the savings in energy usage (as reported by several studies) as well as the cost of a kilowatt-hour in Belgium. Although the empirical studies that estimate energy savings are all situated in the United States, implying longer commuting trips for teleworkers than will be the case in Brussels, these studies give at least a reasonable idea of the magnitude of the effect that can be expected in Brussels. We looked at the scenarios with a 15.3 percent and 16.7 percent additional penetration level and high coefficient for willingness to telework ($W = 0.92$). Furthermore, we assumed 223 workdays per year.

$$TEU = EU \times T \qquad (6.10)$$

TEU = total reduction in energy usage on any particular day due to a particular level and frequency of telework (in kwh),
EU = reduction in energy usage per telework occasion (in kwh),
T   = total number of telework occasions on a particular day.

The two possible tariffs applied by the Belgian electricity company ELECTRABEL were used to assess the monetary savings in energy usage due to a particular level and frequency of telework. We used both the day tariff of 5.94 BEF/kwh ($\approx$ 0.15 Euro/kwh) (4.91 BEF/kwh $\approx$ 0.12 Euro/kwh, value added tax excluded) and the night tariff of 2.72 BEF/kwh ($\approx$ 0.07 Euro/kwh) (2.25 BEF/kwh $\approx$ 0.06 Euro/kwh, value added tax excluded).

$$MTEU = TEU \times M \qquad (6.11)$$

MTEU = monetary savings in energy usage due to a particular level and frequency of telework,

TEU = total reduction in energy usage on any particular day due to a particular level and frequency of telework (in kwh),

M = the cost of a kilowatt-hour.

Table 6.12 and Table 6.13 give an overview of the monetary savings related to a reduction in energy usage for different penetration levels and frequencies of telework, according to three existing studies in this area. In the medium-run, the savings could range between 12.8 million and 61 million Euro per year.

This range is based on our view that, at present, the State of California study provides the most scientifically 'grounded' empirical analysis of telework-related energy savings. However, it is debatable whether energy savings data from California would be valid in Belgium, given the obvious differences in climate, average house size and heating systems used. Hence, this estimate should be considered as only a tentative (and certainly imperfect) approximation of the real situation.

Table 6.12 Savings in energy usage in Brussels on a particular day due to a particular level and frequency of telework

	Telework occasions on a particular day	Savings in energy usage in Brussels on a particular day based on the Puget Sound study	Savings in energy usage in Brussels on a particular day based on the SCAG study	Savings in energy usage in Brussels on a particular day based on the State of California study
Average frequency of 1.5 days per workweek				
Penetration level of telework of 15.3%	14,151	389,153 kwh	615,569 kwh	850,475 kwh
Penetration level of telework of 16.7%	15,446	424,765 kwh	571,901 kwh	928,305 kwh
Average frequency of 3 days per workweek				
Penetration level of telework of 15.3%	28,302	778,305 kwh	1,231,137 kwh	1,700,950 kwh
Penetration level of telework of 16.7%	30,892	849,530 kwh	1,343,802 kwh	1,856,609 kwh

Source: authors' own calculations

Table 6.13a Monetary savings in energy usage in Brussels per year – day tariff

Day tariff of 0.15 Euro/kwh	Monetary savings in energy usage in Brussels per year based on the Puget Sound study in million Euro	Monetary savings in energy usage in Brussels per year based on the SCAG study in million Euro	Monetary savings in energy usage in Brussels per year based on the State of California study in million Euro
Average frequency of 1.5 days per workweek			
Penetration level of telework of 15.3%	12.8	20.2	27.9
Penetration level of telework of 16.7%	13.9	22.1	30.5
Average frequency of 3 days per workweek			
Penetration level of telework of 15.3%	25.6	40.4	55.8
Penetration level of telework of 16.7%	27.9	44.1	61

Source: authors' own calculations

Table 6.13b Monetary savings in energy usage in Brussels per year – night tariff

Night tariff of 0.07 Euro/kwh	Monetary savings in energy usage in Brussels per year based on the Puget Sound study in million Euro	Monetary savings in energy usage in Brussels per year based on the SCAG study in million Euro	Monetary savings in energy usage in Brussels per year based on the State of California study in million Euro
Average frequency of 1.5 days per workweek			
Penetration level of telework of 15.3%	4.8	7.7	12.8
Penetration level of telework of 16.7%	5.3	8.4	14.0
Average frequency of 3 days per workweek			
Penetration level of telework of 15.3%	9.7	15.3	25.6
Penetration level of telework of 16.7%	10.6	16.7	27.9

Source: authors' own calculations

6.5.3 IMPACT OF TELEWORK IMPLEMENTATION ON THE EMISSION OF POLLUTANTS RESULTING FROM COMMUTING TO/FROM BRUSSELS

In order to estimate the impact of the reduction in emissions, two methods can be used. The first method involves multiplying the reduction in commuter vehicle-kilometres by a factor that indicates the external cost per vehicle-kilometre of each pollutant. Here, we use the data from the application of Mokhtarian's model. This reduction can then be related to the emission factor per vehicle-kilometre of NO_x, CO_2, VOC, CO, PM10 and SO_x in a peak period in Brussels for gasoline and diesel cars. Here, we use the calculations of Mayeres et al. (1996) for Brussels (Table 6.14).

Table 6.14   Specific emission factors for Brussels

	NO_x	CO_2	VOC	CO	PM10	SO_x
Emission factors in g per vehicle-kilometre (CO_2 in kg) during peak period						
Gasoline cars	1.56	0.170	0.37	2.92	0.00	0.00
Diesel cars	0.20	0.140	0.02	0.33	0.07	0.13
Monetary valuation in Euro per kg	**13.8**	**0.007**	**2.96**	**0.01**	**83.20**	**95.20**

Source: Mayeres et al., 1996

The reduction in commuter trips needs to be divided between gasoline cars and diesel cars. In 1996, the car flux was composed of 60 percent gasoline cars and 40 percent diesel cars.[88]

Formula 6.12 was used to determine the reduction in emission of pollutants for a specific penetration level of telework in Brussels:

$$TE_i = VN \times E_{iG} \times (G/G+D) + VN \times E_{iD} \times (D/G+D) \qquad (6.12)$$

TE_i = the total reduction in emission for a pollutant i in a peak period on any single day in kg,

VN   = the *reduction* in commuter trips for a specific level of teleworkers. As before, we looked at the scenarios with a 15.3 percent and 16.7 percent additional penetration level and high weight coefficient for willingness to telework (W = 0.92),

E_{iG} = the emission factor for a pollutant i for a gasoline car,

E_{iD} = the emission factor for a pollutant i for a diesel car,

G   = number of gasoline cars in the total car fleet,

D = number of diesel cars in the total car fleet.

To assess the monetary impact of a specific penetration level of telework on emissions reduction in kilograms for Brussels, we use formula 6.13:

$$MVE_i = MVE/g_i \times TE_i \tag{6.13}$$

MVE_i = the total monetary value of the impact of a specific penetration level of telework on the specific emissions of NO_x, CO_2, VOC, CO, PM10, or SO_2,

i = a particular pollutant,

MVE/g_i = the monetary value of the marginal external cost for a specific pollutant i in BEF per kg.

Table 6.15 gives an overview of the monetary savings in external costs related to emissions for different penetration levels and frequencies of telework. In the medium-term, the savings could range between 3.1 million and 6.8 million Euro per year.

Table 6.15 *Reduction in emissions resulting from a specific penetration level of telework*

	Penetration level of telework of 15.3 percent and frequency of 1.5 days per workweek							
	NO_x	CO_2	VOC	CO	PM10	SO_x	total per day	total per year in million Euro
Reduction in emission in kg	608.5	94,625.6	138.2	1,128.3	16.8	31.1	-	-
Reduction in costs in Euro	8,397	704	408	11	1,398	2,961	13,879	3.1
	Penetration level of telework of 16.7 percent and frequency of 1.5 days per workweek							
	NO_x	CO_2	VOC	CO	PM10	SO_x	total per day	total per year in million Euro
Reduction in emission in kg	664.2	103,285.1	150.4	1,231.6	18.3	34	-	-
Reduction in costs in Euro	9,166	768	444	12	1,522	3,237	15,150	3.4
	Penetration level of telework of 15.3 percent and frequency of 3 days per workweek							
	NO_x	CO_2	VOC	CO	PM10	SO_x	total per day	total per year in million Euro
Reduction in emission in kg	1,217	189,251.3	275.5	2,256.6	33.5	62.3	-	-
Reduction in costs in Euro	16,795	1,407	813	22	2,787	5,932	27,756	6.2
	Penetration level of telework of 16.7 percent and frequency of 3 days per workweek							
	NO_x	CO_2	VOC	CO	PM10	SO_x	total per day	total per year in million Euro
Reduction in emission in kg	1,328.3	206,570.2	300.7	2,463.2	36.6	68	-	-
Reduction in costs in Euro	18,331	1,536	887	24	3,045	6,474	30,298	6.8

Source: authors' own calculations

For the second estimate of telework's effect on the emission of certain pollutants, we use the data from the Puget Sound study. In this case, estimates are available only for PM, NO_X, VOC and CO. An estimation of the monetary savings in the external costs related to emissions due to a particular level and frequency of telework can be made using formula 6.14.

$$TE_i = T \times PS_i \times 1/1000 \qquad (6.14)$$

TE_i = the total reduction in emission for a pollutant i in a peak period on a particular day in kg,

T = the number of telework occasions. As before, we examined the scenarios with a 15.3 percent and 16.7 percent additional penetration level and a rather high coefficient for willingness to telework (W = 0.92),

PS_i – the reduction in emission of a pollutant i per telework occasion according the Puget Sound study in grams.

To assess the monetary impact of a specific penetration level of telework on emissions reduction in kilograms for Brussels, we used formula 6.15:

$$MVE_i = MVE/g_i \times TE_i \qquad (6.15)$$

MVE_i = the total monetary value of the impact of a particular penetration level of telework on the particular emissions of NO_X, VOC, CO, or PM10,

i = a particular pollutant,

MVE/g_i = the monetary value of the marginal external cost for a specific pollutant i in BEF per kg.

Table 6.16 gives an overview of the monetary savings. In the medium run, the savings could range between 3.3 million and 7.1 million Euro per year. These results are thus very similar to the results obtained using the first method.[89]

Table 6.16   Reduction in emissions resulting from a specific penetration level of telework

| | Penetration level of telework of 15.3 percent and frequency of 1.5 days per workweek | | | | | |
	NO$_x$	VOC	CO	PM10	total per day	total per year in million Euro
Reduction in emission in kg	386.6	367.4	2,888.9	97.9	-	-
Reduction in costs in Euro	5,335	1,084	29	8,144	14,592	3.3
	Penetration level of telework of 16.7 percent and frequency of 1.5 days per workweek					
	NO$_x$	VOC	CO	PM10	total per day	total per year in million Euro
Reduction in emission in kg	422	401	3,153.3	106.9	-	-
Reduction in costs in Euro	5,824	1,183	31	8,893	15,931	3.6
	Penetration level of telework of 15.3 percent and frequency of 2 days per workweek					
	NO$_x$	VOC	CO	PM10	Total per day	total per year in million Euro
Reduction in emission in kg	515.5	489.8	3,851.9	130.6	-	-
Reduction in costs in Euro	7,114	1,445	38	10,865	19,462	4.3
	Penetration level of telework of 16.7 percent and frequency of 2 days per workweek					
	NO$_x$	VOC	CO	PM10	total per day	total per year in million Euro
Reduction in emission in kg	562.6	534.6	4,204.3	142,5	-	-
Reduction in costs in Euro	7,764	1,577	42	11,855	21,237	4.7
	Penetration level of telework of 15.3 percent and frequency of 3 days per workweek					
	NO$_x$	VOC	CO	PM10	Total per day	total per year in million Euro
Reduction in emission in kg	773.2	734.7	5,777.9	195.8	-	-
Reduction in costs in Euro	10,670	2,167	57	16,289	29,184	6.5
	Penetration level of telework of 16.7 percent and frequency of 3 days per workweek					
	NO$_x$	VOC	CO	PM10	total per day	total per year in million Euro
Reduction in emission in kg	844	802	6,306.6	213.8	-	-
Reduction in costs in Euro	11,647	2,366	63	17,786	31,862	7.1

Source: authors' own calculations

As noted above, the two methods yield similar end results. The first model takes into consideration only the vehicle type and the distance travelled, while the second approach incorporates all determining parameters. However, the first model incorporates a larger number of pollutants. Furthermore, the application of the first model builds upon estimates calculated specifically for Belgian urban areas. Although both approaches have clear advantages, we prefer the first approach, because it incorporates parameters specifically calculated for Belgium (Brussels).

6.5.4 IMPACT OF TELEWORK IMPLEMENTATION ON NOISE POLLUTION CAUSED BY COMMUTING TO/FROM BRUSSELS

In order to estimate monetary savings due to a reduction in noise pollution, we use formula 6.16:

$$MS = VN \times S \tag{6.16}$$

MS = monetary savings in external costs related to noise due to a particular level and frequency of telework,

VN = savings in vehicle-kilometres due to a particular penetration level and frequency of telework. As before, we looked at the scenarios with a 15.3 percent and 16.7 percent additional penetration level and high weight coefficient for willingness to telework (W = 0.92),

S = marginal external cost of noise per vehicle-kilometre. We use the assessment of Mayeres et al. (1997) (0.06 BEF/km ≈ 0.0015 Euro/km).

Table 6.17 gives an overview of the monetary savings in external costs related to noise. In the medium-run, the savings could range between 198,644 and 433,640 Euro per year.

Table 6.17   Monetary savings in the external costs related to noise due to a particular penetration level and frequency of telework

	Reduction in vehicle-kilometres	Monetary savings in the external costs related to noise per day in Euro	Monetary savings in the external costs related to noise per year in Euro
Frequency of 1.5 days per workweek			
Penetration level of telework of 15.3%	598,896	891	198,644
Penetration level of telework of 16.7%	653,703	972	216,820
Frequency of 3 days per workweek			
Penetration level of telework of 15.3%	1,197,793	1 782	397,288
Penetration level of telework of 16.7%	1,307,406	1 945	433,640

Source: authors' own calculations

6.5.5   IMPACT OF TELEWORK IMPLEMENTATION ON ROAD ACCIDENTS CAUSED BY COMMUTING TO/FROM BRUSSELS

In order to estimate the monetary savings related to road accidents we use formula 6.17:

$$MA = VN \times A \qquad (6.17)$$

MA = monetary savings in external costs related to road accidents due to a particular level and frequency of telework,

VN = savings in vehicle-kilometres due to a particular penetration level and frequency of telework. As before, we examine the scenarios with a 15.3 percent and 16.7 percent additional penetration level and a rather high coefficient for willingness to telework (W = 0.92),

A = marginal external cost of road accidents per vehicle-kilometre. We use the assessment of Mayeres et al. (1997) (0.1036 Euro/km).

Table 6.18 gives an overview of the monetary savings in external costs related to road accidents. In the medium-run, the savings could range between 13.8 million and 30.2 million Euro per year.

Table 6.18   *Monetary savings in external costs related to road accidents due to a particular penetration level and frequency of telework*

	Reduction in vehicle-kilometres	Monetary savings in external costs related to road accidents per day in Euro	Monetary savings in external costs related to road accidents per year in million Euro
Frequency of 1.5 days per workweek			
Penetration level of telework of 15.3%	598,896	62,059	13.8
Penetration level of telework of 16.7%	653,703	67,736	15.1
Frequency of 3 days per workweek			
Penetration level of telework of 15.3%	1,197,793	124,115	27.7
Penetration level of telework of 16.7%	1,307,406	135,473	30.2

Source: own calculations

6.5.6   TOTAL MONETARY SAVINGS OF TELEWORK IMPLEMENTATION DUE TO A REDUCTION IN COMMUTING TO/FROM BRUSSELS

By combining the monetary savings resulting from the reduction in external costs related to road congestion, air pollution, noise pollution and road accidents, as well as the monetary savings related to energy savings, we can determine the total monetary savings resulting from a particular penetration level and frequency of telework. To calculate the monetary savings related to a reduction in air pollution, we used the results from the first method, for reasons given above. To calculate the savings in energy usage, we used the estimates based on the State of California study, again for reasons outlined above. We used the day tariff rather than the night tariff, on the grounds that the energy savings normally occur during conventional working hours.

Table 6.19 displays the results. **In the medium run, the total savings due to increased telework implementation could range between 240.4 million and 524.8 million Euro per year.**

Table 6.19   *Monetary savings in external costs related to road congestion,*
                air pollution, noise pollution, road accidents and energy usage
                due to a particular penetration level and frequency of telework

	Monetary savings in external costs related to road congestion, air pollution, noise pollution and road accidents, as well as the monetary savings related to energy savings per day in million Euro	Monetary savings in external costs related to road congestion, air pollution, noise pollution and road accidents, as well as the monetary savings related to energy savings per year in million Euro
Frequency of 1.5 days per workweek		
Penetration level of telework of 15.3%	1.1	240.4
Penetration level of telework of 16.7%	1.2	262.4
Frequency of 3 days per workweek		
Penetration level of telework of 15.3%	2.2	480.8
Penetration level of telework of 16.7%	2.4	524.8

Source: authors' own calculations

6.6 CONCLUSION

In this chapter, we showed that telework has a high potential effectiveness as
a policy tool for alleviating road transport externalities. We first examined
telework's theoretical impact on travel behaviour, energy consumption and
air pollution. Then, applying our results to Brussels, we determined the
monetary savings that increased telework implementation could bring with
respect to road congestion, air pollution, noise pollution, road accidents and
energy consumption. **In the medium run, the total savings due to
increased telework implementation could range between 240.4 million
and 524.8 million Euro per year.**

NOTES

[1] Nilles (1991), Nilles (1977) and Gordon et al. (1991).
[2] Nilles (1988).
[3] Salomon (1985), Salomon (1986), Denayer (2000), Mokhtarian (1990) and La Bella et al., (1990).
[4] Mokhtarian et al. (1995).
[5] Hamer et al. (1991) and Mokhtarian et al. (1995).
[6] Mokhtarian et al. (1995). Although this design is the best one available for assessing telework's travel, energy and air quality effects, even this effective research design faces three problems. First, surveys that include several sequential waves of surveying often have high drop-out rates. There is a high likelihood that drop-outs differ significantly from those who stay in the survey programme; this compromises the generalizability of the research results. Second, the more time that elapses between the first and final surveys, the more likely that participant fatigue will occur, hence the accuracy of the data will drop as time goes by. Finally, participant conditioning may occur. Here, earlier responses influence later ones. See Mokhtarian et al. (1995).
[7] Ibid.
[8] Lyons et al. (1998), Memmott (1963) and Kraemer (1982).
[9] Shopping trips, another prime candidate for substitution, will not be discussed in this book.
[10] Gray et al. (1994), Mannering and Mokhtarian (1995), Salomon (1984), Salomon (1990), Nilles (1976), Nilles (1991), Ritter and Thompson (1994), Polishuk (1975) and Mokhtarian (1998).
[11] Salomon (1984).
[12] Ibid.
[13] For instance, during the 1984 Olympic Games in Los Angeles, a 7 percent reduction in traffic produced a 60 percent decrease in congestion. See Ritter and Thompson (1994).
[14] Sampath et al. (1991) and Nilles (1988).
[15] Lie and Yttri (1999).
[16] Rathbone (1992).
[17] Hamer et al. (1991) and Hamer et al. (1992).
[18] Some critical remarks on these studies are, however, in order. For instance, the ENTRANCE Southampton study found that, even before the introduction of telework, the average number of commuting trips per day was only 1.5 trips, while one would expect this number to be 2. This surprising result can be explained by the fact that if part of the commuting trip is used to attend a meeting or to take care of personal matters, the trip is no longer classified as a commuting trip. Furthermore, the commuting trip is not fully eliminated for the average teleworker after the adoption of telework, although the study only included homeworkers. The fact that an average teleworker still travels eight kilometres as a commuter on a telework day instead of 48 kilometres can be explained by the fact that the majority of the sample (70 percent) occasionally teleworks during only portions of the day. The ERICSSON study revealed that 39 percent of the current teleworkers believe that telework has not changed their number of commuting trips. However, a more in-depth study of this phenomenon revealed that this was probably due to a large proportion of 'half-day' teleworkers in the sample (Skåmedal, 2000). The teleworkers involved still commute to work every day.
[19] Nilles (1991), Ritter and Thompson (1994), Mokhtarian et al. (1995) and Lyons et al. (1998). The ERICSSON study is, so far, the only study that did not find a significant

difference in commuting distance between teleworkers and conventional workers (Skåmedal, 2000). A possible (partial) explanation may be the high percentage of occasional teleworkers in the sample.

When a teleworker 'commutes' to a satellite centre, the situation is reversed, and teleworkers have shorter commutes than their colleagues. The Los Angeles study, conducted in 1973, found that satellite centres reduced one-way average commuting distance by 65 percent (Nilles, 1988). The RABO study, conducted in the 1990s, found that satellite centres reduced personal kilometres travelled by 74 percent, and vehicle-kilometres by 65 percent.

Two time-use studies seem at first glance to go against our generalization; they conclude that the absolute amount of difference in daily travel time between conventional workers and teleworkers is relatively small (Michelson et al., 1999). However, these studies classified every worker who spent at least one hour per day (excluding overtime) performing work at home for a principal employer as a teleworker. Thus, a substantial number of nomadic workers were included in this sample. This type of teleworker does more business-related travel than conventional workers. Hence, this may be the reason for the unusual results regarding travel time.

[20] Rasking (1999).

[21] Ibid.

[22] Nilles (1988).

[23] Nilles et al. (1976) and Salomon (1985).

[24] Salomon (1985) and La Bella et al. (1990). Kraemer (1982) reached similar conclusions regarding substitution. According to that study, 41 percent of travel to business meetings can be replaced by narrowband teleconferencing devices and an additional 9% by videoconferencing. Kraemer's slightly higher percentages may be due to the fact that only travel to business meetings (75 percent of all business travel) was considered.

[25] Salomon et al. (1991).

[26] Kraemer and King (1982).

[27] Gillespie et al. (1995), Gillespie (1998) and Mokhtarian et al. (1995).

[28] Nilles (1988).

[29] Gillespie et al. (1995).

[30] Kitamura et al. (1990).

[31] Pendyala et al. (1991).

[32] Skåmedal (2000), based on the empirical results of the ERICSSON study in Sweden.

[33] Sampath et al. (1991) and Garrison and Deakin (1988).

[34] Kitamura et al. (1990) and Pendyala et al. (1991).

[35] Skåmedal (2000).

[36] Salomon (1985).

[37] Gillespie et al. (1995).

[38] Kitamura et al. (1991), Nilles (1991) and Ritter and Thompson (1994). The State of California study (USA) showed that telework increased the percentage of non-work trips made to destinations within 20 kilometres of the home from 35 percent to 42 percent (Mokhtarian et al., 1995). The ERICSSON study also found indications of a reduction in the length of non-work related trips (Skåmedal, 2000).

[39] Sampath et al (1991).

[40] Balepur et al. (1998).

[41] According to the State of California Pilot study and the Puget Sound study, total travel savings were about 6 percent higher than the savings in commuting. This implies that telework   may actually decrease non-commuting travel (Mokhtarian et al., 1995). Furthermore, the Netherlands studies reported a drop in the number of trips made by

teleworkers for purposes other than commuting or business (experiment 1 showed a reduction of 14 percent, and experiment 2 showed a reduction of 15 percent) (Hamer et al., 1991) (Hamer et al., 1992). The ERICSSON study also reported indications of a reduction of non-work related trips (Skåmedal, 2000). The researchers believed that this could be explained by a streamlining of activities, whereby simple home - activity - home chains were replaced with longer and more complicated ones. However, their own research results tend to undermine this theory, since according to their data teleworkers reduced their average chain length by 12 percent (Hamer et al., 1992).

[42] Mokhtarian et al. (1995).

[43] Sampath et al. (1991).

[44] Gillespie et al. (1995), Lyons et al. (1998) and Kitamura et al. (1990).

[45] To obtain this percentage, we looked at the number of full-time and part-time employees in a household, the number of drivers, the number of available cars and the modal split of the potential teleworker before he/she teleworks.

[46] The empirical results of the two-year State of California Telecommuting Pilot Project (Sampath et al., 1991) (Kitamura et al., 1990) found no evidence that the household members of teleworkers made any additional trips during that time. The same conclusion was drawn by Hamer et al. (1991) based on a pilot project in the Netherlands and by Skåmedal (2000) based on the ERICSSON study. Some evidence even indicates that the non-work trips of household members are reduced. This may be due to participant fatigue and under-reporting, or it may be due to the streamlining of travel patterns by all household members due to the additional flexibility in trip scheduling (Kitamura et al., 1990).

[47] Skåmedal (2000).

[48] Mokhtarian (1988) and Mokhtarian (1990).

[49] Gillespie et al. (1995) and Ritter and Thompson (1994).

[50] Ibid.

[51] The four most important reasons to relocate the residence are (Brown, 1976): (1) a change in composition of the family, (2) a change in the family income, (3) a change in workplace and (4) a change in the real estate market.

[52] van Reisen (1997) and Lyons et al. (1998).

[53] Lund and Mokhtarian (1994).

[54] Mokhtarian (1991b).

[55] Skåmedal (2000).

[56] Lyons et al. (1998).

[57] Salomon (1984).

[58] Kraemer (1982) and Nilles (1976).

[59] Kraemer (1982). Kraemer notes that, in the UK, the transportation sector is responsible for only 15 percent of total energy consumption.

[60] Kraemer (1982).

[61] Salomon (1984).

[62] Gillespie et al. (1995). It has been estimated that each percent reduction in urban commuting in the United States would save about 8.6 billion kilowatt-hours a year. See also Nilles et al. (1976).

[63] Mokhtarian et al. (1995).

[64] Salomon (1984).

[65] Due to the fact that early adopters tend to have a longer commuting trip, this table's 'average reduction in energy use' is likely an overestimation with respect to all potential teleworkers. In order to avoid this problem, an estimation of average fuel saving per kilometre due to telework would be more appropriate (Mokhtarian et al., 1995).

66 Gillespie et al. (1995) and Mokhtarian et al. (1995).

67 Henderson et al. (1996).

68 By 'cold start' we mean that the vehicle's engine is cold. An engine is considered cold if it has been turned off for more than one hour for vehicles with a catalytic converter and four hours for vehicles without a catalytic converter.

69 Henderson et al. (1996).

70 Stop-and-go travel is the most harmful in terms of emission rates of carbon monoxide and hydrocarbons (Salomon, 1984).

71 Sampath et al. (1991) and Henderson et al. (1996).

72 B.I.M. (1994 - 1995 - 1996).

73 Gillespie et al. (1995).

74 Mokhtarian et al. (1995) and Henderson et al. (1996). Both studies indicated that the teleworkers were telecommuters, but the State of California study did not define 'telecommuter.' In the Puget Sound study, the analysis of air quality impact is based on 72 telecommuters (these persons did not necessary participate in all survey waves) of which eight teleworked from a centre and ten teleworked only partial days (Henderson et al., 1996).

75 Mokhtarian et al. (1995).

76 Sampath et al. (1991).

77 The estimates obtained in the Puget Sound study were based on the same type of air quality model, namely EMFAC and BURDEN, but using a later version (7F). Although these models are among the most advanced mobile source emission models available and probably provide the best estimates of the impact of telework implementation on vehicle admission for air basins in California today, they tend to underestimate the amount of emissions caused by vehicle activity (Henderson et al., 1996) (Henderson et al., 1994). The models take into consideration the season as well as the fleet age mix. Summer and winter are the two seasons for which vehicle activity patterns and atmospheric conditions result in the worst air quality. In the summer the greatest concern is ozone precursors (VOC and NO_x), while in the winter the CO level is of greatest concern.

78 Deliege (1993).

79 Nationaal Instituut voor de Statistiek (1999).

80 Ibid.

81 Ministerie van Verkeer en Infrastructuur (1999).

82 Nilles (1988).

83 It should be noted that this figure of 77 percent is higher than the equivalent figure found in Appendix 9, the calculation in Appendix 9 was based on other data.

84 Mokhtarian (1998) points out that this technique is based on the 'demand decomposition' approach commonly adopted in marketing to assess the potential market for a product.

85 Mokhtarian (1998).

86 Nilles (1988) and Balepur et al. (1998). Ideally, part-time telework would also be taken into consideration. Here, the commuting distance stays the same; it simply takes place during off-peak hours. However, since this option was not offered to the surveyed employees, this group is not taken into consideration.

87 Gillespie et al. (1995) and Ritter and Thompson (1994).

88 Febiac (1997).

89 The reduction in emissions per telework occasion assumed in the second model can be criticised for reflecting a 'foreign situation' (e.g., in terms of car fleet composition) not directly comparable to the Brussels case.

APPENDIX 1. TELEWORK IN EUROPE

The penetration level of telework in the EU is still rather low (European Commission, 1998) (European Commission, 1999). In people's minds, telework is still often associated with full-time, unskilled and low-income office work that can be performed at home (Qvortrup, 1998).

However, the penetration level is increasing rapidly. In 1997, approximately two million Europeans were teleworkers. By 1998, this figure had risen to more than four million.

The telework penetration level differs among the EU member states, varying from 18.2 percent in the Netherlands to 0.9 percent in Spain. In fact, Europe can be divided into two groups of countries based on telework penetration level. The northern and western countries (Denmark, Finland, Ireland, Netherlands, Sweden, United Kingdom, Germany and Belgium) have a relatively high penetration level, whereas the southern and eastern countries (Austria, France, Greece, Italy, Portugal and Spain) have a very low telework penetration level. Table Appendix 1.1 gives the penetration levels in 14 EU member states for 1994, 1997 and 1998 - 1999. This table shows that in 1994 the penetration level of telework was extremely low across the EU. Since 1994, however, the penetration level of telework has risen significantly in the northern and western countries while remaining basically flat in the southern and eastern countries. According to Van Ommeren (1998), these differences in the penetration level of telework can be explained through cultural differences in attitude concerning management at a distance, the advancement of communication technology and national government policies.

Table Appendix 1.2 suggests that EU member states with high telework penetration levels also have high levels of investment in information technology (IT) per capita and a high number of PCs per 100 white collar workers. The number of internet users per 1000 inhabitants is also positively correlated with the penetration level of telework in the member states.

Table Appendix 1.1   Telework penetration levels in the EU member states

	Penetration level of telework (informal and formal arrangements		
	1994	1997	1998 - 1999
Northern and Western Countries			
Belgium	0.48	5.3	6.2
Denmark	0.37	9.7	11.6
Finland	2.50	6.3	10.0
Germany	0.41	1.9	5.1
Ireland	1.40	6.1	7.1
Netherlands	1.22	9.1	18.2
Sweden	3.77	5.4	9.0
United Kingdom	2.20	7.0	5.5
Southern and Eastern Countries			
Austria	0.35	1.5	2.0
France	0.98	1.1	1.8
Greece	0.46	0.5	1.3
Italy	0.46	0.9	1.7
Portugal	0.56	1.3	2.2
Spain	0.82	0.6	0.9

Sources: European Commission, 1997, 1998 and 1999

The relationship between telework and population density is complicated; telework has high penetration levels in states where the population density is very high, and also where it is very low. This is not surprising once we realize the many reasons for adopting telework. Generally speaking, EU member states with a low population density are motivated by the possibility that telework may improve the development of rural areas and may lead to a more geographically balanced distribution of wealth. Member states with a high population density, on the other hand, tend to be more motivated by the possibility that telework could reduce road congestion and air pollution (European Commission, 1998). (The UK, the Netherlands, Belgium and Ireland all have severe road congestion problems and clearly hope that telework will help solve these problems.)

We recognize that population density is a relatively crude tool for the generalization in the previous paragraph. A more sophisticated explanation would include the percentage of population living in urban areas, as shown in Table Appendix 1.3. Even countries with a low population density may be attracted by telework in order to alleviate their urban congestion.

Table Appendix 1.2   Variables positively correlated with the penetration of telework implementation

	PC's/100 white collar workers	IT per capta in EURO	Internet users/1000 inhabitants	Population per square kilometre
Austria	62	463	46	94
Belgium	52	495	47	331
Denmark	68	803	131	121
Finland	63	520	146	15
France	54	526	79	106
Germany	51	492	50	227
Greece	37	84	11	79
Ireland	84	333	41	50
Italy	46	268	13	190
Netherlands	64	578	90	371
Portugal	27	128	19	110
Spain	50	168	22	78
Sweden	85	782	152	19
UK	57	627	95	239

Sources: PC's/100 white collar workers, IT per capita in Euro: European Commission, 1998; Internet users/1000 inhabitants and Population per square kilometre: EITO, 1999.

Table Appendix 1.3 Percentage of population in urban areas

Country	Urban population as percentage of total population
International mean	53.28
United States	76.32
Canada	76.78
Australia	84.70
Japan	78.26
Singapore	100
Sweden	83.14
UK	89.26
Germany	86.70
France	74.88
Italy	66.68
Spain	76.24

Source: Huws et al., 1999

Another revealing aspect of an intra-EU comparison is the different drivers and barriers in the different EU member states. Table Appendix 1.4 gives an overview of the abbreviations, Table Appendix 1.5 gives an overview of the barriers, and Table Appendix 1.6 provides an insight into the drivers.

In member states with a high penetration level, the IT infrastructure is clearly a driver, and the needed IT infrastructure is generally present. (Belgium, however, is an exception to this rule. Here, the internet has not been adopted yet by the majority of the workforce, and the investment in IT has, so far, been relatively low.) It is also interesting to note that, in Denmark, the Netherlands and the UK, work arrangements are relatively informal and business is very open to innovations in work methods (European Commission, 1998). These attitudes are also drivers for implementing telework.

In member states with a high telework penetration level, the main barriers are regulations and laws that hinder further telework implementation, management misunderstanding of the concept and management's refusal to implement telework. The first barrier is clearly one that should be addressed by public policy-makers. The other barriers, however, are organizational and should be eliminated at the level of individual organizations.

In most member states with a low penetration level, the main drivers are a high public and governmental awareness, whereas the IT infrastructure is clearly the main barrier. The IT infrastructure is simply not sufficient to allow on-line telework.

Table Appendix 1.4 Abbreviations

Denmark	DK
Netherlands	NL
United Kingdom	GB
Finland	FIN
Ireland	IRL
Sweden	S
Belgium	B
Germany	D
Austria	A
Portugal	P
France	F
Italy	I
Spain	E
Greece	GR

Table Appendix 1.5 *Main current telework barriers in the EU member states*

BARRIERS	DK	NL	GB	FIN	IRL	S	B	D	A	P	F	I	E	GR
Postponing of telecommunication liberalization														X
Geographical settings - a central position between East and West Europe									X					
Situation of the labour market - low or high unemployment rates due to the current economic development lead to risk aversion				X				X	X		X			
Negative attitude of trade unions				X					X					
Regulations and laws that hinder the developments of IT	X	X	X		X	X		X	X		X			
Formal view of work arrangements						X		X	X					
Low investment in IT					X		X	X	X	X	X	X	X	X
Low level of access to internet							X	X	X	X	X	X	X	X
High telephone costs									X	X	X	X		
Low internet usage							X	X	X	X	X	X		X
Relatively autonomous regions but making it difficult to develop and sustain a national and international policy							X				X			
Management misunderstanding	X	X	X	X	X	X	X	X	X	X	X	X	X	X
Low employment participation (= # people employed/# people in the age group between 18 and 65)							X							
Low public awareness										X	X		X	X

Source: authors' analysis based on the European Commission, 1998

Table Appendix 1.5 *(Continued) Main current telework barriers in the EU member states*

BARRIERS	DK	NL	GB	FIN	IRL	S	B	D	A	P	F	I	E	GR
Conservative mentality toward change in general and especially in work methods								X	X					
Low proportion of information workers as compared to the European average								X						X
High PC costs												X	X	X
Small houses			X									X		
Low number of PCs									X					

Source: authors' analysis based on the European Commission, 1998

Table Appendix 1.6 *Main current telework drivers in the EU member states*

DRIVERS	DK	NL	GB	FIN	IRL	S	B	D	A	P	F	I	S	GR
Carry-tthough of telecommunication liberalization			X		X	X		X	X					X
Road congestion in urban areas		X	X		X	X	X							
Geographical settings – an isolated position / presence of EU institutions				X			X			X				
Importance of IT training in education	X	X		X		X			X	X				
Positive attitude of trade unions	X							X					X	

Source: authors' analysis based on European Commission, 1998

DRIVERS	DK	NL	GB	FIN	IRL	S	B	D	A	P	F	I	S	GR
Situation of the labour market - high unemployment rates in a specific region or prolonged high unemployment rates			X						X	X	X			
Adjustment of regulations and laws to developments in IT	X	X				X	X	X				X	X	
Informal view of work arrangements			X											
High level of public interest and awareness	X	X	X	X	X	X	X	X	X			X	X	
High level of governmental interest and awareness	X	X	X	X	X	X	X	X	X	X	X	X		
Presence of a network of telecentres			X		X	X	X							
High investment in IT	X	X	X	X	X	X						X		
Accelerating investment in IT	X												X	
High level of access to internet	X		X	X	X	X	X		X	X				
High/increasing usage of the available internet accesses	X		X	X	X	X								
Demographic diaspora					X					X	X	X		X
High quality telecommunication infrastructure	X	X	X			X	X		X					
Low telephone costs			X											X
An open mentality to innovation in work methods	X	X	X					X		X				
High participation of women in the labour force						X								
High employment participation	X	X				X	X							

Source: authors' analysis based on European Commission, 1998

APPENDIX 2. OCCUPATIONS SUITED FOR TELEWORK

Table Appendix 2.1 Occupations suited for telework

Job title	Full-time home-Based	Part-time home-based	Full-time satellite office or telework centre	Part-time satellite office or telework centre
Accountant		**	**	**
Advertising executive	*	**	**	**
Applications programmer	**	**	**	**
Architect	**	**	**	**
Auditor		**	**	**
Author	**	**	**	**
Central files clerk			*	
Civil engineer	**	**	**	**
Clerk-Typist	*	**	**	**
Clinical psychologist		**	**	**
Computer scientist		**	**	**
Counter clerk				
Data entry clerk	**	**	**	**
Data search specialist	**	**	**	**
Department general manager		**	*	**
Design engineer		**	**	**
Economist	*	**	**	**
Financial analyst	**	**	**	**
General secretary		**	**	**
Graphic artist	**	**	**	**
Industrial engineer		**	**	**
Journalist	**	**	**	**

Table Appendix 2.1(Continued) *Occupations suited for telework*

Job title	Full-time home-Based	Part-time home-based	Full-time satellite office or telework centre	Part-time satellite office or telework centre
Lawyer	*	**	**	**
Mail clerk			**	**
Mainframe operator			*	
Maintenance technician		**	**	**
Manager of managers		**	**	**
Manager of non-managers		**	**	**
Manager, machine systems	*	**	**	**
Market analyst	**	**	**	**
Marketing manager		**	**	**
Natural scientist		**	**	**
Office machine operator			**	**
Personnel manager		**	**	**
Purchasing manager	*	**	**	**
Receptionist			**	**
Risk analyst	**	**	**	**
Software engineer	**	**	**	**
Statistician	*	**	**	**
Stock analyst	**	**	**	**
Supervisor	*	**	**	**
Systems engineer		**	**	**
Systems programmer		**	**	**
Technical writer	**	**	**	**
Telemarketer	**	**	**	**
Telephone operator	**	**	**	**
Theoretical physicist	**	**	**	**
Travelling salesperson		**	**	**
University professor		**	**	**
Word processing secretary	**	**	**	**
Laboratory director		**	*	**
Laboratory scientist			*	*

Notes :
** = OK
* = suitable for some people
Blank space = not suitable

Source: Nilles, 1998

APPENDIX 3. FACTOR ANALYSIS ON THE ADVANTAGES AND DISADVANTAGES FROM THE EMPLOYER'S POINT OF VIEW

The number of variables related to telework's potential drivers and barriers was reduced using factor analysis in order to obtain a clearly structured choice model. A factor analysis was used for the 23 statements related to telework's potential drivers and barriers; this resulted in seven factors after applying principal component analysis. Here, linear combinations of the standardized original responses on the input variables are formed (in this case, the 23 statements) (Norusis, 1994).

In order to determine if a factor analysis is appropriate, the variables must be related to each other. The objective of a factor analysis is to determine the number of dimensions for which variables have a strong correlation with each other (De Pelsmacker and Van Kenhove, 1994). Furthermore the data must be a sample from a multivariate normal population. The data resulted from a 5 point Likert scale. Hence, a priori it is assumed that these variables are measured on an interval scale (De Pelsmacker and Van Kenhove, 1994). Furthermore, based on the tests done, a normal distribution of the variables can be assumed.

The factor analysis was conducted on 83 observations (specifically, the answers of the 83 human resources managers who completed the survey). Following a generally applied methodological rule-of-thumb in market research, ten times more observations than variables should be collected (De Pelsmacker and Van Kenhove, 1994). Hence 230 observations should have been collected. However, if the correlation between the original variables is sufficiently high, a factor analysis is justified (Norusis, 1994b). In order to assess whether there is sufficient correlation between the original variables,

Barlett's test of sphericity can be used. This test assesses whether the correlation matrix is an identity matrix (i.e., all diagonal terms are 1 and all off-diagonal terms are 0). This test assesses the correlation between the original variables (Norusis, 1994b). Based on the results of Barlett's test of sphericity for our 23 variables, the conclusion can be drawn that the correlation matrix is not an identity matrix. Hence, there is a correlation between the orginal variables. Consequently, a factor analysis can be conducted. Another test that can be used to assess whether or not it is convenient to perform a factor analysis is the Kaiser-Meyer-Olkin (KMO) measure. This index compares the magnitude of the observed correlation coefficients to the magnitudes of the partial correlation coefficients (the partial coefficient is low when the variables share common factors) (Norusis, 1994b).

If the KMO measure is close to one, it indicates that common factors between the variables are high. A result below 0.5 indicates that the variables are not suited for factor analysis (Norusis, 1994b). For our analysis a result of 0.659 was obtained. This means that a factor analysis can be used but the KMO measure is only mediocre.

The Principal component analysis resulted in seven factors, explaining 66.3 percent of the variance among the original variables.

In order to obtain a clearer picture of which variables are highly correlated with a particular factor, the factors are orthogonally rotated through the varimax method.

The factors can be interpreted as follows:

1. *Factor 1 (internal operations)* is highly correlated with 'hinders face-to-face interaction' (variable 6), 'hinders training' (variable 7) and 'hinders teamwork' (variable 8).
2. *Factor 2 (human resources problems)* is highly correlated with 'reduces absenteeism' (variable 13), 'enhances recruiting potential' (variable 14), 'reduces staff turnover' (variable 15) and 'reduces the redundancies of staff' (variable 16).
3. *Factor 3 (strategic market position)* is highly correlated with 'more work hours' (variable 2), 'enhanced flexibility' (variable 9) and 'enhanced productivity' (variable 10).
4. *Factor 4 (labour market relations)* is highly correlated with 'opposition of trade unions' (variable 5) and 'clear labour regulations' (variable 23).
5. *Factor 5 (conventional infrastructure)* is highly correlated with 'solution for the lack of adequate office space' (variable 17) and 'gains in office space' (variable 18).
6. *Factor 6 (customer service)* is highly correlated only with 'enhanced customer service' (variable 11).

7.   *Factor 7 (telework infrastructure)* is highly correlated with 'hinders the security of internal data' (variable 19) and 'requires costly investments' (variable 22).

In the next step, t-tests were constructed for the seven factors in order to determine whether there was a significant difference in the perception of these factors between human resources managers of organizations that have implemented telework and human resources managers of organizations that have not yet done so. The same analyses were also conducted from a stated preference perspective, comparing human resources managers of organizations intending to implement telework in the future versus human resources managers of organizations unwilling to do so. From these analyses the conclusion can be drawn that, based on revealed preferences, both groups share the same perceptions regarding factor 1 ('problems with internal operations'), factor 2 ('solution for human resources problems'), factor 5 ('solution for conventional infrastructure') and factor 6 ('customer service'). Differences in perceptions exist for factor 3 ('enhanced strategic market position') (t-test, p = 0.028), factor 4 ('problem with labour market relations') (t-test, p = 0.004) and factor 7 ('problems with telework infrastructure') (t-test, p = 0.024).

If the perceptions of the human resources managers of organizations intending to implement telework in the future are compared with those of human resources managers of organizations not prepared to do so, the perceptions of the two groups differ only for factor 3 ('enhanced strategic market position') (t-test, p = 0.013) and factor 5 ('solution for conventional infrastructure') (t-test, p = 0.084).

APPPENDIX 4. CHOICE MODEL OF THE ADOPTION OF TELEWORK BY EMPLOYERS

The parameters relevant to the adoption of telework by employers (dependent variable) are used as independent variables in the logistic regression model. These independent variables consist of the environmental parameters identified in Chapter 4 and the factors related to the advantages and disadvantages of telework implementation identified in Appendix 3. In order to estimate the binary choice between the adoption of telework and the non-adoption of this practice, a logistic regression model can be used. Logistic regression directly estimates the probability that a particular event will occur (Norusis, 1994), in this case the probability that an organization will implement telework in the future (comparing organizations that will implement telework in the future with organizations that will not implement telework in the future) or the probability that an organization has implemented telework (comparing organizations that have implemented telework with organizations that have not implemented telework). The relevance of the environmental parameters and the relevance of the factors related to the advantages and disadvantages of telework to the probability that an organization will (has) implement(ed) telework can be formulated by using following formula Appendix 4.1.

$$\text{Prob(adopting telework)} = \frac{e^Z}{1 + e^Z} = \frac{1}{1 + e^{-Z}} \qquad \text{(Appendix 4.1)}$$

where Z is the linear combination

$$Z = B_0 + B_1 X_1 + B_2 X_2 + \ldots + B_p X_p$$

The probability that telework is adopted can be estimated as:

Prob (not adopting telework) = 1 – Prob (adopting telework)

In a logistic regression the parameters (B_0, ..., B_p) are estimated using the maximum-likelihood method. That means that the coefficients that make the observed results most likely are selected (Norusis, 1994).

The first logistic regression model was estimated based on revealed preferences. Z was found to be a combination of four parameters, namely a constant, 'the awareness of the concept of telework,' 'coordination and control which is output-oriented' and 'flexible work hours,' which can be represented as indicated in the following formula Appendix 4.2.

$$Z = 2.6391 - 12.4552 \text{ x variable II 6 (flexible work} \qquad \text{(Appendix 4.2)}$$
$$\textit{hours)} - 14.3823 \text{ x variable IV.1 (awareness of the}$$
$$\textit{concept of telework)} - 3.7377 \text{ x variable result2}$$
$$\textit{(coordination and control is output-oriented).}$$

If Z is estimated for an organization not yet in the sample, the probability that this organization has implemented telework can be assessed based on the earlier mentioned formula Appendix 4.1. If the probability is greater than 0.5, telework implementation is predicted. The final model was correct in 96.67 percent of the cases. Another indication of the model's goodness of fit can be obtained by examining how likely the sample results actually are, given the parameter estimates. The probability of the observed results, given the parameter estimates, is known as the likelihood. Since the likelihood is a small number less than 1, it is customary to use –2 times the log of the likelihood (–2LL) as a measure of how well the estimated model fits the data. A good model that results in a high likelihood of the observed results is translated in a small value for –2LL. A perfect fit is obtained when the log likelihood is 0 (Norusis, 1994). The model with only a constant has a –2LL of 67.480 while the end model had a –2LL of 11.847.

The second logistic regression model was estimated based on a comparison of organizations that have implemented telework versus organizations that have not implemented telework, including all significant variables except the one related to awareness. Since the lack of awareness is a strong barrier to telework implementation, Z was found to be a combination of five parameters, namely a constant, 'coordination and control is output-oriented,' 'the organization is active in a knowledge-based sector,' and 'experience with outsourcing and labour-market relations,' which can be represented as indicated in formula Appendix 4.3.

$Z = 0.4672 + 1.9784 \times SECTOR3$ *(the organization is*   (Appendix 4.3)
active in a knowledge-based sector) $- 4.3340 \times result2$
(coordination and control is output-oriented) $- 2.4691 \times$
SOURCE (experience with outsourcing) $- 1.1207 \times$
FAC4_1 (labour-market relations).

If Z is estimated for an organization not yet in the sample, the probability that this organization has implemented telework can be obtained based on the earlier mentioned formula Appendix 4.1. The final model was correct in 85 percent of the cases. The model with only a constant has a $-2LL$ of 67.480 while the end model had a $-2LL$ of 28.020. These results indicate that the model does not fit as well as the previous model.

The third logistic regression model was estimated based on a comparison of organizations that intend to implement telework in the future with organizations that will not implement telework in the future, including all significant variables. Z was found to be a combination of parameters, namely a constant, 'awareness of the concept of telework,' and 'flexible work hours,' which can be represented as indicated in formula Appendix 4.4.

$Z - 2.1196 - 3.2808 \times$ *variable II 6 (flexible work*   (Appendix 4.4)
hours) $- 2.4629 \times$ *variable IV.1 (awareness of the*
concept of telework).

If Z is estimated for an organization not yet in the sample, the probability that this organization is planning to implement telework in the future can be obtained based on the earlier mentioned formula Appendix 4.1. If the probability is greater than 0.5, telework is expected to be implemented in that organization in the future. This model was correct in 76.47 percent of the cases. The model with only a constant has a $-2LL$ of 70.5244 while the end model had a $-2LL$ of 45.341.

The fourth logistic regression model was estimated based on a comparison of organizations that will implement telework in the future with organizations that will not implement telework in the future, in this case including all significant variables except the one related to awareness. Z was found to be a combination of three parameters, namely a constant, 'the availability of electronic communication,' and 'flexible workhours,' which can be represented as indicated in formula Appendix 4.5.

$$Z = 0.7376 - 2.8170 \text{ x variable II 6 (flexible work} \qquad \text{(Appendix 4.5)}$$
$$\text{hours}) - 8.8376 \text{ x variable I 9 (the availability of}$$
$$\text{electronic communication).}$$

This model was correct in 76.47 percent of the cases. The model with only a constant had a –2LL of 70.5244 while the end model had a –2LL of 49.087.

APPENDIX 5. FACTOR ANALYSIS ON TELEWORK DRIVERS AND BARRIERS FROM THE EMPLOYEE'S POINT OF VIEW, PART ONE: EMPLOYEE ATTITUDES

The number of variables regarding drivers and barriers to telework implementation was reduced using factor analysis in order to obtain a clearly structured choice model. After applying principal component analysis, the ten hypotheses regarding employee attitudes (hypotheses 39 - 48 in Chapter 5) resulted in four factors. The original variables were measured on a five-point Likert scale. In order to determine the correlation between the original variables, we used Bartlett's test of sphericity and the KMO measure. Both measures indicate that the correlation between the variables is sufficient to allow a factor analysis.

In order to reduce the number of factors, we used the criterion that the factor should have an eigenvalue of at least one. This produced four factors that explained 64.21 percent of the original variables.

In order to interpret the factors, an orthogonal rotation based on the varimax method was performed.

The factors can be interpreted as follows:

1. *Factor 1 (interaction in the office)* is highly correlated with 'Face-to-face contact with my direct supervisor is important' (variable 4), 'Face-to-face contact with other employees is important' (variable 5) and 'The atmosphere in the office is important' (variable 6).

2. *Factor 2 (commuting trip)* is highly correlated with 'My daily commuting is stressful' (variable 1) and 'Daily commuting has a negative influence on society' (variable 3).
3. *Factor 3 (working without interruptions)* is highly correlated with 'The ability to work without interruptions from colleagues is important' (variable 7) and 'The ability to work without interruptions from household members is important' (variable 8).
4. *Factor 4 (elements related to the two life spheres)* is highly correlated with 'My daily commuting allows to me to make a distinction between family and professional life' (variable 2), 'A distinction between family and professional life is important' (variable 9) and 'The ability to use the organization's restaurant is important' (variable 10).

In the next step, t-tests were constructed for the four factors in order to determine whether there are significant differences in the perception of these factors between current teleworkers and non-teleworkers, as well as between potential future teleworkers and employees not willing to telework, and between potential, future regular teleworkers and employees not willing to become regular teleworkers.

Our analysis suggests that the perceptions of current teleworkers and non-teleworkers differ only with respect to factor 2 ('commuting trip') (t-test, $p = 0.001$). Between potential future teleworkers and employees not willing to telework, perceptions differ for all four factors (factor 1: 'interaction in the office': t-test, $p = 0.000$) (factor 2: 'commuting trip': t-test, $p = 0.001$) (factor 3: 'working without interruptions': t-test, $p = 0.059$) (factor 4: 'elements related to the two life spheres': t-test, $p = 0.037$). We found the same results when comparing potential, future regular teleworkers with employees not willing to become regular teleworkers (factor 1: 'interaction in the office': t-test, $p = 0.000$) (factor 2: 'commuting trip': t-test, $p = 0.000$) (factor 3: 'working without interruptions': t-test, $p = 0.059$) (factor 4: 'elements related to the two life spheres': t-test, $p = 0.011$).

APPENDIX 6. FACTOR ANALYSIS ON TELEWORK DRIVERS AND BARRIERS FROM THE EMPLOYEE'S POINT OF VIEW, PART TWO: EMPLOYEE BELIEFS ABOUT TELEWORK'S CHARACTERISTICS

We conducted a factor analysis on the potential drivers and barriers presented to the respondents. After applying principal component analysis, the 33 statements in Chapter 5 about telework's potential drivers and barriers were reduced to nine factors. The original variables were measured on a five-point Likert scale. In order to determine the correlation between the original variables, we used two tests: Bartlett's test of sphericity and the KMO measure. Both measures indicate that the correlation between the variables is sufficient to allow a factor analysis. The KMO measure of 0.764 can be characterized as acceptable.

In order to reduce the number of factors, the criterion that the factor should have an eigenvalue of at least one was used. This resulted in the identification of nine factors that explained 58.86 percent of the original variables.

In order to interpret the factors, an orthogonal rotation based on the varimax method was performed.

The factors were given the following interpretation:

1. *Factor 1 ('higher responsibility and control')* correlates highly with variable 20 ('Telework would result in easier access of banks and public services'), variable 22 ('Telework would result in more ecologically

responsible behaviour'), variable 23 ('Telework would make it possible to perform daily activities more independently'), variable 30 ('Telework would result in more flexibility in adjusting the work schedule') and variable 31 ('Telework would result in more flexibility in arranging personal free time').

2. *Factor 2 ('connection with organization')* is highly correlated with variable 5 ('Teleworkers are socially isolated'), variable 6 ('Telework has a negative influence on the culture within an organization') and variable 7 ('Teleworkers are less in touch with the organization').

3. *Factor 3 ('requirement for individual discipline')* is highly correlated with variable 17 ('Telework would result in more distractions from other people'), variable 18 ('Telework would result in more conflict situations with other household members'), variable 19 ('Telework would require more self-discipline') and variable 29 ('Telework would make it more difficult to make a distinction between professional and family life').

4. *Factor 4 ('time flexibility')* is highly correlated with variable 8 ('Telework leads to more flexibility'), variable 24 ('Telework would result in more free time for family and friends') and variable 32 ('Telework would result in more personal leisure time').

5. *Factor 5 ('abuse')* is highly correlated with variable 3 ('Telework leads to abuse by the employer') and variable 4 ('Telework leads to abuse by the employee').

6. *Factor 6 ('communication')* is highly correlated with variable 13 ('Telework would result in less social interaction') and variable 14 ('Telework would result in less professional interaction').

7. *Factor 7 ('relocation')* is highly correlated with variable 1 ('A solution if the employer relocates') and variable 2 ('A solution if the employee moves').

8. *Factor 8 ('operational costs')* is highly correlated with variable 12 ('Telework would result in higher personal operational costs').

9. *Factor 9 ('evaluation')* is highly correlated with variable 26 ('Telework would result in a more accurate work evaluation').

In the next step, t-tests were constructed for the nine factors in order to assess whether there are significant differences in the perception of the factors (1) between current teleworkers and non-teleworkers, as well as (2) between potential future teleworkers and employees unwilling to telework and (3) between potential, future regular teleworkers and employees unwilling to become regular teleworkers.

Our analysis suggests that the perceptions of current teleworkers and non-teleworkers differ only with respect to factor 2 ('connection with organization') (t-test, p = 0.000), factor 7 ('relocation') (t-test, p = 0.003) and factor 8 ('operational costs') (t-test, p = 0.020).

Between potential future teleworkers and employees unwilling to telework, the perceptions differ for factor 1 ('higher responsibility and control') (t-test, p = 0.064), factor 2 ('connection with organization') (t-test, p = 0.000) and factor 7 ('relocation') (t-test, p = 0.000).

Between potential, future regular teleworkers and employees unwilling to become regular teleworkers, the perceptions differ for factor 1 ('higher responsibility and control') (t-test, p = 0.033), factor 2 ('connection with organization') (t-test, p – 0.000), factor 3 ('requirements for individual discipline') (t-test, p = 0.076) and factor 7 ('relocation') (t-test, p = 0.000).

APPENDIX 7. CHOICE MODEL OF THE ADOPTION OF TELEWORK BY EMPLOYEES

The parameters relevant to the adoption of telework by individual employees (dependent variable) are used as independent variables in the logistic-regression model. These independent variables consist of both the individual-level characteristics discussed in Chapter 5, and the factors identified in Appendix 5 and Appendix 6.

The dependent variable used should be defined along following dimensions (Bagley and Mokhtarian, 1997):

1. the nature of the alternatives (binary choice (yes or no)) versus multinominal frequency (amount of telework),
2. the type of telework being considered (home, centre or both),
3. whether a stated preference or an actual choice is being measured.

The individual adoption of telework can be explained by a number of variables, which can be formalized as follows (Mannering and Mokhtarian, 1995) (formula Appendix 7.1):

$$U_{ni} = b_{oi} + b_{1i} H_n + b_{2i} T_n + b_{3i} W_n + b_{4i} P_n + e_{ni} \qquad \text{(Appendix 7.1)}$$

U_{ni} = the value of the function determining the probability of individual n choosing frequency i.

H_n = vector of household and socio-economic characteristics.

T_n = vector of household transportation characteristics and individual travel behaviour.

W_n = vector of attributes of an individual's work or attitudes towards work.

P_n = vector of personal attitudes and awareness.

e_{ni} = error term reflecting factors not taken into account by the model. $b_{oi}, b_{1i}, b_{2i}, b_{3i}$ and b_{4i} are vectors of statistically estimated parameters that can vary over the choice alternatives.

However, in the binary logistic regression analysis used in this book, not all variables were used to determine the probability that an employee will adopt telework. Furthermore, all analyses were done twice: once with all significant variables, and once with all significant variables except the two variables related to awareness of the concept of telework (because these variables can be viewed as 'de facto' eliminating the choice to telework).

The first logistic regression model was estimated based on a comparison between current teleworkers and non-teleworkers, including all significant variables. The probability that an individual adopts telework can be calculated using the following formula.

$$\text{Prob(adopting telework)} = \frac{1}{1 + e^{-Z}} \qquad \text{(Appendix 7.2)}$$

Z was found to be a combination of five parameters, namely a constant, 'positive attitude of the direct supervisor,' 'use of the car during work hours,' 'considered the option to telework' and 'clerical occupation,' which can be represented as indicated in the following formula.

$Z = -0.3733 - 2.0807 \times HOUDING6$ *(positive attitude* (Appendix 7.3)
of the direct supervisor) – 1.080 x WAGEN3 (use of the
car during work hours) – 2.2436 x NAGEDACH
(considered the option to telework) + 1.2332 x
BEROEP3 (clerical occupation).

Once Z is determined for an individual, then the probability that the individual will adopt telework can be assessed using formula Appendix 7.2. If this probability is higher than 0.5, he/she is expected to adopt telework. The final model was correct in 84.62 percent of the cases. The $-2LL$ measure also improved from 180.147 to 116.465.

The second logistic regression model was estimated based on a comparison between current teleworkers and non-teleworkers, including all relevant significant variables except the ones related to awareness of the concept of telework.

In this case, Z was found to be a combination of six parameters, namely a constant, 'positive attitude of the direct supervisor,' 'uses a company car,' 'relocation,' 'connection with organization' and 'experience with taking work home,' which can be represented as indicated in formula Appendix 7.4.

$$Z = 0.8393 - 2.0973 \times HOUDING6 \text{ (positive attitude of} \quad \text{(Appendix 7.4)}$$
$$\text{the direct supervisor)} - 1.4972 \times BEDRIJF4$$
$$\text{(availability of a company car)} + 0.8462 \times FAC7\_2$$
$$\text{(relocation)} - 0.5547 \ FAC2\_2 \text{ (connection with}$$
$$\text{organization)} - 1.5820 \times THUISWER \text{ (experience with}$$
$$\text{taking work home).}$$

The final model was correct in 86.39 percent of the cases. Furthermore, the −2LL measure improved from 180.147 to 113.256.

Research by Mokhtarian and Salomon (1996b) shows that where telework is a valid and preferred option, it will be chosen in more than two thirds of the cases (constraints can prevent individuals from acting on their preferences) (Mokhtarian, 1998). Therefore, additional insights can be obtained by looking at **potential** future teleworkers and **potential,** future **regular** teleworkers.

The third logistic regression model was estimated based on a comparison between potential future teleworkers and employees not willing to telework. The model was first determined using all significant variables and then using all relevant variables except the ones related to awareness of the concept of telework. However, the result was the same.

When estimating the probability that an individual is willing to become a teleworker or regular teleworker, Z was found to be a combination of six parameters, namely a constant, 'uses a company car,' 'relocation,' 'connection with organization,' 'interaction in the office' and 'manager,' which can be represented as indicated in formula Appendix 7.5.

$$Z = 3.8328 - 1.4187 \times BEDRIJF4 \text{ (uses a company car)} \quad \text{(Appendix 7.5)}$$
$$+ 1.1121 \times FAC7\_2 \text{ (relocation)} - 0.7979 \times FAC2\_2$$
$$\text{(connection with organization)} - 0.9950 \times FAC1\_1$$
$$\text{(interaction in the office)} - 1.1375 \times BEROEP2$$
$$\text{(manager).}$$

The final model was correct in 82.87 percent of the cases. In addition, the −2LL measure improved from 196.108 to 134.185.

The fourth logistic regression model was estimated based on a comparison of potential, future regular teleworkers and employees not willing to become regular teleworkers, including all significant variables.

Z was found to be a combination of six parameters, namely a constant, 'considered the option to telework,' 'relocation,' 'connection with organization,' 'interaction in the office' and 'a managerial function,' which can be represented as indicated in formula Appendix 7.6.

> $Z = 3.0246 - 0.9773 \times NAGEDACH$ *(considered the*   (Appendix 7.6)
> *option telework) + 1.0056 x FAC7_2 (relocation) –*
> *0.7086 x FAC2_2 (connection with organization) –*
> *0.9041 x FAC1_1 (interaction in the office) – 1.2495 x*
> *BEROEP2 (a managerial function).*

The final model was correct in 80.49 percent of the cases. Furthermore, the –2LL measure improved from 186.611 to 124.694.

The fifth logistic regression model was estimated based on a comparison between potential, future regular teleworkers and employees not willing to become regular teleworkers, including all significant variables except the ones related to awareness of the concept of telework.

Z was found to be a combination of six parameters, namely a constant, 'uses car during work hours,' 'relocation,' 'connection with organization,' 'interaction in the office' and 'a managerial function,' which can be represented as indicated in formula Appendix 7.7.

> $Z = 3.9113 - 1.5522 \times BEDRIJF4$ *(uses a car during*   (Appendix 7.7)
> *work hours) + 1.0905 x FAC7_2 (relocation) – 0.8733 x*
> *FAC2_2 (connection with organization) – 1.0725 x*
> *FAC1_1 (interaction in the office) – 1.2780 x*
> *BEROEP2 (a managerial function).*

The final model was correct in 83.54 percent of the cases. In this case, the –2LL measure improved from 186.611 to 123.179. Note that the quality of the fourth and fifth logistic regression models is almost the same.

APPENDIX 8. TELEWORK IN BELGIUM

In this Appendix, we present the reasoning behind our estimate that the penetration level of telework in Belgium is approximately 3.97 percent, with a frequency of 1.5 days per workweek. We assume that the penetration level in Brussels is approximately the same.

At present, there is no good statistical data on the number of teleworkers in Belgium. Fortunately, though, there is good statistical data on the number of homeworkers. (Belgian law defines a homeworker as an employee who agrees to work as a subordinate of an employer and in return receives a fee and works at a freely-decided location.)

However, the data about homeworkers both overestimates and underestimates the number of teleworkers. It overestimates the number of teleworkers because it includes people for whom the work and home environments are the same (for example, domestic workers and farmers). These individuals are not teleworkers, because their working at home does not reduce work-related travel. Furthermore, the data on homeworkers underestimates the number of teleworkers because individuals employed in satellite offices or local telework centres are not included (Handy and Mokhtarian, 1996). We will now summarize how we start with the data about homeworkers and correct for both the overestimation and the underestimation.

According to the National Institute of Statistics, there were 628,029 homeworkers in 1996, making up 16.56 percent of the Belgian workforce. To determine the number of teleworkers, we first eliminate a number of sectors, because the activities concerned are in principle not suited for telework or because the home and workplace are often identical. Using NACE, the EU classification of economic sectors, we eliminate the following sectors: NACE A/B (Agriculture, hunting and forestry / Fishery), NACE F (Construction industry), NACE G (Wholesale and retail, car repair and household articles), NACE H (Hotels and restaurants), NACE K (Exploitation of and trade in real estate, renting and consultancy), NACE N (Public health and public assistance) and NACE P/Q (Private households with employees /

Extraterritorial organizations and bodies). Hence maintaining following sectors : NACE C (Extraction of minerals), NACE D (Industry), NACE E (Distribution of electricity, gas and water), NACE I (Transport, storage and communication), NACE J (Financial institutions) and NACE L/M/O (Administration and defence, compulsory social security/ education / remaining and welfare facilities and social-cultural and personal services). Data on the exact number of homeworkers employed in NACE N and NACE K is not directly available, in the sense that this data was collected in combination with data on the number of homeworkers in other sectors. For example, the homeworkers' data on sector N is included in a set that covers sectors L, M, N and O. We assume that the proportion of homeworkers in sector N is the same as for the set of sectors L, M, N and O together. We perform a similar calculation for NACE K.

In the second step, we use ISCO, the EU classification of occupation classes. We calculate the number of workers in the occupation classes ISCO 1 (Executive, administration, managerial), ISCO 2 (Professional specialists), ISCO 3 (Technicians and related Sales) and ISCO 4 (Administrative support) as a percentage of the total workforce in Belgium per sector. In most cases, those four activity classes are well suited for telework. Then, we assume that the ratio between ISCO 1, ISCO 2, ISCO 3 and ISCO 4 and the total Belgian workforce will also be found in the total number of homeworkers, so we multiply the number of homeworkers by this ratio. This produces an estimate of the number of workers in ISCO 1, ISCO 2, ISCO 3 and ISCO 4 within the total number of homeworkers.

Finally, we remove the self-employed from the total number of homeworkers, assuming that:

• the same percentage of self-employed individuals is found in all occupation classes, and
• the same ratio between self-employed individuals and the total workforce is found in the total number of homeworkers.

To carry out this correction, we multiply the ratio of the total number of self-employed individuals to the Belgian workforce by the total number of homeworkers left after the previous correction.

The result of all these calculations is an estimated penetration level of 3.97 percent for Belgium (see Table Appendix 8.1). This is a very rough estimate, which should be used only as an approximation. For Brussels, we assume the same penetration level.

Table Appendix 8.1 Penetration level of telework in Belgium

	NACE C	NACE D	NACE E	NACE I	NACE J	NACE L/M/O	TOTAL EMPLOY-MENT
Total number of individuals who usually work at home	259	21,558	218	3,457	17,120*	88,909*	382,556
Total number of individuals who sometimes work at home	386	25,435	1,592	6,310	16,024 *	73,078*	245,473
Total number of homeworkers	645	46,993	1,810	9,767	33,144 *	16,198*	628,029
Total number of individuals per sector according to the occupation	9,945	754,339	29,433	286,182	158,413	844,759	3,791,749
Total number of individuals in activity classes ISCO1, ISCO2, ISCO3 and ISCO4	4,447	280,133	18,820	158,038	136,446*	589,746*	2,102,268
Total number of individuals in activity classes ISCO1, ISCO2, ISCO3 and ISCO4 as compared with the total workforce (in %)*	47.43%	37.14%	63.95%	55.22%	86.13%	69.81%	55.44%
Total number of individuals self-employed	341	33,965	116	13,791	29,149*	65,645*	514,857
Total number of individuals self-employed as compared with the total workforce (in %)*	3.43%	4.50%	0.39%	4.82%	18.40%	7.77%	13.57%
Total number of teleworkers*	295	16,668	1,112	5,133	23,294	104,297	150,799
Penetration level of teleworkers (in %)*	2.96%	2.21%	3.78%	1.79%	14.7%	12.35%	3.97%

Sources: NIS - Sociale Statistieken - 'Enquête naar de beroepsbevolking 1996,' data indicated with a '*' is the authors' own calculations, authors' own compilation of table

At present, there is also no statistical evidence regarding the frequency of telework in Belgium. However, inter alia in the Netherlands, the frequency has been estimated at between 1 and 1.5 days per workweek (van Reisen, 1997). Because the Belgian situation is best compared with the Dutch situation, we assume that the average frequency for Belgium and Brussels is 1.5 days per workweek.

APPENDIX 9. THE FUTURE OF TELEWORK IN BELGIUM

Forecasting the adoption of telework is complex for several reasons. Telework implementation leads to a wide range of direct and indirect effects, to which actors may assign different weights. For instance, different actors will perceive its costs and benefits differently. Furthermore telework's long-term impacts may be different from its short-term impacts. Also, the decision to implement telework is a joint decision of at least two actors (employee and employer); their joint approval is a necessary condition for telework adoption (Salomon, 1998).

To make forecasting even more difficult, the adoption of telework cannot be considered as the mere adoption of a technology, because telework influences a wide set of variables, such as employee-employer relationships, intra-household relationships and the individual's position vis-à-vis his or her social environment (Salomon, 1998).

That being said, we will present three approaches to forecasting the adoption of telework: expert prediction, an analysis of the characteristics of a teleworker, and accounting. These will yield three estimates of the future of telework in Belgium.

APPENDIX 9.1   EXPERT PREDICTION

Halal (1993) used the Delphi method with 11 experts to assess the successful introduction of emerging information technologies and information services, including the adoption of telework. The 11 experts had both academic and professional (and private sector as well as public sector) backgrounds. They concluded that the likelihood of 'successful' telework implementation (whereby half of the workforce would telework from home) is about 0.52 and that the year of occurrence is most likely to be 2009. According to the experts, the adoption of telework will require a change in social patterns that will occur only if individuals are driven by necessity, for example as the result of escalating social costs of travel.

APPENDIX 9.2   ANALYSIS OF THE CHARACTERISTICS OF A TELEWORKER

A forecast of the trend in the number of teleworkers can also be based on the worker characteristics highly correlated with the decision to telework. For example, workers in their thirties have a high willingness to telework, and this group is bound to grow during the next decade. This leads to the conclusion, ceteris paribus, that the number of teleworkers will grow.

Given that the decision to telework is strongly related to the employee's occupation, this makes the occupation a promising characteristic for predicting the adoption of telework. In general terms, the following ISCO occupation classes are suitable for telework:

- executive, administration, managerial,
- professional specialists,
- technicians and related sales, and
- administrative support.

The shift-share technique can be used to analyse the anticipated effect on the number of teleworkers resulting from a change in workforce distribution among the different occupation classes (Handy and Mokhtarian, 1996). Originally, this technique was used to analyse the change in employment in a region compared to the change in the nation as a whole. The growth of the number of teleworkers in an occupation for a region can be divided into a national, an occupational and a regional effect. The national effect reflects the global growth of employment in the nation as a whole. The occupational effect is the growth in an occupation class after deducting the national effect. The regional effect reflects the growth in employment in a region for an occupation class after deducting the national growth in that particular occupation class.

To carry out this analysis, we divided the occupation classes used by the National Institute of Statistics of Belgium into occupation classes suitable and not suitable for telework. For this analysis, we used the data of 'de enquête naar de beroepsbevolking' (the population census) of 1993 and 1996. (We used this data because its occupation classification is based on international standards.) Table Appendix 9.1 reflects the growth of the different occupation classes between 1993 and 1996 for the Brussels-Capital Region and Table Appendix 9.2 gives the same information for Belgium. Table Appendix 9.3 shows the results of the shift-share analysis.

Table Appendix 9.1 Occupational trends in the Brussels-Capital Region

	1993		1996		
	Total	Per-centage	Total	Per-centage	Growth
Executive, administration, managerial	76,407	12.15%	85,404	13.63%	11.78%
Professional specialists	130,429	20.74%	140,579	22.43%	7.78%
Technicians and related sales	72,039	11.46%	61,820	9.87%	-14.19%
Administrative support	165,123	26.26%	169,238	27.01%	2.49%
Subtotal	**443,998**	**70.61%**	**457,041**	**72.94%**	**2.94%**
Service occupations	52,433	8.34%	52,037	8.30%	-0.76%
Agriculture, forestry and fishing and related	2,152	0.34%	932	0.15%	-56.69%
Others	130,185	20.71%	116,602	18.62%	-10.43%
Subtotal	**184,770**	**29.39%**	**169,571**	**27.06%**	**-8.226%**
Total	**628,768**	**100%**	**626,612**	**100%**	**-0.34%**

Source: authors' assessment

Table Appendix 9.2 Occupational trends in Belgium

	1993		1996		
	Total	Per-centage	Total	Per-centage	Growth
Executive, administration, managerial	372,757	10.0%	408,021	10.90%	9.5%
Professional specialists	665,135	17.8%	709,030	18.93%	6.6%
Technicians and related sales	355,551	9.5%	353,762	9.45%	-0.5%
Administrative support	631,123	16.9%	631,455	16.86%	0.1%
Subtotal	**2,024,566**	**54.1%**	**2,102,268**	**56.14%**	**3.8%**
Service occupations	359,152	9.6%	380,029	10.15%	5.8%
Agriculture, forestry and fishing and related	103,389	2.8%	105,214	2.81%	1.8%
Others	1,216,264	32.5%	1,157,073	30.90%	-4.9%
Subtotal	**1,678,805**	**44.9%**	**1,642,316**	**43.86%**	**-2.2%**
Total	**3,741,702**	**100%**	**3,785,905**	**100%**	**1.2%**

Source: authors' assessment

Table Appendix 9.3 may require some explanation. This table shows the factors that produced, for example, the increase of 11.78 percent for the occupation class 'Executive, administration, managerial' in the Brussels-Capital Region. Of that increase, 1.2 percent came from the growth in national employment, 8.3 percent came from the growth in that particular occupation class and 2.28 percent came from the extra growth in employment in that occupation class in the Brussels-Capital Region compared with the nation as a whole. Note that the occupational effect is positive for two of the four occupation classes suited for telework, namely 'Executive, administration, managerial' (8.3 percent) and 'Professional specialists' (5.4 percent).

Table Appendix 9.3 Shift-share analysis of the growth in occupations suited for telework

	Growth				Shift-share analysis	
	(1)	(2)	(3)	(4)	(2) - (1)	(3) - (2)
Executive, administration, managerial	1.2%	9.5%	11.78%	1.2%	8.3%	2.28%
Professional specialists	1.2%	6.6%	7.78%	1.2%	5.4%	1.18%
Technicians and related sales	1.2%	-0.5%	-14.19%	1.2%	-1.7%	-13.69%
Administrative support	1.2%	0.1%	2.49%	1.2%	-1.1%	2.39%

Notes:
(1) = growth in the Belgian workforce,
(2) = growth in the occupation class for the nation as a whole,
(3) = growth in the occupation class for the Brussels-Capital Region,
(4) = national effect,
(2) - (1) = effect produced by the growth in the occupation class,
(3) - (2) = effect produced by the difference between the Brussels-Capital Region and the nation
            as a whole

Source: authors' own calculations

Now that we know the growth in each occupation class for the Brussels-Capital Region, we use that to calculate the future number of teleworkers in the Brussels-Capital Region. In Table Appendix 9.4, we assume that the current penetration level of telework is 3.97 percent for both Belgium and Brussels (see Appendix 8 for this calculation). The employment in occupations suited for telework represents 72.94 percent of the active workforce. Accordingly, we assume that

- 5.44 percent (3.97 percent/0.7294) of the people employed in jobs suited for telework are teleworkers,

- 0 percent of the people employed in jobs not suited for telework are teleworkers, and
- the same ratios will persist in 2004, eight years later.

The growth for each occupation class between 1993 and 1996 was doubled for the period 1997 - 2004 because the time period is twice as long.

A more exact forecast would require data on the percentage of teleworkers per occupation class, as well as data on the evolution of the number of teleworkers per occupation class. However, based on the best data available, the shift-share analysis suggests that, due solely to a quicker growth of the jobs suited for telework compared to the growth in jobs not suited for telework, the numbers of teleworkers in the Brussels-Capital Region will increase by 0.25 percent between 1997 and 2004.

Table Appendix 9.4 *Forecast of the penetration level of telework in the Brussels-Capital Region based on the shift-share approach*

	Growth of the number of teleworkers between 1997 and 2004	1996			2004	
		Percentage of teleworkers in the occupation class	Number of individuals employed in the occupation class	Number of teleworkers in the occupation class	Number of individuals employed in the occupation class	Number of teleworkers in the occupation class
Professions suited for telework						
Executive, administration, managerial	23.56%	5.44%	85,404	4,646	105,525	5,741
Professional specialists	15.56%	5.44%	140,579	7,547	162,453	8,837
Technicians and related sales	-28.38%	5.44%	61,820	3,363	44,275	2,409
Administrative support	4.98%	5.44%	169,238	9,207	177,666	9,665
Professions not suited for telework	-16.45%	0.00%	169,571	0	141,677	0
Total workforce	-0.64%		626,612	24,863	631,596	26,652
Penetration level of telework				3.97%		4.22%

Source: authors' own calculations

APPENDIX 9.3   ACCOUNTING

This third method is very rudimentary. With this method, we calculate a mid-term penetration level of telework for Brussels based on the assumption that the maximum penetration level of telework in the future by the most innovative organizations in a particular sector in the survey of human resources managers can be extrapolated to the sector as a whole. (More in-depth information about the survey of human resources managers is provided in Chapter 3.) If all organizations in a particular sector reported that they could not implement telework, the possible penetration level of telework is assumed to be zero.

This leads to the estimation of a mid-term penetration level of telework of 21.5 percent of the labour force in Brussels. In Table Appendix 9.5, we give an overview of the estimated penetration level of telework in particular sectors.

Table Appendix 9.5 Mid-term estimates of the penetration level of telework in different sectors

	Percentage of employees employed in that particular sector	Absolute number of employees in that particular sector	Percentage of teleworkers in the workforce in that particular sector	Absolute number of teleworkers in the workforce in that particular sector
NACE A:	0.1%	648	0%	0
NACE B:	0.0%	83	0%	0
NACE C:	0.2%	1,068	0%	0
NACE D:	9.9%	62,035	7%	4,342
NACE E:	1.0%	6,146	0%	0
NACE F:	4.4%	27,629	0%	0
NACE G:	11.3%	70,779	3%	2,123
NACE H:	3.3%	20,956	0%	0
NACE I:	7.8%	49,271	4%	1,971
NACE J:	10.9%	68,551	21.3%	14,601
NACE K:	11.7%	73,647	27%	19,885
NACE L:	17.1%	107,326	75.4%	80,924
NACE M:	7.5%	47,186	4%	1,887
NACE N:	7.7%	48,702	0%	0
NACE O:	5.0%	31,467	0%	0
NACE P:	0.1%	891	0%	0
NACE Q:	2.0%	12,352	75.4%	9,313
Total	100%	628,736	21.5%	135,046

Source: authors' own calculations

APPENDIX 9.4 CONCLUSION

As we have said before, telework is a social construct, not a technology. Consequently, forecasting is extremely difficult. Nonetheless, we used three tools to forecast the implementation of telework. Experts suggest that it is entirely possible to see penetration levels of 50 percent by 2009. A shift-share analysis gives us good reason to expect at least a small increase in telework penetration, due merely to the different growth rates in different occupations. The accounting method suggests a mid-term penetration level of 21.5 percent.

REFERENCES

Agres, C., D. Edberg, and M. Igbaria (1998), 'Transformation to Virtual Societies : Forces and Issues', *The Information Society*, **14** (2), 7 - 82.

Aichholzer, G. (1998), 'A Social Innovation in Its Infancy. Experiences with Telework Centres', in P. Jackson and W. van der (eds), *Teleworking, International Perspectives from Telecommuting to the Virtual Organization,* London - New York: Routledge, pp. 292 - 302.

Alvehus, J. and J. Lindström (1998), 'Expression Management in Virtual Environments', in R. Suomi, P. Jackson, L. Hollmén, and M. Aspnäs (eds), *Proceedings of the Third International Workshop on Telework Telework Environments,* Turku Centre for Computer Science General Publications, no. 8, 1 – 4 September, pp. 395 - 407.

Apgar, IV M. (1998), 'The Alternative Workplace: Changing Where and How People Work', *Harvard Business Review*, **76** (3), 121 - 36.

Bagley, M. and P. Mokhtarian (1997), 'Analyzing the Preference for Non-Exclusive Forms of Telecommuting: Modeling and Policy Implications', *Transportation*, **24**, 203 - 26.

Balepur, P., K. Varma, and P. Mokhtarian (1998), 'Transportation Impacts of Center-Based Telecommuting: Interim Findings from the Neighborhood Telecenters Project', *Transportation*, **25**, 287 - 306.

Barker, R. (1994), 'Legitimacy: The Identity of the Accused', *Political Studies*, **42** (1), 101 – 02.

Bator, F. M. (1958), 'The Anatomy of Market Failure', *Quarterly Journal of Economics*, **72** (3), 351 - 79.

Baumol, W. J. and W. E. Oates (1988), *The Theory of Environmental Policy,* 2nd edition, Cambridge, UK: Cambridge University Press.

Bélanger, F. (1999), 'Workers' Propensity to Telecommute: An Empirical Study', *Information & Management,* **35** (3), 139 - 53.

Belgisch Staatsblad (1996), 24-12-1996.

Bergum, S. (1998), 'Telework, Organization and Management. Results from a Research Program in Norway', in R. Suomi, P. Jackson, L. Hollmén, and M. Aspnäs (eds), *Proceedings of the Third International Workshop on Telework Telework Environments,* Turku Centre for Computer Science General Publications, no. 8, 1 – 4 September, pp. 75 - 92.

Bernardino, A., M. Ben-Akiva, and I. Salomon (1992), 'Stated Preference Approach to Modeling the Adoption of Telecommuting', *Transportation Research Record,* (1413), 22 - 30.

B.I.M. (1996), *Luchtkwaliteit in het Brussels Hoofdstedelijk Gewest, Emissiemetingen 1994-1995-1996,* B.I.M. Rapporten -12.

Bohm, P. and C. Russell (1985), 'Comparative Analysis of Alternative Policy Instruments', in A. Kneese and J. Sweeney (eds), *Handbook of Natural Resource and Energy Economics (Vol 1),* North Holland: Amsterdam, pp. 395 - 460.

Boneschansker, E. (1995), 'Externe Kosten Van Het Verkeer', *Tijdschrift Vervoerswetenschap,* (1), 89 - 100.

Brown, H. J. (1976), 'De Betekenis Van Het Veranderen Van Baan Voor Het Verhuisgedrag', *Bouwen en Wonen,* (7).

Buchanan, J. M. and W. C. Strubblebine (1962), 'Externality', *Economica,* **29** (116), 371 - 84.

Bush, W. (1990), 'Telecommuting the Case of Research Software Development', *Technological Forecasting and Social Change,* **37**, 235 - 50.

Büssing, A. (1998), 'Teleworking and Quality of Life', in P. Jackson and J. van der Wielen (eds), *Teleworking, International Perspectives from Telecommuting to the Virtual Organization,* London - New York: Routledge, pp. 144 - 65.

Button, K. J. (1994), *Transportation Economics,* England: Edward Elgar.

Ced.samson (1998), *Human Resource Management Telewerken.*

Chapman, A., N. Sheehy, S. Heywood, B. Dooley, and S. Collins (1995), 'The Organizational Implications of Teleworking', in C. Cooper and I. Robertson (eds), *International Review of Industrial and Organizational Psychology,* New York: John Wiley, pp. 29 - 48.

Coeck, C. (1993), 'Beleidsinstrumenten Voor Een Toekomstgericht Milieubeleid en Hun Repercussies Voor Het Bedrijfsleven', *A & B kwartaalschrift,* **18** (1), 14-35.

Cross, T. and M. Raizman (1986), *Telecommuting the Future Technology of Work,* Homewood, Illinios: Down Jones-Irwin.

Deliege, D. (1993), *Les Absences pour Maladie dans le Secteur Privé.*

Denayer, W. (2000), 'Telewerken als deeloplossing voor mobiliteitsproblemen', in: *Gids op Maatschappelijkgebied,* maart, pp. 15 - 21.

De Pelsmacker, P. and P. Van Kenhove (1994), *Marktonderzoek Methoden En Toepassingen,* Leuven: Garant.

de Vries, H. (1988), 'Legal Aspects of Telework : The Dutch Experience', in F. van Rijn and R. Williams (eds), *Concerning Home Telematics,* North-Holland: Elsevier Science Publishers, pp. 439 - 53.

DG, XIII-B (1995), *Legal, Organizational and Management Issues in Telework,* European Commission.

Di Nicola, P. and R. Parrotto (1998), 'Organisational fitting and Diffusion of new culture.', in P. Jackson and J. van der Wielen (eds), *Teleworking, International Perspectives from Telecommuting to the Virtual Organization,* London-New York: Routledge, pp. 303 - 18.

Duxbury, L., C. Higgins, and R. Irving (1987), 'Attitudes of Managers and Employees to Telecommuting', *Information systems and operational research*, **25** (3), 273 - 85.

Eldid, O. and D. Minoli (1995), *Telecommuting,* Boston: Artech House.

Elkin, S. and B. Cook (1985), 'The Public Life of Economic Incentives', *Policy Studies Journal*, **13** (4), 797 - 813.

Elmore, R. (1987), 'Instruments and Strategy in Public Policy', *Policy Studies Review.* **7** (1), 174 - 86.

Empirica (1985), *Trends and prospects of electronic home working. Results of a survey in four major European countries*, FAST series no. 20, Science and Technology policy, Commission of the European Communities.

Engström, M. and R. Johanson (1998), 'It and Alternative Forms of Working, Living and Communication – by Flexibility in Time, Space and Organization.', in R. Suomi, P. Jackson, L. Hollmén, and M. Aspnäs (eds), *Proceedings of the Third International Workshop on Telework Telework Environments,* Turku Centre for Computer Science General Publications, no. 8 1 – 4 September, pp. 129 - 47.

European Commission (1997), 'Status Report on European Telework Telework 1997'.

European Commission (1998), 'Status Report on European Telework Telework 1998'.

European Commission (1999), 'Status Report on European Telework New Methods of Work 1999'.

EITO (1999), 'European Information Technology Observatory 99'.

Febiac (1997), *Data Digest.*
Feick, J. (1992), 'Comparing Comparative Policy Studies – a Path Towards Integration?', *Journal of Public Policy*, **12** (3), 257 – 85.

Fireman, S. (1998), 'Evolution of the Telecommuting Withdrawal Model a US Perspective.', in P. Jackson and W. van der (eds), *Teleworking,*

International Perspectives from Telecommuting to the Virtual Organization, London - New York: Routledge, pp. 281 - 91.

Gainey, T., D. Kelley, and J. Hill (1999), 'Telecommuting's Impact on Corporate Culture and Individual Workers: Examining the Effect of Employee Isolation', *SAM Advanced Management Journal,* **64** (4), 4 - 10.

Gareis, K. (1998), 'Telework and the Bottom Line – Costs and Benefits of Telework in German Insurance Companies', in R. Suomi, P. Jackson, L. Hollmén, and M. Aspnäs (eds), *Proceedings of the Third International Workshop on Telework Telework Environments,* Turku Centre for Computer Science General Publications no. 8, 1 – 4 September, pp. 107 - 28.

Gareis, K. and W. Korte (1999), 'Benchmarking Progress on Telework and Other New Ways of Working in Europe', *Proceedings of The Fourth International Telework Workshop Telework Strategies for the New Workforce,* 31 August 1999 – 3 September 1999, Tokyo, 346 - 56.

Garrison, W. and E. Deakin (1988), 'Travel, Work, and Telecommunications: A View of the Electronics Revolution and Its Potential Impacts', *Transportation Research A,* **22** (4), 239 - 45.

Gillespie, A. (1998), 'Telework and the Sustainable City', Paper presented at the NECTAR EuroConference on Sustainable Transport: Europe and its Surroundings, Israel, April 19 - 25 1998.

Gillespie, A., R. Richardson and J. Cornford (1995), 'Review of Telework in Britain : Implications for Public Policy', prepared for Parliamentary Office of Science and Technology, Centre for Urban and Regional Development Studies, University of Newcastle upon Tyne.

Giuliano, G. (1992), 'An Assessment of the Political Acceptability of Congestion Pricing', *Transportation,* **19**, 335 - 58.

Gordon, G. (1988), 'The Dilemma of Telework : Technology Versus Tradition', in W. Korte, S. Robinson, and W. Steinle (eds), *Telework : Present Situation and Future Development of a New Form of Work Organization,* North-Holland, Amsterdam: Elsevier Science Publishers, pp. 113 - 36.

Gordon, P., H. Richardson, and M. J. Jun (1991), 'The Commuting Paradox. Evidence from the Top Twenty', *Journal of the American Planning Association*, **57** (4), 416 - 20.

Gray, M., N. Hodson, and G. Gordon (1994), *Teleworking Explained,* New York: John Wiley.

Gray, P. (1997), 'A Demand-Side Approach to Telecommuting: The Integrated Workplace Strategies Concept', *Information Systems Management*, **14** (4), 21 - 8.

Greenberg, J. (1987), 'A Taxonomy of Organizational Justice Theories', *Academy of Management Review*, **12** (1), 9 - 22.

Greenberg, J. (1990), 'Organizational Justice: Yesterday, Today and Tomorrow', *Journal of Management*, **16** (2), 399 - 432.

Gurstein, P. (1991), 'Working at Home and Living at Home: Emerging Scenarios', *The Journal of Architectural and Planning Research*, **8** (2), 164 – 80.

Halal, W. (1993), 'The Information Technology Revolution. Computer Hardware, Software, and Services into the 21st Century.', *Technological Forecasting and Social Change*, **44**, 69 - 86.

Hamer, R., E. Kroes, and H. Van Ooststroom (1991), 'Teleworking in the Netherlands: An Evaluation of Changes in Travel Behaviour', *Transportation*, **18**, 365 - 82.

Hamer, R., E. Kroes, and H. Van Ooststroom (1992), 'Teleworking in the Netherlands: An Evaluation of Changes in Travel Behaviour – Further Results', *Transportation Research Record*, (1357), 82 - 9.

Handy, S. and P. Mokhtarian (1994), *Present Status and Future Directions of Telecommuting in California,* California Energy Commission.

Handy, S. and P. Mokhtarian (1995), 'Planning for Telecommuting. Measurement and Policy Issues', *Journal of the American Planning Association*, **61** (1), 99-111.

Handy, S. and P. Mokhtarian (1996a), 'Forecasting Telecommuting: An Exploration of Methodologies and Research Needs', *Transportation*, **23**, 163 - 90.

Handy, S. and P. Mokhtarian (1996b), 'The Future of Telecommuting', *Futures*, **28** (3), 227 - 40.

Harman, K. and A. Bordow (1998), 'An Exploration of Teleworker –Manager Relationship', in R. Suomi, P. Jackson, L. Hollmén, and M. Aspnäs (eds), *Proceedings of the Third International Workshop on Telework Telework Environments,* Turku Centre for Computer Science General Publications no. 8, 1 – 4 September, pp. 304 - 11.

Heller, W. P. and D. A. Starret (1976), 'On the Nature of Externalities', in S. A. Lin (ed.), *Theory and Measurement of Economic Externalities,* New York: Academic Press.

Henderson, D., B. Koenig, and P. Mokhtarian (1994), '*Travel Diary - Based Emissions Analysis of Telecommuting for the Puget Sound Telecommuting Demonstration Project',* Research Report UCD-ITS-RR-94-26, Institute of Transportation Studies University of California, Davis.

Henderson, D., B. Koenig, and P. Mokhtarian (1996), 'Using Travel Diary Data to Estimate the Emissions Impacts of Transportation Strategies: The Puget Sound Telecommuting Demonstration Project', *Journal of Air and Waste Management Association,* **46**, 47 - 57.

Hickerson, S. R. (1987), 'Instrumental Valuation: The Normative Compass of Institutional Economics', *Journal of Economic Issues,* **21** (3), 1117 - 43.

Holti, R. and E. Stern (1987), *Distance Working: origins – diffusion – prospects,* Tavistock Institute, Commission of the European Communities, FAST programme.

Howlett, M. and M. Ramesh (1993), 'Patterns of Policy Instrument Choice: Policy Styles, Policy Learning and the Privatization Experience', *Policy Studies Review,* **12**, 3 - 24.

Huws, U. (1988), 'Remote Possibilities: Some Difficulties in the Analysis and Quantification of Telework in the UK', in W. Korte, S. Robinson, and W. Steinle (eds), *Telework : Present Situation and Future Development of a New Form of Work Organization,* North-Holland, Amsterdam: Elsevier Science Publishers, pp. 61 – 76.

Huws, U. (1993), 'Teleworking in Britain', A report to the Employment Department, Research Series no. 18.

Huws, U. (1994), 'Teleworking Follow-up to the White Paper, Report to the European Commission's Employment Task Force (DGV)', in European Commission (eds), *Social Europe*, supplement 3, 1995, pp. 1 - 66.

Huws, U. (1996), 'Teleworking: an Overview of the Research', Analytica, A report to the Department of Transport, Department of the Environment, Department of Trade and Industry and Department for Education and Employment.

Huws, U. (1998), *Teleworking and Local Government, Assessing the Costs and Benefits?*, The Local Government Management Board.

Huws, U., N. Jagger, and S. O'Regan (1999), *Teleworking and Globalisation*, IES Report 358.

Huws, U., W. Korte, and S. Robinson (1993), *Telework Towards the Elusive Office*, New York: John Wiley Information Systems Series.

Illegems, V., A. Verbeke, and R. S'Jegers (1999), 'The Implementation of Teleworking: Drivers and Constraints', *Proceedings of the Fourth International Telework Workshop: Telework Strategies for the New Workforce*, 31 August 1999 - 3 September 1999, Tokyo, Japan, pp. 156 - 65.

Illegems V., A. Verbeke, R. and S'Jegers (2000), 'Virtual mobility: Teleworking as an alternative to structural congestion', *Proceedings of the 7th World Congress on Intelligent Transport Systems, From Vision to Reality*, Turin, Italy, 6 - 9 November 2000 (on CD-Rom).

Illegems, V., A. Verbeke, and R. S'Jegers (2001), 'The Organizational Context of Teleworking Implementation', *Technological Forcasting and Social Change*, **68** (3), 275 - 91.

ILO (International Labour Organisation) (1995), *Rapport V (1) Le travail à domicile*.

Imbrechts W., 1995, 'Telewerk in het licht van het ARAB', *Arbeidsblad*, November-December, 27 - 33.

Jackson, P. and J. van der Wielen (1998), 'Actors, Approaches and Agendas: From Telecommuting to the Virtual Organisation', in P. Jackson and W. van der (eds), *Teleworking, International Perspectives from Telecommuting to the Virtual Organization,* London - New York: Routledge, pp. 1 - 20.

Jones, P. and A. Hervik (1992), 'Restraining Car Traffic in European Cities: An Emerging Role for Road Pricing', *Transportation Research A*, **26** (2), 133 - 45.

Kågeson, P. (1993), *Getting the prices right. A European Scheme for making Transport Pay its True Costs*, The European Federation for Transport and Environment (T&E), Katarinatryck AB Stockholm.

Kinsman, F. (1987), *The Telecommuter,* New York: John Wiley.

Kitamura, R., J. Nilles, P. Conroy, and D. Fleming (1990), 'Telecommuting as a Transportation Planning Measure: Initial Results of California Pilot Project', *Transportation Research Record*, 1285, 98 - 104.

Köhler, E., R. Moran, and J. Tansey (1988a), 'The Home as Electronic Work Place an Overview of Research', in F. van Rijn and R. Williams (eds), *Concerning Home Telematics,* North-Holland: Elsevier Science Publishers, pp. 393 - 412.

Köhler, E., R. Moran, and J. Tansey (1988b), 'Telework in the European Community: Problems and Potential', in W. Korte, S. Robinson, and W. Steinle (eds), *Telework: Present Situation and Future Development of a New Form of Work Organization,* North-Holland, Amsterdam: Elsevier Science Publishers, pp. 7 – 19.

Kondo, K. (1999), 'Telework and Telemanagement', *Proceedings of The Fourth International Telework Workshop Telework Strategies for the New Workforce*, 31 August 1999 – 3 September 1999, Tokyo, pp. 19 – 28.

Konno, A. (1999), 'Creating a New Work Life Using Telecommunication Technology : Introducing Telework and a New Organizational Paradigm', *Proceedings of The Fourth International Telework*

Workshop Telework Strategies for the New Workforce, 31 August 1999 – 3 September 1999, Tokyo, pp. 176 – 84.

Korte, W. (1988), 'Telework Potential and Reasons for Its Utilization from the Organization's as Well as the Individual's Perspective', in F. van Rijn and R. Williams (eds), *Concerning Home Telematics,* North-Holland: Elsevier Science Publishers, pp. 373 - 91.

Korte, W. and R. Wynne (1996), *Telework Penetration, Potential and Practice in Europe,* Amsterdam: IOS Press.

Kraemer, K. (1982), 'Telecommunications/transportation substitution and energy conservation part 1', *Telecommunication Policy,* March, 39 - 59.

Kraemer, K. and J. King (1982), 'Telecommunications/transportation substitution and energy conservation part 1', *Telecommunication Policy,* June, 87 - 99.

Kraut, R. (1989), 'Telecommuting: The Trade-Offs of Home Work', in M. Siefert, G Gerbner, and J. Fisher (eds), *The Information Gap. How Computers and Other New Communication Technologies Affect the Social Distribution of Power,* Oxford: Oxford University Press, pp. 19 – 47.

Kubicek, H. and U. Fischer (1988), '(Tele-) Homework in the Federal Republic of Germany Historical Background and Future Perspectives from a Worker's Perspective', in W. Korte, S. Robinson, and W. Steinle (eds), *Telework: Present Situation and Future Development of a New Form of Work Organization,* North-Holland, Amsterdam: Elsevier Science Publishers, pp. 177 – 88.

Kugelmass, J. (1995), *Telecommuting: a Manager's Guide to Flexible Work Arrangements,* New York: Lexington Books.

La Bella, A., A. Morini, and M. Silvestrelli (1990), 'Telematics and Business Travel', *Telematics,* April, 107 - 32.

Lam, S., S. Lim, and M. Loh (1995), 'A Survey of the Status of Teleworking in Singapore', *Proceedings of the 1995 Pan Pacific Conference on Information Systems*, Singapore, pp. 200 – 4.

Lie, C. and B. Yttri (1999), 'AO/DI – The Future Communication Solutions for Teleworkers?', *Proceedings of The Fourth International Telework Workshop Telework Strategies for the New Workforce,* 31 August 1999 – 3 September 1999, Tokyo, pp. 252 – 62.

Limburg, D. (1998), 'Teleworking in a Managerial Context', in R. Suomi, P. Jackson, L. Hollmén, and M. Aspnäs (eds), *Proceedings of the Third International Workshop on Telework Telework Environments,* Turku Centre for Computer Science General Publications no. 8, 1 – 4 September, pp. 93 - 106.

Linder, S. and B. Peters (1989), 'Instruments of Government: Perceptions and Contexts', *Journal of Public Policy,* **9** (1), 35 – 58.

Lund, J. and P. Mokhtarian (1994), 'Telecommuting and Residential Location: Theory and Implications for Commute Travel in Monocentric Metropolis', *Transportation Research Record,* 1463, 10 - 4.

Luukinen, A. (1996), 'A Profile of Finnish Telework: Survey Results Concerning the Nature, Extent and Potential of Telework in Finland', in Luukinen A., J. Pekkola, A. Heikkilä and M. Zamindar (eds): *Directions of Telework in Finland,* Report by the Finnish Experience with Telework Project, Ministry of Labour, Publication of Labour Administration 143, pp. 1 - 22.

Luukinen, A., J. Pekkola, A. Heikkilä and M. Zamindar (1996), 'Directions of Telework in Finland', Report by the Finnish Experience with Telework Project, Publication of Labour Administration 143, Ministery of Labour.

Lyons, G., A. Hickford, and J. Smith (1998), 'The Nature and Scale of Teleworking's Travel Demand Impacts : Insights', in R. Suomi, P. Jackson, L. Hollmén, and M. Aspnäs (eds), *Proceedings of the Third International Workshop on Telework Telework Environments,* Turku Centre for Computer Science General Publications no. 8, 1 – 4 September, pp. 312 – 30.

Mahmassani, H., J. R. Yen, R. Herman, and M. Sullivan (1993), 'Employee Attitudes and Stated Preferences toward Telecommuting: An Exploratory Analysis', *Transportation Research Record,* 1413, 31 - 41.

Mannering, J. and P. Mokhtarian (1995), 'Modeling the Choice of Telecommuting Frequency in California: An Exploratory Analysis', *Technological Forecasting and Social Change*, 49, 49 – 73.

March, J. and J. Olsen (1986), 'Popular Sovereignty and the Search for Appropriate Institutions', *Journal of Public Policy*, **6** (4), 341 - 70.

May, A. D. and C. A. Nash (1998), 'Urban Congestion: A European Perspective on Theory and Practice', *Review paper for the Annual review of Energy and the Environment.*

Mayeres I., S. Proost and K. Van Dender (1997), 'Marginale externe kosten van transport : beschrijving, waardering en meeting', in B. De Borger and S. Proost (ed.), *Mobiliteit : De juiste prijs*, Leuven, Apeldoorn: Garant, pp. 43 – 80.

Mayeres, I., S. Ochelen and S. Proost (1996), 'The marginal external costs of urban transport', *Public Economics Research Paper, no. 51.*

Mayntz, R. (1983), 'The Conditions of Effective Public Policy: A New Challenge for Policy Analysis', *Policy and Politics*, **11** (2), 123 – 43.

Mcgrath, P. and M. Houlihan (1998), 'Conceptualising Telework Modern or Postmodern?' in P. Jackson and W. van der (eds), *Teleworking, International Perspectives from Telecommuting to the Virtual Organization,* London - New York: Routledge, pp. 56 - 73.

Memmott, F. (1963), 'The Substitutability of Communications for Transportation', *Traffic Engineering*, **33**, 20 – 5.

Michelson, W., Palm, L. K. and T. Wikström (1999), 'Forward to the Past? Home-Based Work and the Meaning, Use, and Design of Residential Space', *Research in Community Sociology*, **9**, 155 – 84.

Milliken, F. (1987), 'Three Types of Perceived Uncertainty About the Environment', *Academy of Management Review*, **12** (1), 133 - 43.

Ministerie van Verkeer en Infrastructuur (1999), *Algemene Verkeerstellingen 1998.*

Mirchandani, K. (1999), 'Legitimizing Work: Telework and the Gendered Reification of the Work-Nonwork Dichotomy', *The Canadian Review of Sociology and Anthropology*, **36** (1), 87 – 107.

Mintzberg H. (1981), 'Organizational design : fashion or fit?', *Harvard Business Review*, January-February, 103 – 16.

Mokhtarian, P. (1988), 'An Empirical Evaluation of the Travel Impacts of Teleconferencing', *Transportation Research A*, **22** (4), 283 – 9.

Mokhtarian, P. (1990), 'A Typology of Relationships between Telecommunications and Transport', *Transportation Research A*, **24** (3), 231 - 42.

Mokhtarian, P. (1991a), 'Defining Telecommuting', *Transportation Research Record*, 1305, 273 – 81.

Mokhtarian, P. (1991b), 'Telecommuting and Travel: State of the Practice, State of the Art', *Transportation*, **18**, 319 – 42.

Mokhtarian, P. (1998), 'A Synthetic Approach to Estimate the Impacts of Telecommuting on Travel', *Urban Studies*, **35** (2), 215 - 41.

Mokhtarian, P., M. Bagley, and I. Salomon (1998), 'The Impact of Gender, Occupation and Presence of Children on Telecommuting Motivations and Constraints', *Journal of the American Society for Information Science*, **49** (12), 1115 – 34.

Mokhtarian, P., S. Handy, and I. Salomon (1995), 'Methodological Issues in the Estimation of the Travel, Energy, and Air Quality Impacts of Telecommuting', *Transportation Research A*, **29A** (4), 283 - 302.

Mokhtarian, P. and I. Salomon (1994), 'Modeling the Choice of Telecommuting: Setting the Context', *Environment and Planning A*, **26**, 749 – 66.

Mokhtarian, P. and I. Salomon (1996a), 'Modeling the Choice of Telecommuting 2. A Case of the Preferred Impossible Alternative', *Environment and Planning A*, **26**, 1859 – 76.

Mokhtarian, P. and I. Salomon (1996b), 'Modeling the Choice of Telecommuting 3. Identifying the Choice Set and Estimating Binary

Choice Models for Technology-Based Alternatives', *Environment and Planning A*, **26**, 1877 – 94.

Mokhtarian, P. and I. Salomon (1997), 'Modeling the Desire to Telecommute: The Importance of Attitudinal Factors in Behavioral Models', *Transportation Research A*, **31** (1), 35 - 50.

Mokhtarian, P. and K. Sato (1994), 'A Comparison of the Policy, Social, and Cultural Contexts for Telecommuting in Japan and the United States', *Social Science Review*, **12** (4), 641 – 58.

Moon, C. (1998), 'Factors Affecting the Take-up of Teleworking in the Uk', in R. Suomi, P. Jackson, L. Hollmén, and M. Aspnäs (eds), *Proceedings of the Third International Workshop on Telework Telework Environments*, Turku Centre for Computer Science General Publications no. 8, 1 – 4 September, pp. 257 - 67.

Nationaal Instituut voor de Statistiek (1994), *Statistisch Jaarboek van België*, Boekdeel 112, Ministerie van Economische Zaken.

Nationaal Instituut voor de Statistiek (1999), *Algemene Volks- en woningtelling 1991 : Werk- en Schoolpendel*, Monografie no. 11B.

Nilles, J. (1976), 'Telecommuting: Communications as a Substitute for Commuting', in Grunig (ed), *Decline of the Global Village*, pp. 137 – 57.

Nilles, J. (1977), 'Telecommunications and Urban Structure', *Proceedings of the IEEE 77 International Communications Conference*, **II**, 257 - 60.

Nilles, J. (1988), 'Traffic Reduction by Telecommuting: A Status Review and Selected Bibliography', *Transportation Research A*, **22** (4), 301 – 17.

Nilles, J. (1991), 'Telecommuting and Urban Sprawl: Mitigator or Inciter?' *Transportation*, **18**, 411 – 32.

Nilles, J. (1997), 'Telework: Enabling Distributed Organizations Implications for It Managers', *Information Systems Managers*, **14** (4), 7 – 14.

Nilles, J. (1998), *Managing Telework Strategies for Managing the Virtual Workforce,* New York - Chichester – Weinheim – Brisbane – Singapore -Toronto: John Wiley & Sons Inc.

Nilles, J. (1999), 'Some Common - and Not So Common Telework/Telecommuting Questions', Jala International, http://www.jala.com/faq.htm#forecast.

Nilles, J., J. F. Carlson, P. Gray, and G. Hanneman (1976), *The Telecommunications - Transportation Tradeoff. Options for Tomorrow,* New York: John Wiley & Sons.

Norusis, M. (1994), *SPSS Advanced Statistics 6.1.,* SPSS Inc.

NUTEK (1997), *Telework - Good practice for the future! Telework in Theory and Practice based on 100 European Telework Cases and Telework '97 4th European Assembly on Telework and New Ways of Working Arranged by NUTEK in Stockholm,* September 24 - 26.

Olson, M. (1982), 'New Information Technology and Organizational Culture', *MIS Quarterly,* **6** (4), 71 – 92.

Olson, M. (1988), 'Organizational Barriers to Telework', in W. Korte, S. Robinson, and W. Steinle (eds), *Telework : Present Situation and Future Development of a New Form of Work Organization,* North-Holland, Amsterdam: Elsevier Science Publishers, pp. 77 – 100.

Olszewski, P. and S. H. Lam (1996), 'Assessment of Potential Effect on Travel of Telecommuting in Singapore', *Transportation Research Record,* 1552, 154 – 60.

Olszewski, P. and P. Mokhtarian (1994), 'Telecommuting Frequency and Impacts for State of California Employees', *Technological Forecasting and Social Change,* **45,** 275 - 86.

Pearce, D. W. and R. K. Turner (1990), *Economics of Natural Resources and the Environment,* Hertfordshire: Harvester Wheatsheaf.

Pendyala, R., K. Goulias, and R. Kitamura (1991), 'Impact of Telecommuting on Spatial and Temporal Patterns of Household Travel', *Transportation,* **18,** 383 – 409.

Pigou, A. C. (1932), *1960,* Macmillan & Co Ltd/London: The Economics of Welfare.

Polishuk, P. (1975), 'Review of the Impact of Telecommunications Substitutes for Travel', *IEEE Transactions on Communications,* **COM-23** (10), 1089 – 98.

Porter, M.E. (1985), *Competitive advantage. Creating and sustaining superior performance,* New York: Free Press.

Qvortrup, L. (1992), 'Telework: visions, definitions, realities, barriers', *Cities and New Technologies,* OECD, Paris, pp. 77 - 108.

Qvortrup, L. (1998), 'From Teleworking to Networking Definitions and Trends', in P. Jackson and W. van der (eds), *Teleworking, International Perspectives from Telecommuting to the Virtual Organization,* London-New York: Routledge, pp. 21 - 39.

Rasking, J. (1999), 'Gaan werken kost gemiddeld een half uur', *De Standaard,* 14 September 1999, vol. 76, no. 257, pp. 1.

Rathbone, D. (1992), 'Telecommuting in the United States', *ITE Journal,* December, 40 – 4.

Reichwald, R. and K. Möslein, (1999), 'Telework Strategies: The Diffusion of a Workplace Innovation', *Proceedings of The Fourth International Telework Workshop "Telework Strategies for the New Workforce",* 31 August 1999 – 3 September 1999, Tokyo, pp. 166 - 75.

Ritter, G. and S. Thompson (1994), 'The Rise of Telecommuting and Virtual Transportation', *Transportation Quarterly,* **48** (3), 235 - 48.

Salomon, I. (1984), 'Man and His Transport Behaviour: Part 1a Telecommuting – Promises and Reality', *Transport Reviews,* **4** (1), 103 – 13.

Salomon, I. (1985), 'Telecommunications and Travel. Substitution or Modified Mobility?', *Journal of Transport Economics and Policy,* **19** (3), 219 – 35.

Salomon, I. (1986), 'Telecommunications and Travel Relationships: A Review', *Transportation Research A*, **20** (3), 223 - 38.

Salomon, I. (1990), 'Telematics and Personal Travel Behaviour with Special Emphasis on Telecommuting and Teleshopping', in H. M. Soekkha, P. H. L. Bovy, P. Drewe and G.R.M. Jansen (eds), *Telematics*, pp. 67 – 89.

Salomon, I. (1994), 'How Much Telecommuting Should We Count On? A Forecast for Tel-Aviv in 2020', *Transportation Research Record*, 1463, 26 – 34.

Salomon, I. (1998), 'Technological change and social forecasting : the case of telecommuting as a travel substitute', *Transportation Research Part C*, 6, 17 – 45.

Salomon, I. and M. Salomon (1984), 'Telecommuting: The Employee'S Perspective', *Technological Forecasting and Social Change*, **25**, 15 – 28.

Salomon, I., H. Schneider, and J. Schofer (1991), 'Is Telecommuting Cheaper Than Travel? An Examination of Interaction Costs in a Business Setting', *Transportation*, **18** (4), 291 - 318.

Sampath, S., S. Saxena, and P. Mokhtarian (1991), 'The Effectiveness of Telecommuting as a Transportation Control Measure', *Proceedings of the ASCE Urban Transportation, Planning and Air Quality*, pp. 347 - 62.

Satellite Office Association of Japan (1997), *A Report on the Survey of Telework Population in Japan,* http://egg.tokyoweb.or.jp/soajhome/english/twp96-e.htm.

Sato, K. and W. Spinks (1998), 'Telework and Crisis Management in Japan', in P. Jackson and W. van der Wielen (eds), *Teleworking: International Perspectives from Telecommuting to the Virtual Organization,* London - New York: Routledge, pp. 233 - 44.

SERV (Sociaal-Economische Raad van Vlaanderen) (1999), *Aanbevelingen over telewerken in Vlaanderen,*15 September 1999.

Shamir, B. and I. Salomon (1985), 'Work-at-Home and the Quality of Working Life', *Academy of Management Review*, **10** (3), 455 - 64.

Shin, B., K. Higa, O. Shen, and T. Ide (1999), 'Analyzing the Media Usage Behavior of Telework Groups: A Contigency Approach', *IEEE transactions on systems, man and cybernetics : Part C systems and humans*, **29** (1), 127 - 39.

Skåmedal, J. (2000), 'Telecommuting's Implications on Transportation - Results from a Swedish Study', *Proceedings from the 5th International Telework Workshop*, Stockholm, Sweden, http//:www.ida.liu.se/labs/eis/telework2000/.

Spinks, W. (1991), 'Satellite and Resort Offices in Japan', *Transportation*, **18**, 343 - 63.

Stalmans, W. (1974), 'De Externe Effecten in De Economische Theorie En in De Welvaarts-Economie', *Economische en Sociaal Tijdschrift*, **28** (6), 801 - 24.

Stanworth, J. and C. Stanworth (1991), *Telework: The Human Resource Implications*, Institute of Personnel Management.

Steinle, W. (1988), 'Telework : Opening Remarks on an Open Debate', in W. Korte, S. Robinson, and W. Steinle (eds), *Telework : Present Situation and Future Development of a New Form of Work Organization*, North-Holland, Amsterdam: Elsevier Science Publishers, pp. 7 – 19.

Steward, B. (1999), 'Sickness Absenteeism in Telework : A Sociological Study', *Proceedings of The Fourth International Telework Workshop Telework Strategies for the New Workforce*, 31 August 1999 – 3 September 1999, Tokyo, 61 - 8.

Sturesson, L. (1998), 'The Mis-Match between Suppliers and Users in Telework', in P. Jackson and W. van der Wielen (eds), *Teleworking, International Perspectives from Telecommuting to the Virtual Organization*, London - New York: Routledge, pp. 319 - 28.

Sullivan, M., H. Mahmassani, and J. R. Yen (1993), 'Choice Model of Employee Participation in Telecommuting under a Cost-Neutral Scenario', *Transportation Research Record*, 1413, 42 – 8.

Teo, T., V. Lim, and S. Wai (1998), 'An Empirical Study of Attitudes
    Towards Teleworking among Information Technology (IT)
    Personnel', *International Journal of Information Management*, **18**
    (5), 329 – 43.

Toffler A. (1980), *The Third Wave*, London: Pan Books.

Tomaskovic-Devey, D. and B. Risman (1993), 'Telecommuting Innovation
    and Organization : A Contingency Theory of Labor Process Change',
    Social Science Quarterly, **74** (2), 367 - 85.

Valenduc, G. and P. Vendramin (1999), 'Telework and Non-Standard Ways
    of Working: Trends and Challenges for the Future of Work in
    Europe', *Proceedings of The Fourth International Telework
    Workshop Telework Strategies for the New Workforce*, 31 August
    1999 – 3 September 1999, Tokyo, pp. 40 – 8.

Van Neerven, G. (1991), 'Onderzoek Naar Zin En Onzin Van Telethuiswerk
    Komt Op Gang Heeft Telewerken Een Toekomst?', *Brabant
    Business*, 7 - 8, 64 - 7.

van Ommeren, J. (1998), 'Telework in Europe', in R. Suomi, P. Jackson, L.
    Hollmén, and M. Aspnäs (eds), *Proceedings of the Third
    International Workshop on Telework Telework Environments,* Turku
    Centre for Computer Science General Publications no. 8, 1 – 4
    September, pp. 164 – 83.

van Reisen (1997), *Ruim baan door telewerken? Effecten van flexibele
    werkvormen op ruimtelijke ordening en mobiliteit als gevolg van
    veranderend tijd-ruimtegedrag*, TU Delft: Publikatiebureau
    Bouwkunde.

Varma, K., C. I. Ho, D. Stanek, and P. Mokhtarian (1998), 'Duration and
    Frequency of Telecenter Use: Once a Telecommuter, Always a
    Telecommuter?' *Transportation Research Part C*, **6** (1-2), 47 - 68.

Verbeke, A. and C. Coeck (1995), 'A Note on Economic Rationality in
    Environmental Policy', *International Review of Economics and
    Business*, **42** (6), 495 – 515.

Verhoef, E. T. (1997), *The Economics of Regulating Road Transport,* Cheltenham-Brookfield: Edward Elgar.

Wardman, M. (1988), 'A Comparison of the Revealed Preference and Stated Preference Models of Travel Behaviour', *Journal of Transport Economics and Policy,* **22** (1), 71 – 92.

Watad, M. and F. Disanzo (2000), 'Case Study the Synergism of Telecommuting and Office Automation', *Sloan Management Review,* **41** (2), 85 - 96.

Weijers, T., R. Meijer, and E. Spoelman (1992), 'Telework Remains "Made to Measure". The Large-Scale Introduction of Telework in the Netherlands', *Futures,* **24** (10), 1048 - 55.

Weijers, T. and S. Weijers (1988), 'To Introduce or Not Introduce Telework', in F. van Rijn and R. Williams (eds), *Concerning Home Telematics,* North-Holland: Elsevier Science Publishers, pp. 413 - 21.

Yanabu, K. (1999), 'A Cost Simulation for Working at Home and Sensitivity Analysis', *Proceedings of The Fourth International Telework Workshop Telework Strategies for the New Workforce,* 31 August 1999 – 3 September 1999, Tokyo, pp. 263 – 70.

Yap, C. and H. Tng (1990), 'Factors Associated with Attitudes Towards Telecommuting', *Information & Management,* **19** (4), 227 - 35.

Zamindar, M. (1995), *Telework in Finland: Factors Behind Telework Use as Seen from an Employer Perspective,* Publication of Labour Administration 116, Ministry of Labour.

INDEX